METHODS OF IT PROJECT MANAGEMENT

SECOND EDITION

by
Jeffrey L. Brewer, PMP
and
Kevin C. Dittman

Purdue University Press
West Lafayette, Indiana

Library of Congress Cataloging-in-Publication Data

Brewer, Jeffrey L.
  Methods of IT project management / by Jeffrey L. Brewer, PMP and Kevin C. Dittman. --
Second edition.
    pages cm
  Includes bibliographical references and index.
  ISBN 978-1-55753-663-1 (hardback : alk. paper) -- ISBN 978-1-61249-277-3 (epdf) -- ISBN 978-
1-61249-278-0 (epub) 1. Information technology--Management. 2. Information technology
projects--Management. 3. Project management. I. Dittman, Kevin C. II. Title.
  HD30.2.B74 2013
  004.068′4--dc23
                              2013008147

Credits and acknowledgments borrowed from other sources and reproduced, with permission, in
this textbook appear on appropriate page within text.

Microsoft® and Windows® are registered trademarks of the Microsoft Corporation in the U.S.A. and
other countries. Screen shots and icons reprinted with permission from the Microsoft Corporation.
This book is not sponsored or endorsed by or affiliated with the Microsoft Corporation.

Special permission to use portions of the material contained on the website "What is CMMI?"
located at (http://www.sei.cmu.edu/cmmi/general/index.html) and associated links ©2008
Carnegie Mellon University, in this publication is granted by the Software Engineering Institute.
ANY CARNEGIE MELLON UNIVERSITY AND SOFTWARE ENGINEERING INSTITUTE
MATERIAL CONTAINED HEREIN IS FURNISHED ON AN "AS-IS" BASIS. CARNEGIE
MELLON UNIVERSITY MAKES NO WARRANTIES OF ANY KIND, EITHER EXPRESSED OR
IMPLIED, AS TO ANY MATTER INCLUDING, BUT NOT LIMITED TO, WARRANTY OF
FITNESS FOR PURPOSE OR MERCHANTABILITY, EXCLUSIVITY, OR RESULTS OBTAINED
FROM USE OR THE MATERIAL. CARNEGIE MELLON UNIVERSITY DOES NOT MAKE ANY
WARRANTY OF ANY KIND WITH RESPECT TO FREEDOM FROM PATENT, TRADEMARK,
OR COPYRIGHT INFRINGEMENT. The Software Engineering Institute and Carnegie Mellon
University do not directly or indirectly endorse nor have they reviewed the contents of this
publication. Capability Maturity Model(R), CMM (R), CMMI (R) are registered in the U.S. Patent
and Trademark Office by Carnegie Mellon University.

Project Management Institute *A Guide to the Project Management Body of Knowledge (PMBOK®
Guide)* – Fifth Edition, Project Management Institute, Inc., 2013. Copyright and all rights reserved.
Material from this publication has been reproduced with the permission of PMI.

This book was previously published by: Pearson Education, Inc.

ISBN-13: 978-1-55753-663-1
ISBN-10: 1-55753-663-5

Dedication

To my wife Heidi and children Jessica and David for their love and understanding.

—Jeff

To my family with love.

—Kevin

ABOUT THE AUTHORS

Jeffrey L. Brewer

Kevin C. Dittman

Jeffrey L. Brewer is an associate professor of Computer & Information Technology (CIT) at Purdue University. He received a B.S. degree in Computer Technology in 1982 from Purdue University and an M.S. degree in Management Information Systems from the University of Missouri, St. Louis in 1995. Professor Brewer's teaching and scholarly interests include systems analysis and design, computer-aided software engineering (CASE), agile development methodologies, IT project management, and telecare/ telemedicine technology solutions. Jeff obtained his PMP certification in 2002. Before returning to Purdue to teach, he spent 19 years working in several different industry environments, including specialty retail, manufacturing, and medical association management. He spent most of those 19 years in a project manager role.

Kevin C. Dittman is an associate professor of Computer Information Systems and Technology at Purdue University. He received a B.S. degree in Computer Science in 1981 from Purdue University and an M.S. in Management from the Florida Institute of Technology in 1989. Professor Dittman specializes in information systems analysis and design, systems engineering, requirements engineering, quality process improvement, and project management. He co-authored the leading textbook *Systems Analysis and Design Methods*, and he has published several papers and journal articles on use case modeling, IT quality, and project management. Professor Dittman has over 32 years of industrial and consulting experience in the IT arena, with top corporations such as Catepillar, Cook Medical, and Cummins Engine.

BRIEF CONTENTS

CONTENTS

PREFACE

Information technology (IT) is relatively new as a discipline and relatively new to adopting the concept that project managers need special training and play a unique, important, and strategic role in an organization. Today, more than ever before, organizations are dependent on the successful execution of projects to survive. The profitability of an organization is affected by how successful its projects are and how well they are managed. Due to the size, complexity, and number of IT projects today, organizations face ever-increasing challenges:

The United States spends $2.3 trillion on projects every year, or one-quarter its gross domestic product, and the world as a whole spends nearly $10 trillion of its $40.7 gross product on projects of all kinds.

Worldwide IT spending is expected to rise 3 percent to $3.8 trillion according to Gartner Research. Fueling this spending is the move to the "Big 4" today: cloud, mobile, social, and data analytics. This growth is broken down as follows:

- Computing Hardware—   Growth (6.6%) Total Spending ($448 billion)
- Enterprise Software—   Growth (6.9%) Total Spending ($301 billion)
- IT Services—   Growth (4.8%) Total Spending ($905 billion)
- Telecom Equipment—   Growth (8.3%) Total Spending ($408 billion)
- Telecom Services—   Growth (2.3%) Total Spending ($3,786 billion)

Roger Session, CTO of Object Watch, reports that worldwide the annual cost of IT failure is around $6.18 trillion (that's over $500 billion per month). The culprit: increasing IT complexity.

One key reason for the complexity of IT projects is that IT changes quickly, creating a shortage of the required IT skill sets. As a result, organizations are forced to pay premiums to acquire the needed talent through permanent hires, contracting, or outsourcing. In the past, these resources were required to be onsite (at the organization's office) to work on the project team. Technology advances have enabled today's IT employee to work from home or work in another part of the country or even in separate countries without ever needing to go to the office. Geographically dispersed project teams present unique challenges for the success of a project. For organizations to prosper today, they must embrace project management principles to increase productivity and return on investment (ROI) in order to create a competitive advantage locally and globally. The world, in many ways, has become a much smaller place.

THE PURPOSE OF THIS BOOK

Throughout the United States and much of the rest of the industrialized world, project management practitioners have recognized the need to improve project management in order to improve project success and have done so. Examples of initiatives include the formation of project management certification programs and training, project management offices and mentoring programs in many corporations, the advent of university and college courses dedicated to project management, and, in December 2008, the development of "The Project Management Manifesto in America" by 16 recognized project management experts. An initiative has been directed at President Obama's administration to promote better project management. Why? In addition to the 2008/2009 rash of bank and corporate failures and bailouts, the infamous Standish Group CHAOS reports provide some insights. Starting back in 1995, the Standish Group documented a dismal track record of IT project success of only 16.2 percent, with billions of dollars wasted on canceled projects. An updated study in 2006 indicated a slight improvement, with a 35 percent success rate. Based on this information, most would agree that the IT industry has a long way to go. But how do these facts relate to the profession of project management? The same CHAOS studies also list the top reasons for project failures (many discussed throughout this text), and to no one's surprise, most were project management related. However, the Standish Group report also concluded that better project management is one of the key factors responsible for many of the significant improvements and is a key criterion for project success.

This leads us to the question of why we wrote this book. As authors, we have over 45 years of project experience in the IT field. We have seen the "good, the bad, and the ugly" when it comes to IT projects, and we have the scars to prove it. We started offering project management courses at Purdue University in fall 1999, first at the graduate level, and in spring 2002 at the undergraduate level. Our goal was to provide students an educational experience consisting not only of the concepts, techniques, and methods found in the leading project management reference books but also practical knowledge—lessons learned, if you will—that students could apply immediately at their place of employment. In order to achieve this goal, we needed to find the right resources to assist in our endeavor. First and foremost we selected the Project Management Institute's (PMI's) project management body of knowledge (PMBOK) to use as our guide in providing a project management foundation and to serve as our base for educational content and our framework. Next, we strove to find the ideal textbook that not only covered the PMBOK in detail but presented it such that a practitioner could use it as a guide out in the field—a book that covered the material according to the sequence of the project management life cycle (process oriented, not concept oriented). Finally, we wanted a book that not only presented the concepts but instructed students on the techniques and provided relevant examples on how to do them. Basically, we wanted a textbook that actually guided the reader in applying project management concepts and techniques. We tried several fine books, but none of them was what we ideally were looking for, so we decided to write our own, which you are now holding. Our objective was to have a single textbook that students can use that is written in a lively, conversational tone. Based on our past experience with previous textbooks, we have found that the more traditional, academic tone tends to lose students' interest. Our conversational approach (along with the numerous examples) works well with a wider variety of students.

THIS BOOK'S IT FOCUS

As you may have found, there are many textbooks written on the subject of project management. *Methods of IT Project Management* is different from most others because it presents project management with an IT focus, for the following reasons:

- More and more information systems, IT, management of information systems, and computer science students are required or want to take a project management course, and their instructors are looking for a relevant textbook.
- There is an increasing population of IT professionals who are or strive to be project managers and are looking for information to assist them in their field.

- Many of the techniques used in project management, as well as the methods of their use, are very different from those used in other industries, such as the construction industry or the medical industry.

Unlike many other textbooks, all the examples (such as the one presented below), case studies, discussions, and questions in this textbook are presented with an IT concentration. As authors, we believe that using IT-relevant instruments to demonstrate what we are trying to communicate enhances student understanding and learning.

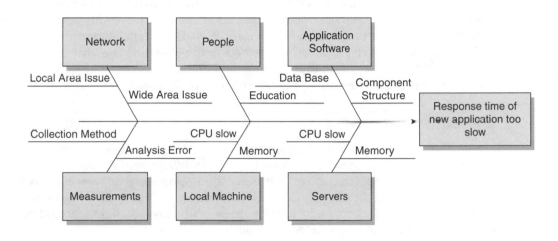

BASED ON THE 2013 FIFTH EDITION GUIDE TO THE PMBOK

We as authors have recognized the increased demand for project management education and the need for a textbook that addresses the practical application of the subject matter as well as content that is based on the PMBOK. The PMBOK, a globally recognized standard for managing projects in today's marketplace, was developed by the PMI, which currently has more than 300,000 members and manages the leading professional certification program. Individuals obtaining this PMI certification are referred to as project management professionals (PMPs). *Methods of IT Project Management* is based on the most current version of *A Guide to the PMBOK*—the fifth edition, released by PMI at the start of 2013.

WHO THIS BOOK IS FOR

Methods of IT Project Management is intended to be the primary text for a practical course in managing an IT project. Such courses are normally taught in colleges and universities at the senior or graduate level. The course is taught to both IT and business majors. The textbook implements the learning outcomes outlined in the IS'2002 Information Systems Model Curriculum, jointly developed by the Association of Computing Machinery (ACM), the Association for Information Systems (AIS), and the Association for Information Technology Professionals (AITP) (IS 2002.10 Project Management and Practice). This book also implements the learning outcomes outlined in the body of knowledge defined by ACM/ SIGITE (Association of Computing Machinery Special Interest Group for Information Technology Education) SIA4.0 Project Management.

Before using *Methods of IT Project Management*, students should have a basic knowledge of the IT discipline. While not required or assumed, courses in systems analysis and design, programming, database design, and telecommunications can significantly enhance the learning experience provided by this textbook.

LIFE CYCLE APPROACH

The focus of the textbook follows the PMBOK sample life cycle. We believe that covering the material in this sequence, as opposed to covering the material by knowledge area, allows students to more fully understand the concepts and more readily apply the material, as they would in real-life projects. This approach is also beneficial to courses in which the students work on a live project while they cover the material. The goal is for students to learn project management concepts and methods and at the same time develop skills they can use immediately during and upon completion of the course.

A RESOURCE FOR THE PMP EXAM

The PMP certification issued by PMI is the world's leading project management certification. Not only are individuals who possess PMP credentials recognized for their skills and knowledge, but the credentials can lead to increased earnings, job opportunities, and advancement. We have recognized the importance of the credentials by dedicating Appendix C to preparing for the PMP exam. This appendix contains helpful advice on studying for and passing the PMP exam, along with practice study questions.

REPOSITORY OF PROJECT MANAGEMENT TEMPLATES

We know how important it is to have access to the templates referenced in the book to be used for assignments, case projects, or exams. Therefore, all the templates referenced in the book are provided in a single place in Appendix B for your convenience, and they can be obtained from the publisher.

HOW THIS BOOK IS ORGANIZED

Methods of IT Project Management is divided into four parts and three appendixes. Past experience indicates that instructors can omit and re-sequence chapters as they feel will work best for the audience. Every effort has been made to decouple chapters from one another as much as possible to make possible this re-sequencing the material—even to the extent of reintroducing selected concepts and terminology.

Part I, "Project Management Overview," provides an introduction to the project management discipline, the project management methodology, and the PMBOK. These chapters introduce the history of project management, the role of the project manager, systems thinking and concepts, the project management life cycle, and the project management framework, which includes the PMBOK knowledge areas and component processes. Part I can be covered relatively quickly.

Part II, "Project Initiation and Planning Methods," covers the project initiation and planning phases of the project management life cycle. Coverage includes selecting a project, creating the project charter, creating the project plan, defining the project scope, building the project team, determining the project schedule and budget, setting quality standards, planning for project risks, and planning for procurement.

Part III, "Project Execution and Control Methods," covers project plan execution, quality assurance, team development and management, information distribution, stakeholder management, and project procurement execution. It includes coverage of change control, cost control, quality control, and performance reporting.

Part IV, "Project Closeout Methods and Advanced Topics," covers the life cycle activities, tools, and techniques used at the end of a project. It also includes coverage of project management offices, outsourcing, ethics, virtual teams, and two maturity models: the Capability Maturity Model Integrated (CMMI) and the Organizational Project Management Maturity Model (OPM3).

Part V, "Appendixes," provides a Microsoft Project help guide, a list of the project management templates used throughout the text, and coverage of the PMP certification exam.

PEDAGOGICAL QUALITIES

Pedagogical Use of Color and Framework

Methods of IT Project Management uses two colors throughout the text and uses a matrix that reflects our framework for applying project management (depicted on the next page) based on the latest version of the PMBOK. We created the framework to provide a comprehensive snapshot of the PMBOK's knowledge areas and process groups and for students to use as a point of reference. This feature, which distinguishes this textbook from others, presents the framework graphic preceding each PMBOK chapter in order to provide a visual reference for the content covered in that chapter. It creates a great roadmap for student learning, helping them see where they have been and where they are going. It also functions as a great study aid in preparing for knowledge assessment activities such as exams and quizzes.

Learning Objectives and End-of-Chapter Summaries

Designed as study aids, the learning objectives in each chapter reflect what students should be able to understand and accomplish after completing the chapter. Each end-of-chapter summary reviews the key areas of the chapter and provides insight into the areas where students should focus their attention.

End-of-Chapter Review Questions, End-of-Chapter Problems and Exercises, and End-of-Chapter Projects and Research

Methods of IT Project Management provides multiple means to assess leaning, aid thinking, and provide additional opportunities for research and learning—through end-of-chapter review questions, end-of-chapter problems and exercises, and end-of-chapter projects and research.

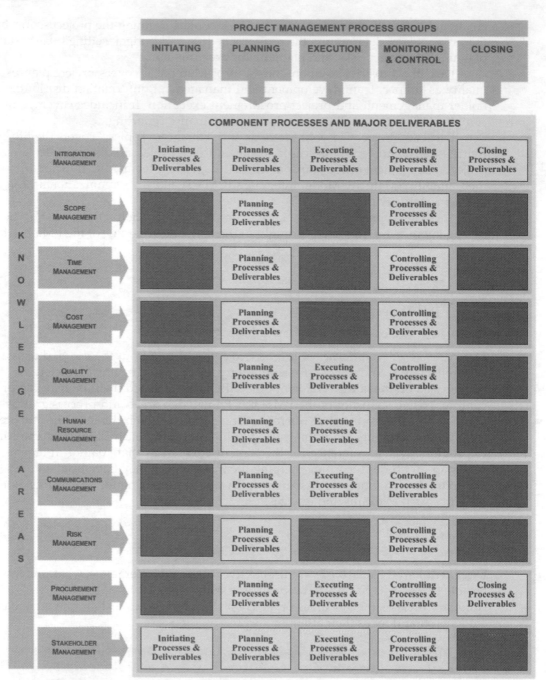

Running Case Study

Each chapter opens with the "The Project Management Chronicles" feature, a running case study that introduces the concepts and techniques discussed within the chapter. This case study, based on a fictitious project management consulting company, walks students through the trials and tribulations of leading a project. This serious but sometimes comical journey is based on real-life experiences and projects, emphasizes the human aspect of the job, and discusses and demonstrates best practices.

Minicases

At the end of each chapter is one or more minicases based on the running case study. Each minicase provides additional opportunities for students to apply project management concepts and techniques and also provides thought-provoking scenarios to challenge more advanced students. It provides material suitable for excellent class discussions and debates.

Suggested Readings

At the end of each chapter is a list of recommended readings that offer additional references for further research. Many of the exercises direct students to those areas in order to complete the exercise.

PROVEN STRATEGIES AND HINTS TO SUCCESS

A new section added in the second edition to many of the chapters, "Proven Strategies and Hints To Success" provides the reader strategies and best practices proven by experts in the field at real companies to aid project managers in delivering successful projects. In many cases, these come from real case studies of live projects.

Key Terms

Each chapter provides definitions and descriptions of some of the key terms related to project management. Every discipline tends to develop its own unique jargon and acronyms. This can become frustrating for students who are unfamiliar with a term. By highlighting key terms in text and providing their definitions in the Glossary, this textbook augments the learning process; the student doesn't have to take a break to look up a definition of an unfamiliar term or skip the term altogether, without knowing what it means.

SUPPLEMENTS AND INSTRUCTIONAL RESOURCES

It is our goal to provide adopters with a complete course, not just a textbook. *Methods of IT Project Management* includes the supplements described on the following pages.

For the Instructor

ALL OF THE FOLLOWING SUPPLEMENTS CAN BE PROVIDED BY CONTACTING THE PUBLISHER: The instructor's guide, templates, PowerPoint presentations, and the image library (text art).

INSTRUCTOR'S GUIDE   The instructor's guide includes course-planning materials, chapter-planning guidelines, teaching notes, and answers to end-of-chapter problems, exercises, and minicases.

POWERPOINT PRESENTATIONS   You'll find a slide show repository in Microsoft PowerPoint (complete with instructor notes that provide teaching guidelines and tips). Instructors can (1) pick and choose the slides they wish to use, (2) customize slides to their own preferences, and (3) add new slides. Slides can be organized into electronic presentations or printed as transparencies or transparency masters.

PART 1

Project Management Overview

1

Introduction to Project Management

R & S Amusements Services

Entry 1

Case Study

This is the continuing account of Jeff Dunbar and Kevin Pullen, senior project management consultants for Premier Project Management Services (PPMS). PPMS is a leading provider of training, mentoring, and consulting services to organizations throughout the United States. The company's headquarters is located in West Lafayette, Indiana, but PPMS maintains regional offices in the areas where it has large client bases, including Orlando, Chicago, and Denver.

R & S Amusements Services has hired PPMS to lead the effort of modernizing its computing resources in order to stay competitive and profitable, as well as to continue to meet the demands of its customers.

Tom Demarco, a noted scholar in the information technology (IT) industry, said it best: "project management is more than concepts, tools, techniques, and methods. It is about people working with people." (Demarco, 1997) Although experience is the best teacher, you can learn a great deal by observing other project managers in action. Mr. Kent Clawson, senior partner for PPMS, has kindly consented to let you watch two of his top managers on a typical project.

Jeff Dunbar, a certified project management professional (PMP), has volunteered for this assignment. He has 23 years of project management experience and has successfully completed many IT projects. Jeff received his certification from the Project Management Institute (PMI), which is the leading provider of education and knowledge and is considered a pioneer in the field of project management. PMI's membership consists of more than 395,000 professionals, representing more than 125 countries. PMI professionals come from virtually every major industry, including aerospace, automotive, business management, construction, engineering, financial services, IT, pharmaceuticals, health care, and telecommunications.

Kevin Pullen, also a certified PMP, has agreed to work with Jeff on this project. He has 20 years of project management experience and has also been extremely successful.

3

Both individuals are highly skilled and bring different strengths to the table, which should provide you with a valuable learning experience.

Jeff and Kevin are meeting with the client today, and they have invited you to observe the meeting. It'll be a good way for you to get acquainted with the project and R & S Amusements Services.

Setting   *In the office of Reid Lewis, president of R & S Amusements Services*

REID   Good Morning Jeff! It's so nice to see you again. How have you been?

JEFF   Fine, thank you. And you?

REID   Couldn't be better.

JEFF   Mr. Lewis, this is my colleague Kevin Pullen, who will be assisting me on this project.

KEVIN   Pleased to meet you, Mr. Lewis.

REID   Nice to meet you, Kevin, and please call me Reid. Kevin, I don't how much Jeff has told you about this opportunity, but allow me to give you a little background about the business.

KEVIN   Super. Please go right ahead.

REID   As you know, we are in the business of distributing amusement machines—pool tables, jukeboxes, video games, pinball games, and the like—to area businesses, with the intent of making money for both the business location and us. I started in the business in 1947, with three machines, and now R & S Amusements Services has grown to be one of the largest amusement machine operators in the Midwest. We employ 125 full- and part-time employees, and we service more than 500 business establishments—our customers. The types of establishments include arcades, restaurants, taverns, clubs, bowling alleys, campgrounds, and numerous others. At each of these establishments, we have installed one or more amusement machines from our current inventory of more than 6,500.

KEVIN   That's quite an accomplishment! Could you please explain how this makes you money?

REID   Sure! The basis of my business is this: We are in the entertainment business. We provide amusement machines to various business locations for their customers to enjoy. Their customers pay money to play a game or listen to music while at the location. The money earned by the machines is divided by the business location and us. That is our fee for installing and maintaining the machines.

JEFF   Is the money divided evenly?

REID   Depends on the contract. With every business location we deal with, we enter into a contract. Basically, it is an agreement between the business establishment and us, on what services we will provide, at what cost, and the time period of the contract. The nature of the business and the value of the machines factor into what the percentage split is.

KEVIN   Do you mainly service the greater Lafayette area?

REID   You could say our headquarters is here but we service almost the entire state of Indiana. We have regional offices in Fort Wayne and Bloomington, Indiana, and I'm looking seriously into opening an office in Cincinnati, Ohio.

JEFF   I had no idea amusement machines could be so profitable.

REID   The peak years were when the Pac-Man video games were first released. That craze was unbelievable. Now, with competition from home video game systems, personal computers, and the Internet, we have to be more creative and intelligent to be competitive and make a profit. This is the primary reason you gentlemen are here.

KEVIN   Please explain.

REID   There is more to the business than emptying quarters or dollars bills out of a machine's cash can—that's what we call the storage device that holds the money that is deposited into a machine. *(Jeff and Kevin laugh)* Even that is a complicated process. You have to plan how often a location will be collected from (weekly, biweekly, or monthly) and on what day. Then you have to determine which locations will be collected from on the same day so that it is most economical for us in terms of travel time and labor expense of the collector. The collector usually has to count the money at the location's site and then divide the proceeds based on the contract and give the location its share. At the end of the day, the money the collector brings in is audited to ensure that no mistakes were made.

JEFF   That in itself sounds like a sophisticated process.

REID   Yes, but it's all the other logistical operations that allow the business to operate smoothly and efficiently that can be extremely challenging.

JEFF   Such as?

REID   The purchasing of new machines and the disposal of the old ones and the repair of machines that break down or need to be upgraded. The solicitation of new customers and the management of those relationships to ensure both sides are happy. The tracking of inventory is also an issue—not only of the machines—but also of parts and other support equipment. The ordering and management of our music inventory—the CDs that are installed in jukeboxes, and believe it or not, we still have people who want the old 45s jukeboxes. Also, there are issues with the management of the prize inventory for redemption games and those games such as cranes and the like where you can win prizes such as stuffed animals.

KEVIN   What do you mean by *redemption*?

REID   Some machines are on a redemption basis—you know, the games that dispense a certain number of tickets based on how many points you score. Then you can redeem all your winning tickets for fabulous prizes—such as candy, bubblegum, a lava lamp. *(They all laugh)* Kids love it—it is a big money maker at skating rinks, bowling alleys, and arcades.

In addition, we sponsor dart and pool leagues and the associated tournaments. Let me explain. One of our most popular games at bars is an electronic dart board game. Typically, the most popular establishments in a town will host a league of 10 or more teams (each team consisting of five individuals) to entice people to come in and play darts, with the hope that they will also spend money to enjoy the location's food and beverages. It's very similar to a bowling alley hosting a bowling league. We benefit because the players have to pay each time they play the dart game. The locations themselves don't have the resources or know-how to manage the league, so we do it for them—for a fee. I have four employees dedicated just to managing leagues. It is a lot of work. At the end of the season, we host an area tournament, and the winners advance to national tournaments, usually held in Las Vegas.

KEVIN   I would never have guessed that this business was so involved.

REID   And I haven't even mentioned things like human resource functions such as payroll, or finance functions such as accounts payable. It is really quite impressive and mind-boggling, if you think about it. *(Both Jeff and Kevin nod their heads)*

The bottom line is that we are doing a very poor job of taking advantage of IT to help us manage and run the business. We have some software to help us. Five years ago we purchased a package to track and manage our machine inventory. It does the job, but it's very limited in meeting the needs of an organization our size.

JEFF   Have you contacted the company that wrote the software about upgrading it to meet your needs?

REID   We tried, but they went out of business two years ago.

KEVIN   That's not good.

REID   Now you are beginning to see the situation we are in. You probably won't believe it, but most of our business functions are still manual. We track our collections in Excel spreadsheets, for heaven's sake! We produce all our reports in Microsoft Word.

JEFF   It's amazing that you have done so well.

REID   Yes, but we won't continue to do well unless we make some major changes. The economy is not as strong as it used to be, and our profits are down. We need to take advantage of what IT can do for us to decrease costs and generate revenue—such as creating a web site for our business so that we can attract new customers and our existing customers can go and get information such as collection history and the like.

KEVIN   You may be one of the few businesses of your size that doesn't have a web site of some sort.

REID   Yes, we are behind the times, and it's downright embarrassing sometimes. But I don't have a staff knowledgeable of these sorts of things, nor do I know who to hire to build software for me. That brings me back to why you gentlemen are here. As I was telling Jeff over the phone a few days ago, I was having lunch with a couple of my friends from Purdue University last week, and I was complaining to them about all my problems. They told me how critical it is to find people who are knowledgeable about these sorts of projects and to do them right in order to be successful. When I asked them where I would find such people, they recommended that I get in touch with PPMS, which has experts in this type of thing; they were highly complimentary of you, Jeff, and you, too, Kevin. That's why I specifically requested both of you, in case you didn't know.

JEFF   That's very flattering.

REID   Now, if I can be frank, what qualifies you gentlemen to be the right people to help me and my company?

JEFF   Good question. First, let me explain that everything that you have described that you want to do is a series of projects that involves IT. A project is a temporary endeavor with a purpose of creating a unique product. We are in the business of managing projects like yours. In fact, we are highly successful at it.

REID   What makes you so successful?

KEVIN   We have created a standard set of processes—or a methodology, if you will—that is based on the PMI's *Guide to the Project Management Body of Knowledge (PMBOK)*. The *Guide to the PMBOK* is a document that contains knowledge and practices that can be applied to most projects, no matter what the discipline. Our standard processes, which have been tested and used on dozens of IT projects and refined over time, enable us to be consistent in our approach to planning, executing, and controlling projects in order to meet customer expectations in terms of content and quality.

REID   So what you are telling me is that you have, for lack of better words, a project management recipe book for doing projects?

JEFF   That's a good analogy, and I'll expand on it: By having a recipe that is proven, we can repeat it several times, knowing what the outcome will be—project success! In addition, both Kevin and I are PMI-certified project managers. To obtain that certification, you must not only have achieved a certain level score on an examination, but you actually have to demonstrate that you have applied project management skills over several years. We have had a lot of experience in these types of projects, Reid, and we will definitely do our best in doing what you believe needs to be done.

REID   I have every reason to believe you will, but you will need to help me determine what needs to be done first.

JEFF   Reid, because we are running short on time, can we schedule another meeting to continue this conversation and start planning how we are going to accomplish your goals?

REID   Absolutely! I will invite a few other key players, Diana Brooks and Mark Lewis, to get their input.

KEVIN   That would be great! Would you happen to have an organization chart so we can become more familiar with the company and the responsibilities of the various employees?

REID   Yes, I do. I will have my secretary email you a copy.

JEFF   Thanks for your time, Reid. See you in a couple days.

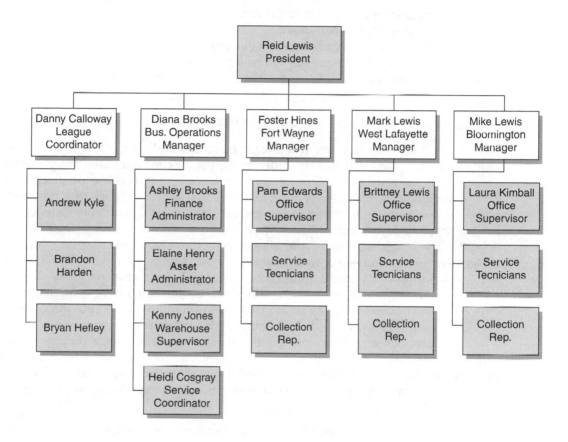

HOW TO USE THE DEMONSTRATION CASE

You've just been introduced to a case study that will be continued throughout this book. The purpose of the continuing case is to show you that tools and techniques alone do not make a project manager successful. Project management involves a commitment to work for and with a number of people.

Each chapter of this book begins with a "The Project Management Chronicles" feature about R & S Amusements Services that introduces new ideas, tools, and/or techniques that are examined in that chapter. Jeff and Kevin will work closely with the client as well as with their team to manage the project to meet its objectives. They will use current best practices and follow procedures and processes that are used by today's most successful organizations when building information systems.

CHAPTER PREVIEW AND OBJECTIVES

Projects exist in everything we do, from trips to the grocery store to building enterprise-level information systems. This chapter introduces you to projects and project management. Before you can begin to understand how to run effective successful projects, you must understand what a project is and the context in which it exists. You will understand projects and project management when you:

- Can define what a project is and is not
- Can define project management
- Understand the history of project management
- Understand the skills necessary to lead projects
- Understand the organizational structures where projects exist

AN INTRODUCTION TO PROJECT MANAGEMENT

Projects have always been and will always be an integral part of the everyday lives of individuals and corporations. For individuals, projects may involve the planning and execution of weekend outings, family get-togethers, spring break trips to Cancun, and even something as simple as preparing a grocery list, which includes allocating a grocery budget and then going to the store to purchase the needed items. Your success with the project of going to the grocery store maybe judged on whether you were able to buy everything you needed, within your allotted time frame, and whether you stayed under budget. Failing to meet one or more of these criteria may mean making certain trade-offs, such as deciding to have hot dogs because you don't have the budget for steak or buying an entrée you can prepare in the microwave because you don't have enough time to prepare a full four-course meal. Managing trade-offs is common in an individual's everyday life, and it is also critical in the daily function of an organization.

Organizations are dependent on the successful execution of projects to survive now more than ever. The profitability of an organization is affected by how successful its projects are and how well they are managed. Due to the size, complexity, and quantity of information technology (IT) projects today, organizations face ever-increasing challenges, as indicated by the following:

- The United States spends $2.3 trillion on projects every year, or one-quarter its gross domestic product, and the world as a whole spends nearly $10 trillion of its $40.7 gross product on projects of all kinds.
- Worldwide IT spending is expected to rise 3% to $3.8 trillion according to Gartner Research. Fueling this spending is the move to the "Big 4" today: cloud, mobile, social, and data analytics. This growth is broken down as follows:
  - o Computing Hardware   Growth (6.6%)   Total spending ($448 billion)
  - o Enterprise Software   Growth (6.9%)   Total spending ($301 billion)
  - o IT Services   Growth (4.8%)   Total spending ($905 billion)
  - o Telecom Equipment   Growth (8.3%)   Total spending ($408 billion)
  - o Telecom Services   Growth (2.3%)   Total spending ($3,786 billion)
- Two-thirds of CEOs (based on a Forester study) believe IT will make a greater contribution to their industry in the next 10 years than any prior decades.

- IDC projects cloud computing will be 27% of all new spending—"cloud computing will spend the next five years as the hottest new IT market in town."
- IDC's updated IT Cloud Services Forecast predicts that public cloud computing will make up $17.4 billion worth of IT purchases and be a $44 billion market by 2013
- Forrester forecasts that overall United States IT spending in 2013 will be $1,266 billion on all goods, services, and staff. The largest categories are IT salaries accounting for $241 billion, and software at $232 billion. Computer equipment spending will be $92 billion.
- Roger Session, CTO of Object Watch, reports that worldwide the annual cost of IT failure is around $6.18 trillion (that's over $500 billion per month). The culprit—increasing IT complexity.

One key reason for the complexity of IT projects is that technology changes quickly, creating a shortage of the required IT skill sets. As a result, organizations are forced to pay premiums to acquire the needed talent through permanent hires, contracting, or even outsourcing. In the past, these resources were required to be onsite (at the organization's office) to work on the project team. Technology advances have enabled today's IT employee to be able to work from home or work in another part of the country or even in separate countries without ever needing to go into the office. Geographically dispersed project teams present their own challenges for the success of a project. For organizations to prosper today, they must embrace

PROVEN STRATEGIES AND HINTS TO SUCCESS

Another reason for the increased complexity is that systems users demand more and more functionality and capabilities in the products that our projects provide. Using Glass's Law[1] as applied to IT: "For every 25% increase in the business functionality of a service, there is a 100% increase in the complexity of that service. For every 25% increase in the connections of a system, there is a 100% increase in the complexity of that system."

[1]Glass's Law comes from Robert Glass's *Facts and Fallacies of Software Engineering*. He did not discover the law. He actually described it from a paper by Scott Woodfield, but Glass did more than anybody to publicize the law.

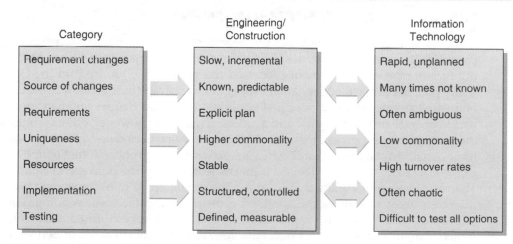

FIGURE 1-1   **Project Differences Between Disciplines**

project management principles to increase productivity and return on investment (ROI) in order to create a competitive advantage locally and globally. The world, in many ways, has become a much smaller place.

This textbook focuses on project management with an IT focus because many of the techniques used and the methods of use are very different than those in other industries, such as construction or health care. We will examine these differences, including the following, throughout the text (see Figure 1-1):

- Traditionally high turnover rates of IT workers
- Level of uniqueness and complexity of each project due to rapid changes in technology
- Difficulty of visualizing software for the developer and the customer
- Difficulty getting accurate customer requirements
- Rate of change in requirements
- Difficulty testing all the possible states of software
- Need for constant training to keep team members current with the technology

Because of the nature of these differences, IT organizations are now changing their approach to IT projects, making organizational structure changes in order to become leaner, adaptable, and better at handling change. Moving to a more supportive model for project management is one way to do this. We will continue our discussion of contemporary IT organizational structures and their impact later in this chapter.

The Project Management Institute (PMI) defines a number of benefits for organizations that use structured project management techniques (we will talk more about PMI throughout this text):

- Improvement in customer satisfaction
- Better cost performance and higher return on investment
- Better schedule performance, better allocation of time commitments, and better utilization of resources, as well as higher productivity
- Increased quality, reducing rework
- Increase in delivering-required features

THE HISTORY OF PROJECT MANAGEMENT

The origins of project management can be traced back to the days of constructing the great pyramids in Egypt; however, the U.S. Department of Defense (DOD) is credited with bringing formal project management processes and tools to the forefront in the United States. Many people believe the Manhattan Project in the early 1940s (involved in the development of the first atomic bomb) was the first application of modern project management because it had a separate project manager and a technical manager; however, others would argue that the roots of current project management tools and practices date to the late 1950s. Finding itself behind in the "space race" when the Soviet Union launched the *Sputnik 1* satellite on October 4, 1957, the DOD devised a means to speed up the delivery of military projects. The result was a discipline that included the definition of roles, tools, and processes that direct a project to achieve the specified goals. First and foremost was defining someone with sole accountability for a project to serve as a single point of contact; so the modern project manager was born. A project manager needed tools to assist in performing the job, and the Program Evaluation and Review Technique (PERT) was developed in 1958. Project

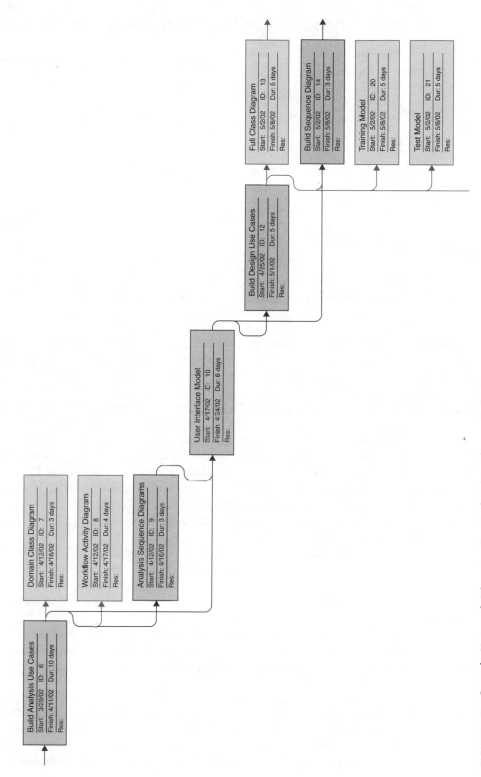

FIGURE 1-2 Sample Network Diagram Created Using Microsoft Project

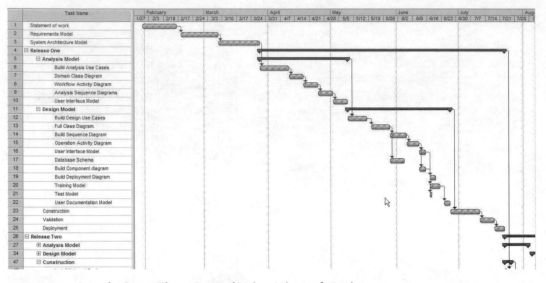

FIGURE 1-3   Sample Gantt Chart Created Using Microsoft Project

managers used PERT for analyzing the time it takes to complete the tasks of a given project and thus determine the minimum time needed to complete the total project. A network diagram—similar to the one shown in Figure 1-2, created using Microsoft Project—is used to display the information. Later, to satisfy a need for formal project decomposition, PERT was enhanced to include the work breakdown structure (WBS), a technique for identifying the items to be performed in a project that is represented by a hierarchical tree structure of tasks and deliverables. Both PERT and WBS will be covered in detail later in this textbook.

A key tool used to this day is the Gantt chart. Figure 1-3 shows an example of a Gantt chart, representing a software development project drawn using Microsoft Project software. Today's project managers use Gantt charts to communicate project status to key project sponsors and the rest of the team. The project manager may also use a Gantt chart to help show the dependency of some tasks on other tasks, assisting to build a good project schedule. The chart was first developed by Henry Gantt in 1917 to help schedule the work in factories.

At roughly the same time as the invention of PERT, the DuPont Corporation invented the Critical Path Method (CPM). CPM is a method that identifies the set of tasks, when performed in sequence, that total the longest overall duration of time; this is called the *critical path*, the shortest time to complete the project. The duration of the critical path determines the duration of the entire project.

PERT and CPM evolved through the 1960s, becoming commonplace in major space (such as NASA's *Apollo* program) and defense programs, but they saw limited use beyond those industries. Even at engineering schools, project management was usually taught on a limited basis.

In the 1970s, the field of project management grew for three primary reasons: (1) There was a growing demand for sophisticated and complex products, (2) companies were growing in terms of size and complex activities, and (3) large companies needed to compete in a global dynamic business environment. These factors contributed to more and more companies adopting formal project management methods in order to successfully complete projects.

In the 1990s, interest in project management soared because of a convergence of several factors. More powerful computers and software made it easier to use the classic project management techniques. Standard practices and processes such as the Project Management Body of Knowledge (PMBOK) and the Capability Maturity Model Integration (CMMI) were introduced in an effort to standardize the practices of software development, making it easier to predict and track performance as well as manage projects.

Today, with the popularity of using the Internet as a data capture and information delivery tool, project management techniques have evolved to manage projects based on "Internet time," meaning projects with short delivery schedules. Using complex models such as PERT or CPM for projects spanning a few days or weeks may prove to be too costly and restrictive to deliver a successful project. Project managers have turned to more agile approaches (called, among other names, *extreme or agile project management*) that focus on the human side of project management rather than the rigid rules of a formal, heavy process. Chapter 2 covers project management methodologies, including extreme project management, in more detail.

PROJECT MANAGEMENT DEFINITIONS

Now that you have an understanding of the history of project management, it is time to define what constitutes a **project** and the act of managing a project.

A project has three key characteristics:

• Temporary
• Unique
• Progressively elaborate

First and foremost, a project is temporary. It must have a beginning and an end. Seems simple, doesn't it? But many of the issues we face in managing projects involve getting people to understand that projects are supposed to end. A project reaches its end when one of the following occurs:

• The project's objectives have been achieved, as agreed by the sponsor.
• It has been determined that the project's objectives will not or cannot be achieved.
• The need for the project no longer exists, and the project is terminated.

Many times projects, especially in the IT industry, turn into "death march" projects that never end. (Yourdon,1997) These projects, for a variety of reasons, will never be successful, but organizations continue to work on them. Maybe the customer has requested additional features; there has been a change in the technical architecture; key resources have left or been reassigned, which have slowed or delayed the project; or no one will terminate a dying project because management does not want to be viewed as a failure. In any of these cases, management fails to grasp the important concept that a project must have an end date: It must have closure in order for its success and performance to be evaluated and for the good of all the stakeholders involved. One of the goals of this text is to help you learn how to get to a "project end status." You will learn to establish at the beginning of the project the user-defined critical success factors that, when achieved, signal the end of the project. You will also learn to get key stakeholders to agree on what these factors are and on what exactly constitutes their fulfillment. You will also learn some techniques to keep user-generated requirements from increasing during the life of a project. If the project allows changes and new requirements to be continually added, referred to as *scope creep*, you will never get done.

The second characteristic is that a project is *unique*, thus producing a unique deliverable. In other words, the project must never have been done before, and it must have a well-defined purpose. This holds especially true in the IT industry, where the underlying technology that a project is based on changes frequently. In addition, other factors, such as different requirements, different customers, different tools, and different platforms, all contribute in making a project unique, thus creating uncertainty and risk.

The third characteristic that defines a project is that it is *progressively elaborate*. This concept refers to the idea that development occurs in steps and then continues in small increments, adding features and definition. For example, a customer and software developer will have a basic understanding of the project in the initial phase of the development life cycle, and during the project's later phases or in later iterations, they will obtain a more detailed understanding of what is to be built, then design how it is to be built in more detail with each iteration, and then actually build it in these increments.

There are also some secondary characteristics that define typical projects:

- Each project must have a primary sponsor or champion.
- A project usually cuts across organizational lines, requiring resources from several different departments or organizations.
- A project must do something, must have an output or a deliverable. The deliverable might not be something physical such as a product that you can hold in your hand; for example, it might be process improvements or education and training.

So why is doing projects in IT so difficult? In repetitive jobs, such as line assembly, quality, productivity, and efficiency are gained due to the repetitive nature of doing the same types of activities over and over again in producing the same product. The more you build something, the better and the faster you become because of repetition. Success is measured by how many of the same type of "widgets" are produced each day. In IT, most of us don't have the luxury of building the same software package over and over again until we become experts in building that type of software (we may, for example, build only one payroll package in our career); thus we don't realize the benefits of product repetition. But we can take advantage of process repetition—the idea of managing a project by following a standard project management process in order to gain repetitive successes.

Project management is accomplished via the project management processes of initiating, planning, executing, monitoring and controlling, and closing, which a project manager performs in order to accomplish the project's objectives.

A project manager manages a project by performing these four high-level activities:

- Setting clear and achievable objectives
- Identifying requirements
- Adapting the project to the various concerns of the stakeholders
- Balancing the demands of the *triple constraint*

The Triple Constraint

Every project is constrained by a list of customer-requested requirements (scope), the amount of time available to produce the system in support of the requirements (time), and the limit of money available (cost). This is referred to as the **triple constraint** of project management.

These three basic criteria are generally used to evaluate the success of a project and its management and are the primary success factors that project managers use to produce successful projects:

- **Scope** is assessed by the degree to which the system satisfies the requirements set forth and agreed upon by the customer and the development team. Functional requirements as well as nonfunctional requirements are defined at the beginning of the project. The development team uses this definition as a blueprint for building an acceptable product for the customer. The extent to which an activity in the development cycle meets these requirements is a measure of the scope. Historically, a large percentage of IT projects have failed because the system has not satisfied the customer's requirements in terms of scope.
- **Time** refers to the amount of time (hours, days, weeks, months) allocated to completing the project. Each activity of a project is estimated to take a certain amount of time in order to complete. All the activities are scheduled in an order best determined by the project manager, with assistance from the team to successfully complete the project. The project manager monitors the schedule to ensure that each activity is being completed within the amount of time allocated and by the date specified.
- **Cost** refers to the resources being spent (usually money) in order to turn the requirements into an acceptable system. It includes costs such as the salaries of the development team and the costs for buying computer hardware and software. A budget is normally established at the beginning of a project, based on estimates of the resources required. A project manager must monitor the budget and associated costs in order to be able to complete the project within budget and to take corrective action, if needed.

Every project is constrained differently, according to the goals of the system owner (sponsor) and the development team. The following are examples of competing constraints a project manager must balance in order to deliver a successful project: (1) how much budget is allocated to complete the project, (2) the need to complete the project by a certain date, and (3) the need for the finished system to include these features. A fourth criterion, **quality**, is often mentioned as an additional key factor of many IT projects. Customers have come to expect a certain level of quality from information systems. For example, "the system is to be implemented with fewer than 3 defects per 10,000 lines of code" and "the user interface must meet corporate standards and federal guidelines for access by the handicapped" are quality objectives that present challenges for a project manager. Many times, in order to satisfy the quality goals of a project, a project manager and project sponsor may have to make decisions that negatively affect the other constraints, such as having to allocate more time and more budget.

Project managers have to juggle the three constraints and come up with a trade-off, based on the priorities placed on the three constraints. For example:

- Reducing time allowed will increase cost (especially if overtime is required) and may reduce the scope (functions and features) of the system.
- Reducing costs (cutting the budget) will increase time (delay schedule) and may reduce the scope (functions and features) of the system.

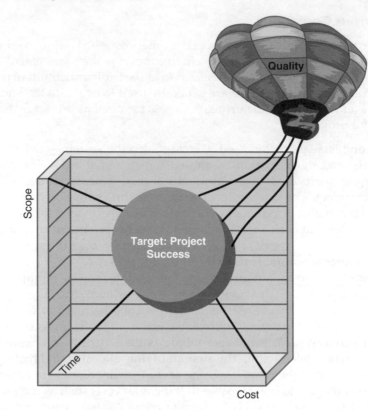

FIGURE 1-4 Project Management Triple Constraint

- Increasing scope (adding features) will certainly increase time and/or cost.
- Reducing scope may reduce time and cost (and it may also negatively affect quality).

These statements reflect how the three constraints—scope, time, and cost—each continuously influences and is influenced by the other two (see Figure 1-4). To deliver a successful project, a project manager must learn to balance the three and make trade-offs. The fourth element, quality, can be adjusted as well to ensure that the other three stay in focus. For example, you may be able to reduce the amount of testing or negotiate with the sponsor for a lower-quality product in order to save money or time in order to complete the project on time. A former NASA official compared the conditions of project management to a "three-legged milk stool consisting of performance, time and cost. If any of the legs are missing, the stool will collapse." (Werderitsch, 1990) For example, a project completed on time and within budget, yet not meeting scope requirements, will not be accepted by the users. In addition, a project that is late and over budget is considered a failure even if it meets the scope requirements.

The Need for Better Project Management

In 1995, the Standish Group conducted a study titled CHAOS. The study surveyed 365 IT executive managers in the United States who managed more than 8,000 IT application projects. The sample contained small, medium, and large companies across several industry segments. The results of the study showed, as the title of the study indicates, that IT projects were in total chaos (see Table 1-1). "A huge portion of the more than $250 billion spent annually on IT application development is wasted because companies fail to utilize effective project management practices." (Chaos, 2005) The study has been repeated several times in 2001 and 2003, as you can see from Table 1-1. Only 16.2% of projects were counted as successful in 1995, and the projects were delivering only 61% of the desired features. Successful projects were defined as meeting all project objectives on time and on budget.

TABLE 1-1 Standish Group Study Results

	1994	1998	2000	2002	2004	2006	2008	2010
Successful IT projects	16%	26%	28%	34%	29%	35%	32%	37%
Failed/cancelled IT projects	31%	28%	23%	15%	18%	19%	24%	21%
Challenged IT projects	53%	46%	49%	51%	53%	46%	44%	42%

The Standish Group repeated the study in 2001 and again in 2003, observing some noteworthy improvements (see Table 1-1). Successful projects increased to 34%, average cost overruns decreased to 43%, and average time overruns decreased to 82%.

One of the major reasons for the improvements indicated in the CHAOS study was attributed to better project management practices and better-trained project managers. Joseph Gulla (2012) of IBM reports that 54% of project failures can be attributed to project management, whereas only 3% are attributed to technical challenges. As you can see from the statistics, the IT profession is still challenged in learning how to deliver successful projects. This text and the classrooms where it is used hopefully can continue to build more successful project managers. The next section discusses the skills a project manager needs in order to be successful.

PROFILES OF PROJECT MANAGERS AND THE PROFESSION

From the results of studies, such as the CHAOS studies, organizations are beginning to understand the importance of well-run projects and the importance of trained project managers. In the early days of IT, individuals were put in charge of projects without the benefit of project management training. People were chosen on the basis of their performance in other positions. They were good programmers or good systems analysts, so it was assumed that they could run a project. Today, we know that successful project managers need to acquire skills much different from just general supervisory skills or just technology skills. Project management has emerged as a separate discipline with its own unique skill set. Many of the "soft skills" required to be successful project managers, are thought to be difficult or impossible to teach; they must be inherent in the individual. Other skills—mainly technical skills—can be taught to help project managers become successful. We do not get into a lengthy debate here about which skills can and cannot be taught; we feel that organizations need to look for individuals who demonstrate many of the abilities listed under "soft skills" and then train them to acquire the other skills, which are explained throughout the remainder of this text.

Soft skills:	Covered in:
• Leadership	Chapter 10
• Team building	Chapter 1
• Negotiation	Chapter 10
• Conflict management	Chapter 10
• Organization for self and others	Chapter 5
• Communication, both oral and written, to both technical and nontechnical audiences	Chapter 7
• Change management	Chapter 11
• Active listening	Chapter 7

Technical skills:	
• Project management software knowledge	Appendix A
• Understanding of the technology being used in the project (software, hardware, network, etc.)	Chapter 6
• Basic knowledge of the business	Chapter 5
• Cost estimating and budgeting knowledge	Chapter 6

How much technical knowledge is necessary for a project manager to have has been debated at length. Some say that anyone who is a good project manager should be able to manage any project without any knowledge of the technology; they believe that sound project management principles should apply. The idea that project managers need an in-depth technical background to manage a technical project has been argued on both sides. We have found, from our collective 40-plus years of industry experience as project managers, that it depends more on the individual and the type of project than on some hard-and-fast rule. The one principle that is consistent across all schools of thought is that a project manager must learn to delegate. A project manager cannot be the chief programmer, chief network analyst, or chief database designer and also run the project. Yourdon (2002) makes the point that project managers need some technical expertise, especially in to-day's Internet development environment, and a manager must be able to evaluate the

PROVEN STRATEGIES AND HINTS TO SUCCESS

The generic rules of thumb for software project managers (this came from their many years of consulting) (Jones, 2007):

- One project manager for every eight technical staff members
- One full-time PM for every 1,500 function points
- One PM for roughly every 150,000 source code statements
- Project management starts before requirements and runs after the project ends
- Project management work = 35% of available management time
- Personnel work (resources) 30% of available management time
- Meetings with other managers or clients = 22% of available management time
- Departmental work = 8% of available management time
- Miscellaneous work = 5% of available management time

hardware/software environment alternatives presented to him or her from the technology folks in order to make or present the information to those who will make the purchasing decisions. The project manager must be able to balance the "excessive optimism" of the technologist with the reality of what is the best way to spend the company's resources.

A project manager must be able to perform six basic functions well in order to run successful projects:

1. *Manage the project scope*—The project manager needs to make sure the team works on what is needed for the project and nothing else.
2. *Manage human resources*—The team must work together. This doesn't just happen; it takes a directed effort.
3. *Manage communications*—This occurs at many levels, such as with team mates, customers, managers, vendors, and others.
4. *Manage the schedule*—The project manager must keep people on schedule and delivering work on time.
5. *Manage quality*—The project manager needs to make sure that all work performed meets with customer-expected levels of quality.
6. *Manage costs*— The project manager must keep an eye on the budget to make sure all the work can be done without exceeding the allocated budget.

Whether project managers are born or made or somewhere in between, none are successful without training and experience. The soft skills they are born with must be honed and improved with each project. Technical skills are often teachable but must be learned over time as well. No one learns everything there is to know about IT. It is a constantly changing field, and project managers must continually update their knowledge.

WHERE IN THE ORGANIZATION DOES A PROJECT MANAGER WORK?

The projects described in this textbook take place in **organizations** that are trying to complete a set of objectives using IT as the enabler. Organizations exist in many sizes, industries, cultures, and structures. To increase your chances of success as a project manager, you must understand how organizations work (and not work, as the case may be). Every organization creates a unique structure, perhaps developed through years of evolutionary adjustments due to many forces. But many similar traits can be found even when terminology and names vary. As the globe continues to shrink, due largely to advances in technology, it becomes critical for project managers to understand their own organizations and how their projects collaborate with external entities.

There is no one best way for organizations to be structured. From a project perspective, organizational structure can have a significant impact on the success of many IT projects. The structure can control the official communications channels; who is hired, fired, or promoted; who gets put on what team; and the directing of activities for subordinates. As a project manager, you may not have much of a say in how the organization is structured, but if you understand the influence a structure may have on your project, you might be able to convince management to make some adjustments, or at the very least, you will know how to function better in the current environment. Each of the three structures discussed in this section (traditional, matrix, and project) has benefits and drawbacks associated with trying to run a successful IT project. No one structure is the best in all situations.

Organizational Structure / Project Characteristics	Functional	Matrix			Projectized
		Weak Matrix	Balanced Matrix	Strong Matrix	
Project manager's authority	Little or none	Limited	Low to moderate	Moderate to high	High to almost total
Resource availability	Little or none	Limited	Low to moderate	Moderate to high	High to almost total
Who controls the project budget	Functional manager	Functional manager	Mixed	Project manager	Project manager
Project manager's role	Part time	Part time	Full time	Full time	Full time
Project management administrative staff	Part time	Part time	Part time	Full time	Full time

FIGURE 1-5   Organizational Structure Influences on Projects

Source: Project Management Institute, *Guide to the Project Management Body of Knowledge,* Fifth Edition, p. 22.

The *Guide to the PMBOK* provides a summary of some key differentiators for organizational structures. Figure 1-5 compares functional, three forms of matrix, and project structures, using the characteristics project management authority, resource availability, project budget control, project manager's role, and project's administrative staff. Each of these characteristics will be used in the discussion of each type of structure later in this section.

Organizational Structures (Formal and Informal)

Many organizations publish, at least internally, their formal structure in the form of a chart similar to those shown in the following pages. The structure shows the official line of authority, all the departments that exist, and (at least by title) the major responsibilities of each. Many small to medium organizations might not have officially created organizational charts for many reasons. If an organization does not have one, a project manager should develop one to make sure he or she understands the authority relationships. The project manager must know who has the proper authority to make decisions, to hire and fire staff, and to affect pay. Just as important to the success of the project are the informal relationships that exist. An informal chart will not exist in any official capacity, but a project manager should discern and draw such a chart. A good practice is to draw an informal chart by drawing dashed lines on top of the existing formal organizational chart. The dashed lines represent the informal relationships. Such informal relationships exist in every organization, at all levels, and they represent how individuals associate based on friendships, shared interests, family, and others. These relationships can create powerful subgroups within the organization and can have a significant impact on a project. Learning what these relationships are and learning to use them can have a major influence on the success of your project.

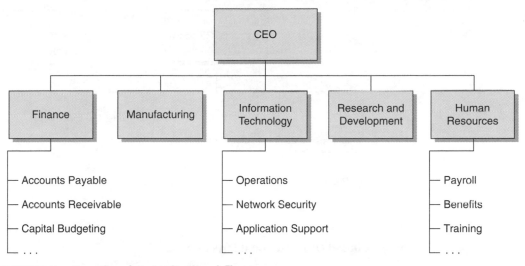

FIGURE 1-6   Functional Organizational Chart

THE TRADITIONAL ORGANIZATIONAL STRUCTURE (FUNCTIONAL, PRODUCT, CUSTOMER, PRO-CESS, GEOGRAPHIC)   A traditional structure is organized around one of these characteristics: job function, end product, customer groups, a specific process, or geographic location. Figure 1-6 represents an organization structured around job function. Organizations have found that this structure has contributed to the poor track record of IT projects discussed earlier including: It is not very adaptable, there is no accountability across department boundaries (large IT projects always cross boundaries), it does not adapt to rapid changes in technology or the supply chain, and customers are spread out across many different departments.

The functional structure has the following benefits:

- An individual can specialize and become proficient in one area. For example, a systems analyst who has spent the past 10 years supporting users with issues related to inventory control applications will know everything there is to know about how the process works and how the computer applications supporting the process work.
- Communication channels are well established. If you look at the chart, you can quickly see who is in charge of what and who you need to talk to about issues and problems.
- There is good control over resources because each has only one boss.
- Budgeting and cost control are relatively easy because all budgets are differentiated by defined department boundaries.
- Traditional advancement occurs within the functional department.

The functional structure has the following drawbacks:

- The project manager holds the least amount of authority compared to the other two organization structures (refer to Figure 1-5). Because of this, getting the right resources, in terms of people and money, can be much more difficult.
- Resources may be underutilized, and resources may be misallocated. If the project manager needs resources from another department, he or she may have little say in which ones are provided. The department providing resources doesn't want to

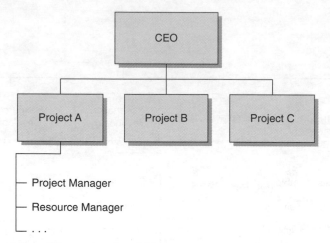

FIGURE 1-7   Project-Based Organizational Structure

lose its best people, even if it is not utilizing them to the full extent possible, and the project manager may get a less-than-optimum choice.

- This model does not take advantage of the economies of scale gained when sharing resources (people and materials) across projects. For example, say your organization has two projects running, and each one needs a senior database analyst on a part-time basis. Each project goes out and hires a consultants from each of two different firms. Many firms discount services based on volume purchases, so if the two projects had combined their requests, they might have gotten a discount and saved money.
- An individual's exposure to knowledge outside one's department is limited which may slow or halt career progression.
- The focus is not always on the project; everyone has his or her own job to do in addition to working on projects.

PROJECT-BASED ORGANIZATIONAL STRUCTURE   The project-based organizational structure is shown in Figure 1-7. This structure is organized completely around projects, and sometimes it exists only for the duration of one particular project. The organization created to host the 2012 Summer Olympic Games held in London, England, and the 2012 presidential election committees for all candidates are examples of teams brought together from many different sources for just one project that were disbanded when the project was completed. Many IT consulting companies are project based. Although a few individuals must perform some administration functions, answer the phones, and so on, most in the firm are billing customers for the time they spend on their projects.

The project-based structure has the following benefits:

- One manager has authority and accountability.
- The project manager has authority for work assignments and staff salary reviews.
- Communication channels are direct and open.
- Adaptability to changes is increased, and decision-making power is put in the hands of the project manager, who is involved in the process daily.

- Project managers can build up considerable expertise from repetition of similar technologies. They can run projects that are based on similar types of applications or technologies, and with each one, they gain critical knowledge and experience.

The project-based structure has the following drawbacks:

- There is the potential for underutilization of resources or misallocation of resources, and the sharing of resources across projects can suffer from issues similar to those of a functional structure.
- It does not take advantage of economies of scale when sharing resources (people and materials) across projects.
- Project myopia can set in: Project managers can see only the project they are working on and may lose sight of the bigger picture when they're focused on only their particular projects.
- Career progression possibilities may be limited. Project-based organizations tend to be flatter because there are fewer levels of management, which means there are also fewer possibilities for promotions. The opportunities for growth are dependent on the number of projects that people are working on.
- Support for administrative functions is more difficult, and the organization must find a way to charge each project for the support functions that span a number of projects, such as office staff, sales and marketing, and support for office computer systems.

MATRIX ORGANIZATIONAL STRUCTURE (WEAK TO STRONG)   Figure 1-8 shows an example of a matrix organizational structure. This structure was created as a way to combine the benefits of the functional structure and the benefits of the project structure into one organization. Organizations have come to realize the importance of adaptability and rapid change. The world is changing at an ever-increasing rate, and organizations must adopt a structure that is dynamic. Workers report to their functional supervisors for matters related to their specialization (accountants report to their accounting manager, manufacturing engineers report to their manager) and annual job performance reviews, and they report to project leaders for work assignments associated with specific projects. Despite the problems associated with this type

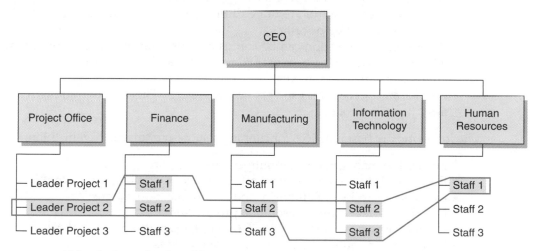

FIGURE 1-8 Matrix Organizational Structure

of structure (for example, workers can have multiple bosses with conflicting agendas), many organizations are moving to this type of arrangement because it also offers many benefits. If implemented correctly, the matrix structure holds great promise for increasing the success of projects. See the section on critical success factors below for building a matrix organization.

Matrix organizations come in three general forms: weak, balanced, and strong. Each type represents a different level of project manager authority and a different time commitment from project team members (Figure 1-5). The determination of a weak to strong matrix structure is primarily determined by two criteria: whether the project manager is assigned to the project full time or part time and the level of authority granted to the project manager. In many balanced and strong matrix organizations, a project office has been created to manage all projects and add visibility to the importance of projects to the organization. (Chapter 14 of this text covers project offices in greater detail.)

The matrix structure has the following benefits:

- There is formal project accountability, and the project is highly visible throughout the organization.
- It is more dynamic and adaptable to change than the other structures.
- Sharing of knowledge across projects is enhanced. The project office is responsible for monitoring all projects across the entire organization, and it becomes the archive for all project information.
- Policies and procedures can vary across projects. The organization can have one project management process, with allowed variations based on the type and size of a project. (Chapter 2 provides more detail on project methodologies.)
- There is less stress about a project ending. In a project-based organization, when a project ends, a person's job may go away as well if there isn't another project waiting.

The matrix structure has the following drawbacks:

- Multiple supervisors have competing priorities. For example, the head of network support in the IT department may need to get the latest security patch applied to all the servers at the same time the manufacturing department needs the best network analyst to do an expansion of the network into the new manufacturing facility.
- Budget and cost control are more difficult, mainly due to having multiple supervisors with competing priorities.
- Project team motivation can be confusing. For example, an employee may wonder whether to listen to her boss who controls her salary or to the project manager who is giving her work assignments.
- Policies and procedures can vary across projects. This is both a strength and a weakness, if not controlled.

The following are best practices for running a successful matrix organization:

- Ensure top management commitment and support.
- Establish a project management office and clearly delineate its role.
- Establish clear lines of authority and communication channels.
- Establish formal conflict-resolution procedures.
- Use a holistic or systems approach to select, execute, and control projects.
- Establish and control the project close-out process.

CHOOSING THE CORRECT ORGANIZATIONAL STRUCTURE   As you can see from this discussion, there are many criteria to consider when making a decision about which organizational structure to use. Much research has been done to determine the best structure to match the type of project being executed. (Sadler, 1971; Argyris, 1967; Youker, 1977) Are you dealing with a research and development project, a major system upgrade, a minor software application update, or a major enterprise resource planning (ERP) system project? All these types of projects fare better or worse under different structures. What does an organization do when it has a number of types of projects going on at the same time?

This same research has shown that different structures work differently in their ability to control elements of the triple constraint: cost versus time versus scope. Research from Kent Crawford at PM Solutions suggests that more and more firms are moving to some form of a matrix organization to try to get the best of both worlds—to gain more formal project control without giving up the benefits of the traditional forms of organizational structure (Crawford, 2002).

Chapter Review

1. Projects exist in every part of our lives, personal and work. At work, IT is growing in importance for every organization, and thus IT-based projects are also growing in importance.

2. IT projects are growing in size, complexity, and strategic importance. For these reasons, IT project management has grown more difficult and requires advanced project management skills.

3. IT projects are unique, requiring special tools and techniques. The following categories demonstrate some of the key differences: requirement changes, sources of changes, requirements themselves, resources required, implementation plans, and testing.

4. The key benefits of a structured project management process are improvement in customer satisfaction, better cost performance, better schedule performance, increased quality, and increased number of delivered features.

5. Project management was devised as a means to speed up the delivery of military projects. The result was a discipline that involves the definition of roles, tools, and processes that, when executed, direct a project to achieve the specified goals.

Some of the early key tools created were PERT, WBS, and the Gantt chart.

6. In the 1990s, interest in project management soared because of a convergence of a number of factors: more powerful computers and software, standard practices and processes being defined and adopted, and widespread use of the Internet and global competition.

7. A *project* is a temporary sequence of related activities that must be completed to create a unique product or service. A project is defined as having three characteristics: temporary, unique, progressively elaborate.

8. *Project management* is defined as a process of applying knowledge, tools, and techniques to a project's activities to deliver stated project requirements within agreed-upon scope, time, cost, and quality constraints.

9. Every project is constrained by its scope, time, and cost, referred to as the *triple constraint*. Project managers must continually balance these three constraints in order to be successful. Some authors add a fourth constraint: quality. If any one of the constraints changes either intentionally or unintentionally, the project manager must negotiate changes in the others to keep the project on target.

10. The results of a number of studies demonstrate a critical need for better project managers and project management processes.
11. Project management requires a diverse set of skills. This chapter lists many of them under the soft skills category and technical skills category.
12. Organizations use many different types of structures to accomplish their goals: functional, project based, and matrix structures. Each offers strengths and weaknesses for the execution of successful projects.

Glossary

organization   A system composed of human and physical resources working together to achieve shared goals.

project   A temporary sequence of related activities that must be completed to create a unique product or service.

project management   The process of applying knowledge, tools, and techniques to a project's activities to deliver stated project requirements within agreed-upon scope, time, cost, and quality constraints.

triple constraint   Scope, time, and cost objectives that have to be balanced in order to deliver successful projects.

Review Questions

1. What factors have the biggest impact on IT project?
2. What are the key differences between IT projects and projects in other disciplines?
3. What changes are organizations making because of the differences mentioned in question 2?
4. What are the potential advantages to using a structured project management approach?
5. What were some of the earliest tools and techniques used by project managers?
6. Who developed the Gantt chart, and what need did it fulfill?
7. What were the primary reasons for the growth in project management during the 1970s?
8. What were the primary reasons for the growth in project management during the 1990s?
9. What is the definition of a *project*?
10. What are the key characteristics that describe a project?
11. What is project management?
12. What is a "death march" project?
13. A project manager manages projects by doing what four high-level activities?
14. What is the triple constraint of project management?
15. What is the fourth constraint of project management that some authors include?
16. What factors mentioned in the Standish Group's CHAOS study were responsible for improvements in project success rates?
17. Good project managers have a combination of skills from which two general skill sets?
18. What are the six basic functions project managers perform to run successful projects?
19. List the three organizational structures described in this chapter.
20. Which of the three organizational structures are organizations gravitating toward in order to improve their project success rates? Why?

Problems and Exercises

1. For organizations to prosper today, they must embrace project management principles to increase productivity and ROI in order to create a competitive advantage locally and globally. Explain why you agree or disagree with this statement.
2. Discuss the reasons why IT projects differ from projects in other disciplines. What implications does this have for modern IT project managers?
3. Describe the events that led up to the beginnings of project management in the United States during the 1950s. Also describe some of the early tools used by project managers.
4. Describe what happened during the 1970s to spur the growth in project management and compare and contrast this with the events that occurred during the 1990s and that are occurring today.
5. In your own words, explain what a project is and describe its key characteristics.
6. Explain what the term "death march" project means and why such projects should be avoided at all costs. In your opinion, why do you believe organizations continue with such projects?
7. This chapter reports some distressing statistics about the success rates of IT projects. Explain why you believe IT projects have such low success rates. What can be done to improve the numbers?
8. Define the project management triple constraint and explain its significance to project managers.
9. This chapter mentions quality as a possible fourth constraint of project management. Explain how quality is affected by and affects the other three constraints.
10. Explain the skills project managers need to possess in order to have repeated successes in running projects both from a soft skill perspective and technical skill perspective.
11. How important is it for a project manager running an IT project to have technical skills in the technology being used in the project he or she is running? Explain.
12. Compare and contrast the three principal organizational structures (traditional, project based, and matrix) described in this chapter and explain the levels of project manager authority that exist in each.
13. Describe the difference between formal and informal organizational charts and their significance to project managers.
14. Based on the project success rates associated with each type of organizational structure, why don't all organizations switch to a project-based structure?
15. Explain the difference between a weak matrix structure and a strong matrix structure.

Projects and Research

1. If you have done an internship or a co-op, or if you are currently working for an organization, explain the company's current organizational structure and why it is in place. You will probably need to interview someone from the human resources department as well as someone from the IT department. You could also use the surrounding community to locate an organization and interview someone from its human resources staff to find out what type of organizational structure it uses and why.
2. Interview someone who is a full-time project manager. Find out what this person feels are his or her strengths and weaknesses and compare this list of skills with the list presented in this chapter.
3. Use the web site of the Project Management Institute, www.pmi.org, as well as other sites to research the creation of the *Guide to the PMBOK* and how it has evolved over time to its current edition. Explain its significance to the project management profession.
4. Write a short paper, describing two projects you have worked on previously either during an internship, in class, or as a full-time employee. Describe one project that went well and why and describe one project that didn't go very well and why. In the summary, explain why you believe IT projects have a poor success rate.

1. *Background:* Mike, a newly hired IT project manager with many years of experience, works for A-Parts, a midsize automobile parts manufacturer located in Kalamazoo, Michigan. The company has experienced major revenue growth over the past couple years and needs to upgrade many of its old software applications. Jeff Smith, the owner and CEO of the privately owned company, has realized that the company needs to do a better job of running projects to cope with the new large upgrade projects, so he hired Mike. A-Parts is organized around job functions (see the following organizational chart). The first major project Mike has been asked to run is the new accounting and inventory control software upgrade. The entire suite of accounting software will be replaced, along with the inventory control software used in the warehouse. The two systems will be linked together such that data updates that occur in either system will be recorded in the other system simultaneously. Therefore, it will be extremely important for the two groups to work together to make sure the project is a success.

Current Situation: The project is 30 days old and is already in some trouble. The two key sponsors, the vice president of accounting and the vice president of manufacturing, can't seem to agree on one application solution. Each wants a solution that fulfills his needs best, and the IT department would need to write custom code to get the applications to share information. The two sponsors are also not very willing to relinquish their best personnel to work on the project because they fear that these individuals will not be able to fulfill their current work responsibilities. Mike has been trying to create an amiable solution, with both parties giving up something, but so far he's had no luck. Jeff has been reluctant to step in; he prefers they handle it themselves. Part of the problem is that Mike reports to the IT supervisor, who reports to the vice president of accounting, so he is feeling pressured to do things that favor the accounting department over manufacturing. Mike decides that maybe a different organizational structure is necessary to help solve some of the issues.

Discussion: Describe the current organizational structure for A-Parts and summarize its strength and weaknesses. What suggestions do you have for Mike to improve the situation at A-Parts? Do you feel that a different organizational structure would help the situation? If so, which one? Explain.

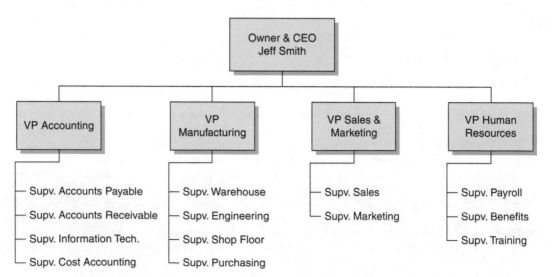

2. *Background:*   Heidi is an excellent experienced systems analyst for State First Insurance Company. She has been with State First for 15 years and has received many excellent annual reviews based on her performance. Her boss, Juan Carlos who has been in the position for a short time, inherited a project from his predecessor to automate the claims processing from the field insurance offices back to the corporate office. The project has been running for nearly a year, with little progress. Juan decides to change the project leader and give the job to Heidi because she has years of experience with the company and has been a good systems analyst. Juan's instructions to Heidi are just go get this project done; it's her number-one priority.

Current Situation: After one week on the project, Heidi has discovered the following: The vendor selected to do the wide area connection has since gone out of business, and another vendor has yet to be selected. The original budget for the project of $400,000 has already been spent—and then some. The initial time line called for a pilot project to start next February, but it is now December, and there is not a chance that the February date can be met. The key component of the system is the custom code that needs to be developed between the field agent's software and the corporate database. The lead software developer for this effort just left the company for a job that offers more pay and fewer hours.

Discussion: This project would certainly fall into the category of a "death march" project. Explain what this means and what Heidi's next steps should be. Can this project be saved? If so, how? Based on what you know from the case study, should Juan have given this project to Heidi? Explain.

Suggested Readings

Argyris, C. (1967). Today's problems with tomorrow's organizations. *The Journal of Management Studies*. February, pp. 31–55.

Barker, J., Tjosvold, D., & Andrews, R. (1998). Conflict approaches of effective and ineffective project managers: A field study in a matrix organization. *Journal of Management Studies* 25(2):167–178.

Bartels, A. (2008). Global IT 2008 market outlook. Retrieved from www.forrester.com/go?docid=44429.

Bozzelli, T. (2007). A global insights report. Retrieved from www.government-insights.com.

Brooks, F.P. 1987 (April). No silver bullet: Essence and accidents of software engineering. *IEEE Computer* 20(4):10–19.

Chabrow, E. (2004). 270K fewer workers will have been hired in 2004. *InformationWeek*. Retrieved from www.informationweek.com/news/global-cio/showArticle.jhtml?articleID=46802605.

Chaos (1995). Chaos chronicles. Retrieved from www.standishgroup.com.

Cook, R. (2008). Closing the governance gap with project portfolio management (PPM). Retrieved from www.cio.com/article/397215/Closing_the_Governance_Gap_With_Project_Portfolio_Management_PPM.

Crawford, J. K. (2002). The strategic project office: A guide to improving organizational performance. Marcel Dekker/Center for Business Practices.

DeMarco, T. (1997). *The deadline*. New York: Dorset House Publishing.

Galbraith, J.R. (1971). Matrix organization designs: How to combine functional and product forms. *Business Horizons* 14, pp. 29–40.

Gross, G. (2005). *White House 2006 budget proposal would boost IT spending*. February 8, 2005. Retrieved from www.computerworld.com/printthis/2005/0,4814,99618,00.html.

Gulla, J. (2012). Seven reasons IT projects fail. *IBM Systems Magazine*. Retrieved from www.ibm systemsmag.com/mainframe/tipstechniques/applicationdevelopment/project_pitfalls/.

Hoffman, T. (2004, September 6). CIOs foresee modest boost in IT spending. *ComputerWorld*. Retrieved from www.computerworld.com/action/article.do?command=viewArticleBasic&articleId=95700.

Jones, C. (2007). *Estimating software costs: Bringing realism to estimating.* New York: McGraw Hill.

Krantz, G. (2004, September 15). *Outsourcing trend touches independents, too.* Retrieved from http://searchcio.techtarget.com/originalContent/ 0,289142,sid19_gci1006375,00.html.

Melymuka, K. (2004, September 20). Sidebar: The keepers. *ComputerWorld.* Retrieved from www.computerworld.com/careers/story/0,10801,959 45,00.html.

Sadler, P. (1971). Designing an organizational structure. *Management International Review.* Vol. 11, No. 6, pp. 19–33.

Sondergaard, P. (2008). Opening keynote address. Gartner symposium/ITexpo, Orlando Florida.

Souder, W.E. 1983. Project evaluation and selection. In D.I. Cleland and W.R. King, eds., *Project management handbook.* New York: Van Nostrand Reinhold.

Werderitsch, A.J. (1990). Project Management Oversight: An independent project assessment. *Cost Engineering* July 32(7):19.

Wilder, C & Davis, B. (1998, November 30). False starts, strong finishes. *InformationWeek.*

Youker, R. (1977). Organizational alternatives for project management. *Project Management Quarterly.* Vol. VIII, No.1, March 1977.

Yourdon, E. (1997). *Death march: The complete software developer's guide to surviving "mission impossible" projects.* Upper Saddle River, NJ: Prentice Hall.

Yourdon, E. (2002). *Managing high-intensity internet projects.* Upper Saddle River, NJ: Prentice Hall.

2

A Systems View and Systems Methodology

R & S Amusements Services

Event 2

Setting *Jeff Dunbar and Reid Lewis are sitting in Reid Lewis's office, having a cup of coffee and talking.*

REID Jeff, I have been meaning to tell you how pleased I am that you and Kevin are working with us on improving our information systems around here. We definitely need the help.

JEFF Thanks, Reid. That's our job, and believe me, you are not alone in needing help with your information technology projects. In fact, because information technology changes so often, it seems like a never-ending process. Businesses have become so dependent on computers and software to help manage and run their operation that any new software release that offers increased functionality or computer hardware that makes a process more efficient, leading to increased profits, must be addressed in order for the organization to be and/or remain competitive.

REID That's definitely true, even in our business. We now have video games—the ones you play in arcades that connect to the Internet so the person playing can play against people playing the same game in other parts of the world. We consistently have to upgrade the game technology we offer to entice people to play and continue to play the games. If we don't, another operator will, and we'll lose business.

JEFF So you have a basic understanding of the environment we work in.

REID I won't give myself that much credit, even though I have had some formal training in information systems development.

JEFF You have. That's good!

REID Yes. When I became interested in computers and started messing around with programming, I foolishly envisioned doing all of our information systems work myself. So I enrolled in a couple courses, one being a systems course that taught me the systems development life cycle, or how

	to follow a process to build a system. "Piece of cake," I thought, until I tried to do it myself. Needless to say, I'm better off in the entertainment game industry.
JEFF	Don't be too hard on yourself; I applaud you for starting out the right way—recognizing that to have the best chance to succeed, you must follow a tried-and-true process or methodology. Not understanding this is a mistake that most beginners make. It takes years of education, training, and experience to be good in this business—that's what makes it so difficult. It's one thing to create a single-user application that only runs on a single computer, but to create a multiuser application that runs on multiple computers, interfaces with other computer systems, and contains complex business rules and logic is a totally different matter. It takes someone or most likely a group of people with a high level of skill and knowledge to do that.
REID	That's what is hard for me to comprehend. It seems that everything that we have to do in systems development is enormous in terms of scope and complexity. And we are not even a Fortune 500 company; I can't imagine the magnitude of their systems. How do you know where to begin? What do we do first? Can't it get out of control and overwhelming?
JEFF	It can if it's not managed properly. That's why we utilize a systems approach, along with sound project management processes and principles.
REID	What do you mean by *systems approach?*
JEFF	It's the process of examining problems or opportunities in their environment or in the entire organization and then decomposing those problems into smaller components, thus making them easier to understand and then solve, and finally managing the resolution of those problems. [*Reid looks confused*] It's utilizing the systems development life cycle you mentioned earlier to plan, identify requirements, design the solution, and then implement it, all the while using a separate methodology to manage it all. The key is using the appropriate systems development life cycle or process, based on the characteristics of the project.
REID	Do you mean there are different types of life cycles?
JEFF	Yes, there are, and the one you use depends on the type of product you are building and your project characteristics, such as team size, criticality of the application, purchased versus custom-made software solution, and so on. Using the right methodology gives you the best chance for a successful project. In addition, there is a life cycle for the management of building the product, which encompasses the product life cycle. This facilitates the building of multiple products in parallel or in sequence.
REID	This is going to be an extreme learning experience for me!
JEFF	It will be for both of us—I will be learning about your business, and you will become more familiar with mine.
REID	I can't wait. Say, let's go get a refill of coffee, and then you can tell me how we are going to get started.

CHAPTER PREVIEW AND OBJECTIVES

Repeatable successes for project managers, the meeting of project objectives over and over again, come from their ability to establish and utilize a standard project management life cycle (PMLC) in all their projects and across the organization and to manage the relationship between the PMLC to the different systems development life cycles (SDLCs) used to create products. A project has a life cycle that is separate from but integrated with the product's SDLC. It's important for project managers to understand their individual project within the context of their entire environment, using the systems approach. This chapter describes the systems approach to project management, the process life cycles associated with projects and various products, and how to integrate the two types of life cycles. You will understand these topics when you can:

- Define the systems approach and its impact on project management
- Define a PMLC and understand how to apply it
- Define several SDLC models and know when to use each different type
- Define the relationship between the PMLC and the SDLC and understand how the two work together

THE SYSTEMS APPROACH TO PROJECT MANAGEMENT

In the early stages of most information technology (IT) education programs, students are taught to examine any proposed issue or opportunity by breaking it down into smaller and smaller parts in order to completely understand the total process and then offer a proposed solution. For example, say that a company's sales and marketing department has approached the IT department about adding a shopping cart feature to the company web site. It would allow customers to place orders online, adding and removing items until they are ready to process their order (check out). The IT department is excited because it would be a very cool technology to work with and put on the site. But someone, ideally senior management and the project manager, needs to take a step back and ask: Before we implement that feature, how will this affect and be affected by other projects already under way? What are our competitors doing? When should this be done in relation to other projects waiting to start or already executing? Someone, the project manager or the organization's decision makers, needs to understand that before the company decides to start a project, it first needs to understand the whole picture. It needs to understand where this project will fit into the group of projects already started or being proposed. What if another group of users had approached the IT department about upgrading the company's inventory control system, and management had decided it was a good idea and that project had already begun? These two systems would probably need to work together, but if no one knows about the other, problems will most certainly appear. In large IT departments, this scenario happens all too often.

The **systems approach** is a process that allows projects to be viewed in the context of the entire environment, including both inside and outside the organization. It is a process that can bring order and discipline to a large, chaotic, unorganized situation. It is the opposite of an analytical process, which takes the whole and breaks it into its component parts. Project managers, to be successful, must learn to use a systems approach.

The systems approach consists of three interrelated components: systems theory, systems analysis, and systems management. In the next section, we define each of these components and draw correlations between systems terms and project management practice. It is not within the scope of this text to give a complete lesson in systems theory, but this chapter provides enough information on the discipline and terminology to understand it and apply it as a project manager.

Systems theory involves a philosophy of or a way of looking at the world—a language or set of principles and interventions for thinking and problem solving. Some of the key terms are described next, along with their implications for project managers.

A project doesn't occur in a vacuum; it exists within a **system**. There are two broad categories of systems: open and closed. A *closed system* is considered to be completely self-contained; to understand it, you merely look on the inside, without regard to the external environment. A machine is a closed system; to understand how it works, you simply open it up and study the internal mechanisms. An *open system* is not self-defining; to understand it, you must also understand its environment. The human body and organizations are examples of open systems. They have the ability to affect and be affected by their environments and adapt. This concept of open systems is very important to project management because it is where projects take place. The following are a few key terms you need to be familiar with in order to understand the systems approach:

- **Subsystem**—A system is made up of subsystems, smaller systems that are part of a larger system. For example, the human heart is a subsystem of the human body, and the accounts receivable subsystem is a part of the financial software system of an organization.
- **Element**—An element is the smallest part of a system. What is defined as an element varies depending on the level of understanding needed at a particular point in time. If you are investigating the detailed workings of an order processing software subsystem, you need to break it down into smaller pieces, such as entering new orders, checking inventory, and checking customer addresses. These pieces become the elements for the order processing software subsystem. The accounts receivable subsystem is considered an element at this time because you don't yet need to understand its inner workings.
- **Attribute**—Attributes are individual characteristics that are part of systems and subsystems. In defining a new software system, you define attributes such as business requirements and database schemas. In project management, you define attributes such as budgets, schedules, and activities or tasks.
- **Boundary**—A boundary surrounds a system and separates it from its environment (see Figure 2-1). Most of what a project manager does exists on the boundary: How

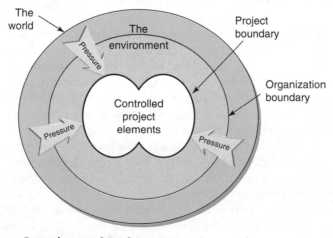

FIGURE 2-1 **Systems Boundary and Environment**

do you keep other projects from taking your key resources away, how do you foresee a new government regulation coming and its affect on your project, and how do you convince management not to cut your budget when there are cash flow issues?

- **Environment**—The environment is everything that exists outside the system or outside the control of the project manager (see Figure 2-1). In this text, when we refer to the *environment*, we are speaking specifically about those factors in the environment that are relevant to the system being studied. The organization, governments, economies, foreign countries, and so on all have roles in the environment.
- **Objectives**—Open systems are designed to do something to change an input into an output via an internal process. The something that the system is designed to do is spelled out in the list of objectives. IT projects consist of customer-driven requirements or outputs needed from the system. Based on the desired outcomes and your knowledge of the inputs, you must build a project plan that describes the process of changing the inputs into outputs (meeting the objectives) and dealing with the changes the environment brings.
- **Constraints**—Every system has limitations forced on it from internal forces or external forces, and sometimes the limits are self-controlled. We would all like to play basketball like Michael Jordan, but most of us have limitations on our abilities. In Chapter 1, we discussed the triple constraint of project management as limits in terms of scope, time, and cost.
- **Integration**—For a system to reach its objectives, all the subsystems and elements must work together effectively. Let's look at the Michael Jordan analogy again: For Michael to perform at his best, he had to condition his body as well as his brain, the two had to work together. In project management, we must make sure to manage the items both inside and outside the boundary.

Figure 2-1 is a depiction of the environment that project managers must understand and learn to work in. Using the systems approach will help project managers to identify and understand all the pressures that the external environment can create. Once identified, these pressures need to be dealt with or at least compensated for to prevent them from wreaking havoc with the project. Too many organizations and project managers in the past have tried to act as if they are isolated from their environment. Cleland and King (1972) state that managers must:

- Appreciate the need to assess forces in the environment
- Understand the forces that significantly affect their organization
- Integrate these forces into the organization's goals, objectives, and operations

Although all projects are influenced by forces in the environment—such as new government regulations, withdrawal of funding, and technology obsolescence—these forces cannot be allowed, if at all possible, to control the outcome of the project. Project managers working on the boundary must strive to keep this from happening on a daily basis. Techniques such as risk analysis and SWOT analysis (both explained in Chapters 3 and 4) are two tools that project managers can use to keep environment forces in check.

Systems analysis is "a problem-solving technique that decomposes a system into its component pieces for the purpose of studying how well those component parts work and interact to accomplish their purpose" (Whitten, Bentley, & Dittman, 2004, p. 38). In traditional systems development projects, a systems analyst studies the needs presented by users and attempts to understand them and have them understood by others by reducing a complex high-level set of requirements down into smaller and smaller elements. The smaller elements can then be defined, estimated, and understood by all team participants. The smaller elements are then purchased or constructed and put together to form the whole. For example, a user comes to the IT department with a high-level list of requirements to build a web site that will represent the entire organization. As is common, this list isn't very detailed or complete: "We want information on the web site that tells potential customers who we are, where we are located, our philosophy, and what products we offer at each site." It's not until the analyst begins breaking this down into its elements that a more complete list of needs can be ascertained (for example, the color schemes, technologies, back-end systems to integrate with, search capabilities, menu styles).

The systems management component is responsible for the management of the whole system—objectives, environment (both internal and external), constraints, resources (both human and other), and the culture and social environment of the organization. This is what project management is all about.

Review "The Project Management Chronicles" feature at the beginning of this chapter and notice how Jeff explains the use of the systems approach to Reid. When you, as a project manager, are handed a project to manage, one of the first things you need to do is put the project in context. Getting answers to the following questions as soon as possible will help your project get off to a great start:

- Who is the project sponsor?
- What other ongoing or pending projects might have an impact on this project?
- What outside influences could have an impact on my project?
- What early constraints, if any, have been placed on the project from scope, time, and cost perspectives?

Learning to take a systems approach is not easy, especially for those new to the working world, but it is possible if you are willing to put time and effort into it. The next section of this chapter explains the processes associated with the PMLC and the SDLC. It also explains how the two must work together to achieve project success.

THE PROJECT MANAGEMENT LIFE CYCLE

Project managers and their project teams divide projects into phases to facilitate better control and communication. When you put these phases together into a prescribed order, you have the project's **life cycle**. Each project life cycle should have a beginning and an end. Each phase should have defined deliverables and criteria that signal that it is time to move from one phase to the next. Having a project broken down into phases also gives the team and management good places to take snapshots of how the project is performing. Many call these gaps between phases **stage gates**. After reviewing a project's progress, management should decide whether to proceed with the project or cancel it and not spend any more time or money on it.

Figure 2-2 shows a generic project life cycle that has six phases: initiate, plan, execute, control, close iteration, and close project. These phases have names similar to those of the five major process groups you will read about in Chapter 3, but their meaning here is different. Every organization should create a standard project life cycle in order to promote communication within the team and stakeholders and across all teams in the organization. A project life cycle should include the following:

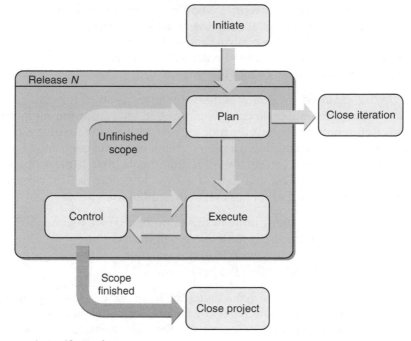

FIGURE 2-2   Project Life Cycle

PROVEN STRATEGIES AND HINTS TO SUCCESS

Bushell (2007) uses a quote from Mike Balle's book titled Systems Thinking: "imagine trying to train a horse to run faster by teaching each of its legs to perform more efficiently." A bit over the top, but point made, and many companies continue to try and make their projects, and thus their companies, better by implementing point solutions—ISO certification, adopt the latest process methodology, or latest fad technique—all in the expectation that each measure in isolation will improve the company. John Parsons wrote in his 2000 paper "Productivity Measurement in the Service Sector," that in the early days of the industrial age it was convenient and advantageous to adopt the traditional philosophy of breaking everything down into its component parts and then studying the parts, but this approach does not work as well in today's complex world. An organization must adopt a systems view of the organization and its projects. The article offers the following key concepts for improvement:

- "Hearts and Minds." Two key facets to improved productivity: the technical (systems, structures, technologies—heart) and the social (culture, quality of work life, organizational climate—mind). Instituting change means formulating a vision, defining core business, ensuring adequate resourcing, and using change management principles providing integrated thinking to make it all happen. The systems approach highlights connections between internal functions, customers and suppliers, organizations and community, and companies and the ecosystem.
- "Measuring What You Manage." Before designing and implementing a performance measurement system, you must understand the nature of the phenomena being measured, why the processes are being measured, who will use the results, and how they will use them.

- What specific work (activities) should be done in each phase
- A definition of each phase's deliverables (outcomes)
- The integrated change control process being used
- What resources are involved with each deliverable
- Criteria that need to be met to complete each phase

In this example, the project is delivered in many small releases, called iterations. Each release follows the life cycle from beginning to end, from the initiate phase to the close phase. Referencing the definition of a project given in Chapter 1 concerning progressive elaboration, each release of a project delivers a small part of the whole, until the entire product is created and you run out of requirements (that is, the scope is complete).

Notice in Figure 2-2 that there are two close phases. The close iteration phase addresses the process steps that happen at the end of each iteration, such as:

- Did we get everything done in this iteration that we planned to?
- If not, what is remaining, and when will this get done?
- What lessons have we learned in this iteration?
- When have we scheduled the next iteration?

The close project phase occurs after the team decides to complete the project. This determination could be attributed to many factors, such as having satisfied all requirements or running out of money. In this final phase, the team updates the project database with the final results, conducts a thorough lessons learned exercise, and releases project resources.

THE PRODUCT SYSTEMS DEVELOPMENT LIFE CYCLE

Many organizations have a formal information systems development process consisting of a standard (repeatable) set of processes or activities that are followed to build a system or product. The **systems development life cycle (SDLC)** is a systems approach to problem solving that organizes these processes into phases and tasks for the purpose of building an information system product, starting with the initial planning processes and carrying through to implementation and support.

Many SDLC methodologies have been developed over the years to guide the development effort. One of the first and most common is the **waterfall model**, which was inherited from the engineering community. Because many aspects of information systems are unique (for example, network infrastructures, hardware, software language, application domain, Internet use, organizational culture, outsourcing), experts in the industry have developed different SDLCs for different types of projects. Examples of these are IBM's *Rational Unified Process (RUP)*, **Scrum**, and **Extreme Programming (XP)**. As you will read in the following sections, there is not one life cycle that's a fit for all; rather, it is up to the project manager and team to select the SDLC that is most appropriate for the project that will give them the best chance for success.

The following sections present several SDLC models and the advantages and disadvantages of each. This is not intended to be an exhaustive list but a representation of the many choices available for building an information system. Project leaders and team members need to learn how to select the best methodology for each project and company culture.

The Waterfall Model

The waterfall model is considered the traditional approach to systems development. It describes a development approach that is linear and sequential, has distinct objectives for each phase, and in which the output of one phase is the input for the next. Boehm and Turner refer to this as plan driven: requirements/design/build paradigm with standard well defined processes that organizations improve continuously (2004). The waterfall model was so named because once water goes over the falls, it can't turn back or go back up. Similarly, in systems development, once a phase has been completed, you can't return to a prior phase (see Figure 2-3). The advantage of waterfall development is that it allows for strict managerial control. The project schedule can be developed with firm deadlines for each phase of the project.

The primary disadvantage of the waterfall model is that it does not easily accommodate changes to requirements. The waterfall approach expects all requirements to be defined in the beginning and to be stable throughout the project. This is not typically the case with today's information system projects; very rarely does the user know 100 percent of what is required upfront, and it is very common for 25 percent to 50 percent of the requirements to change during the course of a project. DeGrace and Stahl (1990) referred to these issues as "wicked problems"—those that are difficult to quantify and for which it is difficult to describe successful solutions. There is generally not a yes/no or true/false answer, but there may be a good/bad distinction. The waterfall approach is typically used because it provides management the most visibility, is easier to manage, and it is best understood within the industry. It lends itself to large, complex applications due to its reliance on documentation and end-of-phase deliverables.

Waterfall Model	
Strengths	**Weaknesses**
• It is well understood.	• It does not accommodate change to requirements very well.
• It is easy to manage.	
• It works with large, complex applications.	• All requirements must be known and defined in the beginning.
• When teams are distributed geographically.	• It does not allow the team to go back and repeat a phase (iterate).
• It does not require experienced IT personnel.	
	• It can not be adapted to different project types very easily.
	• It encourages a communications gap between users and IT personnel.

The Evolutionary Prototyping Model

Evolutionary prototyping focuses on gathering correct and consistent requirements and building a system incrementally through a series of gradual refinements, or prototypes, as indicated in Figure 2-4. In contrast to the traditional waterfall approach, with the evolutionary prototyping model, requirements are discovered throughout the process, and the

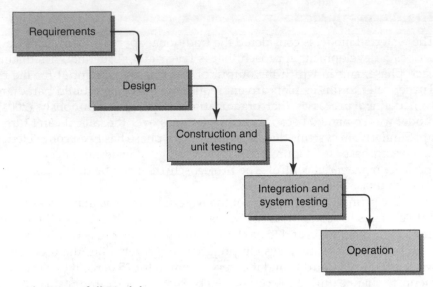

FIGURE 2-3   The Waterfall Model

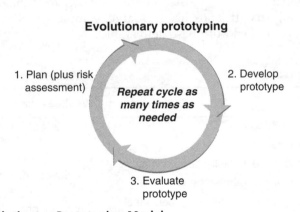

FIGURE 2-4   The Evolutionary Prototyping Model

system is repeatedly refined, based on those discoveries. This approach allows developers to learn from each prototype and apply those lessons to future versions.

The evolutionary prototyping approach is an excellent choice for research and development projects because those types of projects are characterized by having many unknown requirements. In addition, quickly building mockups of system components for user review allows for timely feedback that can be incorporated in the next design or prototype.

The Evolutionary Prototyping Model	
Strengths	**Weaknesses**
• Customers can see steady progress. • This is useful when requirements are changing rapidly, when the customer is reluctant to commit to a set of requirements, or when no one fully understands the application area.	• It is impossible to know at the outset of the project how long it will take. • There is no way to know the number of iterations that will be required. • It is difficult to build an accurate cost estimate.

The Spiral Model

The spiral life cycle model (see Figure 2-5) is based on the classic waterfall model with the addition of risk analysis and iterations. The spiral model emphasizes the need to go back and reiterate earlier stages a number of times as the project progresses. It's actually a series of short waterfall cycles, each producing an early prototype that represents a part of the entire project. This approach helps demonstrate a proof of concept early in the project, and it helps to accurately reflect the complexity of ever-changing technology. The model consists of four main parts, or blocks, and the process is shown by a continuous loop going from the inside toward the outside. The size of the spiral represents the growing size of the application being completed. In Figure 2-5, the angular component represents progress, and the radius of the spiral represents cost.

The Spiral Model	
Strengths	**Weaknesses**
• It is good for large and complex projects. • It accommodates changes well. • It can react to risks very quickly. • Software is produced early in the software life cycle. • It provides increased user visibility.	• It can be a costly model to use. • Risk analysis requires highly specific expertise. • A project's success is highly dependent on the risk analysis phase. • It doesn't work well for small projects.

Iterative and Incremental Model

The iterative and incremental model is an intuitive approach to the waterfall model and is similar to the spiral model. Multiple development cycles (commonly referred to as *timeboxes*) take place in this model (see Figure 2-6). Cycles are divided into smaller, more easily managed iterations. Each iteration passes through the standard life cycle phases. A working version of software is produced during the first iteration, so you have working software early on during the project life cycle. Subsequent iterations build on the initial software produced during the first iteration.

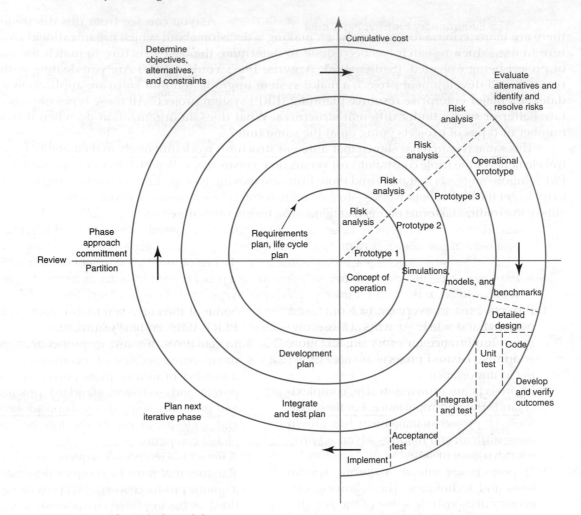

FIGURE 2-5   The Spiral Model

Source: Based on work done by Barry Boehm, A spiral model of software development and enhancement, 1988 Computer Vol. 21, May, pp. 61–72.

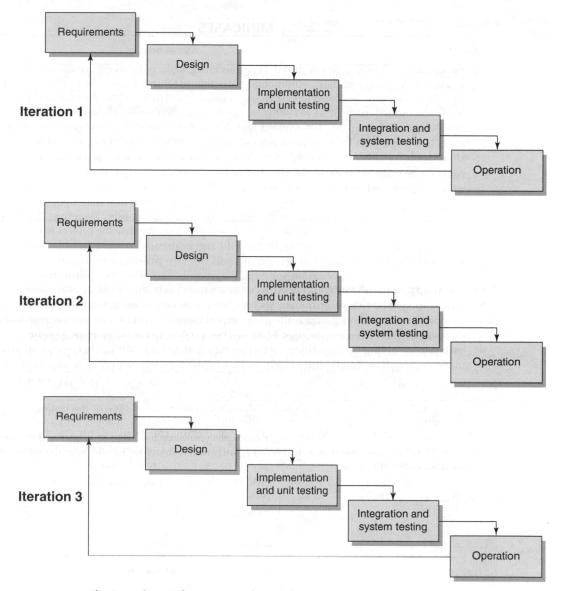

FIGURE 2-6 The Iterative and Incremental Model

Iterative and Incremental Model

Strengths	Weaknesses
• Working software is generated quickly and early during the software life cycle.	• It is not easy to manage.
• It is more flexible than the other methods, and changing scope and requirements is less costly with this model than with others.	• The team must be able to estimate well to plan iterations.
• It is easier to test and debug during a smaller iteration.	• It is difficult to determine cost and time estimates early in the process.
• It is easier to manage risk because risky pieces are identified and handled during the iterations.	• It requires experienced team members.
• Each iteration is an easily managed milestone.	

The Scrum Model

The Scrum approach, developed by Ken Schwaber and Jeff Sutherland, was developed for managing the systems development process. Scrum is based on the concept that software development is not a defined process but an empirical process with complex input-to-output transformations that may or may not be repeated under different circumstances.

The name *Scrum* is essentially derived from the game of rugby. In rugby, a play where two opposing teams attempt to move against each other in large, brute-force groups is called a scrum. Each group must be quick to counter the other's thrust and adjust and exploit any perceived weakness, without the luxury of planning.

The main idea of Scrum is that systems development involves several environmental and technical variables that are likely to change during the process (for example, requirements, time frame, resources, technology). This makes the development process unpredictable and complex, requiring flexibility of the systems development process in order to respond to these changes. As a result of the development process, a useful system is developed. (See Figure 2-7.)

The Scrum Model

Strengths	Weaknesses
• The project is more manageable.	• It doesn't work well with large teams.
• Progress is made even when requirements are not stable.	• It requires experienced developers.
• Everything is visible to everyone.	• It is not good for mission- or life-critical systems.
• Team communication improves.	• It requires hands-on management but not micromanagement.
• The team shares successes along the way and at the end.	• It requires constant monitoring, both quantitatively and qualitatively.
• Customers see on-time delivery of increments.	
• Customers obtain frequent feedback on how the product actually works.	

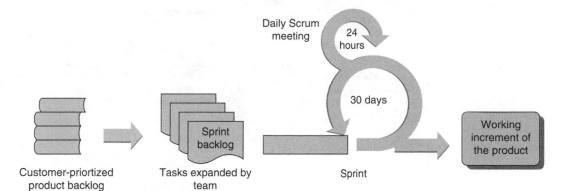

FIGURE 2-7   The Scrum Model

Source: Adapted from Agile Software Development with Scrum by Ken Schwaber and Mike Beedle.

The RUP Model

RUP provides a disciplined approach to assigning tasks and responsibilities within a development organization. Its goal is to ensure the production of high-quality software that meets the needs of end users, within a predictable schedule and budget. RUP is an iterative process that identifies four phases of a software development project: inception, elaboration, construction, and transition. Each phase involves one or more iterations where an executable is produced, but it may be an incomplete system (except possibly in the inception phase). During each iteration, the team performs activities from several disciplines (workflows), in varying levels of detail. Figure 2-8 provides an overview diagram of RUP.

The RUP Model	
Strengths	**Weaknesses**
• Risks are mitigated earlier.	• It is not easy to tailor RUP to smaller projects.
• Change is more manageable.	
• It offers greater reuse.	• It involves a large volume of process guidelines and is very detail heavy.
• The project team can learn along the way.	
• It provides better overall quality.	
• It enhances team productivity by providing every team member with easy access to a knowledge base with guidelines, templates, and tool mentors for all critical development activities.	

The XP Model

Extreme Programming (XP) is arguably the best known of the agile methodologies. XP's basic approach involves short development cycles, frequent updates, dividing business and technical priorities, and assigning user stories. XP has four key values—communication,

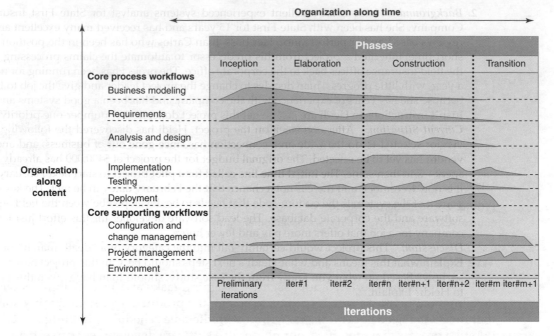

FIGURE 2-8 **The RUP Model**

Source: http://www.ibm.com/developerworks/rational/library/content/03July/1000/1251/
1251_bestpractices_TP026B.pdf

feedback, simplicity, and courage—plus a dozen practices that are followed during XP projects—planning, small releases, metaphor, simple design, refactoring, testing, pair programming, collective ownership, continuous integration, 40-hour week, on-site customer, and coding standards. XP places great emphasis on testing. In fact, XP programmers are required to write tests as they write production code. Because testing is integrated into the build process, a highly stable and expandable product results.

The XP Model

Strengths	Weaknesses
• The project is more manageable.	• It doesn't work well with large teams, geographically dispersed teams, or large projects.
• Progress is made even when requirements are not stable.	
• Everything is visible to everyone.	• It requires experienced developers.
• Team communication improves.	• It is not good for mission- or life-critical systems.
• The team shares successes along the way and at the end.	
• Customers see on-time delivery of increments.	
• Customers obtain frequent feedback on how the product actually works.	

XP is designed to allow small development teams to deliver quickly, change quickly, and change often. XP provides the absolute minimum set of practices that enable small, co-located development teams to function effectively in today's environment of rapid development.

The next section explains how project life cycles and product life cycles work together to reach a successful project solution.

PROVEN STRATEGIES AND HINTS TO SUCCESS

Agile vs. traditional methods (Waterfall) project methodology success rates: successful 42% vs. 14%, challenged 49% vs. 57%, and failed 9% vs. 29%, respectively, as reported from the Chaos reports from the Standish group 2002 through 2010. Scott Ambler found similar results from his annual survey (www.ambysoft.com/surveys): Agile project methodologies delivered higher quality products, higher value, the traditional actually came up with a negative value, and agile had a higher ROI and shorter time to completion. From Ambler, successful agile teams:

- Are more likely to have dedicated business expertise (stakeholders) involved in the project
- Had a working environment and tools that support agile development
- Are organized to support agile development
- Existed in organizations with effective executive sponsorship
- More likely to be measured based on value creation and less likely to be judged based on traditional metrics

From Johnson's (2003) survey of organizations that utilize agile principles in their projects: 93% experienced team productivity improvements, 88% found improved quality of their developed applications, and 83% experienced better business satisfaction with the software.

INTEGRATION OF PROJECT TO PRODUCT LIFE CYCLES

Hopefully you can now see that there is a difference between PMLCs and product SDLCs. Each contains phases, deliverables, and decisions that need to be made before the team can move on to a subsequent phase, but the focus and work product of each are very different. In the IT arena, some of the functions traditionally done in the product development life cycle are now done in the project life cycle, as noted later in this section. Many organizations treat the project life cycle as part of the product life cycle. This text breaks them out separately because they truly are a distinct set of processes and deliverables. The resources responsible for the phase deliverables are also different; the project manager is always ultimately responsible for all deliverables of the project life cycle, and various other resources are responsible for the deliverables of the product life cycle (for example, the database analyst is responsible for the database schema, the network analyst is responsible for the network design).

Figure 2-9 is a diagram of one way to tie together a project life cycle with a product life cycle. After completing the project life cycle initiation phase deliverables, a decision needs to be made about whether to stop the project or to proceed (stage gate). Making a decision to stop a project can be difficult and sometimes a very political decision, but it needs to be done if the project's outcome will not deliver on the stated objectives. The earlier this is known, the more time and money can be saved.

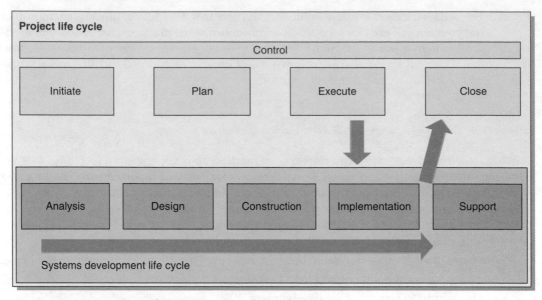

FIGURE 2-9   Integration of Project and Product Life Cycles

If management and stakeholders make the decision to proceed, then you start the planning phase. Again, the team needs to deliver all the required elements for planning the project and then make a decision to proceed or not to proceed. During the execution phase of the project life cycle, the team begins the SDLC analysis phase. Each phase continues, with the same objectives: Deliver all agreed-upon objectives for that phase and, at the end, make a decision about whether to continue the project or stop work on the project. When the product development life cycle begins, both life cycles are executing and have distinct deliverables. For example, when a network analyst finishes building a model of the new network topology, he or she delivers this model to the team for review, and the project manager is responsible for updating the project plan, status reports, and so on.

In the generic example shown in Figure 2-9, at the end of the implementation phase, the product is built and deployed to the users. The product moves into a support phase that is (much of the time) performed by different personnel than the ones who built it. At this step in the life cycle, between implementation and support, the project is officially coming to an end, and the project life cycle close phase begins.

In order to facilitate each of the methodologies discussed in the previous section (Scrum, spiral, XP, and so on), a different approach is needed for the project life cycle. Figure 2-10 shows a project with many subprojects or releases. This is referred to as a **program**. A program can have many related projects, all working together to produce one large product, or the projects can produce different products but be related by some other characteristic, such as the resources involved or the need for the finished products to work together. For example, the building of a new web site might be a program consisting of projects to create the end user design, database integration, security levels and rules, integration with legacy applications, and programming of business rules.

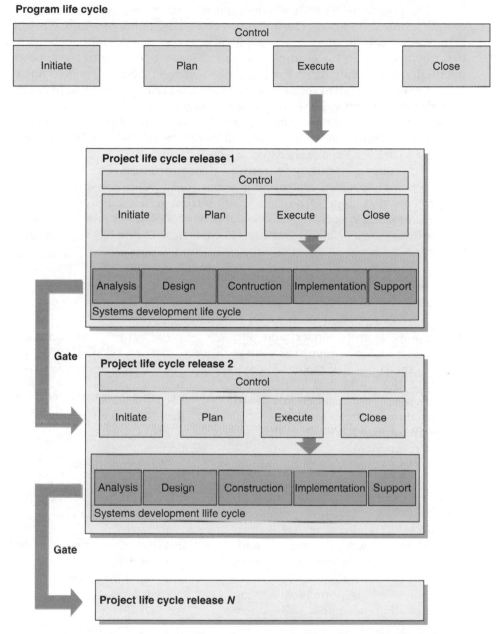

FIGURE 2-10   Integration of Project Life Cycle to Iterative Development Life Cycle

The program follows the same generic project life cycle as before: initiate, plan, execute, control, and close. During the execute phase of the program, work begins on each subproject. Each subproject is itself a project and should follow the project life cycle described earlier. In the example shown in Figure 2-10, each of the subprojects runs sequentially. When subproject 1 is finished, subproject 2 begins, and so on. This is not the case in many projects; to speed up delivery of the entire program, many of the subprojects may run concurrently. For example, a web site interface design team might work on its subproject while the database design team works on its subproject while the network and security team works on its subproject. All these subprojects must be coordinated and work together to deliver a comprehensive, integrated solution.

Each subproject must go through a close procedure, which becomes more complicated when subprojects are running concurrently. Care must be taken to ensure that subprojects that depend on deliverables from other subprojects are aware of any changes or delays. A change in one subproject will affect other subprojects. The close procedures run as before, but careful attention is needed to evaluate any and all changes.

Chapter Review

1. Project managers must understand and utilize the systems approach—view projects in the context of the entire environment, both inside and outside the organization—to get projects designed and planned optimally.
2. The systems approach consists of three interrelated components:
   a. *Systems theory* involves a philosophy of or a way of looking at the world—a language or set of principles and interventions for thinking and solving problems. The following related terms are defined in this chapter: subsystem, element, attribute, boundary, environment, objectives, constraints, and integration.
   b. *Systems analysis* is a problem-solving technique that decomposes a system into its component pieces for the purpose of studying how well those component parts work and interact to accomplish their purpose.
   c. *Systems management* is responsible for the management of the whole system: objectives, the environment (both internal and external), constraints, resources (both human and other), and

the culture and social environment of the organization.
3. The PMLC is a prescribed order of phases—smaller segments of the entire project. Each contains a specific deliverable, and they collectively deliver a result.
4. A PMLC includes the following information:
   a. What specific work should be done in each phase
   b. A definition of each phase's deliverables, plus the change control process for each
   c. What resources are needed and involved
   d. Criteria that need to be met to complete each phase
5. An SDLC is a systems approach to problem solving that organizes a standard set of processes or activities into phases and tasks for the purpose of building an information systems product.
6. Many variations of the SDLC have been used to develop information systems, and each has strengths and weaknesses. This chapter covers the following methodologies:

a. **Waterfall**—This traditional approach describes a development approach that is linear and sequential, has distinct objectives for each phase, and for which the output of one phase is the input for the next.

b. **Evolutionary prototyping**—This model focuses on gathering correct and consistent requirements and involves building a system incrementally through a series of gradual refinements or prototypes.

c. **Spiral**—This model involves a series of short waterfall cycles, each producing an early prototype that represents a part of the entire product.

d. **Iterative and incremental**—In this model, multiple development cycles, called iterations, take place. Each iteration passes through the standard life cycle phases, similarly to the waterfall approach. A small working version of software is produced during the first iteration, so the team has working software early in the process. Subsequent iterations build on the initial software produced during the first iteration.

e. **Scrum**—This model is based on the concept that software development is not a defined process but an empirical process with complex input/output transformations that may or may not be repeated under different circumstances.

f. **Rational Unified Process**—The RUP model is an iterative process that identifies four phases of any software development project: inception, elaboration, construction, and transition. Each phase contains one or more iterations where an executable is produced but that is perhaps an incomplete system.

g. **Extreme Programming**—The XP model includes short development cycles, frequent updates, division of business and technical priorities, and assignment of user stories. XP has four key values: communication, feedback, simplicity, and courage.

7. Product life cycles are integrated with but defined separately from project life cycles because of the differences in deliverables and resources involved.

Glossary

life cycle A prescribed order of phases (smaller segments of an entire project) in which the phases contain specific deliverables that collectively deliver a result.

program A group of related projects, managed in a coordinated way to obtain benefits and control not available when managing them individually.

stage gate A decision-making opportunity between phases or iterations in the project life cycle to determine whether the project should proceed as is, proceed with changes, or be terminated.

system A set of interacting, interrelated, or interdependent elements that work as part of a whole.

systems approach A process of examining a problem or an issue by first understanding its environment and then reducing the problem or issue into smaller components and finally managing the resolution of the problem or issue.

systems development life cycle (SDLC) An approach to building IT systems that consists of a standard set of phases, each of which produces a prescribed set of deliverables.

Review Questions

1. What is a project life cycle, and how is it used?
2. What is a product life cycle, and how is it used?
3. Explain how product life cycles differ from project life cycles. How are they similar to one another?
4. Explain how the integration of project life cycles with product life cycles should work.
5. Describe the systems approach and its significance for project managers.
6. Define each of the three components of the systems approach.
7. Differentiate between the systems approach and the systems analysis approach taught in introductory systems analysis and design courses.
8. Define the concept of *systems* in your own words and give examples of a system in which the sum of its parts is worth more than each part individually.
9. Differentiate between open systems and closed systems. Why is this difference significant to a project manager?
10. This chapter states that much of what a project manager does exists on the boundary of the project. Explain what is meant by this statement.
11. Explain what is meant by the *environment* surrounding a project. How is a project affected by events in the environment?
12. Explain the concept and need for stage gates between project phases.
13. Explain the concept of delivering a project in incremental iterations.
14. Write a brief explanation of each of the following PDLC methods and explain the strengths and weaknesses of each: waterfall, iterative and incremental, spiral, Scrum, XP, and RUP.
15. Specifically compare and contrast the traditional waterfall model with the more modern RUP model. Should one always be used over the other? Explain.

Problems and Exercises

1. You work for a large pharmaceutical company that has offices spread out all over the globe. Your boss comes to your office, excited about a new methodology he just read about called Extreme Programming, and he wants you to use it on the new HR application that your group is getting ready to work on. The HR software will track employee information such as job performance, salary, vacation, and so on for all 12,000 employees in all countries, and it will tie into the corporate payroll system. The project team contains members from the United States, the United Kingdom, Singapore, Japan, and India. Write a memo to your boss, explaining why the use of Extreme Programming might not be such a good idea for this project.
2. Lori is the newly appointed project manager for the Fultz Metal Works Company, a small $30 million tool-and-die manufacturer. To remain competitive, the company is launching a series of projects to upgrade all of its computer-aided machinery. The project will be costly and risky for Fultz Metal. Unfortunately, no one in the company is familiar with the new hardware and software. The company wants all work done in house because they don't trust outsiders. If you were offering advice to Lori on the selection of a methodology, what would you say and why?
3. Based on the following criteria, construct a decision tree to determine the best product development methodology: risk, size both in dollars and effort, company culture, location of team participants, amount of planning and control needed, and rate of environment change.
4. Give some examples of projects you have worked on where you feel the wrong methodology was used and where you feel the right methodology was used. Explain the ramifications of these methodology choices.
5. Which one(s) of the methodologies described in this chapter do you feel would be the most difficult to manage? Explain. Which do you think is the most successful? Why?

6. Write a memo to a nontechnical manager, explaining why a team decided to use an iterative and incremental development methodology on its project.

7. As a student, you generally take more than one course during a given semester. Each course requires different amounts of your time, at varying schedules. Many students spend more time on the courses within their major than on others because generally they are more interested in the subject. But students need to be able to balance their time and demonstrate a solid overall GPA. How might the systems approach aid students in budgeting their time and efforts?

8. Explain the difference between systems thinking and analytical thinking. Also, explain why both are important to a project manager.

9. For an IT project dealing with upgrading all company computers to the latest version of the Windows operating system, list and explain the forces in the environment that may cause problems.

10. Mark, Pam, and Rick all work in the IT department for a large manufacturing company. Mark supports the accounting department, Pam supports the purchasing department, and Rick supports the quality control department. Mark has started working on a new software application to upgrade the financial software to something that runs on a different operating system than the previous version. Pam is in the middle of a project that involves delivering better custom reports, based on purchasing data. Rick has been asked to develop a new custom system for the quality assurance department that will help the company in receiving ISO 9000 certification. Problems began to surface during the implementation of the new accounting software. It turned out that the new accounting software was not compatible with the old purchasing software and required new information to be tracked by the purchasing agents. Pam was nearly done with her new reports when she found out that they would need to be changed, and the work so far has been wasted. Rick was upset because they would have to stop their work on the ISO 9000 certification until the issues were resolved. Explain how the use of the systems approach could have helped avoid many or even all of these problems.

 MINICASE

1. *Background:* Mark Lewis, the son of Reid Lewis, the president of R & S Amusements Services, was having dinner with a good friend, A.J., an independent IT contractor. A.J. specializes in small business application development. He is proficient in custom programming using Visual Basic and Microsoft Access. After awhile, the dinner conversation concentrated on the IT automation project at R & S Amusements Services. Mark was explaining to his friend the scope of the project and that they had contracted with Premier Project Management Services (PPMS) to oversee the project. A.J., being a highly motivated entrepreneur trying to secure more work, was doing his best to convince Mark that using PPMS was a waste of money. He said that PPMS would force R & S to follow a rigid process that would require a lot of extra busywork that would do nothing but kill more trees. A.J. sais that PPMS used a rigid process as an underhanded way to bill additional hours to make more money, and it was a big problem in the industry. A.J. told Mark that if he were smart, he would fire PPMS and hire him, and he could finish the project in one-third of the time and at one-third of the cost. In fact, he could start programming as early as the day after tomorrow.

   Current Situation 1: Mark is in his father's office, reflecting on the previous night's dinner conversation. Mark is trying to convince Reid that PPMS is not needed, and it's a waste of money. After 30 minutes of discussion, Reid calls Jeff Dunbar and Kevin Pullen to his office. Reid asks Jeff and Kevin if he made a mistake hiring them and asked what they had to say in response to A.J.'s claims.

Discussion: Describe how you would convince Reid and Mark of the value of PPMS's services. Defend the allegations of always using a rigid process to increase billable hours. Respond to the statement that Mark could hire a programmer, and the project would be completed in one-third the time and at one-third the cost (even though the requirements haven't even been fully determined yet) and that they could start programming in two days. What compromises might you suggest to make Reid feel more comfortable about his decision?

Current Situation 2: Mark has decided to hire A.J. as a consultant to help with the project in any way he can. But mainly he is there to keep an eye on PPMS and report back to him about any improper practices or costs.

Discussion: You are Jeff and Kevin, and you know there is a risk that A.J. might sabotage the project. How do you approach Reid with your fears, and at what cost? How do you "manage" Mark? You know he doesn't trust you because his beliefs have already been biased by A.J. Is there anything you can do to win him over? Finally, how do you deal with A.J.? Personally, you can't fire him, so how do you manage the relationship so it will not affect the project? How can you convince A.J. that if he stays in line, it can be a win–win situation?

Suggested Readings

Arthur, L.J. (1992). *Rapid evolutionary development: Requirements, prototyping & software creation.* New York: John Wiley & Sons, Inc.

Berinato, S. (2001, July 1). The secret to software success. *CIO Magazine.* Retrieved from www.cio.com/archive/070101/secret.html.

Boehm, B. (1989, May). A spiral model of software development and enhancement. *Computer*, pp. 61–72.

Boehm, B., & Turner, R. (2004). *Balancing agility and discipline: A guide for the perplexed.* Boston: Addison-Wesley.

Budde, R., Kautz, K., & Zullighoven, H. (1992). *Prototyping: An approach to evolutionary system development.* New York: Spring-Verlag.

Bushell, S. (2007). *Taking a systems view.* Retrieved from http://www.cio.com.au/article/print/204657/taking_systems_view/.

Charvat, J. (2003). *Project management methodologies: Selecting, implementing, and supporting methodologies and process for projects.* Hoboken, NJ: John Wiley & Sons, Inc.

Churchman, C.W. (1979). *The systems approach and its enemies.* New York: Basic Books.

Churchman, C.W. (1968). *The systems approach.* New York: Dell.

Cleland, D. & King, W. (1972). *Management: A systems approach.* New York: McGraw-Hill.

DeGrace, P., & Stahl, L.H. (1990). *Wicked problems, righteous solutions: A catalogue of modern software engineering paradigms.* Upper Saddle River, NJ: Prentice Hall.

Johnson, M. (2003). *Shine technologies: Agile methodologies.* Retrieved from http://www.shinetech.com/agile_survey_results.jsp.

Johnson R., Kast F., & Rosenzsweig, J. (1973). *The theory and management of systems.* New York: McGraw-Hill.

Mabel, J. (2004). *Project lifecycles: Waterfall, rapid application development, and all that.* Retrieved from www.lux-seattle.com/resources/whitepapers/waterfall.htm.

McConnell, S. (1996). *Rapid development: Taming wild software schedules.* Redmond, WA: Microsoft Press.

Whitten, J., Bentley, L., & Dittman, K. (2004). *Systems analysis & design methods.* New York: McGraw-Hill.

Wells, D. (2001). *Extreme Programming: A gentle introduction.* Retrieved from www.extremeprogramming. org.

3

The Project Management Framework

R & S Amusements Services

Event 3

Setting   *This is a continuation of Event 2, with Jeff Dunbar and Reid Lewis having just returned from getting another cup of coffee and now sitting in Reid Lewis's office. Kevin Pullen has just entered the office and joined the conversation.*

KEVIN   Hello Reid, Jeff. Do you mind if I join the party?

REID   *[Laughing]* Sure, come on in.

JEFF   Kevin, Reid was just telling me that he attended a class in systems analysis and design, and he knows some programming.

KEVIN   Great! Sign him up! We will need all the help we can get! Seriously, that will make our job easier because you will be able to better understand the concepts and techniques we may be using and how we are applying them in the context of your business.

REID   *[Reid raises his hands]* Hold on there. Don't get too carried away! I know enough to be dangerous, which means I think I know more than I really do. *[Jeff and Kevin start laughing]*

JEFF   You will be fine, a great help. We wish many of our clients had a better understanding of what they know and don't know. Many believe they know a lot about computers and thus delivering computer systems projects.

REID   Jeff, let's revisit what we were talking about earlier. You mentioned that there is a life cycle for building the product and another life cycle for *managing* the building of the product? Could you explain this? I don't think I understand what you mean.

JEFF   Sure Reid. Kevin, feel free to chime in if you want to. As you know, the life cycle for building the product is the typical systems development life cycle (SDLC), which you are already familiar with. The other life cycle is the one project managers use to manage the project—the project management life cycle (PMLC). The phases of the PMLC are initiating, planning, executing, controlling, and closing. PMI also uses these names to refer to its process

55

groups. PMI calls them *process groups* because each contains one or more related component processes—in other words, a set of tasks to be performed to produce a specified outcome. We decided to stick with the names when we created our life cycle.

REID   *[Looking thoroughly confused]* Okay, I guess.

KEVIN   Reid, take the planning phase, for example. One of the component processes is developing the project management plan, which is part of the Integration Management knowledge area.

REID   Okay, now I'm really confused. What is a knowledge area?

KEVIN   A *knowledge area* is an identified area of project management knowledge. There are ten of them, as specified by PMI's PMBOK. *PMBOK* stands for the project management body of knowledge. One knowledge area is called Time Management, and another is Scope Management. Each knowledge area has mapped to it component processes that project managers must be skilled at in order to be accomplished at a particular knowledge area.

REID   I had no idea.

KEVIN   Don't feel bad. Formal project management in the IT field is fairly new compared to other disciplines. So, we have a lot of catching up to do. Jeff and I have developed a framework to help folks like you better understand what we are doing. You will have a grasp of it in no time.

REID   I don't know about that.

JEFF   Sure you will, and you will be on your way to becoming a PMP.

REID   PMP? What . . .

JEFF   Let's hold that discussion for another coffee break and get back to work.

         (to be continued)

CHAPTER PREVIEW AND OBJECTIVES

Before you can begin understanding the practice of managing projects, you need to have a clear understanding of the processes and key tools (methods) that define project management. This chapter describes the project management framework, consisting of process groups, knowledge areas, and component processes. You will understand the project management framework when you can:

- Define the five process groups and understand how they interact over time
- Define the ten knowledge areas
- Define the component processes that exist within each process group
- Know the methods used in each component process and the deliverables produced
- Understand the importance of the Project Management Institute and other professional societies

A FRAMEWORK FOR PROJECT MANAGEMENT

As mentioned earlier in this book, in the late 1950s and early 1960s, the term *project management* emerged as projects began to grow rapidly in scope, size, duration, and resources. In 1969, the **Project Management Institute (PMI)** was founded for the following reasons:

- To create a forum for project managers to discuss emerging concepts and practices
- To officially recognize project management as a profession in and of itself
- To bring together people from all branches of project management to share and learn from each other

In the early 1970s, PMI conducted seminars and symposiums in the United States and overseas, created its first local chapter, and had membership of 2,000 worldwide. By the end of the twentieth century, membership soared from 2,000 to over 50,000, and **special interest groups (SIGs)** were created. In 1994, the first edition of *A Guide to the Project Management Body of Knowledge* **(PMBOK)** was published.

PMI created several publications to assist in the dissemination of project management knowledge during the 1970s through 1990s, such as journals, newsletters, and magazines. At the end of 2012, PMI had more than 395,000 members in more than 125 countries, and it had many SIGs, such as Information Systems and Manufacturing.

PMI offers and controls the leading certification credential today: project management professional (PMP). We will talk more about this and how to get certified later in the text. Certifications can be an important part of ensuring quality in a profession. In 1999, PMI became the first organization in the world to have its certification program receive the International Organization for Standardization (ISO) 9001 recognition. By the end of 2012, PMI had certified more than 500,000 PMPs.

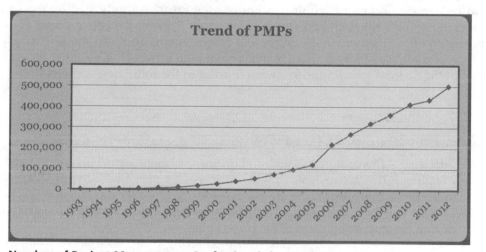

Number of Project Management Professionals by Year

The growth in PMI membership and participation is analogous to the growth in project management awareness and importance and demonstrates the importance that PMI plays in the future directions of this profession. Although PMI is the largest professional project management society, it is not the only one. Several others are growing as well, including the International Project Management Association (IPMA) and APMG-UK, which is a proponent of the Projects in Controlled Environments (PRINCE2) methodology. In addition, because of the increased importance of the project management profession globally, the ISO standards committee in 2012 released standard ISO 21500:2012, titled "Guidance on Project Management." This standard, which closely resembles the PMBOK, is the first in a family of related project management standards scheduled to be released.

The PMBOK is a starting point, not an endpoint. Organizations rarely adopt the entire PMBOK as is; they use it as a starting point and then develop their own **framework**, filled with processes, phases, and methods. We have done the same thing with this book; we started with the PMBOK and have added our own flavor to it to give you added definition and understanding. This chapter introduces the concepts of the framework, and subsequent chapters will explain them in detail.

The basic structure and terminology presented in this text is from *A Guide to the PMBOK*, 5th edition. The methods discussed in subsequent chapters are based on material from the PMBOK, other authors, and this text's authors' own combined 40 years of information technology project management experience.

Why is the structure of our text based on the PMBOK? As stated in earlier chapters, project management has become a strategic necessity in today's organization. Like many other professions, such as computer science, accounting, or engineering, project management needed to create a shared knowledge base from which research and maturity of practices could be established. A common language is needed to allow researchers and practitioners to communicate across departments, organizations, industries, and countries. The PMBOK establishes this common language; more than 3 million copies of it are in circulation, and it has been translated into eight different languages.

The framework used in this text (see Figure 3-1) is structured around five **process groups**, which are made up of **component processes** consisting of tools, techniques, and outcomes, organized within ten **knowledge areas**. As indicated by the solid blue boxes in Figure 3-1, not all knowledge areas apply to every process group. For example, Integration Management and Stakeholder Management apply to the Initiating process group, and all the other knowledge areas have blue boxes. (We will discuss and define each of the process groups and knowledge areas in the following sections.)

The Process Groups

Five basic process groups are used to conduct a successful project:

- *Initiating*—This group deals with authorizing the beginning or end of a project or phase.
- *Planning*—This group deals with ensuring that the objectives of a project are achieved in the most appropriate way.
- *Execution*—This group deals with coordinating all resources (people and material) during the implementation of the project plan.
- *Controlling*—This group deals with monitoring project variances from what was planned to actual progress.
- *Closing*—This group deals with formal acceptance of the project or a phase and updating the project information base with lessons learned.

These process groups consist of several individual component processes that turn inputs into outputs during each phase of the project. Chapters 4 through 13 of this text describe each of these processes and the methods (tools and techniques) used in each.

Throughout the text the process groups are covered in a sequential (linear) format, but in fact the process groups overlap with varying intensity during the execution of a project. For example, in Figure 3-2, the vertical axis displays the varying amount of work or activity for each process group that occurs on many projects, and the horizontal axis depicts how the process groups overlap over time. Soon after the project initiation process group begins, planning processes can begin, and controlling processes should begin. For example, the project charter is one of the main documents created during project initiation. Because this document contains signatures of key stakeholders or project sponsors, the project charter needs to be put under configuration control (a process for controlling

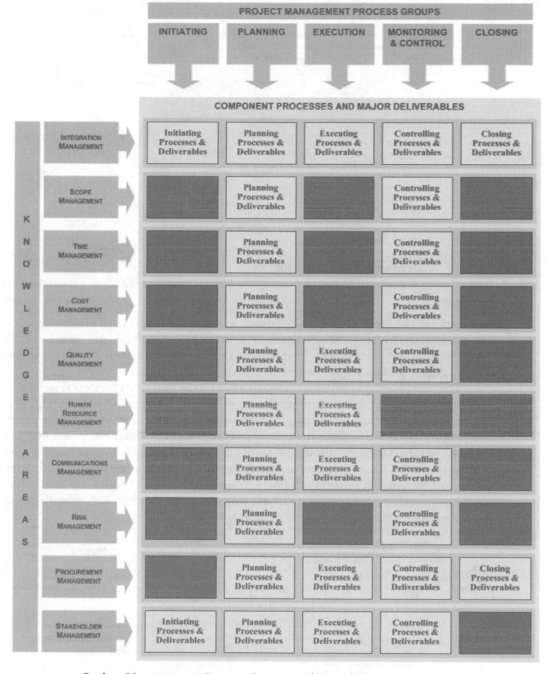

FIGURE 3-1   Project Management Process Groups and Knowledge Areas

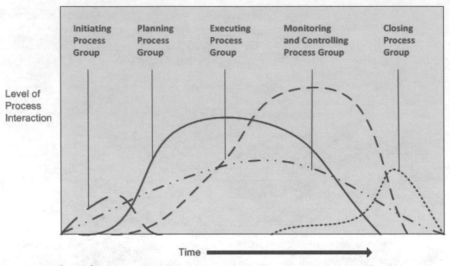

FIGURE 3-2   Overlap of Process Groups

Source: Project Management Institute, *Guide to the Project Management Body of Knowledge*, Fifth Edition, p. 51.

and tracking changes) as soon as it is done, which is a method used within the controlling processes. (Don't worry about what these documents or methods are right now; they will be thoroughly explained later in the text.) During the execution process, the initiating, planning, and controlling processes can also be in operation.

The process groups are linked to each other by the outcomes they produce; the outcome of one group is often the input into another, as indicated in Figure 3-3. For example, the project charter is an output from initiation and is one of the key inputs into the planning process.

Figure 3-3 demonstrates how process groups exist within each phase of an iterative project. (Iterative projects are defined in Chapter 2.) The initiating process group is the process that begins the project as well as each phase. Each phase consists of all five process groups interacting over time. Each phase as well as the entire project ends with the closing process. As each phase ends, the closing process reviews what was accomplished in the previous phase and what needs to be done or redone in the next phase.

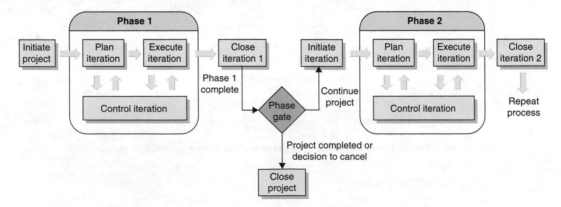

FIGURE 3-3   Process Groups Interacting in a Phase

Process groups supply a roadmap to follow, and the knowledge areas describe the methods (for example, car, plane, bus) of how to get to our destination, which is project success. The next section presents an overview of the ten knowledge areas.

The Knowledge Areas

As defined earlier, a knowledge area describes project management knowledge in terms of its component processes. The ten knowledge areas are:

- Integration Management
- Scope Management
- Time Management
- Cost Management
- Quality Management
- Human Resources Management
- Communications Management
- Risk Management
- Procurement Management
- Stakeholder Management

The knowledge areas represent the body of knowledge that a project manager must have in order to consistently deliver successful projects that meet a customer's expectations in terms of scope, time, cost, and quality of the project deliverables, as depicted in Figure 3-4.

Figure 3-4 depicts the process of project management as an integrated machine. Project requirements/specifications are funneled into the machine to start it running. Project requirements are the raw materials feeding the machine, and the product deliverables are the finished goods. The core knowledge areas of Scope, Time, Cost, and Quality are represented by the large gears that have to be there to make it all work. The facilitating knowledge areas—Stakeholder, Risk, Procurement, and Human Resources—are attached to the fly wheel to help the gears of the key processes along. And connecting the core knowledge area gears to the facilitating knowledge area fly wheel is the Integration knowledge and communication area gears. The output of the machine (product deliverables) is controlled by the customer. They alone are the ones who determine the success or failure of your project. Success is measured by the customer's perception of the quality of the delivered product.

The individual knowledge areas are defined in Table 3-1. Each of these definitions includes a list of tasks (component processes) that are executed to produce the outcomes dictated by the knowledge area. The individual component processes are defined later in the chapter.

The Component Processes

As stated earlier and shown in Figure 3-1, the project management framework presented in this text, which is based on work done by PMI, consists of ten knowledge areas presented on the vertical axis and five process groups organized across the top on the horizontal axis. At the intersection of the two the component processes are presented—the project management processes that are common to most projects and the major

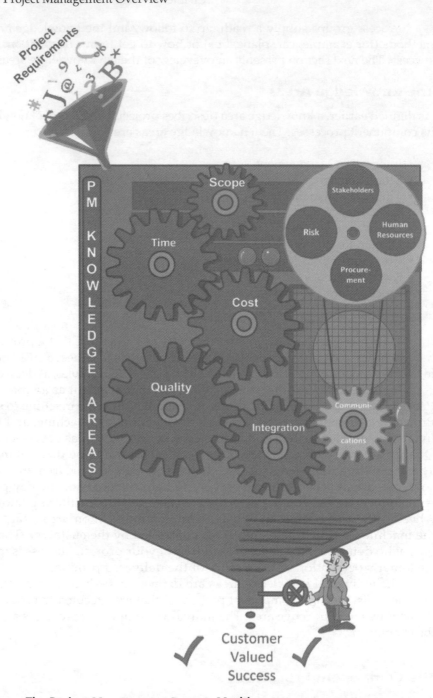

FIGURE 3-4   The Project Management Process Machine

TABLE 3-1   The Ten Knowledge Areas

Knowledge Area	Definition	Component Processes
Integration Management	Describes the processes and methods required to identify, define, combine, unify, and coordinate the various processes with the other eight knowledge areas	Develop project charter, develop project management plan, direct and manage project execution, monitor and control project work, perform integrated change control, and close project or phase
Scope Management	Describes the processes and methods required to ensure that the project delivers exactly what the customer requested and only what the customer requested to create a successful project	Plan scope management, collect requirements, define scope, create WBS, validate scope, and control scope
Time Management	Describes the processes and methods required to create and manage appropriate schedules to complete the project	Plan schedule management, define activities, sequence activities, estimate activity resources, estimate activity durations, develop schedule, and control schedule
Cost Management	Describes the processes and methods required to create and manage the project budget	Plan cost management, estimate costs, determine budget, and control costs
Quality Management	Describes the processes and methods required to ensure that the project delivers the stated and implied needs for which it was designed	Plan quality management, perform quality assurance, and control quality
Human Resources Management	Describes the processes and methods required to effectively use the people associated with the project	Develop human resource plan, acquire project team, develop project team, and manage project team
Communications Management	Describes the processes and methods required to create, collect, disseminate, and store information about the project	Plan communications management, manage communications, and control communications
Risk Management	Describes the processes and methods required to identify, quantify, and control risks associated with the project	Plan risk management, identify risks, perform qualitative risk analysis, perform quantitative risk analysis, plan risk responses, and control risks
Procurement Management	Describes the processes and methods required to acquire and manage goods and resources from a source outside the project team	Plan Procurement Management, conduct procurements, control procurements, and close procurements
Stakeholder Management	Describes the processes and methods required to identify project stakeholders and managing the interaction between them and the project team	Identify stakeholders, plan stakeholder management, manage stakeholder engagement, control stakeholder engagement

deliverables produced by those processes. The following sections introduce the component processes of each process group, as well as the major deliverables produced. Later chapters provide examples of the major deliverables and explain how to create them.

Initiating Component Processes and Major Deliverables

Before the project begins, a critical activity occurs: selecting the project to work on. Chapter 4 helps you determine which project to work on and figure out how best to select the right mix or portfolio of projects for your organization. Even if a project is run perfectly but it turns out the organization is headed in a different direction, valuable resources and time can be wasted. The projects chosen must be in step with the organization's **strategic plan**. Chapter 4 describes some key methods you can use to help with strategic planning.

The Initiating group applies to the Integration Management Knowledge Area and the Stakeholder Management Knowledge Area of the framework. As illustrated in Figure 3-5, it consists of project initiation:

- *Project initiation*—The process of formally authorizing a new project or determining that an existing project should proceed into its next phase. Recall from Chapter 2 that the initiation phase is where these stage gate decisions (to proceed with the project or not) are made.

As a result of the project initiation process, two major deliverables are produced:

- *Project charter*—This document formally authorizes a project. It should include (or may reference another document) the business need that the project must address, a description of the product to be created, critical success factors, and:
  a. *Identification of the project manager*—The project manager should be identified and assigned as early in the project as feasible. In many cases, the project selection process happens first and then, after the project is selected for execution, an appropriate manager is chosen to lead the effort.
  b. *Project assumptions*—These are factors that for planning purposes are considered to be true, real, or certain.
  c. *Project constraints*—These are factors that limit the project management team's options.
- *Stakeholder register*—This document summarizes all the stakeholders (people or organizations) that are affected by some part of the project.

You can think of the project charter as the course syllabus you are handed at the beginning of each semester from each course. The syllabus (hopefully) contains a list of objectives, a high-level schedule, work expectations, policies, and information about the project leader (professor). If all this information is clearly laid out and followed, the chances the course will run smoothly are enhanced. If there is a problem during the semester, and you need to hand in a homework assignment late, you only need to check the syllabus to see if it can be handed in at all and what type of grade penalty will be assessed. With a well-defined syllabus, questions can be answered quickly, and each student is treated fairly and consistently. Projects also rely on a good charter to help in answering questions and knowing what the key deliverables are and when they are needed.

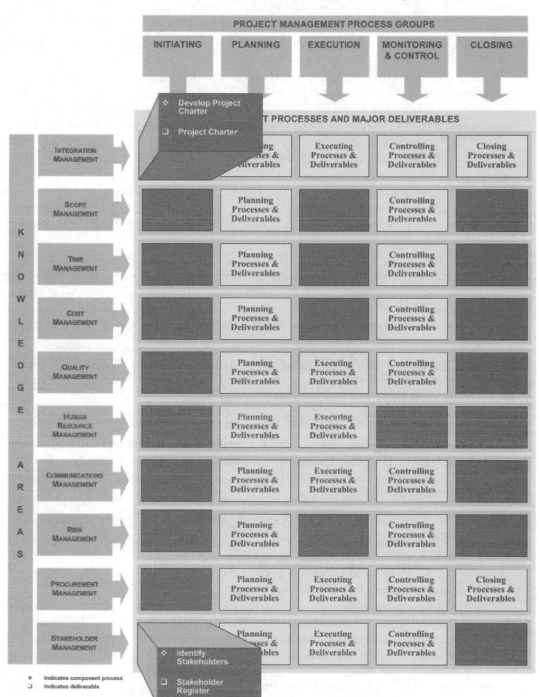

FIGURE 3-5   Initiating Component Processes and Major Deliverables

Planning Component Processes and Major Deliverables

Before jumping into the planning component processes, think about a couple of quotes. First, consider the following, from Lewis Carroll's *Alice in Wonderland*: The king says to Alice, "Begin at the beginning and then go 'til you come to the end; then stop." This is, unfortunately, how many companies do their planning—they don't. They start a project with no idea of what is required to complete it, so they never end. Now think about another famous quote: "Those who fail to plan plan to fail." Doing a good job of planning can't be stressed enough. The largest number of tools for any of the five process groups exists in the Planning group. T. Capers Jones (1998) states:

> The seeds of major software disasters are usually sown in the first three months of commencing the software project. . . . Once a project blindly lurches forward toward an impossible delivery date, the rest of the disaster will occur almost inevitably. (p. 120)

The errors we make in the initiation and planning processes are much more significant than at any other time.

The Planning group consists of component processes and deliverables that are applicable to every knowledge area of the framework, as shown in Figure 3-6. In Integration Management, the process is as follows:

- *Develop project management plan*—This process uses the outputs from the other planning processes to create a consistent and coherent document that can be used to guide both project execution and project control.

The primary deliverable of project plan development is the project plan:

- *Project management plan*—This formal approved document is used to manage project execution. The project plan can be expected to change over time when new information about the project becomes available. A good deal of this text is devoted to building pieces of the project plan.

The planning processes of Scope Management are:

- *Collect requirements*—This is the process of discovering, defining, and documenting stakeholders' needs to meet stated project objectives.
- *Define scope*—This is the process of subdividing the major project deliverables into smaller, more manageable components.
- *Plan scope management*—This is the process of creating a scope management plan.
- *Create work breakdown structure (WBS)*—The WBS is a deliverables-oriented grouping of project components that organizes and defines the total scope of a project. As with the scope statement, the WBS is often used to develop or confirm a common understanding of project scope among the stakeholders. Let's again use the course syllabus example from earlier in this chapter. Many syllabi include a complete list of assignments, number of exams, and so on that a student is asked to complete during the semester. The WBS defines each outcome or deliverable that is required to build the product.

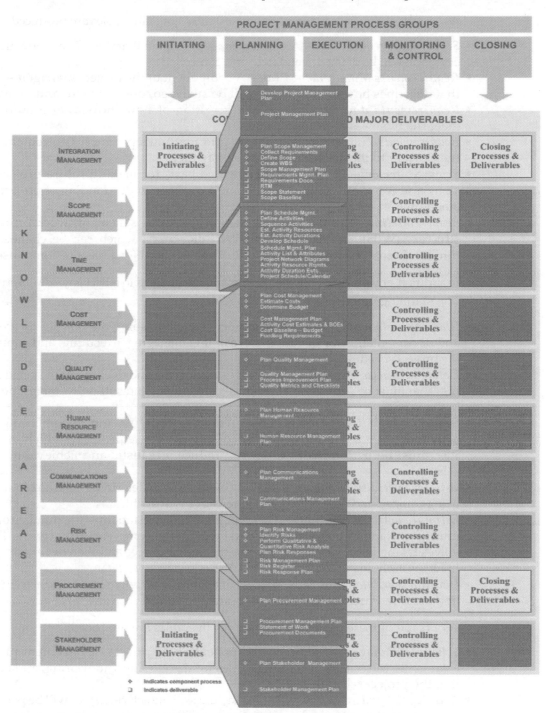

FIGURE 3-6   **Planning Component Processes and Major Deliverables**

As a result of the scope planning processes, six major deliverables are produced:

- *Scope Management Plan*—A scope management plan that documents how the project scope will be defined, validated, and controlled.
- *Requirements Management Plan*—A component of the project management plan that describes how requirements will be analyzed, documented, and managed.
- *Requirements documentation*—A description of how individual requirements meet the business need for a project.
- *Requirements Traceability Matrix*—A grid that links product requirements from their origin to the deliverables that satisfy them.
- *Scope Statement*—Provides a documented basis for making future project decisions and for confirming or developing a common understanding of project scope among the stakeholders.
- *Scope Baseline*—The approved version of the scope statement, work breakdown structure (WBS), and its associated WBS dictionary, which can be changed only through formal change control procedures and is used for a basis of comparison.

In addition, any previously created documents are updated to reflect any new information.

The planning processes of Time Management are:

- *Plan schedule management*—Is the process of establishing the policies, procedures, and documentation for planning, developing, managing, executing, and controlling the project schedule.
- *Define activities*—This process involves identifying and documenting specific activities that must be performed to produce deliverables and sub-deliverables identified in the WBS.
- *Sequence activities*—This process involves identifying and documenting interactive logical relationships—that is, identifying the sequence in which the activities must be performed in order to produce a realistic and achievable project schedule.
- *Estimate activity resources*—This process is used to determine which resources are being utilized and how much of each resource is available.
- *Estimate activity durations*—This process involves estimating the number of work units (for example, hours, days, weeks) required to complete each activity. This involves taking information on project scope and resources and then developing durations for input to schedules.
- *Develop schedule*—This is the process of analyzing activity sequences, activity durations, and resource requirements to create the project schedule.

As a result of these processes, six major deliverables are produced:

- *Schedule management plan*—A component of the project management plan that establishes the criteria and the activities for developing, monitoring, and controlling the project schedule.
- *Activity list and attributes*—This list includes all the activities that will be performed on the project as well as characteristics of each activity. In addition a milestone list may be created which lists all the project milestones and whether they are mandatory or optional.

- *Project network diagrams*—These are schematic displays of the project activities and the logical relationships (dependencies) among them. The most common type of project network diagram is called a PERT (program evaluation and review technique) chart.
- *Activity resource requirements*—These are the hours available from each resource for each task. In addition a resource breakdown structure may be created which illustrates resources by category and type.
- *Activity duration estimates*—These are quantitative assessments of the likely number of work periods (for example, hours, days, weeks) that will be required to complete an activity.
- *Project schedule/calendar*—This approved (base-lined) deliverable includes at a minimum the planned start and expected finish dates for each activity. The project schedule can be presented in tabular form or graphically using a project network diagram or using special types of bar charts called Gantt charts and milestone charts. The schedule should also have a management plan that defines how changes to the schedule will be managed as well as calendars that defines working and non-working times.

In addition, any previously created documents are updated to reflect any new information. The planning processes of Cost Management are:

- *Plan cost management*—Is the process that establishing the policies, procedures, and documentation for planning, managing, expending, and controlling project costs.
- *Estimate costs*—This process involves developing an approximation (estimate) of the costs of the resources needed to complete project activities.
- *Determine budget*—This process involves allocating the overall cost estimates to individual activities or work packages to establish a cost baseline for measuring project performance.

As a result of these processes, four major deliverables are produced:

- *Cost management plan*—A component of the project management plan that describes how costs will be planned, structured, and controlled.
- *Activity cost estimates*—These are quantitative assessments of the likely costs of the resources required to complete project activities. The cost estimates get more accurate over time.(Later chapters discuss the concept of progressive elaboration as it applies to budgets). In addition, basis of estimates (BOEs) may be produced which is supporting documentation detailing what information and process was used to prepare the estimates.
- *Cost baseline*—This is a time-phased budget that will be used to measure and monitor cost performance on a project.
- *Funding requirements*—Both periodic and total funding requirements are needed to deliver all documented requirements on projects derived from cost estimates.

In addition, any previously created documents are updated to reflect any new information. Quality Management has only one planning process:

- *Plan quality management*—This process involves identifying which quality standards are relevant to a project and determining how to satisfy them.

As a result of quality planning, four major deliverables are produced:

- *Quality management plan*—This formal or informal document describes how the project management team will implement its quality policy.
- *Quality metrics*—In very specific terms, what something is and how it is measured by the quality control process.
- *Checklists*—Specific lists are used to verify that a set of required steps has been performed.
- *Process improvement plan*—A component of the project management plan that details steps for analyzing processes to identify activities that enhance their value.

In addition, any previously created documents are updated to reflect any new information. The planning processes of Human Resources Management are:

- *Plan human resource management*—This process involves identifying, documenting, and assigning project roles, responsibilities, and reporting relationships.

As a result of this process, one major deliverable is produced consisting of three sub deliverables.

- *Human resource management plan*—A component of the project management plan that describes how the roles and responsibilities, reporting relationships, and staff management will be addressed and structured. This plan consists of the following components:
    - *Role and responsibility assignments*—These assignments include project roles (who does what), responsibilities (who decides what), and who has what authority that must be assigned to the appropriate project stakeholders.
    - *Staffing management plan*—This formal or informal document describes when and how human resources will be brought onto and taken off the project team. It also describes their available time to work on a project, any training needs, any pertinent human resources policies or regulations, and any safety guidelines.
    - *Organizational chart*—This is a graphical display of project reporting relationships that communicates who works for (or reports to) whom, among the project team members and stakeholders.

In addition, any previously created documents are updated to reflect any new information. Communications Management has only one planning process:

- *Plan communication management*—This process involves determining the information and communications needs of the stakeholders—who needs what information, when they will need it, how it will be given to them, and by whom.

As a result of communications planning, one deliverable is produced:

- *Communications management plan*—This formal or informal document provides:

    a. What methods will be used to gather and store the various types of information
    b. To whom information will flow and what methods will be used to distribute the various types of information
    c. A description of the information to be distributed
    d. Methods for accessing information between scheduled communications
    e. A method for updating and refining the communications management plan as the project progresses and develops

In addition, any previously created documents are updated to reflect any new information. The planning processes of Risk Management are:

- *Plan risk management*—This process involves deciding how to approach and plan the risk management activities of the project.
- *Identify risks*—This process involves determining which risks might affect the project and documenting their characteristics.
- *Perform qualitative risk analysis*—This process involves performing a qualitative analysis of risks and conditions in order to prioritize their effects on project objectives.
- *Perform quantitative risk analysis*—This process involves measuring the probability and consequences of risks and estimating their implications for project objectives.
- *Plan risk responses*—This process involves developing procedures and techniques to enhance opportunities and reduce threats to the project's objectives.

As a result of these processes, three major deliverables are produced:

- *Risk management plan*—This document describes how risk identification, qualitative and quantitative analysis, response planning, monitoring, and control will be structured and performed during the project life cycle.
- *List of analyzed risks (register)*—This list (or multiple lists) include:

  a. Prioritized qualitative and quantified risks
  b. Risks for additional analysis and management

- *Risk response plan*—This document describes what actions will be performed for each risk identified.

In addition, any previously created documents are updated to reflect any new information. The planning process of Procurement Management is:

- *Plan procurement management*—This process involves determining what to procure, when to procure, and a list of potential sellers.

As a result of this process, three major deliverables are produced:

- *Procurement management plan*—This document describes how the remaining procurement processes (from solicitation planning through contract closeout) will be managed.
- *Statement(s) of work*—This document describes the procurement item in sufficient detail to allow prospective sellers to determine if they are capable of providing the item.
- *Procurement documents*—These documents (for example, requests for proposal [RFPs]) are used to solicit proposals from prospective sellers.

In addition, any previously created documents are updated to reflect any new information. The Planning Process of Stakeholder Management is:

- *Plan stakeholder management*—The process of developing appropriate management strategies to effectively engage stakeholders throughout the project life cycle, based on the analysis of their needs, interests, and potential impact on project success.

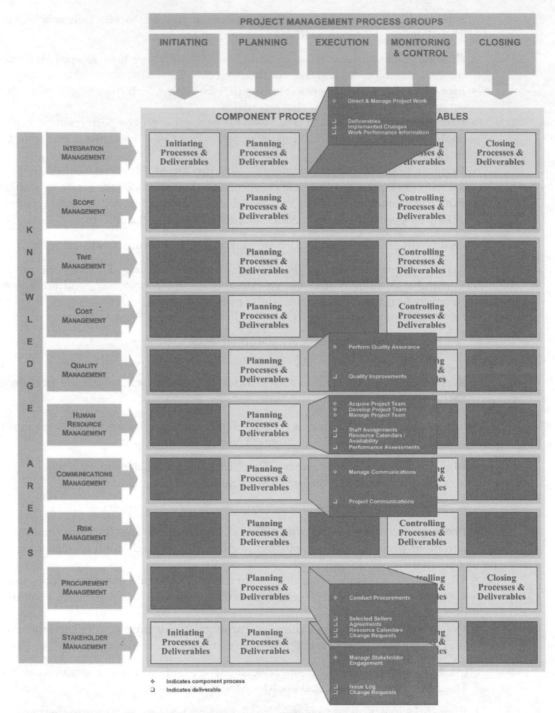

FIGURE 3-7   Execution Component Processes and Major Deliverables

As a result of this process, one major deliverable is produced:

- *Stakeholder management plan*—A component of the project management plan that defines the processes, procedures, tools, and techniques to effectively engage stakeholders in project decisions and execution based on the analysis of their needs, interests, and potential impact.

In addition, any previously created documents are updated to reflect any new information. The Planning group, its inputs and outputs, and the tools and techniques used are explained in detail in Chapters 5 through 10 of this textbook.

Execution Component Processes and Major Deliverables

The Execution group consists of component processes and deliverables that apply to six of the knowledge areas of the framework, as shown in Figure 3-7. Recall from Chapter 2 that this is where the product actually gets built. The product-specific life cycle begins to generate product-specific deliverables. In Integration Management, the process is as follows:

- *Direct and manage project work*—This process is used to carry out the project plan by performing the activities included therein.

As a result of project plan execution, three major deliverables are produced:

- *Deliverables*—These are the outcomes of the activities performed to accommodate the project.
- *Implemented changes*—These are changes to project scope, project costs (budgets), or the project schedule.
- *Work performance information*—This is information collected on the current status of the project activities.

In addition, any previously created documents are updated to reflect any new information. There is only one execution process in Quality Management:

- *Perform quality assurance*—This process involves evaluating overall project performance on a regular basis to provide confidence that the project will satisfy the relevant quality standards.

As a result of the quality assurance process, one primary deliverable is produced:

- *Quality improvement*—This includes taking action to increase the effectiveness and efficiency of the project to provide added benefits to the project stakeholders.

There are three execution processes in Human Resources Management:

- *Acquire project team*—This process involves finding and acquiring the human resources needed to execute the project.
- *Develop project team*—This process involves developing individual and group competencies to enhance project performance.
- *Manage project team*—This process involves tracking each team member's performance during the project and coordinating changes.

As a result of the team development process, three deliverables are produced:

- *Staff assignments*—Appropriate people are assigned to each task on the WBS.
- *Resource availability*—Each person may have different time periods available to work on a project. Many individuals work on more than one project at a time, and they need to split their time.
- *Performance assessment*—Project managers need to continually evaluate the effectiveness of each team member and the team as a whole.

There is one execution process in Communications Management:

- *Manage communications*—The process of creating, collecting, distributing, storing, and retrieving project information in accordance with the communications management plan.

As a result of this process, one major deliverable is produced:

- *Project communications*—Information distributed to the stakeholders using the appropriate media and format.

In addition, any previously created documents are updated to reflect any new information. The execution process of Procurement Management is:

- *Conduct procurements*—This process involves obtaining quotations, bids, offers, or proposals, as appropriate, and choosing solutions from among potential sellers.

As a result of this process, four primary deliverables are produced:

- *Selected sellers*—This is a list of qualified sellers, based on predetermined selection criteria. This is generally more than one after the initial review of the proposals.
- *Agreements*—A document such as a contract that defines the intentions of the project.
- *Resource calendars*—A calendar that identifies the working days and shifts in which the resources are available.
- *Change request*—A formal proposal to modify the procurement agreement.

In addition, any previously created documents are updated to reflect any new information. The execution process of Stakeholder Management is:

- *Manage stakeholder engagement*—This is the process of communicating and working with stakeholders to meet their needs/expectations and address issues as they occur throughout the life cycle.

As a result of this process, two major deliverables are produced:

- *Issue log*—A document used to document and monitor elements under discussion or in dispute between project stakeholders.
- *Change request*—A formal proposal to modify an approved document.

In addition, any previously created documents are updated to reflect any new information. The process group Execution, its inputs and outputs, as well as the tools and techniques used are explained in detail in Chapter 10.

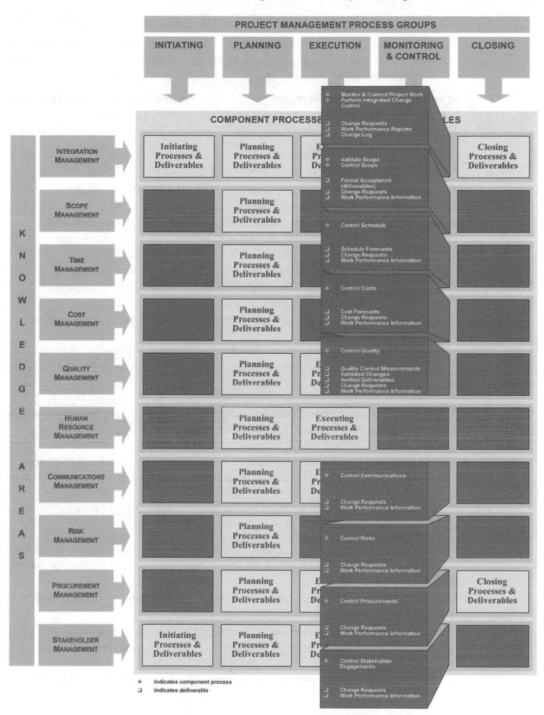

FIGURE 3-8   Control Component Processes and Major Deliverables

Controlling Component Processes and Major Deliverables

The Monitoring and Control group consists of component processes and deliverables that are applicable to all but one of the knowledge areas of the framework, as depicted in Figure 3-8. In Integration Management, the processes are as follows:

- *Monitor and control project work*—This process involves monitoring project progress (scope, time, cost, and quality) throughout the entire life cycle.
- *Perform integrated change control*—This process involves coordinating changes across the entire project.

As a result of this process, three primary deliverables are produced.

- *Change request*—A formal proposal to modify the project management plan.
- *Work performance reports*—Project documents containing information to assist in generating decisions, actions, or awareness. Examples of these include:
  - *Corrective action*—is anything done to bring expected future project performance in line with the project plan.
  - *Forecasts*—estimates of conditions in the project's future based on information available at the time the forecast is made
  - *Lessons learned*—is documentation that details the causes of variances, the reasoning behind the corrective action chosen, and other types of lessons learned.
- *Change log*—A comprehensive list of changes made during the project which include the date the change was made, and the impact in terms of time, cost, and risk.

In addition, any previously created documents are updated to reflect any changes. The controlling processes of Scope Management are:

- *Validate scope*—This process involves formalizing acceptance of the project scope.
- *Control scope*—This process involves controlling changes to the project scope.

As a result of the scope validation and scope change control processes, three primary deliverables are produced:

- *Formal acceptance*—This is documentation that the client or sponsor has accepted the product of the project phase or major deliverable(s) must be prepared and distributed.
- *Change requests*—This is any modification to the agreed-upon project scope, as defined by the approved WBS.
- *Work performance information*—Project performance information as it pertains to scope (how much has been completed, how many changes, etc.).

In addition, any previously created documents are updated to reflect any changes.

The Time Management knowledge area consists of one controlling process:

- *Control schedule*—This process involves controlling changes to the project schedule.

As a result of the schedule control process, three major deliverables are produced:

- *Schedule forecasts*—Estimates of conditions in the project's future based on information available at the time the forecast is made
- *Change request*—A formal proposal to modify the project's schedule.
- *Work performance information*—Project performance information as it pertains to the schedule. Using earned value terms, the schedule variance and schedule performance index values for selected WBS activities.

In addition, any previously created documents are updated to reflect any changes. The Cost Management knowledge area consists of one controlling process:

- *Control cost*—This process involves controlling changes to the project budget.

As a result of the cost control process, three major deliverables are produced:

- *Cost forecasts*—Estimates of conditions in the project's future based on information available at the time the forecast is made
- *Change request*—A formal proposal to modify the project's budget.
- *Work performance information*—Project performance information as it pertains to the cost/budget. Using earned value terms, the cost variance and cost performance index values for selected WBS activities.

In addition, any previously created documents are updated to reflect any changes. Quality Management has only one controlling process:

- *Control quality*—This process involves monitoring specific project results to determine whether they comply with relevant quality standards and identifying ways to eliminate causes of unsatisfactory performance.

As a result of quality control, five major deliverables are produced:

- *Quality control measurements*—These are collected results of quality control activities for evaluation against the quality standards.
- *Validated changes*—Items are re-inspected and approved or disapproved.
- *Change request*—A formal proposal to modify a project activity in order to improve the quality of the project.
- *Verified deliverables*—In the end, all deliverables should meet stated requirements of the stakeholders.
- *Work performance information*—Project performance information as it pertains to the cost/budget. Using earned value terms, the cost variance and cost performance index values for selected WBS activities.

In addition, any previously created documents are updated to reflect any changes. The controlling process of Communication Management is:

- *Control communications*—This is the process of monitoring and controlling communications throughout the life cycle to ensure the information needs of the project stakeholders are met.

As a result of the Communications Management monitoring and control process, two major deliverables are produced:

- *Work performance information*—Project performance information as it pertains to status reporting, progress measurement, and forecasting.
- *Change request*—A formal proposal to modify the project's schedule, scope, or budget (costs).

In addition, any previously created documents are updated to reflect any changes. The controlling process of Risk Management is:

- *Control risks*—This is the process of implementing risk response plans, tracking identified risks, monitoring residual risks, identifying new risks, and evaluating risk process effectiveness throughout the project.

As a result of the Risk Management monitoring and control process, two major deliverables are produced:

- *Work performance information*—Project performance information as it pertains to risk process effectiveness.
- *Change request*—A formal proposal to modify the project's schedule, scope, or budget (costs) because of a risk event.

In addition, any previously created documents are updated to reflect any changes. The controlling process of Procurement Management is:

- *Control procurements*—This is the process of managing procurement relationships, monitoring contract performance, and making changes to contracts as appropriate.

As a result of the Procurement Management monitoring and control process, two major deliverables are produced:

- *Work performance information*—Project performance information as it pertains to contract performance of both the buyer and the seller.
- *Change request*—A formal proposal to modify or correct provisions of the contract between the buyer and the seller.

In addition, any previously created documents are updated to reflect any changes. The controlling process of Stakeholder Management is:

- *Control stakeholder engagement*—This is the process of monitoring overall project stakeholder relationships and adjusting strategies and plans for engaging stakeholders.

As a result of the Stakeholder Management monitoring and control process, two major deliverables are produced:

- *Work performance information*—Project performance information as it pertains to effectiveness of stakeholder engagement.
- *Change request*—A formal proposal to modify a stakeholder management document.

In addition, any previously created documents are updated to reflect any changes.

The Control group, its inputs and outputs, and the tools and techniques used are explained in detail in Chapters 11 and 12.

Closing Component Processes and Major Deliverables

The Closing process group consists of component processes and deliverables that are applicable to two of the knowledge areas of the framework, as shown in Figure 3-9. In Integration, the process is as follows:

- *Close project or phase*—At the official end of one phase of the project or the entire project, collect any remaining project performance metrics.

As a result of the closing project process, five deliverables are produced:

- *Final project or service*—This is the end product as a result of completing the project which includes the confirmation that the project has met all customer requirements for the product or service of the project.
- *Project archives*—This is a complete set of indexed project records.
- *Formal acceptance*—Stakeholders formally acknowledge (signatures) the acceptance of the product.
- *Lessons learned*—This is documentation that details the causes of variances, the reasoning behind the corrective action chosen, and other types of lessons learned.
- *Team member assessments*—These are evaluations of each team member's work performance on the project.

The closing process of Procurement Management is:

- *Close procurements*—This process involves completion and settlement of the contract, including resolution of any open items.

As a result of the contract closeout process, three major deliverables are produced:

- *Contract file*—This is a complete set of indexed records to be included with the final project records.
- *Formal acceptance and closure*—This is a formal written notice that the contract has been completed.
- *Lessons learned*—This documentation details the causes of variances, the reasoning behind the corrective action chosen, and other types of lessons learned.

The process group Closing, its inputs and outputs, and the tools and techniques used are explained in detail in Chapter 13.

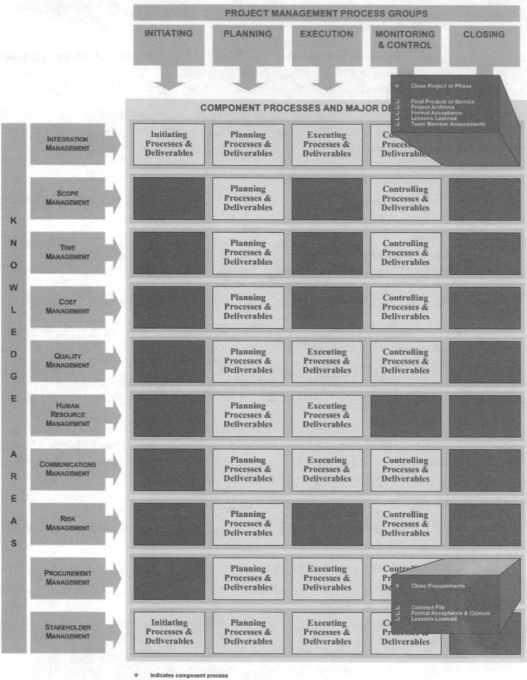

FIGURE 3-9 **Closing Component Processes and Major Deliverables**

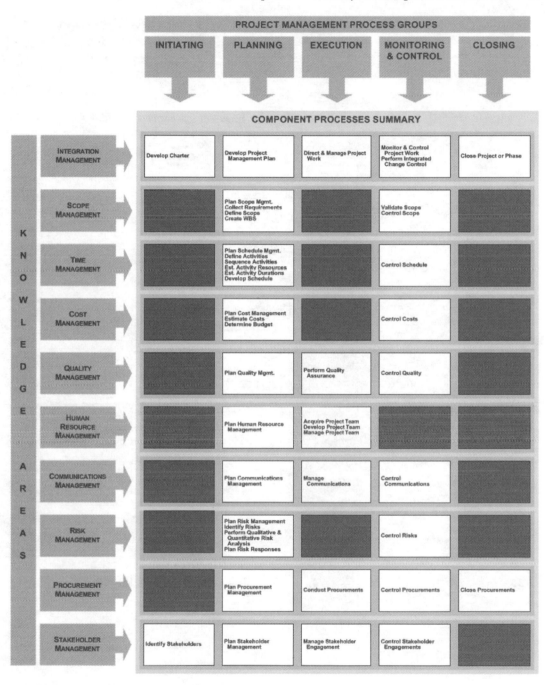

FIGURE 3-10 Component Processes Summary

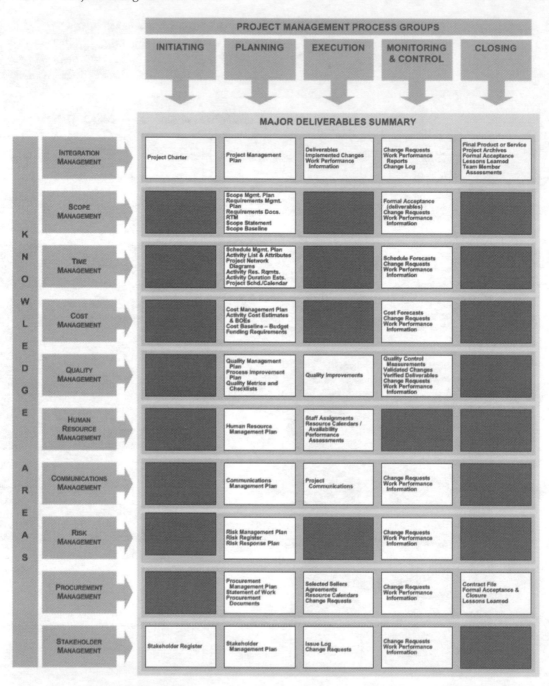

FIGURE 3-11   Major Deliverables Summary

Framework Summary

This chapter presents an introduction to the project management framework based on the PMI's PMBOK. The text uses the framework as a visual guide and reminder about where you have been and where you are going in terms of learning the project management process as well as the tools and techniques that successful project managers use in order to bring projects in on time, under budget, and meeting stakeholders' expectations.

The following chapters discuss in detail the common project management processes, the inputs to those processes, the tools and techniques project managers use, and the outputs (deliverables) produced as a result of the processes. Figures 3-10 and 3-11 provide a summary of the framework introduced in this chapter and the major deliverables described here.

Chapter Review

1. In the late 1950s and early 1960s, the term *project management* emerged as projects began to grow rapidly in scope, size, duration, and resources. In 1969, the Project Management Institute (PMI) was founded for the following reasons:
   - To create a forum for project managers to discuss emerging concepts and practices
   - To officially recognize project management as a profession in and of itself
   - To bring together people from all branches of project management to share and learn from each other

2. In 1994, the first edition of *A Guide to the Project Management Body of Knowledge* (PMBOK) was published. The PMBOK describes the sum of knowledge within the profession of project management, including knowledge of proven traditional practices that are widely applied as well as knowledge of innovative and advanced practices.

3. The project management framework is structured around five process groups that are made up of component processes consisting of tools, techniques, and outcomes, organized within nine knowledge areas.

4. These are the five basic process groups used to conduct a project:
   a. *Initiating*—Authorizing the beginning or ending of a project or phase.
   b. *Planning*—Ensuring that the objectives of the project are achieved in the most appropriate way.
   c. *Execution*—Coordinating all resources (people and material) during the implementation of the project plan.
   d. *Controlling*—Monitoring of project variances from what was planned to actual progress.
   e. *Closing*—Formal acceptance of the project or a phase and updating of the project information base with lessons learned.

5. The process groups overlap with varying intensity during the execution of a project.

6. A knowledge area describes project management knowledge in terms of its component processes. There are ten knowledge areas:
   1. Integration Management
   2. Scope Management
   3. Time Management
   4. Cost Management
   5. Quality Management
   6. Human Resources Management
   7. Communication Management
   8. Risk Management
   9. Procurement Management
   10. Stakeholder Management.

7. The ten knowledge areas represent the body of knowledge that a project manager must have in order to consistently deliver successful projects that meet a customer's expectations for scope, time, cost, and quality of the project deliverables.

8. The project management framework consists of ten knowledge areas presented on the vertical axis and five process groups organized across the top on the horizontal axis. At the intersection of the two, the framework presents the component processes, which are the project management processes that are common to most projects and the major deliverables produced by those processes.

Glossary

component process An organized set of tasks designed to fulfill an explicit outcome within a process group.

deliverable A tangible and verifiable work product.

framework A set of assumptions, concepts, values, and practices that constitutes a way of viewing reality.

knowledge area A description of project management knowledge in terms of component processes.

process group A collection that consists of one or more component processes.

project management body of knowledge (PMBOK) The sum of knowledge within the profession of project management, including knowledge of proven traditional practices that are widely applied as well as knowledge of innovative and advanced practices.

Project Management Institute (PMI) An international professional society created to guide the development of project managers and researchers.

special interest group (SIG) A group organized around a common interest or issue. Examples of current PMI SIGs include Aerospace & Defense, Human Resources, Information Systems, and Women in Project Management.

strategic plan A formal plan generally spanning three to five years for an entire business entity that defines its mission, vision, goals, strategies, and measures of progress.

Review Questions

1. Explain the makeup of the Project Management Institute.
2. List the reasons for the creation of the Project Management Institute.
3. Define what is meant by a PMI special interest group.
4. What is the PMBOK, and what is its importance to the field of project management?
5. What is a PMP?
6. Define the term *framework*.
7. What is a component process? A process group? A knowledge area?
8. List and define the five process groups.
9. List and define the ten knowledge areas.
10. What is a component process?
11. Define the term *deliverable*.
12. Define what the project management framework is and explain what pieces make up the framework.

Problems and Exercises

1. Explain how process groups overlap during the course of a project. Draw a graph similar to the one in this chapter.
2. Give your own interpretation of the analogy that the process groups supply us with a roadmap to follow and the knowledge areas describe the methods (for example, car, plane, bus) of how to get to our final destination.
3. Create a set of interview questions to ask a professional project manager concerning how his or her organization's project management framework was defined and how it has evolved over time. Contact a professional project manager and actually ask these questions. Prepare a two- to three-page paper based on your results.

Projects and Research

1. Visit PMI's web site, at www.pmi.org. Become familiar with the content and location of important information at this site.
2. Research the SIGs listed on PMI's web site, at www.pmi.org. Choose one SIG and research its mission and objectives. Prepare a presentation for the class.
3. Research other professional societies that deal with project management and write a paper discussing the differences from and similarities to PMI.
4. Research other certifications for project management professionals. Do a comparative analysis of your findings. Does one certification offer more benefits than another? Write a paper presenting your recommendation on which one would be the best to pursue and why.

MINICASE

1. *Background:*   Review the background information from the Chapter 2 minicase, where Mark Lewis, the son of Reid Lewis (president of R & S Amusements Services), was trying to convince his father that the hiring of Premier Project Management Services (PPMS) to manage the IT automation project at R & S was a waste of money. He insisted the money would be better used to hire an independent contractor (an acquaintance close to Mark) to do the entire project. This conversation triggered a series of meetings between Jeff Dunbar and Kevin Pullen of PPMS and Reid and Mark Lewis of R & S Amusements Services—meetings that took time away from the real purpose of the project but were required in order for Jeff and Kevin to communicate their value and convince Reid and Mark why it's in their best interests that Jeff and Kevin continue on the project.

    Current Situation 1:   Kevin, Jeff, and Mark were in Reid's office, discussing the future of PPMS with the project. Reid brought up the fact that he had talked to a local consulting firm that provides project management services, and their rates appeared to be quite a bit cheaper than PPMS's. Further in the conversation, Reid stated that the firm made a good impression, but he had learned that those consultants had no experience in managing IT projects, nor did they use the PMBOK. He said the president of the firm had told him that all projects, including IT, were basically the same. In fact, the president said, "If you have managed one project, you can manage them all." The firm's president also made some disparaging remarks about the PMBOK—"Academic mumbo-jumbo that wannabe project managers hide behind because they don't know how to manage real projects."

Discussion: Describe how you would convince Reid and Mark that all projects are not alike. Discuss how IT projects are different from projects in other disciplines and why this matters. Finally, describe how you would convince Reid and Mark of the value of the PMBOK and the benefits it provides. Also discuss why Reid and Mark should be concerned if the other firm they are considering does not follow a standard process.

Current Situation 2:   Mark asked why PPMS costs so much and why Kevin and Jeff think they deserve to be paid so much. Jeff provided several reasons and highlighted the fact that all PPMS's project managers are certified PMPs. Mark replied that he heard that anyone off the street who read the PMBOK could take the exam and get certified, so in his opinion, certifications are basically worthless and provide no value.

Discussion: Respond to Mark's claim about the PMP certification being worthless. What value does this certification provide to an individual project manager and the organization he or she works for? Is Mark correct that anyone can take the PMP exam? If not, how would you correct Mark in his understanding? Explain to Mark the entire PMP certification process and describe the other credentials PMI offers. How is the PMP certification different from other similar certifications?

Suggested Readings

Archibald, R.D. (1992). *Managing high technology programs and projects*. New York: Wiley.

Cleland, D.I., & King, W.R. (1983). *Project management handbook*. New York: Van Nostrand Reinhold.

Fahrenkrog, S. (2000). *Standards committee manager. A Guide to the Project Management Body of Knowledge (PMBOK)*. Newtown Square, PA: Project Management Institute.

Graham, R.J. (1985). *Project management: Combining technical and behavioral approaches for effective implementation*. New York: Van Nostrand Reinhold.

Jones, T.C. (1998). *Estimating software costs*. New York: McGraw-Hill.

Project Management Institute (PMI). (2013). *A guide to the project management body of knowledge*, 5th ed. Newton Square, PA: PMI.

PRINCE2 web site, at www.prince2.org.uk.

Project Management Institute web site, at www.pmi.org.

Schuler, J.R. (1995, October). Decision analysis in projects: Summary and recommendations. *PM Network*, pp. 23–27.

Souder, W.E. (1983). Project evaluation and selection. In D.I. Cleland and W.R. King, eds., *Project management handbook*. New York: Van Nostrand Reinhold.

PART 2

Project Initiation and Planning Methods

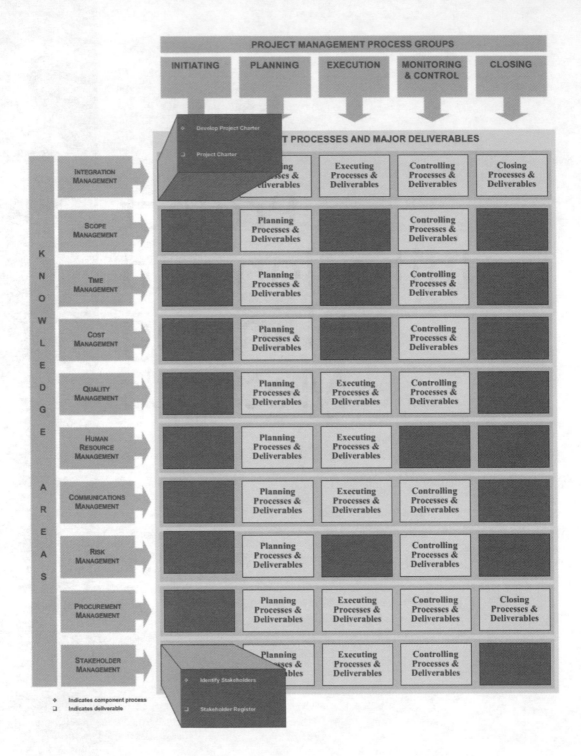

4

Project Selection and Initiation

R & S Amusements Services

Event 4

Setting   A meeting is being held in a conference room at a local hotel. All managers as well as key employees of R & S Amusements Services, as well as Jeff Dunbar and Kevin Pullen, are in attendance. This is the kickoff meeting for the project to modernize R & S's computer applications and systems. Reid Lewis, who is the president of R & S Amusements Services, and the project's executive sponsor, is currently at the podium. Let's join the meeting currently in progress. . . .

REID   I want to thank you all for taking the time from your busy schedules to be here today. As most of you are aware, I have decided to embark on a project to bring our computer systems and operations into the twenty-first century *[applause from everyone]*—or at least equal to or better than those of our competition. In order for this project to be successful, it is imperative that it receive the utmost support from each one of you, starting with today's meeting. Diana has distributed copies of today's agenda, which is now displayed on the overhead projector. As you can see, after the opening remarks, we will have introductions. Let me start by introducing Jeff Dunbar and Kevin Pullen *[Jeff and Kevin stand up]* of Premier Project Management Services. Jeff and Kevin are certified project managers who have a wealth of experience implementing information technology business systems. We are extremely fortunate to have these talented individuals lead and guide our efforts for the development of our new systems. I expect each of you to give Jeff and Kevin total cooperation in the event that they call on your services. *[Reid nods to Jeff and Kevin to sit down]* I'm sure most of you know each other, but let's still go around the room and have everyone stand up and give their name, location, and what role they serve in the company. *[Introductions proceed around the room]*

REID   Now that everyone knows each other, let's move on to the next order of business. Jeff, Kevin, and I have been meeting over the past few months and reviewing our current business processes and assessing our needs for automating those processes. In summary, we have identified nine areas that are in desperate need of attention. They are: *[He motions to Diana to display the next slide]*

1. Customer management (contracts)
2. League management
3. Asset management (asset tracking)
4. Inventory control (parts and supplies)
5. Collection management (revenue tracking)
6. Service and repair management
7. Sales and marketing
8. Internal operations (finance, shipping, receiving, etc.)
9. Human resources (payroll and benefits)

I'm sure that each one of you has strong feelings and opinions about one or more of these areas, and we will solicit those thoughts in due time. For now, though, we have identified three areas, or *projects*, that will receive top priority. We will concentrate our IT efforts on those projects initially, and when those have concluded, we will concentrate on the other areas. The three projects that we will work on first are customer management, asset management, and collection management. *[Heidi Cosgray raises her hand].* Yes, Heidi, you have a question?

HEIDI   Reid, can you elaborate on how you determined which projects would be first?

REID   Sure! But, I think I will ask Jeff to share how we came up with our decision.

JEFF   We evaluated each by following a formal project selection process that took into consideration many things, including return on investment, strategic importance to the company, risks, and available resources. *[This process will be demonstrated later in the chapter]* As a result of the analysis, the three projects Reid mentioned were identified as having the highest priority and enough available resources, in that I mean people.

REID   I might add, Jeff, that those three projects are also highly related to each other. In other words, it would be difficult to do one without the other.

HEIDI   I see, but those other areas are also in great need of help.

REID   I absolutely agree. But you can only do so much at one time, based on the resources you have available. You have my word that those other areas will be addressed also, but at a later time.

HEIDI   Okay, I guess.

REID   And now I am appointing Diana Brooks, Ashley Brooks, and Mark Lewis as the key interface contacts—or, as Jeff and Kevin refer to them, our subject matter experts (SMEs). Diana and Mark are responsible for directly working with Jeff and Kevin throughout the project. It will also be their responsibility to call on your knowledge *[pointing to the audience]* and expertise when the need arises. At this time, I am now going to turn over the meeting to Jeff Dunbar.

JEFF   Thank you, Mr. Lewis. First of all, Kevin and I would like to thank all of you for giving us the opportunity to participate in this project. It will be hard and challenging work, but I'm sure that by working together, we can build a product that will provide great value to the organization. Now, let's review the project charter and the vision of the project. *[Jeff motions to Kevin to bring up the first page of the project charter on the overhead projector]*

(To be continued)

(Instructions for building the project charter and an example of a project charter are presented later in this chapter.)

CHAPTER PREVIEW AND OBJECTIVES

Before a project manager begins working on a project, he or she needs to understand how and why the organization decided to spend valuable resources—money and time—on the project. Chapter 2 describes this process as using the systems approach. It is important for a project manager to understand the reasons a project was selected so that the critical success factors—the tasks that, once completed to the user's satisfaction, mean the project is done and successful—for the project are clearly defined and understood. You will understand the project management initiation process when you can:

- Define the Project Initiation process group, with all its component processes and deliverables
- Understand why selecting the right projects to work on is important and sometimes difficult for an organization
- Learn the tools and techniques of project selection, including:

  1. The strategic planning process for the organization and IT department
  2. Quantitative methods, including the following:

     a. Return on investment (ROI)
     b. Net present value (NPV)
     c. Internal rate of return (IRR)
     d. Payback analysis

  3. Qualitative methods
  4. Balanced scorecard
  5. Real options
  6. The weighted scoring model (WSM)

- Understand the importance and contents of a project charter and the stakeholder assessment matrix
- Understand how to conduct a project kickoff meeting

AN INTRODUCTION TO PROJECT SELECTION AND INITIATION

Chapter 1 defines *project*, and Chapter 2 describes the concept of a project life cycle. With these two concepts understood, we will now move on and discuss in this chapter how projects should be selected. Before launching the start of a project, project managers need to take a step back and figure out what projects the organization *should* be working on. Many projects in the past have been selected because of the "squeaky wheel" syndrome: The person who makes the most noise repeatedly gets his or her projects selected. Hopefully, you can see that this is not the best method to selecting projects. An organization needs to go through a formal process of selecting the right mix of projects before it formalizes the list into a project charter and begins work. In most, if not all, organizations, there are more projects than there are funds and people to run them. Organizations therefore need to be very selective in choosing the projects that will return the most value to the organization. *Value* in this sense relates not only to dollars (profit) but factors such as market share, customer relations, safety issues, environmental concerns, and new government regulations. Why this project? Who selected it? and What else is going on in the organization at the same time? are all questions that need to be asked and answered before work on the project begins.

One only needs to look at the dismal success rates of IT projects, presented in Chapter 1, to see why it's important that organizations begin by choosing the right projects to work on. In the past, IT professionals have done a poor job of understanding and presenting the value of IT projects. The reasons for the poor performance are twofold: First, IT professionals spend more time studying technology than finance and second, they are unable to effectively communicate to management that IT projects are different than projects in other industries and thus require different metrics. IT professionals, especially managers and project managers, must understand the broader picture of the organization and the impact a technology project will have on it from cost and other perspectives. They need to understand and possess the ability to communicate the value of IT projects in terms the rest of the organization can understand. In the sections of this chapter that follow, many techniques are described that will aid a project manager in communicating the value of IT projects. Many of the newer techniques, such as balanced scorecard and real options, have begun to address this issue of finding better ways to define the merits of an IT project.

In today's business climate of tight budgets, limited IT resources, and low IT project success rates, organizations are becoming more and more selective in the IT projects they approve. But most organizations are beginning to realize the strategic importance of IT to their success. In a 2002 survey commissioned by InfoWorld, 70 percent of the respondents said that IT was "absolutely essential to their company's business objectives." (InfoWorld, 2002) To get projects approved, IT managers must learn to align their projects with the company's strategic direction. To accomplish this, project managers need to ask themselves some key questions about a project so they can understand what value it lends to the organization, the risks associated with the project, and the value of the project to the organization if it is successful. Andriole (2001) has identified four key issues that must be considered in order to understand the bigger organizational picture in which IT projects play a role:

1. *Business value*—IT project managers must look at a project from a business perspective by identifying what business process(es) will be most affected. They must understand the process thoroughly and the impact the project will have on these processes. They must also understand what impact the project will have on associated processes. Using the systems approach assists in learning what impact a project will have on all parts of the organization.
2. *Technology*—The technology used for a project needs to be well tested, scalable, secure, modifiable, and usable. Has the technology been used in the organization before, and do we have experience with it? What technology is the competition using, and how might technology allow this organization to see what works and doesn't work in their specific industry?
3. *Cost/benefit questions*—An organization needs to understand whether the complete costs—including acquisition, development, and ongoing support costs—of the project outweigh its benefits.
4. *Risk*—IT project managers must do a thorough risk assessment for the project. They must know what kinds of issues or problems might surface during the project—such as the software vendor going out of business in the middle of the project or funding for the project being cut in half during execution—and be sure to have appropriate safeguards or workarounds in place so the project can still be completed.

All this information needs to be presented in the project's **business case**. (The next section of this chapter demonstrates how to gather and use this information to build the business case.)

PROVEN STRATEGIES AND HINTS TO SUCCESS

Eilertsen (2004), a principal at the Kollner Group, provides the following list of "Best Practices" to aid organizations in their project selection process:

- Be formal and ongoing, and integrated into the strategic planning system, the process management system and other continuous business cycles.
- Ensure that the executive leadership team is keenly involved with the Project Selection process.
- Include a Project Steering Committee or function that is constituted by the executive leadership team to assist with project evaluations and recommendations.
- Require that projects are evaluated against an objective business criteria aligned with the strategic goals and receive scoring based on associated weighted factors.
- Include an activity step that allocates resources for feasibility analysis to projects that achieve a threshold score (business importance) but require additional information for decision-making.
- Use a well-defined threshold to separate small projects from larger strategic projects in order not to overload smaller projects with unnecessary evaluations and ensure thorough analysis of larger projects.
- Establish clear project decision-making authority levels between organizational entities such as the executive leadership team, the project steering committee, business units, and functional departments.
- Reinforce mechanisms that support project decisions that are for "the good of the company" versus "private interests."
- Provide easy access to selection criteria, project definition and evaluation as well as project portfolio and status.

Business Case

The contents of the business case may change, depending on the size, cost, level of risk, or strategic importance of the project. The levels of each of these factors and others will determine the amount of time and information required for the business case. For example, if you need to build a business case for a small feature to be added to the company web site that was projected to cost $5,000 and take only two weeks to complete using one person, the business case would be short and probably not very detailed. But if you were asked to build a business case for a project that had early estimates of over $500,000 and 20 people and would take the next six months, your business case would need to be much more detailed and complete.

Key parts of the business case may include the following:

- Key objectives
- Methods and sources used to obtain information for the business case
- Benefits to the organization if the project is successful
- Consequences if the project is not done

- Full life cycle costs
- Qualitative models
- Quantitative models
- Risks

All of these parts are defined in later sections of this chapter.

Input is needed from a variety of people to build the business case. The business case should not be developed by one person in a vacuum. The team responsible for putting together the business case should be representative of all affected stakeholders. IT professionals should also participate on the team to aid in information gathering. The benefits of building such a team for the business case development process are many:

- *Credibility*—Credibility is achieved because the information comes from many different sources, allowing for checks and balances.
- *Accuracy*—Accuracy is improved for the same reasons as credibility, as well as the fact that the information comes from the people who are best equipped to provide it. For example, to get salary data for key resources needed for the project, you go to the human resources department, which can provide the basic salary data plus overhead rates (insurance, vacation, and so on), or to get market impact, you solicit input from the marketing and sales department.
- *Thoroughness*—Thoroughness is aided by this approach if all team members are allowed input into the process.
- *Ownership*—It's important that IT projects not be viewed as solely the property of the IT department. All stakeholders from all affected departments need to feel like part of the process and take some ownership in making sure the project is successful.

The main purpose of the business case is to aid decision makers in selecting the best projects possible for the benefit of the organization. The business case must demonstrate how an IT project will add value to the organization.

PROJECT MANAGEMENT CONCEPTS: PROJECT SELECTION AND INITIATION

This section introduces the tools and techniques of building each part of the business case mentioned in the previous section, as well as the two key deliverables from the Initiation process—the project charter and the stakeholder assessment matrix (referred to as "stakeholder register" in the fifth edition of the PMBOK).

Strategic Planning

One of the key considerations for making project selection choices is the answer to the question Does the proposed project aid the organization in the fulfillment of its strategic plan? Organizations use many strategies to execute the **strategic plan**; this text concentrates on technology as an enabler of an organization's success. In today's organization, IT has become the key piece to success. You would have to look really hard to find a project an organization is executing today that doesn't involve IT in some way. Most of the objectives in an organization's strategic plan include an IT strategy.

The main goal of any project should be to deliver some form of business value: higher market share, new product or market, better customer support, higher productivity, lower operating costs, and so on. All these are typically defined in the company's strategic plan as goals and objectives. Listed next to each goal or objective is a list of strategies that will fulfill the objective. The development of strategies (projects) must focus on what is needed to meet the strategic plan's goals and objectives. This development involves an analysis of the external environment to identify economic, social, and technological opportunities and potential threats. It also involves a **SWOT analysis** of the internal environment.

SWOT stands for *strengths, weaknesses, opportunities,* and *threats.* An organization needs to understand the external opportunities and threats that exist and their internal strengths and weaknesses in order to face them. Each of these categories is defined as follows:

- *Strength*—A strength is an organizational resource (money, people, location, equipment, IT) that can be used to meet an objective.
- *Weakness*—A weaknesses is a missing or limited resource that bears on the organization's ability to meet an objective.
- *Opportunity*—An opportunity is a circumstance that may provide the organization a chance to improve its ability to compete.
- *Threat*—A threat is a potentially negative circumstance that, if it occurs, may hinder an organization's ability to compete.

The deliverable from all identified analysis is a set of strategies (projects) designed to best meet the needs of all stakeholders.

Because today's organizations face an ever-growing number of opportunities and threats, they must be able to successfully execute multiple projects in multiple departments. A technique that assists organizations in managing multiple projects is called **portfolio management**. IT project portfolio management organizes a group of IT projects into a single portfolio consisting of reports that capture project goals, costs, time lines, accomplishments, resources, risks, and other critical factors. Chief information officers (CIOs) and other IT managers can then regularly review entire portfolios, allocate resources as needed, and adjust projects to produce the highest returns.

With IT project portfolio management, you group projects so they can be managed as a portfolio, much as an investor would manage stocks, bonds, and mutual funds. Benefits of this approach include the capability to identify redundancies, allocate resources across all projects appropriately, and monitor project progress. An additional benefit that's highly regarded by CIOs is the capability to view projects as investments, thus analyzing not only how much a project will cost but also its anticipated risks and returns in relation to other projects. This allows entire portfolios to be managed in order to produce the highest returns. Project portfolio management is covered in more depth in Chapter 14.

Many studies have been conducted to research the most used and most appropriate project selection methods in various industry segments (Bacon, 1992; Cabral-Cardoso & Payne, 1996; Jiang & Klein 1999; Souder 1983). All the tools discussed in this chapter were rated highly by most of the studies, depending on project characteristics—strategic value, risk, size (both in time and cost), and industry. The bottom line is that organizations need to follow a formal structured, repeatable process to ensure that they are working on the best mix of projects to match their current economic and strategic situation. Also, the importance and size of the project should drive the amount of time and money used in building the business case. For example, an inexpensive one-week project should not take three weeks to justify, and a one-year, 20-person, high-value and high-cost project should not take 10 minutes to justify.

Project Selection Models

A project selection model is a simplified representation of project characteristics. Evaluating something that hasn't happened yet can be a very difficult and complex task. Models allow you to emphasize key parts of the puzzle and see them more clearly. When you look at just one project at a time, the complexity issues are small, but organizations must continually evaluate many projects that consist of different costs, schedules, risks, importance, and so on. But remember that these models are partial representations of reality, and final decisions need to be made by informed decision makers. There are two basic types of project selection models: qualitative and quantitative.

The next two sections walk through the process of adding qualitative and quantitative models to the business case. Then, later in this chapter, information from the case study is used to build the business case and demonstrate how the top three projects were selected for the R & S Amusements Services case study.

QUALITATIVE MODELS   The following are some examples of **qualitative models**:

- **Subject matter expert (SME)** judgments
- "Sacred cow" decisions
- Mandates

SMEs are individuals either within a company or outside the company who possess expertise or unique knowledge in a particular facet of the business, either because of work experience, education, or a combination of the two. SMEs can evaluate projects with or without more complex quantitative models and can categorize projects with low, medium, and high priority rankings. Some use colors to code projects, with high priority getting green, medium getting yellow, and low getting red. High-priority projects tend to be scheduled and initiated before medium- and low-priority projects.

Sacred cow decisions are made because someone—generally in upper management—really wants a particular project to be done. These decisions are not always in the best interest of the organization but of one individual or a group. Unfortunately, many organizations still operate today using this method. The scenario usually goes something like this:

- A senior manager from a non-IT department picks up a trade magazine and reads about how all the best companies are doing XYZ to be competitive. He then schedules a meeting with an IT manager and explains that XYZ is something we have to implement.
- The IT manager, not knowing any better, launches a project, gathers resources, and begins to operate under the directive to "get it done ASAP (as soon as possible)."
- Other projects that these individuals are working on are all delayed, as they work on the "sacred" one.

Now, it may be that this is a worthwhile project, but maybe some other worthwhile projects were dropped. Companies need to make sure they follow a systems approach and evaluate any new projects against other potential projects and currently running projects.

The third qualitative method is mandates. Mandates can come from vendors, government agencies, industry sectors, or markets. Vendors may in the case of computer software release a new version and stop support for previous versions: You either upgrade or risk losing support. Some vendor contracts stipulate that you will keep the software current. A project may be mandated by key customers. Many consumer goods retailers are mandating that all suppliers be capable of conducting business—including orders, shipping information, and inventory control—completely electronically. If your company doesn't have this capability but wants to do business with the customer, you will be required to add these capabilities.

Other mandates may come from a government agency or legislative body that passes a new law. For example, the Family and Medical Leave Act allows individuals to take a leave of absence from work to care for a family member. The employee is guaranteed a position with the company upon returning to work—maybe not the same position, but a job. Companies were forced to update their human resources software and systems in order to track and manage this type of event.

The industry segment or market pressures may force companies to make changes to remain competitive. For example, if a primary competitor offers a new service or product that is well received by customers, you may be forced to follow suit or risk losing market share. Some examples include U.S. banks offering automatic teller machines (ATMs) with access to cash withdrawals and deposits and major brick-and-mortar retailers such as Sears and Wal-Mart needing to create online services, including product catalog searches and purchasing.

QUANTITATIVE MODELS Every IT project will have some level of financial benefit to the organization as well as some level of cost. The bottom line is that IT projects cost money. The reason we create financial models for project selection analysis is simply to ascertain whether the benefits outweigh the costs and to what degree. Each organization uses different combinations of these models. No organization uses every one of them during each selection process. Some determine the mix of models to use based on the type and significance of the project. High-risk, high-dollar projects get more scrutiny than low-risk, low-dollar projects.

Before examining each of the **quantitative models**, it's important that you understand that the numbers generated are estimates of future occurrences. Just because they look finite and complete doesn't mean that they are the whole story. These numbers are just one of the project characteristics you need to look at when deciding the merits of a new project.

One item of business you need to understand before looking at the financial models is the idea of the **time value of money**, which affects the quantitative models. Projects of any size occur over long periods of time—many span multiple years. Consequently, any evaluation of benefits and cost must be done over several time periods. A typical IT project will have costs from day one but may not see any real benefits until much later. The key issue with quantitative models in this regard is that money has a time value. A dollar earned today has more buying power than a dollar earned later, due to many factors, such as inflation and risk.

If you give someone a dollar today, she can invest it in a savings account and increase the value of the dollar, making it worth more than the dollar she receives a month from now. Organizations must operate in the same fashion. Organizations can invest the money they have today in a bank account or in other projects to increase its value. Before you invest money in a project, you must compare its rate of return against other opportunities (other projects). The following formula and example will help you understand the time value of money.

$$FV = PV(1 + i)^n$$

Where

FV = future value of an investment (project)

PV = present value of that same investment

$\quad i$ = interest rate or discount rate or cost of capital

$\quad n$ = number of years

The following simple example shows how this formula works. An organization invests $1,000 today ($PV$) for 1 year ($n$) at an interest rate of 10 percent (i), which means the investment is worth $1,000(1+.1)^1$, or $1,100, at the end of the first year. The problem arises when you have multiple investments with varying rates of returns. One investment might start making money in one year and another in five years. You need to find a way to evaluate different investments equally. You do this by evaluating the present value of each of the investments. This is called *discounting future values to the present*, or *discounted cash flows*. The formula above becomes:

$$PV = \frac{FV}{(1 + i)^n}$$

The following example demonstrates the value of a promise of $1,000 in benefits one year from today:

$$PV = \frac{\$1,000}{(1 + 0.1)^1} = \$909$$

The results show that the promise of $1,000 a year from today is worth only $909 today due to risk, inflation, and other factors. Understanding the concept of the time value of money is necessary before tackling the quantitative project selection models in the next section.

All of the following quantitative models can be calculated using a spreadsheet program such as Microsoft Excel or just a handheld calculator. The following sections explain the four quantitative models: net present value (NPV), internal rate of return (IRR), return on investment (ROI), and payback period. Later in the chapter, these formulas are used in the R & S Amusements Services case study to demonstrate how you can use these formulas during the project selection process.

Net Present Value   NPV is one of the most often used quantitative models for project selection. NPV is a method of calculating the expected net monetary gain or loss from an investment (project) by discounting all future costs and benefits to the present time. If the NPV turns out to be a positive value, the project has surpassed the cost of capital or return available by investing the same money in other ways. All other project characteristics being equal, the project with the highest NPV should be chosen.

To calculate NPV, you first determine the total costs of the project each year and the total benefits each year over a set number of years. Many organizations dictate the evaluation period you must use for your calculations, such as three or five years. Sometimes, this period might depend on the length of the project. The person or team responsible for determining the costs and benefits must do a thorough job of examining all known values to make the NPV calculation meaningful. (Finding these benefits and costs is covered in greater detail in Chapter 6.) The second step in the process is to determine the interest or discount rate. This number is based on the cost of obtaining capital to fund the project or the amount of return an organization can get from other investment opportunities with similar risks. Next, you calculate the NPV using the following formula:

$$NPV = \sum_{t=0\ldots n} = CF/(1 + i)^t$$

Where:

t = year of the cash flow

n = last year of the cash flow

CF = cash flow at time t

i = interest rate or discount rate

Let's look at an example that illustrates how to calculate NPV. There are two projects you might choose. The costs or cash outflows and the benefits or cash inflows are listed below for five years. Year 0 numbers are the initial costs and benefits. In many but not all IT projects, the year 0 values for benefits are zero.

	Year 0	Year 1	Year 2	Year 3	Year 4	Year 5
Project 1						
Costs (cash outflows)	$120,000	$100,000	$75,000	$50,000	$50,000	$20,000
Benefits (inflows)	$0	$60,000	$100,000	$120,000	$180,000	$100,000
Net cash flow	($120,000)	($40,000)	$25,000	$70,000	$130,000	$80,000
Project 2						
Costs (cash outflows)	$75,000	$90,000	$30,000	$30,000	$20,000	$20,000
Benefits (inflows)	$0	$85,000	$100,000	$75,000	$50,000	$25,000
Net cash flow	($75,000)	($5,000)	$70,000	$45,000	$30,000	$5,000

Setting the discount rate to 8 percent, an example of how to calculate NPV for this example is located in the chart at the top of the following page.

When you look at the NPV for both projects, you see that Project 1 has the higher value, making it more attractive. Both projects have a positive NPV, so both could be done if enough resources are available.

INTERNAL RATE OF RETURN   IRR is similar to NPV in process but is slightly more difficult to calculate. The IRR is the discount rate at which NPV is zero. Finding an IRR solution involves trial and error: You keep plugging in different discount rates and see which one drives the NPV to zero. You can compare the IRR value to other projects or to a company standard to see which projects should get priority. If the organization has set a minimum value of 8 percent and the project IRR is 15 percent, you have a positive situation, and you should do the project. If the project IRR turns out to be 6 percent, you might not get permission to do the project.

	Do the Math	Discounted Cash Flow
Project 1		
Year 0	($120,000)	($120,000)
Year 1	($40,000)/(1 + 0.08)^1	($37,037)
Year 2	$25,000/(1 + 0.08)^2	$21,433
Year 3	$70,000/(1 + 0.08)^3	$55,569
Year 4	$130,000/(1 + 0.08)^4	$95,553
Year 5	$80,000/(1 + 0.08)^5	$54,448
NPV	**Add Them Up**	**$69,966**
Project 2		
Year 0	($75,000)	($75,000)
Year 1	($5,000)/(1 + 0.08)^1	($4,630)
Year 2	70,000/(1 + 0.08)^2	$60,014
Year 3	$45,000/(1 + 0.08)^3	$35,723
Year 4	$30,000/(1 + 0.08)^4	$22,051
Year 5	$5,000/(1 + 0.08)^5	$3,403
NPV	**Add Them Up**	**$41,561**

Using the same example as before for NPV, the IRR turns out to be 19.8 percent for Project 1 and 26.6 percent for Project 2. With the discount rate set at 8 percent, both projects return a positive value. If you must choose one project over the other, then choose Project 2, which has the higher IRR.

RETURN ON INVESTMENT   ROI provides the percentage return expected over the life of the project, using the following formula:

ROI = (Total discounted benefits - Total discounted costs)/Total discounted costs

Let's look at an example using the same numbers from the example used to calculate NPV. You first determine the discount factor for each year and then multiply each benefit and cost for that year by its discount factor:

Year	Do the Math	Discount Factor
0	$1/(1 + 0.08)^0$	1
1	$1/(1 + 0.08)^1$	.93
2	$1/(1 + 0.08)^2$	.86
3	$1/(1 + 0.08)^3$	.79
4	$1/(1 + 0.08)^4$	.73
5	$1/(1 + 0.08)^5$	.68

Then you calculate discounted benefits and costs:

Project 1	Discounted Costs	Discounted Benefits
Year 0	(1) * $120,000 = 120,000	(1) * $10 = 0
Year 1	(0.93) * $100,000 = 93,000	(0.93) * $60,000 = 55,800
Year 2	(0.86) * $75,000 = 64,500	(0.86) * $100,000 = 86,000
Year 3	(0.79) * $50,000 = 39,500	(0.79) * $120,000 = 94,800
Year 4	(0.73) * $50,000 = 36,500	(0.73) * $180,000 = 131,400
Year 5	(0.68) * $20,000 = 13,600	(0.68) * $100,000 = 68,000
Totals	$367,100	$436,000

Project 2	Discounted Costs	Discounted Benefits
Year 0	(1) * $75,000	(1) * $0
Year 1	(0.93) * $90,000	(0.93) * $85,000
Year 2	(0.86) * $30,000	(0.86) * $100,000
Year 3	(0.79) * $30,000	(0.79) * $75,000
Year 4	(0.73) * $20,000	(0.73) * $50,000
Year 5	(0.68) * $20,000	(0.68) * $25,000
Totals	$256,000	$335,000

Finally, inserting the project's total discounted benefits and discounted costs into the ROI formula results in the following:

ROI Project1= ($436,000 - $367,100)/$367,100 = 19%

ROI Project2= ($335,000 - $256,000)/$256,000 = 31%

If you must choose one project over the other, then choose Project 2, which has the higher ROI.

PAYBACK PERIOD   The payback period is the amount of time it will take a project before the accrued benefits surpass accrued costs, or how much time an investment takes to recover its initial cost. As with the other quantitative models, many organizations have a maximum number in mind that all projects must meet or beat. If an IT project has a payback period of four years but the organization demands two years, then either you won't be allowed to proceed with the project or you must make adjustments to change the equation.

Using the numbers from the NPV model example earlier, you calculate the payback period by first tracking the net cash flow across each year to determine the year when net benefits overtake net costs. For Project 1, this occurs sometime in year 4, and for Project 2 sometime in year 3. See the following numbers:

Year	Year 0	Year 1	Year 2	Year 3	Year 4	Year 5
Net cash flow Project 1	($120,000)	($160,000)	($135,000)	($65,000)	$65,000	$145,000
Net cash flow Project 2	($75,000)	($80,000)	($10,000)	$35,000	$65,000	$70,000

The payback period ignores the time value of money but offers a glimpse at the potential risk associated with each of the projects. A longer payback period generally infers a riskier project. The longer it takes before a project begins to make money for the organization, the greater the chances that things can go wrong on the project. Because of these drawbacks, the payback period is not generally used in isolation but is combined with other measures or is used as an initial deal breaker. Organizations can set a maximum number of periods, such as 18 months, and any project that doesn't break even before the maximum is not considered further.

In the next section, all the project selection methods are brought together and used to build a weighted scoring model to help management make project selection decisions.

Weighted Scoring Model

The WSM is a culmination of all the other models discussed so far in this chapter. It is used to evaluate all projects on as equal a basis as is humanly possible. It attempts to remove human bias in the project selection process. The criteria used to compare projects differs from one organization to another and may differ between types and classes of projects within the same organization. For example, some organizations use different models based on the size and length of their projects. The projects are rated small, medium, and large, and each group has its own set of criteria. Many times medium-size projects use the entire criteria set from a small project's set of elements with some additional elements, and large projects use the medium-size project's set of criteria with additional elements.

Figure 4-1 shows an example of the WSM for a large project. The criteria used to make decisions are listed in the first column of the table. These are by no means the only elements an organization might use to base their decision. As stated earlier, if you had a small system upgrade project that was being done because the vendor was dropping support on the current software, the chart would look quite a bit different. The second column contains the weight assigned to each criterion. Notice that some have higher weights (more importance) than others.

At different times or for different types of projects, organizations change the importance of each criterion. For example, for all IT projects, an organization might emphasize strong customer support and strategic plan alignment, as shown in the example in Figure 4-1. During tough economic times, the organization might want to stress the financial measures (NPV, IRR, and ROI) for all projects. Using these weights allows the organization to change the priorities and use the appropriate priorities in the decision-making process.

The assignment of weights to each criterion can become a lengthy and sometimes heated process, as each person tries to get a high rating for his or her own favorite criterion. Care must be taken to not alienate individuals and to come to a consensus of opinion.

	Criterion	Weight	Project			
			1	2	3	4
1	Market share effect	10%	70	70	50	30
2	Competition	5%	30	70	70	70
3	Risk	10%	10	30	50	30
4	Product fit	5%	70	70	50	0
5	Strategic plan alignment	15%	50	50	70	30
6	Customer support	20%	50	50	30	30
7	Payback	10%	70	70	30	10
8	NPV	15%	70	50	30	30
9	ROI	10%	50	50	30	10
	Totals	100%	53	54	43	26.5

FIGURE 4-1 **Weighted Scoring Model Example**

TABLE 4-1 WSM Rates

Rating	Score
Poor/not satisfied	0
Below average	10
Average	30
Above average	50
Excellent	70

The final set of columns in Figure 4-1 contains the results for each project, based on a standard scale. The same rates must be used on all projects under consideration. The rates used aren't as important as the uniform application of those rates. Table 4-1 shows the rates that were used in this example. If a criterion is rated high for a particular project, it receives a score of 70, and if it is rated poor, it receives a score of 0.

Next, let's look at some examples from Figure 4-1 and Table 4-1 in more detail. For the criterion market share effect, if the project will raise the organization's market share significantly, it receives a 70. If the project will have no effect or a negative effect, it receives a 0 score. For the criterion risk, the numbers work in the opposite direction: If the project has a high amount of risk, it receives a low score, and if it has relatively low risk, it receives a high score. Risk is discussed in more detail in Chapter 8, but for now, just know that although you can never get rid of all the risk in a project, there are ways to reduce risk and its effect on a project.

Finally, you assign each criterion a score across all projects and enter those numbers in the table. Some of these scores are subjective, but as long as the SMEs are evaluating them consistently, you should end up with consistent results. Some organizations set up ranges for some of the criteria. For example, if the NPV is within certain ranges, you assign an appropriate score; if NPV is between $500 and $1,000 (some use a percentage of the project cost instead of an exact dollar amount), you assign a score of 10; if it is between $1,000 and $5,000, you assign a score of 30; and so on. The last step is to multiply each score by its weight and then sum the results. In Figure 4-1, you can see that Project 1 received a score of 53, Project 2 got a score of 54, Project 3 was scored 43, and Project 4 received a score of 26.5. Based on these results, Project 2 has the highest score and should be done first, but Project 1's score was so close that it should also be looked at if enough resources exist to do both.

Two final thoughts need to be discussed about the WSM before we move on. First, notice that there are no descriptive names attached to the projects—just numbers are used. Many organizations prefer that the names be left off this chart to help reduce bias in the final decision. The decision should be based on the merits of the results presented in the chart. Second, even though we have seemingly reduced the decision down to a table of numbers, humans must make the final decisions. Each of these numbers is based on subjective evidence and thus will always require humans in the process.

Before moving on to the creation of the first project deliverable and the project charter, and how to conduct a stakeholder analysis, let's discuss two alternative methods organizations can use to aid in the process of making project decisions: the balanced scorecard and real options.

Additional Project Valuation Techniques

BALANCED SCORECARD   The balanced scorecard approach was developed in the early 1990s by Drs. Robert Kaplan (Harvard Business School) and David Norton (cofounder and president of Balanced Scorecard Collaborative Inc., based in Boston, USA). This approach gives a company the ability to identify what it should measure in order to balance the financial perspective of the organization.

The balanced scorecard approach suggests that the organization be viewed from four perspectives (see Figure 4-2):

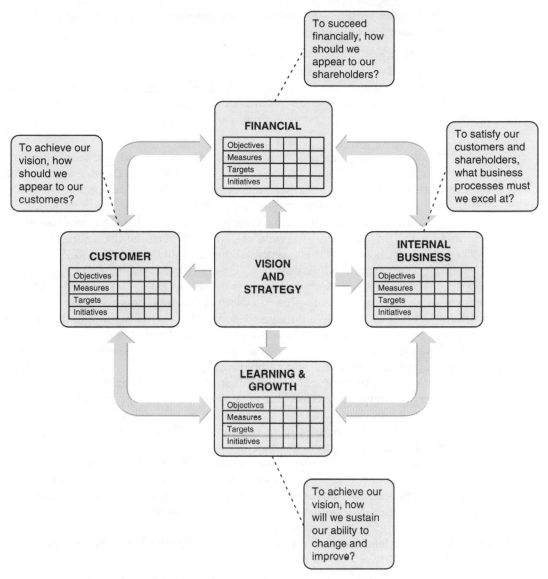

FIGURE 4-2 The Balanced Scorecard Perspectives

Reprinted by permission of Harvard Business School Press. From "The Balanced Scorecard: Translating Strategy into Action" by Robert S. Kaplan and David P. Norton. Boston, MA 1996, p. 9. Copyright ©1996 by the Harvard Business School Publishing Corporation; all rights reserved. *Source:* "Using the Balanced Scorecard as a Strategic Management System," by Robert S. Kaplan and David P. Norton, Harvard Business Review, January-February 1996.

- *Financial*—The strategy for growth, profitability, and risk, viewed from the perspective of the shareholder.
- *Customer*—The strategy for creating value and differentiation, from the perspective of the customer.
- *Internal business*—The strategic priorities for various business processes, which create customer and shareholder satisfaction.

• *Learning and growth*—The priorities for creating a climate that supports organizational change, innovation, and growth.

In addition, the organization needs to develop metrics, collect data relative to each of these perspectives, and analyze the data.

The balanced scorecard model is widely implemented across many diverse industries and organizations for alignment to business strategy and vision. Studies indicate that more than 60 percent of the Fortune 500 companies currently use the balanced scorecard in some form.

REAL OPTIONS   The movement toward the real options methodology for IT project portfolio management derives from a financial model that considers the management of a portfolio of stock investment options. This theory became most widely acknowledged outside the finance sector when Professor Robert C. Merton, Harvard University, and Professor Myron S. Scholes, Stanford University, were jointly awarded the Nobel Prize in Economic Sciences for the development of a new method to determine the value of derivatives in 1995 from the application of their computational formula developed in 1973.

Today, only around 30 percent of CFOs are using a real options approach to make investment decisions, although real options theory is widely acknowledged as achieving better results than traditional valuation methods. It has, however, so far not gained as much importance in practice as it maybe deserves. This is mainly due to the options theory being very mathematical and rather difficult to understand.

A fundamental definition of *option* is "the right, but not the obligation, to buy (call option) or sell (put option) an investment holding at a predetermined price (called the exercise price or strike price) at some particular date in the future." [Latimore, D. (2002) p. 2] Real options allows an organization to value IT projects in a manner similar to the way we value stock options. A stock option lets us make a small investment today in order to reduce our risk later on. At the same time, it keeps open the possibility of making a bigger investment later, if the future goes the way we expect it to. Applying that thinking to IT projects through a relatively new approach, the real options methodology, can lead to better project valuation, capital budgeting, and strategic planning. The more uncertain the times, the more valuable an options approach becomes. The use of real options in IT is still in its infancy, but other industries have used real options valuation for some time. In the fast-moving world of IT, demand, technology changes, factor prices, and many other parameters vary widely. A real options approach lets managers consider that uncertainty and how they might best react to it.

IBM defines two types of real options:

> *Growth options* give a firm the ability to increase its future business. Examples include research and development, brand development, mergers and acquisitions, leasing or developing land, or—most pertinent—launching a technology initiative.
> *Flexibility options*, on the other hand, give a company the ability to change its plans in the future. Management can purchase the option to delay, expand, contract, switch uses, outsource or abandon projects. [Latimore, D. (2002) p. 3]

Viewing an investment as an option allows projects to be evaluated and managed in respect to future value and a dynamic business environment. The acknowledgement of a dynamic business environment introduces the concept of an iterative valuation process that reflects changing business objectives or environmental conditions and opportunities.

In order to make real options easier to understand, T.A. Leuhrman (1998a) used the analogy of a tomato garden: In a tomato garden, not all the tomatoes are ripe at the same time; some are ready to pick right now, some are rotten and should be thrown away, and some will be ready to harvest at a later date. We can apply this line of thinking for evaluating investments. Traditionally, the evaluation of investments has been limited to a yes/no "ripe or rotten" decision based solely on NPV. With real options, an investment with a negative NPV may still be good, but perhaps it's just not the right time—it's not ripe yet. If you can delay until the proper time (now ripe), your once-negative NPV would be positive.

Figure 4-3 divides a tomato garden (option space) into six regions, with definitions of the types of options that fall into each region and directions about how to handle them. The regions are defined as follows:

- *Region 1*—This region is a now-or-never area, where either all the unknowns about an investment have been determined or the time to decide is up. If the investment has a value-to-cost greater than 1, you should invest.
- *Region 2*—Investment in this region is currently showing a value-to-cost greater than 1, but it is still not time to invest. The line dividing Region 2 and Region 3 equates to the NPV of the option. In Region 2, the NPV is greater than 0.
- *Region 3*—Investment in this region is currently showing a value-to-cost greater than 1, but it is still not time to invest. In Region 3, the NPV is less than 0.
- *Region 4*—Investment in this region has a value-to-cost ratio of less than 1. This would not be pursued unless conditions are improved to make it a worthy investment before time runs out.
- *Region 5*—Investment in this region has a value-to-cost ratio of less than 1. This would not be pursued unless conditions are drastically improved to make it a worthy investment before time runs out.

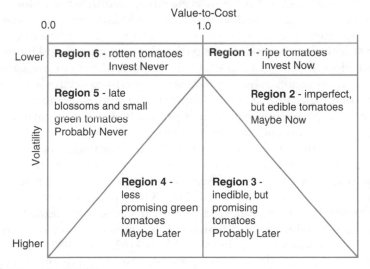

FIGURE 4-3 The Tomato Garden

- *Region 6*—This region is a now-or-never area, where either all the unknowns about an investment have been determined or the time to decide is up. If the investment has a value-to-cost below 1, you should not invest.

Based on this model, managers should nurture the investments in Regions 3 and 4 to attempt to increase their value or reduce their cost, thus improving their locations to Regions 1 or 2. Plotting related options in the tomato garden will help managers understand where they need to focus their attention. As in a real tomato garden, managers need to constantly monitor and reevaluate the options and their locations in order to strive for the best yields.

This completes our section on project selection techniques. As you can see, a variety of choices are available to help organizations become better at selecting the right projects. Many studies have been done to review the use and effectiveness of these techniques. The problem in trying to draw any conclusions from these studies is that they all address different industry segments, over different time periods, using different technologies. The choice of which techniques to use is based on many factors: company culture, financial position, industry segment, technology proposed, length of project, size of project, and so on. Organizations should use a method that builds a weighted scoring model which consists of elements and weights that are pertinent to the organization at a point in time and circumstances. It is not the mission of this text to prescribe which methods must be used but to give a number of choices to choose from to enable the best selection of projects. The next section assumes that a selection of projects has been made and it is time to begin working on them. The next step is to conduct a stakeholder analysis to identify stakeholders and assess their attitudes and involvement with the project.

Stakeholder Analysis

A **stakeholder analysis**, which identifies the stakeholders process from the Project Stakeholder Management Knowledge Area, identifies the influence and interests of the various stakeholders and documents their needs, wants, and expectations. These needs and wants form the basis of the scope statement described in Chapter 5. Another part of the stakeholder analysis deals with influence, power, and interest in the project. This second piece of information plays an important part in the success of most projects. Successful project managers must learn to perform accurate stakeholder analyses. The results of doing a stakeholder analysis are best doucmented in a spreadsheet that should be kept and reused on each project that shares a particular stakeholder. Much of the information collected (see Figure 4-5) is of a very personal nature and can be reused from project to project. Most of the information is shared with the rest of the team, but some of the information, such as items of a very personal nature, are best kept private. A long time ago, Sun Tzu, a Chinese general, said the following concerning knowing your stakeholders: "If you know the enemy and know yourself, you need not fear the result of a hundred battles. If you know yourself but not the enemy, for every victory gained you will also suffer a defeat. If you know neither the enemy nor yourself, you will succumb in every battle" (Clavell, 1983). We don't want to insinuate that stakeholders are the enemy; quite the contrary, if dealt with correctly, they become your best allies.

The stakeholder analysis process consists of the following steps:

1. Identify all potential stakeholders.
2. Determine interests, expectations, and influence for each.
3. Build a stakeholder assessment matrix (see Figure 4-5).
4. Analyze appropriate stakeholder approach strategies and update the matrix.
5. Update throughout the project.

The first step, before collecting information from stakeholders, is to correctly identify who the stakeholders are and where they come from. Figure 4-4 shows the many places you should look to find stakeholders. Usually, the easiest stakeholders to

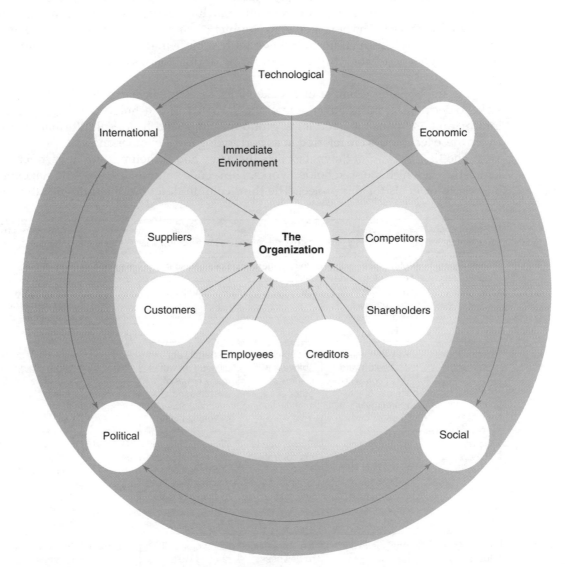

FIGURE 4-4   Sources of Project Stakeholders

Source: Adapted from Grover Starling, (1996). "The Changing Environment of Business." Reprinted by permission.

locate are those internal to the organization. For example, if you're installing a new software package for the accounting department, you first look for stakeholders in the accounting department. Then, you might need to include the CFO, CEO, and related IT personnel (operations, analysts, developers, and so on). Next, you can move on to the immediate environment of potential suppliers of the software and maybe additional hardware vendors, customers, creditors, shareholders, and competitors. When all these have been documented, you can move on to the broader environment, which includes international concerns; political concerns (if the accounting package was purchased to meet Sarbanes-Oxley compliance, for example); and social, economic, and technological concerns. A concerted effort is needed to include everyone who might have an interest in the project. The next step is to conduct research to complete the matrix shown in Figure 4-5 by conducting interviews with subject matter experts and referring to previous notes generated during the building of the business case or on previous projects.

Figure 4-5 is an example of a stakeholder assessment matrix (or referred to as the stakeholder register in the 5th edition of the PMBOK). The techniques used for getting the information are: personal interviews, group meetings, and historical information. Collectively these techniques are referred to as performing a stakeholder analysis.

The first column of the matrix lists the name and sometimes the department or organization in which the stakeholder works. The second column describes the stakeholder's interest in or goals for this project. The third column describes the influence this person

Stakeholder/ Organization	Interests	Influence	Unique Information	Role	Approach Strategies
Mike Smith Accounting	Major user of the new information, been with company 15 years	Voice is heard all the way up to the CEO	Loves Nascar, has four children, likes camping	Key end user	Family oriented, needs to work straight time with no overtime to take care of family
John Doe Shipping	Key end user of the software, most computer literate of the company	His opinion of software will influence other users	Generally against all change, works many hours of overtime, no children, always seems stressed	End user	Approach carefully about changes, schedule first for training
George Rogers Warehouse	Against using computers due to his lack of knowledge	Some, due to his control of the warehouse and staff	Well liked but will need many hours of computer training; well liked by his warehouse staff	Key end user	Slowly work with him to bring computer skills up to date; careful not to insult due to computer knowledge
Mark Kane Inventory	Anxious to use new software	Not much, due to newness with company	Major baseball fan and Colts football fan	Observer	Periodic status updates

FIGURE 4-5   Stakeholder Assessment Matrix

will have on decisions and ultimately the outcome of the project. The fourth column is one you might want to keep private, depending on the nature of the information. Unique information can be job related but often is information about stakeholders' personal lives— anything that may aid the project manager in formulating an approach strategy. The fifth column is the official role the stakeholder will play during the project, and finally the last column describes the approach the project manager and the team should take in working with each stakeholder.

The final step in the stakeholder assessment process is to make sure to update this information throughout the life of the project so it is as accurate as possible for future projects. If it is accurate, there is no need to start from scratch to generate this information the next time you work with a particular stakeholder. Depending on the length of time between encounters, you might need to update the information, but this should give you a great start.

After completing the stakeholder analysis, the team is ready to turn its attention to the first deliverable of *every* project, regardless of characteristics such as size and risk: the project charter.

Project Charter

The **project charter** is the first tangible work product created in all projects, regardless of size and type. Even the smallest projects can benefit from doing an abbreviated charter. Figure 4-6 shows an example of a standard project charter format. Don't panic if you don't understand some of the sections in the charter; the text has covered only a few of its elements. During the next several chapters, the other elements will be explained, and you will learn exactly how to fill out each part of the charter. The project charter is the first work product that is placed under *configuration control*, the process that controls any and all changes made to a project after the charter has been signed. Notice toward the bottom of the charter that a section has been reserved for approvals. The key stakeholders of the project are required to sign the project charter before any work begins and the project proceeds. The key stakeholders are the executive sponsor and any manager who has resources involved in the project. Once the charter is signed, no one should be allowed to make changes to it unless it goes through the formal change control process.

Let's talk about a couple of best practices when it comes to creating project charters. First, it should not be created in isolation. Like the project selection process, the charter requires input from many sources. Information is retrieved from the business case, the organization's strategic plan, SMEs, sponsors, project leaders, and so on. Second, it is not a novel; it should be short and to the point. It should not be any longer than is absolutely necessary. For a simple project, a page or less may be sufficient. For a longer project with more risk, time, and dollars, several pages will be required to capture the required information. But remember that in order to get full sponsor support, sponsors must understand and agree to everything contained in the project charter. The main purpose of the project charter is to first get a sponsor to take ownership of the project and second to make sure that at the outset of the project, everyone is on the same page and agrees to the project objectives.

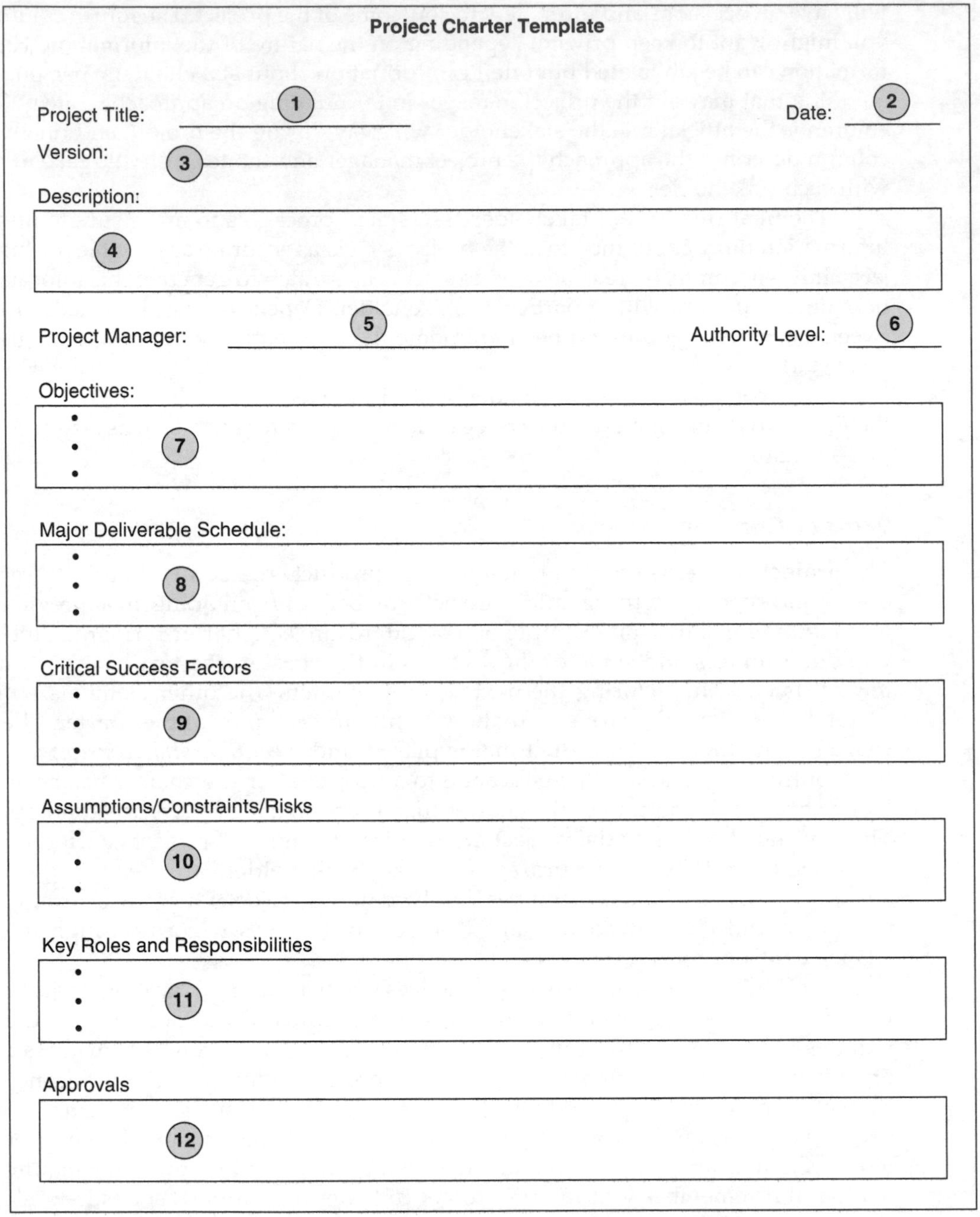

Project Charter Template

Project Title: _____ ①   Date: _____ ②

Version: _____ ③ _____

Description:

┌──┐
│ ④   │
│   │
└──┘

Project Manager: _____ ⑤ _____   Authority Level: ___ ⑥

Objectives:

┌──┐
│ •   │
│ •   ⑦   │
│ •   │
└──┘

Major Deliverable Schedule:

┌──┐
│ •   │
│ •   ⑧   │
│ •   │
└──┘

Critical Success Factors

┌──┐
│ •   │
│ •   ⑨   │
│ •   │
└──┘

Assumptions/Constraints/Risks

┌──┐
│ •   │
│ •   ⑩   │
│ •   │
└──┘

Key Roles and Responsibilities

┌──┐
│ •   │
│ •   ⑪   │
│ •   │
└──┘

Approvals

┌──┐
│   ⑫   │
│   │
└──┘

FIGURE 4-6   Project Charter Template

In some organizations, the project charter is used as a formal contract between the sponsor and IT department or an outside vendor. In these instances, the project charter tends to be much longer, containing a complete statement of work (SOW) and a detailed budget. Chapter 9 covers the concept and contents of the SOW in detail. For now, all you need to know is that a SOW is a detailed narrative description of the work needed to be performed as part of a project. This is necessary so contractual agreements can be reached on each specific deliverable and its associated cost.

The project charter template has three main sections: project identification, key project characteristics, and resource responsibilities and approvals. The project identification section includes the project title, date, version identifier, description, name of the project manager, his/her authority on this project, and the description. The key project characteristics include objectives, major deliverable schedule, critical success factors, and assumption, constraints, and risks. The third section consists of the key roles and their responsibilities and the project approvals. Each section is more fully defined next:

1. *Project title*—A project charter needs a short, action-oriented title, usually starting with an action verb. Many organizations like to create a short form of the title, using the first letter of each word, such as Upgrade Project Software (UPS). The title needs to be long enough for people to differentiate from others but short enough to be remembered.
2. *Project date*—This is the date the charter was completed and ready for authorized signatures.
3. *Version*—Once signed, the project charter is under configuration version control. If anything in the project changes and affects this document, a new version should be created, and a new version number should be assigned.
4. *Description*—This includes business needs, project purpose, justification for the project based on market demand, business need, customer request, technological advance, legal requirement, social need, and information that will tie in with the organization's strategic plan.
5. *Project manager*—This is the name of the person assigned as the manager of the project, who could be internal or external to the organization.
6. *Authority level*—The charter needs to specify the amount of authority the project manager and others have to make project decisions without approval from others. The authority level covers all aspects of the project, including scope, time, and cost. For example, a certain authority level may allow the project manager to make decisions that have an impact on cost of less than 10 percent of the entire budget and/or less than a fixed dollar amount of, say, $1,000.
7. *Objectives*—Objectives are written at a high level and cover the major project objectives. The template contains bullet points to reinforce the idea that these do not need to be complete sentences. The key purpose in the objectives section is to clearly state the boundaries of the project. It is just as important to state what is *not* included as it is to state what is included. The objective statements should be future outcome based (for example, "the update to the inventory control software will allow the warehouse to cut overhead expenses by 25 percent").
8. *Major deliverable schedule*—Each objective needs to be listed in this section, along with a projected delivery date. Keep in mind that you are very early in the process and haven't even begun the project, so coming up with a specific date will be difficult or even impossible. If the sponsor or the organization's management team requires a date, you should try to use a month (April) or quarter (third quarter) and not get

locked into an exact date. This section also shows the order in which the objectives will be worked on and completed. For some projects, customers have exact "need by" dates for parts of the project due to government regulations, interdependencies with other projects, or competitive pressures. In these cases, you need to make sure these dates are noted and explained. The explanation should include the negative consequences of not meeting the due dates.

9. *Critical success factors*—This is a list of metrics that will be tracked to measure success. The metrics may be different on every project and need to be generated by the project sponsor. Like the objectives, these need to be short and to the point. They should be defined in the form of goals. George Doran coined the acronym SMART (for specific, measurable, assignable [preferably to one person or at a minimum one group], realistic, and time related) as a way to aid in the goal creation process. When all the goals or success factors have been achieved, the project is complete and successful.

10. *Assumptions/constraints/risks*—The project charter needs to contain a list of issues that can affect the outcome of one or more of the objectives and thus the project and need to be monitored or mitigated. These are items significant enough that they need to be brought to the attention of the sponsor and upper management. Relevant regulatory agency policies and procedures should be noted in this section. Any specific security issues should be described in this section.

11. *Key roles and responsibilities*—The project charter needs to list the names, roles, and responsibilities required to complete the project successfully. The names at this stage in the project are generally tied to job function or departments and not individuals. For example, the names might be "database support," "network support," or "human resources management." The roles describe what the named person or function will be doing on this particular project. The responsibilities are more specific, such as "schedule staff," "perform appraisals," or "perform logical and physical data modeling."

12. *Approvals*—Finally, a project charter needs a list of names and signatures of people who agree with the stated objectives and critical success factors and who authorize the start of the project.

Kickoff Meeting

With the completion of the stakeholder analysis and the signing of the project charter, it's time to schedule and conduct the kickoff meeting. It seems at first glance to be a trivial event, but the kickoff meeting needs to be well planned to ensure that the project starts on the right foot. A project can be difficult enough during execution; you don't want to make it even harder by skipping the kickoff meeting.

The first step is to make sure to invite the right people, which you can determine from your updated stakeholder assessment matrix (refer to Figure 4-5). If someone who should be at the kickoff is not invited, that person might turn against the project and not participate. It is easier to invite everyone connected and run the risk of inviting someone who doesn't need to be there than to forget someone. The meeting should be called, organized, and run by the key sponsor, with support from the project manager. Many times in the past on IT projects, the IT project manager did the scheduling, and the project quickly became an "IT" project that lost key support. The kickoff meeting allows everyone to hear the same message and agree publicly to provide support. Finally, the kickoff meeting can be a festive event, complete with hats, mouse pads, coffee mugs, and other items with the project name or acronym printed on them to get everyone excited about the project. It is a good way to get the project off to a great start. In the "How to Conduct the Project Initiation Process" section, later in this chapter, a sample kickoff meeting agenda is provided.

PROVEN STRATEGIES AND HINTS TO SUCCESS

A common wiki tool, created by the Information Technology division of the Commonwealth of Massachusetts to propose a common methodology for project management in the state, offers the following best practices for conducting the kick-off meeting:

- Every project requires a formal kick-off to bring together the team and stakeholders
- Make sure to invite the right people
- Material needed before organizing the meeting: project charter, skills needed in the team, roles and responsibilities at a high level, communication plan
- Develop and disseminate the meeting agenda well before the meeting. The agenda includes: project goals and objectives, high-level plan with deliverables
- Critical success factors and project complete acceptance criteria
- Early risks and issues identified
- Communication strategy
- Change management plan

PROJECT SELECTION AND THE INITIATION PROCESS

This section describes the steps necessary to complete the selection process. The project selection process is as follows:

Step 1. Project sponsors prepare the business case for the project, including qualitative and quantitative information, as appropriate or required by the organization. This is performed for each project being considered.

Step 2. The business cases for all the projects are collected by the organization's steering committee staff and separated into categories (research, mandates, strategic direction, market advantage, and so on). The projects can then be compared to others in the same categories. The categories are specific to the organization's industry and mission.

Step 3. The steering committee meets physically or virtually to review the organization's strategic plan and current environment and economic situation. The plan may have been written as much as one or two years earlier, so before project decisions are made, the organization's current situation needs to be reviewed and evaluated.

Step 4. The steering committee builds a WSM for each project within each category, using the appropriate metrics.

Step 5. The steering committee reviews the resource availability needs of each project and compares them to what is currently available. It would be great to always select the best projects, but this might not be feasible if two projects require the same resource full time. The company must then decide not to do both projects or to acquire additional resources. If additional resources are acquired, the project cost structure must be updated.

Step 6. The steering committee selects the projects and commits the associated resources.

Step 7. The selected project manger conducts the stakeholder analysis, with aid from selected SMEs.

Step 8. The steering committee staff creates the project charter, with the aid of the selected project manager. The project manager should be picked based on the needs of the project. A complex critical project should have a senior project leader assigned, and a simple, noncritical project should have a less senior project leader assigned. The project manager's experience should also be taken into consideration. If the project is to update the organization's accounting software, a project manager with accounting background should be selected.

Step 9. The project manager must get the project charter signed by the appropriate stakeholders, securing their support for the project.

Step 10. The project manager, in association with the project sponsor, conducts the kickoff meeting. Many organizations have the sponsor run the meeting and make the invitations to increase the visibility of the sponsor to all stakeholders.

HOW TO CONDUCT THE PROJECT SELECTION AND INITIATION PROCESS

In this section, let's use the R & S Amusements Services case study to demonstrate the process of project initiation. Subsequent chapters follow a similar pattern building on the examples presented here. This section walks through the 10-step project initiation process presented in the previous section. Before proceeding, review the case study at the beginning of this chapter, which depicts the last step in the process: the project kickoff meeting. Before hosting the kickoff meeting, the consultants from PPMS and key members of the R & S Amusements Services team had a lot of work to do. Let's go back in time and begin with the building of the business case and the other deliverables that are created during project initiation and used during the kickoff meeting.

Step 1: Preparing the Business Case

Jeff and Kevin from PPMS are helping decide which projects it should tackle first. Jeff and Kevin, working with Reid Lewis, built a three-year strategic plan for the organization. After the strategic plan was put together, a detailed analysis of the business was conducted, with all members of R & S, to determine which areas needed the most attention. The team came up with nine areas that needed immediate work. Jeff and Kevin discussed with Reid the pitfalls of taking on too many projects and not having enough resources to do them properly, and it was decided to let the projects speak for themselves through a business case and a WSM for each of the nine projects.

Jeff and Kevin worked with key R & S associates from each area to build the business cases. Each business case was written using the same format. The business case for the asset management project is presented here, and it has the following sections:

- Key objectives and benefits
- Key sponsor
- The consequences of not doing the project
- Three years' worth of financial benefits and costs
- All identified risks
- The financial models: NPV, ROI, and payback
- How well the project supports the strategic plan of the business

Business Case: Asset Management
Objectives:

- System will have the ability to track the location of every amusement asset (onsite or in the field) and its level of usability (active, repair, obsolete, etc.)
- Items in inventory include game machines, dollar bill changers, external speakers, maintenance parts
- Inventory information is updated continually in real-time
- Generate requisitions
- Ability to generate ad hoc reports generated by users
- Track vendor information
- Track asset performance

Primary Sponsor: Mark Lewis
Consequences of Not Doing the Project:

- Lost revenue due to not having the correct items at the correct time at the correct location
- Continue to incur expenses for overordering or underordering
- Will not gain productivity enhancements the new automated system will provide
- Customer dissatisfaction continues to increase leading to lost sales

Benefits and Costs (Three-Year Estimates)

- Estimated costs: Year 1, $50,000; Year 2, $10,000; Year 3, $4,000
- Estimated revenue: Year 1, $5,000; Year 2, $50,000; Year 3, $50,000

Risks:

- Low end-user involvement
- Clear statement of requirements
- Proper selection of software product, vendor, and implementation
- Technology selected
- Cost and time estimate errors

Financial Models:

NPV: $25,957
ROI: ($94,500 − $62,740) / $62,740 = 51%
Payback: Occurs early in year 3

Strategic Plan Alignment:

- Asset management has a direct tie to several items on the strategic plan, reducing cost through better management of resources, increasing productivity, and improving the quality of decisions by increasing the quality of information.

Step 2: Creating the Steering Committee

Jeff and Kevin assisted Reid Lewis with the selection of the IT project steering committee, making sure that all business departments were represented fairly. They selected Reid Lewis; Danny Calloway, league coordinator; Diana Brooks, business operations manager; Mark Lewis, manager of the West Lafayette location; and Ashley Brooks, finance administrator. Each member of the steering committee was given one vote and an equal say in the decisions.

Step 3: Reviewing the Strategic Plan and the Current Situation

The steering committee held its first meeting and discussed the process and procedures it was to follow. Each person had been given a copy of the strategic plan and was being asked for any questions. Each person presented a current state-of-the-business report from the perspective of his or her department. This brought everyone up to speed on the many challenges the company as a whole was facing and the nine projects submitted for consideration to help solve these challenges.

Step 4: Building the WSM

Once everyone was satisfied that they were on the same page and understood the company's strategic plan, they were ready to begin building the WSM. The first task was to build the list of selection criteria and then assign weights. After many hours of organized discussion, the committee decided that the following items would appear on the list: strategic plan alignment, ROI, NPV, risk, and customer support. Jeff and Kevin had warned Reid that selecting the categories was the easy part, and assigning the weights could be a long process, as each committee member voices an opinion. Reid was great at letting the committee come to a consensus without enforcing his will as the president. Each member was asked to try to keep the future of the entire business at the center of his or her thoughts. The committee, after several hours of debate, was able to assign weights to the criteria, making sure the total was equal to 100 percent:

Strategic plan alignment—30 percent

Customer support—15 percent

Risk—20 percent

NPV—20 percent

ROI—15 percent

The next step was to decide how to assign scores to the information presented in each of the business cases. In order to assign values to the results, some qualitative and some quantitative value assignments needed to be made and be used uniformly across all projects. Jeff and Kevin explained to the team that it was important to use the same relative values for each criterion. The team decided to use a three low, three medium, and three high assignment value system. The low-range values are 0, 10, and 20; the medium-range values are 40, 50, and 60; and the high-range values are 80, 90, and 100. For example, using the strategic plan alignment criterion, if the project didn't directly support an initiative on the strategic plan or if there was a very weak link, it would receive one of the low scores; if the project directly supported an item on the plan and was integral to its success, it would

Criterion	Weight	Projects								
		1	2	3	4	5	6	7	8	9
Strategic plan alignment	30%	90	70	80	70	90	50	70	90	50
NPV	20%	70	30	70	70	70	50	30	20	30
ROI	15%	70	30	70	80	70	60	40	20	20
Risk	20%	70	50	80	30	80	70	60	70	80
Customer support	15%	100	80	80	20	80	30	90	20	20
Totals	100%	80.5	53.5	76.5	56	79.5	52.5	58.5	51	43

FIGURE 4-7   R & S Amusements Services Weighted Scoring Model

receive one of the high scores; and if it was linked to an item on the strategic plan but played a very minor role, it would receive one of the medium scores. When scoring one of the financial results, the team set up more quantitative ranges. For example, if the ROI was more than 25 percent, the project received a high-range value; if the ROI was between 10 percent to 24 percent, it received a medium-range score; and if the payback was lower than 10 percent, it received a low-range value. Each criterion is evaluated using a similar process. The trick is to use the same thought process for each project for each criterion. Figure 4-7 shows the WSM for R & S Amusements Services.

The project numbers refer to the projects outlined in the case study. The three projects receiving the highest scores were:

- Project 1: customer contract management
- Project 3: asset management
- Project 5: collection management

R & S will therefore work on these three projects first. The decision of which one is done first or which ones can be done at the same time is based on three main factors:

1. Availability of funds
2. Availability of resources
3. Interdependencies of projects

Step 5: Reviewing Resource Needs and Availability

When the committee reviewed the WSM, it found that three projects scored significantly higher than the other six: Projects 1, 3, and 5. The next step for the steering committee was to review resource requirements for the top projects and assess R & S's resource availability to determine how many projects can be done at once and in what order. For example, if Project 1 and Project 3 both required the same resource full time, R & S couldn't do both projects at the same time unless it acquired additional resources (either by hiring new people or hiring temporary services) or it took much longer to do each one.

Step 6: Selecting Projects

After reviewing the resource requirements, R & S decided that it could do all three of the projects at the same time. Information collected while building each project's business case was then used to generate the project charters. The steering committee then had to select a project manager who was the best fit for each project. The selected project manager would then be utilized to help build the project charter. Because R & S Amusements Services has very little experience running IT projects, Jeff and Kevin were asked to run each of these projects, with the assistance of selected R & S associates. It was hoped that in addition to running successful projects, Jeff and Kevin could help train R & S associates in the art of running projects. The three R & S Amusements Services associates chosen to lead the projects are Mark Lewis, the manager of West Lafayette location (Project 3); Diana Brooks, the business operations manager (Project 1); and Ashley Brooks, the finance administrator (Project 5).

Step 7: Conducting a Stakeholder Analysis

Kevin and Jeff worked with members of the steering committee to conduct a stakeholder analysis. They followed the process described earlier in this chapter. A sample of the results of the analysis is contained in Figure 4-8.

Step 8: Creating the Project Charter

A project charter was created for each of the selected projects. The project charters were created by Jeff and Kevin from PPMS, with assistance from R & S Amusements Services associates. As stated earlier in this chapter, a project charter serves several purposes. Because R & S is new to project management, it was very important that the charter spell out the

Stakeholder	Interests	Influence	Unique Information	Role	Approach Strategies
Elaine Henry	Major user of the new information, been with company 15 years	Voice is heard all the way up to the CEO	Loves Nascar, has four children, likes camping	Key end user	Family oriented, needs to work straight time with no overtime to take care of family
Heidi Cosgray	Key end user of the software, most computer literate of the company	Her opinion of software will influence other users	Generally against all change, works many hours of overtime, no children, always seems stressed	End user	Approach carefully about changes, schedule first for training
Kenny Jones	Against using computers due to his lack of knowledge	Some, due to his control of the warehouse and staff	Well liked but will need many hours of computer training; well liked by his warehouse staff	Key end user	Slowly work with him to bring computer skills up to date; careful not to insult due to computer knowledge
Foster Hines	Anxious to use new software	Not much, due to newness with company	Major baseball fan and Colts football fan	Observer	Periodic status updates

FIGURE 4-8   Stakeholder Assessment Matrix, Asset Management Project

exact authority and role of each participant. It was also decided that R & S would move to a matrix style of organization to replace the original functional style. The following is an example of one of the charters.

R & S Project Charter

Project Title: <u>Asset Management</u>   Date: <u>3/1/2008</u>
Version: <u>2008-V1</u>

Description:

> Purchase an asset management software package that comes closest to meeting R & S needs. Then, perform a gap analysis and write custom code to deliver what is missing from the package. Finally integrate this software into the other software solutions of R & S.

Project Manager: Mark Lewis and Premier Consultants   Authority Level: ⇐ 10% of budget

Objectives:

> • Ability to track the location of every amusement asset (onsite or in the field)
> • Inventory: game machines, maintenance supplies, dollar bill changers, external speakers
> • Inventory information is updated continually in real time
> • Generate purchase requisitions
> • Ability to generate ad hoc reports
> • Track vendor information
> • Track asset performance

Major Deliverable Schedule: Duration Estimates

> • Requirements documentation with statement of work   2 months
> • Software/hardware purchase and install   6 months
> • Gap analysis document   2 months
> • Deliver custom software   2 months

Critical Success Factors

> • Find software solution that satisfies a minimum of 75% of stated requirements
> • Improves productivity by 50%
> • Reduces inventory carrying costs by 20%
> • Improve customer satisfaction ratings

Assumptions/Constraints/Risks

> • Low end-user involvement
> • Clear statement of requirements
> • Finding software which matches user requirements and budget

Key Roles and Responsibilities

> • Mark Lewis, project manager
> • Reid Lewis, executive management support
> • Kenny Jones, user requirements from warehouse
> • Elaine Henry, user requirements and software verification

Approvals

Mark Lewis _____   Elaine Henry _____
Reid Lewis _____   Jeff Dunbar   _____
Kenny Jones _____   Kevin Pullen _____

R & S Amusements Project Charter

Step 9: Securing Sponsor Signatures on Charter

Jeff Dunbar and Kevin Pullen explained the importance of getting user buy-in to make these projects successful. After the creation of the project charters, Jeff and Kevin made individual appointments with each of the key stakeholders to make sure they understood all the information presented in the charter and to answer any questions they might have. At the end of each meeting, Jeff and Kevin were able to get the stakeholders to sign the charter, showing their full support.

Step 10: Conducting the Kickoff Meeting

Finally, it was time for the kickoff meeting, which is where we began in the opening of this chapter. You now have an appreciation for all the work that goes into the decisions about what projects to work on and the information presented at a kickoff meeting.

The three projects presented in this chapter will be used throughout the remainder of the text. We present tools and techniques appropriate for each phase of the project and then use these projects to show concrete examples of what the deliverables look like and how to build them.

Chapter Review

1. In most organizations, there are more projects than there are resources to support them. Organizations need to follow a disciplined project-selection process to ensure that they are working on the correct mix of projects.

2. IT professionals must understand the systems context in which the project they are working on exists. The following four key issues will assist in understanding the business context: business value, technology, cost/benefit questions, and risks.

3. A business case is a document composed of a set of project characteristics that aid organization decision makers in deciding what projects to work on. The key parts are objectives, methods and sources, benefits, consequences, costs, qualitative and quantitative models, and risks.

4. A project may be undertaken to fulfill an initiative as part of an organization's strategic plan. IT has become a strategic enabler of most or all of the items on strategic plans.

5. Project selection techniques fall into two groups: qualitative models and quantitative models. Qualitative models consist of relying on SME judgments, sacred cow decisions, and mandates. The quantitative models are NPV, IRR, ROI, and payback period.

6. The WSM is used to compare the merits of projects based on the organization's specific priorities, such as risk, financial concerns, strategic plan initiative, and competition. Each project is evaluated fairly, based on its relative score in the model.

7. The balanced scorecard approach was developed in the early 1990s to enable companies to identify what they should measure in order to balance the financial perspective of the organization. The organization should be viewed from four perspectives: financial, customer, internal business process, and learning and growth.

8. Real options is a methodology that allows an organization to select a mix of projects derived from a financial model of managing a portfolio of stock investment options.

9. A stakeholder analysis is used first to identify all possible stakeholders for the project and then to document their influence, wants, expectations, needs, and interests in the project. This information will form the basis of the scope statement.

10. A project charter is the key deliverable of the initiation phase of every project, regardless of size. The charter officially recognizes the start of a project for all stakeholders. Once signed, the charter should be placed under configuration control. The charter consists of the project title and active date, the version number, a short project description, the project manager's name and authority level, project objectives, major deliverables, critical success factors, assumptions, constraints, risks, and key role responsibilities. The last section consists of key project stakeholder signatures, signifying their approval of the charter and thus the project.

11. The kickoff meeting is organized by the project sponsor to officially announce the start of the project. The project charter should be used to provide information for all participants. Many times, the key stakeholders are asked to sign the charter at the conclusion of the meeting.

Glossary

business case A document composed of a set of project characteristics—costs, benefits, risks, and so on—that aids organization decision makers in deciding what projects to work on.

portfolio management Control and monitoring of an organization's mix of projects to match organizational objectives for risk and investment returns.

project charter A document that formally authorizes the work to begin on a project and provides an overview of objectives and resource requirements.

qualitative model A model that involves making selection decisions based on subjective evaluation using nonnumeric values of project characteristics.

quantitative model A model that involves making selection decisions based on objective evaluation involving numeric values of project characteristics.

stakeholder analysis A process used to find all stakeholders and then identify the influence and interests of the various stakeholders and to document their needs, wants, and expectations.

strategic plan A formal document that outlines an organization's three- to five-year mission, vision, goals, objectives, and strategies.

subject matter expert (SME) A person who has the level of knowledge and/or experience in a particular facet of the business needed to support decision making.

SWOT analysis An analysis of strengths, weaknesses, opportunities, and threats; an information gathering and analysis technique to evaluate external influences against internal capabilities.

time value of money The concept that a sum of money is more valuable the sooner it is received: A dollar today is worth more than the promise of a dollar tomorrow. The worth is dependent on two variables: the time interval and rate of discount.

Review Questions

1. Explain the advantages and disadvantages associated with each of the following project selection methods: mandates, sacred cow decisions, NPV, IRR, payback period, and ROI.
2. Explain the importance of an organization's strategic plan to the selection process.
3. Why is it important for an organization to conduct a project selection process?
4. Define and describe the key components of a business case.
5. Explain why the contents of a business case might change, depending on the project.
6. Describe the stakeholders who should participate on the project selection team.
7. Explain the differences between qualitative and quantitative models and where each may be appropriate for project selection decisions.
8. Using your own words and example, explain the concept of the time value of money.
9. Explain the process of creating a WSM. Include an explanation of the selection of weights for each criterion.
10. How does the real options approach apply to the selection of IT projects?
11. List and explain the four perspectives the balanced scorecard uses to analyze an organization's performance. How does this relate to project selection?
12. What is a project charter, and what are its principal uses?
13. List and explain the major components of a project charter.
14. What type of information is collected through a stakeholder analysis? Explain the process.
15. Describe the contents of a stakeholder assessment matrix.
16. Who should be the individual responsible for planning and organizing (scheduling, sending out the invitations, and so on) the kickoff meeting. Justify your answer.
17. Who should be invited to attend the kickoff meeting?
18. Describe the 10-step project selection process.
19. In your opinion, what are some of the major drawbacks to qualitative models?
20. What does the acronym SWOT stand for? Explain its use.

Problems and Exercises

1. Using a discount factor of 8 percent, calculate the current value of an investment that is worth $20,000 two years from today.
2. As payment for programming services your consulting company provided, a client offers you two choices: (1) $10,000 now or (2) a share in the company, which you are fairly sure will be worth $15,500 four years from now. Using a discount factor of 10 percent, which offer should you choose?
3. You work for a large, successful organization, but lately many of the IT projects have experienced disappointing results. You have been put on the steering committee to improve the selection process. The organization has decided that any new projects selected for implementation must first meet strict financial measures. It has set minimum values for ROI, NPV, IRR, and payback period. Based solely on the financial numbers presented below, answer questions 3A through 3E to determine which of the following projects should be implemented by the organization:

Project 1 costs, Year 1 through Year 4: $100,000; $10,000; $10,000; $10,000
Project 1 revenue: $0; $5,000; $50,000; $110,000
Project 2 costs, Year 1 through Year 4: $50,000; $20,000; $5,000; $5,000
Project 2 revenue: $0; $6,000; $70,000; $100,000
Project 3 costs, Year 1 through Year 4: $120,000; $15,000; $5,000; $5,000
Project 3 revenue: $2,000; $50,000; $100,000; $150,000
Project 4 costs, Year 1 through Year 4: $50,000; $50,000; $10,000; $10,000

Project 4 revenue: $5,000; $70,000; $70,000; $50,000

3A. Calculate NPV for each project, using a 10 percent discount rate.

3B. Calculate IRR for each project.

3C. Calculate ROI for each project, using a 10 percent discount rate.

3D. Calculate payback period for each project.

3E. If the steering committee can choose only one project to work on, which should it be?

4. Use the same project information presented in question 3 but change the discount rate to 7 percent. Does the choice of which project to work on change?

5. As someone who has taken a project management course using this text and understands the need to select projects using a variety of factors, you have finally convinced your organization's steering committee to use a WSM to select its projects. The steering committee has decided to use the following criteria for the decision on the four projects from question 3: NPV, ROI, risk, strategic plan alignment, competition, and resource availability. The relative weights are 25 percent, 15 percent, 15 percent, 20 percent, 15 percent, and 10 percent. Risk for the four projects was determined to be Project 1, very high; Project 2, medium; Project 3, medium; and Project 4, low. Strategic plan alignment was determined to be Project 1, high; Project 2, high; Project 3, medium; and Project 4, medium. Need based on competition was determined to be Project 1, low; Project 2, low; Project 3, high; and Project 4, very high. Resource availability was determined to be Project 1, good; Project 2, good; Project 3, poor; and Project 4, poor.

5A. Use the information above and from question 3 to build a WSM, using a spreadsheet program such as Microsoft Excel. Make up your own scale to rate each project.

5B. Graphically depict the final score for each project, using a bar chart.

5C. If you can select only one project, which one should it be?

5D. Does your choice change if the relative weights change to 10 percent, 10 percent, 30 percent, 30 percent, 10 percent, and 10 percent?

6. The final section of the chapter presents the project charter for one of the projects that R & S Amusements Services chose to work on. Write up a project charter for one of the other projects.

7. Agraj Gokhale has just been promoted and is running his first IT project. The kickoff meeting, run by Agraj and his lead software developer, has taken place, and Agraj is very excited as he explains the results to his manager (who was not at the meeting) one week later. Agraj says, "The meeting was a huge success. We invited the managers from each of the key areas in finance and marketing. We presented a short version of the project charter because you can't put up on a computer overhead display 100 pages of information, can you? We then showed them the detailed Gantt chart of the 22 project deliverables. Finally, we gave each of them a copy of the charter to sign once they finish reading it. I think they were all impressed and liked our presentation because we didn't get much discussion. The meeting lasted only 30 minutes." Agraj's boss asks, "How did Mr. Jenkins respond?" Mr. Jenkins is the controller to whom each of the finance managers report. He has expressed concerns about the budget and aggressive schedule. Agraj responds, "Huh, we didn't invite him because he isn't directly working on the project." Agraj's boss then asks, "How many of the signatures have you gotten on the charter?" Agraj tells him, "Well, none yet, but it has only been a week."

7A. Do you agree with Agraj that he should be excited about this project's chances? Explain.

7B. What should Agraj do next?

8. Olivia, a PMP with 20 years of experience, has been working for the Bank of Lafayette for only a few months when her boss, Glenn, the director of IT, asked her to step in and get a project scope statement finalized and start the project. Olivia spoke with the current IT project leader, Jill, to find out what the issues were. Jill explained that the issues centered around two key and loud stakeholders and their different opinions on what the new technology should support: Lonnie, director of the loan department, and John, director of customer service. The project was to replace the current outdated software applications with a new integrated ERP package. The team had decided to use a phased approach, bringing up different parts of the application at different times. Of course, both user managers felt their respective applications were the most

important and should be done first. What advice would you give Olivia to help get this project moving? What information would you use to help schedule the phased approach?

9. Create a stakeholder assessment matrix based on the following scenario. Be sure to build a list of all stakeholders. Use the format shown in Figure 4-8.

J&B Enterprises is the second-largest maker of Mylar balloons in the world. It is headquartered on the south side of Indianapolis. The company makes and ships, on average, 2 million balloons a month. Hugo is the newly hired project manager in the IT department to aid the company in its ERP implementation, using Microsoft Dynamics AX software. The new system includes the following components: customer relationship management (CRM), general ledger, accounts payable, accounts receivable, sales order processing, and manufacturing resource planning (MRP II). In addition, the software uses the Microsoft SQL Server database program. Your first step is to conduct a meeting with CFO Mary Frett and discuss the upcoming project.

MARY   Hello, Hugo. I hope you're here to give me some good news about the new software. We are really struggling to close our books on the old system. We spend so much time just trying to fix errors and keep the old system running. So, how fast can we get the new stuff up and running?

HUGO   Hello, Mary. Well, I'm here to try to get it started, but I must remind you just how big a job this is going to be. It will take some time to get everyone trained, software installed, and any changes made. Since I'm somewhat new, my main purpose in meeting with you today is to get a list of potential users who will need to be involved in the implementation.

MARY   Well, I can tell you who I want involved and how, but you will need to meet with each one of them individually to make sure they are up to the task. Also, you will need to meet with the CEO, Bill, and keep him up to date with the project since this is the largest IT project the company has ever undertaken. He doesn't know much about computers but will want to be kept in the loop occasionally to make sure things are running smoothly.

HUGO   Okay, I will schedule individual meetings with him and the others. Let's go over the list.

MARY   I am turning over the day-to-day running of the project to the key managers in each of the three major areas: finance, sales, and manufacturing. Marcie will be your main contact in the finance department, George in the sales department, and Julien in the manufacturing department. I would like weekly updates on the status of the project. I will delegate decisions to these three unless something major comes up. If that happens, then Bill and I will make the decisions. I have worked with ERP software before in a previous company, but the software was there when I started, so I have never been through a major upgrade like this. Based on the amount of money we are spending on this, I hope it works the first time.

HUGO   Can you give me some brief information about Marcie, George, and Julien, to give me a place to start?

MARY   Sure. They have been with the company for several years, and they know their jobs very well. Marcie is probably the most knowledgeable about this kind of software. She came to us from a large accounting firm and has been the most vocal about getting the software installed. Julien has been here the longest and knows the most about how the company currently operates. He thought we should have spent the money on improving the automation of the manufacturing process, so you might need to be careful when talking to him. You will need to schedule your meeting early in the morning to catch him; he likes to start work at 6:30 a.m., so he can leave early to go home and work on his small farm. George has been here the shortest time but has already started making some good things happen with sales; but he has complained regularly about issues with tracking customers and getting more information available to him and his sales staff over the web while they travel. Well, good luck.

HUGO   Thanks for your help. I'll send you my first status report at the end of next week.

Projects and Research

1. Write a research paper, reviewing the project selection methods that today's organizations from various industries are using. Also look into the WSM criteria and the relative weights different organizations are using.
2. Compare the results from question 1 to those you get from your university's or college's IT department. What differences did you find, and why do you think a university's criteria might differ from the criteria used by a corporate organization?
3. Search the web or use other means to find examples of project charters. Then do a comparative analysis across industry segments and project types. What items have these charters included that this chapter doesn't describe?
4. Build a list of characteristics that can be used for a WSM. Discuss how different organizations might set the weights based on good and bad economic conditions and highly competitive situations.
5. Can a nonprofit organization receive any value from quantitative selection methods? Explain.
6. Statistics have shown that many organizations today still don't fully utilize a project selection process. Explain why you think this is the case.
7. Describe a well-planned and well-executed project you were a part of either in school or outside school. Describe a project that wasn't as well planned. Explain what was different about the two and what led to success or failure.
8. Define a preliminary scope statement for a project to build a simple interactive web site for this class. The web site should be accessible only by current students and instructors. The web site should allow students access to all the material presented in the class, including lecture slides and notes, extra reading, the course schedule, a chat room, a frequently asked questions section, grades, informative links, and the syllabus.

MINICASES

1. *Background:* Heidi Cosgray of R & S Amusements Services has just left the project kickoff meeting. She is upset and is getting more upset as she walks back to her office. Heidi, as the service coordinator for R & S, is responsible for the prioritization, scheduling, and tracking of service calls to service or repair amusement machines. She deals with the customers (business locations where amusement machines are installed) daily, hearing their complaints and criticisms and making promises she knows she can't keep in an attempt to keep them happy. She has been complaining for months to Reid Lewis about providing her some sort of service management software that would enable her to better serve the customers. Having an automated system to better log calls, assign technicians, track the status of calls, and a host of other things that would make her life less stressful and her job more fulfilling.

   Current Situation 1: Now, after learning that her project wasn't among the top three selected for implementation, Heidi is sitting at her desk, contemplating her next move. She has decided it's time for drastic action and marches into Reid Lewis's office. As the office door is closing, Reid's assistant Leslie hears, "Mr. Lewis, I am handing in my resignation, effective today!" Heidi reminds Reid that he has promised her for months that he'll give her help. He had agreed that her needs were very pressing and would receive top priority. He'd even said that if the company can't keep customers happy, it risks losing their business—so that should be the company's top priority! Now, with the arrival of so-called project manager experts from PPMS (Jeff Dunbar and Kevin Pullen), Reid has totally ignored Heidi's input and needs. Heidi tells Reid she believes he really doesn't value what she does for the company; therefore, she has no other choice but to quit.

Discussion: Put yourself in the shoes of Reid Lewis. How should he respond to Heidi? When Jeff and Kevin asked for participation from all the key stakeholders in order to prepare the business case, what if Reid had refused, allowing only Mark Lewis and Diana Brooks to participate? Would this have been a mistake? Why?

Current Situation 2: After Heidi's outburst, Reid convinces her to meet with Jeff and Kevin. Reid has instructed Jeff and Kevin to work with Heidi to revalidate the order of the project selection and to see if anything can be done to help Heidi.

Discussion: Heidi is a key asset to the organization and the team. She has a wealth of knowledge and is traditionally one of R & S's top performers. Losing her would be a severe blow to the project. Jeff and Kevin definitely do not want to lose her. How should Jeff and Kevin handle this delicate situation? What compromises are available that Heidi may be open to? Heidi claims that she can buy over the Internet a $995 service management software package that would solve 75 percent of her problems. Should Jeff and Kevin let her buy it to keep her happy and occupied (temporary solution) in order to give them time until they can actually address her needs during a future project? What are the risks and benefits of buying the package? Debate the pros and cons of your suggestions.

2. *Background:* Jeff and Kevin are sitting in their office at PPMS, discussing the R & S project. Overall, they have been pleased with the progress so far, but there have been surprises due to the nature of the stakeholders involved. Because of this, Jeff and Kevin are placing great emphasis on doing the stakeholder analysis. Recall that the stakeholder analysis creates a document that should be kept and reused on each project that shares a particular stakeholder. Much of the information collected is of a personal nature and can be reused from project to project. Most of the information is shared with the rest of the team, but some of the information, such as very personal items, is best kept private.

Current Situation 1: Jeff and Kevin are discussing with one another the dynamics of working with Reid Lewis, the president of R & S Amusements Services; his son, Mark Lewis; Mark's friend A.J., the independent contractor; and Heidi, the service coordinator for R & S. One of the issues they may have underestimated was the impact of dealing with a group of stakeholders who had very limited knowledge of computers, systems, and systems development. Because of this, they are documenting these "lessons learned" for reference on future projects of this type.

Discussion: Review the minicases at the end of Chapters 2, 3, and 4. Based on what you read in these minicases, what issues do you think have affected the project so far? What recommendations can you offer Jeff and Kevin in order for them to avoid such issues on future projects?

Current Situation 2: Jeff and Kevin are compiling information about the stakeholders. They will keep this information internally (to themselves).

Discussion: Based on what you have learned so far (from previous minicases and the opening cases), discuss what you believe should be listed on the stakeholder assessment matrix for the following stakeholders: Reid Lewis, Mark Lewis, A.J., and Heidi. Most of the stakeholders who have been identified so far are employees of R & S. Are there other potential stakeholders who haven't been identified as of yet? If so, who are they?

Current Situation 3: Kevin is recording the results from the stakeholder analysis, using an electronic spreadsheet that he will store electronically in the project repository. One of the reasons for storing it electronically is so it can be reused on future projects.

Discussion: Assume that when the project with R & S has been completed, there are no plans for any additional work. How long should Kevin and Jeff keep the stakeholder assessment matrix they prepared for R & S? Is there any potential value in using the stakeholder assessment matrix prepared for R & S on another project for another company? Explain.

Suggested Readings

Andriole, S. (2001). The organization of IT. Retrieved from http://itmanagement.earthweb.com/columns/bizalign/article.php/11080_936101_2.

Archibald, R.D. (1992). *Managing high technology programs and projects.* New York: Wiley.

Bacon, J. (1992). The use of decision criteria in selecting information systems/technology investments. *MIS Quarterly* 16(3):335–353.

Cabral-Cardoso, C., & Payne, R. (1996). Instrumental and supportive use of formal selection methods in R&D project selection. *IEEE Transactions in Engineering Management* 43(4):402–410.

Clavell, J. (1983). *The art of war.* New York: Penguin Group.

Cleland, D.I., & King, W.R. (1983). *Project management handbook.* New York: Van Nostrand Reinhold.

Commonwealth of Massachusetts. Effective project kick-off meetings. Retrieved from https://wiki.state.ma.us/confluence/download/attachments/69894234/Effective+Project+Kick-off+Meetings.pdf?version=1.

Diab, P. (1998, July). Strategic planning + Project management = Competitive advantage. *PM Network*, pp. 25–28.

Doran, G.T. (1981, November). There's a S.M.A.R.T. way to write management goals and objectives. *Management Review*, pp. 35–36.

Eilertsen, S. (2004). The art of project selection. Kollner Group. Retrieved from www.kollnergroup.com.

Fahrenkrog, S. (2000). *A Guide to the Project Management Body of Knowledge (PMBOK).* Newtown Square, PA: Project Management Institute.

Graham, R.J. (1985). *Project management: Combining technical and behavioral approaches for effective implementation.* New York: Van Nostrand Reinhold.

Hinton, M., & Kaye, R. (1996). Investing in information technology: A lottery? *Management Accounting* 74(10):52.

InfoWorld (2002). 2002 Infoworld Compensation Survey. Retrieved from http://www.infoworld.com/cto/ctcompensation2002.html.

Jiang, J., & Klein, G. (1999). Information System Project: Selection criteria variations within strategic classes. *IEEE Transactions in Engineering Management* 46(2):171–176.

Kaplan, R., & Norton, D. (1996). *The balanced scorecard: Translating strategy into action.* Boston: Harvard Business School Press.

Kulatilaka, N., Balasubramanian, P., & Storck, J. (1996). Using Real options to frame the IT investment problem. Retrieved from http://people.bu.edu/nalink/papers/ITRisk.pdf.

Latimore, D. (2002). *Calculating value during uncertainty: Getting real with "real options."* Retrieved from www-1.ibm.com/services/uk/igs/pdf/esr-calculating-value-during-uncertainty.pdf.

Luehrman, T.A. (1998a). Investment opportunities as real options: Getting started on the numbers. *Harvard Business Review* 76(4):51–60.

Luehrman, T.A. (1998b). Strategy as a portfolio of real options. *Harvard Business Review* 76(5):89–99.

Project Management Institute web site, at www.pmi.org.

Schmidt, M.J. (1999). *The IT business case: Keys to accuracy and credibility.* www.solutionmatrix.com

Schuler, J.R. (1995, October). Decision analysis in projects: Summary and recommendations. *PM Network*, pp. 23–27.

Souder, W.E. (1973, August). Utility and perceived acceptability of R&D project selection models. *Management Science*, pp. 1384–1394

Souder, W.E. (1983). Project evaluation and selection. In D.I. Cleland and W.R. King, eds., *Project management handbook.* New York: Van Nostrand Reinhold.

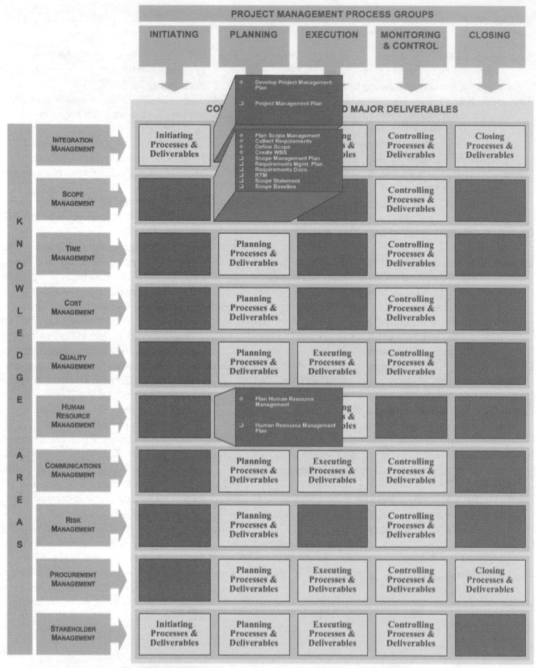

PROJECT MANAGEMENT PROCESS GROUPS

	INITIATING	PLANNING	EXECUTION	MONITORING & CONTROL	CLOSING

CO... ...D MAJOR DELIVERABLES

K N O W L E D G E A R E A S	INTEGRATION MANAGEMENT	Initiating Processes & Deliverables	...ng ...s & ...bles		Controlling Processes & Deliverables	Closing Processes & Deliverables
	SCOPE MANAGEMENT				Controlling Processes & Deliverables	
	TIME MANAGEMENT		Planning Processes & Deliverables		Controlling Processes & Deliverables	
	COST MANAGEMENT		Planning Processes & Deliverables		Controlling Processes & Deliverables	
	QUALITY MANAGEMENT		Planning Processes & Deliverables	Executing Processes & Deliverables	Controlling Processes & Deliverables	
	HUMAN RESOURCE MANAGEMENT		...ng ...s & ...bles			
	COMMUNICATIONS MANAGEMENT		Planning Processes & Deliverables	Executing Processes & Deliverables	Controlling Processes & Deliverables	
	RISK MANAGEMENT		Planning Processes & Deliverables		Controlling Processes & Deliverables	
	PROCUREMENT MANAGEMENT		Planning Processes & Deliverables	Executing Processes & Deliverables	Controlling Processes & Deliverables	Closing Processes & Deliverables
	STAKEHOLDER MANAGEMENT	Initiating Processes & Deliverables	Planning Processes & Deliverables	Executing Processes & Deliverables	Controlling Processes & Deliverables	

Callout (Integration/Planning):
- Develop Project Management Plan
- Project Management Plan

Callout (Scope/Planning):
- Plan Scope Management
- Collect Requirements
- Define Scope
- Create WBS
- Scope Management Plan
- Requirements Mgmt. Plan
- Requirements Docs.
- RTM
- Scope Statement
- Scope Baseline

Callout (Human Resource/Planning):
- Plan Human Resource Management
- Human Resource Management Plan

◆ Indicates component process
❑ Indicates deliverable

5

Project Scope and Human Resources Planning

R & S Amusements Services

Event 5

Setting *A small conference room located outside Reid Lewis's office. Those in attendance include Reid Lewis, Diana Brooks, and Mark Lewis from R & S Amusements Services, and Jeff Dunbar and Kevin Pullen from Premier Project Management Services (PPMS).*

REID   Well, I don't know about all of you, but I think the kickoff meeting went really well. Everyone seemed very excited about the new system and the new and expanded possibilities.
[Everyone in the room nods in agreement]

REID   So, Jeff and Kevin, what's next? I called this meeting at your request and made sure to include the two key user contacts.

JEFF   Thanks, Reid, for scheduling the meeting. Our next steps all have to do with documenting the product requirements for the customer management, asset management, and collection management systems. We need to build a scope statement and a WBS.

REID   A WB . . . what?

JEFF   A WBS, or work breakdown structure. The WBS is a list of tasks that defines all the work that must be completed in order to finish the project.

DIANA Okay, but how do we know what all the tasks are? This seems like such a large undertaking. How can we know everything that needs to be done before we have even started?

KEVIN I'll take this one. You're right. It is a large undertaking, and we probably won't know every single task that is needed at the beginning. Our goal is to get as close as we can at the start and then add to it as we go.

JEFF   Kevin is exactly right. We have done many similar projects for other companies, so we will start with a WBS from a previous similar project so we don't have to start from scratch.

DIANA I get it. We can just use a WBS from one of your previous projects and get started right away.

KEVIN Not quite. We first need to generate a list of detailed requirements before we will know which similar project to use. After that, we will need to change the WBS so it is specific to your project.

REID Excellent. Let's get started.

JEFF Great, this is why we wanted to make sure you were here today, Diana and Mark. We will need your help in building a detailed scope statement and then the WBS. Finally, we will need your input in selecting the right people to work on the project.

(To be continued)

(Instructions for building the scope statement and WBS plus an example of each are presented later in the chapter.)

CHAPTER PREVIEW AND OBJECTIVES

This chapter begins a series of chapters on project management planning. In this textbook, the process for planning is defined as having the following steps: (1) discover the requirements and define the scope (what); (2) define who you need to do each of the things identified in the scope statement (who); (3) put together a schedule based on work priorities and the availability of people (when); (4) estimate cost and time, based on the work required and the experience level of the person assigned (how much), and build your budget; (5) select or create a communications plan and a quality control plan; (6) perform a risk assessment; (7) plan stakeholder management; and (8) if needed, put together a procurement plan. Throughout the next several chapters, you will learn about the tasks required in each process to build the respective deliverables.

The first step in planning is identifying the requirements at a greater level of detail than you did for the project charter and then identifying the right skill sets needed to work on each of the tasks.

In this chapter you will:

- Acquire a general understanding of the parts of the project management plan
- Understand the importance of discovering and documenting stakeholder requirements
- Understand how to create a detailed scope statement and WBS
- Learn how to match the right person, with the needed skill set, to the appropriate activity
- Understand the importance of both formal and informal organizational charts
- Understand past and current research associated with effective human resources management

AN INTRODUCTION TO SCOPE AND HUMAN RESOURCES PLANNING

Project planning starts with the project plan development process, which is part of the Integration Management knowledge area (see the opening chapter map figure). The single deliverable from this process is the project management plan, which consists of deliverables from each of the other nine knowledge areas. Remember from Chapter 3 that the Integration Management knowledge area describes the processes and methods required to identify, define, combine, unify, and coordinate the various processes with all of the other nine knowledge areas (from the project management body of knowledge [PMBOK]). The project plan consists of the following topics:

- Scope management plan (Chapter 5)
- Work breakdown structure (WBS) (Chapter 5)
- WBS dictionary (Chapter 5)
- Staffing management plan (Chapter 5)
- Schedule management plan (Chapter 6)
- Cost management plan (Chapter 6)
- Quality management plan (Chapter 7)
- Process improvement plan (Chapter 7)
- Communication management plan (Chapter 7)
- Stakeholder management plan (Chapter 7)
- Risk management plan (Chapter 8)
- Procurement management plan (Chapter 9)

As you can see, this is quite a list. This text simply can't cover the entire project management plan in one chapter, so the contents of the plan are developed throughout the next several chapters. Even though this is quite a long list, it doesn't necessarily take a long time to develop each piece of the plan. Organizations that are successful at project management have examples and templates already set up for each deliverable. A project manager should be able to start with the default cost management plan or a plan from a prior project and just customize it for the current project. Organizations and project managers who use standard processes and templates have a significant advantage (in terms of cost, time, and accuracy) over those who create a new plan from scratch for each and every project.

Many organizations not only have documented templates for each part of the plan but also may have slightly different standard formats, based on different project characteristics, such as size, complexity, length, and risk level. For example, a small, low-risk project would have a shorter and less formal project planning document than a large, complex project with members of the project team spread out all over the world. In addition, many organizations base their plans on a published methodology such as PMI's PMBOK or IEEE/EIA 12207 and then customize it to fit their culture and/or industry segment. (To find more information on these methodologies and others, see the reading list at the end of the chapter.)

Project teams make their most expensive (in terms of both time and money) mistakes during the planning phase of a project. A project team may do little or no planning, or it may plan incorrectly. By definition, a project is unique and has never been done before, so planning is crucial. McConnell (1998) states that errors found "upstream" during the planning phase cost on the order of 200 times less to fix than errors found "downstream," during the building of the product. Therefore, more time spent upstream reduces the number of costly mistakes later on, reducing the overall cost of the project. Cleland and Ireland write that "the most important responsibility of the project team is to develop the project plan in consort with other supportive stakeholders" (2002, p. 309). Decisions made during the initiation and planning phases of a project set the direction as well as the boundaries within which the project is executed. Planning is not an easy part of the project management process. Few people have the ability to see into the future and plan for the unexpected. Some refer to it as an art more than a science.

Although planning is crucial, project teams must be careful to avoid over-planning; the planning must be appropriate to the size, complexity, and risk of the project. Project managers must be careful to avoid what many systems analysis text books refer to as "analysis paralysis"—getting stuck in the analysis phase, trying to get everything defined perfectly. Planning requires time, resources, and cost, so care must be taken to do it correctly. Because we can't see far into the future, planning must be done as a progressive elaboration process, with each iterative cycle becoming more accurate and more complete. T. Capers Jones summed it up this way: "The seeds of major software disasters are usually sown in the first three months of commencing the software project. Hasty scheduling, irrational commitments, unprofessional estimating techniques, carelessness of the project management function are the factors that tend to introduce terminal problems" (1998, p. 120).

The authors of this text often tell students and organizations that if we don't plan anything, then we can never be late or wrong (how cool), but then how do we know when we are right or when we are done with a project? Inadequate planning is one of the major reasons that many projects never get completed.

Kerzner writes "The project manager is the key to successful project planning. It is desirable that the project manager be involved from project conception through execution. Project planning must be systematic, flexible enough to handle unique activities, disciplined through reviews and controls, and capable of accepting multifunctional inputs. Successful project managers realize that project planning is an iterative process and must be performed throughout the life of the project" (2003, p. 378). Remember from the project life cycle presented in Chapter 2 and the iterative approach to running a project that planning isn't done just once but is a continuous process of adaptation and change.

Project planning activities at this point move from the Integration Management knowledge area into the Scope Management knowledge area, which consists of these processes: plan scope management, collect requirements, define scope, and create the WBS. Examining the project charter can tell you why you are working on the project, but it doesn't give you enough detail about the actual work activities needed to deliver the stated objectives. The first step in building the project management plan is to break down the high-level objectives from the project charter into smaller and smaller requirement pieces, otherwise known as performing systems analysis.

PROJECT MANAGEMENT CONCEPTS: SCOPE MANAGEMENT PLANNING

As discussed in Chapter 1, one of the keys to delivering a successful project is having a complete statement of the product requirements. By building on the objectives listed in the project charter, you can build a more complete **scope statement**. Before or in conjunction with building the scope statement, the team should document the scope management plan consisting of how the project scope will be defined, validated, and controlled. The building of the scope statement, like other project artifacts, should not be done in isolation. A project manager should involve the project team and stakeholders where appropriate. The project manager must use a process that allows and encourages stakeholder involvement in the definition of the product scope. As depicted in the opening chapter map figure, the key deliverables from scope planning are the requirements documents, scope statement, WBS, and the WBS dictionary. Each of these deliverables should be created for every project, regardless of size.

A project's scope comes from many sources. In addition to stakeholders and the other members of the team contributing ideas, other sources of scope may be existing industry standards, organizational culture, or government regulations. For example, in 2002, the U.S. Congress enacted a new set of corporate governance and financial reporting requirements, referred to as the Sarbanes-Oxley Act. This act established, among other items, financial reporting requirements for all publicly traded organizations. Because most financial data exists in one or more computer applications, compliance with the act has required many new IT projects. The act describes what information is to be reported but leaves it up to individual companies to figure out how to produce the information. Another example of project scope being driven by government regulations is the 1996 Health Insurance Portability and Accountability Act (HIPAA). HIPAA provides national guidelines on the privacy of electronic health care records. The legislation is broken down into three parts: privacy, code sets, and security.

The size and depth of the scope statement depends on the following characteristics (Cleland, 2002):

- Project size, including the number of people, dollar value, duration, and geographic span
- Degree of risk to the business
- Cash requirements, such as length of time for return on investment and initial cash requirements
- Technology utilized (for example, maturity, experience of current staff with the technology)
- Project team experience with technology, business, and industry
- Nature of the deliverables, such as whether this is a new product or service, an upgrade, or a repair
- Strategic importance of the project to the organization
- Project definition (for example, whether the requirements are undefined, partially defined, or poorly defined)

This list helps frame the information project managers include in the scope statement and also helps describe items that won't be included in the project, which can be just as important as describing what is included. Everyone needs to be very clear on what requirements are included and what requirements are not included. Specifically listing the items not included helps ensure that stakeholders understand the boundaries of the project, improve communications, and aid project managers in managing stakeholder expectations.

The scope statement appears within the scope management plan, which is used to describe how the project team will define the project scope, develop the detailed project scope statement, define and develop the WBS, verify the project scope, and control the project scope. So far in the discussion of scope planning, the text has explained how the team begins to define the detailed project scope statement. The next section contains a description of how to build the WBS, and Chapter 12 presents several ways to control project scope using an integrated change control process. One of the key uses for the scope management plan is to prevent **scope creep**. Remember from Chapter 1 that the main goal of a project is to deliver the successful finished project within scope, time, and cost constraints. It is nearly impossible to meet any of these targets if the scope is continually growing and changing. Scope creep happens for many reasons; for example: the marketing department may want to get ahead of the competition, the software developers might want to learn about the latest new tool or technique, or the key stakeholder may have recently read an article about the next great feature and want it added to the application. If scope is defined correctly and the team follows a disciplined change control process, scope creep can be minimized or avoided.

Collecting Requirements

Scope definition is accomplished by conducting a requirements discovery and analysis exercise, getting help from subject matter experts (SMEs), and using the results of the stakeholder analysis. The assumptions and constraints first identified on the project charter can now be updated and expanded as well. The requirements discovery and analysis process is done not by the project manager but by skilled systems analysts, who have many tools to aid them in their job. It is not the intent in this text to cover the aspects of the systems analysis profession; we leave that up to the many fine systems analysis and design textbooks on the market. But one technique that bears mentioning is called PIECES (Wetherbe, 1994), which describes different categories of potential requirements:

- *Performance*—Fixing or improving performance, work throughput issues, transactions, or request response times
- *Information*—Fixing or improving all forms of information, including stored data elements, input processes and data, output processes, format, timing, and content
- *Economics*—Fixing or improving a company's economic situation, with expenses and revenue, new markets, new products, faster product releases, and so on
- *Control and security*—Fixing or improving control and security of all company electronic assets
- *Efficiency*—Fixing or improving resource (people, machines, computers, networks) productivity and efficiency
- *Service*—Fixing or improving service usability, accuracy, reliability, adaptability, and compatibility

The list is not exhaustive but offers a framework to aid the analyst in capturing requirements.

Subject matter experts (SMEs) aid the systems analysts in their quest for an accurate list of requirements, including both project requirements and product requirements. Project requirements may consist of business requirements, communication requirements, levels of status reporting, and so on. Product requirements may consist of technical requirements, security requirements, safety requirements, performance requirements, and so on. (See the discussion earlier in this chapter about the PIECES framework.) SMEs can be from inside or outside the organization. They are individuals who have intimate knowledge of how the product of the project is supposed to function. They should be consulted throughout the entire project for input into and acceptance of the requirements. Capturing input of SMEs and other interested project stakeholders is done via the stakeholder analysis, using a variety of techniques: brainstorming sessions, interviews, focus groups, workshops, questionnaires and surveys, observations, and system prototypes.

The requirements should be documented using a requirements management system, preferably an electronic system to aid the team in improving communication, traceability, and visibility. The requirements documentation may consist of the following:

- Functional and nonfunctional system requirements
- Business rules
- Impacts on any other systems and/or departments
- Support and training requirements
- Specific acceptance criteria for each requirement or set of requirements
- Quality requirements

The final step in collecting requirements is to document how requirements will be managed throughout the project. The following questions need to be addressed and then input into the requirements traceability matrix defined next:

- Who has authority to update the list of requirements?
- What process will be used to manage the changes to the requirements?
- How are requirements prioritized? In other words, which ones are done first or are done at all?
- How are requirements traced from discovery to system design to prototype to finished product?

The requirements traceability matrix (RTM) is used to document the links between the requirements for the product that is being built and the artifacts developed to implement and verify those requirements (see figure 5-1). These artifacts may include use cases, user stories, design specifications, software components, test plans, and test cases. Tracing requirements assist the project team to understand which parts of the design and software implement the user's requirements, and which tests are necessary to verify that the user's requirements have been understood and implemented correctly. A good RTM provides forward and backward traceability. Meaning, a requirement can be traced to a test, and a test can be traced to a requirement.

A requirements traceability matrix is created when the requirements are first approved or baselined. It is then updated and reviewed throughout the project's life cycle whenever new artifacts are produced that are related to the requirements. In addition, changes to the requirements are also tracked in the RTM. This assists the project team in assessing the impact a change may have by tracing the affected requirement to all the artifacts to which it is linked.

Work Breakdown Structure

When the product and project requirements have been discovered and documented and the scope statement has been created, the next step is to begin building the **work breakdown structure (WBS)**, which organizes the total scope of the project.

A project is created to *do* something—to produce an outcome or a **deliverable**. The WBS exists and is organized around the project deliverables. Haugan (2002) describes what he calls the *100 percent rule*: The WBS represents 100 percent of the work required to produce the product, and all subtasks must add up to 100 percent of the total scope and shouldn't go over 100 percent. As soon as you define more than 100 percent of the scope,

REQUIREMENTS TRACEABILITY MATRIX									
Project Name: <optional>									
Project Manager Name: <required>									
Project Description: <required>									
Requirement ID	Requirement Description	Status	Architectural/ Design Document	Technical Specification	System Component(s)	Software Module(s)	Test Case Number	Verification	Additional Comments
001									
002									
003									
004									
005									
006									
007									
008									
009									
010									
011									
012									
013									
014									

FIGURE 5-1   **Requirements Traceability Matrix**

you have committed to doing more than you agreed to do, given current resources—and thus scope creep has begun.

The WBS is used for many different purposes throughout the project, so it is extremely important to get it as accurate as possible. The following is a list of uses for the WBS:

- Guide the work of the entire project team
- Facilitate communication between all stakeholders and the project team
- Aid the team in building the schedule and budget
- Assign the right person to the right task
- Get the project to a completed state
- Aid in quality control
- Assign responsibility for each task
- Reduce scope creep
- Aid in budget and schedule progress reporting and performance reporting
- Aid in examining alternative steps in building a product

BUILDING THE WBS   Many techniques exist for aiding a project team in building a complete and accurate WBS. Many people believe that building an accurate WBS that meets the 100 percent rule is more of an art than a science, and it takes years of experience to become proficient at it. The techniques described next (analogy, top-down, bottom-up, and the thread method) are used by novices and professionals alike to aid in creating a complete WBS. Regardless of the technique used, the WBS is an evolving, dynamic artifact as the project moves forward, the WBS gets more detailed and more accurate. Three of the four techniques (analogy, top-down, and the thread method) use the concept of **decomposition** to break down the work into its component parts. The bottom-up technique does decomposition in reverse. Regardless of the technique you use, the 100 percent rule exists at every level of the WBS. Each set of tasks created should deliver 100 percent of the work required to create the deliverable.

THE ANALOGY TECHNIQUE   A WBS is first created by looking for a similar project done in the past and using its WBS as a starting point. The team simply copies the WBS from the previous similar project and changes the name. The team must then begin reviewing the

WBS to make any necessary changes for the new project. IT projects fall into three broad categories: new functionality; maintenance; or conversion of an existing system to a new platform, a new vendor, or a new user interface. Identifying an IT project as one of these three categories can help you find similar projects to use in building a WBS.

The analogy technique:

- Is the fastest path to a completed WBS
- Is a valuable tool for brainstorming a new project and looking for deliverables
- Enhances cross-project consistency
- Improves budget and time estimates
- Improves resource allocations

The following issues are associated with using the analogy technique:

- The team needs to ensure that the previous WBS is completely understood and similar.
- The team needs to make sure the previous WBS is accurate and updated.
- The team needs to critically review the previous WBS and its appropriateness for the new project.

THE TOP-DOWN TECHNIQUE If a similar project's WBS doesn't exist, you must start from scratch. You can use the top-down approach during a brainstorming session, with SMEs, stakeholders, and team members. The team first looks at the list of objectives from the project charter and uses them to determine a high-level list of deliverables that will be used to build the final product. Each deliverable is then decomposed into smaller and smaller steps needed to create that deliverable. This process continues until all objectives have been decomposed sufficiently (see Chapter 6 for more definition on the level of decomposition necessary).

The top-down technique:

- Ensures that a project is organized logically, based on the nature of the project
- Promotes stakeholder participation in the planning phase of the project
- Can help all participants better understand the entire project

The following issues are involved in using the top-down technique:

- The team needs to ensure that major objectives are not forgotten.
- The team needs to decompose the tasks to appropriate levels.
- It can be time-consuming, so it's important to guard against "analysis paralysis."
- Cost and time estimates are more difficult to create and generally less accurate than with the analogy approach.

THE BOTTOM-UP TECHNIQUE If a similar project's WBS doesn't exist but the team is very familiar with this type of project, you can start from scratch with the bottom-up technique. Like the top-down approach, this approach is also generally done during a brainstorming session, with SMEs, stakeholders, and team members. The team first looks at the list of objectives from the project charter and generates a list of low-level activities that will be needed to complete the objectives. The team then groups together the tasks by deliverable. This process continues until all relevant tasks have been grouped into subgroups that directly tie to a major objective. Often, multiple levels of subgroups must be created to create a tie between the low-level task and the project objectives. The bottom-up technique:

- Promotes stakeholder participation in the planning phase of the project
- Can create a greater understanding of the entire project by all participants
- May lead to a more complete list of tasks

The following issues are involved in using the bottom-up technique:

- It can be difficult to organize the process into logical steps or phases.
- The team needs to ensure that objectives are not forgotten.
- It is difficult to retain the focus on the big picture.
- It is difficult to generate a complete list of tasks.

THE THREAD TECHNIQUE   The thread technique is generally used in conjunction with one of the other three techniques. Instead of looking at all of the project's objectives, the group concentrates on them one at a time (generally evaluating the most complex issues or highest-priority objectives first) and decomposes it into lower levels of detail (or higher levels, if using the bottom-up approach). The objectives are evaluated one at a time.

The thread technique:

- Promotes stakeholder participation in the planning phase of the project
- Can help all participants better understand the project
- Provides greater control and focus in brainstorming sessions
- Generally tackles the most important stakeholder objectives first

The following issues are involved in using the thread technique:

- The team needs to be careful not to lose focus of the big picture.
- The team needs to be careful not to lose sight of the effect one objective may have on another.
- It increases the need for communication.
- It is most successful when the project leader and team have a good understanding of the project's objectives.

This list of techniques is not meant to be all encompassing; there are many other possibilities. For instance, when working on U.S. government contracts, contractors are generally given a standard format to follow so that each contractor's piece of the overall project follows the same format. Which technique you use to create the WBS depends on the following:

- *The existence of a similar project*—If a similar project exits, you would use the analogy approach.
- *The experience level of the project manager and team*—If the project manager and team have little experience, you'd choose the top-down approach. Conversely, if they have many years of experience, you'd choose the bottom-up approach.
- *The uniqueness of the product or process*—If the product or process is unique—that is, has never been done before in this company or by this team—you might choose the top-down approach.

PROVEN STRATEGIES AND HINTS TO SUCCESS

The University of Wisconsin administrative support website help guide to project managers (www. pma.doit.wisc.edu/plan/2-1/print.html) has resources for each part of the project life cycle in what they call "DoIT: Project Management Advisor." They offer the following advice in building your WBS:

- Step 1. Determine your strategy for developing a work breakdown structure. The PM should include project team members in all steps.
- Step 2. Identify the highest level components of work to be accomplished, such as: product deliverables (project charter or project plan), life cycle phases (initiate, analyze, design, build, deploy), or functions (create, update).
- Step 3. Next break each of these higher level components of work down into smaller units of work until each component is defined to a level of detail that allows accurate estimating for time and cost.
- Step 4. Adequately describe the task with a component name that is understood by all stakeholders using a noun-verb format (such as Document User Manual, Install Network).
- Step 5. Make sure work has been broken down to the lowest level desired.

WBS Structure

A WBS can be structured in different formats, depending on the type and needs of the project. A WBS can be structured around the product or around process phases. Figures 5-2A, 5-2B, and 5-2C are examples of WBSs. Figure 5-2A is an example of a WBS structured around the subparts of a web development product, Figure 5-2B is a WBS structured around the phases of a generic systems development methodology, and Figure 5-2C is an example of a WBS presented in outline form.

Notice in Figure 5-2C that only one of the Level 1 tasks is decomposed into Level 2 tasks. This is perfectly okay; not all legs of the WBS must be decomposed down to the same level. The amount of decomposition depends on the needs of the individual tasks. One may need to be broken down further than others to make sure it delivers one outcome, can be assigned to one person, and can be budgeted for in terms of time and cost. (Chapter 6 describes how far you should go in decomposing tasks.)

The following are some best practices to keep in mind when building the WBS, regardless of technique or format:

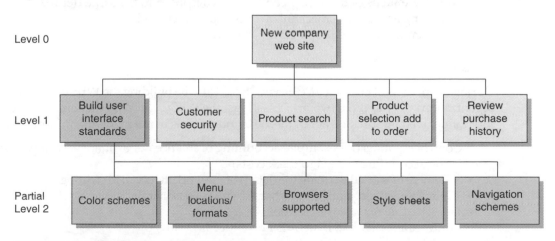

FIGURE 5-2A   WBS by Product Subparts

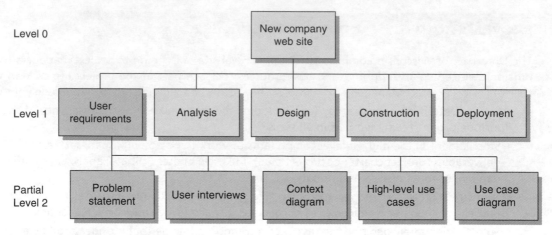

Level 0 — New company web site; Level 1 — User requirements, Analysis, Design, Construction, Deployment; Partial Level 2 — Problem statement, User interviews, Context diagram, High-level use cases, Use case diagram

FIGURE 5-2B   WBS by Phase

```
0       New company web site
1.0       Build user interface standards
1.1         Color schemes
1.2         Menu locations/formats
1.3         Browsers supported
1.4         Style sheets
1.5         Navigation schemes
2.0       Customer security
3.0       Product search
4.0       Product selection–add to order
5.0       Review purchase history
```

FIGURE 5-2C   WBS in Outline Form

- Each WBS element represents a single deliverable.
- The 100 percent rule applies to all levels.
- Each deliverable is distinct.
- Accountability for each task can be assigned to one team member.
- Not all elements of the WBS need to be decomposed to the same depth.
- Reporting and control mechanisms need to be included.
- The team needs to be prepared for changes.

WBS Dictionary

During the process of creating a WBS, you should also be building the WBS dictionary. (Many organizations refer to these two artifacts as just the WBS.) The WBS dictionary is the repository for detailed information about the WBS and consists of the following information:

- Control accounts (for example, accounting or finance department account codes used in the accounting system to track costs)
- Statement of work describing the details of the work involved in creating each deliverable
- The responsible organization (that is, who is responsible for each deliverable)
- The schedule for major milestones
- Contract information, if an outside vendor is involved

- Quality requirements
- Estimates of costs and resources required

When you have the WBS and the WBS dictionary created, the next activity is to find the right resource(s) to assign to each task, based on budget requirements, time availability, skill sets, motivation, and other criteria. The process of human resources planning is discussed in the next section.

PROJECT MANAGEMENT CONCEPTS: HUMAN RESOURCES PLANNING

Project human resources planning involves identifying and then documenting the project roles that must be staffed (for example, database analysts, software developers, systems analysts, SMEs, network engineers, user interface designers), identifying who has what authority (for example, to make staffing decisions, budget decisions, scope decisions), and producing the staffing management plan deliverable. This section describes the managerial knowledge and skills that a project manager needs in order to be successful.

In Tom DeMarco's fictional work *The Deadline*, he tells the story of an experienced project manager who is kidnapped and forced into managing an extremely large IT project. The large IT project experiences nearly every type of major problem imaginable. The story is told in a very humorous way, with just enough reality to make some excellent points about managing IT projects. One of the key statements DeMarco makes is that one of the most difficult tasks a project manager performs is matching project tasks to the appropriate resources. Some individuals love to be challenged and want to take on the hardest tasks. Others just want to come to work, do what they need to do, and then leave—they don't really like to be pushed and challenged. A project manager needs to figure out what motivates each individual on the team and assign just the right amount and type of work to each person.

Unfortunately, just assigning the right task to the right individual might not be enough. A project manager must also understand how to continually motivate and influence members of the team to get work accomplished on time and on budget within quality requirements; a major problem is that team members officially report to someone else in the organization for their performance appraisals, which determine their pay rates. Functional managers (for example, accounting manager, warehouse supervisor) have the luxury of working with the same individuals over greater lengths of time, which allows them to build relationships and get to know each worker; in addition, they are responsible for the pay raises of those who work for them. Project managers in a functional organization or a matrix organization don't have the luxury of time; some team members may be assigned to them for very short periods, making it more difficult to figure out what motivates each team member. The next section of the chapter answers the following questions:

- Assign the right tasks to the right person?
- Motivate the team to perform at peak performance, with the highest quality?
- Obtain the needed power and authority to manage the entire project?

Human Resource Research

Finding ways to motivate workers has been a major concern for managers throughout history. In the early 1900s researchers began exploring and formalizing concepts and theories of human behavior. Many of these original theories are still being studied and expanded upon today. Successful project managers must understand human behavior in order to motivate team members to achieve project objectives. The following sections review the research work of some key individuals in the area of human behavior: Abraham Maslow, Douglas McGregor, William Ouchi, and Frederick Herzberg.

ABRAHAM MASLOW: THE HIERARCHY OF NEEDS   Abraham Maslow identified a prioritized hierarchy of needs that motivate workers to do their best work. The levels, from lowest to highest, are physiological needs, safety needs, social needs, esteem needs, and self-actualization needs. The levels are often depicted in a triangle with physiological needs listed on the bottom and self-actualization at the top point.

The essence of the hierarchy is that a worker will not be motivated by any higher-level needs until his or her lower-level needs have been satisfied. Once a lower-level need is satisfied, a worker will seek satisfaction at the next level. The following are brief definitions of the levels:

- *Physiological*—Air, food, water, clothing, shelter, and sleep.
- *Safety*—Economic security, protection from harm and violence, and secure employment.
- *Social*—Love, belonging, togetherness, approval, group inclusion, and friendship.
- *Esteem*—Self-respect, reputation, recognition, and self-confidence.
- *Self-actualization*—Need to make the most of unique abilities and to strive to perform maximally.

A project manager must understand the needs of all members of the team in order to help them perform at their best. To do this, the project manager must understand where on the hierarchy a team member is currently located. In the IT industry in the United States, workers are generally paid fairly well in comparison to those in other industries, so a worker's basic physiological needs are probably being met.

The next level is safety needs. As a project comes to a close, workers may be nervous about what their next project is going to be and may not be concentrating on the current task. In an organization that has recently done some outsourcing (moving jobs outside the organization), workers may be concentrating more on finding ways to keep their job than on performing well on the nearly finished project. Techniques to aid in the project closing process and outsourcing issues are both covered in Chapter 14 of this text. For now, a project manager needs to be aware of the obstacles to team performance and address them to satisfy the safety needs of the team.

The next level on the hierarchy is social needs. Workers at this level are trying to satisfy their need for a sense of belonging and acceptance by the team. (Chapter 10 covers several techniques to aid project managers in improving team interaction.) Most workers want to be accepted by their peers, want to form friendships, and need the approval of others. Project managers need to learn to build inclusive teams, which will allow acceptance to occur. Most of the time, these social activities have nothing to do with building the actual product but are necessary to meet the needs of the team members, which should translate into a better-functioning team and a higher-quality product.

Next on the hierarchy is the esteem level. At this level, workers are looking for individual recognition for their efforts from the team and organization. IT workers tend to especially need peer recognition. They strive to be known as experts in their particular fields of expertise. Software developers want to be the first to write tricky bits of code, and network engineers want to solve difficult throughput issues. Recognition can be accomplished in a myriad of ways, many of which are discussed in Chapter 10. For example, one technique that has worked is the use of an old bowling trophy. In one project, the software developers were working in a fourth-generation language that had a few shortcomings. They were constantly fighting the language to deliver the final product. Each week during status meetings, they would discuss the latest workarounds they had built. As the weeks passed, it became a competition to see who could come up with the best fix. The project manager decided to start recognizing the person who came up with the best, most imaginative solution; he used as a prize an old small bowling trophy, with a small piece of paper attached, labeled "best bug fixer." Each week during the status meeting, the traveling trophy was awarded to the person who had created the most beneficial workaround, and it turned out to be a highly sought recognition. A simple technique had a huge impact on the morale of team members and on project outcomes.

The final level on the hierarchy is self-actualization. At this level, workers have managed to satisfy all their lower-level needs and they are striving to make themselves better at what they do either at work or outside of work. For team members at this level, the project manager needs to supply a work environment that allows time for training and personal growth. For a project manager, team members at this level are generally the most rewarding to work with.

DOUGLAS MCGREGOR: THEORY X AND THEORY Y EMPLOYEES The work of Douglas McGregor can help a project manager understand how to use an appropriate leadership style to approach workers. McGregor placed workers into two distinct categories: Theory X and Theory Y. Theory X workers are inherently lazy and require constant direct supervision in order to perform work. Theory X workers dislike work and avoid it whenever possible. To get them to work, a supervisor must use punishment as the motivator. A manager with this type of worker uses an authoritarian approach to decision making. Theory Y workers are the opposite: They enjoy work and can be trusted to work efficiently without direct supervision. These workers are motivated by the work itself and need little motivation from their manager. Managers with these workers exercise a participative style of group decision making.

FIGURE 5-3 **Theory X, Theory Y Worker Continuum**

Workers come in many forms, some leaning toward Theory X, some toward Theory Y, and everything in between (see Figure 5-3). A project manager needs to figure out where on this line each team member sits and treat them all appropriately. Making this difficult job even harder, workers change over time and move to different points on the continuum. Just because you have worked with someone before doesn't mean his or her needs will remain the same.

Some individuals work extremely well on their own and need little supervision. They are very responsible and tend to flourish in the right situations. Other workers need daily supervision. They are less organized and need someone to help prioritize their work. This doesn't mean that one worker does better or more work than the other; it just means that one will require more of the manager's time. The sooner a manager understands each worker and accepts that different individuals require different attention and management styles, the more successful a project manager will be running projects.

WILLIAM OUCHI: THEORY Z EMPLOYEES   William Ouchi added a third dimension or theory of workers: Theory Z. Theory Z workers emphasizes a more Japanese cultural-based approach. These workers are more participative and are capable of performing many and varied tasks at different levels of responsibilities. Management techniques with Theory Z workers emphasize things such as job rotation, broadening of skills, generalization versus specialization of skills, and the need for continuous training.

FREDERICK HERZBERG: MOTIVATION HYGIENE THEORY   Frederick Herzberg, whose research was based somewhat on Maslow's hierarchy of needs, found that the factors causing job satisfaction (implying motivation) are different from those causing job dissatisfaction. Herzberg combined the three lower levels of Maslow's hierarchy into one category, called hygiene factors. These hygiene factors include the company, management philosophies, security, status, salary, and interpersonal relations. Herzberg found that these items, if present, don't motivate employees to perform better, but if they are missing, the employees are dissatisfied with their jobs and are not motivated. The second category involves more of the actual work that people do on the job and falls into the two upper levels of Maslow's hierarchy—esteem and self-actualization. If workers experience these levels, they tend to be more satisfied, happier, and more productive.

A key component of Herzberg's research for managers to realize is that the factors are not simply opposites of each other. For example, a bad salary is definitely a de-motivator to most, but a good salary is not necessarily a strong motivator. If the worker dislikes the job, her coworkers, and company policies, salary will not be enough to keep her motivated. Managers must find factors that not only increase worker satisfaction and motivation, but also prevent dissatisfaction. The following lists present such factors:

Factors leading to Dissatisfaction

- Too much supervision
- Company policies
- Relationship with supervisor
- Work conditions
- Relationship with peers
- Salary

Factors leading to Satisfaction

- Recognition
- Work itself
- Achievement
- Responsibility
- Growth in and outside of the job
- Advancement

Getting to know each member of the team and finding out what motivates each is a difficult task, especially on short-term projects. But the ability to accomplish this feat separates average project managers from great ones. Some best practices to follow when directing the work of others include:

- Taking the time to know each individual one-on-one
- Keeping and communicating a positive attitude about the project, the team, and the company
- Assigning the appropriate level of work to each worker
- Communicating often and openly
- Making each worker feel appreciated for his or her particular contribution to the project
- Making sure each worker has the proper training
- Rewarding members of the team fairly and consistently

Authority, Influence, and Power

Most project managers must run projects with cross-functional workers who don't report to them in the official company organizational chart. In this situation, workers on the project have two bosses: the project manager and a functional manager. To further complicate the issue, many workers are part of more than one team, giving them yet another voice to listen to. As a result, workers face conflicting priorities and demands. To be successful, in addition to discovering individual worker needs and motivations, project managers must have the needed authority and power to direct the work required to accomplish the goals and objectives of the project. *Authority* is defined as either legal or acquired authority. In the traditional theory of management, authority is granted from a superior to a subordinate or is legal authority. Legal authority is granted to an individual by virtue of their position in the company or given by a senior member of the management staff. Acquired authority or power is gained from one's peers, based on the perceived knowledge of the individual, his or her interpersonal skills, or work experience on similar projects. Unfortunately, in many IT projects, project managers are not granted the needed legal authority to be successful and so must become good at acquiring authority.

Thamhain and Wilemon identified the following project manager influence types (1999):

- *Expertise*—The project team may see the project manager as having superior content knowledge of the business, past project success, and an appreciation of the technology.
- *Work challenge*—The project manager may have some control over who gets assigned what work.
- *Salary influence*—The project manager may have input (directly or indirectly) into the worker's salary.
- *Friendship*—Personal relationships may be established between the project manager and others.
- *Future work assignments*—The project manager may have influence on a worker's future work assignment.
- *Promotion*—The project manager may have input (directly or indirectly) on a worker's future position promotions.
- *Authority*—Superiors may delegate or give power to a project manager.
- *Fund allocations*—The project manager may have influence on how the project budget is spent.
- *Penalty*—The project manager may be able to penalize nonperforming team members.

Of these nine influence types, three were found to offer the project manager the best chance for success: expertise, work challenge, and salary influence. The influence types least likely to help a project manager succeed are fund allocation, authority, and penalty. The other types fall somewhere in the middle. What this means to project managers is that to obtain higher productivity commitments from workers assigned to their projects, they should strive to influence the team by using their business and technology expertise, assign the right amount of challenging work to the right workers, and try to create an environment in which they have influence on salaries. Many companies have added a section to their yearly salary review process that includes input from project managers on the work an individual performed.

Project managers can receive **project authority** in several ways. It can be delegated to them from senior management, it can be earned from running many prior successful projects, or they may hold a senior position in the company. Because project managers are generally not given a lot of delegated authority, they must learn to use interpersonal influences. Managers may have five interpersonal influence types:

- *Legitimate or formal*—These managers receive support because the project team perceives that the project manager has the right to issue directives.
- *Reward*—These managers receive support because the project team perceives that the project manager has the ability to influence financial rewards such as salaries, bonuses, and promotions.
- *Penalty*—These managers receive support because the project team perceives that they have the ability to punish workers by withholding rewards or assigning non-rewarding work.
- *Expert*—These managers receive support because the project team perceives that they have the knowledge and skills needed to be successful.
- *Referent*—These managers receive support because the project team has great faith in their abilities, based on their personal presence. Examples of individuals who held referent power are John F. Kennedy and Martin Luther King, Jr.

To sum up this part of the chapter on human resources planning, Stephen Covey, a respected management researcher and author of *The 7 Habits of Highly Effective People* (1990), offered some great advice for individuals to become better team participants and project leaders. His work was not directed specifically at project leaders, but it definitely applies and offers guidance on becoming an effective leader without sacrificing your personal life and growth. The major points from his book are summarized here, with their implications for project managers and teams:

1. *Be proactive*—Individuals should focus their efforts and attention on the long term and to think in terms of the long-term consequences of their actions. Individuals have options about how they respond to different situations and should adopt an attitude of understanding the power they have to respond to what happens and make the most of their opportunities. Successful project managers adopt the attitude that they can make a positive difference in almost everything they experience during a project: changes, late work, problem stakeholders, and so on. The other six habits require that this proactive attitude be adopted.

2. *Begin with the end in mind*—Covey refers to this as the habit of *personal leadership*—setting goals for where you want to take your life and then tracking your progress. Before you can reach your goals, you must set them, which requires introspection. An effective project manager continually sets goals for himself and his projects and aids members of his team to set goals as well.

3. *Put first things first*—Individuals need to organize and plan their path to reaching their goals. Project managers must be excellent time managers. They must learn to manage their own time as well as the time of others. Successful project managers learn to concentrate their efforts on activities that maximize their chances of reaching their goals.

4. *Think win–win*—This habit is the first that directly speaks to being a better project manager. Project managers can't deliver projects by themselves; it takes a team effort, with everyone working toward the goals of the project to be successful. Project managers learn the art of compromise and constantly seek win–win decisions.

5. *Seek first to understand and then to be understood*—This is a great philosophy for all. Think about the fact that a physician must first understand the symptoms thoroughly before prescribing a medication. Similarly, project managers must learn to be excellent listeners, seeking first to listen and understand stakeholders and team members.

6. *Synergize*—Synergy means that the whole is greater than the sum of the parts. Project managers learn techniques for getting teams to perform as teams and not as a bunch of individuals. The final solution is always better when everyone is involved and allowed to contribute.

7. *Sharpen the saw*—This is called the habit of self-renewal. It is broken down into four parts: spiritual, mental, physical, and social. Being a project manager can be very stressful and time-consuming. A project manager must take the time to rejuvenate, doing the things he or she likes to do away from work (for example, sailing, golfing, reading). A project manager also needs to find time for continued training/learning to reach the personal goals he or she set as part of the first habit.

Human Resources Planning Deliverables

The three deliverables from the human resources planning part of the project plan are: the project roles and responsibilities matrix, the project organizational chart, and the staffing management plan. For every project, regardless of size, the project manager should create a roles and responsibilities matrix to be sure everyone knows their tasks. The project organizational chart and staffing management plan may not need to be formal documents unless the size of the project requires it. Generally, once the project gets above 10 team members, the project manager should consider creating these project artifacts.

ROLES AND RESPONSIBILITIES MATRIX   One important deliverable during the planning phase of the project is the roles and responsibilities matrix (RRM, also called a RACI matrix, referring to the legend in figure 5-4). After the initial WBS is created, the project manager needs to decide who is needed to perform the individual activities. Based on new knowledge gained in the preceding section, the project manager will be able to assign the right work to the appropriate individuals. Early in the project, at the time of the project charter or the initial

PROVEN STRATEGIES AND HINTS TO SUCCESS

Bob Kantor is an IT management consultant and principle at Kantor Consulting Group. RACI is another name for the roles and responsibilities matrix. RACI stands for the roles that a person or group may play on the project: responsible, approval, consult, inform. Kantor writes, "This is the first assessment I conduct when addressing a project rescue. In almost 100 percent of these rescue efforts, I have found that there is no shared understanding of participant roles and responsibilities." Kantor offers the following critical analysis that should be done when building the matrix, first for each stakeholder:

- Are there too many R's: Are you overloading a particular resource with too much work?
- No empty cells: Not every stakeholder must have something filled in for every task.
- Buy-in: Do you have full support from the stakeholder for each assigned role?

Analysis for each deliverable:

- No R's: This is a problem; someone must take ownership for each deliverable.
- Too many R's: Shared responsibility rarely works. One person, if possible, needs to be the key contact on the work.
- No A's: This is a problem; someone must be held accountable to make sure work is accomplished.
- More than one A: Can cause issues when decisions are needed.
- Every box filled in: Not always needed. Be sure each role is needed; don't just fill something in to complete the matrix.
- A lot of C's: Again, don't fill it in unless needed. It has the potential to create a communication problem.

draft of the WBS, the project manager might not have enough details to assign an individual person to each activity, and it is perfectly acceptable to use a title (systems analyst) or a department name (finance) instead of names of individuals. Figure 5-4 shows an example of an RRM using role names. Another important function of the RRM is to define the level of responsibility that each person, title, or department will have for each objective or activity.

The activities listed on the RRM are generally at a summary level initially (early in the project), and as the project proceeds, they are expanded to include lower-level activities.

| Activity | Responsible Party | | | | | |
	Project Manager	Database Analyst	Accounting Supervisor	CFO	Lead Systems Analyst	Inventory Control Supervisor
Task 1	R	I	A	A	C	C
Task 2	A	C	C	R	C	C
Task 3	R	C	C	A	I	C
Task 4	R	C	C	C	R	I
Task 5	C	R	I	C	I	I

Legend: R = Responsible
A = Approval
C = Consult or review
I = Inform or act as SME

FIGURE 5-4   Roles and Responsibilities Matrix

A responsible party is assigned to each activity or task at one of four levels: getting the activity completed, getting approval of the work product created in each activity, consulting or reviewing, or informing as an SME. The RRM is first generated for the project charter and evolves into finer levels of detail as the project evolves. The RRM is not a static document but changes as facets of the project change.

The benefits associated with having an RRM created for the project are:

- Better communication with stakeholders and team members
- Ability to make decisions more quickly due to roles being clearly spelled out
- Ability to more quickly familiarize new members of the team with the project
- Ability to gain commitment from all
- The potential to see and deal with conflict early
- Improved teamwork

The RRM does have some drawbacks, including the following:

- Just because the project manager has it in writing doesn't make it happen; the project manager must still manage the effort.
- It can look overly simplistic.
- It can sometimes be difficult to define or get a responsible party to agree on a particular role.

The RRM is especially important when part of the project is outsourced and/or offshored. In these cases, the RRM must clearly delineate who is doing what on the project. (We discuss this topic in more detail in Chapter 14 of this text.)

PROJECT ORGANIZATIONAL CHART   After completing an RRM, a project manager is ready to create the project organizational chart, which is similar in concept to the organizational chart for the entire company but is specific to a project or program. Not every project will have its own project organizational chart; generally, it is used only when the project is of sufficient size to warrant its use (see Figure 5-5). A project organizational chart has many of the same benefits as an RRM in documenting roles and aiding communication. A key suggestion when dealing with project organizational charts is not to forget about the informal relationships that exist between individuals, just like on the organizational chart for the entire company (described in Chapter 2). These informal relationships can cause the project leader many headaches if they are unknown or ignored.

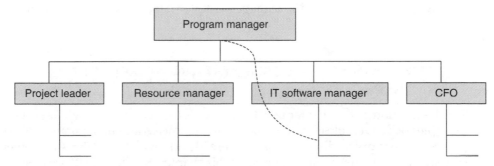

FIGURE 5-5   Project Organizational Chart

STAFFING MANAGEMENT PLAN   The final deliverable from human resources planning is the staffing management plan, which consists of the following elements:

- The process to follow when adding or removing people from the project
- The process to follow in assigning work and managing different groups of workers
- A list of training needed and the process for scheduling and funding the training
- The process for awarding bonuses (both monetary and non-monetary)
- Any safety issues that need to be followed
- Any specific human resources policies that need to be included
- Specific risks associated with assigned human resources

When crafting the initial or early staffing plan and project schedule, never start with a plan that requires resources to work overtime to complete the project successfully. Working overtime—whether compensated or not—on a prolonged basis will very soon begin to cause disharmony in the team. Working overtime once at the end of a project to deliver on time will work once or twice, but if it becomes the norm, stakeholders and your team will soon begin to avoid your projects and not trust the schedules you develop. Always start with a plan that can be accomplished without requiring workers to work long hours over extended periods of time.

THE SCOPE AND HUMAN RESOURCES PLANNING PROCESS

The process for scope and human resources planning involves the following steps:

Step 1. Use an existing scope management plan from a previous similar project. If one is not available, you must begin building one from scratch with the elements mentioned earlier in this chapter.

Step 2. Perform the requirements discovery and documentation process and begin building the requirements traceability matrix.

Step 3. Begin building the scope statement, starting with the project charter and the preliminary scope statement, if one exists.

Step 4. Build the WBS, using a WBS from a similar project or one of the other methods mentioned in the chapter, depending on the nature of the project and the team resources.

Step 5. With the assistance of SMEs, assign resources to tasks and build the roles and responsibilities matrix.

Step 6. If needed, build the project organizational chart.

Step 7. Build the staffing management plan, starting with one from a similar project or a template.

HOW TO CONDUCT THE SCOPE AND HUMAN RESOURCES PLANNING PROCESSES

This last section of the chapter uses the process outlined in the previous section to provide examples of deliverables for the scope planning process and the human resources planning process. Before proceeding, take time to reread and review the R & S Amusements Services case study. In Event 5 at the beginning of this chapter, Kevin and Jeff are meeting with Reid Lewis to discuss the next steps in the process of implementing the three applications: asset management, collection management, and customer management. Kevin and Jeff begin explaining the next steps in the project management process. Let's now work through each of these next steps for the asset management project.

Step 1: Create the Scope Management Plan

Jeff and Kevin will supply a plan that they have used on similar projects and tailor it to this project. The changed plan is outlined below:

- *Definition of scope*—The project team leaders are the steering committee members established in Chapter 4: Reid Lewis, Danny Calloway, Diana Brooks, Mark Lewis, and Ashley Brooks. These will also be the primary decision makers in decisions regarding the scope of the project. This group will meet to discuss what is and is not included in the scope of the asset management project. Each member has one vote, but the group will need to have four out of five votes to pass any issue. This will help alleviate major issues related to split votes and morale on the team. The group will meet daily until the scope statement and WBS are completed. When the project begins, the group will meet virtually every day but in person only once per week.
- *Development of the WBS*—Kevin and Jeff supplied a WBS from a similar project they worked on previously. The group reviewed the WBS and changed it to fit the asset management project at R & S Amusements Services. A brainstorming session will be held to identify all needed changes. The team will then review the current document for one week and write up reasons and justifications for any further changes. The group will meet again and make decisions on all requested changes. This process will continue until a consensus decision is made on the final content of the scope statement and resulting WBS.
- *Scope verification*—A final verification of the scope statement will be done by selecting key individuals from each relevant functional area of the company. The team leaders will meet with their respective departments and conduct similar brainstorming sessions to make sure nothing has been missed.
- *Change control*—Kevin and Jeff supplied a standard integrated change control process that has been used on many previous projects. The process will need to be changed slightly to fit this project and, most importantly, this company. (The integrated change control process is explained in detail in Chapter 12.)

Step 2: Perform the Requirements Discovery and Documentation Process

PPMS has several skilled systems analysts on staff to help R & S discover and document all the needed requirements for the new asset management system. These requirements will be used to build the requirements traceability matrix, the scope statement, and subsequent WBS. Jeff and Kevin have selected a systems analyst, David Irwin, who has four years of experience working with small to medium businesses. Because David hasn't worked with a business quite like R & S, he will need a little extra time to get up to speed and learn about the business and the project. David plans to use small group discussions and individual interviews to build the initial list of requirements.

Step 3: Create the Scope Statement

Starting with the project charter and the requirements documentation developed earlier, the team put together the following scope statement:

SCOPE STATEMENT

Project: Asset Management System (AMS)   **As of Date:** April 2, 2009

Functional Requirements

- System shall have the ability to track location and inventory amount of every item in current inventory as well as in the field. The tracking of inventory will be done by bar-code scanner. The warehouse workers and service technicians will all have portable wireless scanners. Anytime inventory is moved, it will be scanned into the system for real-time data updates.
- Item codes need to support 25 alphanumeric characters
- Track up to two item codes for each item to support vendor numbers and internal numbering
- Inventory amounts: on hand, on order, available, reorder quantity, lead time, discrepancy alerts
- Maintain history of cost changes and turn rates
- Items in inventory include game machines, maintenance supplies, dollar bill changers, and external speakers. All items to be labeled with bar codes.
- Support cycle counting, stock count calendars, inventory snapshots
- Multiple units of measure: each, ounce, and so on.
- Warranty information
- Inventory information is updated continually in real-time. Each worker in the field will have a portable unit that will store changes until the worker returns to the office. Once back in the office, the worker will plug in the unit to update the central database.
- Ability to store up to 500 changes in memory of each unit
- Backup battery packs and auto chargers
- Generate purchase requisitions when inventory reaches minimum levels. Each inventory item will have its own minimum and maximum inventory levels.
- Purchase amounts to receive discounts
- Vendor information
- Pricing information, quantity breaks, percentage of list, percentage markup
- Contract information
- Vendor ratings
- Multiple shipping methods
- The system shall allow authorized users of the system to create ad hoc reports on an as-needed basis
- Reports can be printed or displayed online
- The system shall track vendor information such as name, address, merchandise, prices, quality, delivery options, and timeliness.

Non-Functional Requirements

- System shall be secure from inside and outside the organization
- User will need a user ID and password for access to the system
- User roles will be set up in the system

- System shall have the ability to support a 40 percent per year growth rate in assets
- System shall be available from 7:00 a.m. until 5:30 p.m. Monday through Friday 100 percent of the time and other hours 90 percent of the time.

Success Criteria

- Find and purchase an asset management software package that fulfills at least 75 percent of the stated requirements within given budget constraints that is integrated or can be easily integrated with general ledger, customer management, and collection management
- Improve productivity of warehouse staff, asset management staff, service technicians, and collections representatives by 50 percent collectively
- Reduce inventory carrying costs by 20 percent
- Improve customer satisfaction ratings, based on an annual survey mechanism
- Implementation within 18 months

Constraints

- Stay within stated budget numbers
- R & S staff are not 100 percent dedicated to this project
- Delivery of this project needs to be done in parallel with collection management and customer management

Assumptions

- A software vendor solution can be found to meet user requirements and budget constraints
- Each member of the R & S staff is in support of the new software

Risks

- Maintaining end-user involvement
- Obtaining a clear and comprehensive statement of requirements
- Finding suitable software package with reliable vendor within budget constraints

High-Level Schedule

- Requirements documentation (statement of work), 2 months
- Software/hardware purchase and install, 6 months
- Gap analysis, 2 months
- Custom software, 2 months

High-Level Cost Estimate (first year)

- Additional hardware needed, $40,000
- Software package, $25,000
- Custom code, $30,000
- Overhead contribution, $5,000

Step 4: Create the WBS

As mentioned earlier, a similar project was used to obtain the first pass at a complete WBS. Jeff and Kevin, working with the R & S staff, made changes reflecting the needs of the asset management software implementation project. They followed a similar process

1.0	Project initiation
1.1	Develop project charter
1.2	Review and signoff
1.3	System context diagram
1.4	High-level use case model diagram
1.5	High-level use case narratives
1.6	Adopt change management process
1.7	Preliminary scope statement
2.0	Project plan
2.1	Requirements definition
2.2	Build project schedule
2.3	Build cost estimates
2.4	Quality management plan
2.5	Communications plan
2.6	Risk management
2.7	Procurement plan
3.0	System procurement process
3.1	Make vs. buy decision
3.2	RFP process
3.3	Gap analysis
4.0	System architecture model
5.0	Acquire project team
6.0	Iteration 1
6.1	Analysis model
6.2	Design model
6.3	Construction
6.4	Deployment
6.5	Project status reporting
6.6	Quality assurance
6.7	Closeout
6.7.1	Lessons learned
6.7.2	Corrective actions needed
6.7.3	Resource performance reviews
7.0	Iteration 2

FIGURE 5-6   **Partial Work Breakdown Structure**

to the one they used in defining the scope statement: Key users reviewed the scope statement and the WBS from a similar project, and a brainstorming session was held to identify changes. The new WBS was created and disseminated. Again, team members were given a chance to review and comment. The group was brought back together for final comments and changes. Figure 5-6 shows a part of the WBS created from this process.

Step 5: Create the Roles and Responsibilities Matrix

After completing most or all of the WBS, the team needs to begin assigning the appropriate resources to WBS tasks. Figure 5-7 shows a partial roles and responsibilities matrix for the asset management software project.

The R & S Amusements Services team has now created the requirements documents, scope statement, WBS, and the roles and responsibilities matrix for its asset management software project. Chapter 6 continues with the planning phase of the project, including time management planning and cost management planning.

Activity	Responsible Party							
	Project Manager	Reid Lewis	Diana Brooks	Mark Lewis	Ashley Brooks	Elaine Henry	Heidi Cosgray	Kenny Jones
1.1	R	A	C	C	C	C	I	I
1.2	C	R	A	A	C	C	I	I
1.3	R	A	A	A	C	C	I	I
1.4	R	A	A	A	C	C	I	I
1.5	R	A	A	A	C	C	I	I
1.6	R	A	A	A	C	C	I	I
1.7	R	A	A	A	I	I	I	I
2.1.1	R	A	A	A	C	C	I	I
2.1.2	R	A	A	A	C	C	I	I
2.1.3	R	A	A	A	C	C	I	I
2.1.4	R	A	A	A	C	C	I	I
2.1.5	C	A	R	A	C	C	C	C
2.2	R	A	A	A	I	I	I	I
2.3	C	A	R	A	I	I	I	I
2.4	C	A	A	R	I	I	I	I
2.5	C	A	A	A	R	I	I	I
2.6	C	R	A	A	C	C	I	I

Legend: R = Responsible
A = Approval
C = Consult or review
I = Inform or act as SME

FIGURE 5-7 **Roles and Responsibilities Matrix for the Asset Management Software Project**

Chapter Review

1. The project scope statement describes the characteristics of the product that the project was created to deliver. Team members and stakeholders should be involved in building the scope statement. The size and depth of the scope statement is determined by many factors, such as the size, risk, technology, experience, and strategic importance of the project.

2. Scope definition is accomplished by conducting a requirements discovery and analysis exercise, obtaining help from

SMEs, and using the results of the stakeholder analysis.

3. The results of the scope definition are documented in the requirements traceability matrix and the roles and responsibility matrix.

4. A WBS is an outcome-oriented list of tasks executed by a project team to accomplish stated project objectives. A WBS should represent 100 percent of the work required to produce the project's product. Because the WBS is used for many purposes, it is extremely important to get the WBS as accurate as possible as the project proceeds from start to finish.

5. A project manager can use several different techniques to create a WBS: analogy, top-down, bottom-up, and thread techniques.

6. A WBS can be organized in many ways. The two most popular are around the subparts of the product or by life cycle phase.

7. Project human resources planning involves identifying and documenting the project roles that must be staffed in order to produce the product of the project.

8. To be successful, a project manager must learn to assign the right task to the right person, motivate and influence members of the team who generally officially report to someone else in the organization, and obtain the needed power and authority to manage the entire project.

9. In order to successfully manage human resources, project managers will find it helpful to understand the research conducted by Maslow, McGregor, Herzberg, and others.

10. During the process of assigning human resources to tasks on the WBS, a project manager should begin building a roles and responsibilities matrix, which defines which individual or group is responsible for each task on the WBS.

Glossary

decomposition The act of breaking down a task into smaller and smaller parts until the component parts are at a level that can be assigned, monitored, and controlled.

deliverable A unique and verifiable product, result, or capability to perform a service that is a requirement to produce the end result product of a project.

project authority The delegated, earned, legal, or rightful power to command, act, or direct the activities of others.

project planning Establishing a predetermined course of action, team participants, and delivery dates, based on a project's goals and objectives.

scope creep The unanticipated gradual growth of information systems requirements during the life of a project, causing budget and time overruns.

scope statement A statement that describes the characteristics of the product that the project was created to deliver.

subject matter expert (SME) A person who, through experience, has intimate knowledge of a certain piece of information needed for a task.

WBS An outcome-oriented list of tasks executed by a project team to accomplish the stated project objectives.

Review Questions

1. Explain what is meant by the following: "The project scope statement should not be built in isolation."
2. List and briefly explain the key deliverables for the scope planning process.
3. Describe two sources of project scope elements besides stakeholders and team participants.
4. List and explain the characteristics that determine the size and depth of the scope statement.
5. Discuss project management related problems created due to "scope creep."
6. Explain what subject matter experts are and why they are important to a project.
7. Describe each of the components of the PIECES framework and its uses.
8. Describe each of the methods for creating a WBS and describe advantages and disadvantages of each.
9. What is the 100 percent rule?
10. Describe several uses for a WBS.
11. Describe the contents of the WBS dictionary and its purpose.
12. List and explain the five levels of Abraham Maslow's hierarchy of needs.
13. Explain the difference between a Theory X employee and a Theory Y employee.
14. Describe Frederick Herzberg's hygiene theory of employee needs.
15. List and explain the factors that lead to job dissatisfaction and those that lead to satisfaction according to Herzberg.
16. Differentiate between legal authority and acquired authority.
17. Describe the three influences that Thamhain and Wilemon found to offer the project manager the best chance for success and the types that may cause the opposite effect.
18. Project managers can possess five types of interpersonal influence. Name and describe them.
19. Explain the main benefit of generating a roles and responsibilities matrix (RRM) and describe the contents of this matrix.
20. Explain the main benefit of generating a requirements traceability matrix and describe the contents of this matrix.

Problems and Exercises

1. Perform a self-assessment: Do you prefer to work in a team or on your own? Why? Does your answer depend on the task or project? Explain.
2. Describe the factors that you believe will motivate you to do your best work when you graduate and get your first job. Will these factors change over time? If so, how?
3. Meet with a group of four or five classmates and brainstorm to come up with a list of characteristics that describe the worst teammates (no names!) you have ever worked with either in class or on a job. Discuss ways you might exercise power over these individuals to change their behavior.
4. Build a WBS for the short case study in question 9 in Chapter 4. The project should be organized by short iterations, not trying to deploy all modules at the same time. You should first implement the general ledger component in release 1; release 2 will include the other financial modules, release 3 the sales component, and release 4 the manufacturing software. Each release should follow the general life cycle Project Initiation, Requirements Discovery, Analysis, Design, Construction, Integration Testing, Deployment, and Project Closeout. You should include within each phase at least three tasks and one major deliverable.
5. Develop a WBS to at least two levels of detail for the complete hardware upgrade of the computers in one of your university's computer labs. Be sure to identify critical success factors for the upgrade.
6. Develop a WBS to at least two levels of detail for a spring break trip to Florida by car with three of your closest friends. Be sure to identify critical success factors for the trip.
7. Build a WBS for one of the chapter case study projects other than asset management—either customer relationship management or collection management. You may need to do some research on the Internet about how such software pack-

ages work. The project should use an iterative approach and be organized into the following phases: project initiation, requirements discovery, analysis, design, construction, integration testing, deployment, project closeout. You should include within each phase at least three tasks and one major deliverable.

8. The good news: You have been promoted into a project leader position. The bad news: The software development team you need to manage has been having problems with missed deadlines and morale. The previous project leader was fired for not being able to get things turned around. The team is made up of 15 developers, all very well trained and with several years of experience. Four of them are from India on a sponsored visa, and the other 11 are U.S. citizens from different parts of the country. The team was pulled together from many different parts of the organization to complete a large addition to the company web site. What are you going to do to get things turned around? List some tactics you will use to get the individuals to work better as a team and to begin meeting deadlines.

Projects and Research

1. Research the statement from McConnell (1998) that errors found "upstream" during the planning phase cost on the order of 200 times less to fix than errors found "downstream," during the building of the product. Therefore, more time spent upstream reduces the number of costly mistakes later on, reducing the overall cost of the project. Also, why are the most expensive errors created during the requirements/analysis phase?

2. Research several organizations either in your community or over the web to find out how they go about building a WBS and what their WBSs look like. Are these WBSs organized by phase or product component?

3. Research the impact that the Sarbanes-Oxley Act and HIPAA are having on U.S. companies' IT departments.

4. Do a product search for applications that are designed to document requirements and describe some of the key benefits they describe.

5. Conduct a comparative analysis between the United States and other countries (India, Russia, China) to determine at what level of Maslow's hierarchy of needs workers fresh out of college generally start. What implication does this have for project managers in the United States and in those other countries?

6. The U.S. military has a specification (MIL-HDBK-881) written to describe what a WBS should look like. Use the Internet to look up the standard and write a comparative analysis between it and what is described in this chapter.

MINICASE

1. *Background:* The definition of requirements is one of the most important activities of any IT systems project. Studies have shown that the incorrect definition and mismanagement of project requirements is one of the primary causes of failed projects. In addition, studies have shown that defects introduced during requirements definition can be the most expensive to fix if left undetected until the system is in production. The project leadership team of R & S Amusements Services has convened in Reid Lewis's office to discuss the manner in which they are going to elicit and define the requirements for the project.

Current Situation 1: Jeff Dunbar and Kevin Pullen of PPMS are discussing ways to effectively perform the requirements definition process. Kevin tells the group (Reid Lewis, Mark Lewis, and Diana Brooks) that in his experience, the best way to do this is to convene all the key stakeholders in a room and perform a joint requirements planning session. After Kevin explains the nature of a joint requirements planning session, he informs them that sessions of this type can typically last one to three days but have proven to drastically reduce the time required to elicit and define requirements over using traditional methods. Mark Lewis balks at this suggestion, saying there is no way that they can effectively run the business for three days without the key members of the company. Mark says, "For Pete's sake! We are in the amusement services business, not the systems development business. We have been doing business for 35 years without IT, and we can do 35 more if we have to!"

Discussion: Research the benefits of joint requirements planning sessions (also called joint application design sessions) and then respond to Mark's comment. How do you convince him it is more cost- and time-effective to do a joint requirements planning session? Is there a way to compromise with Mark in order to minimize the time that the employees would be away from their day-to-day jobs? Also explain to Mark and the others about the importance of getting the requirements as complete and accurate as possible at the beginning of the project as opposed to discovering them later in the process.

Current Situation 2: Jeff and Kevin have finally convinced Mark Lewis that a joint requirements planning session is the best course of action, and now they are planning the event. Jeff asks Diana Brooks if she would contact the local hotel and reserve their conference room for up to three days. In addition, he wants her to ask what the hotel will charge to cater drinks and refreshments for the meeting. Reid Lewis overheard the conversation and asked Jeff why this was necessary. He told Jeff that he would rather hold the meetings here in the office to save cost and that he also wanted himself and his employees to be available if any customers called with questions or if any other business matters arose that required their immediate attention.

Discussion: How should Jeff respond to Reid? Based on your research of joint requirements planning sessions, is it a good idea to hold the meetings at a location where there could be frequent interruptions? What rules or guidelines would you enforce on Reid and his employees during these three days of meetings? Include in your discussion a set of best practices for conducting joint requirements planning sessions.

Suggested Readings

Cleland, D., & Ireland, L. (2002). *Project management: Strategic design and implementation.* New York: McGraw-Hill.

Covey, S. (1990). *The 7 habits of highly effective people.* New York: Simon & Schuster.

Demarco, T. (1997). *The Deadline: A novel about project management.* New York: Dorset House Publishing.

Flannes, S., & Levin, G. (2001). *People skills for project managers.* Vienna, VA: Management Concepts.

Haugan, G.T. (2002). *Effective work breakdown structures.* Vienna, VA: Management Concepts.

Herzberg, F. (1968, February). One more time: How do you motivate employees? *Harvard Business Review*, pp. 51–62.

Jones, T.C. (1998). *Estimating software costs.* New York: McGraw-Hill.

Kantor, B. (2012, May 22). How to design a successful RACI project plan. *CIO*. Retrieved from www.cio.com/article/706836/How_to_Design_a_Successful_RACI_Project_Plan.

Kerzner, H. (2003). *Project management: A systems approach to planning, scheduling, and controlling.* Hoboken, NJ: John Wiley & Sons, Inc.

Maslow, A. (1954). *Motivation and personality.* New York: Harper and Brothers.

McConnell, S. (1998). *Software project survival guide.* Redmond, WA: Microsoft Press.

McGregor, D. (1960). *The human side of enterprise.* New York: McGraw-Hill.

Project Management Institute (PMI). (2002). *Practice standard for work breakdown structures*. Newtown Square, PA: PMI.

Project Management Institute (PMI). (2004). *A guide to the project management body of knowledge*, 3rd ed. Newtown Square, PA: PMI.

Rad, P.F. (2002). *Project estimating and cost management*. Vienna, VA: Management Concepts, Inc.

Starling, G. (1996). *The changing environment of business*. Cincinnati, OH: International Thomson Publishing.

Thamhain, H.J. (2005). *Management of technology: Managing effectively in technology-intensive organizations*. Hoboken, NJ: John Wiley & Sons.

Thamhain, H.J. & Wilemon, D.L. (1999). Building effective teams for complex project environments. *Technology Management 5(2.)*

University of Wisconsin. DoIT project management advisor" Retrieved from www.pma.doit.wisc.edu/plan/2-1/print.html.

Whitten, J., & Bentley, L. (2006). *Systems analysis & design methods*. New York: McGraw-Hill.

Worley, C.G., & Teplitz, C.J. (1993, March). The use of expert power as an emerging influence style within successful U.S. matrix organizations. *Project Management Journal*, pp. 31–34.

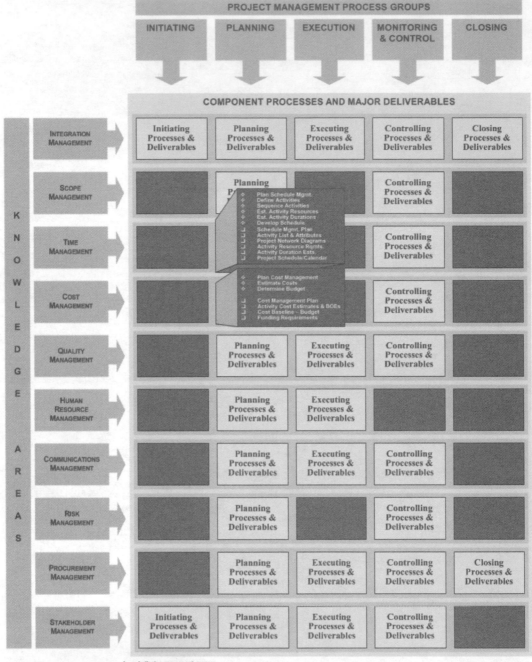

PROJECT MANAGEMENT PROCESS GROUPS

INITIATING	PLANNING	EXECUTION	MONITORING & CONTROL	CLOSING

COMPONENT PROCESSES AND MAJOR DELIVERABLES

KNOWLEDGE AREAS					
INTEGRATION MANAGEMENT	Initiating Processes & Deliverables	Planning Processes & Deliverables	Executing Processes & Deliverables	Controlling Processes & Deliverables	Closing Processes & Deliverables
SCOPE MANAGEMENT		Planning Processes & Deliverables		Controlling Processes & Deliverables	
TIME MANAGEMENT				Controlling Processes & Deliverables	
COST MANAGEMENT				Controlling Processes & Deliverables	
QUALITY MANAGEMENT		Planning Processes & Deliverables	Executing Processes & Deliverables	Controlling Processes & Deliverables	
HUMAN RESOURCE MANAGEMENT		Planning Processes & Deliverables	Executing Processes & Deliverables		
COMMUNICATIONS MANAGEMENT		Planning Processes & Deliverables	Executing Processes & Deliverables	Controlling Processes & Deliverables	
RISK MANAGEMENT		Planning Processes & Deliverables		Controlling Processes & Deliverables	
PROCUREMENT MANAGEMENT		Planning Processes & Deliverables	Executing Processes & Deliverables	Controlling Processes & Deliverables	Closing Processes & Deliverables
STAKEHOLDER MANAGEMENT	Initiating Processes & Deliverables	Planning Processes & Deliverables	Executing Processes & Deliverables	Controlling Processes & Deliverables	

Detail callout (Time Management Planning):
- Plan Schedule Mgmt.
- Define Activities
- Sequence Activities
- Est. Activity Resources
- Est. Activity Durations
- Develop Schedule
- Schedule Mgmt. Plan
- Activity List & Attributes
- Project Network Diagrams
- Activity Resource Rqmts.
- Activity Duration Ests.
- Project Schedule/Calendar

Detail callout (Cost Management Planning):
- Plan Cost Management
- Estimate Costs
- Determine Budget
- Cost Management Plan
- Activity Cost Estimates & BOEs
- Cost Baseline – Budget
- Funding Requirements

◇ Indicates component process
❑ Indicates deliverable

6

Project Time and Cost Planning

R & S Amusements Services

Event 6

Setting *The project leaders have convened once again, in a small conference room located outside Reid Lewis's office at R & S Amusements Services. Those in attendance include Reid Lewis, Diana Brooks, and Mark Lewis from R & S and Jeff Dunbar and Kevin Pullen from Premier Project Management Services.*

REID   I want to start the meeting by expressing my appreciation for all the hard work so far on the project. I have the results of all the interviews that everyone conducted, and the list of requirements—I believe Jeff called this the *scope statement*—looks very complete.

JEFF   I agree, Reid; everyone did a great job of getting me the required information so I could prepare the scope statement. This also allowed us to finish the first pass at the WBS.

DIANA   I'm surprised that once we got going, it really didn't take as long as I thought it would. Tracking everyone down and getting time to sit with us and meet was the hardest part.

JEFF   It almost always is because people are very busy getting their day-to-day jobs done. But we got it done and are now ready for the next step.

REID   You read my mind. What next?

JEFF   The next step is to look at the WBS and decompose the tasks into finer levels of detail.

[Everyone looks very confused]

KEVIN   Jeff, you'll need to explain exactly what you mean by *decompose*.

JEFF   Sorry about that. What I mean is we need to break down each task into smaller and smaller elements of work so they can be understood and assigned to someone.

MARK   How do we know when to stop?

JEFF   Great question, and I wish I had a definitive answer for you, but it really depends. Our guidelines are that a task is broken down far enough when it serves one purpose—meaning it has one deliverable, it can be assigned to one person, and the amount of work can be estimated.

MARK   Do we need to break down every task?

JEFF   No. Many of them will already be at the right level, and many others we won't be able to break down until we know more about the project.

REID   I thought we had the scope statement defined so we knew everything about the project?

KEVIN   Well, we can never, this early in the project, know all the details. This project also involves the purchasing of software, making it difficult to know how much work will be involved until we select a vendor's product and see how well it fits your requirements. Unfortunately, in most of these situations, you aren't going to find a software product that matches 100 percent of your requirements. You find the best product that matches the closest and then you need to fill in the gaps. Until we know what the gaps are, we can't quite complete the WBS. The WBS we chose to start with was for a similar type of project, so it has most of the upper-level tasks defined, but it won't be complete until a decision is made.

REID   I think I'm starting to understand but probably won't entirely until we get there.

JEFF   Don't get too wrapped up in all this now. It will become very clear by the time we get done. After we get done decomposing the tasks, our next job will be to decide on a sequence—which tasks need to follow other tasks. The final step will be to come up with an estimate to complete the work.

DIANA   Won't the estimate depend on who is doing the work?

KEVIN   Excellent observation, Diana. You are correct. We will do as much as we can and then use some numbers that Jeff and I have experienced in other projects until we know more about the project.

REID   Well, sounds like we have more work to do, so let's get started.

(To be continued)

(This chapter provides instructions for decomposing tasks in the WBS, sequencing them, and then estimating effort for them.)

CHAPTER PREVIEW AND OBJECTIVES

This chapter begins with the assumption that the initial work breakdown structure (WBS) has been created for a project. (See Chapter 5 for an explanation of the WBS.) The WBS must now be broken down into finer and finer levels of detail so that work can be estimated, budgeted, and assigned to the right resource to complete. This chapter defines the other two parts of the triple constraint: time and cost. This chapter also describes the processes needed to build a thorough list of activities needed to complete the entire scope of the project, sequence them, and cost them.

As you read this chapter, you will:

- Understand the process of activity decomposition
- Understand the level of detail required for activities
- Understand the process of sequencing activities and the four types of activity dependencies

- Define and understand key cost management terms
- Understand all the components of a project budget

Time is the most precarious element of the triple constraint. Scope and cost can be adjusted to make allowances for issues that occur during the project. Regardless of what you try, you can't make time stand still or back up. Time is a critical commodity and usually in short supply during IT projects. A project manager must learn to plan time accurately to avoid major problems later, during project execution.

As reported in the CHAOS report from the Standish Group (1995), the IT industry has been very poor at managing time during projects. Although time overruns have improved since the initial reports done in the mid-1990s, the study conducted in 2006 concluded that, on average, IT projects were 72 percent overrun on time. The numbers for cost overruns were only slightly better at 47 percent over on average. These numbers signal the importance of doing a better job of time and cost planning.

The reasons for the IT industry's poor track record for time and cost estimate accuracy are numerous and are addressed throughout this chapter, but one key observation made by Ed Yourdon in his work *Death March* (1997) is that IT professionals tend to be overly confident in their abilities or too simplistic in their approach to estimating effort. The IT profession must begin to use a more disciplined approach to estimating time and cost for projects if they are to improve their track record. That is what this chapter is all about.

This chapter is composed of two major sections, the first covering processes for time planning and the second describing processes for cost planning. We then bring these two areas together and build a unified step-by-step process for doing time and cost planning, followed by examples of each technique, using the R & S Amusements Services case study.

PROJECT MANAGEMENT CONCEPTS: TIME PLANNING

The job of a project manager is filled with "time robbers"—activities that at first seem to be short and unobtrusive but when they are all added together can completely fill an entire workday. Project managers must become adept at spotting time robbers and dealing with them effectively. Each one will require a slightly different approach to control. The key is recognizing when they are occurring and having a plan to deal with them. Some examples follow:

A user wanders into your office to talk about the latest project issue first thing in the morning, before most others have arrived, because he figured out that you come in early to try to get some work done. He has an issue and is trying to make it your issue.

Your boss read an article from her favorite business journal while flying back from a business trip. The article was about a new project management methodology, and your boss wants you to review the article and give her some feedback on how to make it work in the organization.

Scenarios like these happen often, and you must learn to budget your time. Harold Kerzner and others (Kerzner, 2001) offer these examples of additional time robbers:

- Task rework
- Telephone calls, e-mail, and hardcopy mail
- Incomplete work

- Lack of needed authority
- Inefficient change procedures
- Waiting on people
- Day-to-day administration
- Excessive levels of review
- Casual office conversations
- Poorly run meetings
- Executive meddling, or micromanagement
- Poorly motivated or educated customers
- Vague goals and objectives
- Poor time management
- Ill-defined project scope
- Company politics
- Working on underfunded projects

The project management body of knowledge (PMBOK) includes the Time Management knowledge area, which contains the following processes: plan schedule management, define activities, sequence activities, estimate activity resources, estimate activity durations, and develop schedule. On many projects, these steps can happen all at the same time, especially when the WBS was created for a project using a WBS from a previous similar project because many of the activities are already defined. The following sections cover them one at a time for clarity.

Plan Schedule Management

The plan schedule management process is used to document the policies, procedures, and documentation requirements for planning, developing, managing, executing, and controlling the project schedule. The plan is created mostly from historical information from the organization and previous projects concerning resources, organization structure, history with similar projects, and experience of the project manager. The key deliverable from this process is the schedule management plan, which should contain at a minimum the following information:

- How some schedule contingencies are to be handled defined by the risk discovery process (defined in Chapter 8). Items such as use of overtime, use of parallel activities when and what, change of task sequences those tasks that have discretionary dependencies.
- What scheduling techniques will be used to track progress such as critical path method or critical chain. What project buffers may be used and how tracked.
- How schedule performance will be monitored and controlled such as using earned value, what accounting codes are significant to record activity for the project .

Define Activities

The **activity definition** process identifies the lowest level of work on the WBS, called **work packages**, that needs to be performed to create the finished product deliverable. Depending on the technique used to create the WBS (refer to Chapter 5), typically the work packages are built by decomposing parent activities down into smaller and smaller units of work. Each activity is decomposed into smaller and smaller units until the task can be assigned to one person who is responsible for the completion of the task, a time and cost estimate can be accurately generated, and the task can be scheduled.

After all activities have been broken down into their respective work packages, keep in mind a couple of helpful thoughts:

- The 100 percent rule is in effect: All the work packages defined must add up to 100 percent of the total scope of the project.
- Not all of the work packages will be defined at the same level of detail.

Following these guidelines on the level of detail for each activity makes monitoring and control of the project easier and more accurate (see Chapter 11). Wysocki and McGary (2003) sum up the decomposition process as follows:

- Status and/or completion is measurable and can be reported easily at any time.
- Start and end events are clearly defined and easily communicated.
- Each activity has a single deliverable.
- Time and cost are easily estimated.
- Activity duration is within acceptable limits—no longer than 10 work days. This is not a hard, unbreakable rule but a suggested guideline that no activity be defined as having an effort longer than two weeks.
- Work assignments are independent; you shouldn't need to interrupt the work in the middle of an activity because another activity does not work as planned.

The completed work product from this process is the complete activity list. It should follow the 100 percent rule and consist of a short name for each activity, along with a longer, detailed explanation of the work and final deliverable. Many companies also attach a cost accounting code to each activity for financial reporting. Other attributes include predecessor and successor information defined in the schedule section of this chapter, assumptions, constraints, lag or lead times, resource requirements, and any imposed schedule start or completion dates.

Sequence Activities

Activity sequencing involves identifying and documenting the logical and sometimes physical relationships among schedule activities. This process is generally carried out and shared with the aid of project management software. Project constraints—such as resource availability, geography restrictions, holidays, and an organization-imposed timetable—often determine the sequence of events. For example, at most universities, major application system upgrades must take place when classes are not in session.

Based on our experiences, project management students tend to grossly underestimate the importance of activity sequencing. The dependencies that are created between activities will control a project manager's ability to make adjustments to the schedule during the execution of the project. Several tools and techniques simply won't work if a project manager doesn't do a good job of establishing dependencies. Between any two activities there exist three possible types of dependencies:

- *Mandatory dependencies*—These dependencies are inherent in the type of work that is being done in each activity. When using these dependencies, a project manager must be very careful that they are the correct choice. For example, you might need to actually write the software code before you can test it, or you might need to build a segment of the network before you can connect clients and test. But be careful not to label items as mandatory that are really discretionary, such as building the entire network before you begin testing it or writing the entire requirements document before proceeding with analysis and design artifacts of the system. Creating mandatory dependencies greatly limits your ability to alter the project schedule during project execution, when changes occur and flexibility is needed to adjust the schedule.

- *Discretionary dependencies*—These dependencies are defined based on a preferred sequence of activities and give the greatest amount of flexibility but need to be documented as such so that changes can be made later in the project, if needed. For example, a project team may decide to wait until the software developers are completely done coding the system before the quality assurance team is scheduled to start reviewing their work, based on projected resource availability.
- *External dependencies*—These dependencies are based on the work being performed by an entity outside the organization or business unit. For example, a project team may decide to outsource the updates to a web site or may want to purchase and install a new development server before beginning software development. These tasks need to be scheduled just as they would be scheduled if they were being done internally because the project manager will still need to track and control them.

All of these scheduling methods involve graphically demonstrating the sequential relationships between activities. According to work by Meredith and Mantel (2003), building and using these scheduling techniques has the following advantages:

- Provides a consistent framework for repeatable project successes
- Effectively illustrates the interdependence of all tasks
- Clearly denotes the dates when resources need to be available
- Determines milestone and project completion dates
- Identifies critical path activities that, if delayed, will delay the project completion date
- Identifies which activities are not on the critical path and thus can be delayed if needed without affecting the project completion date
- Identifies resource availability
- Shows which tasks can or are being done in parallel

The two techniques of activity sequencing covered in this text are the precedence diagram method and the activity on arrow diagramming method. Each is described next, with examples.

THE PRECEDENCE DIAGRAM METHOD The precedence diagram method (PDM) of constructing a project network diagram uses boxes to represent activities (nodes) and lines with arrows to represent the dependencies. In the example shown in Figure 6-1, the task names are shortened to just letters, and the lines with arrows are not labeled. Notice that some of the activities (C, F, G, and H) have more than one predecessor; one (Begin) has only a successor, and one (End) has only a predecessor.

The PDM illustrates four types of dependencies between activities:

- *Finish-to-start*—The beginning of a task is dependent on the completion of all its predecessors.
- *Finish-to-finish*—The completion of a task is dependent on the completion of all its predecessors.

- *Start-to-start*—The start of a task is dependent on the start of all its predecessors.
- *Start-to-finish*—The completion of a task is dependent on the start of all its predecessors.

Finish-to-start is the method most commonly used in projects, and it is generally the default condition in project management software. The least used type is start-to-finish. A word of caution when using different dependency types: Don't use them just to use them. Make sure there is a sound reason for applying any relationship other than finish-to-start. When a project starts and a project manager is trying to track a project of any size, changes that affect the schedule are sure to happen. The more variability in dependency types used, the more complicated the schedule becomes, making changes harder to enter and track. Simplicity is best here.

When you use a project management software package such as Microsoft Project, the PDM is created for you, based on the information you enter (see Figure 6-2). In Microsoft Project, all the information that appears in the task boxes is user configurable. The critical path, described later in this chapter, is indicated by boxes that have bold borders.

THE ACTIVITY ON ARROW METHOD   With the activity on arrow (AOA) diagramming technique, as illustrated in Figure 6-3, the lines with arrows represent the tasks, and the circles are the start and end points. The arrows point in the direction of precedence. One drawback of this technique is that it can show only finish-to-start relationships between activities and not the other three.

To draw an AOA diagram, you draw the Begin circle or node and then proceed with the tasks that do *not* have a predecessor, usually the first tasks to be done on the project. These are shown in Figure 6-3 as lines A, K, and F. Then you move to the next tasks listed in the WBS, in order of precedence. Activity B has a predecessor of A, Activity C has a predecessor of B, and so on. Tasks M, G, and L have no successors, so you draw their arrows to the End node. Next, you add a circle at the end of each arrow as an end point. Finally, you number each circle. Be prepared as you draw this diagram to draw and then erase and redraw as you work your way down the task list.

One final note about drawing AOA diagrams: "Dummy" lines may be needed when a task has multiple predecessors. Dummy lines are drawn in Figure 6-3 as dashed lines. Dummy activities consume no resources and have no time allocated to them. Task E from Figure 6-3 has predecessors Task K, F, and A, but Task H has only Task F as a predecessor and likewise task B has task A as its only predecessor. To make the drawing accurate, you must introduce dummy activities.

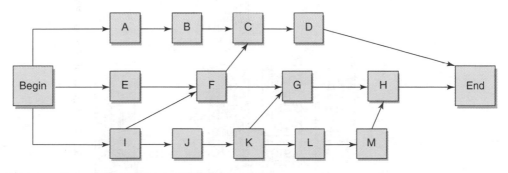

FIGURE 6-1   Precedence Diagram Method Example

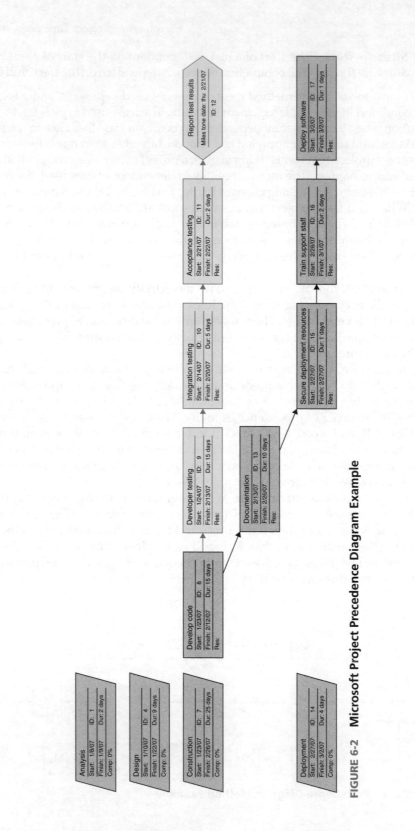

FIGURE 6-2 **Microsoft Project Precedence Diagram Example**

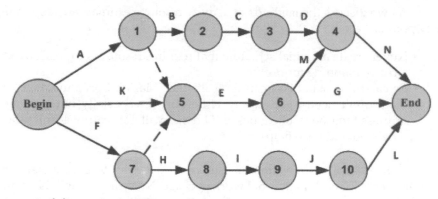

FIGURE 6-3   Activity on Arrow Diagram Example

The final deliverable from the activity sequencing process is the initial, or preliminary, activity schedule; this schedule is called *preliminary* because later in the process you add to it resources based on availability and the duration of each activity to complete the planned schedule.

Estimate Activity Resources

The activity resource estimating process consists of the following deliverables: activity resource requirements, resource calendars, and assigned resources. As happens with many of the processes discussed in this text, activity resource estimating, activity duration estimating, and cost estimating generally occur at the same time on many projects. They are broken out here to aid in the understanding of each and emphasize the different methods used. Estimating resource needs involves determining what resources—including people, computers, electricity, and so on—are needed and in what quantities, and in the case of human resources, what level of expertise. The quality or experience level of the resource will determine the cost and amount of time needed to complete the activity. The decision of which resources to choose may need to be determined by their availability. Just because you want the best network engineer in your company to work on your project doesn't mean you will get him or her. That person is probably working on several other projects and will need to schedule time to work on your project.

Because of the difficulties and inaccuracies of prior IT project estimates for most companies (see the CHAOS report statistics for cost and time overruns reported in Chapter 1), many companies are spending the time to get their workers trained in the art of estimating and/or employing professional estimators. A professional estimator's primary job is to aid the project team in accurately defining time and cost estimates. (From this point forward, the chapter will use the term *estimator* to represent the person who is building the resource, time, and cost estimate for the project. Keep in mind that this could be several different people for the same project.) This person employs many of the methods discussed in this chapter to produce accurate estimates. Individuals doing estimating need to be familiar with an organization's policies related to human resources staffing, make versus buy decision making, rentals or leases, outsourcing, and so on. The techniques used in activity resource estimating are expert judgment, the analogous approach, and alternatives analysis.

As we discuss the methods of activity resource estimating, keep in mind a couple of key points:

- Never create an initial schedule that requires resources to work overtime, or you are already planning for problems.
- Be careful of what Ed Yourdon calls the "Marine Corps mentality": Real programmers don't need sleep. Many IT resources, especially new young ones trying to impress their new colleagues and bosses, will not readily admit when they are overwhelmed and need help.

EXPERT JUDGMENT   An estimator uses *expert judgment* to gain insight into the resource requirements for each individual work package. No estimator will have all the knowledge needed to assess an entire project. The estimator will need to consult IT SMEs—network engineers, database designers, software developers, and user SMEs—accountants, engineers, marketing people, and so on. The estimator seeks to determine what expertise is needed and what level of knowledge is required to complete the deliverable of the work package. (Do we need a senior network engineer with 10 years of experience? Or is this a task that a junior network engineer with 2 years of experience can handle?)

THE ANALOGOUS APPROACH   If the WBS was created using the analogous approach—that is, building the WBS using a similar project first and then editing to fit the uniqueness of the current project—the required resources have already been determined. Adjustments will be needed based on the lessons learned from the previous project and the uniqueness of the current project. For example, say that in the previous analogous project, a junior systems analyst with just one year of experience was assigned to develop the specifications for a small key piece of the application. The junior analyst who was struggling to complete the work didn't want to look bad in front of his boss, so he worked very long hours and weekends to complete the assignment but didn't report the extra effort. The task ended up getting done, but the quality was not up to expectations. The junior analyst then confessed his difficulties to his boss. If this information is not recorded and communicated, the same mistake will be made again and again.

ALTERNATIVES ANALYSIS   Each work package will have alternative ways in which the work can be accomplished. Some examples include different skill levels of resources, internal versus external resources, technology selected, and time constraints. Some of these alternatives are voluntary choices, and others are required. For example, say that a new software package selected is written in Java, and no one on the current staff has Java experience. Or say that the added functionality needed for a student registration system must be done while the students are on break, so time is critical.

Many times the individual tasks that are needed for each work package are not defined to a low enough level of detail to assign resources. These tasks need to be decomposed into lower levels of detail before resources can be estimated. All the tasks are then combined to give a complete picture of the number of needed resources.

The deliverables from the activity resource estimating process are a list of activity resource requirements for each activity within all the work packages, a project resource organization chart and WBS, a hierarchical breakdown of resources by category and type, updated resource calendars showing the availability of each resource (detailing vacations, holidays, and days available to work on the project), and resource loading. Resource loading lists the amount of each resource that the project schedule requires during specific time periods. According to Meredith & Mantel, "Resource loading gives a general understanding of the demands a project or set of projects will make on a firm's resources" (2003, p. 455). Project managers can use loading to make sure that resources are not overutilized; for instance, project management software will notify you that you have someone working 24 hours a day, but it will allow you to do it.

Estimate Activity Durations

When the WBS is more complete and a preliminary schedule and list of resources needed have been created, the project manager is ready for the last step before building the initial project schedule: activity duration estimating. The estimate activity durations process is concerned with determining the time required to complete the work associated with each work package on the WBS. Time is estimated in two dimensions: effort and duration. *Effort* is defined as the actual amount of time, usually in hours, that a particular resource requires to complete a given task. *Duration* is defined as the amount of elapsed time it will take the resource to complete the work. For example, you are a software developer and have estimated that it will take you 24 hours to change and test the software application, based on the requirements you were given. Unfortunately, most IT workers are required to work on more than one project at a time, and you must split your time. Other time robbers, such as email, meetings, and phone calls, also make it difficult to work continuously on one task. The 24 hours you estimated to complete the task actually requires 48 hours in duration. The project schedule must reflect both of these numbers: The 24 hours is used for costing, and the 48 hours applies to the schedule. A project manager needs to know how to estimate the amount of effort required to complete work. Where did the 24-hour estimate come from, and why does it actually take 48 hours to complete?

As we discuss the methods of activity duration estimating, keep in mind a couple of key points about estimating work effort:

- Time and cost estimates should be done in a "progressive elaboration" process, meaning they start out general and less accurate and over time become more detailed and accurate as the project proceeds. Estimates done very early in the life of a project (sometimes referred to as a *rough order of magnitude (ROM) estimate*) can contain as much as -25 percent to +75 percent variance. Estimates done after much of the early planning has been completed contain a variance of -10 percent to +25 percent (sometimes referred to as the *budget estimate*), and as the project moves closer to completion, within the last several months the variance narrows to -5 percent to +10 percent (referred to as the *definitive estimate*). Estimates provided by the *PMBOK Guide*, fifth edition, page 200.
- Steve McConnell (1998) demonstrates the need for progressive elaboration by using a "cone of uncertainty" diagram (see Figure 6-4). In most projects, IT projects especially, the decisions made early on have profound effects on decisions made later, such as which software development tools to use (Java or .NET Framework, for example) or which type of architecture to design (for example, two-tiered, three-tiered, or N-tiered). As you move through the stages/iterations of the project, the cone of uncertainty grows smaller or narrower.

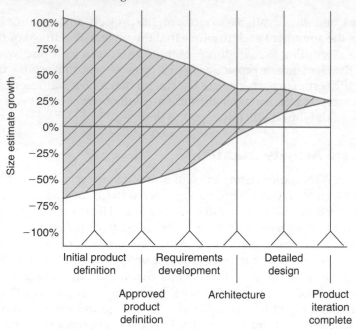

FIGURE 6-4   The Cone of Uncertainty

Source: Adapted from Steve McConnell, "Software Project Survival Guide," reprinted by premission from Microsoft Press.

- McConnell states, "The job of the average manager requires a shift in focus every few minutes. The job of the average software developer requires that the developer not shift focus more often than every few hours" (1998, p. 45). When estimating time and setting up a schedule, try to set up your teams to succeed by giving them the schedule that best maximizes their productivity.
- Brooks's *The Mythical Man-Month* (1975) is a classic book that all project managers should read. It offers the following insights:
  - Techniques that most estimators use are poorly developed. Many are based on a flawed assumption that all will go well. Problems and changes are sure to happen to the project and need to be considered.
  - Many techniques confuse effort with progress, assuming that a person and time are interchangeable.
  - Adding manpower to a late software project makes it later. Just putting more people on a task does not necessarily reduce the time it takes to complete it, and in many cases in IT projects, it will lengthen the time due to communication needs, training, and so on.
  - A *man-month* (referred to today as a *person-month*) in estimating refers to how much work can be done by a worker in a given month. A common error is thinking that because there are, on average, 20 work days a month, there are actually 160 hours of available work time to schedule. However, most workers don't have this much time available due to the time robbers mentioned earlier.

Activity duration estimating consists of the following methods: analogous, top-down, bottom-up, three-point, simulation, and COCOMO. The final deliverable, regardless of method used, is some estimate of effort in time for a particular work task. To arrive at an estimate of time, you first determine which estimate of work size is needed. As Capers Jones, a noted author in this area, points out, the first step in accurately estimating an IT application is determining its size. Over the years, many different techniques have been used, including lines of code, function points, feature points, and so on. After the effort has been sized using one of these methods, time estimates can be applied. Let's examine two methods-lines of code and function points.

TASK SIZING

Lines of Code (LOC)   Lines of Code (LOC), also called source lines of code (SLOC), has been one of the most used metrics in determining the size of a software development project. With the advent of object-oriented software development tools, other measures have emerged that are slowly replacing LOC, such as function points or feature points. The verdict is still out about which method yields the most accurate time and cost estimates; each method has advantages and disadvantages.

LOC estimates are based on historical results. The longer the history of results, the more accurate the new estimates. LOC is generally used very early in the estimating process to get a rough order of magnitude effort estimate. Much research exists that can aid companies in determining project characteristics based on LOC, provided that the technology environments are similar. Some of the key project characteristics that can be determined via historical experience are effort, financial cost, documentation, software bugs, and number of resources. For example, say that you have been asked to generate time estimates to add new functionality to the company web site for the marketing department. Your software development group has done web programming before, but not for the marketing department. The functionality being asked for is similar in breadth to that of other projects you have done, so you look at the results of earlier projects to see how many lines of code it took and the actual results. The previous project required 6,000 lines of code. Based on historical results, you know the following conversion numbers for each 1,000 lines of code using two midlevel software developers:

- Effort = 250 hours, yielding 1,500 hours or just over 9 person-months
- Documentation = 45 pages, yielding 270 pages
- Bugs = 2.1 bugs, yielding 12.6 bugs
- User-instructed rework = 6.1, yielding 36.6 items needing rework
- Financial cost = $18,750, yielding $112,500

The following are some advantages of using LOC as a project sizing method:

- It can be very quick and inexpensive to generate.
- It can be done early in the process.
- It is a universal metric because all application software contains some form of code line.
- It can be easily gathered because many development environments will produce the number for you.
- It can facilitate a lessons-learned process at the end of the project, when comparing what was estimated to what was actually done.

The following are some disadvantages of using LOC as your project sizing method:

- You must be sure to compensate for technology differences. For example, generating a line of Cobol code is different from generating a line of Java.
- It can't be done well unless history exists, but history is generated only through time and many projects.
- You must determine what counts as a line of code (comments, declaratives, and so on) and be consistent.
- If LOC is used as a metric of developer productivity for performance assessments, you need to be careful to measure actual output because it would be easy for a developer to start generating many lines of documentation instead of working code to improve the numbers.
- You must include a process complexity factor to keep projects equal.
- You need to know what level of resource your numbers are based on (for example, experienced versus inexperienced workers).
- No industry standards (such as ISO) exist that describe a line of code.
- You need to distinguish between auto-generated code and original work.
- LOC needs to be continually updated as older records may not be relevant in today's new environments.

Even with its long list of disadvantages, LOC continues to be used as a project sizing metric. The function points method was created to help alleviate some of the issues surrounding using LOC as a metric. It is explained next.

Function Points   The function points method was created in the 1970s by A. J. Albrecht to estimate time and dollars, based on the generated system requirements specification. The key to counting function points is to have a good requirements statement. A function point measures the size of a business function that the new system needs to have, such as an input screen or a report. A large body of research exists on the use of function points as an estimating tool. Like LOC, this method requires historic information to be accurate. Unlike LOC, a standard has been adopted for function points, and this standard is supported by the International Function Point User Group (IFPUG).

Function point analysis can be done at any point in a project but is not considered accurate until late in the planning phase or, if following an iterative approach, until several iterations of the project have been concluded and the system requirements specification is accurate. Function point analysis is only as accurate as the system requirements document.

Calculating function points involves the following process:

Step 1. Count the number of business functions within each of the following categories: user inputs, user outputs, inquiries, data structures, and external interfaces.

Step 2. Determine the complexity level of each function as simple, medium, or complex. For example, output complexity is determined by the number of elements involved, any complex calculations or complex process logic, and the number of data structures.

Step 3. Assign weights for each level of complexity within each category.

Step 4. Multiply each function by its weight and then sum the products to obtain the total unadjusted function points.

Step 5. Compute the value adjustment factor (VAF).

Step 6. Compute the adjusted function point total by using the formula

[Unadjusted total x (0.65 + 0.01 x VAF)]

The following example illustrates this process. Let's use the previous LOC calculation example. A systems analyst creates a requirements document that yields the results of user needs reported in Table 6-1.

TABLE 6-1 Function Point Results

Category	# of Low	Weight	# of Average	Weight	# of High	Weight	Total
			Complexity Calculations				
User inputs	22		5		2		98
User outputs	30		5		1		152
User inquiries	15		15		5		135
Files/structures	70		10		2		620
External interfaces	2		5		0		45
					Grand Total		1050

The function point analysis yields 1,050 function points for this application development project. For steps 1 and 2, you count the number of each type of function category and evaluate them as either low complexity, average complexity, or high complexity. For example, for user inputs there are 22 evaluated at low complexity, 5 evaluated at average complexity, and 2 evaluated at high complexity. In step 3, you assign a weight for each category at each level of complexity. User inputs have a weight of 3 at low complexity, 4 at average complexity, and 6 at high complexity. Next, in step 4, you multiply each number of items by their weight and sum the totals to get the total unadjusted function points.

Step 5 is to compute the VAF by assigning a rating on a scale of 0 to 5 for each of the 14 system characteristics listed in Table 6-2, where the rating scale is as follows:

0 = no effect

1 = incidental

2 = moderate

3 = average

4 = significant

5 = essential

From Table 6-2, the adjustment factor of 40 is calculated and used in the last step of the process. Step 5 is to calculate the total adjusted function points:

Unadjusted total x (0.65 + 0.01 x VAF)
1050 x (0.65 + 0.01 x 40) = 1076.4

TABLE 6-2 Function Point System Characteristics

System Characteristic	Scale (0–5)
Data communications required	2
Distributed processing	1
Performance needs	5
Heavily utilized operating environment	4
On-line data entry	4
Backup and recovery	4
Master file access online	3
Transaction input complexity	2
Internal processing complexity	2
Reusable code	2
Input, outputs, files, inquiries complex	2
Designed for multiple sites	4
Designed to facilitate change	3
Installation complexity	2
Total	40

Now that you know the number of adjusted function points, you can, based on past projects within your organization or similar organizations, make the following estimates:

Effort = (1.49 hours of effort per function point) × (1,076.4) = 1,603.8 hrs
Documentation (0.25 pages per function point) × (1,076.4) = 269.1 pages
Bugs (0.025 bugs per function point) × (1,076.4) = 26.91 bugs
User-instructed rework (0.04 per function point) × (1,076.4) = 43.06
Dollars ($105.10 per function point) × (1,076.4) = $113,129.64

The following are some of the advantages of using the function points method:

- It is independent of programming language and technology.
- It can be used early in the project life cycle, at the end of the requirements discovery phase or design phase.
- A wealth of research exists to support the process.
- The impact of scope changes is easier to comprehend and track.
- Organizations can track their own results and improve the function point estimates.
- It can be used in any development environment.

The following are disadvantages of using the function points method:

- It requires many subjective evaluations (complexity ratings and environmental factors).
- Accuracy is greatly increased only after the detailed design phase or after a few project iterations have been performed.
- It takes some time (training) to perfect and can vary, depending on who is doing the calculations, due to personal bias.

Despite the disadvantages, function point analysis is used on many projects as an estimation tool. Many updates and changes have occurred since the initial research first appeared. One such new technique that has been used in specialized situations is called *feature points analysis*, which was created to deal with different kinds of applications—real-time applications, systems software, embedded software, and so on. Another adaptation, called *object points*, was created to deal with sizing of object-oriented technology projects.

ANALOGOUS ESTIMATING Analogous estimating is mainly used early in the project planning stages, when many of the details of the current project are not known. This method bases a current work package time estimate on the actual time of a work package from a similar project already completed. If it makes sense to do so, you first compare LOC or function points to make sure the tasks are equivalent and then adjust to use the actual time for the new estimate. Analogous estimating can be an excellent technique, provided that the two work packages are similar enough in scope, size (LOC or function points), technology, and complexity. SMEs generally need to be involved to verify the similarity. If the WBS was created using this technique, you already have the information available, although you will need to adjust the numbers based on known differences.

TOP-DOWN OR BOTTOM-UP ESTIMATING Both top-down and bottom-up estimating rely on SMEs being intimately involved during the estimating process. The top-down method, conducted first by higher-level managers in the organization, starts at the top of the WBS and, using analogous techniques or some other technique, creates ROM estimates very early in the planning process. The process proceeds by breaking each upper-level WBS summary item into lower levels of detail and assigning workers familiar with the activity to create estimates. The bottom-up method is the opposite: It starts at the bottom detail level of the WBS and uses three point, simulation, or COCOMO II to create estimates. Done toward the end of the project, it creates a definitive estimate. Each work package receives an estimate that is then rolled up into summary tasks until you reach the top of the WBS.

THREE-POINT ESTIMATING Three-point estimating adds the element of risk into its calculations. For parts of the project that are exceedingly risky (for example, new technology, new vendor, short time frame required), using a three-point estimate may be required. The three-point estimate is based on using SMEs to determine three types of estimates:

- *Most likely*—The work package effort based on the *likely* level, availability, and number of resources, with known work interruptions.
- *Optimistic*—The work package effort based on the *best-case scenario* of resources and interruptions.
- *Pessimistic*—The work package effort based on the *worst-case scenario* of resources and interruptions.

For example, Joe, a network engineer, has been asked to give a time estimate for setup of a new Cisco switch that he has never worked with before. How long will it take Joe to configure, test, and deploy the switch? The last time he did something similar with an earlier model of Cisco switch, it took him a total of 40 hours, so Joe assigned a most likely estimate of 40 hours. But now that Joe has done it once and he expects this process to be similar, he might be able to get it done faster, so Joe's optimistic estimate is 20 hours. But recently Joe read an article stating that Cisco had completely changed the configuration module for this upgrade, so it may take longer than it did last time; Joe therefore assigns a pessimistic estimate of 56 hours.

The next step is to create an average of the three estimates—or, to be more accurate, a weighted average—using the formula $(a + 4m = b)/6$ where a = optimistic time estimate, b = pessimistic time estimate, and m = most likely time estimate. Joe therefore calculates $(20 + (4)40 + 56)/6 = 39.3$ hours as the time estimate for this task.

This process can be time-consuming. It is generally done only on risky sections of the WBS. And then many times it is done only on a summary basis, not on every low-level task. The results can be very accurate, provided that the person doing the estimates is knowledgeable about the task being estimated.

SIMULATION   In situations where an organization or a project manager has very limited or no experience with the product being built or tools to be used, as well as in many research and development projects, using simulation techniques offers an excellent way to assess how different variables will affect the project schedule, including different time estimates, cost estimates, risk, resources, and so on. **Monte Carlo simulation** is a technique that can be applied in such a situation.

A Monte Carlo simulation goes through a set number of iterations and records the outcome. The output shows a project manager and decision makers the distribution of outcomes. Many software products exist today, many tied to Microsoft Project, that will perform simulation for you. Because risk exists in every project, there is a probability distribution associated with the time and cost estimates created. Using the previous example of 20 hours for the optimistic time, 40 hours for the normal time, and 56 hours for the pessimistic time, the team can assign probabilities to each. For example, the team believes there is a 50 percent chance of a normal duration, 25 percent chance of an optimistic estimate, and 25 percent chance of a pessimistic estimate. The software will then simulate the execution of the project, using the associated probability distributions. Figure 6-5, which was created using Crystal Ball (which works as an add-in to Microsoft Excel), shows the frequency distribution for completion dates. To run the simulation, you first create the WBS and then complete time estimates for each activity and enter them into a spreadsheet. Finally, you enter the duration of each path through the network diagram. The final piece of information needed before Crystal Ball can run the simulation is the probability distribution of the time estimates. For this example, you can choose a normal distribution.

The simulation shown in Figure 6-5 tells you that the project can be completed in 79.91 days with a 100 percent probability. The software also allows a specific number of days to be entered for project completion and shows the corresponding probability. As shown in Figure 6-6, the probability of finishing the project in 75 days is 87.2 percent.

Monte Carlo simulation can be time-consuming and should be used only where it makes sense. It can be used for any situation that contains uncertainty, such as during project selection, with time and cost estimation, and during the risk analysis process.

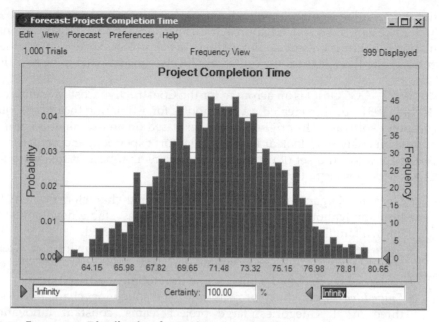

FIGURE 6-5   **Frequency Distribution for Project Completion**

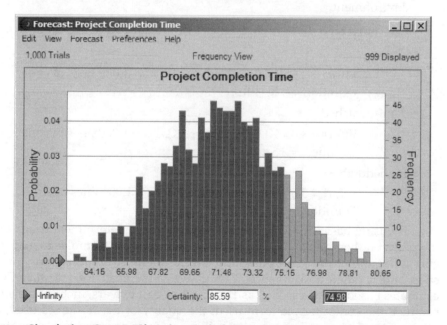

FIGURE 6-6   **Simulation Output Showing Probability of Finishing the Project in 75 Days**

A few words of caution about using simulation software: Although it looks really cool and official, with all its fancy graphs and statistics, the software is oblivious to any assumptions (right or wrong) that the estimators made when they fed it information. The old adage "garbage in/garbage out" certainly applies here. Be careful when using simulation information to make project decisions; keep in mind how the numbers were created and make sure a disciplined approach was used to define the distributions. Also, the simulation is accurate only at a point in time. As the project executes and actual information is entered into the schedule, the estimates will change and need to be reevaluated.

COCOMO   COCOMO is an acronym for the Constructive Cost Model developed by Barry Boehm (1981). Boehm created a set of models for estimating the effort required to develop computer software. His original work was based on an examination of 63 projects, using regression analysis to look at LOC, actual effort expended, and actual schedule duration. Boehm developed a set of exponential equations that best fit this historical information. COCOMO consists of three project types:

- *Organic*—Organic projects have the following characteristics: small project teams, little innovation, few constraints and deadlines, stable development environments, known familiar technology, and few changes expected.
- *Semi-detached*—Semi-detached projects have the following characteristics: medium-sized project teams, some innovation, few constraints, tighter deadlines, more changes expected, and a fairly stable development environment.
- *Embedded*—Embedded projects have the following characteristics: largest of the three in all categories, large project teams, constant innovation, many constraints, very tight deadlines, many changes expected, and a complex development environment.

Each project type has its own formula for calculating effort and duration in person-months:

- Organic:

    Effort = $2.4 \times \text{KLOC}^{1.05}$, where KLOC = 1,000 lines of code
    Duration = $2.5 \times \text{Effort}^{0.38}$

- Semi-detached:

    Effort = $3.0 \times \text{KLOC}^{1.12}$, where KLOC = 1,000 lines of code
    Duration = $2.5 \times \text{Effort}^{0.35}$

- Embedded:

    Effort = $3.6 \times \text{KLOC}^{1.2}$, where KLOC = 1,000 lines of code
    Duration = $2.5 \times \text{Effort}^{0.32}$

By using basic COCOMO, an organization can determine a rough estimate early in the project rather quickly, and over time it can adjust the formulas to match its own experiences. But to get more meaningful answers for most organizations, two other models, called intermediate and advanced COCOMO, can be used. Intermediate COCOMO creates estimates based on size as well as 15 subjective cost drivers, including elements of the end product, the computer platform used, the quality of the resources used, and the project environment. These 15 cost drivers will increase or decrease the estimated project duration and need to be added to the formulas used in basic COCOMO. Advanced, or detailed, COCOMO builds on the cost drivers used in intermediate COCOMO and separates their impact over four major development phases: requirements, product design, detailed design, and code/test development. A version called COCOMO II attempts to take into consideration the following:

- Newer development environments, such as object-oriented software
- Commercial off-the-shelf software projects or reusable software components
- Degree of understanding of architectures
- Shorter development cycles and spiral or new agile iterative incremental development projects

COCOMO II consists of three process models that can be chosen, depending on the development phase of the project. The Early Application Composition model uses object point estimates very early in the process, when the first prototypes are being developed. The Early Design model uses function points to estimate effort early in the project life cycle, when software and system architectures are still being developed. The Post-Architecture model uses LOC or function points plus 17 cost drivers to determine effort. The following are advantages of using COCOMO:

- It is quick.
- It can be used early in the project.
- It can be tailored to fit any organization.
- It can be applied at different phases of the life cycle.
- Many models exist to aid organizations in getting started.

Disadvantages of using COCOMO include the following:

- It ignores documentation and other requirements.
- It involves no compensation for customer attributes (for example, availability, knowledge, cooperation).
- It ignores personnel turnover issues.
- It is based on historical data that may be obsolete.
- It is used only to estimate the development effort; other phases of the project (for example, planning, implementation) are not accounted for.

FINAL THOUGHTS ON ESTIMATING ACTIVITY DURATIONS   Estimating a project's effort is a difficult process, and becoming proficient at it requires many years of training and experience. Many call it an art more than a science. This chapter demonstrates many techniques that can be used. Depending on the organizational size and culture and the type of project, the size and risk associated with each project will determine which estimating techniques to use. The key, regardless of the technique used, is to understand that your early attempts at estimating may not be very accurate, but if you continually evaluate the estimates against actual results on every project, you will begin to get better and better.

At this point of the planning phase of the project, you have a signed project charter authorizing work to begin and listing the major objectives, a WBS (project scope), defined resource needs, a network diagram, and an estimate of effort and duration for each task, based on resource selected (time needed). Next, you need to create the project schedule to get the final duration estimates of time for the entire project.

PROVEN STRATEGIES AND HINTS TO SUCCESS

Spencer Lamoreaux, in "Project Scheduling in Large Organizations: Shifting the Culture," originally published at the 2009 PMI Global Congress Proceedings in Orlando, Florida, describes how Intel deployed a successful schedule management system and practice across the 6,000-person organization. "Advanced scheduling is tough work," Lamoreaux writes. Intel defined the following key components of an advanced project schedule:

- A detailed list of tasks and milestones
- Cost (dollars), effort (person hours), and duration estimates for each task
- Dependencies matched for each task
- Resource leveling each task (extending duration, delaying, or optimizing to ensure no individual is overloaded)
- Determine a proper risk contingency fund (for cost, effort, and duration)
- Build the final high-confidence (90% +) schedule, critical path, and critical resource path that is baselined

The approach Intel used to train and move their project managers off of spreadsheets and napkins to a unified advanced software tool is listed below:

- Focused training (grassroots effort, focus on value)
- Simplified tools (make adjustments to the software tool to facilitate ease of use and consistency)
- Track correct usage (make sure project managers are following the methodology using detailed compliance reports)
- Metrics that matter (after all the training, configuring, and tracking usage, now begin tracking real value-add metrics about the project, such as earned value and resource utilization)

Develop the Project Schedule

Project schedule development determines the planned start and completion dates for each activity listed on the WBS. The deliverable from this process is the project schedule. Before telling individuals what activities to work on and specifically when, a project manager must add the duration estimates to the schedule, along with the resource constraints. Key project sponsors and interested stakeholders will also be very interested in the results of this process. The first two questions stakeholders always ask after making a request for an IT project are When can I get it? and How much will it cost? Project managers must be very careful in managing stakeholder expectations, especially when the project is just getting started and the estimates are still very rough. A project manager must remind stakeholders that attempting to create a precise forecast early in the project will be precisely wrong. As soon as the project manager finishes and communicates the project schedule, stakeholders will start counting the days until the new product is delivered. Project managers can use several different analytical techniques to determine the project schedule: PERT, the critical path method, critical chain, and resource leveling. Using these analytical techniques and creating a schedule provide the following benefits:

- It creates a consistent framework that can be followed from project to project and during the execution of the project.

- It illustrates the interdependencies of the activities on the WBS.
- It facilitates communication within the project team and between the team and stake-holders.
- It aids in the identification of critical activities.
- It helps the project manager evaluate all alternatives and their impact when making scheduling changes during the project.
- It reduces the number of resource scheduling conflicts.
- It helps identify tasks that can or must be run in parallel to keep the project on track.
- It facilitates what-if analysis.

PERT The Program Evaluation and Review Technique (PERT) was developed by the U.S. Navy, in cooperation with the consulting firm Booz Allen Hamilton, for the Polaris missile/submarine project in 1958 to help organize the activities of 11,000+ contractors. PERT uses the network diagramming techniques described earlier in this chapter to build a final schedule. PERT uses a weighted average approach, or beta probability distribution, to capture the three-point estimates discussed earlier (optimistic, most likely, and pessimistic) for activity duration. Figure 6-7 shows an example of the beta distribution, which is used because it is a more realistic representation of how most IT people do estimating—favoring their optimistic estimates.

The following formula is used for calculating the PERT weighted average:

(Optimistic estimate + 4 (Most likely estimate) + Pessimistic) / 6

The PERT weighted averages for each activity are added to the network diagram to show the start dates and finish dates for each and the final project end date. As discussed earlier in this chapter, generating three estimates for every task and then calculating a weighted average is a lengthy and time-consuming process. For this reason and the fact that more accurate and quicker methods exist, PERT is not used as much today as it was in the past.

The next technique described, CPM, is used today for a variety of projects. And, when used in conjunction with the critical chain method, discussed later in this chapter, it is a very effective tool for scheduling and monitoring projects.

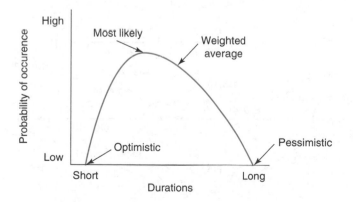

FIGURE 6-7 Beta Distribution of Three-Point Estimates

CPM   The critical path method (CPM) was developed by DuPont, Inc., during the late 1950s (at basically the same time as PERT). CPM uses the sequence and duration of activities to determine the total project duration. CPM produces two key pieces of information. First, it determines the amount of **slack**, or *float*, for each activity in the schedule. Second, it produces the **critical path**, which is the longest path through the schedule or the shortest time in which the project can be completed. All activities that fall on this path are referred to as *critical path activities*.

In most projects, there are several paths through the network diagram that are not the longest path. Theoretically, a project can have paths with identical lengths that are the longest, yielding dual critical paths. But in most projects of any size, there is typically only one critical path, which means that all the other paths have tasks with slack or **free slack**. If a task has free slack it means that the task can be delayed in starting without affecting any other tasks on the schedule. Knowing this information is extremely valuable to a project manager. Learning the proper use of slack time in many projects can determine success or failure. Later in this section, we'll talk about two techniques that allow a project manager to make use of slack time: fast tracking and crashing. But first, let's discuss how to calculate slack time by finding the earliest start time (ES), earliest finish time (EF), latest start time (LS), and latest finish time (LF) for each activity.

Figure 6-8 shows an example of an AOA network diagram with duration and slack calculations included. Figure 6-9 identifies the elements represented in the full diagram. The slack time for each activity can be easily calculated by finding the difference between ES and LS or EF and LF. For Task D, slack is zero because EF - LF = 0 which tells us that Task D is on the critical path. For Task F, slack equals 3, calculated as EF - LF, or 8 - 5 = 3 Notice that using ES – LS yields the same slack. This means that you could delay the start of task F up to 3 days and not affect the end date of the project.

So how are ES, EF, LS, and LF calculated? The calculation is performed for each activity in two passes through the entire network diagram for each path. The first pass through starts at the Begin node and moves to the End node through each path, calculating the ES and EF. The second pass through starts at the End node and moves to the Begin node through each path, calculating the LS an LF.

For the first pass through each task with a predecessor of the Begin node, you assign a zero for ES (see Tasks A, B, and C in Figure 6-8). Then you add the duration to each to

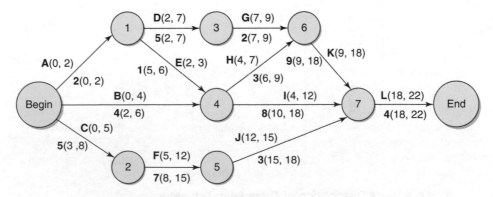

FIGURE 6-8   Activity on Arrow Network Diagram with Schedule Information

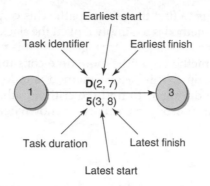

FIGURE 6-9   Duration with Slack Identification

calculate the EF. Task A receives a 2, Task B receives a 4, and Task C receives a 5. For this example, assume that all task durations are measured in days. The next step is to move to the next successor node for each task and assign ES equal to the EF number for its predecessor. Task D has a predecessor of Task A, so it is assigned an ES of 2; Task E has the same predecessor, so it is assigned an ES of 2 as well; and Task F has a predecessor of Task C, so it is assigned an ES of 5. Task H has two predecessors, so you must decide which EF to use. When making the first pass, you always select the EF of the predecessor task that is greater, so for Task H you select the EF of Task B of 4 days. Task E, the other predecessor, has an EF of 3. Thus Task H is assigned 4 days for its ES, and when you add its duration, you get 7 days for EF. All the other activities are calculated in a similar manner.

The second pass begins with the End node and assigns the EF duration of the project to the LF of all tasks that have the End node as a successor. In this example, only Task L has the End node as a successor, so L is assigned an LF of 22. Next, you calculate the LS by subtracting the activity duration from the LF. Task L has a duration of 4 days, so LS = LF - duration = 22 - 4 = 18. Moving to all predecessor tasks, you assign the LF equal to the LS of the successor. This involves Tasks K, I, and J. Notice that each receives the same LF date of 18. This process continues until you reach the Begin node. As in the first pass, when you encounter a task with multiple successors like Task B, how do you decide which LS to use? When doing the second pass, you take the LF of the task that is shortest or smallest. Task B has successor Task H with an LS of 6 and Task I with an LS of 10, so you use Task H and assign 6 as the LF of Task B. Then, as before, you subtract the duration from the LF to calculate the LS.

What does knowing this information mean to you on a project? Well, suppose that as the project manager, you get in the middle of a project and find out that one of the tasks is taking longer than it was supposed to take; if that task is on the critical path, if it doesn't get done on time, the whole project will be delayed. Due to the nature of the activity, adding an additional resource to it would speed it up and enable the team to get it done on time, but the project doesn't have any resources available because they are all working on other tasks. But what if one of the resources needed is working on a task with slack, so it could be delayed and its resources could be used on the task that is behind? When the task that is behind schedule is back on track, the project manager can move the shared resource back to their originally assigned task. Without having knowledge of slack, how would anyone know which resources could be moved, when they could be moved, and for how long without affecting the end date of the project?

The last step is to find the critical path. This can be accomplished using one of two methods. The first method is to simply look at the slack of each activity. If slack is zero, then the activity is on the critical path. In Figure 6-8, this would be the path of activities: A, D, G, K, L. The other method is a little more time-consuming but can be done before you calculate all the slack time. This second method is to look for the longest path through the network, based on duration. To find the critical path, you simply list each possible path and add up the duration of each activity, as shown here:

Paths:

A, D, G, K, L = 2 + 5 + 2 + 9 + 4 = 22

A, E, H, K, L = 2 + 1 + 3 + 9 + 4 = 19

A, E, I, L = 2 + 1 + 8 + 4 = 15

B, H, K, L = 4 + 3 + 9 + 4 = 20

B, I, L = 4 + 8 + 4 = 16

C, F, J, L = 5 + 7 + 3 + 4 = 19

Following this logic, path A, D, G, K, L is the longest path (that is, the critical path), at 22 days; this yields the same result as looking for tasks with zero slack.

Using knowledge of the critical path and slack, a project manager can use two schedule compression techniques, called *crashing* and *fast tracking*. In most projects, schedule compression is one of the most often requested changes project managers are asked to perform.

Crashing   **Crashing** a project schedule is generally done because it is required by some outside force, such as management or a government regulation. Using the project schedule, you begin looking at tasks on the critical path that would deliver the most compression for the least incremental cost. You make this determination simply by looking at the tasks that could be done faster if more resources were added. For example, say that the quality assurance team has estimated that it will take 3 weeks to complete testing of the new software, using two midlevel people. But the task could be completed in 1.5 weeks if they added two additional midlevel workers. If this activity was on the critical path, adding the two additional midlevel people could shorten the project by 1.5 weeks but might increase your costs only slightly, depending on where the resources come from.

Crashing a project often adds or removes critical path tasks. It's important to reevaluate your critical path schedule after each activity is completed. Also, you need to be careful when trying to crash too many activities at once. Your schedule and costs can grow out of control very quickly.

Fast Tracking   Fast tracking is similar to crashing, with all of the same benefits and drawbacks. This technique, however, looks specifically for activities that can be done in parallel if the resources are available. For example, when a project schedule was initially created, say that the project manager set up a discretionary dependency between two tasks because the same resource needed to work on them both. The output of one task is not required for the other task; it was only based on the fact that the same resource was doing both. If another resource is found or hired, the project manager could do both tasks at the same time and shorten the schedule. Many of the product development methodologies described in Chapter 2 of this text are based on the idea of short iterative phases of development.

Fast tracking looks to see if any of these short phases can be done in parallel or at least overlap somewhat instead of being linear.

CRITICAL CHAIN   The **critical chain method**, unlike the critical path method, looks at more than just time and does not assume that you have unlimited resources to accomplish the activities on your project. The ideas for the critical chain method were first introduced by Dr. Eliyahu Goldratt (1997), in his book *Critical Chain*. The method is based on the theory that every project has constraints: time, resources, cost, scope, and so on. The goal of a project manager is to build and run projects so that they best work with the constraints they face. The importance of each constraint varies from project to project.

The critical chain is a path through the project schedule that shows activities with scarce resources assigned. The critical chain technique assists a project manager to focus on critical resources. Figure 6-10 is a network diagram with the critical chain highlighted using a dashed line.

The activity on node (AON) network diagram shows the critical path as shaded nodes of Activities B, D, F, J, and K. Goldratt's critical chain introduces the ideas of using feeding buffers before tasks with scarce resources (FB in the diagram) and using a project buffer to handle many other project constraints at the end of the project designated PB in the diagram. The feeding buffers are created just prior to the task. For example, Tasks C, E, H, and J are all set up to be done by the same resource, so feeding buffers FB1, FB2, and FB3 were set up to keep the schedule on plan in case one of the tasks lasts longer than was scheduled. Because only one of these tasks, Task J, is on the critical path, you might not pay any attention to the other tasks until it was too late and the schedule had slipped.

Another major benefit of using buffers is to remove or reduce the impact of project team member gaming associated with many activity estimates. For example some project managers, when soliciting estimates from IT professionals, know that certain individuals always underestimate their work. The project manager doubles the estimate provided by the individual in order to compensate for the estimating error. Other IT professionals are

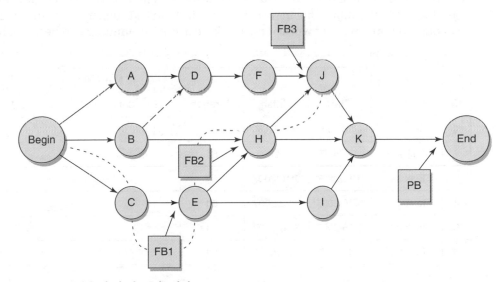

FIGURE 6-10   Critical Chain Schedule

always generating inflated estimates to cover themselves in case of problems; these estimates are way over what is necessary to complete the work. Project managers then know that they must always reduce these estimates to come up with a more accurate estimate. This type of gaming (over estimating and under estimating) doesn't provide good results when you're trying to set up realistic schedules. Feeding buffers and a project buffer give you a way to remove the gaming from the estimates. When you've built up trust within the team, and individuals begin giving accurate numbers, these can be used for the individual activities. Then, looking for critical or constrained activities, feeding buffers are set up with the appropriate amount of time, according to the amount of risk and uncertainty each is buffering. When the project is executing, as time is needed and borrowed from the buffers, it is documented and communicated to all stakeholders. No one is punished for using the time to make sure that accurate reporting is achieved. Incentives are offered to the project team for not using the buffers and awarded at the end of the project.

This process facilitates a much cleaner, better-communicated, and better-run project. Schedules are maintained, and stakeholders are kept informed of progress. A major side benefit of using a critical chain this way is that the project team gets smarter about estimating future work.

Another issue presented by Goldratt that adds to the benefit of using buffers is the problem of resources multitasking, with the idea of reducing idle time between tasks. Figure 6-11a shows an example of resources that are asked to multitask versus a project on which resources are not multitasking displayed in Figure 6-11b. Each example shows three tasks each taking 10 days to complete. In Figure 6-11b, Task 1 is completed in 10 days, Task 2 is completed 10 days after that (or in 20 days), and Task 3 is completed in 30 days.

Now look at Figure 6-11a and see that Task 1 is split into two tasks for demonstration purposes: Task 1-a (the first 5 days before being interrupted) and Task 1-b (the concluding 5 days of work) now take 20 days to complete; Tasks 2-a and 2-b take 25 days of duration to complete; and Tasks 3-a and 3-b take the same time as in Figure 6-11b, 30 days, to complete. Task 1 (split into 1-a and 1-b) is delayed by 10 days compared to not multitasking to finish and Task 2 (split into 2-a and 2-b) by 5 days to finish from Figure 6-11a. This simple example ignores the fact that multitasking in real life causes tasks to take longer than if they were worked all at once. If you have ever worked on a task such as programming and been really involved

ID	Task name	Start	Finish	Duration	2/25	3/4	3/11	3/18	3/25	4/1	
							Mar 2007			Apr 2007	
1	Task 1-a	2/26/2007	3/2/2007	5d							
2	Task 2-a	3/5/2007	3/9/2007	5d							
3	Task 3-a	3/12/2007	3/16/2007	5d							
4	Task 1-b	3/19/2007	3/23/2007	5d							
5	Task 2-b	3/26/2007	3/30/2007	5d							
6	Task 3-b	4/2/2007	4/6/2007	5d							

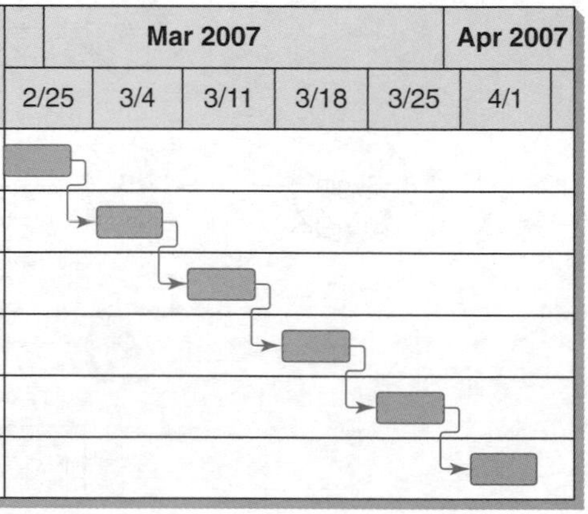

FIGURE 6-11a   Gantt Chart Showing Multitasking

ID	Task name	Start	Finish	Duration	2/25	3/4	3/11	3/18	3/25	4/1	
						Mar 2007				Apr 2007	
1	Task 1	2/26/2007	3/9/2007	10d							
2	Task 2	3/12/2007	3/23/2007	10d							
3	Task 3	3/26/2007	4/6/2007	10d							

FIGURE 6-11b   Gantt Chart Showing One Task at a Time

in the details of some tricky code, gotten interrupted for a couple days for something else, and then returned to the tricky code, you know that it takes a bit of time to pick up where you left off, causing more time to be spent on the task than was probably originally estimated.

The reality of critical resource issues and assigning resources to a schedule leads into the next section of the chapter: resource loading and leveling, the smoothing out of resource demands over the entire schedule for optimum utilization.

RESOURCE LOADING AND LEVELING   Resource loading defines the amount of time a specific resource is needed over each time period. Project management software is good at producing loading reports (see Figure 6-12). A report can list, by day, who is needed and how much time is needed, or it can show, by resource, which days they are needed and how much time across all activities is needed per day. A report is great at highlighting issues of overloading a resource—having a resource working more time in a day than is available. For example, the testers in Figure 6-12 have been asked to work 16 hours during several days in April. If this is 16 hours for two resources (8 hours each), then you are okay, but in this example, only one resource from testing has been assigned. The project manager must either change the schedule or get more testers. The case for trainers is even worse: The schedule has this person working on three separate tasks on the same day, each taking all day to finish. Something is going to have to change to make the schedule workable, or you will get to this part in the project and wonder why you are behind schedule. A project manager needs to make sure the right resource is available on the right day, working the right task. A project manager can fix issues similar to the overloading situation in Figure 6-12 by using a technique called *resource leveling*.

Resource leveling is the process of rescheduling on the project schedule activities that have available slack to achieve a more balanced distribution of resource usage. Project management software can aid a project manager in leveling, but the manager will still need to review the changes to make sure resources are being utilized effectively.

A project manager who is ultimately responsible for the effective use of resources may have to manually perform some or all of the following activities in order to level resources:

- Move activities (manually move activities by changing the discretionary dependencies or entering hard dates)
- Split (manually split activities such that only part of the activity is done at one time)
- Reduce resource availability (change the resources so they are not working full time on the task, which will have the effect of lengthening the activity duration)
- Change/add resources to the task
- Authorize the resource to work overtime

	Resource Name	Work	Details		Sep 8, '02							Sep 15, '02							Sep 22, '02		
				S	S	M	T	W	T	F	S	S	M	T	W	T	F	S	S	M	T
1	⊟ Project Manager	16 hrs	Work																		
	Project Clos	*16 hrs*	Work																		
2	⊟ Developer 1	200 hrs	Work																		
	Install Netwc	*8 hrs*	Work																		
	Install Intern	*8 hrs*	Work																		
	Security	*8 hrs*	Work																		
	Unit Method	*8 hrs*	Work																		
	Unit Class T	*8 hrs*	Work																		
	User Accept	*16 hrs*	Work																		
	Integrate Ac	*24 hrs*	Work			8h	8h	8h	8h	8h			8h			8h	8h				
	Security	*8 hrs*	Work																		
	Unit Method	*8 hrs*	Work																		
	Unit Class T	*8 hrs*	Work																		
	User Accept	*16 hrs*	Work																		
	Integrate Inv	*16 hrs*	Work																		
	Integrate Sa	*16 hrs*	Work																		
	Security	*8 hrs*	Work			8h	8h	8h													
	Unit Method	*8 hrs*	Work						8h												
	Unit Class T	*8 hrs*	Work							8h											
	User Accept	*16 hrs*	Work										8h								
	Enable Sale	*8 hrs*	Work													8h	8h				
3	⊟ Developer 2	144 hrs	Work																		
	Test Model	*8 hrs*	Work																		
	Test Model	*8 hrs*	Work																		
	User Accept	*16 hrs*	Work																		
	Train/Turn o	*8 hrs*	Work																		
	Review Use	*8 hrs*	Work																		
	Test Model	*8 hrs*	Work																		
	User Accept	*16 hrs*	Work													8h	8h			8h	8h

FIGURE 6-12 Microsoft Project Resource Usage Screen

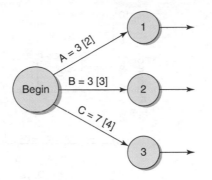

FIGURE 6-13a   A Simple Network Diagram

One or all of these techniques may be required to bring a schedule into reality. Properly leveling resources generates many benefits for the project:

- Greater team productivity
- Greater team morale
- Reduced costs (less overtime and less multitasking)
- Leveled costs with less erratic swings from period to period
- Less management (which is especially important when hiring outside the organization to fully utilize the managers while they're assigned to the project)
- Better use of resources across projects

Figure 6-13a presents the beginning of a simple project network diagram with just three tasks. Task A requires 2 resources working 3 days. Task B requires 3 resources working 3 days, and Task C requires 4 resources and 7 days.

Figure 6-13b shows the resource loading if all tasks are started as soon as possible. It requires 9 resources on day 1, 7 resources on day 3, and 4 resources for the remainder of the project. Figure 6-13c shows all tasks getting done in the same amount of time but using fewer resources at the beginning. Six resources are required at the beginning, 7 resources are needed for days 3 through 5, and 4 resources are needed for days 5 through 7. By moving tasks around and not starting all of them as soon as possible, the project manager can redistribute the resource requirements potentially making resource management easier.

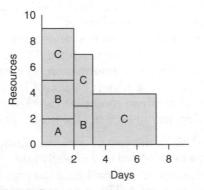

FIGURE 6-13b   A Project Before Leveling

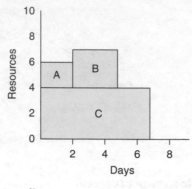

FIGURE 6-13c   A Project After Leveling

When the schedule is built, activities are estimated, and resources are leveled, the next step, as discussed in the next section, is to assign costs to each activity and create a budget.

PROJECT MANAGEMENT CONCEPTS: COST PLANNING

Project cost management is concerned with planning, estimating, budgeting, and controlling the costs of project resources needed to complete 100 percent of the activities of the project. This chapter concentrates on planning, estimating, and budgeting, and Chapter 11 focuses on cost control. Like most of the rest of the project management processes, the cost planning processes will overlap and should be reevaluated throughout the life of the project. For small projects, these three processes (cost planning, estimating, and budgeting) occur at the same time performed by the same person. On larger projects, each process is done sequentially and often times by different people. The text covers them here as separate processes to emphasize the key methods used in each. The output from cost planning is used as part of the overall project plan and can consist of one or all of these elements: budget estimates, units of measure, links to accounting control accounts, allowable variances, methods used to track progress such as earned value (defined in chapter 11), and stakeholder reporting formats.

The judicious use of project resources is extremely important. Organizations have a finite amount of resources, including people, money, and equipment. Not having enough resources or the right resources can have a major impact on every part of a project. Cost overruns, although better than when the CHAOS reports from the Standish Group (1995) first appeared, are still averaging 47 percent.

In this section, the time estimates developed in the preceding section are used to develop a big part of the cost estimates for the project. Next, these cost estimates will be added, along with all other cost information, to create the project budget. But first, it is worth spending a little time to review basic cost terminology before proceeding. A project manager must understand these concepts to work with other departments, such as finance and accounting, to develop and control the project budget:

- *Burden rate*—This is the cost of a human resource, and it takes into consideration more than just a person's salary or hourly rate, including benefits, vacation, holidays, and so on. The accounting department can provide the burden rate, which should be used to determine accurate HR costs for the project.

- *Direct versus indirect costs*—Direct costs are directly attributable to the activities of a project (for example, purchase of hardware or software, labor cost of workers on the team). Indirect costs are costs that are not directly attributable to the activities of the project (for example, overhead rates such as management salaries, energy costs, rents).
- *Recurring versus nonrecurring costs*—Recurring costs appear more than once throughout the life of a project (for example, annual hardware and software maintenance). Nonrecurring costs appear only once (for example, initial purchase cost of hardware and software).
- *Fixed versus variable costs*—Fixed costs are expenses whose total does not change in proportion to the activity of a business or project, within the relevant time period or scale of production (for example, rent, insurance). Variable costs change based on the activity of a business or project (for example, project employee costs).
- *Opportunity costs*—This is a measure of the anticipated return of the project against the anticipated return the organization would receive on a highest-yielding alternative investment that contains a similar risk assessment. The opportunity cost is used during project selection because when choosing one project over another, the organization is giving up the potential opportunities the unselected projects offer.
- *Sunk cost*—This is the cost expended that cannot be retrieved on a product or service. It is money already spent that cannot be recovered.
- *Life cycle costs*—These are all costs incurred over the lifetime of the product or service.

Estimate Costs

The cost-estimating process is used to develop accurate cost estimates for the resources needed to complete each activity of a project. The human resources time estimates have already been done, so in this part of the process, the project manger simply applies the relevant burden rate for each selected resource. Cost estimates are generally expressed in units of currency (dollars, euro, yen, rupees, and so on). Accurate cost estimates need to be created for all types of resources, not just human resources, such as materials, equipment, and facilities.

A key concept to remember is that an estimate is just that—a guess about a future unique event. Therefore, cost estimating and re-estimating should be done throughout the course of the project to improve accuracy and aid management in making decisions. Many issues related to projects coming in overbudget could be answered if everyone understood the accuracy issues involved with early cost estimates. In many organizations, management wants to know exactly what a project is going to cost before the project even begins. Organizations need to understand the numbers presented previously in this chapter and summarized in Table 6-3 when making decisions on projects.

It is important to know the purpose of a cost estimate before communicating the results. Harold Kerzner (2001), a noted project management author, points out that there

TABLE 6-3 Accuracy of Project Cost Estimates

Reference Name	Timing	Accuracy
Rough order of magnitude	Very early (project charter)	−25% to +75%
Budget	Toward the end of project planning process	−10% to +25%
Definitive	Toward the end of project execution	−5% to +10%

can be many uses for cost estimates, with each one needing a different answer. For example, if a consulting company is bidding on a one-time-only project (no follow-on business planned), it might want to build in sufficient contingency amounts, depending on the amount of risk, and bid accordingly. Or if the project is the first of many potential projects for the same organization, it might want to price the first project very aggressively to ensure that it wins the contract. Regardless of the end use of each estimate, they all require the same thing: the creation of an accurate cost estimate.

PROVEN STRATEGIES AND HINTS TO SUCCESS

Mary Brandel, in "Budgetary Black Holes," conducted interviews with many professional project managers and other experts to find where the major problems exist with project budgets. What she found is listed below:

- A detailed list of tasks and milestones
- Scope creep; keep to core functionality by defining requirements as must haves, should haves, and nice to haves.
- Building a too-sophisticated GUI too early in the project, keep it simple
- Lack of negotiation skills on the part of project managers
- Not understanding project finance, which is different from project accounting
- Implementing large, big-bang projects, reduce each large project into many smaller projects
- Overtesting of software
- Duplicate or overlapping tasks
- Poor estimating
- Lack of cost-to-date and estimate-to-complete data
- Many projects should never have been authorized to start; poor project selection practices

Determine Budget

The budget determination process presents to the stakeholders and project team the entire picture of costs for the project, taking into account all the following cost categories: direct and indirect, recurring and nonrecurring, fixed and variable, and all life cycle costs. The results are shared using a baseline table similar to the one presented in Figure 6-14. A table such as this should be maintained and updated throughout the project. At a minimum, it should be accurate and communicated at the end of each phase of the project to aid stakeholders in their decision about whether the project should proceed to the next phase or be cancelled. This becomes the project cost baseline against which to measure.

THE TIME AND COST MANAGEMENT PLANNING PROCESS

The following is the process for project time and cost planning:

Step 1. Define project activities to the correct level of detail in the WBS (decomposition) so that they are assignable, assessable, and controllable.

Sample Project Budget			
	One Time	**Recurring**	**Description**
Human Resources			
Internal Costs	$20,000.00	$10,000.00	Includes all dollars allocated for internal resources
Consultants	$15,000.00		Dollars for SAP consultants
Temporary Services	$2,000.00		Temporary workers needed during implementation
Hardware			
Servers	$16,000.00		2 servers plus network storage device
Network Equipment	$4,000.00		Routers and switches for internal LAN
Workstations	$20,000.00		10 new workstations mainly needed in Accounting
Maintenance		$2,000.00	Yearly maintenance contracts all hardware
Software			
OS Server	$2,000.00		Windows Server
OS Workstations	$3,000.00		Windows Vista Enterprise
SAP Financials	$20,000.00		SAP Business One (Financials)
Microsoft SQL Server	$5,000.00		Database Used for SAP Implementation
Maintenance		$5,000.00	Covers all Software Maintenance Agreements
Project Management			
10% of Budget	$13,000.00		Calculated as percent of total budget
Training			
IT Resources	$5,000.00		Cost of classes, travel, housing, etc.
Accounting Resources	$12,000.00		Cost of classes, travel, housing, etc.
Overhead			
Based on Internal Resources	$3,000.00	$1,000.00	12% of internal costs
Based on Material Needs	$2,000.00	$1,000.00	10% on material needs
Misc.			
Travel	$1,000.00		Not covered in training
Project Buffer	$28,600.00		Critical Chain Project Buffer
Totals	$171,600.00	$19,000.00	

FIGURE 6-14 **Project Budget Baseline Example**

Step 2. Define the sequence of activities and also the type of dependencies (mandatory, discretionary, external) between all tasks on the WBS.

Step 3. Assign the right resources to work on each activity, based on the skills needed to perform the work, resource availability, and budget restrictions.

Step 4. Create time estimates for each activity; the accuracy of these estimates depends on need and the capabilities of the estimator.

Step 5. Build the project schedule and understand and identify the critical path, critical chain, and available slack for each activity.

Step 6. Perform resource leveling to ensure a workable schedule and maximize worker productivity.

Step 7. Assign costs for all resources throughout the project schedule.

Step 8. Build and finalize the initial project budget (including all elements of the budget) to establish your project baseline.

Step 9. Obtain sponsor approval to proceed.

HOW TO CONDUCT THE TIME AND COST PLANNING PROCESSES

This last part of the chapter provides examples of deliverables for the time planning process and the cost planning process. Before proceeding, take time to reread and review the R & S Amusements Services case study. In Event 6 at the beginning of this chapter, Jeff and Kevin are meeting with Reid Lewis and the other members of the project team. The team has recently completed the initial scope statement and WBS for each of the three projects: asset management, collection management, and customer management. The next step in the project, as explained by Jeff and Kevin, is to conduct time and cost planning. The results of these two processes are described next for the asset management software project.

Step 1: Perform Activity Decomposition

Figure 6-15 shows the next level of detail for the asset management software project WBS. The entire WBS has not been included due to space limitations, but notice that the team has begun to decompose each of the activities into smaller, more manageable tasks. For example, the system context diagram has been broken down into three subtasks: conduct user interviews, construct context model, and obtain user agreement.

Step 2: Identify Activity Dependencies

When the list of activities has been created, the next step is to build a list of activity dependencies. Jeff and Kevin wanted to make sure the project team understood the ramifications of how the task dependencies were established. Figure 6-16 is a partial list of the WBS, with associated dependencies. In Microsoft Project, you set up dependencies by establishing a task predecessor that ties one task to another within the software. A "—" means that the task has no predecessor activity, or none has been assigned. Generally, predecessors are not assigned to summary tasks, such as high-level use case narratives. The project software will allow it to be done, but it is better to let the subtasks within each summary task control the flow of events. Because no actual work is being done at the summary task levels, don't assign dependencies to them.

Step 3: Perform Resource Assignments

The entire project team was involved in assigning resources to tasks. The individuals assigned to each task had to agree to perform the activity. As a best practice, it is a good idea to get teams to buy in to the activities they will perform on the project. Figure 6-17 shows a partial list of the resource assignments made by the team.

Step 4: Generate Time Estimates

The entire project team was involved in establishing time estimates. Jeff Dunbar and Kevin Pullen conducted training sessions on doing accurate time estimating. Recall from

```
1.0      Project initiation
1.1          Develop project charter
1.2          Review charter and obtain sponsor signoff
1.3          System context diagram
1.3.1            Conduct user interviews
1.3.2            Construct context model
1.3.3            Obtain user agreement
1.4          High-level use case model diagram
1.5          High-level use case narratives
1.5.1            Inventory updates manual/bar code
1.5.2            Field agents inventory tracking
1.5.3            Purchase requisitions
1.5.4            Track contract information
1.5.5            Pricing schemes
1.5.6            Reporting
1.6          Adopt change management process
1.6.1            Find suitable previously used process and adapt
1.6.2            Obtain user agreement
1.6.3            Training on change control
1.7          Preliminary scope statement
2.0      Project plan
2.1          Requirements definition
2.1.1            Refined use case diagram
2.1.2            Requirement level use case narrative
2.1.3            Scope statement
2.1.4            Work breakdown structure
2.1.5            Roles and responsibilities matrix
2.2          Build project schedule
2.2.1            Define task dependencies
2.2.2            Identify critical activities
2.3          Build cost estimates
2.3.1            Define time estimates
2.3.2            Assign cost rates
2.3.3            Define preliminary budget
2.4          Quality management plan
2.5          Communications plan
2.6          Risk management
2.7          Procurement plan
3.0      System procurement process
3.1          Make vs. buy decision
3.2          RFP process
3.3          Gap analysis
4.0      System architecture model
5.0      Acquire project team
6.0      Iteration 1
6.1          Analysis model
6.2          Design model
6.3          Construction
6.4          Deployment
6.5          Project status reporting
6.6          Quality assurance
6.7          Closeout
6.7.1            Lessons learned
6.7.2            Corrective actions needed
6.7.3            Resource performance reviews
7.0      Iteration 2
```

FIGURE 6-15   Asset Management Software Project WBS

		Predecessor	Type
1.0	Project initiation		
1.1	Develop project charter	—	
1.2	Review charter and obtain sponsor signoff	1.1	Mandatory
1.3	System context diagram	—	
1.3.1	Conduct user interviews	1.2	Discretionary
1.3.2	Construct context model	1.3.1	Mandatory
1.3.3	Obtain user agreement	1.3.2	Mandatory
1.4	High-level use case model diagram	1.3	Discretionary
1.5	High-level use case narratives	—	
1.5.1	Inventory updates manual/bar code	1.3	Mandatory
1.5.2	Field agents inventory tracking	1.3	Mandatory
1.5.3	Purchase requisitions	1.3	Mandatory
1.5.4	Track contract information	1.3	Mandatory
1.5.5	Pricing schemes	1.3	Mandatory
1.5.6	Reporting	1.3	Mandatory
1.6	Adopt change management process	—	
1.6.1	Find suitable previously used process and adapt	1.5	Discretionary
1.6.2	Obtain user agreement	1.6.1	Mandatory
1.6.3	Training on change control	1.6.2	Mandatory
1.7	Preliminary scope statement	1.5	Discretionary

FIGURE 6-16   WBS with Dependencies

		Resources
1.0	Project initiation	
1.1	Develop project charter	Reid Lewis
1.2	Review charter and obtain sponsor signoff	Reid Lewis
1.3	System context diagram	
1.3.1	Conduct user interviews	Jeff Dunbar
1.3.2	Construct context model	Jeff Dunbar
1.3.3	Obtain user agreement	Reid Lewis
1.4	High-level use case model diagram	Kevin Pullen
1.5	High-level use case narratives	
1.5.1	Inventory updates manual/bar code	Elaine Henry
1.5.2	Field agents inventory tracking	Kenny Jones
1.5.3	Purchase requisitions	Ashley Brooks
1.5.4	Track contract information	Ashley Brooks
1.5.5	Pricing schemes	Heidi Cosgray
1.5.6	Reporting	Diana Brooks
1.6	Adopt change management process	
1.6.1	Find suitable previously used process and adapt	Jeff Dunbar
1.6.2	Obtain user agreement	Reid Lewis
1.6.3	Training on change control	Jeff Dunbar
1.7	Preliminary scope statement	

FIGURE 6-17   WBS with Assigned Resources

Chapter 5 that the initial WBS was done using the analogous approach. Jeff and Kevin used a WBS from a previous similar project. That WBS also contained time estimates for activities. These time estimates will be the starting point for R & S Amusements Services. Adjustments to these time estimates were made for this project based on current rates for Jeff and Kevin's services, plus other contractors, as needed. They have also been updated for current salary rates for R & S. Other adjustments made were due to the size and complexity of the current project. Figure 6-18 shows a partial list of the assigned time estimates for each task. The time estimates are effort numbers, not total duration. Duration is determined in the next step, when the schedule is developed.

Step 5: Create Project Schedule

Jeff Dunbar was responsible for using all the elements created so far to build the schedule in Microsoft Project. Jeff used the time estimates and resource availabilities to generate the schedule represented in Figure 6-19 as a Gantt chart. Figure 6-19 is just a partial listing, and the entire project is estimated to take 22 months, which is slightly longer than the original estimate presented in the project charter. The team now has more accurate information about what will be involved in the project and has adjusted the schedule. The project charter should be updated to reflect the changes and approved by the original stakeholders who signed it in the first place: Mark Lewis, Reid Lewis, Kenny Jones, Elaine Henry, Jeff Dunbar, and Kevin Pullen. Included in the 22-month estimate is 2 months of project buffer time.

Step 6: Perform Resource Leveling

The project schedule created in step 5 must next be evaluated to make sure that human resources are being used effectively and not overused. A resource is overused (overloaded) when it has been scheduled for more work in a given time period than it has available. For example, the project charter task was assigned to Reid Lewis. The time estimate to complete the work was 10 days, but notice on the Gantt chart that it will take 20 days to complete because Reid can work on the project only half time. He must continue to manage the company and other matters, so it will take 20 days to get 10 days worth of work accomplished. The

		Time Estimate (Days)
1.0	Project initiation	
1.1	Develop project charter	10
1.2	Review charter and obtain sponsor signoff	2
1.3	System context diagram	
1.3.1	Conduct user interviews	10
1.3.2	Construct context model	1
1.3.3	Obtain user agreement	1
1.4	High-level use case model diagram	1
1.5	High-level use case narratives	
1.5.1	Inventory updates manual/bar code	1
1.5.2	Field agents inventory tracking	1
1.5.3	Purchase requisitions	1
1.5.4	Track contract information	1
1.5.5	Pricing schemes	1
1.5.6	Reporting	3
1.6	Adopt change management process	
1.6.1	Find suitable previously used process and adapt	1
1.6.2	Obtain user agreement	1
1.6.3	Training on change control	3
1.7	Preliminary scope statement	

FIGURE 6-18 WBS with Time Estimates

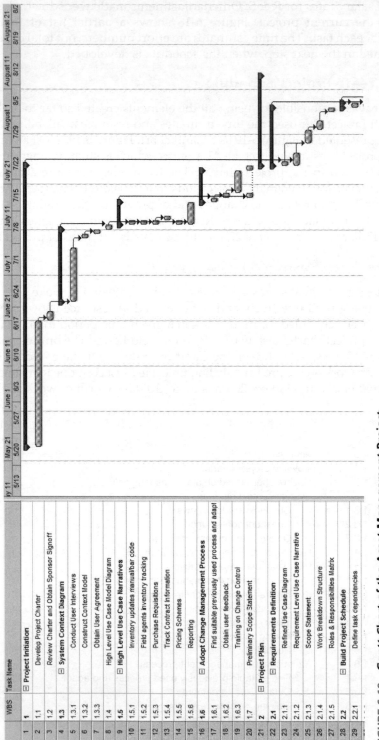

	WBS	Task Name
1	1	⊟ Project Initiation
2	1.1	Develop Project Charter
3	1.2	Review Charter and Obtain Sponsor Signoff
4	**1.3**	⊟ **System Context Diagram**
5	1.3.1	Conduct User Interviews
6	1.3.2	Construct Context Model
7	1.3.3	Obtain User Agreement
8	1.4	High Level Use Case Model Diagram
9	**1.5**	⊟ **High Level Use Case Narratives**
10	1.5.1	Inventory updates manual/bar code
11	1.5.2	Field agents inventory tracking
12	1.5.3	Purchase Requisitions
13	1.5.4	Track Contract Information
14	1.5.5	Pricing Schemes
15	1.5.6	Reporting
16	**1.6**	⊟ **Adopt Change Management Process**
17	1.6.1	Find suitable previously used process and adapt
18	1.6.2	Obtain user feedback
19	1.6.3	Training on Change Control
20	1.7	Preliminary Scope Statement
21	**2**	⊟ **Project Plan**
22	**2.1**	⊟ **Requirements Definition**
23	2.1.1	Refined Use Case Diagram
24	2.1.2	Requirement Level Use Case Narrative
25	2.1.3	Scope Statement
26	2.1.4	Work Breakdown Structure
27	2.1.5	Roles & Responsibilities Matrix
28	**2.2**	⊟ **Build Project Schedule**
29	2.2.1	Define task dependencies

FIGURE 6-19   Gantt Chart of the Asset Management Project

second objective of this step in the process is to ensure that resource productivity is as high as possible. After reviewing the schedule, the project manager discovers that if they move a couple of tasks around, the team can make better use of a single resource's time by having the tasks done back-to-back instead of having a gap of several days. Knowing the slack of each task and the task dependency types allows for better loading and leveling of resources.

Step 7: Generate Cost Estimates

Ashley Brooks, finance administrator for R & S Amusements Services, was given the task of assigning the resource-burdened labor rate for each member of the project team. These rates were entered into the project management software, which multiplies the rate against the estimated time to complete each task. The numbers are then entered into the project budget under the Human Resources Internal Cost line item. A contract for the cost of services from Jeff Dunbar and Kevin Pullen is also added to the project budget as Human Resources—Consultants.

Sample Project Budget			
	One Time	Recurring	Description
Human Resources			
Internal Costs	$25,000.00	$10,000.00	Includes all dollars allocated for internal resources
PM Consultants	$20,000.00		Dollars for SAP consultants
Custom Code	$20,000.00		Estimate for custom code identifed from gap analysis
Hardware			
Servers	$8,000.00		2 servers plus network storage device
Network Equipment	$1,500.00		Routers and switches for internal LAN
Workstations	$4,000.00		10 new workstations mainly needed in Accounting
Maintenance		$1,000.00	Yearly maintenance contracts all hardware
Software			
OS Server	$2,000.00		Windows Server
OS Workstations	$1,500.00		Windows Vista Enterprise
Package	$15,000.00		Asset Management Software Package
Database	$5,000.00		Database Used for SAP Implementation
Maintenance		$2,000.00	Covers all Software Maintenance Agreements
Training			
IT Resources	$5,000.00		Cost of classes, travel, housing, etc.
Accounting Resources	$12,000.00		Cost of classes, travel, housing, etc.
Overhead			
Based on Internal Resources	$3,000.00	$1,000.00	
Based on Material Needs	$2,000.00	$1,000.00	
Misc.			
Travel	$1,000.00		Not covered in training
Project Buffer	$28,600.00		Critical Chain Project Buffer
Totals	$153,600.00	$15,000.00	

FIGURE 6-20   Asset Management Software Project Budget

Step 8: Prepare Project Budget

A portion of the rough order of magnitude budget for the asset management software project is listed in Figure 6-20. Jeff and Kevin have spent many hours with the team, helping them understand the difference between a rough order of magnitude budget and a definitive budget to be sure to manage expectations. Dollar values are separated into one-time costs and recurring costs. At this point in the project, the budget is as accurate as it can be, but it could still be as much as -25 percent to +75 percent off.

Step 9: Obtain Sponsor Approval to Continue

The final step is to assemble all project artifacts created during the time and cost planning processes and present the findings to the sponsors of the project. A simple one-page memo should be drafted that highlights each artifact. Each artifact then requires a sponsor signature to authorize the project to continue. The project was initially selected based on certain criteria, such as net present value and return on investment. Before the project proceeds, the team should reevaluate the selection criteria to make sure it still makes sense to continue with the project before more time and money is expended.

If the sponsors sign the project continuation document, the next steps are to build the quality management plan and the communication management plan, as discussed in Chapter 7.

Chapter Review

1. The day-to-day job of a project manager is plagued with time robbers that must be kept to a minimum. Time robbers, activities that steal precious time away from value-added activities, include personnel conflict issues, impromptu meetings with customers, and long, recurring conversations with vendors.

2. The activity definition process is used to decompose the initial WBS into assignable units of work that can be estimated and monitored.

3. The 100 percent rule for activities within a WBS states that the total of activities must define 100 percent of the work needed to complete the product of the project.

4. The next step in the completion of the WBS is to sequence the activities documenting into logical and sometimes physical (mandatory) relationships among all the activities.

5. An activity dependency can be classified as mandatory, discretionary, or external.

6. Two techniques that can help project managers with sequencing activities are the precedence diagram method and the activity on arrow diagramming method.

7. The precedence diagram method permits four types of dependencies: finish-to-start, finish-to-finish, start-to-start, and start-to-finish.

8. After the WBS is decomposed to its lowest necessary levels, resource needs must be determined, found, and then assigned responsibility for the completion of tasks. Finally, a resource's availability must be assessed and tracked.

9. Based on the proficiency level of a resource, a time estimate for each activity is created, and its associated cost is estimated. Many techniques can be used in estimating,

including the lines of code, function points, analogous, simulation, and CO-COMO methods.

10. PERT (Program Evaluation and Review Technique) uses a weighted-average approach with three time estimates for each activity or group of activities. The three estimates that subject matter experts make are: most optimistic time to complete, most pessimistic time to complete, and the normal time to complete the activity.

11. The critical path method (CPM) uses the sequence and duration of activities to determine the total project duration. CPM is the shortest time in which a project can be completed. Each activity on the critical path, by definition, has zero slack.

12. The critical chain method gives project managers a process that tracks critical activities and scarce resources. Based on the theory of constraints, it identifies and tracks the activities that may be in greatest jeopardy of missing their time/cost estimates or are critical to the success of the project.

13. The cost estimating process is used to develop accurate cost estimates for each activity. An estimate becomes more accurate as the project executes and approaches completion.

14. Cost budgeting attempts to build a complete picture of all costs associated with executing a project.

Glossary

activity definition   The process of identifying and documenting the work that needs to be performed to deliver a product.

crashing   A schedule compression technique in which cost and schedule trade-offs are analyzed to determine how to obtain the greatest amount of compression for the least incremental cost.

critical chain method   A network schedule analysis technique that examines the changes to the schedule that are needed based on limited resources.

critical path   The list of activities that, if delayed, will delay the completion date of the project. By definition, these activities have zero slack.

free slack   The difference between the earliest time an activity can begin and the latest time an activity can begin without changing the completion date of any successor task.

Monte Carlo simulation   A technique that randomly generates specific end values for a variable with a specific probability distribution.

slack   The difference between the earliest time an activity can begin and the latest time an activity can begin without changing the completion date of the project.

work package   An artifact that describes the work needed to produce a deliverable at the lowest level of the WBS.

Review Questions

1. Explain the concept of time robbers and list some that you experience on a daily basis as you try to complete homework and study for exams.
2. Explain the rationale and process for decomposing tasks into smaller and smaller units of work.
3. How do you know when to stop decomposing a task?
4. Explain the difference between logical and physical task relationships.
5. List and explain the four types of dependencies possible between tasks on a precedence diagram.
6. Explain the activities that occur during the activity resource estimating process.

7. Explain the analogous approach to assigning resources to a WBS. List its advantages and disadvantages.
8. Explain why it is important to define time estimates in two dimensions: effort and duration.
9. What does it mean and why is it important to follow a progressive elaboration process when creating time and cost estimates?
10. Why is it important at the beginning of project planning to build resource estimates, assuming that resources will not be required to work overtime to complete their assignments?
11. Briefly describe the task sizing methods lines of code and function points.
12. Explain what is meant by this statement: "The function point analysis is only as accurate as the system requirements document."
13. Compare and contrast the estimating techniques presented in the chapter, being sure to review advantages and disadvantages of each. You might want to create a table listing each technique and associated advantages and disadvantages.
14. Define and explain each of the three project types described within COCOMO.
15. Compare and contrast COCOMO and COCOMO II.
16. Describe the benefits associated with doing good project scheduling development.
17. Explain the process followed when using the PERT approach to scheduling.
18. Explain the CPM process for schedule development.
19. Explain the difference between slack and free slack.
20. Can a project have multiple critical paths? Explain.
21. Define and compare the schedule compression techniques crashing and fast tracking.
22. Describe the critical chain method and compare it to CPM.
23. Briefly describe and compare resource loading and resource leveling.
24. Explain timing and accuracy of the three levels of cost estimates: rough order of magnitude, budget, and definitive estimates.
25. Briefly describe the contents of the schedule management plan.

Problems and Exercises

1. Explain the potential impact to project costs and schedules when assigning the following task relationships (mandatory, discretionary, and external).
2. Describe the advantages and disadvantages of the precedence diagram method and activity on arrow techniques for modeling task dependencies.
3. Create an activity on arrow diagram based on the following information:

   Task A, duration 6, dependent on none
   Task B, duration 5, dependent on none
   Task C, duration 3, dependent on none
   Task D, duration 12, dependent on Task B and Task C
   Task E, duration 2, dependent on Task A
   Task F, duration 5, dependent on Task B
   Task G, duration 1, dependent on Task B
   Task H, duration 9, dependent on Task E and Task F
   Task I, duration 7, dependent on Task G
   Task J, duration 7, dependent on Task H
   Task K, duration 3, dependent on Task I
   Task L, duration 5, dependent on Task D

4. Using the diagram you created in question 3, calculate ES, EF, LS, and LF for each task and the amount of slack. (Refer to Figure 6-8 for an example.) List the tasks that appear on the critical path.
5. Create an activity on arrow diagram based on the following information:

   Task A, duration 2, no dependency
   Task B, duration 4, no dependency
   Task C, duration 7, no dependency
   Task D, duration 5, depends on Task A
   Task E, duration 3, depends on Task B and Task C
   Task F, duration 8, depends on Task C
   Task G, duration 10, depends on Task D and Task E
   Task H, duration 4, depends on Task E
   Task I, duration 7, depends on Task F
   Task J, duration 12, depends on Task H and Task I

6. Using the diagram you created in question 5, calculate ES, EF, LS, and LF for each task and the amount of slack. (Refer to Figure 6-8 for an example.) List the tasks that appear on the critical path.

7. What happens to the critical path in the network schedule created in question 5 if the duration of Task E changes to 11 days?

8. Create a spreadsheet similar to Table 6-1 and find the number of function points for the following application description:

    User inputs = Low complexity = 25, Medium complexity = 5, High complexity = 2

    User outputs = Low complexity = 30, Medium complexity = 10, High complexity = 1

    Files/structures = Low complexity = 50, Medium complexity = 8, High complexity = 5

    User inquiries = Low complexity = 15, Medium complexity = 2, High complexity = 2

    External interfaces = Low complexity = 25, Medium complexity = 10, High complexity = 3

    Use a VAF of 42

9. Use the schedule created in question 5 but adjust the durations using PERT calculation from the three-point estimates below and recalculate slack.

    Task A, Optimistic = 1, Normal = 2, Pessimistic = 5
    Task B, Optimistic = 2, Normal = 4, Pessimistic = 8
    Tack C, Optimistic = 3, Normal = 7, Pessimistic = 12
    Task D, Optimistic = 3, Normal = 5, Pessimistic = 10
    Task E, Optimistic = 1, Normal = 3, Pessimistic = 6
    Task F, Optimistic = 3, Normal = 8, Pessimistic = 15
    Task G, Optimistic = 7, Normal = 10, Pessimistic = 22
    Task H, Optimistic = 3, Normal = 4, Pessimistic = 6
    Task I, Optimistic = 5, Normal = 7, Pessimistic = 12
    Task J, Optimistic = 10, Normal = 12, Pessimistic = 15

10. Bob is a project manager for a small consulting company, Quickie Software Developers, Inc., and is preparing a bid for an outsourcing project for a large Fortune 200 company to develop a new web-based order entry software module. Quickie Software Developers is small and can't afford to lose money on this contract. What suggestions do you have for Bob, as he prepares his budget estimate for the contract? Which estimating techniques would you encourage Bob to use?

11. You have been tasked with selecting and deploying a new Enterprise Resource Planning (ERP) software application for your organization. Unfortunately, the project is already under way, and much of the initial planning has been completed. The initial WBS has been created in Excel because the original project manager didn't know how to use project management software. Management has asked you to step in and get the project moving quickly. They would like to know how quickly you can get the project completed. Use the following table to create an AOA diagram and then identify the critical path. The project is scheduled to be done in four iterations (60-day time box), with each iteration delivering a different module of the ERP package. The WBS has been defined down to the activities during the initial release, but Releases 2 through 4 have been left to later, when more is known about the activities that will occur during those iterations.

12. Using information from problem 11, management has gotten your assessment of when the project will be completed, assuming a linear path. Management is not happy with how long the project is going to take and wants suggestions on how to get it done sooner. What steps could you potentially take to shorten the schedule?

WBS Code	Task Description	Predecessors	Duration (days)
1.0	Project charter	—	5
2.0	Statement of work	—	
2.1	Context diagram	1.0	2
2.2	Use case model diagram	2.1	1
2.3	High-level use case narratives	2.1	10
3.0	Requirements definition		

(continued)

WBS Code	Task Description	Predecessors	Duration (days)
3.1	Refined use case diagram	2.2, 2.3	2
3.2	Requirement-level use case narratives	2.3	10
3.3	System sequence diagrams	3.2	5
4.0	Procurement process	—	
4.1	Create RFP	3.3	5
4.2	Create evaluation criteria	4.1	3
4.3	Conduct vendor search and mailing	4.1, 4.2	10
4.4	Evaluate responses	4.3	10
4.5	Negotiate contract and sign	4.4	5
5.0	Iteration 1		
5.1	Analysis phase and GAP analysis	4.5	8
5.2	Design phase	5.1	8
5.3	Installation	4.5	3
5.4	Construction	5.2, 5.3	20
5.5	Training	5.4	10
5.6	Validation	5.4	5
5.7	Deployment	5.6	4
5.8	Iteration closeout	5.7	2
6.0	Iteration 2	5.8	60
7.0	Iteration 3	6.0	60
8.0	Iteration 4	7.0	60
9.0	Proect closeout	9.0	3

Projects and Research

1. Research the techniques companies are using today for estimating time and cost in their projects.
2. Use the Internet to research the other two projects R & S is doing—customer relationship management and collections management—by looking at similar projects other companies have done. Build a high-level WBS and build a rough order of magnitude budget.
3. Research new developments and directions for the COCOMO II estimating technique.
4. Build a WBS and schedule for a spring break trip to Florida. Identify all dependencies as either mandatory, discretionary, or external.

5. Discuss a project you have worked on where cost was not an issue (unlimited budget) and time was the major factor. Was the project successful?
6. Build a complete budget and write a scope statement for a project that would outfit a university computer lab, complete with hardware, software, and network connectivity. The project will be completed over the course of one summer. Be sure to include one-time costs and recurring costs.

☑ MINICASE

1. *Background:* (Refer to the R & S Amusements Services case study at the beginning of the chapter.) Jeff Dunbar and Kevin Pullen of Premier Project Management Services (PPMS) plan to arrive early at R & S Amusements Services. Jeff wants to further define the project's WBS activities into work packages by analyzing the notes of the interviews with the stakeholders. His goal is to have most of this work complete by the time the rest of the team arrives for work. It is now 5:30 a.m. Jeff, with his usual extra-large coffee, is going through a stack of interview notes between bites of a donut. Kevin, a coffee addict also, is refilling his cup from a thermos he brought from home while waiting for his laptop to boot up and start Microsoft Project. Kevin wants to update the project files with the activity estimates of effort and duration that they documented the previous day. It is his intent and Jeff's to show the updated WBS to the team during the team meeting at 8:30. Based on their time estimates, they will have 15 minutes to spare before the meeting began.

   Current Situation 1: Reid Lewis has decided to come to the office early. He was out of the office last week, attending the National Conference for Amusement Machine Distributors in Las Vegas. While at the conference, he saw demonstrations of software and hardware "guaranteed" to make his life easier and give his company a competitive edge to gain additional business and produce greater profits. The more Reid saw, the more excited he became. He can't wait to tell Jeff Dunbar and Kevin Pullen about his findings. He's sure they will be impressed. On the flight home, in preparation for the meeting, Reid used the time to study all the pamphlets and trade magazines he picked up. He read the testimonials from satisfied users and analyzed the product evaluations. He wrote notes to himself about what he was going to recommend to Jeff and Kevin. He has decided that this information is just too important to wait, and he has to meet with them first thing this morning. As he is pulling in the parking lot, he is elated that they have already arrived. He grabs his briefcase, rushes into the conference room where they are working, and says, "Jeff, Kevin, I'm so glad you're here! Follow me to my office because I want to show you what I learned at the conference. I guarantee it will be a significant boost to the project. It shouldn't take any longer than an hour and a half."

   Discussion: This is a classic case of a time robber. If you were Jeff and Kevin, how would you respond to Reid? Keep in mind that he is the president of the company and the one signing checks. What other policies or guidelines, if any, would you put in place concerning other time robbers, such as the following:

- Reading email
- Personal calls
- Bathroom breaks
- Smoking (which is not allowed in the building; individuals who smoke must do it outside)
- Lunch breaks
- Nonproductive meetings
- Personal time (to run errands, go to doctor appointments, pickup kids at school, and so on)

As you answer, keep in mind employee morale. You don't want disgruntled employees.

Current Situation 2: Reid is looking over Kevin's shoulder while Kevin is working with the project schedule. One of the milestones for selecting a software vendor is scheduled three weeks later than Reid has anticipated. Upon further analysis, Reid notices that the resource scheduled to do the product evaluation work (the key activity for the milestone) is allocated 100 percent to the task, but Kevin has only scheduled the person to work on the task 6 hours a day. This must be an error. Everybody puts in an honest 8-hour day at his company. In fact, at his company, everyone does what it takes to get the job done on time. If that means working 12-hour days, so be it. Reid brings this to Kevin's attention, saying the milestone will be three weeks earlier because overtime will be required!

Discussion: If you were Kevin, how would you respond to Reid? How would you explain the scheduling of 6-hour days even though employees are required to work an 8-hour day? If you were Kevin, how would you convince Reid that mandatory overtime is not always a good idea?

Current Situation 3: Together, Jeff and Kevin have convinced Reid that it's important to do proper scheduling. Reluctantly agreeing, but not satisfied, Reid returns to his office. Five minutes later, Reid rushes back and exclaims, "I know how we can bring the schedule in! I will bring in one more person to work on the product evaluation. If it was going to take one person six weeks to do it, two people should be able to do it in three!" Jeff and Kevin just look at each other and sigh.

Discussion: How should Jeff and Kevin respond to Reid? Can you explain to Reid that adding another person might cause the schedule to expand, not be reduced? Help Jeff and Kevin explain the "mythical man-month" to Reid.

Suggested Readings

Albrecht, A.J. (1979, October 14–17). *Measuring application development productivity*. Proceedings of Share/Guide IBM Applications Development Symposium. Monterey, CA.

Boehm, B.W. (1981). *Software engineering economics*. Englewood Cliffs, NJ: Prentice Hall.

Brandel, M. (2004, August 16). Budgetary black holes. *Computerworld*. Retrieved from www.computerworld.com/s/article/print/95196/Budgetary_black_Holes.

Brooks, F.P. (1975). *The mythical man-month*. Reading, MA: Addison-Wesley.

Corcoran, C.T. (1997, May 26). Cost–benefit analysis: IS managers need to put a price tag on productivity. *InfoWorld*, pp. 65–66.

De Marco, T. (1982). *Controlling software projects: Management, measurement and estimation*. New York: Yourdon Press.

Goldratt, E. (1997). *Critical chain*. Great Barrington, MA: North River Press.

Jones, T.C. (1998). *Estimating software costs*. New York: McGraw-Hill.

Kerzner, H. (2001). Project management: A systems approach to planning, scheduleing, and controlling. 7th edition. New York: John Wiley & Suns.

Lamoreaux, S. (2009). Project scheduling in large organizations: Shifting the culture. PMI Global Congress Proceedings, Orlando, FL.

McConnell, S. (1998). *Software project survival guide*. Redmond, WA: Microsoft Press.

Meredith, J., & Mantel, S. (2003). *Project management: A managerial approach*. New York: John Wiley & Sons.

Standish Group (1995). *CHAOS chronicles*. Retrieved from www.standishgroup.com.

Wysocki, R., & McGary, R. (2003). *Effective project management*. Indianapolis: Wiley Publishing, Inc.

Yourdon, E. (1997). *Death march: The complete software developer's guide to surviving "mission impossible" projects*. Upper Saddle River, NJ: Prentice Hall.

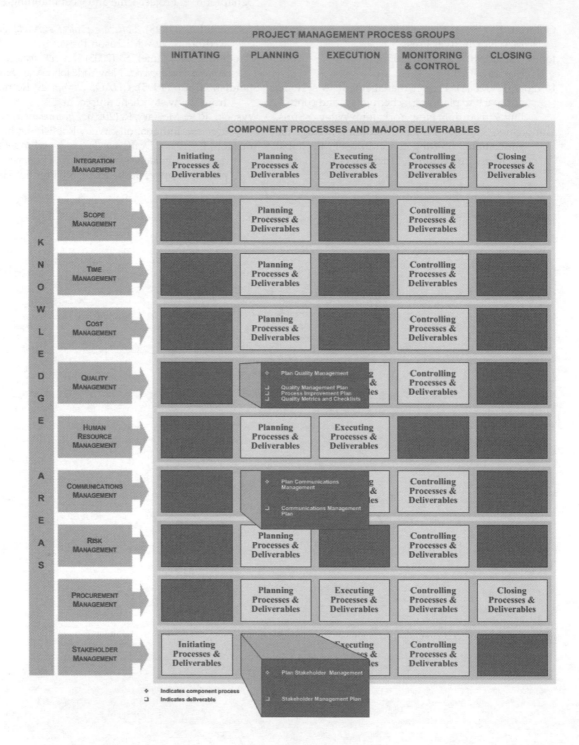

7

Project Quality, Communications, and Stakeholder Planning

R & S Amusements Services

Event 7

Setting   *It is now one week since the meeting described in Event 6, and the project leaders have convened in a small conference room located outside Reid Lewis's office at R & S Amusements Services. Those in attendance include Reid Lewis, Diana Brooks, and Mark Lewis from R & S and Jeff Dunbar and Kevin Pullen from Premier Project Management Services.*

JEFF   At last week's meeting, we finished up work on the WBS, made resource assignments, and finished the preliminary budget. We almost have the project plan completed. I know we have already started some parts of the project, such as looking for vendor products, but we still need to complete the rest of the plan.

REID   Well, Jeff and Kevin, let's discuss exactly what is left so we can get all the plans finalized and get the project moving.

KEVIN   Reid, we are just about done with all the planning. We have the quality management plan and communication management plan to finish, which is what we are hoping to get started on today and finish by next week's status meeting. Then we need to work on the risk management plan and the procurement management plan to finish it all up.

MARK   It sounds like we still have a lot to get done.

REID   I agree. Just how much more time is this going to take?

JEFF   Not as long as you might think. Kevin and I have been doing this for quite some time and have several versions of these plans already done. We will, as we did for the WBS, use a plan we have used on similar projects. We brought the quality and communication plan examples with us today to be used for discussion. We will need to make some changes to them, but starting with them will shorten our work considerably. Our quality management plan is based on Six Sigma.

MARK   Six what? What's a Sigma?

KEVIN   Six Sigma is a quality management process that helps in setting standards for quality and in monitoring the process. Sigma is a Greek letter used in statistics to mean standard deviation. But don't worry about this too much today. We will schedule Six Sigma training for everyone on the project team and then eventually for the whole company.

REID   Well, that does make me feel better about how much time this is going to take.

JEFF   Yes, we have found this to be a major time saver. Unfortunately, many organizations don't maintain a library of past project documents, and so they have to make up new ones each time they start a project.

MARK   Boy, that sounds like a major waste of time and effort!

KEVIN   You are so right. As organizations mature in their project management processes, one of the keys is learning from previous projects and reusing the best parts.

REID   I'm all for anything that speeds this up and gives us something of quality to start with.

JEFF   Okay, let's get started by reviewing the quality management plan that Kevin and I brought with us. We can then move on to the communications management plan.

(To be continued)

(This chapter provides instructions for building the quality management plan and the communications management plan, along with examples.)

CHAPTER PREVIEW AND OBJECTIVES

This chapter begins with a discussion about the quality movement that has taken place over the past several years for IT projects. To fully appreciate the current status of quality management today, the chapter includes a short history of the most noted work done by Deming, Juran, Crosby, Ishikawa, and others. Next, the chapter covers topics related to planning for project communications in all forms. This chapter describes the processes of quality management, communications management, and stakeholder management planning.

As you read this chapter, you will:

- Understand the work done by several noted quality experts and their impact on project management practices
- Understand the definition of *quality* and the different costs of quality
- Know how to build a quality management plan
- Understand the importance of possessing excellent communication skills
- Understand the communication process
- Know how to build a communication management plan
- Know how to build a stakeholder management plan

PROJECT MANAGEMENT CONCEPTS: QUALITY PLANNING

No other topic covered in this text approaches the Quality Management knowledge area for acronyms, buzzwords, and catchy phrases; Business Process Management (BPM),

Business Process Improvement (BPI), Continuous Process Improvement (CPI), Six Sigma, and Kaizen are just a few. Most authors start the discussion of quality by describing the quality movement. The quality story at Wal-Mart, the world's largest retailer, still reflects the founder's philosophy. Sam Walton wrote, "The secret of successful retailing is to give your customers what they want. And really, if you think about it from your point of view as a customer, you want everything: a wide assortment of good-quality merchandise; the lowest possible prices; guaranteed satisfaction with what you buy; friendly, knowledgeable service; convenient hours; free parking; a pleasant shopping experience" (www.walmart. com). At General Electric, a process called *Six Sigma* is used to achieve quality success: "Globalization and instant access to information, products and services continue to change the way our customers conduct business. Today's competitive environment leaves no room for error. We must delight our customers and relentlessly look for new ways to exceed their expectations. This is why Six Sigma Quality has become a part of our culture" (www.ge.com). Quality for every organization today must be of utmost importance and include a strong customer influence. Many examples of project failures can be attributed to poor quality:

- The Sustainable Computing Consortium, a collaboration of major corporate IT users, university researchers, and government agencies, estimated that flawed (or buggy) software cost organizations $175 billion worldwide in 2001.
- In the United States, software bugs cost organizations nearly $60 billion per year, according to the Commerce Department's National Institute of Standards and Technology (NIST). According to NIST, one-third of these costs could be eliminated with improved testing methods, especially early in the development cycle. (Newman, 2002)
- Faulty baggage-handling software at the then-new Denver International Airport delayed the opening of the airport from October 1993 until February 1995, at an estimated cost of $1 million a day. (Li, 1994)
- Therac-25 was a radiation therapy machine produced by Atomic Energy of Canada Limited and CGR MeV of France. It was involved with at least six known accidents between 1985 and 1987, in which patients were given massive overdoses of radiation because of a software bug. At least five patients died of the overdoses. (Gallagher)
- The Pentium FDIV bug was a bug in Intel's original Pentium floating-point unit. Certain floating-point division operations performed with these processors would produce incorrect results. Intel eventually had to recall all the initial chips and replace them. (Janeba, 1995)
- The 2003 blackout of the U.S. Northeast was a massive power outage that occurred throughout parts of the Northeastern and Midwestern United States and Ontario, Canada. It affected an estimated 10 million people in Canada and 40 million people in the United States. Outage-related financial losses were estimated at $6 billion. The initial cause of the outage was not a computer flaw, but if the software had been operating correctly, the outage would have been greatly reduced. (Poulsen, 2004)

As you can see, quality is extremely important to the success of all IT projects; it is so important that many authors add it to the triple constraint (refer to Chapter 1). Figure 7-1 is repeated here from Chapter 1 to demonstrate how quality plays a role in the triple constraint. In all projects, you have a choice about the amount of work that goes into producing a quality product (the amount of air used in the quality balloon). This chapter describes the cost associated with producing (or not producing) a quality product.

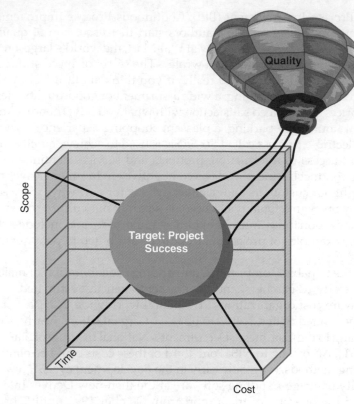

FIGURE 7-1   Triple Constraint, Including Quality

What does it mean to produce a quality product? The definition of **quality** varies, depending on many factors, such as who you are (stakeholder or software developer), type of project, industry, dependability, fitness for use, and safety. For example, a software developer may consider some work he's done to be of high quality because it passed all the quality assurance tests and met all of the defined functional requirements. But the key customer is not in complete agreement because the new system runs more slowly and requires more steps to complete the same process than the old system. The project management body of knowledge uses the American Society for Quality's definition for quality as: "the degree to which a set of inherent characteristics fulfill requirements" (PMI, p. 228). The International Organization for Standardization (ISO) defines *quality* as "the totality of features and characteristics of a product or service that bears on its ability to satisfy stated or implied needs." Notice two key points about these definitions: The product must satisfy the system requirements (stated needs), and it must satisfy the customer's (stakeholder's) implied needs. Project managers must make sure that both are met to ensure a successful project. Earlier in the text, the tools necessary to define the product's requirements were described, in the form of a scope statement and work breakdown structure (WBS). The implied needs are more difficult because many times they don't show up in any official documents. Soliciting the implied needs requires excellent interview techniques, which is an important topic later in this chapter.

The ISO created eight quality management principles that provide a framework for organizations to follow (www. iso. org):

1. *Keep a customer focus*—Because organizations rely on their customers, they must understand customer needs, they must meet customer requirements, and they must exceed customer expectations.
2. *Provide leadership*—Leaders must establish a unity of purpose and set the direction the organization should take by using a unified mission and vision. They must create an environment that encourages people to achieve the organization's objectives.
3. *Involve people*—The organization must involve people from all levels to promote ownership and support.
4. *Use a process approach*—Each activity within an organization must be managed as a process, leading to a more predictable outcome and lowering costs and cycle time.
5. *Take a systems approach*—An organization should approach each activity with knowledge of how each process affects and is affected by other processes in the organization.
6. *Encourage continual improvement*—An organization must create a permanent process that encourages continual improvement, not take a "one and done" approach.
7. *Take a factual approach to decision making*—Decision making should be based on actual, reliable, and current data.
8. *Cultivate mutually beneficial supplier relationships*—Organizations are dependent on their suppliers to be successful, so they should foster relationships built on trust and information sharing to create value for both parties.

Quality must be a continuous process from the beginning of the project until the end. All project management methodologies and product development methodologies stress the importance of quality throughout. In the creation of software products, multiple authors over the past 20 years have stressed the importance of finding errors early in the process, during requirements discovery. A cost and time disparity estimate exists that it's 50 to 200 times more expensive to find an error after the system is deployed than to find that error during requirements discovery. It has been estimated that between 50 to 80 percent of the time in a software development application project is spent in the maintenance phase and not during the initial release of the product. Creating a process that prevents errors from occurring versus the old process of finding them during or near the end of the project inspection step aids organizations in avoiding more costly mistakes. This approach of prevention and early discovery is especially important for organizations that are using an iterative/incremental development methodology because each successive iteration builds on the one before it. If an error goes undetected at the end of the first iteration, the cost increases exponentially the later it is found during subsequent iterations.

To achieve repeatable successes, IT projects must satisfy both the stated and implied needs of the product and stakeholder. Many IT projects, due to their uniqueness and other factors, are prone to missing many of the implied needs of the stakeholders or must carefully balance the costs of meeting stakeholder expectations. Either a systems analyst didn't ask the right questions, or a customer didn't supply the right or complete information. In the earlier example of the product that didn't meet the customer's expectations, the software developer either delivered a great product with zero bugs but it was not the correct solution or delivered the solution but the software was full of bugs. This part of the chapter is about aiding the project manager in creating a quality management plan that will balance the costs of building quality software.

Needed Definitions

The following are definitions of some key quality management concepts:

- *Cost of quality*—This cost is the total cost incurred by an organization to prevent a faulty product or development of a system that does not meet system requirements. Costs include costs related to assessment, rework, lost time, injury, and death, as well as the following:
  - *Prevention costs*—These are up-front costs associated with satisfying customer requirements (for example, costs for design reviews, all forms of system testing, training, surveys).
  - *Appraisal costs*—These are costs associated with ensuring that all requirements have been met (for example, costs for customer acceptance tests, demonstrations, lab tests).
- *Cost of nonconformance*—This is the total cost incurred by an organization because the product does not meet user requirements (for example, rework, poor user productivity).
- *Internal failure costs*—These are the costs associated with system defects before a system is fully deployed (for example, scrap, rework).
- *External failure costs*—These are the costs associated with system defects after the system is fully deployed (for example, scrap, rework, returns, market share, lawsuits).
- *Rework*—Poor quality sometimes requires the same task to be repeated to correct an identified error.
- *Fitness for use*—The product needs to be usable as it was originally intended.
- *Conformance to requirements/specifications*—A product must conform to the written specifications.
- *Reliability*—This is the probability of a product performing as specified without failure over a set period of time.
- *Maintainability*—This is the time and expense needed to restore the product to an acceptable level of performance after it has failed or begun a trend toward failure.

History of and Key Contributions to Quality

Over the past 100 years or so, organizations' view of quality has changed dramatically. There has been a movement away from inspection and toward prevention, the use of statistical process control measures, and a focus on the customer. These changes have been brought about thanks to the work of a number of quality pioneers, including Shewhart, Deming, Juran, Crosby, Ishikawa, Humphrey, and Taguchi.

WALTER A. SHEWHART   In 1918, Walter Shewhart joined Western Electric Company, a manufacturer of equipment for Bell Telephone. Bell Telephone's engineers had been working to improve the reliability of their transmission equipment due to the high cost of the equipment, especially the cost of repair after the equipment was buried. In 1924, Shewhart created the control chart (see Chapter 12) to better understand variation and to distinguish between assignable cause and chance cause. In order to aid a manager in making scientific, efficient, economical decisions, Shewhart developed statistical process control methods. He also believed that quality must be a continuous process and developed the PDSA cycle—Plan, Do, Study Act—which was later extended by W. Edwards Deming.

W. EDWARDS DEMING   During the 1920s, W. Edwards Deming worked at Western Electric in Chicago and developed his early thoughts on quality issues related to processes, not to the workers. He felt that managers spent more time worrying about the problems of the day and not enough on the future. Deming estimated that as much as 85 percent of all quality problems could be corrected by making changes in the process and only 15 percent could be controlled by the workers on the line. Deming met Shewhart while working at Bell Laboratories in the 1930s in New Jersey and became interested in his statistical process control work. Deming extended the PDSA cycle and applied it to all types of processes that exist in the organization. Much of Deming's work is summarized in his 14 points for quality (Deming, 1982):

1. Create constancy of purpose toward improvement of products and services, with aims to become competitive, to stay in business, and to provide jobs.
2. Adopt the new philosophy of cooperation (win–win) from management on down to all employees, customers, and suppliers.
3. Cease dependence on inspection to achieve quality. Reduce the need for inspection by building the product right the first time.
4. End the practice of awarding business on the basis of price alone. Instead, minimize total cost over the long run. Move toward a single supplier for any one item and a long-term relationship of loyalty and trust.
5. Improve constantly and forever every process for planning, production, and service. This will improve quality and productivity and, thus, continually reduce costs.
6. Institute training on the job.
7. Adopt and institute leadership for the management of people, recognizing their different abilities, capabilities, and aspirations.
8. Drive out fear and build trust so that everyone can work effectively.
9. Break down barriers between staff areas (departments). Abolish competition and build a win–win system of cooperation.
10. Eliminate slogans, exhortations, and targets for the workforce asking for zero defects or new levels of productivity. Such programs lead to adversarial relationships as the bulk of issues for improvement are found in the overall process and lie outside the scope of control for most workers.
11. Eliminate numeric quotas for the workforce and numeric goals for management and substitute leadership.
12. Remove barriers that rob people of workmanship. Eliminate the annual rating or merit system and create pride in the job being done.
13. Institute a vigorous program of education and self-improvement for everyone in the organization.
14. Put everybody in the company to work to accomplish the transformation.

JOSEPH JURAN   Dr. Juran started out as an engineer in the 1920s. He has often been credited with adding the human element to quality control, as well as statistical methods. In 1951 he published the *Quality Control Handbook*, which says that quality should be viewed more from the customer's "fitness for use" perspective than from the manufacturer's adherence to specifications. Dr. Juran has also been credited with the Pareto principle, or 80/20 rule. As a general rule, a small number of issues—about 20 percent—cause the most problems (80 percent) on a project. For example, 80 percent of the rework time spent on a product may be caused by 20 percent of the requirements. (Chapter 12 explores this principle in more detail.)

In 1986, Dr. Juran published the Juran Trilogy, which focused on the three areas of quality: planning, quality improvement, and quality control. The three areas coincide with Juran's 10 steps to quality improvement (Juran, 1998):

1. Build awareness of the need and opportunity for improvement.
2. Set goals for improvement.
3. Organize to reach the goals (establish a quality council, identify problems, select projects, appoint teams, and designate facilitators).
4. Provide training.
5. Carry out projects to solve problems.
6. Report progress.
7. Give recognition.
8. Communicate results.
9. Keep score.
10. Maintain momentum by making annual improvement part of the regular systems and processes of the company.

PHILIP CROSBY   Crosby is probably best known for the phrases "zero defects" and "doing it right the first time." He wrote many books, the most famous of which is *Quality Is Free*, published in 1979. Crosby spent most of his career educating managers about the fact that preventing defects is cheaper than fixing them later. Crosby believed in a top-down approach to quality management, in which management must set a good example for the rest to follow. He believed that quality is free because the cost of conformance should be counted as the normal cost of doing business and that the cost for nonconformance is the only cost of quality. Crosby relied less on statistical methods than Deming and Juran and more on motivation and management influence. Crosby developed four absolutes of quality:

1. Quality is conformance to requirements.
2. Quality is prevention over inspection and rework.
3. The standard should be "zero defects."
4. Quality is measured by the cost of nonconformance.

Crosby also developed the following 14 steps to quality improvement: (Crosby, 1979)

1. Make it clear that management is committed to quality.
2. Form quality improvement teams with representatives from each department.
3. Determine where current and potential quality problems lie.
4. Evaluate the cost of quality and explain its use as a management tool.
5. Raise the quality awareness and personal concern of all employees.
6. Take actions to correct problems identified through previous steps.
7. Establish a committee for the zero-defects program.
8. Train supervisors to actively carry out their part of the quality improvement program.
9. Hold a "zero-defects day" to let all employees realize that there has been a change.
10. Encourage individuals to establish improvement goals for themselves and their groups.

11. Encourage employee communication with management about obstacles to quality.
12. Recognize participants' efforts.
13. Establish quality councils to communicate on a regular basis.
14. Do it all over again to emphasize that the quality improvement program never ends.

KAORU ISHIKAWA Ishikawa studied under Deming and likewise believed in a continuous approach to quality improvement, involving all workers from top management down to the lowest-level employee. He is best known for his work *Guide to Quality Control*, published in 1972. In this work, he created quality circles and developed the Ishikawa diagram, commonly referred to as a fishbone diagram because of its resemblance to the skeleton of a fish (see Figure 7-2). The fishbone diagram is a cause-and-effect tool that helps workers discover the true root cause of quality issues. (Chapter 12 describes Ishikawa's fishbone diagram in more detail.) Quality circles are led by non-managers within a single department or as a step in the overall process of producing a product. The team is made up of frontline workers who attempt to improve the effectiveness of their own processes. Ishikawa supported the idea that quality could always go one step further in a continuous approach to affect not only the product but suppliers, customers, and all workers.

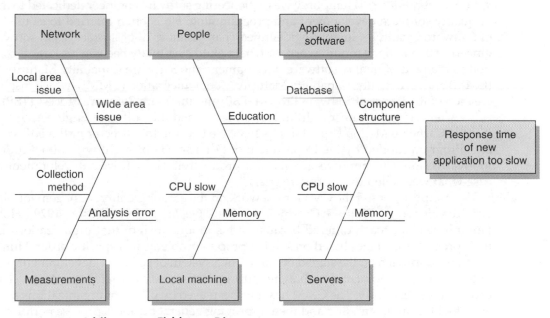

FIGURE 7-2 Ishikawa, or Fishbone, Diagram

GENICHI TAGUCHI Taguchi, as the director of the Electrical Communication Laboratories (ECL) in Japan (the Japanese equivalent to the U.S.-based Bell Labs research organization), developed what are referred to as the Taguchi methods. These methods attempt to optimize the process of engineering experimentation to improve product quality. Taguchi, like Deming, believed that 85 percent of poor quality is attributable to the process and only 15 percent to the individual workers. Many practitioners and academics have had some issues with Taguchi's mathematical approach to his design of experiments, but few argue against the accompanying philosophy based on the following concepts:

- Quality should be designed into the product and not inspected into it.
- Quality is best achieved by minimizing the deviation from a defined target, reducing the effect of uncontrollable environmental factors.
- The cost of quality should be measured as a function of deviation from the standard and collected systemwide (for example, scrap, rework, inspection, returns, warranty service calls, product replacement).

Robust design methods, the modern name given to the Taguchi methods, continually stress the importance of monitoring manufacturing "noise factors"—environmental variation during the product's usage (machine wear), manufacturing variation, and component deterioration. Also, monitoring the total cost of failure during the entire process helps ensure customer satisfaction. The timing of methods work is one of the major drawbacks to the Taguchi methods. They are effective only when applied early in the design of a product.

WATTS S. HUMPHREY   Humphrey was a pioneering software engineer dedicated to the field of quality software development and programming. He is often referred to as the "Father of Software Quality." Humphrey identified characteristics of best practices in software engineering that laid the groundwork for what would eventually become his largest contribution to the field of quality software development: the Software Capability Maturity Model (CMM) and, eventually, Capability Maturity Model Integration (CMMI), which inspired the creation of the Personal Software Process (PSP) and the Team Software Process (TSP).

After a lengthy career at IBM, Humphrey joined the Software Engineering Institute (SEI) at Carnegie Mellon University in 1986. He became the director of the Software Process Program funded by the Department of Defense. He brought with him a number of innovative ideas to improve quality and productivity in software development and to ease what was called the "software crisis."

Humphrey based the CMM framework on the earlier Quality Management Maturity Grid developed by Philip B. Crosby in his book *Quality is Free* (Crosby, 1979). However, Humphrey's approach differed because of his unique insight that organizations mature their processes in stages based on solving process problems in a specific order. Humphrey based his approach on the staged evolution of a system of software development practices within an organization, rather than measuring the maturity of each separate development process independently. The CMM has thus been used by different organizations as a powerful tool for understanding and then improving general business process performance.

Current Quality Initiatives and Standards

Organizations today have discovered that obtaining quality in their IT projects doesn't happen on its own but requires a concerted effort by all project participants, from top management down to the lowest-level employee. Several standards or approaches to achieving quality exist today to aid organizations in improving their product quality and can serve to differentiate one company's product from another. In the world of outsourcing, achieving a high level of certification can give an organization a decisive advantage in winning contract awards. The remainder of this section highlights some of the most prominent standards and initiatives. This overview is not intended to be all inclusive but to give an introduction to some of the most prominent topics.

ISO 9000 In 1987, the ISO instituted the ISO 9000 standard. The ISO, based in Geneva, Switzerland, is a consortium of more than 100 of the world's industrial nations. The American National Standards Institute (ANSI) is the U.S. representative. ISO 9000 is a generic management systems process standard that is applicable to any product, service, or process anywhere in the world. One of the most widely used standards in the world, it consists of the following categories:

- *ISO 9000*—This category defines the key terms and acts as a roadmap for the other standards.
- *ISO 9001*—This category defines the model for a quality system when a contractor demonstrates the capability to design, produce, and install products or services.
- *ISO 9002*—This category is the quality system model for quality assurance in production and installation.
- *ISO 9003*—This category is the quality system model for quality assurance in final inspection and testing.
- *ISO 9004*—This category is the quality management guidelines.

One of the major misconceptions surrounding the ISO 9000 standard is that it ensures that an organization creates a product or service of high quality. In reality, it only confirms that the appropriate systems or process is in place. A company could produce a parachute out of lead and still be ISO certified, for example. To obtain the certification, an organization must develop and adopt a quality management system. Generally, an organization of any size will not try to get the entire organization certified all at once; it will be broken down into departments, stages of development or manufacturing, and so on. When the new quality management system is in place and working, the organization should carry out an internal audit to make sure it is in compliance with relevant standards. When ready, the organization then contacts a registrar (someone certified to do audits) to come and conduct an external audit. If all goes well, the registrar will certify that the organization has met the relevant ISO standards and will register the company. The organization can then tell the world that it is ISO certified.

TOTAL QUALITY MANAGEMENT (TQM) There is no one definition for TQM. This section describes some of the key concepts that most authors agree are a part of it. TQM is a management approach that originated in Japan during the 1950s and has become steadily more popular in the West since the early 1980s. *Total quality* describes the culture, attitude, and organization of a company that strives to provide customers (internal and external) with products and services that satisfy their needs. The culture of the organization requires a focus on quality for all operations, with an emphasis on doing each process right the first time, eliminating defects and waste. TQM requires management and all levels of employees to become involved in continuous improvement in the production of goods and services. It is a combination of quality tools and management-specific tools for achieving increased business while reducing costs and waste. Key principles of TQM include:

- *Employee empowerment*—This involves training, commitment, and full participation with reward and recognition programs tied to quality performance.
- *Management involvement*—This involves leadership commitment, involvement, leading by example, and support for workers.
- *Decisions based on facts*—Statistical process control, rational versus emotional decision making, and accurate and timely data collection are examples of such decisions.
- *Continuous improvement*—This involves eliminating waste and non-value-added activities, recognizing that quality improvement is never complete, continuously collecting data, and continually refining standards.
- *Customer-driven*—An organization should ensure that the customer comes first, continuously assess satisfaction and needs, and strive to meet and exceed customer requirements.
- *Culture*—Establish an open, cooperative, trusting, communicative environment where information can be easily shared up and down the management chain.

BALANCED SCORECARD   The balanced scorecard, developed by Robert Kaplan and David Norton, is an approach for managing and measuring business performance that takes into consideration factors beyond typical financial metrics. This approach has been called a management system in addition to a measurement system that enables organizations to clarify their vision and strategy and translate them into action (Arveson, 1998). The key element of this approach is focusing on the human issues that drive financial outcomes to force organizations to focus on the future. Kaplan and Norton said:

> The balanced scorecard retains traditional financial measures. But financial measures tell the story of past events, an adequate story for industrial age companies for which investments in long-term capabilities and customer relationships were not critical for success. These financial measures are inadequate, however, for guiding and evaluating the journey that information age companies must make to create future value through investment in customers, suppliers, employees, processes, technology, and innovation. (Kaplan & Norton, 1996, p. 7)

The balanced scorecard approach suggests viewing organizational activity from four perspectives:

- *Learning and growth*—This involves training, continuous improvement, and investment.
- *Business process*—This involves reducing non-value-added activities, improving the number of opportunities, and improving the success rates.
- *Customer perspective*—This involves customer satisfaction and needs as well as delivery performance.
- *Financial*—This includes ROI, shareholder value, return on equity, and cash flow.

Organizations must develop metrics for each of these perspectives, based on strategic plans, collect data, and then analyze the data. Many different metrics have been developed—some simple and others more complicated. An organization should list each metric, establish goals and objectives for each, measure results, and establish initiatives to adjust results if issues are found. The key issue with implementing a balanced scorecard is to make sure you pick the right metrics. The things that are tracked are the things that will get company focus and be improved. You must make sure to choose the correct metrics that are tied to the organization's strategic plan.

SIX SIGMA The purpose of the Six Sigma quality methodology is to reduce variation, thus reducing the number of product or service defects. The term *Six Sigma* as it applies to quality was created at the Motorola Corporation in the 1980s. Faced with competition from foreign firms that were able to produce higher-quality products at a lower cost, Motorola developed the Six Sigma methodology to improve quality and reduce the cost of its manufacturing process.

Six Sigma is a rigorous and disciplined methodology that uses data and statistical analysis to measure and improve a company's operational performance by identifying and eliminating defects in manufacturing and service-related processes. Originally used just in manufacturing companies, it has recently been applied to projects in all disciplines including IT. The Greek letter sigma (σ) is used in the field of statistics to represent standard deviation, to measure variability from the mean or average. A small standard deviation means that data cluster closely around the middle (mean), and there is little variability among the data. A normal distribution (see Figure 7-3) is a bell-shaped curve that is symmetrical about the mean. Using a normal curve, if a process is within six sigma, there would be no more than 2 defects per 1 billion items produced. A defect is any instance in which the product or service fails to meet customer requirements.

Translated into IT projects from manufacturing, variation is often the cause of defects or an indicator of process issues. The sigma value indicates how often defects are likely to occur. The higher the sigma value, the lower the probability of a defect occurring in the process. Six Sigma for IT projects is calculated based on the number of defects per million opportunities. An application system has many opportunities for defects. A simple invoice produced from an accounting system's accounts receivable module may have 50 opportunities for defects in just one document (customer information, pricing, product information, shipping information, and so on). In Table 7-1, notice that the goal is to reach six sigma, which means no more than 3.4 defects per 1 million opportunities.

Six Sigma is a business-driven approach to reducing costs by eliminating waste and improving the process of creating a product or service. The Six Sigma methodology follows the following process, referred to as DMAIC (pronounced "dee-may-ic"):

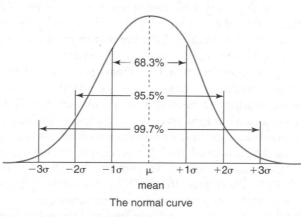

The normal curve

FIGURE 7-3 Standard Deviation Normal Curve

TABLE 7-1   Sigma Values and Defects per Million Opportunities

Sigma (σ)	Defects per Million Opportunities
1	690,000
2	308,537
3	66,807
4	6,210
5	233
6	3.4

- *Define*—Determine customer quality goals.
- *Measure*—Set up relevant metrics, based on customer goals, and collect data.
- *Analyze*—Evaluate data results for trends, patterns, and relationships.
- *Improve*—Make changes, based on facts.
- *Control*—Don't slip backward once targets are reached but set up control methods to maintain performance.

Process Improvement Maturity Models (CMMI and OPM3)

This section describes models for assessing an organization's quality and project maturity. For each maturity model, we describe the needed outcomes that allow an organization to reach a certain maturity level. For organizations, achieving a higher level of maturity means an improvement in quality processes and a reduction of waste and rework. Two maturity models—CMMI and OPM3—are briefly discussed here and are more fully explained in Chapter 14.

THE CAPABILITY MATURITY MODEL INTEGRATION (CMMI)   The Software Engineering Institute (SEI), located at Carnegie Mellon University, was sponsored by the U.S. Department of Defense through the Office of the Under Secretary of Defense for Acquisition and Technology in 1984. SEI was created to aid organizations in the advancement of software engineering practices. Software had become a critical component of every U.S. defense system, and issues with quality and assessment became of paramount importance. SEI determined that the quality of a system is highly influenced by the quality of the process used to acquire, develop, and maintain it. This premise implies a stronger focus on process, which was also supported by the earlier work of Shewhart, Juran, and Deming. To aid organizations in the improvement of their IT systems projects and to aid the U.S. government in selecting qualified vendors, a framework was developed to assess and evaluate an organization's processes, and this framework evolved into the Capability Maturity Model (CMM). The CMM was broken out into several disciplines to facilitate the use of best practices specific to each discipline. In complex environments where several of these disciplines are used, the collective use of individual models has resulted in redundancies, additional complexity, increased costs, and discrepancies. To improve the efficiency of model use and increase an organization's ROI, SEI created the CMMI (I for *integrated*) project to provide a single integrated set of models. Because not all organizations employ every discipline, CMMI also provides guidelines for individual disciplines and discipline combinations.

A maturity model is a structured collection of elements that describe characteristics of effective processes. According to the SEI web site, a maturity model provides:

- A place to start, a benchmark to know if things are improving
- The benefit of a community's prior experiences
- A common language and a shared vision
- A framework for prioritizing actions
- A way to define what improvement means for your organization

A maturity model can also be used as a benchmark for assessing different organizations for equivalent comparison. The text covers this topic in more detail in Chapter 14; for now, you just need to know that the CMMI has become a strategic marketing tool for outsourcing firms. Organizations have used CMMI certification as an excellent way to separate themselves from the competition. The U.S. government has mandated that all technology vendors who aspire to perform work for the U.S. government must be CMMI certified.

The CMMI defines five levels of process maturity: (1) initial, (2) managed, (3) defined, (4) quantitatively managed, and (5) optimizing. Maturity levels provide a defined evolutionary path for achieving a better, more mature systems development process. Levels 2 through 5 contain several key process areas that an organization must have in place and working in order to achieve a particular level of maturity. A process area is a collection of best practices specific to a project phase or related set of activities, such as configuration management or quality assurance. Immature organizations appear at Level 1 and are characterized by software processes that are ad hoc or not present at all. Each project team makes up its own process or doesn't use one at all. Successful projects are possible only if the team is very talented and dedicated. Because there are few or no defined processes, these organizations often operate in "fire fight" mode, running from one problem (fire) to the next. If a project schedule or budget is created, it is grossly inaccurate. Without defined processes that are measurable, these organizations have nothing to measure and improve. They will stay in this state perpetually.

In stark contrast, organizations that have moved up the maturity scale, even from Level 1 to a Level 2, have seen tremendous improvements. Mature organizations have more predicable outcomes and repeatable successes. At Level 2, project schedules and budgets are prepared for every project and are based on previous projects, helping to make them more accurate. Metrics are established, and the organization strives for improvements on every project. The processes become consistent across all projects, aiding in training, communication, and staffing.

Benefits attributed to achieving CMMI-defined maturity are as follows:

- Improved schedule and budget predictability
- Improved cycle time
- Increased team productivity
- Improved product quality
- Increased customer satisfaction
- Improved team morale
- Increased ROI

CMMI is not a guarantee of success and is not without drawbacks:

- It is not a "silver-bullet" and will not magically fix all errors.

- There is no guarantee of a quality product just because the organization follows a quality process. As is true with ISO 9000, a company could make a parachute out of lead and still be certified at CMMI Level 5
- Once an organization is certified, there is no expiration of the certification—the company is certified for life. There is no provision for periodic audits to make sure the company is maintaining its level of performance.

THE ORGANIZATIONAL PROJECT MANAGEMENT MATURITY MODEL (OPM3)   The Project Management Institute (PMI) created the OPM3 maturity model to aid organizations in their maturity progress specifically in terms of project management. The PMI standard says, "OPM3 seeks to create a framework within which organizations can reexamine their pursuit of strategic objectives via best practices in **organizational project management**" (OPM3, 2003, p. xi). OPM3 is intended to guide organizations in the assessment of their current state of project management practices in relation to the standard. It also provides guidance to organizations on how to improve their maturity ratings. The standard was written to be universal, supporting all types of projects and organizations, across the world.

The OPM3 maturity model has four levels of maturity, and each level can exist at a different domain of project management. The three domains of project management are portfolio, program, and project. A project, as described in Chapter 1, is a unique temporary endeavor undertaken to create a product or service. It should be focused on the creation of one single product or service. A program is generally a collection of related projects that are being managed in a coordinated way to obtain benefits and control not available from managing them individually. Likewise, a portfolio is a collection of project and/or programs that are grouped together to obtain benefits and control not available from managing them individually. Organizations can move up the maturity stages or levels, standardize, measure, control, and continuously improve, at each project domain.

As a general rule, organizations new to organizational project management maturity are encouraged to begin at the individual project stage and gain maturity before moving on to maturity in their project management practices for programs and then portfolios. The four stages of maturity are defined below:

1. *Standardize*—A standard process, with defined deliverables, is adopted.
2. *Measure*—Metrics are created and measured.
3. *Control*—Actions are taken, based on facts gathered to improve the project.
4. *Continuously improve*—Modifications are made to improve the process with each project.

The cycle consists of five steps:

    Step 1. *Prepare for assessment*—Organizations must understand the contents of the model and the operation of the OPM3. Contents of the standard include the narrative text, the self-assessment tool, and the three directories that contain detailed data on best practices.

    Step 2. *Perform assessment*—The organization's current maturity state is compared with those described by the model. The first phase of the process looks at which of the best practices the organization is using and plots their use on a continuum of organizational project management maturity. During the second phase, the organization gathers further information at a more detailed level to determine which specific capabilities associated with each best practice the organization currently does and does not demonstrate.

Step 3. *Plan for improvements*—The results from the previous step are used to form the basis of a plan for improvement. The set of best practices that the organization does and does not do forms the basis of the needs.

Step 4. *Implement improvements*—Actual organizational and process change takes place over time.

Step 5. *Repeat the process*—The organization can return to the initial step and perform a reassessment or to step 3 to act on other deficiencies already identified.

The cycle is very similar to the PDSA process described earlier in the chapter. Both are intended to be continuous processes for quality improvement. An organization doesn't just go through the process once, improve a few metrics, and then stop. An organization must always be striving for continuous improvement, and the OPM3 is one method to assist an organization in improving its strategic initiatives through better-run projects.

PMI attributes the following potential benefits to using the OPM3:

- It provides a way to advance an organization's strategic goals through the application of project management principles and practices.
- It provides a comprehensive body of knowledge of best practices in organizational project management.
- It highlights the most critical areas of organizational project management that need improvement for each individual organization.
- It assists organizations in prioritizing and planning strategies for improvement.

At this point in the chapter, after studying the history of quality initiatives and the review of current quality initiatives, it is time to move to actually building the quality management plan for a project.

Plan Quality

Project quality applies to all projects, regardless of the product or process created. All customers, stakeholders, and team members want to create a quality product. But the definition and consequences of poor quality can vary, depending on the audience and the industry. A company that creates a new web site to convey information about its new line of door handles will probably survive if a few minor bugs are found in the software; a new nuclear power plant finding bugs in its software might not fare so well. This section outlines a generic quality management plan format that supports a variety of IT projects. The size and breadth of the plan is determined by the size, importance, and safety issues of the project. The plan can be both formal and informal but should always support the organization's strategic objectives, regardless of whether it is looking to meet ISO, CMMI, or OPM3 standards.

A quality management plan consists of metrics (thresholds such as the number of software bugs allowed), missed requirements, system response time, failure rates, checklists (verifying that a required set of steps was completed), improvement plan (identifying non-value-added steps and removing or improving them), and finally a baseline of where the organization is currently operating. Deciding which metrics to track is an extremely important process because the items tracked are the items that will get attention and will hopefully be improved.

The organization and project team must choose metrics which are of high importance to the project and the organization. Useful metrics, according to Futrell, Shafer, and Shafer (2002) are:

- Simple and easy to understand
- Inexpensive to use
- Robust
- Consistent and used over time
- Unobtrusively collected
- Easily accessible online by all stakeholders

Elements of a quality management plan are listed below, along with examples:

- Philosophies and principles:
  - Authority level of each individual
  - The organization's quality process, defined on its own or one of the popular methodologies identified earlier in the chapter (Six Sigma, TQM, and so on)
  - Overall objectives and timing of corrective actions
- Standards and metrics:
  - "-ilities" of software developed by Barry Boehm (1978) and others:
    - Adaptability
    - Flexibility
    - Generality
    - Installability
    - Interoperability
    - Maintainability
    - Modifiability
    - Portability
    - Reliability
    - Replaceability
    - Reusability
    - Scalability
    - Testability
    - Understandability
    - Usability
  - ROI goals (economy)
  - Efficiency
  - Documentation
  - Customer satisfaction criteria
  - Performance criteria
  - Number of change requests and time to implement
  - Earned value
- Data acquisition and validation:
  - Sampling
  - Surveys
  - Outside assessments
  - System test results
  - When data should be gathered, stored, and by whom
  - Automated testing tools being used or needed

- Configuration management plan
- Roles and responsibilities:
  - Who collects data and who verifies the accuracy of the data
  - Who receives and acts on the data
  - Who makes final decisions on changes
- Status reports:
  - Who is responsible for producing them, what they look like, and how often they are produced
  - Who receives which reports

The following tools and techniques are used to build a **quality management plan**:

- *Cost/benefit analysis*—This method is used to determine the trade-off between the costs of building a quality product or service and the benefits obtained from a product that meets defined quality standards. Many of the costs of quality are defined earlier in the chapter (cost of conformance), as are the benefits (less rework, higher productivity, and so on). The trick is to balance the two so that the benefits received equal or surpass the cost to achieve them. For example, say that a manufacturing organization is just starting a project to add functionality to its online human resources information system. The application is accessible only to current employees on the company's intranet. In an effort to reduce the number of calls made to human resources concerning pay information, the IT department is building an application that will allow access to a person's current and next paycheck information. It has been estimated that this application will save the company 5 phone calls a day for each of the 20 human resources department staff at an estimated 5 minutes for each call, or a total of 500 minutes per day. This amounts to a savings of $3,320 per month, or approximately $39,840 per year. The application will also generate good feelings among the employees. The cost of building the application is fairly minimal because existing hardware can be used. The estimated cost to build the new application is $40,000. The project team is trying to decide how much additional money should be spent to test and deploy the new application. Should the team invest money in hiring an outside firm to do usability analysis to make sure the user interface is intuitive and easy to use? How much time should be invested in testing? Should the team purchase simulation software to make sure the application can support multiple users on the current network? All these questions need to be answered, keeping in mind how important the project is to the stakeholders and organization, the complexity of the project, and the costs of doing the extra testing compared to the anticipated benefits.
- *Brainstorming with or without affinity diagrams*—Brainstorming is a technique used to gather information and ideas from a variety of sources. When a project team is confronted with an unstructured or new issue, it can use several brainstorming techniques to aid in gathering information. Affinity diagrams are one such technique. An affinity diagram is a group decision-making technique designed to sort a large number of ideas, concepts, and opinions into a set of organized groups. A brainstorming session is held about the specific topic under investigation, either online or with everyone present in one room. Each person generates a list of ideas and writes them on small cards or sticky notes. The cards are then randomly laid out or stuck to the wall, and then they are sorted into logical groups. The cards are

moved around until consensus is reached on the groups and which cards belong in each group. The technique can help to clarify and organize a large brainstorming session.

- *Benchmarking*—Benchmarking is the study of a competitor's product, service, or business practice for the purpose of improving an organization's own performance. By studying the quality results of key competitors, an organization can determine the amount of quality needed to become the best in class or to at least match the competition.
- *Design of experiments*—This is a statistical method to help identify the factors that have influence on the quality of a product or process. It allows a team to change certain parameters (more than one at a time) and observe the results. In addition, controlled tests can be conducted and analyzed to evaluate the factors that control the value of a parameter or group of parameters. This technique allows for a statistical framework to be used to change multiple factors that are important to a specific project and review the results instead of changing just one parameter at a time and having to wait for the results before proceeding with another change.

Quality management planning is so important that many authors add it to the triple constraint of projects (scope, time, cost). A quality management plan is generated at the same time as other planning documents because of its influence on all the other planning artifacts. Later in the chapter, we provide an example of a quality management plan for the R & S Amusements Services case study. The next section of this chapter describes the quality planning process steps followed by the process of building the project quality plan with examples from the opening chapter case study.

THE QUALITY PLANNING PROCESS

Assuming that an organization has already established a quality initiative such as Six Sigma or TQM, the process used to build a quality management plan is as follows:

Step 1. Obtain commitment and shared understanding from stakeholders on the quality standards to be used on this specific project.

Step 2. Conduct training for all on the organization's quality initiative (for example, Six Sigma, TQM, CMMI).

Step 3. Define the quality standards, which consist of metrics (goals) to be measured and the acceptable result parameters.

Step 4. Determine how each metric result will be collected and who is responsible for collecting each data item.

Step 5. Conduct project team training on the chosen metrics and the defined process for control and monitoring.

Step 6. Build checklists to aid the project team in collecting and monitoring quality standards.

Step 7. Define and report the current baseline of metrics for the organization.

Step 8. Build process improvement plans and disseminate and execute them.

Step 9. Accumulate information from previous steps and build a quality management plan.

HOW TO CONDUCT THE QUALITY PLANNING PROCESSES

In this section of the chapter, the R & S Amusements Services case study is used to demonstrate the process of building a quality management plan. This section walks through each of the process steps defined in the previous section. Before proceeding, you might want to take time to reread and review the R & S Amusements Services case study. Jeff and Kevin, the consultants from PPMS, are working with the leadership team at R & S Amusements Services to explain the quality management plan and the communication management plan. Jeff and Kevin will also be introducing to the company the Six Sigma quality initiative to help them improve quality on the current projects as well as across the entire organization.

Quality Planning

STEP 1: OBTAIN COMMITMENT   With the aid of Jeff Dunbar and Kevin Pullen, Reid Lewis has been conducting short meetings with each key project stakeholder to convey his commitment and the organization's commitment to the Six Sigma quality process for these projects and all other areas within the company. It is extremely important that the quality message be delivered by upper management and not just by outside consultants. Research has shown that everyone in the organization must be a part of the quality process, especially upper management. Jeff and Kevin wanted to make sure that Reid Lewis led the meetings and explained how important the quality initiatives were to the projects and the organization. It is best to conduct these commitment meetings in person as much as possible. The meetings were done in small groups to allow attendees the opportunity to ask questions and promote discussion to make sure everyone understood the process. These meetings are the direct precursor to the upcoming training and the remaining steps in the quality planning process.

STEP 2: HOLD TRAINING   The training for each stakeholder and team member was done in several four-hour seminar-style classes in order to minimize the impact on their ability to get their everyday jobs done. The goal was to bring every member of the team up to at least a green-belt level and have several reach the black-belt level. (The color of the belt is an indication of the amount of training received.) The training was done by both Jeff and Kevin, who are Six Sigma black belts as well as certified project management professionals. Having Jeff and Kevin do the training worked out well due to their familiarity with the project and the organization. The training initially covered the Six Sigma process at R & S Amusements Services. The second part of the training covered the specific metrics and standards used for the asset management, collection management, and customer management projects.

STEP 3: DEVELOP QUALITY STANDARDS   The project leaders from R & S Amusements Services as well as Jeff and Kevin met to discuss the key quality standards that would need to be used for the current projects. Jeff and Kevin provided a starting point for the brainstorming session, based on previous similar projects they had worked on and the current organization's needs. They also reiterated to the group that the power and value of a tracked metric depends on its ability to aid in decision making. In other words, a team shouldn't just track a metric in order to be tracking. It needs to make sure to measure the items that will provide benefit to the project and organization. The following list consists of the relevant standards the group decided on for the three selected projects:

- The overarching goal is to continue the use of the organization's Six Sigma process with 3.4 defects per 1 million opportunities.
- Strategic metrics:
  - Current (weekly) accurate project status, available to all relevant stakeholders via online reports
  - Project time and cost estimate accuracy and adherence to schedule
  - Adherence to project and product development process
  - Training effectiveness, as measured by surveys
  - Risk identification and management
  - Earned value management (cost performance index and schedule performance index)
- Operational metrics:
  - Number of requirement defects (fixed and outstanding)
  - Time and cost to fix requirement defects
  - Number of software defects by module (fixed and outstanding) by severity level
  - Time and cost to fix software defects
  - System response time
  - Mean time between software or system defects (reliability)
  - System availability
  - Average time to complete a change order

Some of these items may look familiar, and some may not. Don't be too worried about the items the text hasn't covered yet. Later chapters cover the other items, such as risk management and earned value management, in detail. Also, a short note about the type of values collected for each of these metrics: Some will be collected as raw numbers; some will be collected as a scale, such as very high or very low; and some will be collected as percentages. The type of value tracked doesn't matter as much as communicating the relative values, being consistent, and making sure that data are collected and reported appropriately.

STEP 4: COLLECT DATA   The project team worked together to assign a responsible resource for each metric. Just as it is important to have one resource responsible for each task on the WBS, it is equally important to have one resource responsible for collecting metric data. The resource closest to the data should be responsible for collecting it. For example, when collecting data on software defects, the supervisor in charge of the quality assurance team—not the programmer who created the code—should collect the data. Second, the team should strive to make the collection of data as easy as possible. The easier the data are to collect, the greater the chances for accuracy and compliance. For example, Jeff and Kevin encouraged R & S Amusements Services to invest in a software program that works with Microsoft Project and allows team members to easily enter their time spent on each task of the project. The time can be tracked either in the new software or within Microsoft Project.

STEP 5: HOLD SPECIFIC PROJECT TEAM TRAINING   When the metrics have been established for the project, the next step is to make sure everyone on the team understands what metrics are being tracked and why. Acceptable levels of performance are established and communicated as well. The training for R & S Amusements Services was conducted by the team leaders for their respective departments in small groups.

TABLE 7-2   Daily Quality Checklist

	Activity	Responsible	Flagged for Follow-up
☐	Verify time entry for each active task by module	Project leader	(Yes/No)
☐	Verify resource calendars	Project leader	(Yes/No)
	. . .		

TABLE 7-3   Monthly Quality Checklist

	Activity	Responsible	Flagged for Follow-up
☐	Distribute monthly status reports	Project leader	(Yes/No)
☐	Review quality metrics by category	Project leader	(Yes/No)
	. . .		

STEP 6: BUILD CHECKLISTS   The project team, with assistance from Jeff and Kevin, created checklists for each metric by calendar and process phase. The checklist is a simple list of each metric used to verify that each step has been completed. The checklist consists of how data are to be collected, when data are to be collected, and by whom. The checklist is generated based on the calendar: daily tasks, weekly tasks, and monthly tasks. It can also be generated by phase of the project. Some metrics have meaning only during the project execution phase, for example. Some examples of checklists for the R & S Amusements Services projects are shown in Table 7-2 and Table 7-3. (The text will revisit the quality checklists in the quality control section of Chapter 12)

STEP 7: DEFINE AND REPORT BASELINE METRICS   The project team worked together to define the key specific quality metrics to use for each of the selected projects. A list of some of the key metrics selected is included in Table 7-4 for the asset management project. The table contains the specific metric being tracked, the name of the person responsible for collecting the information, how often the data are collected, and the timing of the distribution and who needs to receive the information.

STEP 8: CREATE PROCESS IMPROVEMENT PLANS   The process improvement plans are created and executed in the hope of correcting problems as quickly as possible so as not to affect the project and the final deliverable. Improvement plans are written for each metric being tracked. The entire team must not only be educated on the quality metrics being tracked and why but also must know how the organization intends to improve the process to correct quality issues when they occur. (Chapter 12 covers some specific cases.) The improvement plan contains information on the part of the project team directly involved in the quality issue, the data trends, corrective actions, and incremental improvement data targets. For example, Mark Lewis and Diana Brooks, after reviewing the schedule performance

TABLE 7-4   Project Quality Metrics Tracking Plan

Metric	Responsible	Timing	Distribution
System reliability	Mark Lewis	Weekly	Reid Lewis—weekly Diana Brooks—weekly Ashley Brooks—weekly
Number of changes	Diana Brooks	Daily	Reid Lewis—weekly Mark Lewis—monthly Ashley Brooks—monthly
Requirement defects	Diana Brooks	Daily	Reid Lewis—weekly Mark Lewis—monthly Ashley Brooks—monthly
Time and cost to fix defects	Diana Brooks	Weekly	Reid Lewis—monthly Ashley Brooks—weekly
Earned value—cost performance index	Ashley Brooks	Weekly	Reid Lewis—monthly Mark Lewis—weekly Diana Brooks—weekly
Earned value—schedule performance index	Ashley Brooks	Weekly	Reid Lewis—monthly Mark Lewis—weekly Diana Brooks—weekly

index, noticed that the percentage changed from 101 percent last week to 88 percent this week. This was a significant change for the asset management project, and they asked Ashley Brooks to produce the detailed data that generated the index. After review, they noticed that the key contributor to the slip in schedule was due to the late delivery of computer workstations. The vendor was late getting the shipment delivered due to internal quality issues with the monitors they received from one of the vendors, which pushed back the delivery to R & S Amusements Services. Because the workstations were not delivered on time, the computer installations and training for personnel were also delayed. Because the same vendor was also selected for another shipment of workstations later in the schedule, the team scheduled a meeting with the vendor to make sure future shipments would be on time, and they decided to get bids from other vendors just in case the vendor was late again. The team updated the relevant schedules for the project and made sure to check all other vendor-supplied materials to make sure they began managing these relationships more aggressively.

STEP 9: BUILD A QUALITY MANAGEMENT PLAN   As a final step, the team assembled all of the previously defined information into its quality management plan. The plan for R & S Amusements Services contains the following sections:

    I. General Principles
        1. Authority Levels
            a. Reid Lewis, President R & S, final approval of all changes
            b. Diana Brooks and Mark Lewis, R & S, senior project leaders with authority to make changes that are 10 percent or less of overall project budget and schedule

        2. Quality Approach
          a. Six Sigma
        3. Overall Objectives
          a. See earlier explanation, Step 3: Goals
     II. Standards and Metrics (See earlier explanation, Step 3)
   III. Data Acquisition (See earlier explanation, Step 4)
   IV. Configuration Management
        1. This is covered in Chapter 12.
    V. Roles and Responsibilities (See earlier explanation, Step 6 check lists)
   VI. Status Reports (See earlier explanation, Step 7)

PROVEN STRATEGIES AND HINTS TO SUCCESS

Judy McKay has 20 years of software management experience for a variety of companies, and she is the author of the book *Managing the Test People: A Guide to Practical Technical Management.* The article published in CIO online magazine by McKay summarizes from her book 14 lessons learned on controlling the quality of our IT projects:

- Don't reward for shipping on schedule. Anyone can ship garbage. Base rewards on quality metrics.
- Don't reward heroes for their herculean effort late in the project to fix problems that could have—and should have—been fixed by the same people much earlier in the life cycle.
- If you expect to work your people inordinate hours, you might want to consider corporate-sponsored flu shots. Meaning you will have little leeway when things start going wrong or your key people get sick.
- Always include QA and other project team members in all reviews to get the most well-rounded input possible.
- It's easy to ignore documents that are sent by e-mail for approval. No response does not equal approval: No response means, "I didn't have time to read it."
- Don't start coding until the requirements are stable and understood, or else budget time for subsequent rework.
- Code isn't complete until it works. Good unit testing is part of the development effort, not an optional item to be jettisoned when the schedule is tight.
- Is your test team always grumpy? Maybe it has good reasons! Meaning you are probably doing a very poor job of building a quality product the first time, requiring too much QA testing and rework.
- To maximize team efficiency the project plan must consider testing efficiency. This may determine feature implementation order.
- Buggy software takes longer to ship—on-time doesn't equal a "satisfied customer."
- Hire the right people and build a strong QA team.
- If requirements are testable, they provide enough details for the developers to accurately implement the functionality.
- A cross-functional requirements review will always save more money by preventing bugs than it costs in time and manpower.
- Cost of quality metrics are easy to gather and help to focus a team on the high-return activities.

PROJECT MANAGEMENT CONCEPTS: COMMUNICATIONS PLANNING

Effective project communication is paramount to success on all projects and especially on IT projects, due largely to the language gap that occurs on many projects. The computer industry, more so than some others, uses its own language, often referred to as *computereze*. On many IT projects, the technical workers speak what seems like a different language (computer jargon) than the users of the system. All IT team members as well as the project manager must learn to communicate with stakeholders and be understood. It has been estimated that as much as 90 percent of a project manager's time is spent in some form of communication. An old adage in project management is "if the organization's management team knows nothing of what you are doing, they will assume you are doing nothing." This is truer today than ever before, with an ever-increasing use of offshoring partners and highly complicated technical solutions. When it comes to IT projects, no one likes surprises, especially your boss.

IT programs of higher learning are stressing or should be stressing in their curriculums the importance of learning to communicate in both oral and written forms. This is so important that the special interest group for IT Education of the Association for Computing Machinery (ACM) has stressed in its undergraduate model curriculum the importance of communication skills. The 2005 IT Staffing Report issued by *CIO Magazine*'s executive council reported that 99 percent of IT executives who participated in the survey rated communication a critical or very important skill for senior IT management hires, and 93 percent gave it the same high priority for middle IT management and technical staff. "Among the soft skills, communication is a significant enabling skill that improves team performance at all levels" (CIO Executive Council, 2005, p. 3). The report surveyed 303 senior IT executives from various industries and company sizes. These survey results and others verify the importance that communication skills have for the success of IT projects.

Communication can include several definitions: an exchange of information, a verbal or written message, a technique for expressing ideas effectively, and a process by which meanings are exchanged between persons through a common system of symbols and/or sounds. Figure 7-4 shows the communication process. The medium represents the vehicle transporting the message (telephone, email, and so on). There is a sender of the message and a receiver of the message. Both sender and receiver have their own encode and decode processes, which can be different, based on their individual characteristics, such as age, sex, culture, language, and education. The sender encodes (that is, translates thoughts into language) the message and then sends it via the medium to the receiver, who must then decode the message. In between, noise can affect the ability of the receiver to correctly

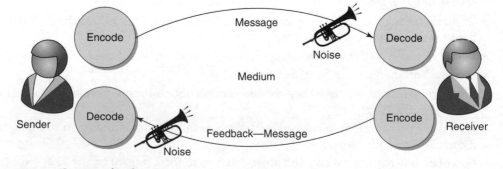

FIGURE 7-4   Communication Process

interpret the message. Noise is anything that interferes with the transmission and understanding of the message (for example, technology issues, language issues, third-party disruptions, attitudes, beliefs, perceptions, values, emotions, cultures, use of computereze). The process is then reversed for the feedback message.

During IT projects, a project manager must learn to communicate with all levels of teammates, managers, stakeholders, and external entities. IT project managers on a project of any size are not going to be the technical experts on most of the project, so they must rely on team members to communicate accurate status information, estimates, and so on. During the course of a project, which can last a year or more, many things can change and need to be communicated. An IT project manager who masters all these forms of communication will have a much better chance at project success.

The Stakeholder Management knowledge area in the PMBOK contains four processes: Identify Stakeholders, Plan Stakeholder Management, Manage Stakeholder Engagement, and Control Stakeholder Engagement. The remainder of this section describes the contents of a communications management plan and the stakeholder management plan. The other processes are described later in the text.

A project **communications management plan** includes information on when and how to prepare and distribute written reports to team members and stakeholders. It should also describe known oral exchanges of information, as well, such as when and where status meetings will occur. The Stakeholder Management plan is the process of developing appropriate strategies to effectively work with all stakeholders throughout the project, based on their needs, interests, and potential impact on the project. The plans must answer the following questions:

- Who are the stakeholders?
- What information do the stakeholders need, when do they want it, at what level of detail do they need the information, and in what form do they need it?
- Who on the project team is responsible for collecting data, creating the reports, and disseminating the reports?
- Who on the project team is the first contact for stakeholders who have questions and issues?
- Who on the project team is the first contact for external vendors who have questions and issues?

Much of the information contained in these two plans is taken from the stakeholder register already completed in an earlier process. Table 7-5 shows an example of a stakeholder register that shows each of the stakeholders and their need for information.

The next section of the chapter describes the processes a team should follow when building a communications management plan and the stakeholder management plan. The final section of the chapter provides examples of each plan for the R & S Amusements Services case study.

THE COMMUNICATIONS PLANNING PROCESS

The process for building the two plans is as follows:

Step 1. Review the stakeholder analysis and add information, if necessary, pertaining to communications management and complete the stakeholder communications matrix.

PROVEN STRATEGIES AND HINTS TO SUCCESS

From Rajkumar's (2010) presentation at the PMI Research and Education Conference, he offers the following tips for Individuals to communicate to achieve success in a team:

- Recognize and understand the differences of each team member and stakeholder and yourself as project leader. Differences in culture, background, familiarity with the project, biases, motivations, etc.
- Create the appropriate message to communicate, be very clear on the content, medium used, reason, or goal for the message
- Deliver the message in the most appropriate format. Should you use an instant message, e-mail, phone call, voicemail, face-to-face?
- Obtain feedback to confirm understanding and ensure the message was accurately received.

TABLE 7-5 Stakeholder Register

Stakeholder	Document	Detail Level	Delivery Format	Frequency	Team Contact
John Smith	Status report	Summary—2	Email—PDF	Monthly	Laura Smith
Mike Dunbar	Status report	Detail	Email—PDF	Weekly	Laura Smith
Becky Ploss	Earned Value Management report	Summary—1	Intranet	Weekly	Larry Cosgray
Dir. Finance	Budget/Actuals	Detail	Hard copy	Monthly	Carlos Rodriguez
Dir. Human Resources	Staffing plan	Detail	Email—PDF	Weekly	Larry Cosgray

Step 2. Define content for status reports and timing.

Step 3. Establish who on the project team is responsible for collecting data for status reports.

Step 4. Establish who on the project team is responsible for creating the reports and disseminating the reports.

Step 5. Establish key project team contacts for each stakeholder to serve as first contact references.

Step 6. Accumulate information from previous steps and build the communications management plan.

Communications and Stakeholder Planning

STEP 1: UPDATE THE COMMUNICATIONS MATRIX Table 7-6 is a portion of the stakeholder communications matrix for the R & S Amusements Services projects. The communications matrix builds on information gathered in the stakeholder register. The key stakeholders are mentioned here, along with which reports they receive, the level of details they want reported, how the report should be delivered to them, and how often the report should

TABLE 7-6 R & S Amusements Services Stakeholder Communications Matrix

Stakeholder	Document	Detail Level	Delivery Format	Frequency	Team Contacts
Reid Lewis	Weekly status Monthly status Staffing	Summary	Hard copy	Monthly	Diana Brooks Mark Lewis
Diana Brooks	Weekly Status Monthly Status Staffing	Detail	Email—PDF	Weekly	Ashley Brooks Heidi Cosgray
Mark Lewis	Weekly status Monthly status Staffing	Detail	Email—PDF	Weekly	Laura Kimball
Ashley Brooks	Weekly status	Detail	Hard copy	Weekly	Kenny Jones
Jeff Dunbar and Kevin Pullen	Weekly status Monthly status Staffing	Summary	Email—PDF	Weekly	Mark Lewis Diana Brooks

be delivered. It also contains a list of key team contacts for each person. The matrix was generated by Jeff Dunbar and Kevin Pullen, after conducting face-to-face interviews with key stakeholders.

STEP 2: CREATE STATUS REPORTS Figure 7-5 is the template the R & S project team uses for the monthly status reports. The report consists of the following information:

- Report date
- Project name
- The name of the person responsible for generating the report
- Current phase of the project at the time of the report (initiating, planning, executing, closing)
- Activity CTP—A list of activities completed during the current time period (CTP), along with associated budget dollars, actual dollars, original schedule date, and actual completion date of each activity
- Activity STP—A list of activities scheduled for work during the scheduled time period (STP), along with associated budget dollars, actual dollars, original schedule date, actual completion date and percentage complete of each activity
- The project's current cost performance index and schedule performance is calculated and shown, along with a color coding of red, yellow, or green. If the project is green, then everything is on schedule and on budget. If either the Cost Performance Index (CPI) or Schedule Performance Index (SPI) is 10 percent or less from ideal, the project is coded yellow, meaning some explanation is necessary but no management intervention is necessary. If the CPI or SPI is greater than 10 percent then a detailed explanation is necessary and intervention by management is required.
- List of any rework needed, based on defects or scope changes requested, along with a type code (resource issue, missing requirement, requirement change, new require-

R&S Amusements Services
Monthly Status Report
Date:

Project Name: Prepared by:
Current Project Phase:

Activity CTP	Budget $	Actual $	Completion Date Schedule	Completion Date Actual

Activity STP	Budget $	Actual $	Completion Date Schedule	Completion Date Actual	% Complete

Current Earned Value
CPI
SPI

Project Status
Red
Yellow
Green

Rework/Changes

Description	Type	Cost Impact	Time Impact

Known Obstacles	Impact

FIGURE 7-5 Monthly Project Status Report Template

ment, workaround needed) plus the cost impact and time impact anticipated due to the rework or scope change

- List of any known obstacles that may inhibit the project from reaching any of its scope, time, cost, or quality goals

STEP 3: COLLECT DATA Before status reports and any other project information can be generated and reported to stakeholders, the data must be collected. The goal is to collect accurate and complete data with the least amount of effort possible. Each data element must be assigned to a person for collection, and a determination needs to be made about when it should be collected. For the asset management project monthly status report, Mark Lewis, the project manager, is responsible for generating the report. Data are collected from each individual working on the project via project management software to which they all have access for activity reporting. The project management software generates the CPI and SPI. The project status color is automatically set based on the CPI and SPI numbers. Rework information and change information come from the integrated change control software application the project team is using. Known obstacles are reported based on the daily status meetings held by each project team.

STEP 4: CREATE REPORTS   As mentioned earlier, it is advantages to have the status reports automated as much as possible to save time and increase accuracy. The communication plan identifies the person responsible for each report, when the report is generated, and how it is assembled. For example, in the asset management project for R & S, the weekly status report is generated every Monday morning by Mark Lewis, and the monthly status report is the responsibility of Mark Lewis and is generated the first working day of each month. Each report automatically pulls data from several sources: project management software, change control software, and the daily issues tracking software, which tracks any obstacles brought up during the daily stand-up meetings. (Stand-up meetings are short daily meetings held by the team, usually lasting no longer than 15 minutes and in a place that does not have chairs.)

STEP 5: ESTABLISH KEY PROJECT TEAM CONTACTS   The team reviewed the stakeholder communications matrix and made sure that all key stakeholders had someone identified. It is very important that each stakeholder have a key contact for information he or she is most interested in. It is also important that each stakeholder have one and only one contact person, to reduce confusion and simplify communications.

STEP 6: BUILD THE COMMUNICATIONS PLAN   The communications plan consists of each deliverable from step 1 through step 6. Like many of the other project plan documents, the communications plan is a dynamic document that should change as the project changes and progresses. It is the project manager's responsibility to ensure its continued accuracy. For many companies, the building of the stakeholder management plan will be just a part of the communications plan, which is what the authors suggest. Some additional information that you may want to include in the communications plan: scope and impact of stakeholder changes and identified interrelationships between stakeholders.

Chapter Review

1. Quality is so important to the success of IT projects that many authors add it to the triple constraint of scope, time, and cost.

2. Quality is defined as the degree to which a set of inherent characteristics fulfill requirements or the degree to which a product satisfies both stated and implied requirements.

3. A cost and time disparity estimate says that it's 50 to 200 times more expensive to finding an error after the system is deployed than to find that error during requirements discovery

4. Over the past 100 years, organizations have changed their view of quality from inspection to prevention and the use of statistical process control measures and a focus on the customer.

5. Some of the key contributors to the change in thinking on quality are Walter A. Shewhart, W. Edwards Deming, Joseph Juran, Philip Crosby, Kaoru Ishikawa, and Genichi Taguchi.

6. Quality planning identifies which quality standards are relevant to a project and an organization and then determines the activities necessary to meet the established

standards in order to deliver the product, fit for customer use. The key tools are cost/benefit analysis, brainstorming, benchmarking, and design of experiments.

7. Communications management consists of processes necessary to ensure timely and accurate generation, distribution, storage, retrieval, and disposition of project information. It must answer the questions Who are the stakeholders? What information do they need? When do they need it and at what level of detail? Who is responsible for generating the report, disseminating the report, and collecting the data? and Who are the main project contacts for each stakeholder?

Glossary

communications management plan The processes necessary to ensure timely and accurate generation, distribution, storage, retrieval, and disposition of project information.

Stakeholder Management Plan The processes of developing appropriate strategies to effectively work with all stakeholders throughout the project, based on their needs, interests, and potential impact on the project.

organizational project management Application of knowledge, skills, tools, and techniques to organizational and project activities to achieve the strategic goals of the organization through projects.

quality The degree to which a product satisfies both stated and implied requirements.

quality management plan Identifying which quality standards are relevant to a project and an organization and determining the activities necessary to meet the established standards in order to deliver the product fit for customer use.

Review Questions

1. Define quality management in your own words and stress the importance of satisfying both stated and implied stakeholder needs.
2. List and explain the eight quality management principles defined by the ISO.
3. What is the cost of quality?
4. What is the cost of nonconformance?
5. What does it mean to do rework?
6. What does it mean for a product to be "fit for use"?
7. Define what is meant by product reliability.
8. Define what is meant by product maintainability.
9. Define the different categories of the ISO 9000 standard.
10. Define and list the key principles of TQM.
11. What is the balanced scorecard?
12. What is Six Sigma?
13. What does CMMI stand for, and how is it used?
14. List and explain each level contained in the OPM3.
15. List and describe the sections of the quality management plan.
16. What is a cost–benefit analysis?
17. What is a design of experiments?
18. Define communications management.
19. List and describe the sections of a communications management plan and the questions this plan must answer.
20. What is the purpose of a stakeholder communication matrix? Describe its contents.

Problems and Exercises

1. The chapter describes the viewpoint of many authors that quality should be included in the triple constraint. Explain why you believe quality should or should not be included in the triple constraint. Support your answer with examples.

2. Build a quality management plan for the other two R & S Amusements Services projects: customer contract management and collection management.

3. Discuss what is meant by the cost of quality or the cost of not producing a quality product.

4. Errors that are created during the early phase of a project, during requirements discovery, are much more expensive to fix the later in the project they are found. Explain why this is and explain its implications for project managers.

5. Explain why the quality movement is going away from inspection to prevention and the use of statistical process control measures. Also explain what impact this has on quality management plans.

6. "Each of the standards ISO 9000, CMMI, and OPM3 prescribes a process to aid organizations in producing a quality product, but an organization can obtain certification at any level and still produce a bad product." Explain whether you agree or disagree with this statement.

7. Using Six Sigma, organizations strive to have 3.4 defects per 1 million opportunities. Explain what this means in terms of IT projects.

8. Using the model of communications depicted in Figure 7-4, for an IT project, explain the issue of noise and its implications for a successful project.

Projects and Research

1. Research the CMMI and write a paper that summarizes the maturity steps, what organizations are using the model, and its implications for project management. Also discuss any drawbacks or issues with the CMMI.

2. Research the OPM3 and write a paper that summarizes the steps, who is using the model, and its implications for project management. Also discuss any drawbacks or issues with the OPM3.

3. Review work from any of the accomplished quality experts mentioned in this chapter and write a more detailed paper to summarize their contributions to the current quality movement. You could instead generate a paper that compares and contrasts the views of each noted author/researcher.

4. Review one or more of the project failures mentioned early in this chapter and write a paper that

explains in detail what happened and why quality was an issue.

5. Research the ISO 9000 standard and write a paper on the different certifications, how the certifications are awarded, and the implications for project management. Also discuss any drawbacks or issues with the standard.

6. Research the balanced scorecard and write a summary paper that defines what it is, who is using it, and its implications for project management. Also discuss any drawbacks or issues with the balanced scorecard.

7. Research Six Sigma and write a summary paper that defines what it is, who is using it, and its implications for project management. Also discuss any drawbacks or issues with Six Sigma.

1. *Background:* (Review the R & S Amusements Services case study at the beginning of the chapter.) Reid Lewis was sitting in his office, reviewing the information concerning quality management he had learned from Jeff Dunbar and Kevin Pullen of Premier Project Management Services (PPMS). He was impressed with the focus on quality and the measures taken to ensure quality not only in the product but also in the processes used to build the product. Because he was a successful businessperson, he was thinking about how he could leverage the training (Six Sigma) and the quality management skills his employees were acquiring while working on the system automation project and improve the processes and the quality of service provided by his company. He decided that he would ask Kevin and Jeff about this. Reid knew Jeff was very sensitive about project time robbers (items that take up time unrelated to the project), so he decided it would be better to discuss the matter over lunch. He decided to take them to an area restaurant, where they could discuss the matter while they were eating.

Current Situation 1: Reid, Jeff, and Kevin were having lunch together at a diner downtown. After about 20 minutes, Reid finally admitted the reason he wanted to have lunch with them: "Guys, I'm sure you're aware that with the economy the way it is and the increasing cost of doing business (mainly fuel prices), we at R & S have really struggled these past two months. Our customer base is down 15 percent, and our revenue is down 25 percent. Don't get me wrong, I am totally committed to the system automation projects—we need those to survive. But I need help in my regular business. I was thinking . . ." Reid went on to tell Jeff and Kevin how impressed he was with all the quality management activities they were using on the project and that he now wants to apply those same techniques to his regular business. He wants to know why R & S is losing customers and why they are making lower revenues. Also, complaint calls have increased 30 percent, but why?

Discussion: Place yourself in Kevin's and Jeff's shoes. How do you respond to Reid concerning this delicate situation? Jeff and Kevin's first and only priority is the system automation projects, but if there is no company, there are no projects to work on. What type of compromise might you suggest?

Current Situation 2: Jeff and Kevin have suggested to Reid a plan of utilizing R & S personnel not directly involved in the project (such as Heidi Cosgray) to work on these quality initiatives; in addition, they could provide an additional resource from PPMS, Gaurav Shah, to assist and mentor in the matter. Reid wholeheartedly agrees and wants to put the plan in action at the start of the week.

Discussion: How do you suggest that Heidi and Gaurav begin? What techniques should be used to analyze the problems of lost customers and increased customer complaints? What are the appropriate metrics that should be tracked, and what techniques should be used to identify them? What about Heidi's issues with her job as service coordinator (refer to the minicase from Chapter 6)? Could this effort not only help her but also provide future benefits when the IT team addresses the service management project?

Suggested Readings

Archibald, R.D. (1992). *Managing high technology programs and projects*. New York: Wiley.

Arveson, P. (1998). *What is the balanced scorecard?* Retrieved from www.balancedscorecard.org/Portals/0/PDF/BSC_for_City-County03.pdf.

Boehm, B., et al. (1978). *Characteristics of software quality*. New York: Elsevier.

Breyfogle, F.W. (1999). *Implementing Six Sigma*. New York: Wiley.

Caputo, K. (1998). *CMM implementation guide: Choreographing software process development*. Reading, MA: Addison-Wesley.

CIO Executive Council. (2005). *IT staffing report*. Retrieved from www.cioexecutivecouncil.com/pub/content/itstaffing_execsumm.pdf.

Cleland, D.I., & King, W.R. (1983). *Project management handbook*. New York: Van Nostrand Reinhold.

Crosby, P.B. (1979). *Quality is free: the art of making quality certain*. New York: McGraw-Hill.

Deming, W.E. (1982). *Out of the crisis*. Cambridge, MA: MIT Press.

Futrell, R.T., Shafer, D.F., & Shafer, L.I. (2002). *Quality software project management*. Upper Saddle River, NJ: Prentice Hall.

Gallagher, T. *Computerized radiation therapy*. Retrieved from http://neptune.netcomp.monash.edu.au/cpe9001/assets/readings/www_uguelph_ca_~tgallagh_~tgallagh. html.

Humphrey, W. (1988). Characterizing the software process: A maturity framework. *IEEE Software* 5(3):73–79.

Ishikawa, K. (1985). *What is total quality control?* (Lu, D. J., trans.) Upper Saddle River, NJ: Prentice Hall.

Janeba, M. (1995). *The Pentium problem*. Retrieved from www.willamette.edu/~mjaneba/pentprob.html.

Juran, J. (1998). *Quality control handbook*. New York: McGraw-Hill.

Kaplan, R.S., & Norton, D.P. (1992). *The balanced scorecard: Translating strategy into action*. Boston: Harvard Business School Press.

Li, A., et. al. (1994). *New Denver airport: Impact of the delayed baggage system*. Retrieved from http://ntl.bts.gov/docs/rc9535br.html.

McCall, J.A., et al. (1977, September 19). *Metrics for software quality evaluation and prediction*. Proceedings of Second Summer Software Engineering Workshop, Greenbelt, MD.

McKay, J. (2007, May 24). Quality doesn't just happen. *CIO*. Retrieved from www.cio.com/article/112800/Quality_Doesn_rsquo_t_Just_Happen.

Newman, M. (2002). *Software errors cost U.S. economy $59.5 billion annually*. Retrieved from www.nist.org.

OPM3 (2003). *Organizational project management maturity model*. Newton Square, PA: PMI.

Poulsen, K. (2004). Software bug contributed to blackout. Retrieved from www.securityfocus.com/news/8016.

Project Management Institute (PMI). (2013). *A guide to the project management body of knowledge*, 5th ed. Newton Square, PA: PMI.

Pyzdek, T. (1999). *The complete guide to Six Sigma*. Quality Publishing.

Rajkumar, S. (2010). Art of communication in project management. PMI Research and Education Conference 2010 Proceedings.

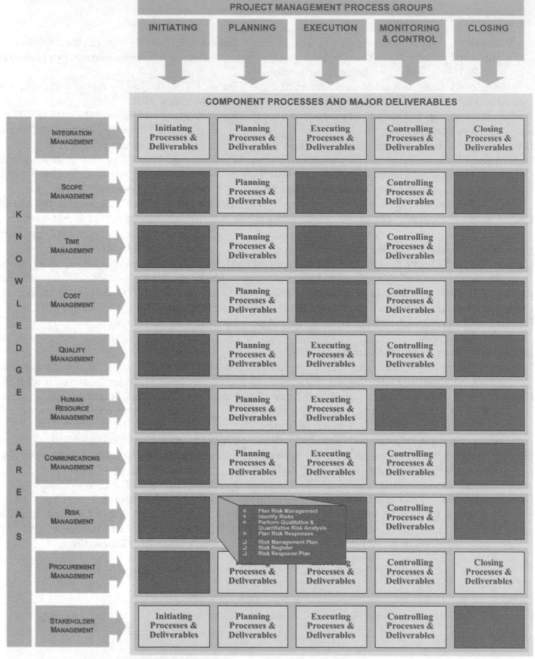

Project Risk Management Planning

R & S Amusements Services

Event 8

Setting   *It is now one week since the meeting described in Event 7, and the project leaders have convened in a small conference room located outside Reid Lewis's office at R & S Amusements Services. Those in attendance include Reid Lewis, Diana Brooks, Elaine Henry, Heidi Cosgray, and Mark Lewis from R & S and Jeff Dunbur and Kevin Pullen from Premier Project Management Services.*

JEFF   Everyone has worked extremely hard, and we had a very productive week. We completed the quality plan as well as the communications plan, so our project plan is on its way toward completion.

REID   Fantastic! Is the planning now completed, so we can get this project started? I am really anxious to get going.

JEFF   Almost. I want you to understand, Reid, as well as the other members of the team, that the work we have been doing is vital to the success of this project. It is in your best interests, as well as ours, to make sure we prepare ourselves in order to complete the project to your expectations and satisfaction. That includes planning for unexpected events that could affect our ability to finish this project on time, within budget, and with the functionality you require.

DIANA   Plan for the unexpected. How do we do that? This sounds like a never-ending exercise!

KEVIN   Great question, Diana, and that is the purpose of today's meeting. We in project management call it *risk management*. It is where we as a team try to identify as many risks as we can that, if they occurred, would adversely affect the project. We then analyze each risk, determining the probability that each could occur and the associated impact to the project if it did. Next, we prioritize the risks based on the ones that have the highest probability of occurring or the greatest impact on the project. For those risks that have high priorities, we formulate strategies to deal with them if they occur.

MARK   Strategies like what?

JEFF   Strategies such as avoiding the risk by eliminating its cause or mitigating the risk by performing activities that will reduce the probability of it occurring. There is also more to it that we will talk about later.

HEIDI   This sounds like it could get very complicated very quickly.

KEVIN   It's not really. The reason you are all here is to help us identify the risks so we can begin preparing the risk management plan.

ELAINE   I doubt if we will be much help; we have never done anything like this before.

JEFF   Oh, but you will. You are the ones who play the "what if" game every day. For example, what if Diana was to call in sick and had to be out of the office for two weeks? Who would be her backup? Who would assume her duties while she was sick? I'm sure the office would not close down while she was away. Somebody would probably be identified—probably Heidi or Mark—who has already been trained to perform Diana's work in case that happened. The planning for that is an example of risk management.

REID   Makes perfect sense to me now. So how do we get started? I can think of a couple risks right now. They are . . .

JEFF   Slow down, Reid. Please keep those to yourself for the time being.

REID   But. . . . (*Looking confused*)

JEFF   (*Laughing and holding up his hands*) You will get your opportunity; right now I don't want your answers influencing the other members of the team.

REID   But . . .

JEFF   Let me explain. We are going to perform an exercise called *brainstorming*, where everyone will write down all the risks that they can think of, based on a given category that Kevin or I will explain. Once everyone is finished, we will collect them and list them all on the board to discuss. It is important that you list everything, no matter how silly it may seem. Your submissions will be confidential in order to avoid embarrassment or any influence one team member may have on another.

(Both Jeff and Kevin look at Reid)

REID   (*Looking astonished*) Wh-wh-wh-what? But I would never . . .

JEFF   Kevin is going to get us started by handing out a stack of yellow sticky notes to each of you.

KEVIN   Please list only one risk per sticky note.

REID   What if I run out of sticky notes?

KEVIN   That is a risk we will have to assume. (*Laughing*) I'm sure we have more.

JEFF   You will have five minutes to list all the risks you can think of for the category . . .

(To be continued)

(This chapter provides instructions for building the risk management plan, along with examples.)

CHAPTER PREVIEW AND OBJECTIVES

This chapter describes the process of building a risk management plan. Organizations must perform risk management planning on every project, regardless of size or complexity, so it is very important to learn how.

As you read this chapter, you will:

- Define and recognize risk
- Define the contents of a risk management plan
- Conduct a risk identification and prioritization process
- Define the correct risk response strategy for the organization

AN INTRODUCTION TO RISK MANAGEMENT PLANNING

Several project deliverables defined previously in this text, such as the project charter and the communications management plan, rely on accurate assessment of project **risk**. Every IT project, regardless of size, complexity, location, or organization, contains some measure of risk, so it is extremely important that a formal risk management process be followed on every project. A project manager's objective is not to remove all risk from a project—that simply can't be done—but to identify and manage risks to the benefit of the project. In fact, according to DeMarco and Lister, risks on a project can be a good thing if managed appropriately: "If a project has no risks, don't do it. A project without risk also is without any real value" (2003, p. 9). In other words, there are risks that provide new opportunities that will affect a project in a constructive way, and there are risks that threaten the success of the project.

The main objectives of risk management are to increase the probability and impact of positive outcomes and decrease the probability and impact of negative outcomes. Unfortunately, many organizations don't follow a formal risk management process; rather, they operate in a perpetual state of crisis management. Crisis management, the opposite of good risk management, involves trying to figure out what to do about a problem after it has occurred instead of planning for issues in advance. This is also referred to as perpetual *fire fighting*.

According to the dictionary, *risk* is simply defined as the possibility of loss or injury. In IT projects, this can mean many things, from a slip in the project schedule of a few days, to the need for additional money or resources, to the possibility of injury or even death. Risk can also be defined as a function of the project impact and the likelihood of an event occurring. This last definition is the one this chapter explores in more detail. Understanding the process of risk management described in this chapter will help a project team in assessing the impact a negative event will have on a project and how likely (generally expressed as a percentage or qualitative term) the event is to occur.

The reasons to perform risk management planning are as follows: (based on DeMarco and Lister, 2003)

- *Risk management makes aggressive risk-taking possible*—An organization operating from a position of knowledge, with mitigation strategies in place, can afford to be more aggressive and take on a higher level of risk.

- *Risk management decriminalizes risk*—It allows an honest and open evaluation of risk to occur, without fear of being labeled as a negative thinker or thought of as being against the successful completion of the project.
- *Risk management sets up projects for success*—It provides a clear understanding of what is possible within normal operating procedures and what might be a stretch to achieve.
- *Risk management bounds uncertainty*—It helps a project team understand what it doesn't know (known unknowns).
- *Risk management provides minimum-cost downside protection*—Armed with the knowledge of each risk's impact and likelihood, the team can develop an accurate justification for the amount of money and time to be spent on mitigation strategies.
- *Risk management protects against invisible transfers of responsibility*—An element of the risk register is the identification of who owns each risk. Risk management identifies each stakeholder's share of the identified risks (customer, vendor, project team, and so on) to allow a conscious effort on the part of the project team to understand who has what risks and who should have the risks that make the most sense for the success of the project and stakeholder.
- *Risk management can save part of a failed effort*—The key here is to not let the failure of a part of a project destroy the whole project.
- *Risk management maximizes opportunity for personal growth*—Organizations exposed to bad projects can tend to become risk adverse, from then on taking on only small, simple projects offering little benefit or job growth for the participants.
- *Risk management protects management from getting blindsided*—As mentioned in Chapter 7, in project management, no one likes surprises.
- *Risk management focuses attention where it is needed*—The objective is to utilize resources (human and monetary) where they are needed most to benefit the project and organization.

Executing the process to build the risk management plan should be done on every project, regardless of size, complexity, length, or importance. However, the effort expended should be complementary to these same metrics. The size, complexity, length of schedule, or strategic importance of the project should dictate the time and energy spent on the risk management process. For a small, non-complex, semi-important project, a team will identify risks and perform a quick qualitative assessment of impact and likelihood. For a large, complex project, a team will perform a more comprehensive search for risks and utilize techniques discussed later in this chapter under the heading "Performing Quantitative Risk Analysis."

As in the other project management processes described in this text, in risk management, many of the processes take place at the same time instead of in a linear fashion. It is too confusing to describe the processes along with the tools and techniques all at once, so this chapter explains them in a linear fashion and points out when they are often done at the same time.

The Project Management Institute's project management body of knowledge (PMBOK) describes the following risk management processes: plan risk management, identify risks, perform qualitative risk analysis, perform quantitative risk analysis, plan risk responses, and control risks. This chapter explores all these processes except for control, which is described in Chapter 12.

PROJECT MANAGEMENT CONCEPTS: RISK MANAGEMENT PLANNING

The primary deliverable from the risk management planning process is the risk management plan. The PMBOK defines *risk management* as "the systematic process of identifying, analyzing, and responding to project risk." An organization identifies, in its risk management plan, the approach, plan, and who will execute the risk management activities. The risk management plan is created early in the planning phase of the project and updated throughout the life of the project.

The following are some industry best practices to keep in mind during the risk management process (DeMarco, 1997):

- Manage projects by managing their risks.
- Create and maintain a census of risks for each project.
- Track the causal risks, not just the ultimate undesirable outcomes.
- Assess each risk for probability and likely cost.
- Predict for each risk the earliest symptom that might indicate materialization.
- Appoint a risk officer, one person who is not expected to maintain a "can-do" attitude, to ensure that negative information gets communicated.
- Establish easy (perhaps anonymous) channels for bad news to be communicated up the hierarchy.

The risk management plan consists of the following information:

- Methodology—approaches (process steps), tools, and data sources that may be used to perform risk management
- Roles and responsibilities to manage risks throughout the entire project
- Budgeting for risk management activities (mitigation strategies)
- Timing of risk management activities (how often the risks are reviewed, when mitigation strategies will be implemented)
- Risk categories—high level used during identification (technology, customers, performance, and so on)
- Risk probability and impact scales (five levels from very likely to very unlikely or just the three levels—low, medium, high) that are defined for consistency across projects and project managers
- Format for the risk register and its use—how risks are communicated and tracked

Before information about risks can be assessed and dealt with risks first have to be found. The next section of this chapter describes the tools and techniques a project team can use to find the potential risks in a project.

Identifying Risks

The first step in the risk management planning process is to identify as many risks as possible for the upcoming project, with the knowledge that you can never see them all. But the more risks a team identifies and quantifies, the more the team reduces the amount of uncertainty on the project and gives the project manager the information necessary to build in sufficient contingency reserves (defined more specifically later in this chapter, but for now simply extra money and time) to help ensure that a product is delivered as defined. Risk identification is not a one-time process done only at the beginning of a project but

Risk Register					
Project: Project Name					Date: Current Date
Risk	**Trigger Event**	**Responsible**	**Consequence**	**Probability**	**Mitigation**
(name and short description)	(action(s) preceeding the risk occurring)	(person or group responsible for monitoring and mitigation)	(key project impact if risk occurs)	(qualitative or quantitative probability of occurrence)	(strategy being used to reduce likelihood)

FIGURE 8-1   Risk Register

should be a continuous process of team members and stakeholders—not just the project manager—looking for new issues that may affect the success of the project.

A project team can use several techniques to identify potential risks. In most cases, a combination of techniques can be used to produce the best, most complete list of risks. While reviewing each technique, keep in mind that many times, identifying risks and quantifying them occur at the same time. While a project leader has the team assembled and thinking about risks is a great opportunity to also do a qualitative assessment of the risks. The key deliverable from the risk identification process is the risk register (see Figure 8-1). Qualitative and quantitative assessment techniques are explained in the next sections of the chapter. The identification tools and techniques discussed next include broad organizational categories, analogy, brainstorming, interviews, Delphi technique, and SWOT analysis.

USING BROAD ORGANIZATIONAL CATEGORIES   Teams often use brainstorming sessions to help organize and channel ideas into broad categories. Risks are examined using broad categories such as people, technology changes, quality and performance issues, customers, vendors, management, funding, political issues, legal issues, and market forces. During a brainstorming session, a team is directed to generate ideas surrounding these categories, one at a time. For example, a team may be asked to generate every risk it can think of that exists with current people involved in the project, such as customers located in another location separate from the development team or a newly installed application written in Java, with few IT staff having Java experience.

ANALOGY   The analogy approach uses information from past similar projects or the experience of team members to look for risks. Studies have shown that IT projects share risks related to the following:

- User involvement/commitment
- Management commitment/support
- Technology evolution
- Scope definition and management
- Time management
- Cost estimation and management
- Management of end-user expectations
- Staffing

- Security
- Disaster Recovery

Using the analogy approach gives a team an excellent head start in finding and accessing risks in a project.

BRAINSTORMING   Brainstorming is a non-structured or semi-structured method of eliciting ideas from a group, with the goal of generating a complete list of ideas. The key to running a successful brainstorming session is to foster an atmosphere that allows all ideas to be spoken, regardless of likelihood. If everyone feels able to contribute to the discussion, free from persecution or harassment of their ideas, a better, more complete list of ideas will be generated. When all ideas have been documented (for example, on a whiteboard or flipchart), the group then begins discussing the merits of each. If the group is new or participants are unfamiliar with each other, participants may be more hesitant to put forth ideas. In this case, a process that allows ideas to be expressed in secret can be very effective. The following process illustrates one example of an anonymous brainstorming technique using sticky notes:

Step 1.   During a short time interval, such as five minutes, have each participant write down on sticky notes as many ideas as they can think of, writing one idea per sticky note. This is best done if ideas are generated about one general category at a time, such as technology issues or resource issues. Participants do not write their names on the notes.

Step 2.   Participants hand their sticky notes to the moderators, who stick them on a chalkboard or whiteboard in the front of the room. If duplicate ideas are found, they are stuck on top of each other to reduce the number of entries. A list of ideas is then quickly generated, and the team discusses the merits of each.

Step 3.   Ideas that have close to zero probability of occurring or zero impact to the project are removed from the board.

Step 4.   The ideas that remain are then rated for likelihood and impact. (This process is discussed in more detail later in this chapter.) Sticky notes are an important part of this process because they can be moved around easily. The team can draw a large matrix on the chalkboard or whiteboard, similar to the probability and impact matrix shown in Figure 8-2. The sticky notes can then be moved around inside the matrix until the team agrees on the placement of each.

Step 5.   The team generates the start of the risk register (refer to Figure 8-1) from the sticky notes.

Impact ⟶	Low	Low Med.	Medium	Med. High	High
Probability Low					
Low Medium					
Medium					
Medium High					
High					

FIGURE 8-2   Probability and Impact Matrix

DELPHI TECHNIQUE   The Delphi technique is another technique that helps a project team brainstorm ideas anonymously. In this technique, the participants do not know who proposed each idea, so ideas can be generated without fear of ridicule. A moderator presents the question electronically to each participant, who then generates ideas and sends them electronically to the moderator. The moderator accumulates all responses into one list, which is then distributed for team comment. The comments are returned to the moderator for accumulation and dissemination. This process continues until a general consensus is reached. The technique is somewhat time-consuming and labor-intensive, but it is a good way to generate a list of ideas, especially if the participants are dispersed geographically.

INTERVIEWS   Interviewing is a useful technique used on many projects. The project leader and other key members of the team who have interview skills conduct personal one-on-one discussions with key stakeholders. The crucial aspect of successful interviewing is to make sure the stakeholders feel comfortable sharing ideas with the interviewer. The success of this technique is heavily dependent on the skills of the interviewer.

SWOT ANALYSIS   SWOT—an acronym for strengths, weaknesses, opportunities, and threats—was first defined and used during project selection in Chapter 4. SWOT analysis offers a framework with which to conduct a brainstorming session, sticky-note exercise, or a Delphi technique session. A key benefit of this technique is the focus on both sides of each issue: strengths versus weaknesses and opportunities versus threats. The brainstorming group is asked to list the strengths and weaknesses of the company surrounding the current project. Next, the group looks at potential threats or risks and the opportunities that exist from a successful project.

The **risk register** is the main deliverable from the risk identification and analysis process (see Figure 8-1). The risk register is a dynamic document that must be continually updated as a project progresses. The risk register consists of the following elements:

- *Risk*—This is the name of the risk, along with a short description. Some like to include a numbering scheme to make it easier to reference.
- *Trigger event*—This is an explanation of the event or events that signal to the person monitoring that this risk is about to happen or has happened; it involves looking at the root cause of the risk. For example, if a vendor hired to create a sizable portion of the code needed for the new application has been experiencing larger-than-normal turnover rates among employees, trigger event will be any missed or late milestones or software quality issues.
- *Responsible*—This is the name of the person (preferred) or group/department responsible for monitoring the risk and executing mitigation activities. Using the previous example, a software development project leader may be assigned responsibility for tracking a vendor's progress.
- *Consequence*—This is an explanation of the impact to the project if the risk occurs. Using the previous example, if a vendor is late with its part of a system, the entire project schedule will be delayed, also raising the project budget.
- *Probability*—This is an estimation of the likelihood that the risk will materialize and affect the project. The probability is often a qualitative rating (low, medium, high) or could be a more quantitative number.

- *Mitigation*—This is an explanation of the strategy being used to reduce the chances that the risk will occur. Using the previous example, say that the team decided to set up multiple two-week milestones for the vendor to keep an eye on the vendor's progress and make sure it doesn't start slipping.

Now that we've looked at some risk identification tools and techniques, let's look at the methods associated with performing a qualitative risk analysis (more subjective based) and a quantitative risk analysis (more mathematical and statistical based).

Performing Qualitative Risk Analysis

Qualitative risk analysis consists of subjective techniques used to determine the probability of occurrence and the project impact of identified risks. This usually involves a method that can be done quickly in a short period of time, with few resources. The output of this process updates the probability column of the risk register and aids a project team in prioritizing **mitigation strategies**. Not every risk identified needs to have a mitigation strategy. Mitigation requires time and money and should be reserved for risks that have a high probability of occurring and/or have a significant impact on a project. The following sections describe two techniques for performing qualitative risk analysis: interviews with subject matter experts (SMEs) and probability and impact matrixes.

INTERVIEWS   Just as interviews are used to identify risks in the first place, they can be used to assess the impact and probability of risks. A team can find more information about identified risks by interviewing individuals who have expertise in the affected areas. SMEs can come from anywhere in the company and potentially outside the organization. For example, say that an organization has decided to launch a major software initiative to install a SAP ERP application consisting of financial software, manufacturing software, and sales analysis software. The organization has never before implemented a system like this, so it decides to consult with outside experts, skilled in this type of software implementation, to build the risk register.

PROBABILITY AND IMPACT MATRIX   A probability and impact matrix aids a project team in prioritizing the risks that need more attention than others, based on either their probability of occurring or the size of the impact to the project or both. The matrix clearly shows what risks should be tracked and possibly have mitigation strategies created. Figure 8-2 shows an example of a probability and impact matrix. The columns represent the degree of impact to the project's scope, time, cost, and quality goals. This matrix example uses a five-level scale: low impact, low medium impact, medium impact, medium high impact, and high impact. SMEs determine the scores based on historical data. Table 8-1 describes the possible scores. Point values are sometimes used as scores (for example, a risk may be given a .1 instead of a low rating or both).

The next step is to use expert judgment and historical data to determine the probability that a risk will materialize. The values are the same as those used to assess the impact. A low rating means less than a 10 percent chance, a low medium rating means an 11 to 30 percent chance, a medium rating means a 50 percent chance, a medium high rating means a 70 percent chance, and a high rating means a 90 percent or higher chance.

TABLE 8-1   Risk Rating Scores

Risk (Rating Factor)	Category Description
Low (.1)	Little to zero impact on scope, time, cost, and/or quality objectives
Medium Low (.3)	Has some impact less than 5%; able to meet project objectives with minimal addition of resources
Medium (.5)	Impact in the range 10 to 20%; unable to meet all project objectives without additional resources or time
Medium High (.7)	Impact in the range 20% to 40%; unable to meet many of the project objectives; major changes in scope, time, cost required
High (.9)	Catastrophic impact; project will not be completed with 40% or higher effect on scope, time, cost, and/or quality objectives

Once a risk has been given both a probability score and an impact score, it should be placed in the proper cell in the matrix. If the risk falls into one of the shaded areas, the team should prepare mitigation strategies and monitor them closely. The team may decide that if the risk appears in the high/high cell that further quantitative analysis is required. The number of shaded cells depends on the organization's culture and risk utility (or the organization's support/tolerance of or need for risk).

The key issue with qualitative risk assessment is estimator bias. Estimator bias may include relationships with other experts and their ratings, personal motivation, predispositions, and bias toward the initial value. A disciplined approach to risk assessment can help avoid or reduce the impact of many of these biases.

Performing Quantitative Risk Analysis

Much like qualitative risk analysis, quantitative risk analysis attempts to estimate the impact a risk may have on a project as well as the probability that it will occur in order to assist project team members in preparing mitigation strategies. The key difference between the two analysis methods is that quantitative analysis is based on mathematical or statistical techniques to model the behavior of a particular risk. The decision about whether to use quantitative or qualitative analysis techniques is made on a project-by-project basis and even within a single project can be made on a risk-by-risk basis. For example, for its major ERP software project, the XYZ organization has decided that all 10 of the top risks must have quantitative analysis performed because the project is of major significance to the success of the organization. If the project fails, the company may have to file for bankruptcy. The XYZ organization is also involved in a small project to upgrade the company's virus protection software, using the same vendor's product. This project will only perform qualitative risk analysis on all identified risks.

The tools and techniques described in this section include decision tree analysis with expected monetary value (EMV) and Monte Carlo simulation.

DECISION TREE ANALYSIS WITH EMV   Decision tree analysis is generally used along with a graphical representation (Figure 8-3) that describes a set of options under consideration along with estimated implications of each option. The analysis consists of costs, revenues (or benefits), and probabilities for each option path. Notice that each of two options contains different paths that may be followed, with different probabilities. The EMV analysis technique

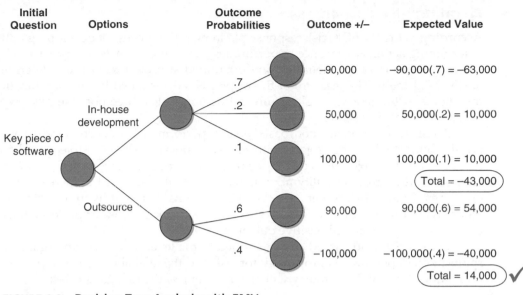

FIGURE 8-3 Decision Tree Analysis with EMV

is a statistical concept that calculates the average outcome when dealing with unknown future scenarios. Positive outcomes are expressed as positive values and negative outcomes as negative values. The sum of the probabilities for each option must equal 100 percent.

The decision depicted in Figure 8-3 is whether to outsource or develop in-house a key piece of software. If the in-house option is chosen, there are three possible outcomes: outright failure of the system, with a 70 percent probability and a negative outcome of –90,000; a partial success in meeting scope, time, and cost goals, with a 20 percent probability and a positive outcome of 50,000; and a 10 percent chance of complete success with a 100,000 outcome. The outcomes are then multiplied against their respective probabilities of success to obtain the EMV of each. The same calculations are conducted for each path in the second option of outsourcing. The EMVs are then added together for each path, and the total shows that the second option (outsourcing) is the better choice, with an EMV of 14,000.

MONTE CARLO SIMULATION Monte Carlo simulation was introduced back in Chapter 6 as an aid in building accurate time estimates for WBS activities. It can also be used during quantitative risk analysis to simulate the impact a risk may have on project goals. Based on the probabilities of various outcomes, similar to the decision tree analysis example, a simulation can be run multiple times, based on the frequency distribution, to determine the expected outcomes with probabilities. Simulation during the risk management process is generally used to determine cost and schedule outcomes using three-point estimates of task durations. The three-point estimates are based on the task's associated risks. For example, a simulation may show that the current project has a 95 percent chance of getting done in 15 months but only a 10 percent chance of getting done in 12 months, which is what was requested.

The risk values are then added to the appropriate column in the risk register. Remember that the process of risk management is an ongoing process and not done just at the beginning. Risks are monitored throughout the project, and, if needed, qualitative assessments and quantitative assessments are repeated.

Planning Risk Responses

According to the PMBOK, risk response planning is the process of developing options and determining actions to enhance opportunities and reduce threats to a project's objectives. Basically, once risks are identified and quantified, a project team must determine what to do about them. The measure of the response is determined by the organization's risk thresholds or tolerance for risk. Figure 8-4 demonstrates three possible risk preferences: averter, neutral, and seeker.

A risk averter organization, based on past performances or current industry segment, is only comfortable doing projects with small amounts of risk. As a project's risk increases, its utility for the project goes down, regardless of expected outcomes. Organizations that are risk neutral grow in utility at an equal pace with risk and the increase in expected outcomes. Finally, risk seekers may be organizations that exist in an industry or culture where risky projects are required to survive. Risk seekers look for projects that are risky due to their high expected positive outcomes.

Once a risk is identified and quantified to the level necessary, an organization's response will depend on its propensity for risk and the availability of resources to build a mitigation strategy. The strategy will be part of one of the four categories:

- *Risk avoidance*—Avoidance entails eliminating a specific threat or risk, usually by eliminating its causes, making a change in the design, making a change in requirements, or changing technology to remove the risk entirely. It's important to recognize that avoiding the risk may also avoid associated benefits.
- *Risk acceptance*—An organization can decide to accept the consequences if a risk occurs without trying to control it. In this situation, no mitigation strategy is deemed necessary, although you may set aside some contingency reserves for cost and schedule.
- *Risk transference*—An organization can shift the consequence of a risk and responsibility for its management to a third party that is internal or external to the organization (outsourcing), or it can move it to another department within the same company.
- *Risk mitigation*—An organization can reduce the impact of a risk event by reducing the probability of its occurrence. Organizations are making heavy use of prototyping and newer agile product development methodologies that include short development phases with heavy customer involvement and continuous testing as a mitigation strategy to lessen the risks associated with systems development projects.

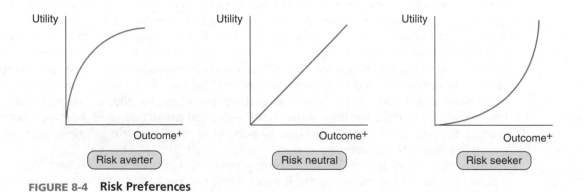

FIGURE 8-4   Risk Preferences

The final step after the risk response has been chosen is to update the risk register with the mitigation strategy, including fallback plans, contingency plans, and contingency reserves deemed appropriate. *Fallback plans* are used if the project cannot be completed as originally planned so an alternate destination needs to be sought. *Contingency plans* are put in place to allow for fluctuations that will allow the project to finish as originally planned. *Contingency reserves* are excess amounts of time, money, resources, and so on that are approved for the project and are used only if necessary in order for the project to finish as originally planned. Contingency plans use the contingency reserves to meet project objectives.

PROVEN STRATEGIES AND HINTS TO SUCCESS

The following is a list of ten items that many project managers overlook when performing risk management (Shacklett, 2012):

- Key personnel losses in user areas as they are reassigned or take a new job with a different company
- Merger and acquisition fallout, from a resource and technology perspective
- Poor communications (hurried, fragmented, incomplete, garbled, misunderstood)
- Carelessness with vendors, thorough research of key vendors is needed for performance, and what happens if they are acquired or go out of business
- Board engagement in decision making, sometimes upper management can get "too involved" in project decision making
- Distributed servers in remote locations, distributed support, improper environments
- Expert knowledge hoarding, either another department refuses to assist or the one key resource with all the answers is already allocated 150% on other projects
- Employee dating and spouses, need the right guidelines in place to make sure the project is unaffected when these go wrong
- Lack of documentation
- A poor disaster recovery plan, during and after the project

RISK MANAGEMENT PLANNING PROCESS

This section of the chapter lists the steps in the risk management planning process:

Step 1. **Build/choose the risk management plan format.** Organizations that have established guidelines and templates for a risk management plan simply choose the best one for the current project, based on selected metrics, such as project length, size, complexity, resources, and so on. For an organization that doesn't have a standard plan, a format similar to the one presented in this chapter needs to be defined.

Step 2. **Identify risks.** The project team and stakeholders are involved in identifying risks to the project.

Step 3. **Conduct risk assessment.** The team needs to assess each potential risk for impact and likelihood. Most risks will receive just a qualitative assessment, and others will need a more accurate detailed quantitative assessment.

Step 4. **Complete the risk register.** The team uses the list of risks identified in step 2 and the assessments created in step 3 to build the risk register.

Step 5. **Complete the risk management plan.** Now that risks have been identified, other elements of the plan can be completed: roles and responsibilities, risk register, methodology, schedule of activities, budget, and a list of any specific tools.

HOW TO CONDUCT THE RISK PLANNING PROCESSES

In this final section of the chapter, the R & S Amusements Services case study is used to demonstrate the process of building a risk management plan. This section walks through each of the process steps defined in the previous section. Before proceeding, take time to reread and review the R & S Amusements Services case study. Jeff and Kevin, the consultants from PPMS, are working with the leadership team at R & S Amusements Services to explain the risk management planning process.

Step 1: Build the Risk Management Plan

Jeff and Kevin brought to the meeting a copy of a risk management plan template they've used on several previous projects. Starting with a template greatly reduces the amount of time needed to begin building the plan. The sections of the template are as follows: revision history, statement of purpose, roles and responsibilities, documentation, methodology, risk categories, schedule for risk management activities, budget for risk management activities, risk management tools. After reviewing the template with R & S Amusements Services, the team began brainstorming ideas for risks on the asset management project.

Step 2: Perform Risk Identification

Kevin and Jeff conducted a sticky-note brainstorming session with the R & S Amusements Services leadership team, with the goal of identifying the risks that could potentially adversely affect the project. As a result of the session, the list of risks shown in Figure 8-5 was created, sorted by category.

Step 3: Perform a Risk Assessment

After the R & S Amusements Services leadership team identified the project risks, Jeff and Kevin facilitated the assessment of each risk by performing a quantitative analysis. A team member was assigned one or more risks, with the task of determining the probability of the risk occurring and the impact the risk would have on the project. Using the scale presented earlier in the chapter, Figure 8-6 presents the results of the analysis and a calculation of the resulting risk exposure.

Figure 8-7 shows the results of the analysis transferred to the probability and impact table. The shaded areas represent a risk exposure greater than .07, which is the threshold that the leadership team determined for mitigating risks. As indicated in Fig-

Risk List		
Risk No.	**Category**	**Risk Description**
①	Internal—Resources	Unavailable subject matter experts—The staff at R & S will not be dedicated to this project alone; they will still have to perform their regular duties.
②	Internal—Inexperience	Inexperienced team—Jeff and Kevin have many years of experience running IT projects but all of the team members do not.
③	Internal—Schedule	Schedule changes—With the possibility of scope changes and other issues, schedule changes may also be needed.
④	Technical—Requirements	Poor scope definition—Because the workers are new to project management and the use of technology to aid them in their asset management process, Jeff and Kevin need to make sure those requirements are captured accurately and reflect the true requirements of the project.
⑤	Project Management (PM)—Scope Risk	Scope creep—Jeff and Kevin need to make sure that a formal change control process is in place and is followed. This may be a challenge since the workers at are new to project management practices.
⑥	PM—Scope Risk	Scope changes—Due to the difficulties mentioned above in getting all of the requirements identified, scope changes will be inevitable.
⑦	PM—Plans	Unclear objectives—same issues as poor scope definition
⑧	PM—Plans	Unclear SOW or WBS—same issues as poor scope definition
⑨	External—Vendors & Suppliers	Because management has directed that a package will be purchased to implement the asset management requirements, there exists a risk that the purchased solution does not meet management's expectations in terms of functionality, cost, technical feasibility, or support.

FIGURE 8-5   **Asset Management Project Risk List**

ure 8-7, risks 1, 4, and 6 need to be managed. It is important to note that this may change based on future assessments because risk management planning is a reoccurring, continuous process.

Step 4: Complete the Risk Register

The next step in the risk management planning process is to complete the risk register with the prioritized risks. Figure 8-8 shows a risk register documenting the event that triggers a risk, the consequence of the risk happening, and the mitigation plan.

Risk Exposure				
Risk No.	Assignee	Risk Probability (RP)	Risk Impact (RI)	Risk Exposure RP * RI
●	Reid Lewis	High (.9)	Medium (.5)	.45
●	Team	Medium (.5)	Medium low (.3)	.15
●	Jeff Dunbar & Kevin Pullen	Medium (.5)	Medium low (.3)	.15
●	Jeff Dunbar & Kevin Pullen	Medium (.5)	Medium (.5)	.25
●	Jeff Dunbar & Kevin Pullen	Medium (.5)	Medium low (.3)	.15
●	Jeff Dunbar & Kevin Pullen	Medium (.5)	Medium (.5)	.25
●	Jeff Dunbar & Kevin Pullen	Medium low (.3)	Low (.1)	.03
●	Jeff Dunbar & Kevin Pullen	Medium low (.3)	Low (.1)	.03
●	Reid Lewis	Low (.1)	Medium (.5)	.05

FIGURE 8-6   **Asset Management Project Qualified Analysis Results**

Impact ⟶	Low	Low Med.	Medium	Med. High	High
Probability Low		❼ ❽			
Low Medium			❷ ❸ ❺		
Medium	❾		❹ ❻		❶
Medium High					
High					

FIGURE 8-7   **Asset Management Project Prioritized Risks**

Risk Register

Project: R & S Asset Management Project Date: October 21, 2006

Risk No.	Risk	Trigger Event	Responsible	Consequence	Probability	Mitigation
1	Unavailable subject matter experts—The staff at R & S Amusements Services will not be dedicated to this project alone; they will still have to perform their regular duties.	Each team member has been assigned a number of hours per week to be dedicated to the project. If the actual hours spent are less than 80% of the assigned hours, mitigation should occur.	Reid Lewis	Lack of team involvement will have an adverse affect on schedule	High (.9)	Temporary personnel will be hired for low skilled jobs. Skilled employees will be transferred from other sites to handle overflow.
4	Poor scope definition—Because the workers at R & S are new to project management and the use of technology to aid them in their asset management process, Jeff and Kevin need to make sure those requirements are captured accurately and reflect the true requirements of the project.	Requirements defects greater than 25%.	Jeff Dunbar & Kevin Pullen	Adverse effect on schedule, cost, & quality	Medium (.5)	Project will employ newer agile methodologies which include short development phases with heavy customer involvement and continuous testing.
6	Scope changes—Due to the difficulties mentioned above in getting all of the requirements identified, scope changes will be inevitable.	Change requests greater than 25%.	Jeff Dunbar & Kevin Pullen	Adverse effect on schedule & cost	Medium (.5)	Project will employ newer agile methodologies which include short development phases with heavy customer involvement and continuous testing.

FIGURE 8-8   Asset Management Project Risk Register

Step 5: Complete the Risk Management Plan

The final step in risk management planning is to complete the risk management plan. A full risk management plan for the asset management project for R & S Amusements Services is provided below.

Asset Management Project
Risk Management Plan

Prepared by:

Jeff Dunbar &
Kevin Pullen
Of
Premier Project Management Services

October 31, 2007

Version 1.0 Draft 1

Risk Management Plan for Asset Management   *10/31/07*

TABLE OF CONTENTS

1. REVISION HISTORY

Author(s)	Date	Reasons For Changes	Version
Jeff Dunbar & Kevin Pullen	10/31/07	Initial Draft	1.0 Draft1

2. STATEMENT OF PURPOSE

This document describes the risk management approach and procedures that will govern the risk management process for the Asset Management project. This includes descriptions of the methodology used, the roles and responsibilities of team members, budget, timing and schedule of risk management activities, risk categories, risk probability and impact scales, and how risks will be tracked and communicated.

3. ROLES AND RESPONSIBILITIES

Project Manager   The Project Manager will assign a Risk Officer to the project, and identify this individual on the project's organization chart. The Project Manager and other members of the Project Management team, *Reid Lewis, Diana Brooks, Elaine Henry, Helen Futz, Mark Lewis from R & S and Jeff Dunbar and Kevin Pullen,* shall meet biweekly to review the status of all risk mitigation efforts, review the exposure assessments for any new risk items, and redefine the project's priority risk list.

Risk Officer   The Risk Officer will coordinate the risk identification and analysis activities, maintain the project's risk register, notify project management of new risk items, and report risk resolution status to management.

Project Member Assigned a Risk   The Risk Officer will assign each newly identified risk to a project member, who will assess the exposure and probability for the risk factor and report the results of that analysis back to the Risk Officer. Assigned project members are also responsible for performing the steps of the mitigation plan and reporting progress to the Risk Officer biweekly.

4. DOCUMENTATION

Risk Register
The risk factors identified and managed for this project will be accumulated in a risk register, which is located in a document called *Asset Management Risk Register*. The format of the Risk Register is presented in Appendix A.

Risk Data Items
The following information will be stored for each project risk:

Risk-   name and short description
Trigger-   action(s) preceding the risk occurring
Responsible-   person or group responsible for monitoring and mitigation
*Consequence-*key project impact if risk occurs
Probability-   qualitative or quantitative probability of occurring
Mitigation-   strategy being used to reduce likelihood

Closing Risks
A risk item can be considered closed when it meets the following criteria:

The planned mitigation action has been successfully completed eliminating the risk or has changed the impact and/or probability such that it currently poses no issue to the project.

5. METHODOLOGY

Risk Identification

Task	Participants
The project leadership team will conduct brainstorming sessions (utilizing the Delphi Technique) to identify project risks. These sessions will be conducted at the beginning of each project phase. The candidate risks will be analyzed producing the final list which will be documented in the Asset Management Risk Register.	*Reid Lewis, Diana Brooks, Elaine Henry, Helen Futz, Mark Lewis from R & S and Jeff Dunbar and Kevin Pullen.*

Risk Assessment

Task	Participants
The Risk Officer will assign each risk to an individual project member, who will estimate the probability the risk could become a problem (scale of 0.1 (low), 0.3, 0.5, 0.7, 0.9 (high)) and the impact if it does (scale of 0.1(low), 0.3, 0.5, 0.7, 0.9 (high)).	*Assigned Project Member*

The individual analyzed risk factors are collected, reviewed, and adjusted if necessary by the team. The list of risk factors is sorted by descending risk exposure (probability times impact).	*Risk Officer*

Risk Mitigation Planning

Task	Participants
The project leadership team will meet and select one of four risk mitigation strategies (risk avoidance, risk acceptance, risk transference, risk mitigation) for each of the top priority risks, or those risk factors having an estimated exposure greater than .07.	*Reid Lewis, Diana Brooks, Elaine Henry, Helen Futz, Mark Lewis from R & S and Jeff Dunbar and Kevin Pullen.*
For each of the top priority risks, the project leadership team will determine actions that will reduce either the probability of the risk materializing into a problem, or the severity of the exposure if it does.	*Reid Lewis, Diana Brooks, Elaine Henry, Helen Fuitz, Mark Lewis from R & S and Jeff Dunbar and Kevin Pullen.*
The mitigation plans for the assigned risk items are documented in the risk register.	*Risk Officer*

Risk Monitoring & Control

Task	Participants
The status and effectiveness of each mitigation action is reported to the Risk Officer every two weeks.	*Assigned individual*
The probability and impact for each risk item reevaluated and modified if appropriate.	*Risk Officer*
If any new risk items have been identified, they are analyzed as were the items on the original risk register and added to the risk register.	*Risk Officer*
The *Risk Register* is regenerated based on the updated probability and impact for each remaining risk.	*Risk Officer*

	Any risk factors for which mitigation actions are not being effectively carried out, or whose risk exposure is rising, may be escalated to an appropriate level of management for visibility and action.	*Risk Officer*

Risk Response

Task	Participants
Each individual who is responsible for executing a risk mitigation plan carries out the mitigation activities.	*Assigned individual*

Lessons Learned

Task	Participants
On a monthly basis the Risk Officer documents risk related lessons learned.	*Risk Officer*

6. RISK CATEGORIES

Risk Breakdown Structure   The following figure depicts the high-level risk categories and subcategories that will be used on the Asset Management project.

7. SCHEDULE FOR RISK MANAGEMENT ACTIVITIES

Risk Management Plan	The risk register will be completed and made available to the project team by *11/15/07.*
Risk Identification	A risk workshop will be held on approximately *11/20/07.*
Risk Register	The risk register will be completed and made available to the project team by *11/30/07.*
Review	The Risk Management Plan and Risk Register will be reviewed and approved by the Project Manager approximately by *12/05/07.*
Risk Tracking	The status of risk management activities and mitigation success will be reviewed at the conclusion of each life cycle phase and be a factor in the decision to proceed. The risk management plan will be updated at that time.

8. BUDGET FOR RISK MANAGEMENT ACTIVITIES

Labor	$12,500.00 with a reserve of $5,000.00 has been budgeted for risk management activities. Individuals performing risk management tasks should log their time against account number RS-AM-2007-1035.

9. RISK MANAGEMENT TOOLS

Microsoft Word will be used to document the Risk Management Plan and Risk Register. Both documents will be stored in the project repository.

Appendix A.

Risk Register					
Project: Project Name				Date: Current Date	
Name	Trigger Down	Responses	Consequence	Probability	Mitigations
***	***	***	***	***	***

Risk Register Format

Chapter Review

1. Every IT project, regardless of size, complexity, location, or organization, faces risks and must follow a formal risk management process.

2. The main objective of managing risk on a project is to increase the probability and impact of positive outcomes and to decrease the probability and impact of negative outcomes.

3. Risk is defined as the possibility of loss or injury, or it can be defined as a function of project impact and likelihood of occurring.

4. The PMBOK from PMI defines the following processes as part of risk management planning: risk identification, qualitative risk analysis, quantitative risk analysis, risk response planning, and risk monitoring and control.

5. The key deliverable from the risk management planning process is the risk management plan, which consists of the following elements: methodology, roles and responsibilities, budgeting information, timing of risk management activities, risk categories explored, list and definition of risk probability and impact scale formats, and explanation of each element of the risk register.

6. The risk identification process attempts to identify all risks associated with a given project, utilizing the following techniques: broad organizational categories, analogy, brainstorming, interviews, Delphi technique, and SWOT analysis.

7. A key risk-tracking tool is the risk register, which consists of the following elements: risk name and description, trigger event, responsible person, consequence to project, probability of occurrence, and mitigation strategies, if any.

8. Qualitative risk analysis is a subjective method for qualifying each risk for impact and probability of occurrence. It involves conducting interviews with SMEs and creating a probability/impact matrix.

9. Quantitative risk analysis is a mathematical, statistically based approach to assessing a risk's impact and probability of occurrence. It consists of decision tree analysis with EMV and Monte Carlo simulation

10. Risk response planning is the process of developing options and determining actions to enhance opportunities and reduce threats to a project's objectives. A risk response should fall into one of the following choices: risk avoidance, risk acceptance, risk transference, or risk mitigation.

Glossary

mitigation strategy   A process that attempts to reduce the likelihood and/or impact of a risk to the success of a project goal.

qualitative analysis   A process that involves using subjective methods to qualify each risk for impact and probability of occurrence.

risk   An event that, if it occurs, will have a negative impact on one or more of the following: project scope, time, cost, quality, or resources.

risk register   Contains the outcomes from the risk identification and assessment analysis processes.

Review Questions

1. Explain why projects have risks.
2. What are the two major components of risk?
3. List and explain the two main objectives of risk management.
4. Explain how risk management can allow an organization to be more aggressive and take on riskier projects.
5. Explain why risk management should be done on every IT project but the amount of risk management varies by project.
6. Explain what is meant by crisis management and why many organizations continue to exist in this type of environment.
7. List each of the key pieces of information that make up a project risk management plan and briefly describe each piece.
8. List and explain the common risks that all IT projects share.
9. Explain why it can be difficult to find and define all risks on a project.
10. Explain how broad organizational categories are used to help identify risks.
11. Describe how a brainstorming session should be conducted to get the best results.
12. Describe the steps of the Delphi technique.
13. List the contents and explain the function of the risk register.
14. Describe the key differences between doing a qualitative risk assessment and doing a quantitative risk assessment.
15. Describe the process of building a probability and impact matrix and how the results are used to aid in risk management planning.
16. Describe the drawbacks to using qualitative risk analysis techniques.
17. Define and explain how to assess risks with the decision tree analysis technique using EMV.
18. Define and explain how Monte Carlo simulation is used to assess risks.
19. Explain what is meant by an organization's risk utility.
20. Explain each of the four categories of risk response.

Problems and Exercises

1. Explain the statement made by Tom DeMarco and Timothy Lister in their book *Waltzing with Bears* (2003): "If a project has no risks, don't do it. A project without risk also is without any real value."
2. Explain the process of SWOT analysis and then conduct a SWOT analysis for the R & S Amusements Services case study, adding to information already addressed in this chapter.
3. Obtain a free copy of simulation software (see Appendix B for suggestions on where to find one) and conduct your own trials for the R & S Amusements Services project.
4. Explain the difference between a fallback plan and a contingency plan. Create one of each for the R & S Amusements Services case study in this chapter, based on the risks identified in this chapter. Pick one of the risks and explain its impact to the project and your fallback and contingency plans.
5. You have been asked to use decision tree analysis with EMV to assess the risk in selecting among three different projects, each with unique expenses, risks, and expected monetary outcomes, with estimates shown below:

	Probability/Outcome Complete Success	Probability/Outcome Partial Success	Probability/Outcome Complete Failure
Project 1	20% / $60,000	40% / $50,000	40% / $65,000
Project 2	15% / $75,000	55% / $35,000	30% / $70,000
Project 3	10% / $150,000	20% / $75,000	70% / $80,000

a. Draw a decision tree analysis chart with values from the table shown here, filling in the amounts for EMV totals.

b. Which project presents the best alternative, based on this information, for a risk-averse organization?

c. Which project presents the best alternative, based on this information, for a risk-seeking organization?

6. Change the probabilities in question 5 to the following and reevaluate your answers.

Project 1 = 25, 30, 45
Project 2 = 20, 40, 40
Project 3 = 20, 35, 45

7. Following are four short case study scenarios that represent risk response category choices. Match each scenario with one of the four possible risk responses (accept, avoid, transfer, mitigate) and explain your answer.

a. Two critical tasks in the project you are running deal with complex database design issues. You have negotiated with the supervisor of the data management group to get the group's best worker in this area, John. The problem is that a rumor has surfaced that John is looking for a new job and may leave the company at any time. To make sure your project will be less affected if John leaves, you have built some contingency funds and extra time into the schedule. You have also contacted several local consulting companies that have expertise in database design, just in case.

b. The current project is to add a new information section to the company's public web site for the marketing department. The project is not particularly complex, but you have worked with the marketing department before and know that the people there are difficult to work with because of their lack of technology experience and their travel schedules. As the project leader, you have decided to adopt a more agile development methodology with short development time intervals. You have also asked the marketing department to dedicate one individual as a key contact.

c. After researching all the possible software applications on the market, your team has reduced the list to just two choices. The first application delivers on 95 percent of the needed requirements, but the vendor is very new and has a small customer base. The second application delivers on 85 percent of the needed requirements; the vendor has been in business for many years and has a large customer base. The company, being risk averse, decides on the second application package.

d. The current proposed project is to create a custom software application, which will add functionality identified during the recent gap analysis between the purchased accounting software package and the user requirements. The custom software must interface with the new software, but your organization has no one trained in the new software application. The project team has decided to hire a consulting company to develop the new application.

8. Create a probably/impact matrix based on the information below. Explain which of the risks needs to be further analyzed and/or watched closely during the project.

	Impact	Probability
Key piece of code construction outsourced	Medium high	Medium high
Budget constraints	Medium	Medium low
Poorly understood requirements	Medium low	Low
Change management	Low	Medium
Some key users located in a different location from IT staff	Medium	High
Technology used for development is new to IT staff	Medium high	High
Project manager assigned to project is new to the company	High	High

9. List each of the nine knowledge areas defined in the Project Management Institute's PMBOK. List and explain at least one risk per knowledge area that IT projects might experience.

Projects and Research

1. Research articles written about IT projects that failed and discuss the risks that, if addressed, could have potentially changed the outcome.
2. Outsourcing portions of IT projects is an increasingly common practice. Research the risks inherent in projects for which all or some of the tasks are outsourced. Are there any additional issues related to projects whose tasks are outsourced to firms outside the United States? Explain.
3. Search the Internet for examples of risk management plans and compare them to the one presented in this chapter.
4. Research the risk management software applications available on the market and write a paper summarizing their features/capabilities. List some of the disadvantages of using these tools.
5. Research and then write a paper describing mitigation strategies for the following IT project risks:
   a. Scope creep (continually expanding requirements)
   b. Software quality issues
   c. Customer involvement
   d. Management commitment
   e. Unachievable project schedule and/or budget
   f. High project team turnover

MINICASE

1. *Background:* As stated in this chapter, a project manager's objective is not to remove all risk from a project—that simply can't be done—but to identify and manage risks to the benefit of the project. The leadership team at R & S Amusements Services has just spent several hours going through the process of identifying project risks, assessing their probability and impact, and preparing the resulting risk management plan—a plan that will hopefully help ensure the success of the project.

   Current Situation 1: Jeff Dunbar and Kevin Pullen of PPMS were sitting in Jeff's office, reviewing the risk management plan they just completed with the help of Reid Lewis, Diana Brooks, Elaine Henry, Heidi Cosgray, and Mark Lewis of R & S Amusements Services. Both Jeff and Kevin were wondering if the team had performed an adequate job of not only identifying all the possible risks concerning the project but also correctly assigning the probability of occurrence.

   Discussion: Review the minicases at the end of Chapters 2, 3, 4, and 7. What additional risks, if any, should be identified concerning the working relationship with Mark Lewis, the hiring of A.J., the problems with Heidi Cosgray and service management, and the current business problems with R & S Amusements Services? If there are additional risks, what is your estimate of the probability of their occurrence? What is your estimate of the impact to the project?

   Current Situation 2: Diana Brooks and Mark Lewis of R & S Amusements Services were discussing with Reid Lewis of R & S and Jeff Dunbar and Kevin Pullen from PPMS the identified risk "Unavailable subject matter experts—the staff at R & S Amusements Services (R & S) will not be dedicated to this project alone; they will still have to perform their regular duties." Diana had been assigned the task of assigning the probability of occurrence of the risk and assigned it a .9 probability. Mark had disagreed with that assessment, saying that it was way out of line and should be no higher than .3. Mark told those present that keeping the probability at .9 was a mistake and doing so would create a flawed risk management plan.

   Discussion: How would you explain to Mark that the plan is not flawed? How would you resolve the disagreement between Mark and Diana? What technique(s) would you use to determine the proper probability of this risk and any other risk on the project?

Suggested Readings

Boehm, B. (1989). *Software risk management*. Los Alamitos, CA: IEEE Computer Society Press.

Charette, R.N. (1989). *Software engineering risk analysis and management*. New York: McGraw-Hill.

Conrow, E.H. (2003). *Effective risk management: Some keys to success*. Reston, VA: American Institute of Aeronautics and Astronautics.

DeMarco, T. (1997). *The deadline: A novel about project management*. New York: Dorset House Publishing.

DeMarco, T., & Lister, T. (2003). *Waltzing with bears: Managing risk on software projects*. New York: Dorset House Publishing.

Fairley, R. (1994). Risk management: For software projects. *IEEE Software* 11(3):57–67.

Jaafari, A. (2001). Management of risks, uncertainties and opportunities on projects: Time for a fundamental shift. *International Journal of Project Management* 19(2):89–101.

Jones, C. (1994). *Assessment and control of software risks*. Upper Saddle River, NJ. Yourdon Press Prentice Hall.

Keil, M., Cule, P., Lyytinen, K., & Schmidt, R. (1998). A framework for identifying software project risks. *Communications of the ACM* 41(11):76–83.

Project Management Institute (PMI). (2004). *A guide to the project management body of knowledge*, 3rd ed. Newton Square, PA: PMI.

Shacklett, M. (2012, December 10). 10 IT risk management issues that are often overlooked. Retrieved from www.techrepublic.com/blog/10things/10-it-risk-management-issues-that-are-often-overlooked/3516?tag=content;siu-container.

Wideman, R.M. (1992). *Project and program risk management: A guide to managing project risks and opportunities*. Newton Square, PA: Project Management Institute.

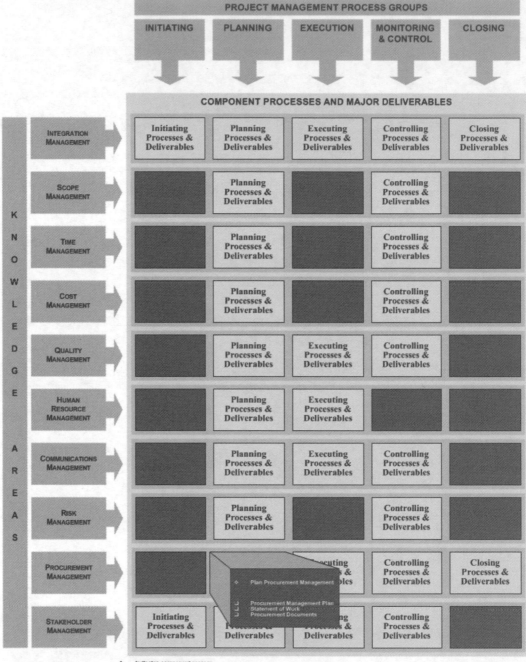

9

Project Procurement Planning

R & S Amusements Services

Event 9

Setting *It is now two weeks since the meeting described in Event 8 and the project leaders have convened in a small conference room located outside Reid Lewis's office at R & S Amusements Services. Those in attendance include Reid Lewis, Diana Brooks, and Mark Lewis from R & S and Jeff Dunbar and Kevin Pullen from Premier Project Management Services.*

REID   Good morning, everyone. How is everything going?

JEFF   Extremely well, actually. We've made great progress so far.

REID   That's good news! So I believe the topic for today's meeting is planning what we want or have to buy—is that correct?

KEVIN   *[Laughing]* In a way you're right, Reid! We call it *procurement planning*, and it involves planning for those elements of the project that will be bought or created from someone outside the project team or R & S Amusements.

MARK   More planning! Ugh!

[Jeff and Kevin laugh]

JEFF   I can assure you, Mark, that there is light at the end of the tunnel. When we identified and documented the requirements for this project, we talked about the fact that certain elements potentially would have to be pur-chased. Once we performed the analysis—we call it make/buy analysis—we determined that we will have to procure the software that will provide the asset tracking functionality as well as the hardware that is required to run the software that the technicians will use.

KEVIN   In addition, because one of the required functions of the new system is the mapping capability—as you recall, it is the ability to produce maps and directions to the locations where your equipment is installed as well as determining the most cost- and time-effective routes to service and collect from the locations—this functionality will need to be outsourced to an external development company.

MARK   *[Looking puzzled]* What does *outsourcing* mean?

KEVIN   Basically, outsourcing means hiring someone from outside R & S Amusements to perform work. For example, Reid outsourced the management of this project to Jeff and me, and hopefully he still thinks that was a good idea. *[All laughing]*

MARK   I see. But why do we have to go outside for the mapping functionality?

JEFF   Good question! It is because we don't have the means or know how to write the software ourselves, and it doesn't make sense to hire a full-time employee to do it. That would be very expensive, and after the project was done, what would you have that person do?

MARK   That makes sense. But who is going to maintain the software after it is written? What if it has bugs? Or what if we need changes?

JEFF   More great questions! Those are issues we will have to work out with the company we contract with. That is why it is important that we plan for it now. It is in your best interests to create the proper documents such as contracts to protect you in case someone can't deliver as promised or the hardware and software don't function as advertised. We want to minimize the risk of the project not being successful.

REID   Makes perfect sense to me. So how do we start planning for all this?

JEFF   Let's start by discussing what documents are going to be required, such as the statement of work and . . .

MARK   The statement of what? You and Kevin always like to speak in a foreign language, don't you? Do you call it *PM speak*? I've learned so many new terms, my head has been hurting for months.

KEVIN   Jeff this one is all yours. *[Smiling]*

JEFF   Thanks! *[Laughing]* Mark, the statement of work is a document that describes . . .

(To be continued)

(This chapter provides instructions for building the procurement plan, statement of work, and other procurement documents as well as providing completed examples.)

CHAPTER PREVIEW AND OBJECTIVES

This chapter, which discusses the procurement management plan, is the final chapter that deals with building parts of the project management plan. *Procurement* refers to all the elements of a project that will be bought or created from someone outside the project team or organization. In order to create the procurement management plan, several other project artifacts must already exist, including the work breakdown structure (WBS), the WBS dictionary, the project schedule, and the scope statement.

As you read this chapter, you will:

- Understand how to create an accurate and complete statement of work (SOW)
- Understand how to create project procurement documents, such as the request for proposal (RFP) and request for quote (RFQ)

- Understand what a contract is and how to decide which type to use
- Be able to identify and understand the risks involved in the procurement process

AN INTRODUCTION TO PROCUREMENT MANAGEMENT PLANNING

A project team must decide, in the course of planning, what activities and items it will need to purchase or buy from a vendor or seller in another department in the company or in another organization on the other side of the planet. (This chapter describes the process used to make this decision.) The team members might change their minds about this decision halfway through the project—and that's okay. Unfortunately, many projects miss deadlines or run over budget because the team tries to do something in-house only to find out that it doesn't have the time or the expertise to complete the work and must then procure the product or service. The reverse also happens: A team may first decide to hire a vendor to do the work and then have to do the work in-house because the vendor can't deliver. After learning the tools and techniques of procurement management planning, you can avoid these changes during the execution of the project and achieve a successful procurement process result.

Outsourcing for organizations in the United States and all over the rest of the world is continuing to increase, utilizing more and more of an information technology (IT) department's budget. IDC, a leading market research firm, reports that the global market for services (for example, data center management, help desk support, network operations, applications maintenance, disaster recovery services) was $84.6 billion in 2004 and is estimated to reach $112.5 billion by the end of 2009. The top three outsourcing firms in the world are IBM, EDS, and Computer Sciences Corporation (CSC). (Gilbert, 2005) U.S. federal spending on IT outsourcing increased from $6.6 billion in 2002 to nearly $15 billion by the end of 2007. Gartner predicts that offshore IT services spending will grow by 40 percent in the United States and by as much as 60 percent in Europe. (Gartner, 2008) Based on these current trends, the project procurement process is becoming a major competency at which organizations must become proficient and excel.

The term **procurement** has several synonyms, such as purchasing or outsourcing. The project management body of knowledge (PMBOK) from the Project Management Institute (PMI) defines the processes of the Procurement Management knowledge area as plan procurement management, conduct procurements, control procurements, and close procurements. This chapter covers the processes involved in planning procurements.

The procurement planning process is used to determine what to procure, when to procure it, and how to procure it. It also involves documenting requirements, which is usually done in a procurement document, such as a SOW, RFQ, or RFP. This process also involves identifying potential sellers—groups or organizations that offer a service or product for rent or sale. Not all projects have a procurement process; sometimes a project is small enough that all work is handled using the organization's current hardware, software, and personnel. If the procurement process is needed, all steps in the process defined later in this chapter must be completed to help ensure a successful result. As in other planning processes described in this text, many of the processes occur at the same time, but they are discussed here one at a time to aid in reader understanding. How the steps of the process may overlap is explained, where appropriate, in the chapter.

PROJECT MANAGEMENT CONCEPTS: PROCUREMENT MANAGEMENT PLANNING

Many project teams view the procurement process as a "project within a project," meaning that the entire procurement process is run as a project, with initiation, plan, execute, control, and closeout steps. As you learn more about the procurement process, you might agree. The remainder of this chapter deals with initiation and planning for procurement. Chapter 11 covers the execution of the procurement process, and Chapter 13 covers the closeout step.

Planning Procurements

The key goal of the procurement planning process is to determine which project needs can best be met by sellers or vendors outside the project team. Sellers can exist within the same organization or in different organizations nearby or on the other side of the globe. Creating and signing contracts with organizations outside the project team's company is referred to as *outsourcing*, and if the seller is located in another country, it is referred to as *offshoring*. (Some other recent trends, such as nearsourcing and rural sourcing, are discussed in Chapter 14.) The process described in this chapter will work in any procurement situation, regardless of where the seller is located. But even though the overall process is the same, there are some unique tools and techniques needed when dealing with sellers located in other countries; these are covered more fully in Chapter 14.

As mentioned earlier in this chapter, the first step in the procurement process is deciding whether you need to procure something. To make this decision, a project team conducts a **make-or-buy analysis**, making sure to include subject matter experts (SMEs). A make-or-buy analysis will help the team determine whether it makes more sense to perform the activities within the project team or to contract with a seller. Key decision points include cost, human resources, time, strategic direction, and risk. The final make-or-buy decision is generally a combination of all five decision points.

In order to make an informed decision, a complete cost analysis must be done. The following are some cost considerations for both decisions:

- Make:
  - Labor costs (that is, internal cost of human resources)
  - Human resources knowledge; if needed knowledge is not present, training will be needed
  - Cost to prepare and maintain all product artifacts (progress reports, testing, schedules, and so on)
  - Rework costs, such as costs for requirements changes and fixing bugs
  - Ongoing support costs, such as day-to-day maintenance and updates after implemented
  - Opportunity costs (because while team members are working on this project, other items are not getting done)
- Buy:
  - Cost associated with the procurement process
  - Cost to manage the relationship
  - Initial purchase cost, along with ongoing support costs

IT human resources are, for most organizations, in short supply; that is, most organizations don't have enough qualified resources to perform all the projects they have requests to execute. During a make-or-buy analysis, an organization must look objectively at the skills required to make the product and then evaluate current resources for a match and availability. If no skill match is found, the choices are to train current human resources, hire new resources that already have the relevant skills, or outsource the work to a seller who has the relevant skills.

IT projects today are time critical for most organizations. If a project can't be done fast enough, its value is diminished, as the competition will gain a market advantage. In order to meet time constraints, a project team may need resources from outside the organization.

The long-range strategic direction of the organization must be used in the decision process. The project team performing a make-or-buy decision must also look at the needs of the organization in the future. What makes sense for one project in isolation may not make the most sense for the future of the entire organization. For example, an organization might need to concentrate all of its efforts into research and development of new products to keep pace in the market and not invest resources in software development. In this scenario, the organization has decided to concentrate on core competencies. Therefore, it would be best to outsource any new development or new software purchase.

Based on the information from the other decision criteria, the team needs to assign a risk value to each of the outcomes—one for a make decision and one for a buy decision. Understanding the organization's culture for risk (adverse, neutral, or seeking) will help the team make this choice.

Consider this final note on the make-or-buy analysis: Organizations have several choices available when deciding to purchase a product or service from a seller: lease, rent, or buy. Each choice will have different cost considerations. Leasing or renting is generally done to lessen the upfront cost and the disposal cost of the product. A lease or rent returns the product back to the seller at the conclusion of the contract. If the organization will have no further use for the item past the end of the contract, then this may be preferred over purchasing the product. Leasing or renting might also present an attractive choice for organizations that need to be very conservative with their cash on hand.

The rest of this chapter assumes that a decision has been made to procure a product or service. The next questions that need to be answered are: How much? When? and From whom to purchase? The "how much" question is answered based on the scope statement and the WBS and then defined in the SOW. The "when" question is defined using the previously defined project schedule, which may need to be adjusted, based on vendor selection and availability. Finally, the "from whom" question is answered by following the conducting procurements process, which is explained in Chapter 11 of this text.

Understanding Types of Contracts

The seller/buyer relationship is based on a signed contract. There are many different types of contracts, and unfortunately, many seller/buyer relationships have become difficult because the wrong type of contract was used. In fact, in many documented cases, a whole outsourced project has failed due to the wrong contract being used or key concepts being left out of the contract. In most IT outsourced projects, it is extremely important to use the correct type of contract for both the seller and the buyer.

Contracts generally fall into one of three broad categories: fixed-price or lump-sum, cost-reimbursable, and time and material. Each of these categories is explained next, along with a description of where each is most appropriate.

FIXED-PRICE, OR LUMP-SUM, CONTRACTS   A fixed-price, or lump-sum, contract is appropriate when the SOW is sufficiently detailed and stable and the seller can prepare an accurate fixed price for completing the work. The seller is obligated to complete 100 percent of the work at the negotiated contract value. Because of this, the seller assumes a large portion of the risk. This type of arrangement presents some negative issues for the buyer as well if the seller builds into the price an excessive amount of contingency funds. The buyer would end up paying a larger price than may be needed to complete the work. Another issue for the buyer concerns the financial viability of the seller. If the seller grossly underestimates the time and cost to complete the work and partway through the project must stop work or dissolve the business, the buyer is faced with a decision. The organization can agree to pay extra fees to get the seller to complete the project, cancel the contract and select a new seller, or take the seller to court in an attempt to get the project completed, but this process is usually very long and expensive. All three choices result in product delays and additional cost. For these reasons, this type of contract should be used only in small, well-defined, non-critical projects.

COST-REIMBURSABLE CONTRACTS   Some contracts specify reimbursement (payment) of the seller's actual costs plus a fee, typically representing the seller's profit. The seller's costs contain both direct and indirect costs. In many cases, the indirect costs are calculated as a percentage of the direct costs. Cost-reimbursable contracts include incentive clauses based on the seller meeting certain project objectives, such as schedule targets or cost targets. The seller is rewarded with bonus payments. There are three common types of cost-reimbursable contracts:

- *Cost-plus-fee (CPF) or cost-plus-percentage of cost (CPPC)*—The seller is reimbursed for allowable (agreed to by buyer) costs plus a fee, calculated as a percentage (again agreed to by the buyer) of the actual costs. The extra fee will vary, based on the actual cost of the project. The buyer typically has the option to audit the books of the seller to confirm costs expended. This type of contract does not provide much of an incentive for the seller to reduce costs because the buyer has agreed to pay a percentage of them above the fixed amount.
- *Cost-plus-fixed-fee (CPFF)*—The seller is reimbursed for allowable costs plus a fixed fee, calculated as a percentage of the allowable costs. The fee is determined at the time the contract is signed. For example, a project originally estimated to cost $50,000 may also involve a fixed fee of $5,000. If the project is completed by the seller at a cost of $60,000, the seller would receive only the $50,000 plus the $5,000, for a total of $55,000.
- *Cost-plus-incentive-fee (CPIF)*—The seller is reimbursed for allowable costs plus a predetermined fee, an incentive bonus, based on meeting certain time and cost objectives. In many CPIF contracts, both the buyer and seller benefit when the actual final cost is less than expected, based on a predetermined sharing formula. CPIF offers a

seller more profit if costs are reduced or performance is improved and less profit if costs are raised or performance goals are not met. The following two examples illustrate how CPIF contracts work.

1. Sharing formula 85/15 (85 percent by buyer and 15 percent by seller)
   Allowable cost: $50,000
   Target fee: $3,750
   Maximum fee: $6,750
   Minimum fee: $1,500
   Project result:
       Seller completes the project at a cost of $45,000.
       Seller is paid $45,000 + ($50,000 − $45,000* .15) + $3,750 = $49,500
       Seller profit = $4,500

2. Sharing formula 85/15
   Allowable cost: $50,000
   Target fee: $3,750
   Maximum fee: $6,750
   Minimum fee: $1,500
   Project result:
       • Seller completes the project at a cost of $55,000.
       • Seller is paid $55,000 + $1,500 = $56,500
       • Seller profit = $1,500

Cost-reimbursable contracts work best in situations when the size of the project makes it difficult to define 100 percent of the tasks, thus making the budget estimate less accurate. This category of contracts offers the opportunity for the buyer and seller to share some of the project's risks.

TIME AND MATERIAL (T&M) CONTRACTS   Time and material contracts assign all the risk to the buyer and virtually none to the seller. The seller is reimbursed for all previously defined costs and additional material costs of the seller to complete the product. The defined costs are generally determined on a per-unit basis, such as the hourly rate charge for a resource multiplied by the number of hours the resource works on the project. Many of these projects have no upper limit assigned, so the seller has little incentive to complete the project at a minimal cost. These contracts are mainly used when the scope of the work cannot be defined up front and a seller is hired and works until the project/problem is completed. For example, say that a company's Microsoft Exchange email server is not working, and the current staff have been unable to figure out the problem. A consultant is hired at $200 per hour to work until the problem is fixed.

Choosing the Correct Contract Type

As mentioned earlier, the type of contract signed, along with the specific contract terms and conditions, establishes the degree of risk borne by the buyer and seller. Figure 9-1 summarizes the risk for the buyer and seller for each type of contract.

FIGURE 9-1   **Risk Burden by Contract Type**

Establishing the correct set of terms and conditions, regardless of contract type, is crucial for the success of the buyer/seller relationship. In most IT procurement contracts, a set of specific quality metrics are created and monitored; this is generally referred to as a service-level agreement (SLA). An SLA is a key part of a contract between a buyer and a seller that specifies, usually in measurable terms, what specific services are to be provided. The following are some of the metrics that may be included in an SLA:

- Specific times that a service, such as an application that the buyer is using from an application service provider, must be available
- Response times and latency
- Mean time to respond to issues
- Mean time to repair
- Problem notification/escalation procedures
- Application maintenance upgrades
- Number of users who can be served simultaneously
- Reporting content and frequency
- Change management procedures
- Security provisions
- Data backup procedures

The specific requirements depend on the service being provided and the size and strategic importance of the service. An organization that is preparing to outsource its complete help desk function will want to write a very detailed and complete SLA. An organization that is using an Internet-based application to aid in conducting customer satisfaction surveys on a periodic basis will have a much shorter SLA requirement. The key is to determine what levels of service the organization actually needs to do its business. Requiring too much may create unneeded complexity and cost. (The more service guarantees requested from the seller, the higher the cost.) Finally, along with each service-level requirement, there must be an associated cost to the seller if the seller fails to deliver. These costs need to be significant enough to provide an incentive to the seller to deliver the services.

Creating the right type of contract with the right terms and conditions will help an organization and a project team to transfer some of the project's risks and also to give the buyer a better means of managing the buyer/seller relationship. From the perspective of the buyer, the contract documents become the planning input documents to the project of delivering the required product or service. Before the contract can be decided on and terms negotiated, the seller must know exactly what is expected, which must be documented by the buyer in the form of a SOW.

Creating a Statement of Work (SOW)

The **statement of work (SOW)** is a document that describes the procurement item in sufficient detail to allow prospective sellers to determine whether they are capable of providing the item and potentially at what cost. The more complete and accurate the SOW, the greater the chance for a successful result. Similar to developing a complete WBS, developing a complete, concise, and clear SOW is a difficult task. Many organizations employ skilled experts to write the contract SOW. Because the SOW represents 100 percent of the contract requirements, it is important for the project team to get confirmation about its contents from the organization's management and SMEs. It is also imperative that the seller have a complete understanding.

The SOW may contain all or some of the following information: a dictionary, standards and specifications, period of performance, critical success factors, deliverables, and special requirements. Figure 9-2 shows an example of a SOW template.

The language used in the SOW should be understandable by all participants (project team, seller, buyer, management, and so on). Requirements should avoid words that allow for multiple interpretations. Use active voice for all requirements and use *shall* whenever a provision is mandatory (for example, "The seller shall deliver a user interface that . . ."). Avoid using the words *any*, *either*, and *and/or* because these words imply that the seller has

Project Title:
Origination Date:

Details

Dictionary	(terms, acronyms, and abbreviations)
Requirements (Scope of Work)	(complete list of clear, specific requirements written in active voice)
Period of Performance	(begin date and end date of contract, major milestone deliverable dates, cost implications for early/late work)
Critical Sucess Factors	(similar to those presented in the Project Charter, listed here are those critical factors which will determine the success of the procurement process)
Deliverables	(key deliverables, conditions of acceptance, dates, format, etc.)
Applicable Standards	(reference any required standards that must be followed)
Special Requirements	(location of work and personnel, constraints, assumptions)

FIGURE 9-2   Contract Statement of Work Template

a choice. Also, avoid using jargon and slang, which may not be understood by a seller in a different part of the country or in a different country.

The size and complexity of the SOW will vary with the characteristics of the product requested. A SOW written to procure a new ERP software application with associated consulting needs will be more complex and thorough than the SOW for the procurement of a couple custom reports. The SOW is a dynamic document that needs to change as the procurement process moves along, keeping in mind that after the contract is signed, there must be a formal change control process in place to control any changes to the SOW.

The SOW must be completed before moving on to the creation of the next procurement documents, the RFP and the RFQ. These documents are described in the next section.

Creating the Request for Proposal (RFP) and Request for Quote (RFQ)

The last objective of the procurement planning process is to prepare the documents needed to complete the procurement process—namely the request for proposal (RFP) and the request for quote (RFQ)—to build evaluation criteria, and to find and request seller responses to the RFP or RFQ. There are many other types of procurement documents, but the most used on IT projects are the RFP and RFQ.

Buyers use RFPs and RFQs to purchase services or products; they promote a fair and competitive process for suppliers. The same RFP or RFQ is shared with all potential sellers. Once a seller is selected, this document then becomes a major part of the contract. See Figure 9-3 for the RFP/RFQ template.

The procurement document format and content vary by industry and organization. The template presented in Figure 9-3 contains the following information:

1. *Purpose/background*—This section contains information about the company and background concerning the product or service being requested. Also lists the qualifications for an acceptable proposal, including where, how, and when to submit the response. It should also contain all contact information and whether it is permissible for the seller to directly contact the organization with questions. To keep the process fair to all, many times an organization will hold one or more formal meetings with all interested sellers to answer questions.
2. *Objectives*—This is a high-level list of procurement objectives.

```
1.      Purose/background
2.      Objectives
3.      Schedule
4.      Statement of work
5.      Technology constraints
6.      Evaluation criteria
7.      Contract and license agreement
8.      Supplier qualifications and customer references
9.      Pricing (RFQ only)
10.     Appendices (maybe)
10.1        Sample contract
10.2        Diagrams
10.3        Outline for submission/response
```

FIGURE 9-3 RFP/RFQ Template

3. *Schedule for procurement and project*—This is a time line of events for the procurement process and final delivery of the end product or service.
4. *SOW*—The RFP or RFQ includes the complete SOW, as described in the previous section of this chapter.
5. *Technology constraints*—This is a description of technical constraints and requirements that the sellers will have to be able to supply or work within. For example, if a buyer's technology infrastructure consists of only Microsoft Windows Server and a Windows client machine, the seller must deliver a solution that will work in this environment. If strict performance requirements are needed, they should be explicitly described here.
6. *Evaluation criteria with explanations*—This is a list of criteria that will be used to judge the seller responses, along with the associated importance of each criterion.
7. *Contract intentions (type)*—This section describes the specific type of contract the buyer will be asking the seller to sign. A sample contract could be included in the appendices.
8. *Supplier qualifications and customer references*—This is information about the seller that helps the buyer determine whether the seller is qualified and has the resources to deliver the product or service. This information may contain financial information, customer references, and total number of similar products or services delivered.
9. *Pricing (RFQ)*—If this section is needed, it provides a detailed format for pricing. Depending on the type of product or service, the price may need to be broken down into its detailed components. For example, say that a buyer has written an RFQ for a new customer relationship management system. The seller provides pricing on the software, installation, yearly licensing, training, consulting, and integration charges.
10. Appendices
    10.1 Sample contract
    10.2 Diagrams (UML, network, and so on)
    10.3 Outline for submission format

DEVELOPING AND COMMUNICATING THE PROPOSAL EVALUATION CRITERIA The final step in the RFQ or RFP preparation process is to develop and communicate the proposal evaluation criteria. The evaluation criteria, which are used to rate and evaluate seller proposals, should be included in the procurement documents delivered to potential sellers. Providing this information will make clear exactly how the proposals will be judged. It will also help the seller determine whether sellers can supply the product or service. The evaluation criteria may change from one project to the next, based on the relevant project criteria size, complexity, criticality, risk, and so on. The following is a list of sample criteria:

- Initial and life cycle price
- Seller's ability to address each item in the SOW
- Seller's experience with similar projects
- Seller's customer references
- Seller's financial stability
- Seller's technical approach
- Seller's production capacity and interest
- Who owns intellectual property rights, if applicable

Developing the Procurement Management Plan

The final deliverable from the purchase planning and acquisitions process is the procurement management plan, which consists of the following:

- types of contracts to be used,
- who is responsible for preparing evaluation criteria and assessing proposals,
- delegation of authority,
- templates for procurement documents,
- constraints and assumptions,
- handling of the interface between the procurement process and the other project schedule activities,
- and procurement metrics to be used to manage sellers.

The results of the procurement management process will have far-reaching consequences for the rest of the project in the areas of budget, schedule, resources, and scope. A poorly run procurement process could cause cost escalation issues, require resources to be pulled from other areas of the project to complete uncompleted seller work, or cause other major schedule issues. Other affected areas of the project may include risk management, communications management, and quality management. The issues raised during this section of the chapter stress the importance of following a formal procurement process with all types of procurement; however, this process is especially important when the seller is offshore. (The unique challenges inherent in an offshore procurement process are discussed in Chapter 14.)

PROVEN STRATEGIES AND HINTS TO SUCCESS

Gruman (2007) offers the following advice to set up a vendor management office. Several companies have found success creating a vendor management office (VMO) to aid them in procurement management. Jeff Dixon, Cisco Systems, estimates a tenfold return in the staffing investments of a vendor management entity—from better deals through consolidated purchasing, and from avoiding the costs of straightening out piecemeal or short-term deals later. The key goal of creating a VMO is not to create a firewall between IT and the vendor, but to be smart and consistent within the enterprise about managing multiple aspects of any vendor relationship. There are many ways to create a formal VMO. The most common is a virtual approach consisting of legal staff and procurement professionals to IT vendor management, and use IT "account managers" to coordinate all aspects of specific vendor relationships and IT "scouts" to assess technology and market trends that may change needs later. Not every purchase should be managed through the VMO. The size, complexity, and risk of the purchase should determine whether the VMO is involved.

THE PROCUREMENT MANAGEMENT PLANNING PROCESS

The following are the process steps to follow during the procurement management planning process:

> **Step 1.** Review the requirements, WBS, schedule, and so on.
> **Step 2.** Decide what needs to be procured, how, and when.
> > a. Make-or-buy decision
> **Step 3.** Develop the SOW.
> **Step 4.** Develop procurement documents (RFQ, RFP, and so on).
> **Step 5.** Build the procurement management plan.

HOW TO CONDUCT THE PROCUREMENT PLANNING PROCESSES

In this final section of the chapter, the R & S Amusements Services case study is used to demonstrate the process of building a procurement plan. This section walks through each of the process steps defined in the previous section. Before proceeding, take time to reread and review the R & S Amusements Services case study. Jeff and Kevin, the consultants from PPMS, are working with the leadership team at R & S Amusements Services to explain and guide them through the procurement planning process.

Step 1: Review Existing Planning Artifacts

Jeff and Kevin from PPMS reviewed the project requirements, the current project WBS, and the current project schedule with the leadership team of R & S Amusements Services. The following items represent an abbreviated list of identified candidates for procurement from an outside agency:

- Twenty tablet PC devices for use by technicians and collectors for data collection
- Twenty thermal imaging printers for use by technicians and collectors
- Development of the location mapping component, which will be integrated with the asset tracking and management system
- Procurement of the commercial off-the-shelf (COTS) package for asset tracking and management

For this iteration of the procurement planning process, the team will concentrate on the necessary activities to procure the tablet PCs.

Step 2: Decide What Needs to Be Procured, How, and When

The team decided that the tablet PCs will need to be purchased within the next 60 days. This will allow time for R & S Amusements Services employees to be trained and become familiar with the devices before formal testing and production begin. The team considered possible vendors both locally and nationally for the devices. The team determined that a national vendor may be able to offer a slightly lower price, but the vendor would have to reside locally in order to fulfill the employee training, warranty, and repair requirements.

Step 3: Develop the SOW

Jeff and Kevin from PPMS brought to the meeting a copy of a SOW template used on several previous projects. As in other situations, starting with a template will greatly reduce the amount of time it will take to create the SOW. The finished SOW is shown in Figures 9-4a through 9-4d.

Step 4: Develop the Request for Quote (RFQ)

In addition to the SOW template, Jeff and Kevin also brought a copy of a RFQ template used on a past project. Along with the other leadership team members, they prepared the RFQ for the tablet PCs. This document is shown in Figures 9-5a through 9-5f.

Statement of Work *1/31/08*

Asset Tracking & Management Project
Statement of Work

Prepared by:

Jeff Dunbar &
Kevin Pullen
Of
Premier Project Management Services

February 14, 2008

Version 1.0 Draft1

R & S Amusements Services Page: 1

FIGURE 9-4a SOW for R & S Amusements Services, Page 1

Statement of Work *1/31/08*

TABLE OF CONTENTS

 R & S Amusements Services

Page: 2

FIGURE 9-4b   SOW for R & S Amusements Services, Page 2

---

1. REVISION HISTORY

Author(s)	Date	Reasons For Changes	Version
Jeff Dunbar & Kevin Pullen	1/31/08	Initial Draft	1.0 Draft1

2. INTRODUCTION

R & S Amusements Services has a requirement for tablet personal computing devices. These devices will enable R & S Amusements Services technicians to use mobile computing to diagnose machine problems, enter repair and move orders, track inventory, and manage machine collections. These devices will be used to collect data that will be input into the new Asset Tracking and Management System which R & S Amusements Services will use to track their coin-operated amusement machines and other assets.

3. OBJECTIVE

The objective of this SOW is to acquire tablet personal computing devices used to collect data that will be input into the new Asset Tracking and Management System.

4. SCOPE

The scope of this effort includes the following:

4.1   MS Windows compatible Tablet PC

    4.1.1   The device shall contain an Intel Pentium M Processor at a minimum of 1.1GHz.

    4.1.2   The device shall be capable of running the Microsoft Windows XP operating system.

    4.1.3   The device shall have at a minimum 1.0 GByte RAM.

    4.1.4   The device shall have at a minimum 32.0 GBytes of hard disk storage.

    4.1.5   The device shall weight no more than 2.5 pounds.

    4.1.6   The device shall be of a size no larger than 9" by 7" by 1".

    4.1.7   The device shall have USB connectivity capability (2 ports minimum).

R & S Amusements Services   Page: 3

FIGURE 9-4c   SOW for R & S Amusements Services, Page 3

Statement of Work   *1/31/08*

4.1.8   The device shall have Ethernet connectivity.
4.1.9   The device shall have a digitizer pen capability.
4.1.10 The device shall have a Lithium-ion battery with 29WHr capacity.

5.   SERVICES REQUIRED

The vendor shall perform the following tasks listed below as required:

5.1   Delivery and setup of twenty tablet PCs for operation.
5.2   Provide training to 18 R & S Amusements Services employees on the maintenance and operation of the table PC.
5.3   Provide on site repair service within 24 hours of a service call.
5.4   Provide a loaner device if the device being repaired is unavailable for a period of more than 38 hours.

6.   DELIVERABLE

The vendor shall provide at a minimum the operating manual of each tablet PC as well as the operating documents for all included software.

7.   PERIOD OF PERFORMACE

The vendor shall deliver the tablet PCs no later 4/1/2008.
The vendor shall provide training no later than 5/1/2008.

8.   CRITICAL SUCCESS FACTORS

Success of this procurement activity is based of the following:
- Procurement of a tablet PC that meets the requirements stated above.
- Using the procured PC enables R&S Amusements Services technicians and other employees to perform the required tasks efficiently and effectively.

R & S Amusements Services   Page: 4

FIGURE 9-4d   SOW for R & S Amusements Services, Page 4

Request For Quote *2/14/08*

Asset Tracking & Management Project
Request For Quote

Prepared by:

Jeff Dunbar &
Kevin Pullen
Of
Premier Project Management Services

February 14, 2008

Version 1.0 Draft1

Disclosure of this document is limited to R & S Amusements Services employees and others who have been authorized by a R & S Amusements Services representative

R & S Amusements Services Page: i

FIGURE 9-5a RFQ for R & S Amusements Services, Page 1

Table of Contents

R & S Amusements Services Page: ii

FIGURE 9-5b RFQ for R & S Amusements Services, Page 2

1 Background and Purpose

R & S Amusements Services is in the business of distributing amusement machines – pool tables, jukeboxes, video games, pinball games, and the like to area businesses with the intent of making money for both the business location and us. The business started in 1947 with three machines and now R & S Amusements Services has grown to be one of the largest amusement machine operators in the Midwest. They employ 75 full and part-time employees and service over five hundred business establishments which include arcades, restaurants, taverns, clubs, bowling alleys, campgrounds, and numerous others. At each of these establishments R & S Amusements Services has installed one or more amusement machines from their current inventory of over 6500.

R & S Amusements Services has embarked on a multi-phasedplan for automating their business processes. This effort will be a multi-phased project with phase 1 of the project focusing on Asset Tracking and Management.

The purpose of this document is to request a quote for the procurement of twenty tablet personal computers and associated services outlined in detail later in this document.

2 Objectives

The objective of this SOW is to acquire tablet personal computing devices used to collect data that will be input into the new Asset Tracking and Management System.

3 Schedule

Bids shall be firm offers and shall remain valid for acceptance by R & S Amusements Services 60 days following the RFQ closing date.

RFQ closing date: March 31, 2008

4 Statement of Work

Reference associated SOW document.

5 Technology Constraints

Reference associated SOW document.

6 Evaluation Criteria

6.1 Contract Award In Best Interest

R & S Amusements Services reserves the right to accept or reject proposals on each item separately or as a whole, to reject any or all bids without penalty, to waive any informalities or irregularities therein, and to contract as the best interest of R & S

  R & S Amusements Services   Page: 3

FIGURE 9-5c   RFQ for R & S Amusements Services, Page 3

Amusements Services may require to best meet the needs of R & S Amusements Services, as expressed in this RFQ. R & S Amusements Services reserves the right to award any resultant contract(s) as a whole, or split award between competing bidders.

6.2 Rejection of Bids

Reasons for rejection of bids by R & S Amusements Services include the following:

    a. Failure to use the bid form furnished by R & S Amusements Services

    b. Late or incomplete bids will not be accepted. Bids may also be rejected for failure to conform to the rules or requirements contained in the RFQ;

    c. Failure to sign the bid by an authorized representative;

    d. Proof of collusion among bidders, in which case all bids involved in the collusive action will be rejected;

6.3 Contract Award

R & S Amusements Services reserves the right to negotiate modification of the bid prices, terms and conditions with the lowest responsive, responsible bidder in conjunction with the award criteria contained herein, prior to the execution of a contract, to ensure a satisfactory procurement.

7 Contract and License and Agreement

The materials, supplies or services covered by this document shall be furnished by Seller subject to all the terms and conditions set forth in this document including the following, which Seller, in accepting the contract, agrees to be bound by and to comply with in all particulars and no other terms or conditions shall be binding upon the parties unless hereafter accepted by them in writing. Written acceptance or shipment of all or any portion of the materials or supplies, or the performance of all or any portion of the services, covered by this document shall constitute unqualified acceptance of all its terms and conditions. The terms of any proposal referred to in this document are included and made a part of the order only to the extent it specifies the materials, supplies, or services ordered, the price therefor, and the delivery thereof, and then only to the extent that such terms are consistent with the terms and conditions of this document.

The services, materials and supplies furnished shall be exactly as specified in this document free from all defects in Seller's performance, design, workmanship and materials, and, except as otherwise provided in this document, shall be subject to inspection and test by R & S Amusements Services at all times and places. If, prior to final acceptance, any services and any materials and supplies furnished therewith are found to be incomplete, or not as specified, R & S Amusements Services may reject

 R & S Amusements Services

Page: 4

FIGURE 9-5d **RFQ for R & S Amusements Services, Page 4**

them, require Seller to correct them without charge, or require delivery of such materials, supplies, or services at a reduction in price which is equitable under the circumstances. If Seller is unable or refuses to correct such items within a time deemed reasonable by R & S Amusements Services, R & S Amusements Servicesmay terminate the contract in whole or in part. Seller shall bear all risks as to rejected services and, in addition to any costs for which Seller may become liable to R & S Amusements Services under other provisions of this order, shall reimburse R & S Amusements Services for all transportation costs, other related costs incurred, or payments to Seller in accordance with the terms of this contract for unaccepted services and materials and supplies incidental thereto.

8   Vendor References

The vendor shall provide on request by R & S Amusements Services the names, address, and phone numbers of three references who have procured products and services from said vendor.

9   Evaluation Criteria

Each RFQ response will be evaluated on the bases of the following criteria list in order of importance: price, support, experience, timely deliverable of product.

10 Pricing

Item	Description	Unit Cost	Extended Cost
1.	MS Windows compatible Tablet PC		
2.	Delivery and setup of twenty tablet PCs for operation		
3.	Training to 18 R & S Amusements Services employees on the maintenance and operation of the table PC		
4.	Provide on site repair service within 24 hours of a service call		

Total Bid: _____

11 Send Completed Bids to:

Reid Lewis
R & S Amusements Services
1512 Main Street
West Lafayette, IN 47907-0001
(765) 843-5534

FIGURE 9-5e   **RFQ for R & S Amusements Services, Page 5**

Request For Proposal *2/14/08*

12 For Additional Information or Clarification, Contact:

Reid Lewis
R & S Amusements Services
1512 Main Street
West Lafayette, IN 47907-0001
(765) 843-5534

R & S Amusements Services Page: 6

FIGURE 9-5f RFQ for R & S Amusements Services, Page 6

In addition to the RFQ, the team prepared a cover letter that will accompany the RFQ to each prospective vendor. The letter invites each vendor to respond to the RFQ, and it summarizes the evaluation criteria for the RFQ, which in this case are the lowest total bid and satisfactory reference responses.

Step 5: Develop the Procurement Management Plan

The procurement management plan describes how the process will be managed, from development of procurement documentation through the end of the contract. The plan may consist of many of the following elements:

- The type of contract (the purchase of the tablet PCs will use a fixed price contract with penalty clauses for late delivery)
- Roles and responsibilities (Reid Lewis will be in charge of monitoring the contract and communicating with the seller. Mark Lewis is in charge of the initial quality assurance for each computer.)
- Authority levels
- Prepared procurement documents (that is, the RFQ)
- Constraints and assumptions
- Procurement metrics used to manage and evaluate sellers (for example, delivery schedule, quality of machines when delivered, support if needed)

Steps 1 thru 5 will be repeated for each product or service that needs to be procured from an outside agency. The evaluations of the RFQ seller responses are covered in Chapter 10.

Chapter Review

1. *Procurement* refers to all the elements of a project that will be bought or created from someone outside the project team or organization.
2. The procurement planning process is used to determine what to procure, when to procure it, and how to procure it and to prepare the procurement documents, such as a SOW, RFQ, and RFP.
3. Key decision criteria involved in making a make/buy decision are cost, human resources, time, strategic direction, and risk.
4. The seller/buyer relationship is based on a signed contract. A contract can take many forms, including fixed-price, cost-reimbursable, and time and material.
5. Types of cost-reimbursable contracts are cost-plus-fee, cost-plus-fixed-fee, and cost-plus-incentive-fee.

6. The buyer of a product or service has the least amount of risk in a fixed-price contract and the most risk in a time and material contract. The situation is reversed for the seller.
7. A service-level agreement (SLA) specifies as part of the contract what specific services are to be provided, in what amounts, and at what levels.
8. The SOW document is used to describe a procurement item in sufficient detail to allow prospective sellers to determine whether they are capable of providing the item and potentially at what cost.
9. A request for proposal (RFP) or request for quote (RFQ) is a document that buyers use to purchase services or products. This system promotes a fair and competitive process for suppliers.

Glossary

contract   A mutually binding agreement entered into by two or more parties that is enforceable in a court of law. It obligates the seller to provide the specified products, services, or results. It also, in most cases, obligates the buyer to provide financial compensation.

make-or-buy analysis   A process used to determine whether a project team should produce a product or service itself or purchase it.

procurement   The purchase or acquisition of products, services, or results needed from an entity outside a project team to perform work defined on the project, possibly under a contract.

statement of work (SOW)   A document that describes 100 percent of the work or services required to be completed under contract by a seller.

Review Questions

1. What are the PMBOK-defined processes for the Procurement Management knowledge area?
2. What does *procurement* mean?
3. What is a make/buy analysis?
4. List and explain each of the key decision criteria used in a make/buy analysis.
5. Define the uses for and the content of a SOW.
6. Define the uses for and the content of an RFP.
7. Define what a contract is and how it should be used.
8. What is a fixed-price contract, and how does it differ from a cost-reimbursable contract and a time and materials contract?
9. Describe what a service-level agreement is and how it should be used in a procurement process.
10. Explain the contents of a procurement management plan.

Problems and Exercises

1. List each type of contract described in this chapter and build a matrix that describes their similarities and differences.
2. The consulting company you are working for is negotiating a contract with a large hospital to conduct a security assessment of its wireless network to confirm that it complies with federal privacy regulations and, if it doesn't, to aid in fixing any issues. The customer is proposing a fixed-price contract, but due to the potential complexity and unknown issues that may materialize, your consulting company would like to propose a solution that would limit their risk. What type or types of contracts would you suggest that your consulting company use and why?
3. Calculate the organization's total cost for the following scenario:
   - The organization has signed a cost-plus-fixed-fee contract.
   - The seller estimate of expenses is $150,000.
   - The fixed fee is set at $10,000.
   - Calculate the result if the project is completed by the seller at a cost of $155,000.
   - Calculate the result if the project is completed by the seller at a cost of $140,000.
4. Calculate the organization's total cost for the following scenario:
   - The organization has signed a cost-plus-incentive-fee contract.
   - The sharing formula is 90/10 (90 percent by buyer).
   - The seller estimate of allowable expenses is $150,000.
   - The target fee is set at $10,000.
   - The maximum fee is $19,750.

- The minimum fee is $5,000.
- Calculate the result if the project is completed by the seller at a cost of $146,000.
- Calculate the result if the project is completed by the seller at a cost of $190,000.

5. The medium-size manufacturing organization XXX Corporporation has written a very complete SOW and included it in the recent RFP it sent out to prospective sellers. The project is estimated to take two months and is very low in complexity. The problem is that the XXX Corporation is short on staff and hasn't been able to free up anyone to work on a new project involving adding some new static marketing information to the public portion of the web site. The marketing information has already been written and approved by all levels of management. The XXX Corporation has decided to outsource this project. Due to the nature of the project, the company would like to find a seller willing to sign a fixed-price contract. Do you think the company will be successful? Is this the right type of contract to sign for this project? Explain.

6. Explain why the buyer has more risk in a time and materials contract than in a fixed-price contract.

7. In which type of contract is the seller least likely to be concerned with controlling costs? Explain.

Projects and Research

1. Research a recent "mega deal" outsourcing contract (defined as being over $1 billion) and study the type of contract signed, any special clauses added, and the process followed.

2. Find an example of an outsourcing agreement in which something went wrong and explain why.

3. Research different organizations' templates for writing an RFP. (Look online or use your past experience.) Explain the differences and similarities in these templates and why you think they are different.

4. Practice building an RFP or RFQ for a project, using the template provided in Figure 9-3. The company you should practice on is thinking of adding a shopping cart feature to its web site, which supplies parts to the plumbing industry. Research how several of your favorite Internet-based shopping sites have implemented this feature and write the RFP.

5. Research the largest outsourcing sellers and describe the types of services and products they provide.

MINICASE

1. **Background:** (Review the R & S Amusements Services case study material.) Diana Brooks, business operations manager for R & S Amusements Services, has come to work early Monday morning so she can talk with Reid Lewis about some information she learned over the weekend while attending a family party. Diana was talking to several members of her family about new projects at work and especially about all the new computers the company was going to be buying for the asset management system, as well as the other new projects. Diana's husband's nephew, John, happened to overhear the conversation and asked about the new computers and specifically what they were going to get. It turns out that John works for a small computer storefront company that builds PCs for sale. Diana was recalling what Jeff and Kevin from PPMS discussed at the last meeting about finishing the requirements documents and then writing the procurement documents to be sent out to prospective vendors.

   Current Situation 1: Diana is on her way to see Reid to tell him that John, her husband's nephew, offered to build the computers they need, make them a great deal, and enable them to keep the business local. John said they could start right away, and it would save R & S lots of time working on procurement documents—and he wasn't really even sure what those were. All he needed was a short list of requirements, and he would start getting the parts in and building the computers. He said that they didn't normally work with big orders or these types of machines, but a computer is a computer, right?

Discussion: What issues do you see with this process of buying the computers from John's small computer company? If you were Reid Lewis, how would you respond to Diana when she comes to your office with the news? How would you explain to Diana the importance of getting all the requirements documented thoroughly first before deciding on a vendor? How would you explain to Diana the importance of getting competitive bids for the computer hardware?

Current Situation 2: After the requirements have been gathered and the RFQ is generated (see Figures 9-5a through 9-5f), R & S sends the RFQ to several vendors, most of which were found based on research that PPMS provided. Diana insisted that the RFQ also be sent to John's small local computer store.

Discussion: After the requirements have been gathered and the RFQ is generated, discuss how you think John's company would stack up against the larger, more established, companies that aren't local. How important is it, in your opinion, that the company R & S procures the equipment from be local? How important is it, in your opinion, that the company have experience dealing with these types of hardware systems?

Suggested Readings

Applegate, L., Austin, R., & McFarlan, F. (2007). *Corporate information strategy and management: Text and cases.* New York: McGraw-Hill.

Burkholder, N. (2006). *Outsourcing: The definitive view, applications, and implications.* New York: John Wiley & Sons.

Cleland, D., & Gareis, R. (2006). *Global project management handbook: Planning, organizing, and controlling international projects.* New York: McGraw-Hill.

DiPaolo, A. (2004, November 11). Outsource, but train those who remain. *Chief Executive.* Retrieved from www. chiefexecutive. net.

Gartner (2008). *Gartner identifies top 30 countries for offshore services.* Retrieved from www.gartner .com/it/page.jsp?id=565107.

Gilbert, A. (2005). *Study: IT outsourcing services multiply.* Retrived from www.zdnetasia.com/news/ business/0,39044229,39297069,00.htm.

Gruman, G. (2007, October 29). Why you should create a vendor management office. Retrieved from http://www.cio.com/article/149700/Why_ You_Should_Create_a_Vendor_Management _Office.]

Halvey, J., & Melby, B. (2005). *Information technology outsourcing transactions: Process, strategies, and contracts.* New York: John Wiley & Sons.

Harney, J. (2002). *Application service providers (ASPs): A manager's guide.* Boston: Addison-Wesley.

Hofmann, H.F., Yedlin, D.K., Mishler, J.W., & Kushner, S. (2007). *CMMI for outsourcing: Guidelines for software, systems, and IT acquisitions.* Boston: Addison-Wesley.

Hyman, G. (2003, March 19). Overseas outsourcing hurts U.S. economy, says firm. *AspNews.* Retrieved from www. aspnews. com/news/ print/0,,4191_2118191,00. html.

Klepper, R., & Wendell, J. (1997). *Outsourcing information technology systems, and services.* Upper Saddle River, NJ: Prentice Hall.

Mainville, M. (2003, June 25). Russia poised to benefit from outsourcing. *InfoWorld.* Retrieved from www. infoworld. com/article/03/06/25/ HNrussiaout_1.html.

Porter-Roth, B. (2002). *Request for proposal: A guide to effective RFP development.* Boston: Addison-Wesley.

Project Management Institute (PMI). (2004). *A guide to the project management body of knowledge,* 3rd ed. Newton Square, PA: PMI.

Rosencrance, L. (2003, January 9). Federal IT outsourcing spending to hit $15 billion in fiscal '07. *Computerworld.* Retrieved from www.computerworld. com/printthis/2003/0,4814,77391,00.html.

PART 3

Project Execution and Control Methods

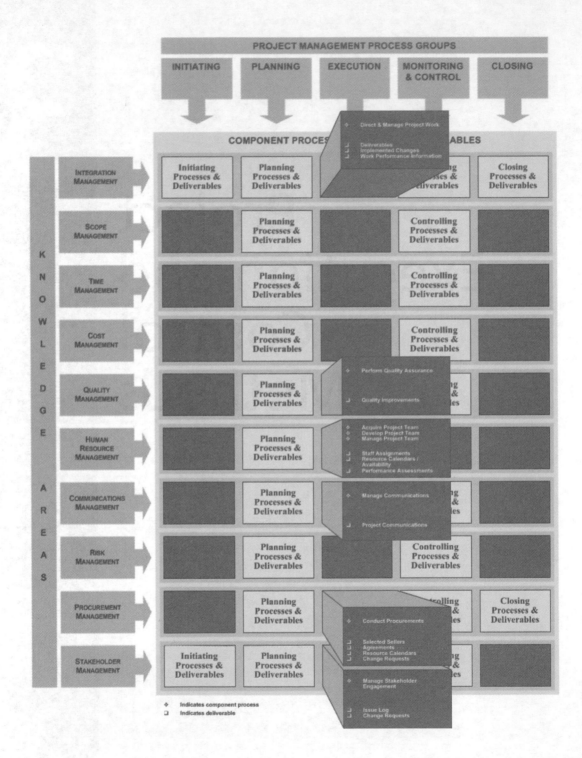

10

Project Execution

R & S Amusements Services

Event 10

Setting   *It has been two months since the formal project kickoff meeting, and the project leaders have convened in a small conference room located outside Reid Lewis's office at R & S Amusements Services. Those in attendance include Reid Lewis, Diana Brooks, Mark Lewis, Mike Lewis, Foster Hines, Elaine Henry, and Heidi Cosgray from R & S and Jeff Dunbar, Kevin Pullen, Jessica Langston, and Teresa Jenkins from Premier Project Management Services.*

JEFF   Good morning, everyone. Thank you for taking time out of your busy schedules to attend this monthly project status meeting, as outlined in our communication plan. Here is the agenda for today's meeting:
[The following bullets are being displayed on an overhead projector.]

- Introductions
- Status of the upcoming quality audit
- Team building
    Meyers/Briggs test
    Offsite face-to-face (F2F) meeting at Camp Cherokee

- Status of asset tracking core team
- Status of vendor selection for the tablet PCs
- Issues and concerns

JEFF   First and foremost, I'm sure everyone has noticed that two new individuals have joined us this morning. Please welcome Jessica Langston and Teresa Jenkins from Premier Project Management Services.

JESSICA/
TERESA Hello, everyone. Nice to meet you all.

GROUP Hello.

JEFF   In a moment we'll quickly go around the room and introduce ourselves to Jessica and Teresa. But first let me explain why they are here. Jessica is skilled in performing quality audits, so I have invited her here to help conduct the requirements process assessment.

REID   Forgive me for asking the question, but isn't that something you or Kevin could do?

KEVIN   That's a fair question, Reid. True, Jeff and I could conduct the audit because we both have been trained and have experience in those efforts, but if we perform the assessment, we run the risk of not having a nonbiased, impartial evaluation. Because both Jeff and I have worked so closely with the project, we may unknowingly be biased one way or another. By having an "outsider" perform the audit, we hope to avoid such biases.

REID   I see. *[Nodding]* That makes sense.

JEFF   And Teresa is PPMS's education coordinator. She will be responsible for administering the Myers-Briggs Type Indicator (MBTI) test to all the project team members.

MARK   What? We have to take a test? *[Laughing]* Reid, I didn't sign up for this! *[Reid shrugs his shoulders helplessly]*

HEIDI   What happens if we fail?

JEFF   *[Laughing]* Hold on, everyone. Calm down. It's not that kind of test. In fact, I'm willing to bet that you will find it quite interesting.

MARK   I'll be the judge of that! *[Laughing]*

KEVIN   Jeff, allow me come to your rescue. *[Grinning]*

JEFF   By all means. By the way, Jessica and Teresa, we have a great group here that is never afraid to speak their minds. *[Laughing]*

DIANA   *[Addressing Teresa and Jessica]* Don't you two worry. We just have to keep Jeff and Kevin in line. They are always speaking "project manager-ese" and trying to convert us.

JESSICA/
TERESA *[Laughing]* We know what you mean!

KEVIN   *[Trying to look annoyed]* Can we get back to the agenda? *[Everyone stops laughing but keeps grinning]* Thank you. As I was saying, the MBTI has been in use for over 50 years. It was originally developed during World War II in order to help women, who were entering the industrial workforce for the first time, identify the sort of war-time jobs for which they would be most comfortable and suited. Companies today use the test to provide guidance on how well an employee will work with other team members both socially and professionally. In addition, it provides useful insight to a project manager about how to manage an individual. For example, the test can indicate whether a person performs best in a structured or nonstructured work environment. Teresa can explain in more detail at the employee face-to-face meeting, where the test will be given.

JEFF   As Kevin said, Teresa can address any other questions at our offsite face-to-face meeting next Saturday. Okay, now let's take a minute to go around the table and introduce ourselves to Jessica and Teresa.

        [Everyone around the table says their name and their duties with R & S]

JEFF   Thank you. Item number 2.

HEIDI   Jeff, I have a question. Why do you and Kevin use the term *face-to-face*?

KEVIN   I'm sorry, Heidi, Jeff and I are guilty of PM speak again. *[Nodding to Diana]* Face-to-face is a term we use for meetings where the team actually meets in person. Today, many meetings are conducted electronically, through teleconferencing, videoconferencing, instant messaging over the Internet, or even chat rooms. In fact, at some companies that have locations worldwide, you could be on a team and never meet the other team members in person. You know them only by their voice or image. It has always been our practice to ensure that all the team members meet each other in person—*face-to-face*. It truly makes for a better work relationship and environment. Jeff, back to you.

JEFF   Now back to the quality audit.

        (To be continued)

        (This chapter discusses the agenda presented in this case.)

CHAPTER PREVIEW AND OBJECTIVES

This chapter covers the tools and techniques that project managers use during the project execution phase of an information technology (IT) project. The execution phase consists of tools and techniques from five of the nine knowledge areas from the Project Management Institute's project management body of knowledge (PMBOK): Integration Management, Quality Management, Human Resource Management, Communications Management, Stakeholder Management, and Procurement Management (as depicted in the opening chapter map).

As you read this chapter, you will:

- Understand the integration of the project management life cycle and the product development life cycle
- Understand how to perform a quality audit
- Understand how to build and lead successful project teams
- Understand how to keep stakeholders informed about a project's progress
- Understand how to manage stakeholder expectations
- Know how to lead a successful procurement seller selection process

AN INTRODUCTION TO PROJECT EXECUTION

Figure 10-1 depicts the project management life cycle used throughout this text, which was first explained in Chapter 2. The project management life cycle and the product life cycle are most visibly integrated during the project execution phase. Just as the phases in the project management life cycle overlap, so do the project management and product life cycles. The first step of a product life cycle is generally to identify and document the user requirements for a new IT project. But much of this work has already been done during the planning phase of the project management life cycle, with the definition of the requirements document and

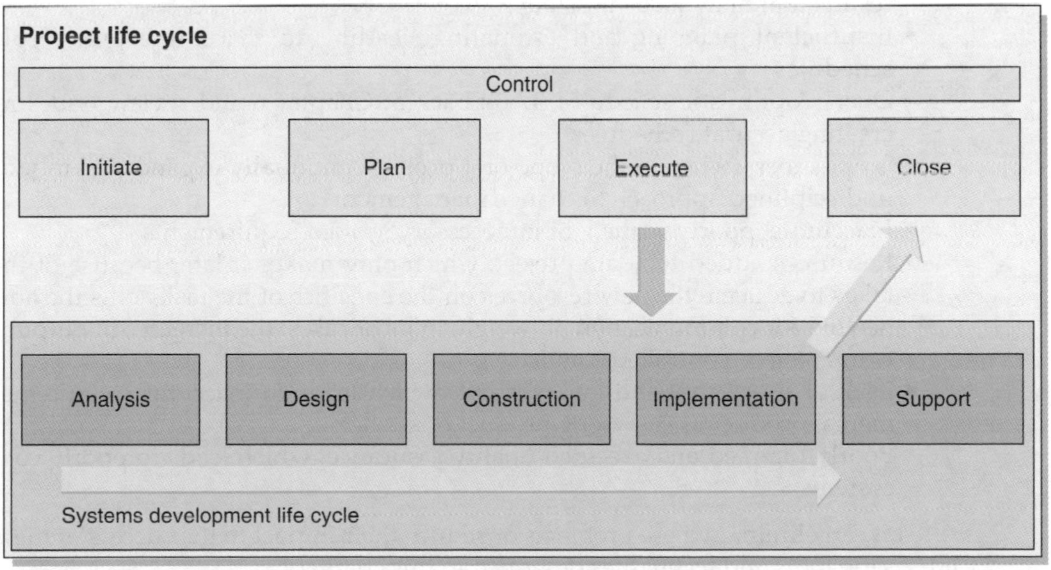

FIGURE 10-1 Integration of Project Management and Product Life Cycles

scope statement. When the product life cycle starts, the scope statement needs to be broken down into a finer level of detail, depending on the type of product being created. Understanding how the two life cycles interact and overlap is an important concept to review as the project execution phase begins.

The highest percentage of time on a project—hours worked—occurs during the project execution phase, as work begins on building the product or service. All members of the project team will be involved in the execution portion of the project at one time or another, so it is important that project managers understand how to lead, manage, and direct the project team as the execution phase begins. Building a great project management plan means little at this point of the project if project and product deliverables are not managed properly during execution.

During project execution, it is not uncommon for a project manager and team to get overwhelmed with trying to get the product or service completed to meet time, cost, scope, and quality goals; often, time is not spent on other key processes, such as communication, risk management, change management, and seller management. To help prevent this from happening, the process described throughout the text demonstrates the proper project planning techniques to help ensure that when execution begins, the project team is prepared. This chapter and the next two chapters focus on how project managers can manage the quality of a project and product deliverables, build and manage the project team, successfully communicate project information, manage sellers, control the triple constraint (scope, time, and cost), and monitor and control risk.

The following list describes some of the most common IT project-related problems encountered during the execution phase:

- Human resources problems, such as lacking needed skills, being given the wrong work assignments (either too difficult or not difficult enough), not being trained correctly or at all, not being motivated properly
- Poor management of stakeholder expectations (The project manager must communicate with stakeholders honestly about the status of the project and not promise results that may not be possible.)
- Insufficient planning and estimating, leading to inaccurate project plans and schedules
- Overly optimistic schedules (Look back at Chapter 6 and review issues related to creating accurate schedules.)
- Scope creep (wherein the scope of a project continually expands, mainly due to an undisciplined approach to change management)
- Inaccurate, poorly written, or unnecessary system requirements
- Resources added to a late project, which only makes it later because of the time it takes to educate the new resources on the specifics of the tasks plus the added time needed for communication outweigh, in most cases, the increases in output
- Unmanaged/controlled conflict
- Lack of user input and involvement, which leads to inaccurate requirement statements, producing the wrong product or service
- Poorly planned and executed quality assurance, which leads to poorly constructed systems

A team can eliminate these problems or reduce their impact to the success of the project if it uses the tools and techniques described in this chapter.

PROJECT MANAGEMENT CONCEPTS: PROJECT EXECUTION

The tools and techniques of a project's execution phase exist in the following PMBOK knowledge areas (KA), listed below along with their associated processes:

- *Integration Management*—Direct and manage project work
- *Quality Management*—Perform quality assurance
- *Human Resources Management*—Acquire, develop, and manage a project team
- *Communications Management*—Manage communications
- *Procurement Management*—Conduct procurements
- *Stakeholder Management*—Manage stakeholder engagement

These knowledge area processes are covered in detail in this section of the chapter, followed by examples of tools and techniques using the R & S case study.

The Integration Management Knowledge Area

The Integration Management knowledge area consists of the following processes: develop project charter, develop project management plan, direct and manage project work, monitor and control project work, perform integrated change control, and close project or phase. Directing and managing project work is the only process performed during project execution.

During project execution, the product or service deliverables begin to materialize based on the scope statement defined in the project management plan. The goal of the execution phase is to work on each task defined in the work breakdown structure (WBS) to produce the identified outcomes and to follow the defined or as-changed project schedule. The processes concerned with monitoring and controlling changes to these plans is covered in Chapters 11 and 12.

The deliverables from the execution phase are primarily product driven, such as lines of code, user interface elements, training, and process definitions. The discussion of the product deliverables is beyond the scope of this text. This chapter focuses instead on the project deliverables of quality audit results, change requests, issue logs, human resources assignments, human resources performance information, dissemination of project performance information, and, if needed, the selection of sellers to handle outsourced work. All these deliverables except the last one are required on every IT project.

The Quality Management Knowledge Area

The Quality Management knowledge area consists of the following processes: plan quality, perform quality assurance, and control quality. The quality assurance process is performed during project execution.

The **quality assurance** process is focused on the processes required to produce the desired results defined in the quality plan. There is a subtle difference between the quality assurance process and the quality control process, discussed in Chapter 11. Because quality assurance is focused on the processes that lead to the creation of quality products, it is focused on preventing errors or defects before they occur. The quality control process is concerned with monitoring project/product results to determine whether the quality standards have been met. Chapter 11 explains several tools a project team can use to assist in monitoring results.

To understand the difference between quality assurance and quality control, it might help to think of quality assurance as the management section of quality management and quality monitoring and control as the process to highlight the activities that need to be managed. According to *A Guide to the PMBOK* (PMI, 2013), quality assurance is the area where a project manager can have the greatest impact on project quality. A project manager has more control over the processes that are used than over the product deliverables, such as each line of code. On most, if not all, medium to large IT projects, a project manager will never see any of the application code generated by the software developers and must spend time influencing the processes that will lead to better-written software.

In many organizations, quality assurance and the **quality audit**, discussed next, are done by a separate department, referred to by several different names, including quality assurance, quality control, or quality management. The role of this group is to ensure that everyone on the project team is following the defined quality processes. Moving this responsibility away from the resources that are actually creating the product will help to promote a nonbiased, impartial evaluation. These individuals have received specialized training in quality assurance tools and techniques, which enables them to conduct the quality audits.

Quality audits are generally scheduled in advance but can also occur randomly. The objective is to find non-value-added or inefficient processes and procedures within a project. Eliminating non-value-added processes or inefficient procedures should increase the overall quality of the project and product deliverables. Persons doing the audits must be trained in doing process analysis, including root cause analysis, to make sure the source of the issue—not just the symptoms—is found and fixed. For example, during a recent quality audit, a quality assurance team found that the software development group responsible for writing the integration application between the company's new general ledger application and the legacy customer billing application was experiencing higher-than-normal software defects. The quality assurance team reviewed the quality processes the software development group was following, and everything seemed to be okay. Upon further investigation, the team started noticing that the results of the peer code reviews were not documenting having found many errors. Upon digging a little deeper into the issue, the quality assurance team discovered that the software development team leader doing the peer reviews thought they were a waste of time and only went through the motions and wasn't doing a good job of reviewing the work. When this was discovered, the leader and the team were given training on the importance of the peer reviews and how to properly conduct a team code review. They were also trained on how to document issues found.

The deliverables from the quality assurance process are requested process changes, corrective actions, and updates to any project documentation affected.

Human Resources Management Knowledge Area

The Human Resources Management knowledge area consists of the following processes: plan human resource management, acquire project team, develop project team, and manage project team. During project execution, these processes are performed: acquire project team, develop project team, and manage project team. These processes are described next.

ACQUIRING THE PROJECT TEAM   Before work can begin on a project, human resources (people) have to be selected and assigned to work on the project. Unlike in many school situations, where a project team is selected by an instructor, in organizations, selecting the right people is critical to the success of a project. In some situations, the selection process is limited to who is available or the decision is made by upper management, and the project manager must conduct the project as assigned. In situations where the project manager is given the opportunity to select the best people for each part of the project, several techniques should be used to find the right people who have the correct technical skills as well as the nontechnical skills to be successful on the team.

The first step in the process is to understand the skills necessary to perform the technical functions required. Does the position require a seasoned veteran with many years of experience, or can it be done by someone fresh out of school? How much experience should this person have in the particular technology? For example, Jim, a new project manager, has been asked to staff a project to add functionality to the organization's purchased customer relationship management (CRM) package. The package uses an Oracle database, which the new software will need to access. The organization uses the .NET Framework for custom software projects. The new functionality is not currently included in the purchased package due to its unique and complex nature. When the project is completed, it will give the organization a strategic advantage in its industry. Jim will want to get the best people possible due to the complexity and importance of the project. But what if the best aren't available because they are involved in other projects?

One of the key skills a project manager must possess is negotiation. Negotiation is a discussion intended to produce an agreement—in this case, how the project manager can get the services of a busy key resource. In these situations, the two parties (the project managers) should be striving for a win–win situation for both projects the key resource is working on and, of course, the organization. Both project managers might be able to rework their schedules to accommodate the other, using available slack or other available resources. If the situation can't be resolved, the project manager will need to look for a resource from outside the organization. Outsourcing part of the project and hiring a consultant to provide the needed expertise on the project are both possibilities for resolving the issue. If sufficient time is available before the resource is needed, the project manager may be able to get a less experienced resource trained to fill the role. Regardless of which scenario is selected, the project manager will need to adjust the project documentation (schedules, budgets, and so on) accordingly. Negotiation skills are covered in more detail in Chapter 12.

The second step in the process of resource selection is looking at a prospective team member's nontechnical skills, consisting of personality traits, communication skills, interest and motivation factors, and business knowledge. If a resource selected doesn't possess the needed business domain experience, extra time will need to be built into the schedule for the person to learn the business. In general, resources who are interested in a project are much easier to motivate and will produce higher-quality work at a higher productivity rate. Depending on the nature of a project and a person's position in the organization, the ability to communicate with team members is important. Historically, IT resources have not been very good communicators. When this is the case, extra time is needed in the project schedule to develop this skill to make the team more productive.

The final trait mentioned above and one of the most difficult to ascertain is a prospective team member's personality traits—factors that determine whether this resource will fit in with the current team and project. Many times, a project manager must conduct individual interviews and then use judgment about how well a person will work with other team members both socially and professionally. Many organizations have had some success using personality type models, the most popular being the Myers-Briggs Type Indicator (MBTI) and the follow-on study, the Keirsey Temperament Sorter.

The MBTI has been in use for over 50 years. (www.MyersBriggs.org) The original developers of the indicator were Katharine Cook Briggs and her daughter, Isabel Briggs Myers, who initially created the indicator during World War II, believing that a knowledge of personality preferences would help women who were entering the industrial workforce for the first time identify the type of war-time jobs where they would be most comfortable and suited. Based on his or her responses to multiple-choice questions, a person who takes the MBTI is identified as having personality preferences that fit into 1 of 16 different personality types, or natural tendencies in a given situation. The MBTI defines four dimensions of behavior (see Figure 10-2):

• *Extrovert/Introvert (E/I)*—Extroverts draw energy from the external world of people and activities, while introverts draw energy from internal factors such as ideas, emotions, or impressions. Extroverts tend to act, then reflect, and then act further, while introverts tend to reflect before acting, act, and then reflect again. The general population is split with 50 percent being extroverts and 50 percent being introverts.

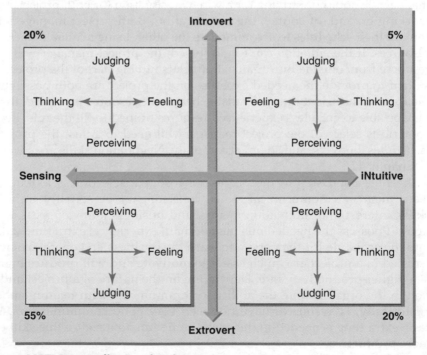

FIGURE 10-2   MBTI Personality Tendencies

- *Sensing/Intuitive (S/N)*—These are referred to as the *information-gathering (perceiving)* functions. They describe how new information is understood and interpreted. Individuals with a preference for sensing prefer to trust information that is in the present and tangible (facts)—that is, information that can be understood by using the five senses. Those with a preference for intuition tend to trust information that is more abstract or theoretical and that can be associated with other information (either remembered or discovered by seeking a wider context or pattern). Intuitive workers, who comprise about 32 percent of the population, tend to be great at brainstorming sessions.
- *Thinking/Feeling (T/F)*—These are referred to as the *decision-making (judging)* functions. Both thinking and feeling types strive to make rational choices, based on the data received from their information-gathering functions (S or N). Neither type is necessarily better at making decisions; they just get to solutions in slightly different ways. Thinking individuals make decisions based on their intelligence and thoughts, and they follow a logical objective path. Feeling individuals tend to make decisions based on what is best for everyone to promote harmony within the group. Thinkers tend to appreciate logical structure and clarity in communication that is more focused on work and not personal emotions. Sixty percent of the U.S. male population falls into the thinking category, and 40 percent of females in the United States are in the thinking category.
- *Judgment/Perception (J/P)*—These represent ways in which individuals realize and live with processed information. Judgment people tend to organize all life events and act according to their defined plans. They focus on goals, planning, and strategies designed to reach their defined goals; 58 percent of the U.S. population falls into this category. Perception people lean toward a life designed around improvisation, spontaneity, and continually looking for alternative paths.

Figure 10-2 also shows the general population percentages of who fits into each general category. As you can see, 55 percent of the general population demonstrates tendencies that fall in the Extrovert/Sensing personalities, while only 5 percent demonstrate tendencies that would fall in the Introvert/Intuitive personalities. The personality traits or styles and associated preferences placed in each section of the graph represent the interaction of various combinations of temperaments rather than just the individual traits.

The results of the MBTI are reported using just the four letters representing the four sections of the graph, such as ISTJ for Introvert/Sensing/Thinking/Judgment or ENFP for Extrovert/Intuitive/Feeling/Perception. Knowing the tendencies of each member of the team will help aid a project manager in team selection, communication types and levels of detail, and organizing types of meetings. Some individuals do better in less structured, free-thinking situations, such as brainstorming sessions, while others need a more formal structure. IT workers tend to be categorized as ISTJ types.

Wideman (1998) did some interesting work, mapping project management skills into each of the 16 MBTI temperament cells. The basic premise of the research was to determine which types of temperament tendencies make better project leaders and project participants. The first step was to match project leader traits to each of the 16 different MBTI personality types. The traits were then associated with successful project leader traits in different phases of the project. Wideman concluded that about 40 percent of the general population is suited for project management positions of one kind or another and another 25 percent of the population falls into the follower position and make good team members. Based on these numbers, about 35 percent of the general population was not suited for project work of any kind.

The Keirsey Temperament Sorter (KTS) is based on the early work of the MBTI but contains just 4 temperaments, not 16. The work is based on observable patterns of behavior that have been studied for centuries. Hippocrates, a Greek physician, proposed the four humors, which are related to the four temperaments: Artisan, Guardian, Idealist, Rational. Keirsey grouped the 4 types against the MBTI as follows: Guardians as Sensing/Judgment; Artisans as Sensing/Perception; Idealists as Intuitive/Feeling; and Rationals as Intuitive/ Thinking.

Organizations today are more frequently employing virtual teams for IT projects. A *virtual team* is a group of team members who are working on the same project but are geographically dispersed, such that they may never meet face-to-face. The term can also be stretched to include team members who are on different ends of a building and rarely meet face-to-face. Technologies such as videoconferencing, email, instant messaging, groupware, and teleconferencing are all used to aid project communications. The uses of virtual teams presents some new challenges for project leaders in acquiring and developing project teams. Most project leaders prefer collocated teams, where everyone on the team is located in one place, simplifying team formation, communication, and the development of trust within the team. Chapter 14 presents more information on the successful use of virtual teams.

The key deliverables of the process of acquiring project teams are defined staff assignments and updates to the staffing management plan. If project management software is being used, these staff assignments can be tracked and assigned to individual tasks in the WBS. After the project team has been selected and assigned to tasks on the projects, the next challenge for the project leader is to get the group to perform as a team to deliver a product of high quality that meets stakeholders' needs.

DEVELOPING THE PROJECT TEAM   The two key objectives of the process of developing a project team are to improve the competencies (skills) of each team member and to promote teamwork to enhance project performance. It has been estimated that project managers spend 75 to 90 percent of their time communicating, making communication one of the key skills needed during team development. Many techniques are available to help project managers build better, more cohesive, high-performing teams. Before we explore them, let's first look at the sources of conflict on project teams and the stages of team development, as defined by Tuchman (1965).

Conflict on IT projects is inevitable, so it is extremely important for project managers to learn where conflict is coming from and to understand the type of conflict and the most effective ways of dealing with it. A project manger needs to understand the potential sources of conflict, based on project phase, and then build time into the schedule to address team conflict issues. Thamhain and Wilemon (1975) published some of the earliest research on conflict and teams. The results of their study of 150 project managers and the way they managed conflict showed where the highest number of conflicts occurred during different phases of the project. The primary source of conflict changes from one phase to the next. During the initial project formation stage, the main source of conflict is priorities and then procedures. The primary source of conflict changes slightly during the early stages of project execution, as the overall amount of conflict increases; priorities is still number one, followed by schedule issues. During the longest portion of a project, execution, the highest source of conflict changes to issues with the project schedule, followed by technical issues. Finally, during the closing stages of the project life cycle, the main source of conflict is focused on the schedule, with labor and personality coming in a distant second.

Thamhain and Wilemon (1975) computed conflict intensity by using two factors from their survey: the total frequency of the type of conflict and the magnitude of the conflict, as rated by the project managers in the survey. The research discovered that the average total conflict is highest across all categories during the early execution phase of the project.

Several more recent research studies have shown a slight change in the sources of conflict. Kezsbom's (1992) findings show that goals and priority definition is the highest-ranking conflict category, followed by personality and interpersonal conflict, followed by problems in communication and information flow. Kezsbom attributes this shift in conflict to changes in technology, organizational structures, markets, and the more widespread use of cross-functional teams. Posner's (1986) research listed conflict over schedules as number one, followed by cost and budget issues and then project priorities.

The bottom line on conflict for project managers is that it will happen, and you need to learn to manage it to the benefit of the project. Successful project managers are very good at managing conflict. Another important topic helpful in understanding teams and getting them to work productively deals with understanding the process of group development. Tuchman (1965) developed a five-stage maturity model through which all groups move: forming, storming, norming, performing, and adjourning. Each of these stages is explained further in Table 10-1.

A project manager's main objective is to get to the performing stage as quickly as possible. The time and methods needed to reach the performing stage vary from project to project, as the human resources vary from project to project. The following factors contribute to the length and difficulty of the maturation process: familiarity of the team members with each other, familiarity of the team with the project and technology, team member culture differences, the physical location of team members, and the nature of the project to the team and the organization.

Team-building activities are used to improve the skills of each team member and to promote better teamwork (moving through Tuchman's maturity stages). The principal goals of team building are to help the team to be more interdependent, establish agreeable reasons to work together, and be accountable as a unit, and to allow for a moderate level of conflict, promote shared goals and objectives, and build trust. Team-building activities might consist of short sessions held in the organization's office or may include events held away from the organization's office, lasting several days and run by a professional. Some examples of activities that can be used include paintball competitions, mountain climbing, scavenger hunts, and group problem-solving exercises. (Before deciding to use one of these team-building activities, make sure the team is physically capable of the activity, such as mountain climbing, and be sensitive to gender and cultural issues.)

Team-building activities can be used at any stage of a project. Building trust among team members is the most important aspect of team maturation. Building trust in groups that have never worked together before or that consist of cultural differences is very difficult, so time spent doing team-building activities is needed early in the process. Team-building activities should not be done just once at the beginning of a project and forgotten; they should be done throughout the project to promote continuous team development.

TABLE 10-1   Team Maturation Process Stages

Stage	Activity	Characteristics
Forming	• Members get to know each other • Members find out what they will be doing • Some of the team ground rules are established	• Courtesy • Caution • Confusion • Quiet • High morale
Storming	• Members begin resisting any group influence • Conflict arises on competing goals and approaches • Hidden agendas and prejudices begin to appear	• Tension • Confrontational • Alienation • Criticism • Low morale
Norming	• Rules and standards are established • Task standards and expectations are delineated • Team agrees on operating procedures • Team members develop closer relationships	• Development of team skills • Confrontation of issues • Rebuilding of morale • Cooperation • Collaboration • Commitment
Performing	• Focus shifts to task accomplishment • Division of tasks is established	• Trust • Consideration of members • Efficiency • High morale • Flexibility
Adjourning	• Group is disbanded following project completion or reassignment • Project is either completed or cancelled	• Compromise • Communication • Closure

Whenever possible, project teams should be physically located close together. Of course, this is not always possible; part of the software development team may be in California and the other part in Bangalore, India. For large projects, organizations have had success moving the team to a neutral site, away from their usual day-to-day offices. This not only aids in team maturation but also helps team members focus on the project and not on their previous job responsibilities.

A final note on team development has to do with reward for and recognition of desirable team behavior. The ground rules for any type of reward or recognition need to be established as early in the project as possible and clearly communicated and evenly applied across all project teams. In many cases, rewards work best when they are given to the entire team and not select individuals; however, there are times when an individual goes above and beyond and should be recognized. To obtain maximum effectiveness, rewards need to be appropriate to the culture and needs of the team.

The outputs from the develop team process are mostly indirect, such as lower team turnover rates, higher productivity, and higher quality of deliverables. Some organizations use a formal team-based performance assessment instrument to help determine the team members' annual performance review.

MANAGING THE PROJECT TEAM   As stated earlier in the chapter, a project manager will spend between 75 to 90 percent of their time communicating and working with others. This involves leadership, negotiation, performance evaluation, motivation, education, and **conflict management**, to name just a few activities. Managing a project team involves tracking team member performance, providing feedback, resolving issues, and coordinating changes to enhance project performance. The monitoring and control tools discussed in Chapters 11 and 12 show a project manager what is wrong and even in what area a problem exists, but the tools can't tell why something occurred if it has anything to do with human resources. The tools can't tell why a team member is very productive one day and not productive the next when all things are the same at the job. Maybe the team member had a bad night, with little sleep, or maybe he is coming down with a cold. The techniques discussed so far might tell you that this team member's productivity is down but not why. The process of managing project teams is about finding out why the numbers are what they are by knowing what is going on with members of the team and, if needed, implementing corrective actions to improve performance.

One of the most common performance-damaging activities that a project manager needs to learn to control is conflict. A project manager will spend 20 percent of his or her time dealing with some form of conflict. Therefore, conflict management is a key skill for a project manager to have.

Conflict management involves preventing, managing, or resolving conflicts as they occur throughout a project. Before proceeding any further in the discussion of conflict, three things need to be understood about conflict. First, from Thamhain and Wilemon (1975), we understand that the reasons for or sources of conflict are dynamic; they change over time. Second, whether one party has actually wronged another or whether they disagree on something is not the point; the *perception* of the conflict is what matters. In some cases, a person may not have done or said anything to cause conflict, but another person may believe he or she was wronged and has the perception that the conflict exists. For a project manager, it's important to understand exactly what type of conflict exists before deciding how to resolve it. Third, not all conflict is bad. The right kind of conflict, if managed properly, can actually make the project and the end product better. The trick is to understand the different types of conflict and manage them properly. There are three general categories of conflict on projects:

- *Task-oriented conflict*—This type of conflict is associated with disagreements regarding end results or outcomes and results from multiple perceptions of a project stemming from vague or incomplete scope statements or requirement specifications.
- *Administrative, or process, conflict*—This type of conflict is associated with disagreements about reporting relationships or who has authority to make decisions. This is especially evident in matrix organizations, when a team member has several managers—project leader(s) and a functional supervisor.
- *Interpersonal, or relationship, conflict*—This type of conflict is associated with personality differences between project team members, such as work ethics, egos, or individual personalities.

Remember that some conflict is good; if managed, it can have a positive effect on a project's outcome. If managed properly, task-related and administrative conflict can be good. Interpersonal conflict is almost always bad. The trick is to find the optimal level of conflict; too little leads to low amounts of innovation, and too much leads to problems.

There are a number of ways to handle conflict. The choice of which one depends on the type of conflict, time pressures for resolution, the intensity of the conflict, the importance of the problem to project success, the level of cooperation possible, and the physical location of the individuals. Each of the techniques listed below can be used and successful in reaching a decision. Each item in this list is followed by what is often times the final result for each party involved in the conflict. *Win–win* means that both parties win, and lose–lose means that both parties lose something in the result. Win–lose means that one party gets what he or she seeks from the conflict, and the other loses. The goal, if possible, is to always find a win–win solution.

- *Good project management*—Nothing is a substitute for good project management in the first place. It can head off detrimental conflict before it can occur. (win–win)
- *Avoidance*—Avoidance involves leaving the conflict (the individuals) alone, hoping that it will work itself out without intervention. (lose–lose)
- *Problem solving*—Problem solving consists of face-to-face meetings between a moderator and the parties involved. (win–win)
- *Shared goals*—The moderator creates shared goals for both parties that can be achieved only by working together (win–win)
- *Smoothing*—The moderator plays down differences while emphasizing common interests (lose–lose)
- *Compromise*—Each party gives up something. (lose–lose)
- *Authoritative command (forcing)*—The boss issues orders about the outcome. (win–lose)
- *Altering behavior*—For this solution, which takes time, a person must be willing to get training or counseling to alter behaviors or attitudes. (short term: lose–lose; long term: win–win)
- *Altering team structure*—This solution takes time, and a team may lose productivity while in transition. Some people just can't work together, so sometimes it's necessary to either remove a member from the team entirely or change work assignments. (win–lose)

Performing team member performance appraisals is another function performed by a project manager during the process of managing the project team during the execution phase. Organizations have struggled with the best way to review individual team member performance when it comes time for their annual reviews, especially in a matrix organization, where the functional supervisor is responsible for doing the annual review. A technique that many organizations have used successfully is to add a section to the performance review that addresses the individual's contribution to projects and have the representative project manager contribute the details. The percentage of time devoted to projects should determine the weight assigned to this part of the annual review.

Thamhain and Wilemon (1975) describe the following characteristics of team performance, which can be used to help compare one team against another or against a benchmark to aid in rating team performance and determining whether some form of intervention is necessary:

- Work and team structure:
  - Team participation in project definition and dynamic evolution of work plans
  - Evolution and change in team structure and responsibilities as needed
  - Broad information sharing
- Communication and control:
  - Effective cross-functional channels and linkages
  - Ability to seek out and process information
  - Clear sense of purpose and direction
- Team leadership:
  - Minimal hierarchy in member status and position
  - Internal team leadership based on situational expertise, trust, and need
  - Clear management goals, direction, and support
- Attitudes and values:
  - Commitment of members to established objectives and plans
  - Shared goals, values, and project ownership
  - Capacity for conflict resolution and resource sharing
  - Team building and self-development
  - High morale and team spirit
  - High commitment to established project goals

Leadership

The *Guide to the Project Management Body of Knowledge* defines leadership as "focusing the efforts of a group of people toward a common goal and enabling them to work as a team." Quite simply, leadership is the ability to get things done through others. For a project manager, leadership is the process (inspiring, motivating, influencing, altering behaviors) he or she uses to influence the project team to get the project completed. Project leaders demonstrate the following skills:

- Embrace change
- Excellent problem solvers
- Manage conflict well
- Pursue effectiveness in all they and others do
- Innovate
- Build trust
- Highly self-motivated
- Excellent communicators
- Decisive

Einsiedel (1987) conducted a study that identified five characteristics closely associated with effective project leaders:

- Credibility—the project manager must be trustworthy and taken seriously
- Creative problem solver—think outside the box to solve problems during the project
- Tolerance for ambiguity—must be skilled at working in complex and often ambiguous situations
- Flexible management style—must be able to handle rapidly changing situations, especially in IT projects
- Effective communication skills—ability to communicate with all levels of workers from the CEO down to the lowest paid staff members

One of the most important characteristics of a good project leader is the ability to use adaptive techniques of leadership. Unique to project management is the need to adapt leadership style not only to the individual, but also to the team structure and team maturation stage (see Table 10-1 in the text), as well as the life cycle phase of the project. Different leadership techniques for motivation, as an example, are required early in the project as opposed to later in the project life cycle, or for a team that is in the forming stage as opposed to in the performing stage. In no other discipline is a leader required to adjust as often and varied as in project management. For further study, review the work of Hersey and Blanchard (1979) and Kerzner (2006).

Negotiation

The ability to negotiate win-win resolutions is a critical skill for project managers to develop. Negotiation, according to the *Guide to the Project Management Body of Knowledge*, is a strategy of conferring with parties of shared or opposed interests (such as project team members and key stakeholders) with a view toward compromise or reaching an agreement. The goal is for both parties to "win" something, even if compromise is required from one or both. Negotiations take place in all walks of life, but the basic structure of negotiations is fundamentally the same whether it be in an IT project or a construction project—all negotiations share four common characteristics (Raiffa, Richardson, and Metcalfe, 2002). First, there are two or more parties; second, the parties can be creative and cooperate to arrive at a joint decision; third, the payoffs to any party depend either on the consequences of the joint decision or alternatives external to the negotiations; and fourth, the parties can reciprocally and directly exchange information, honest or not. Their research also demonstrated that contrary to common belief, people on average are not very good at negotiating optimal outcomes. Yet, most project managers have had little formal training on negotiating, and individuals predominantly rely on implicit knowledge, personal capabilities, and situational factors in crafting agreements (Ertel, 1999). Project managers need to get formal training in becoming better negotiators for resources internal and external, working with stakeholders, working with upper management and members of the team. The following skills and behaviors are useful in becoming a successful negotiator:

- Analyze the situation thoroughly from all sides. How much trust do you have in the other party, how much power do you have in the situation, and what, if any, real-time pressures are present?
- Differentiate between wants and needs, both theirs and yours.
- Focus on interests and issues rather than on positions; separate the people from the problem, put yourself in their shoes, recognize emotions and deal with them.
- Ask high and offer low, but be realistic.
- If necessary, invent options for mutual gain.
- When you make a concession, act as if you are yielding something of value, don't just give in.
- Both parties should feel as if they have won. This win-win negotiating style is preferred but not always achievable. If possible, don't let the other party leave feeling as though he or she has been taken advantage of.
- Listen attentively and actively; communicate articulately.

The Communications Management Knowledge Area

The Communications Management knowledge area from the PMBOK consists of the following processes: identify stakeholders (see Chapter 4), plan communications (see Chapter 7), distribute information, manage stakeholders, and report performance (see Chapter 12). This chapter describes the processes of distributing information and managing stakeholders.

DISTRIBUTING INFORMATION   The main objective of a project manager during the process of distributing information is to provide designated project information to the appropriate stakeholders in a timely manner, based on the requirements identified in the communications management plan. Chapter 4 describes how a project manager conducts a stakeholder analysis and identifies the information, format, and timing required for each stakeholder. This process requires the use of all forms of communication skills, including written, oral, listening, and speaking skills. Collecting the information, formatting reports, and delivering reports in the right format can all be very time-consuming, leading many organizations to purchase automated systems to help collect and disseminate project information. Many software solutions exist to assist team members in tracking their work on projects. The time required, along with work status, should be collected daily. Tools also provide report-building assistance or directly link with other tools that allow sophisticated report generation. Reports can be set up one time and then executed as needed manually or automatically, based on date and time. The more automated the reports, the less time required of the project manager.

Many technologies exist today for disseminating project information, including email, instant messaging, text messaging, videoconferencing, teleconferencing, telephone, voice mail, fax, and tools collectively referred to as Web 2.0 tools (for example, blogs, wikis, podcasts, vidcasts, and web conferencing). The trick is to use the appropriate tool in each situation. Each tool has strengths and weaknesses. For example, if a project manager were trying to assess the commitment level of a stakeholder, a face-to-face meeting would be best so that all nonverbal communication could be evaluated. Using other methods can work in some situations but not as affectively. However, face-to-face meetings are not always the best answer. If a project manager needs to convey some simple instructions or project status, then an email or a web posting that the stakeholder could retrieve might be the best solution. The bottom line is to evaluate the type of information that needs to be conveyed, the response needed, and the timing of both before selecting the correct media choice.

If information distribution occurs correctly, stakeholders are kept up-to-date on the project with the information they need to make decisions or to just be informed about progress. Project managers should never underestimate the importance of communicating with stakeholders as they will ultimately determine the success or failure of a project.

The Stakeholder Management Knowledge Area

MANAGING STAKEHOLDER ENGAGEMENT   Managing stakeholder engagement refers to managing communications to satisfy the needs of and resolve issues with project stakeholders. The success of any project is in the eyes of the stakeholders, so all facets of communication with them need to be carried out with care. Stakeholders deserve and require accurate information on the status of the project, even if the information consists of bad news. Project managers need to use the stakeholder analysis and the roles and responsibilities matrix created earlier in the project to help determine the level of communication necessary and the interests of each stakeholder. As the project progresses, the needs of stakeholders will change, and these documents need to be updated to reflect the most current information. For example, say that because of certain risk events that have occurred during a project, the team needs to put in place a fallback plan that requires a different set of stakeholders to become involved. In this situation, the current stakeholders need to be informed before and during the change process of exactly why the fallback plan has to be implemented. The key pieces of information to communicate will vary across projects, but the main items are: issue logs, change requests, performance data, and progress reports.

The Procurement Management Knowledge Area

The Procurement Management knowledge area from the PMBOK consists of the following processes: plan procurements (see Chapter 9), conduct procurements, control procurements (see Chapter 12), and close procurements (see Chapter 13). The process of conducting procurements is covered in this chapter.

CONDUCTING PROCUREMENTS   The first objective of the process of conducting procurements is to obtain responses from sellers who were selected in the planning phase of the project and given a copy of the procurement documentation—the request for quote (RFQ) or request for proposal (RFP). To make sure all sellers have equal access to information they need before generating a response, organizations should host question-and-answer sessions (sometimes referred to as a *bidder's conference*) either face-to-face or electronically and invite all potential sellers. All sellers need to be allowed time to ask questions, and the information needs to be shared with everyone at the same time. Each seller can then determine whether it can offer a competitive response to the RFP or RFQ.

After the organization has answered all questions, the sellers prepare their responses and submit their documents by the assigned due date. It is very important that all sellers be treated equally and that no one be given extra information or extra time to prepare responses. Once the seller responses are received, the organization must then follow a formal evaluation process to determine who should be selected.

This next part of the process involves using previously documented seller evaluation criteria to select the best seller proposal; this removes or reduces the opportunities for bias. To reduce the opportunity for bias on the part of the selection committee, the names of the sellers can be removed from the proposals. A weighted scoring model is created to view the final assessments (see Figure 10-3). The weighted scoring model used to select the best proposal is similar in format to the one used for project selection (see Chapter 4). The criteria and the weights are part of the procurement documents that the sellers received. Supplying this information to the sellers accomplishes two objectives: First, it communicates to the sellers exactly how their proposals will be evaluated, allowing them to communicate accurately their strengths and weaknesses, and second, it forces the selection committee to identify these criteria before the procurement documents are sent. The selection committee consists of SMEs who can accurately evaluate the information supplied by the sellers. For example, deciding how well the proposal adheres to requirements needs to involve those who are most familiar with the system's requirements, which may include individuals from outside the IT department. To accurately evaluate the seller's financial stability, the committee should involve someone with a finance or accounting background.

The selection committee strives to rate each seller's proposal consistently. For example, in Figure 10-3, the price category should have ranges applied to determine the rating. For example, using the criterion adherence to requirements, each proposal should be rated consistently, using established formulas. Proposals meeting only 50 percent to 60 percent of the stated requirements should receive a rating of 30, those matching 60 percent to 70 percent of the stated requirements should receive a rating of 50, those matching 70 percent to 80 percent should receive a rating of 70, and those proposals matching 80 percent and above should receive a rating of 90. Establishing these documented guidelines for ratings for each criterion will aid the selection committee in evaluating each proposal fairly.

As is true for the weighted scoring model used during project selection, the criteria used for procurement proposal selection are subject to change. Each type of product or service being procured may need to have a different set of criteria applied. The list in Figure 10-3 is not meant to be exhaustive of all possibilities but represents a common set of criteria found on many scoring models.

The job of selecting a seller is not quite finished when the selection is made from the weighted scoring model process. The next step concerns contract negotiations. Chapter 9 covers the multitude of contract types, and now the selection committee or a team of professional contract negotiators must work with the seller to produce a successful contract. Many organizations have a team of individuals with a law background to handle the contract negotiations to make sure the organization is safeguarded against bad contracts. The final step in the

| | | | Seller Proposal | | |
Criterion	Weight	1	2	3	4
1 Price	15%	70	50	90	30
2 Adherence to requirements	20%	30	70	50	90
3 Seller experience	10%	30	70	90	90
4 Past customer list	5%	0	70	90	70
5 Specific skill sets	10%	50	70	70	70
6 Seller approach	10%	50	70	50	30
7 Seller financial stability	10%	50	90	90	90
8 Contract choices	10%	90	70	30	30
9 Interest level	10%	90	70	30	50
Totals	100%	52.5	69	64	62

Rating	No/worst answer	0
	Below average	30
	Average	50
	Above average	70
	Excellent	90

FIGURE 10-3 **Weighted Scoring Model—Seller Proposal Review**

process of contract negotiation is to work out how the contract will be managed between the seller and the organization. The contract management plan consists of the following:

- The period of performance, including dates when the project begins and ends as well as dates of important milestones
- Change management (that is, the integrated change control process, explained in Chapter 11)
- Required documentation that details the information and timing of key project status information
- Delivery and performance requirements

The last step in this process is to make sure that when the contract and contract management plan are negotiated and signed, any other affected project documents are updated, such as the risk management plan, the project schedule, and the project budget.

PROVEN STRATEGIES AND HINTS TO SUCCESS

Implementing agile methodologies to help projects during the execution process greatly improves performance as mentioned in Chapter 2. The techniques listed below help especially during project execution (Griffiths, 2004):

- Daily short stand-up meetings where development team members briefly answer three questions: what have you been working on since the last meeting; what are you working on today; and do you have any problems, issues, or impediments to making progress today?
- All software projects contain requirements and technical uncertainty, plans (WBS) should be feature-based instead of developer task-based.
- Build software iteratively and incrementally.
- Use meaningful metrics that are aligned to the true goal, such as features-delivered and project time remaining.
- Empower the team and do not micromanage the developer teams. This means, "engaging the team and business representatives in the planning of features, then letting the team select and develop the features for that iteration as they see fit."

THE PROJECT EXECUTION PROCESS

Previous chapters list the steps in the process that is the focus of the related chapter, but for the project execution life cycle phase described in this chapter, it is impossible to describe one general process. As the project plan unfolds during execution, the project and product artifacts are created, based on the established plan. The project deliverables, such as status and performance reports, are generated on a regular schedule, based on the needs of the project. In the next section, each of the project execution processes is further explained, using the R & S Amusements Services case study for examples.

HOW TO CONDUCT THE PROJECT EXECUTION PROCESS

In this final section of the chapter, the R & S Amusements Services case study is used to demonstrate the activities of the execution process. This section provides examples

Name	Time Allocation (per Week)
Elaine Henry, asset administrator	80%
Heidi Cosgray, service coordinator	20%
Kenny Jones, warehouse supervisor	20%
Ashley Brooks, finance administrator	20%
Brittney Lewis, office supervisor	40%
*Gene Gentry, service technician	40%
*David Young, collector	40%

FIGURE 10-4   R & S Amusements Services Project Team Members

and walks through many of the processes defined in the previous sections. The processes tend not to occur in a sequential order and are not presented in that manner here. Before proceeding, take time to reread and review the R & S Amusements Services case study.

Process 1: Acquire the Project Team

The leadership team of Reid Lewis, Diana Brooks, and Mark Lewis from R & S and Jeff Dunbar and Kevin Pullen from PPMS have identified additional team members and made time allocations for each (see Figure 10-4).

Because Gene Gentry and David Young (marked by an * in figure 10-4) are both from offsite locations and are key employees at their site, Reid Lewis has agreed to the following concessions in order to allow them to participate:

- Both Gene and David will be given a $30.00 per diem to cover food and gas and a $125.00 lodging allowance per week.
- Both the Fort Wayne and Bloomington sites can hire part-time help, as necessary.
- Saturday overtime is authorized on a volunteer basis for business-critical issues.
- Each employee will be sure to record his or her time in the provided application.

Process 2: Develop the Project Team

Kevin Pullen has contracted with the Camp Cherokee Leadership Center, located in Brookfield, Indiana, as the site for the project team's face-to-face meeting, to be held March 15, 2008. This will be a day-long event, with the morning session consisting of communicating project information and Teresa Jenkins administrating the MBTI. After lunch (provided by Camp Cherokee), the team will participate in team-building exercises as part of the leadership program of Camp Cherokee. These activities are designed to encourage effective teamwork, communication, and interpersonal skills. Most exercises, affectionately called *games with a purpose*, will take place outdoors, and casual clothing is recommended. A sample exercise from The Leaders Institute is provided below:

Tennis Balls

Divide the participants up into small groups of about eight to ten people and have them arrange themselves in a circle. Give a tennis ball to one person and explain the rules of the game:

1. Each group is in competition with the other groups in the room. The group that can complete the most "circuits" in a given time will be the winner.
2. A completed circuit occurs when every person in the group has touched the tennis ball.
3. Only one person in the group can touch the tennis ball at one time (therefore, the ball must be tossed rather than passed).
4. If the ball ever touches the floor, then production must stop for one minute.

Have the teams complete a few circuits to get comfortable and begin creating patterns that make them more efficient. The facilitator may want to stop the groups and get feedback as to how they are becoming more efficient and help them understand that this is a natural progression in business as well. Have the groups continue to complete circuits, but as time progresses, the facilitator will add additional rules to make the process more difficult:

- *A co-worker calls in sick*—Remove one of the group participants and tell the group that the participant called in sick. After they complete a few circuits, remind them that just because someone calls in sick doesn't mean that that person's work doesn't need to be completed. (They will probably have just continued to complete the circuit just as they had before the person left.) Remind them that each of their last few circuits had one fewer touches than before, so they do not count. Someone will have to pick up the slack for the absent person. After a new pattern is established, have the person come back.
- *Double Production*—Throw a second ball into the mix and tell the group that the client wants them to double production. Only one ball can be held by any one person at a time. You can add a third or even fourth ball later.
- *Diversity*—New federal legislation states that you need to include more minorities and women in your production line, so every other person who touches the ball must be either a woman or a minority.

Process 3: Manage the Project Team

Jeff and Kevin assisted Reid Lewis in implementing a formal performance appraisal process in which each employee would be evaluated at least annually and newer or poor-performing employees would be evaluated more frequently. These appraisals would be the basis for merit raises as well as promotions. In addition, Jeff and Kevin advised Reid on other human resource management factors, such as rewards systems, employee motivation, and conflict management. A formal seminar was held with the project leadership team on conflict management and how it affects project success. This was a one-day seminar that was held offsite at a local hotel.

Process 4: Conduct Procurement

Reid Lewis, Diana Brooks, and Mark Lewis from R & S and Jeff Dunbar and Kevin Pullen from PPMS met to review the vendors that responded to the RFQ for tablet PCs. Three responses were received in total, with one being disqualified because it was not complete and was not signed by an authorized individual. The team reviewed and evaluated each response. The results of the evaluation are shown in Figure 10-5.

		Seller Proposal	
Criterion	**Weight**	**Computer Warehouse**	**COMPTEC**
1 Price	15%	70	90
2 Adherence to requirements	20%	30	90
3 Seller experience	10%	30	90
4 Past customer list	5%	0	90
5 Specific skill sets	10%	50	70
6 Seller approach	10%	50	50
7 Seller financial stability	10%	50	90
8 Contract choices	10%	90	30
9 Interest level	10%	90	50
Totals:	**100%**	**52.5**	**74**

	Rating:		
		No/worst answer	00
		Below average	30
		Average	50
		Above average	70
		Excellent	90

FIGURE 10-5 **Seller Selection Matrix**

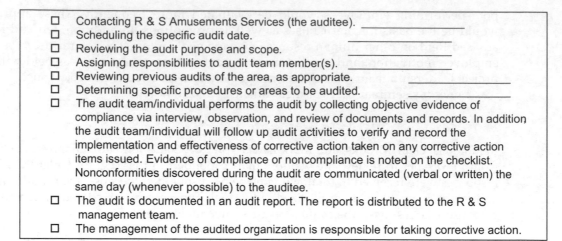

☐   Contacting R & S Amusements Services (the auditee). _____

☐   Scheduling the specific audit date.   _____

☐   Reviewing the audit purpose and scope.   _____

☐   Assigning responsibilities to audit team member(s).   _____

☐   Reviewing previous audits of the area, as appropriate.

☐   Determining specific procedures or areas to be audited.   _____

☐   The audit team/individual performs the audit by collecting objective evidence of compliance via interview, observation, and review of documents and records. In addition the audit team/individual will follow up audit activities to verify and record the implementation and effectiveness of corrective action taken on any corrective action items issued. Evidence of compliance or noncompliance is noted on the checklist. Nonconformities discovered during the audit are communicated (verbal or written) the same day (whenever possible) to the auditee.

☐   The audit is documented in an audit report. The report is distributed to the R & S management team.

☐   The management of the audited organization is responsible for taking corrective action.

FIGURE 10-6   Quality Audit Checklist

As shown in the matrix in Figure 10-5, COMPTEC will be awarded the contract, based on its high score. Computer Warehouse will be mailed a formal letter indicating that it was not chosen for the contract. In the event that Computer Warehouse requires additional information, Kevin Pullen will draft the correspondence.

Process 4: Quality Audit

Jessica Langston of PPMS was brought in by Jeff Dunbar to perform a quality assessment of the procurement process. Jessica used the checklist presented in Figure 10-6 to guide and track her efforts.

Jessica interviewed each team member who participated in the procurement of the tablet PCs. In addition, she reviewed all documentation, including the statement of work and RFQ, plus the letters of contract award and denial. Her findings are recorded in the audit report shown in Figures 10-7a through 10-7d.

Process 5: Distribute Information

Recall that the main objective of a project manager during the manage communications process is to provide designated project information to the appropriate stakeholders in a timely manner, based on the requirements identified in the communications management plan and the stakeholder management plan. One of the requirements of the plan is that Reid Lewis is to receive a monthly summary status report prepared by Diana Brooks and Mark Lewis. A copy of this report is shown in Figure 10-8.

The report shown in Figure 10-8 indicates that the team is in the analysis phase of iteration 1 and has completed the activity of refining the system requirements document to include a refined definition of both functional and nonfunctional requirements. In addition, during this time period, the team has started refining the high-level use cases into more detailed essential use cases and is on schedule, having completed 35 percent of the estimated

Request For Quote   *2/14/08*

Audit Report
of
The Procurement Process

Prepared by:

Jessica Langston
of
Premier Project Management Services

For
R&S Amusements Services

April 11, 2008

Version 1.0

Disclosure of this document is limited to R & S Amusements Services employees and others who
have been authorized by a R & S Amusements Services representative

 R & S Amusements Services   Page: i

FIGURE 10-7a   Audit Report, Page 1

Table of Contents

 R & S Amusements Services

FIGURE 10-7b   Audit Report, Page 2

1   Subject

Quality audit of the R & S Amusements Services procurement activities associated with the Asset Tracking and Management System project.

2   Purpose

To verify that the requirements established by the R & S Amusements Services QA Program are being effectively implemented for the procurement activities. And if not effectively implemented, document any and all discrepancies for disposition.

3   Scope

The audit included the procurement activities conducted during the time frame of January 1, 2008 through March 31, 2008 for the Asset Tracking and Management System project. The auditor interviewed cognizant personnel in person when possible and others over the phone, examined relevant documentation, reviewed procedures, and evaluated procedure implementation to determine adequacy and effectiveness of compliance with R & S Amusements Services QA Program requirements.

4   Background

R & S Amusements Services has embarked on a multi-phased plan for automating their business processes. This effort will be a multi-phased project with phase 1 of the project focused on Asset Tracking and Management. A requirement of this project is to purchase 30 tablet personal computing devices used to collect data that will be input into the new Asset Tracking and Management System. The specifications for the tablet personal computing devices are known and written as part of the procurement documentation. Premier Project Management Services (PPMS) was hired to conduct the quality audit.

5   Summary

The auditor determined that there was one violation of policy requirements listed below.

> Failure to send denial of contract letter to vendor that was disqualified.

6   Date of Audit

April 8-9, 2008

 R & S Amusements Services   Page: 3

FIGURE 10-7c   Audit Report, Page 3

7   Personnel Contacted

Reid Lewis, Diana Brooks, and Mark Lewis from R & S Amusements Services and Jeff Dunbar and Kevin Pullen from PPMS.

8   Observations, Findings, and Recommendations

    a. Big Johns House of Electronics was disqualified from the bidding process due to the response it submitted not being complete and not signed by an authorized individual. In accordance with policy a letter was to be drafted and sent to the vendor informing them of their disqualification.
Finding: Failure to send correspondence.
Recommendation: Draft and send letter by April 30, 2008.

 R & S Amusements Services

Page: 4

FIGURE 10-7d   Audit Report, Page 4

R & S Amusements Services
Monthly Status Report
Date: 5/28/08

Project Name: Asset Tracking   Prepared by: Diana Brooks
Current Project Phase: Analysis – 1

Activity CTP	Budget $	Actual $	Completion Date Schedule	Actual
Refine SRD	5.5K	4.2K	5/24/08	5/25/08

Activity STP	Budget $	Actual $	Completion Date Schedule	Actual	%Complete
Use Cases	6.5K	2.3K	6/10/08	TBD	35%

Current Earned Values

CPI = .989
SPI = 1.00

Project Status

	Red
	Yellow
✓	Green

Rework/Changes

Description	Type	Cost Impact	Time Impact
None at this time			

Known Obstacles   Impact

None at this time

FIGURE 10-8 Monthly Status Report

effort. However, the cost has been slightly higher than budgeted. Based on the earned value indicators (see Chapter 11), the project has a green status. The team reports no rework or obstacles at this time. This report will be printed and hand delivered to Reid Lewis. Table 10-2 lists the other reports that are generated, as called out in the communications plan.

TABLE 10-2   Stakeholder Communications Matrix

Stakeholder	Document	Detail Level	Delivery Format	Frequency	Team Contacts
Reid Lewis	Weekly status Monthly status Staffing	Summary	Hard copy	Monthly	Diana Brooks Mark Lewis
Diana Brooks	Weekly status Monthly status Staffing	Detail	Email—PDF	Weekly	Ashley Brooks Heidi Cosgray
Mark Lewis	Weekly status Monthly status Staffing	Detail	Email—PDF	Weekly	Laura Kimball
Ashley Brooks	Weekly status	Detail	Hard copy	Weekly	Kenny Jones
Jeff Dunbar and Kevin Pullen	Weekly status Monthly status Staffing	Summary	Email—PDF	Weekly	Mark Lewis Diana Brooks

Chapter Review

1. The execution phase of a project consumes the greatest percentage of hours worked compared to all other phases in the project life cycle.
2. The goal of the execution phase of a project is to create all deliverables identified in the WBS, in the defined time frame established in the project schedule.
3. Project deliverables during the execution phase consist of the following: quality audits, human resources task assignments, human resources performance information, dissemination of project performance information, and selection of seller proposals.
4. Quality assurance is focused on the processes that prevent errors or defects before they occur.
5. The role of a quality assurance department is to ensure that the defined quality processes are being followed by everyone on a project team.
6. The first step in the human resources team acquisition process is to understand the technical skill requirements for each task. The second step is to evaluate a potential team member's nontechnical skills, consisting of personality traits, communication skills, interest and motivation factors, and business knowledge.
7. Two instruments used to aid a project manager in understanding personality traits are the Myers-Briggs Type Indicator and the Keirsey Temperament Sorter.
8. The objectives of the project team development process are to improve the competencies of each team member and to promote teamwork to enhance project performance.
9. Managing a project team involves tracking team member performance, providing feedback, resolving issues, and coordinating changes to enhance project performance.

10. Conflict management involves preventing, managing, or resolving conflicts as they occur throughout a project.
11. Project teams develop in varying lengths of time through a five-stage maturity process: forming, storming, norming, performing, and adjourning.
12. The process of managing stakeholders' expectations involves managing communications to satisfy the needs of and resolve issues with project stakeholders.
13. A project manager is responsible for making sure that information is disseminated to stakeholders correctly and in the time and format requested.
14. To reduce the opportunity for bias when selecting a seller's proposal, the procurement selection team should use a weighted scoring model. This model uses decision criteria that the selection committee created when the procurement proposals were created and sent to the sellers.

Glossary

conflict management   A process that seeks to prevent, manage, or resolve conflicts as they occur throughout the life of a project.

quality assurance   The implementation of all planned activities to ensure that a project will employ all processes needed to meet stated quality requirements.

quality audit   An independent review of executing processes to ensure that they are being followed and that they will enable the project team to meet the established quality standards.

Review Questions

1. List and explain several of the common problems that occur in many projects during the execution phase of the project life cycle.
2. What is the main goal of the quality assurance process?
3. What is the quality audit used for?
4. List and explain the first step in the process of acquiring a project team. Also list and explain the second step.
5. List the four dimensions of the Myers-Briggs Type Indicator model and describe characteristics of each.
6. List and describe the activities a project manager conducts in managing a project team's human resources.
7. Define *conflict management* and describe why it is dynamic and not always bad for a project.
8. Define the three different categories of conflict on projects and discuss which ones generally are and are not for a project's success.
9. What is a virtual team?
10. List the goals for the process of developing a project team.
11. List the areas in which conflict is most prevalent during the execution phase.
12. List and define each stage of the Tuchman model for team maturation.
13. List the principal goals of team-building activities.
14. List several of the team-building activities described in this chapter and explain why they would be used during the execution phase.
15. Describe the importance of managing stakeholder expectations.
16. Describe the main objective of the manage communications process.
17. Describe the resources that are required to work on the procurement proposal selection committee.
18. Describe how weights are used in a weighted scoring model for seller proposal selection.

Problems and Exercises

1. The project execution phase contains fewer processes and deliverables than the project planning phase, but the execution phase consumes more time and resources. Explain.

2. Discuss the integration and overlap that exist between the project management life cycle and the product life cycle, especially during the execution phase of the project.

3. Jim is a project manager for a large Midwestern insurance company recently assigned to get on track a project that has been executing for several months. The project is slightly behind schedule and overbudget. One of the key problems has been that the project team put together for this project has experienced some turnover and has had to add new people who are unfamiliar with the project and the other team members. In addition, most of the original team members had not worked together much before they joined this team. The project requires the creation of a new application using software that the team was unfamiliar with in the beginning. The current team consists of 12 people, 4 females and 8 males, with 3 of the individuals born outside the United States. If you were Jim, what types of team-building techniques would you use to get the project back on track?

4. You are the project manager for a team of 25 people assigned to upgrade all 250 workstations in the company to the Windows Vista operating system. Stacy, a new hire in the procurement department, has been assigned to your project. During a recent team meeting, you mention to Stacy that your group is doing a phased roll-out and that you will need pricing from Microsoft on the 250 new copies of Vista that you'll need.

   Two weeks later, you receive a phone call from the receiving department that several large boxes containing Vista just arrived, and they need to know what to do with them. This is not what you had in mind, and it creates several issues. The project team needed only one copy of the media, which they were going to install on the server and push out to all the networked computers. Also, the project budget was set up for a purchase but not for several months as the team is preparing to image all the current computers and understand the software requirements for each. What type of communication techniques should have been used to avoid this situation? Explain.

5. Create a weighted scoring model in Microsoft Excel or your favorite spreadsheet program, based on the following information: The Garcia Property Management (GPM) Company has seen its business grow from two employees operating out of Nadia Garcia's garage to a company with 50 employees and significant office space. The time has come for GPM to invest in an integrated software package to help run the business, including financial software, sales and marking, and inventory. GPM, not having the expertise to run this project itself, has hired a professional consulting company to find the right software and hardware. The consulting company sent out an RFQ to five different vendors. Each seller proposal was reviewed using the following criteria: contract choices, price, requirements satisfied, experience, previous customers, and financial stability. Because the company is still somewhat small and is growing with slim profit margins, price was deemed to be very important, followed by requirements, experience, previous customers, financial stability, and then contract choices. Create a weighted scoring model for this case, supplying your own results for each of the five sellers.

6. The following weighted scoring model results were reported for a project to install a new help desk software application for the IT department. Unfortunately, after all the results were tabulated, two of the seller proposals ended up with exactly the same total score.

   What further analysis/decision making could be used to make a final determination in selecting the best proposal?

Criterion		Weight	Project			
			1	2	3	4
1	Experience	15%	70	70	70	30
2	Requirements match	20%	30	70	50	70
3	Contract choices	10%	10	10	70	30
4	Price	20%	30	70	70	30
5	Seller interests	10%	50	30	70	30
6	Seller approach	10%	50	50	50	30
7	Customer list	15%	70	70	30	10
	Totals	100%	44	58	58	35

	Rating		
	Poor/not at all	0
	Below average	10
	Average	30
	Above average	50
	Excellent	70

Projects and Research

1. Research, using the Internet, several real examples of weighted scoring models that organizations have used to select seller proposals. Compare the selected criteria and the weights used. Discuss why the criteria and weights vary between organizations and industries.

2. Research the Myers-Briggs Type Indicator (MBTI), how it is used, and who is using it. Also, look for newer studies that have evolved since this test was first introduced. Conduct interviews with professional project managers, asking how often they get to select their own project team members as opposed to having them selected for them. If they get to choose their own teams, research which methods they use to select members.

3. Conflict on IT projects is inevitable, but the nature of the conflict has changed over the past 10 years. Research how the areas generating the most conflict have shifted over time.

4. Use the Internet to search for conflict management training and describe the results, including who is doing the training and how the training is done.

5. Research team-building activities that several organizations have used to aid their project teams. Describe the individual situations, and why each particular activity was chosen, and whether the activity was successful.

MINICASE

1. **Background:** (Review the R & S Amusements Services case study.) The whole project team from R & S Amusements Services is at its offsite face-to-face meeting, beginning the team-building activities. The first activity is an outdoor scavenger hunt. Each team of three is given a list of items to find and bring back.

   Current Situation 1: Danny Calloway is the league coordinator for R & S. As the groups are announced and given their lists, Danny speaks just loud enough for everyone around him to hear: "Boy, this has to be the biggest waste of time. I have a ton of work to get done, and I'm here doing this? I don't even know most of these people very well since I travel so much to each of the businesses we support. Can I be excused to go get some real work done?"

   Discussion: Reid Lewis, president of R & S, and Kevin Pullen from PPMS have overheard Danny's comments. Put yourself in their place. How would you reply to Danny, and how would you explain the importance of getting the team to function as a team? What arguments could you offer to convince Danny that the team-building activities are worthwhile?

Current Situation 2: Toward the end of the all-day session, the results from the MBTI are reported to Jeff, Reid, and Kevin. The results demonstrate that, based on his answers, maybe Danny shouldn't be a team leader. This information, coupled with his response to the team-building activities and with some other negative comments, has created a challenging situation for Reid.

Discussion: Put yourself in Reid's position. What should you do with Danny? Should you fire him? Do you relieve him of project leader responsibilities but keep him involved, knowing this might continue to affect the team? or Do you leave him as the team leader but get him some additional training (and, if so, what kind)?

Suggested Readings

Brooks, F. (1995). *The mythical man-month*. Reading, MA: Addison-Wesley.

Cleland, D. (1996). *Strategic management of teams*. New York: Wiley.

Cleland, D. (1997, January). Team building: The new strategic weapon. *PM Network*, pp. 29–31.

DeMarco, T., & Lister, T. (1987). *Peopleware: Productive projects and teams*. New York: Dorset House.

Einsiedel, A. (1987). Profile of effective project managers. *Project Management Journal*, 18(5):51–56.

Ertel D. (1999). Turning negotiation into a corporate capability. *Harvard Business Review*, 77(3): 55–70.

Ford, R., & McLaughlin, F. (1992, November). Successful project teams: A study of MIS managers. *IEEE Transactions on Engineering Management*, pp. 312–317.

Griffiths, M. (2004). Utilizing agile principles alongside a guide to the project management body of knowledge for better project execution and control in software development projects. PMI Global Congress Proceedings, Anaheim, CA.

Hersey, P., & Blanchard, K. (1979). *Management of organizational behavior*. Englewood Cliffs, NJ: Prentice-Hall.

Keirsey, D., & Bates, M. (1984). *Please understand me: An essay on temperament styles*. Amherst, NY: Prometheus Books.

Kerzner, H. (2006). *Project management: A systems approach to planning, scheduling, and controlling*. Hoboken, NJ: John Wiley & Sons, Inc.

Kezsbom, G. (1992). Re-opening Pandora's box: Sources of project conflict in the '90s. *Industrial Engineering* 24(5):54–59.

McConnell, S. (1996). *Rapid development*. Redmond, WA: Microsoft Press.

Nelson, B. (1998, July). Energized teams: Real world examples. *PM Network*, pp. 43–46.

Posner, B. (1986). What's all the fighting about? Conflicts in project management. *IEEE Transactions on Engineering Management* EM-33:207–211.

Project Management Institute web site, www. pmi.org.

Project Management Institute (PMI). (2004). *A guide to the project management body of knowledge*, 3rd ed. Newton Square, PA: PMI.

Raiffa, H., Richardson, J., & Metcalfe, D. (2002). *Negotiation analysis: The science and art of collaborative decision making*. Cambridge: Harvard University Press.

Stuckenbruck, L., & Marshall, D. (1985). Team building for project managers. In John R. Adams et al., eds., *The Principles of Project Management: Collected Handbooks from the Project Management Institute*. John R. Adams et., al., eds. 1997. Sylva, NC: PMI Publication Division.

Thamhain, H., & Wilemon, D. (1975, Summer). Conflict management in project life cycles. *Sloan Management Review*, pp. 31–49.

The Leaders Institute. *Tennis Ball*. Retrieved from: http://www.leadersinstitute.com/teambuilding/team_building_tips/tennis_balls.html.

Tuchman, B. (1965). Development sequence in small groups. *Psychological Development Bulletin* 63(6):384–399.

Wideman, R.M. (1998). Project teamwork, personality profiles and the population at Large: Do we have enough of the right kind of people? Proceedings of the 29th Annual Project Management Institute Seminar/Symposium "Tides of Change," Long Beach, California, USA, 1998.

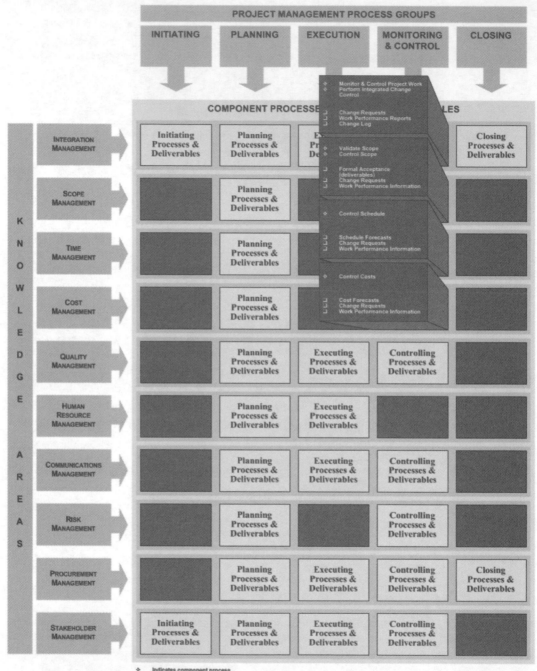

PROJECT MANAGEMENT PROCESS GROUPS

	INITIATING	PLANNING	EXECUTION	MONITORING & CONTROL	CLOSING

COMPONENT PROCESSES AND DELIVERABLES

KNOWLEDGE AREAS	INITIATING	PLANNING	EXECUTION	MONITORING & CONTROL	CLOSING
INTEGRATION MANAGEMENT	Initiating Processes & Deliverables	Planning Processes & Deliverables	Executing Processes & Deliverables	◆ Monitor & Control Project Work ◆ Perform Integrated Change Control ❏ Change Requests ❏ Work Performance Reports ❏ Change Log	Closing Processes & Deliverables
SCOPE MANAGEMENT		Planning Processes & Deliverables		◆ Validate Scope ◆ Control Scope ❏ Formal Acceptance (deliverables) ❏ Change Requests ❏ Work Performance Information	
TIME MANAGEMENT		Planning Processes & Deliverables		◆ Control Schedule ❏ Schedule Forecasts ❏ Change Requests ❏ Work Performance Information	
COST MANAGEMENT		Planning Processes & Deliverables		◆ Control Costs ❏ Cost Forecasts ❏ Change Requests ❏ Work Performance Information	
QUALITY MANAGEMENT		Planning Processes & Deliverables	Executing Processes & Deliverables	Controlling Processes & Deliverables	
HUMAN RESOURCE MANAGEMENT		Planning Processes & Deliverables	Executing Processes & Deliverables		
COMMUNICATIONS MANAGEMENT		Planning Processes & Deliverables	Executing Processes & Deliverables	Controlling Processes & Deliverables	
RISK MANAGEMENT		Planning Processes & Deliverables		Controlling Processes & Deliverables	
PROCUREMENT MANAGEMENT		Planning Processes & Deliverables	Executing Processes & Deliverables	Controlling Processes & Deliverables	Closing Processes & Deliverables
STAKEHOLDER MANAGEMENT	Initiating Processes & Deliverables	Planning Processes & Deliverables	Executing Processes & Deliverables	Controlling Processes & Deliverables	

◆ Indicates component process
❏ Indicates deliverable

11

Project Monitoring and Control, Part I

R & S Amusements Services

Event 11

Setting *It is about midway through the R & S Amusements Services project, and the project leaders have convened in a small conference room located outside Reid Lewis's office at R & S Amusements. Those in attendance include Reid Lewis, Diana Brooks, and Mark Lewis from R & S and Jeff Dunbar and Kevin Pullen from Premier Project Management Services.*

REID   Good morning, everyone. I hope you all had a good weekend.

JEFF   Mine was nice, thank you. The reason we are here is that everyone in this room is a member of the change advisory board.

MARK   Refresh my memory, Jeff. What is that?

JEFF   Gladly, Mark. As you recall, one of the most critical factors in being able to deliver a successful project is managing the requests for change that affect the time, cost, and scope of the project. For projects that don't have a formal process in place, cost and schedule can easily spin out of control with additional requirements and other changes that were not in the initial plan.

DIANA   That's easy: The project manager should just say no!

KEVIN   That's a lot easier said than done, Diana. Because of political ramifications and other factors, it may be difficult for a project manager to say no. If a request came from a company vice president or president, sticking your neck out and saying no might be political suicide. Most likely, if the VP was adamant about the request, he or she would go over the project manager's head and make a very strong recommendation to the project manager's boss. The project manager would probably not have much choice: Do the work or find another job. We all know that here at R & S, Reid would never pull rank and do that. *[Everyone laughs]*

JEFF   Kevin's right. When you have a committee of leaders to review change requests, analyze the impacts, and make approve/deny decisions, those decisions tend to be respected by all parties, and the responsibility and stress are not levied on just one person.

DIANA   That makes sense to me.

JEFF   With that said, let's talk about a request for change (RFC) we received from Elaine Henry. *[Jeff projects a copy of the RFC on the screen so everyone can view it]* I'll summarize: During the data migration activity to the new system, Elaine found that at least 30 percent of the data were inaccurate or missing.

MARK   What data are we talking about, Jeff?

JEFF   The data describing each asset—ID number, serial number, name, and so forth—as well as the data related to where that asset is currently installed and its installation history.

MARK   Okay, how does that impact the project?

KEVIN   According to Elaine, she is requesting full inventory of the company's assets—approximately 6,500 items—and the locations where they are installed—approximately 500 customer sites plus our warehouses and repair shops. She estimates that it will take three people 10 days to perform the inventory and an additional 5 days for one person to ensure that all the data have been input into the system.

JEFF   Based on our analysis, if we approve this and start tomorrow, we are looking at a three-week schedule delay because the next three tasks are dependent on those data being loaded and accurate. In terms of cost, we are looking at a $4,000 labor cost plus the cost of driving to the customer locations we didn't plan for.

REID   Wow! Do we have any alternatives?

DIANA   I don't think so. We definitely need the data, and the data have to be accurate, or we are just wasting our time. I do have an idea, though, that might decrease the time and cost a little bit.

REID   Let's hear it.

DIANA   It's possible that we have data collectors and technicians already scheduled to visit many of those locations. We can request that when they are onsite, they do the inventory.

MARK   Won't that slow them down or increase their daily work hours?

DIANA   Yes, which means we might have to pay some overtime hours or offer some other form of compensation. But, in my opinion, that will more than offset the savings in time, labor, and driving expenses. Why pay for a trip to just do inventory if we don't have to? In addition, it will give us an opportunity to install the new bar-code ID labels on each asset. We had that task scheduled for later in the project, but why not do it now?

MARK   That's true. I think it would work.

REID   I definitely agree. Sounds like a plan. Diana, I want you to check the collection schedules and . . .

JEFF   Reid, before you do that, let's make sure we follow proper protocol and make sure the group all agrees with the approval to proceed. If I may call for a vote. . .

(To be continued)

CHAPTER PREVIEW AND OBJECTIVES

This chapter describes the tools and techniques required to perform the monitoring and control processes for the project management body of knowledge (PMBOK) areas Integration Management, Scope Management, Time Management, and Cost Management. Monitoring and control involves a set of processes from nine of the ten knowledge areas. Chapter 12 will cover the remaining five knowledge areas.

Throughout this chapter, the material is presented such that the techniques of monitoring are intertwined with the techniques of control. The two represent opposite functions: Monitoring is collecting and reporting information concerning previously defined project performance elements, and control uses the information supplied by the monitoring techniques in order to bring project actual results in line with stated project performance standards.

As you read this chapter, you will:

- Understand what is meant by monitoring and control
- Understand the integrated change control process
- Understand how to conduct the scope verification process
- Understand how to monitor and control scope time and understand cost issues

AN INTRODUCTION TO PROJECT MONITORING AND CONTROL, PART I

This chapter is the first of two chapters on the techniques used during the monitoring and control phase of the project life cycle. Monitoring and control processes are used to measure and report progress; handle changes to scope, time, cost, and quality; manage risk mitigation strategies; and administer procurement contracts. Refer to Figure 3-2, which demonstrates the time and effort overlap of project process, and remember that the monitoring and control process begins very early in the life of a project and overlaps all other processes. Monitoring and control should begin as soon as work begins on the project charter, to coordinate the work of several people to produce a well-written charter that will be accepted by the project stakeholders.

The process of monitoring and control occurs in a continuous fashion throughout a project. The whole project team should be involved in the daily monitoring and control of the project. All the following elements should have been defined during the planning phase of the project: the items to be monitored, who is assigned to monitor them, how the data will be collected, and the frequency of monitoring.

The keys to making this process work are listed below:

- The organization and project manager must foster an environment that allows for the honest reporting of results. The old adage "don't shoot the messenger" definitely applies in this situation. Project managers need to have accurate information in order to manage a project optimally and to make the right decisions when data indicate that something is going wrong.
- To reduce the chances for biased reporting, the process should be as automated as possible, and there needs to be a separation of responsibilities. For example, the person monitoring the quality of a section of software code should not be the same person who wrote the code.
- Time must be allocated in the project schedule to perform the tasks of monitoring and control demonstrated in this chapter and Chapter 12.
- Finally, all members of the project team, stakeholders, and other management resources should receive training on effective monitoring and control techniques.

Monitoring and control consists of processes from nine of the ten PMBOK knowledge areas. This chapter covers the following processes: perform integrated change control, monitor and control project work, validate scope, control scope, control schedule, and control cost.

The remainder of this chapter discusses the tools and techniques needed to perform monitoring and control for these processes. The other knowledge area processes concerned with the monitoring and controlling of the project will be discussed in Chapter 12.

PROJECT MANAGEMENT CONCEPTS: PROJECT MONITORING AND CONTROL

The Integration Management Knowledge Area

The Integration Management knowledge area consists of the processes that coordinate all the various processes and activities contained in all five process groups—Initiate, Plan, Execute, Control, and Closing. Integration management processes become extremely important during monitoring and control due to the amount of overlap with other process groups and the continuous nature of the activities. All the techniques explained for this process group are used repeatedly throughout the life of a project. Not every technique is used on every project, as noted in the explanations of each, but those that are used are used repeatedly.

MONITOR AND CONTROL PROJECT WORK   Successful monitoring and control depends on accurate and current project work performance information. The types of information, with examples, are listed below:

- *Daily raw numbers*—These numbers are related to resource time expended per task assignment, milestones achieved, cost information, and resource calendar updates.
- *Frequency numbers*—The numbers deal with product bugs or quality issues reported, user issues reported, and communication issues.
- *Qualitative assessments*—These are assessments such as user-reported likes/dislikes about the product and team member–reported task completion percentage estimates.

Because of the amount of information needed for larger projects, many organizations try to automate the data collection process as much as possible. Many different tools exist to aid a project manager in collecting this information. Where appropriate in the text, these tools are mentioned.

To achieve repeatable successes from project to project, the tools and techniques used for monitoring and control must be instilled into the organization's culture as part of the project methodology. Every employee must understand the importance and need for accurate data collection to keep a project under control.

PERFORMING INTEGRATED CHANGE CONTROL   Every IT project that lasts more than a couple days will experience a variable amount of change. In the past, many tried to run IT projects using predictive system development methodologies, thinking that they could completely eliminate or greatly reduce the number of changes. More recently developed agile methodologies, as discussed in Chapter 2, understand that change is inevitable and that change can be a good thing that makes technology projects better, if they are managed correctly.

The management of change so that changes benefit a project instead of hurt the project is what the **integrated change control** process is all about. The integrated change control process is a formal process used to ensure that only approved necessary changes are made to a project or product. The change management process is performed from the beginning of the project through completion. It is extremely important to the success of any project that needed changes be allowed to happen but within a defined formal process that is communicated to all stakeholders and team members. The integrated change control process consists of the following key activities:

- Identifying that a change needs to occur or has occurred
- Establishing a governance structure for reviewing and approving requested changes
- Managing the approved changes when and as they occur, by regulating the flow of requested changes
- Maintaining the integrity of project artifacts, as changes occur (for example, all schedule information is updated to reflect the results of the changes to time, cost, budgets, schedules, quality, human resource needs, and risks)
- Communicating and documenting all changes to all stakeholders
- Configuration management to identify, document, and control changes to the work product

Figure 11-1 provides an example of a generic integrated change control process. It's important to understand who should control the process. Every documented requested change must be either accepted or rejected by an authority from the project management team; the proper authority is called a change advisory board (CAB) or a change control board (CCB). The CAB is a cross-functional group consisting of key members of the user and IT management teams. The chair of the CAB should be the key project sponsor or that person's designee. The chair, membership, and size of the CAB may vary, based on the requirements of each project. How often the group meets (in person or electronically) to discuss proposed changes depends on the needs of the project but should not exceed two weeks on any project. The team can meet and make decisions (reject, approve, defer, or analyze further) electronically—so it doesn't necessarily need to meet in person. The estimated size of the team is recommended to be between three and six persons, depending on the size and needs of the project.

The steps in the integrated change control process shown in Figure 11-1 are explained below:

Step 1. *Create the RFC*—Any person (the initiator) in the organization or another approved stakeholder can write a request for change (RFC). The RFC could also be written by a designated representative of an outsourcing partner. The information required for this form (Figure 11-2) is described later in the chapter. The completed form is sent to the designated change screener. The change screener can be more than one person but generally is just one person who has knowledge of the area affected by the change.

Step 2. *Initial review RFC*—The screener's first job is to make sure that the RFC is completely filled out, with all required information. If the RFC is not complete, it is returned to the initiator.

Step 3. *Review and assign priority*—The screener reviews the priority assignment suggested by the initiator to make sure it is accurate, based on his or her knowledge of the project and the initiator. Some individuals may submit all their requests with the highest priority and urgency, thinking this is the only way to get their issue passed.

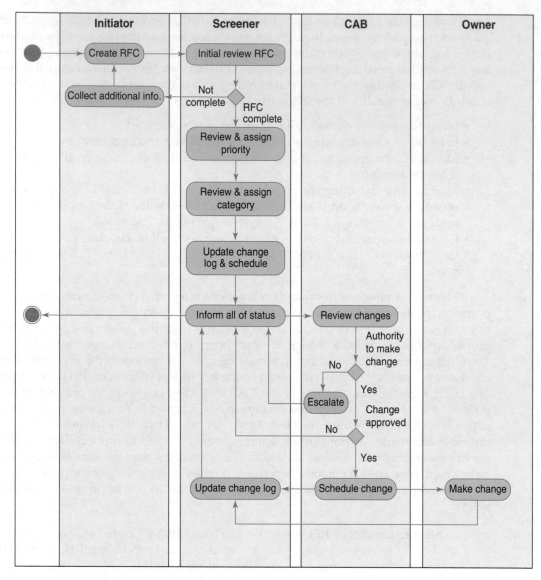

FIGURE 11-1 **Integrated Change Control Process**

Step 4. *Review and assign category*—The screener reviews the category assignment suggested by the initiator to make sure it is accurate, based on his or her knowledge of the project and the initiator.

Step 5. *Update change log and schedule*—An update is made to the master change control log, with all relevant information. Based on the priority and category of the change, it is scheduled for CAB review.

Step 6. *Inform all of status*—The screener is responsible for communicating all actions to the initiator, CAB, and other concerned stakeholders.

Step 7. *Review changes*—The CAB meets either in person or electronically to review any and all RFCs that have been scheduled for review:

- First, the CAB must determine whether it has the authority to make the change. If it does not, the RFC is elevated to the proper senior person(s).
- Second, the CAB reviews the change and has the option to do one of the following:
  - *Reject*—The change, in its current form, will not be made.
  - *Approve*—The change is scheduled, based on priority and category.
  - *Defer*—The change is deferred to a later meeting.
  - *Analyze further*—More information is needed about the change before a decision can be made.
- If rejected, the change is sent back to the initiator, with an explanation.
- If deferred, the change remains pending and is reviewed at a later meeting.
- If sent for further analysis, the change is sent back to the initiator with an explanation of needed information.
- If approved, the change is scheduled for incorporation into the project.

Step 8. *Schedule change*—When scheduled, the change is assigned to a change owner, who is the person responsible for making sure the change is made, tested, and communicated to the screener.

Step 9. *Make change*—Once the change is completed and verified, the screener updates the master change log accordingly.

The RFC shown in Figure 11-2 contains the following elements:

- *Project name*—If the change concerns an ongoing project, the project name; otherwise, the name of the application that the change applies to.
- *Date submitted*—The date the change is submitted and sent to the screener.
- *Submitted by*—The name and contact information of the change initiator.
- *Change req. #*—The change request number assigned by the screener, which is simply a unique sequential identifier. If using an automated system, the number is assigned automatically.
- *Priority*—One of the following options:
  - *Emergency*—Used only in the most severe cases, when day-to-day working of the business is affected or the business is at risk, such as after a major security breach
  - *High*—Important for the business, either financially or legally, and must be implemented soon
  - *Medium*—A needed change with good to excellent benefits to the business but without a critical need date
  - *Low*—A needed change with fair to good benefits to the business but without a critical need date
- *Description of change*—A complete, detailed description of the requested change, including examples and relevant affected parts of the project and/or system. This is any and all information needed to help the CAB make a decision about the merits of the change.
- *Category*—The change's impact on the infrastructure, users, or business. The choices are:
  - *Major*—Requires major changes to several executables and/or database tables

Request For Change

Project Name: Monthly Financial Status Reports   **Date Submitted:**   10/1/2008

Submitted by: Sally Jones   **Change Req. #:**
(name, contact information)

Priority: H   (E,H,M,L)   **Status:**

Description of change:

Due to the timing of the reports, the inventory carrying costs are not getting calculated correctly. In most cases the costs are submitted after the report generation causing the financial statements to be in error. The change is to delay the start of monthly report generation until most recent cost data is input. Change the system to add a check to make sure that the cost information has been input before generating the reports.

Category: Minor   (Major, Significant, Minor, Operational)

Business Reason for change: (cost benefit analysis)

To improve the accuracy of the monthly financial statements so that better decisions can be made in a more timely fashion.

Business Impact if change denied:

Late or poor decisions made because they are based on inaccurate information

Indicate Impact on:

Scope		Cost	X
Schedule		HR	
Risk		Quality	X
Other			

Suggested Implementation Schedule

I would suggest the change be made as soon as possible, and until done a note needs to be attached to the reports explaining the situation

Required Approvals:

Name	Date	Approve/Reject
Jim Golden		
Mark Kane		
Mike Rogers		

FIGURE 11-2 Request for Change Form

- *Significant*—Requires minor changes to several executables and/or database tables
- *Minor*—Requires minor changes to one executable or database table
- *Operational*—Needs minor upgrade to software version, security patch, and so on
- *Business reason for change*—The return on investment (ROI) justification for the change
- *Business impact if change denied*—Impact to the business if the change is not made
- *Indicate impact on*—One or more project characteristics that the change will affect (for example, cost, scope, schedule, quality, risk, budget)
- *Suggested implementation schedule*—Suggestions from the change initiator about when the change needs to be put in place, any task or project dependencies, or any required mandated dates
- *Required approvals*—If the CAB is authorized to make the change, signatures of the initiator and each member of the CAB. If the CAB is not authorized, then it is escalated to the appropriate senior person(s) of the organization for a decision and signature.

If possible, the RFC should be created electronically, especially for medium to large projects. This will expedite the process and reduce the chances for errors and misinterpretation. Several software packages allow the entire process to be automated and managed.

Using a formal integrated change control process offers the following benefits:

- Increased awareness of the impact of a proposed change
- Assurance that only needed or required changes are made
- Increased visibility
- Communication and documentation of changes
- Better schedule management
- Increased accountability on the part of both the requester of the change and the person assigned responsibility to complete the change
- Better control of project quality, based on established standards

The downside to using a formal process is the potential for a poorly run process giving the impression of control when little exists. If not managed properly, it could lead to longer delayed projects.

During many IT projects, a key part of the integrated change control process is managing the configuration of the product. Working with any of the software development tools today requires a plan to control configuration. As objects are developed by different individuals, teams, and organizations (outsourced), someone or something needs to make sure that they will fit together to create a working product. A configuration management process (or system) with change control provides a standardized, effective, and efficient process to centrally manage changes within a project. The configuration management process consists of the following:

- *Identification*—Identifying the structure of the product, its components, and their type and making them unique and accessible in some form to the team. For example, what version of the file/code/object is needed? The goal is to be able to identify any and all parts that make up/compose a single released/deployed version of the system or process.
- *Control*—Controlling the release of a product and changes to it throughout the product life cycle by having in place controls that ensure consistent releases via the

creation of a baseline product. Said another way, controlling each and every piece of the application within each formal release. An error found after a product is released needs to be evaluated for impact on other versions and maybe for other customers.

- *Status accounting*—Recording and reporting the status of the system components and change requests and gathering vital statistics about the system components in the product for auditing. The team must be able to reproduce each release of the system with complete documentation.
- *Verification and audit*—Validating the accuracy and completeness of a product against stated objectives and requirements and maintaining consistency among the components by ensuring that the product is configured with all the correct pieces.

Configuration management is best controlled using an automated process. Many software solutions are available on the market to aid a project team in managing the product configurations and communicating with all project teams.

All proposed changes need to be identified, recorded, and either accepted or rejected with valid sound business reasons. Performing the integrated change control process correctly is an important weapon in the war against scope creep.

The Scope Management Knowledge Area

Remember that the scope management knowledge area is responsible for ensuring that the project includes all the work needed and only the work needed to complete the project successfully in the eyes of the stakeholders. In this chapter, the processes concerned with monitoring and control are described: validating scope and controlling scope.

VALIDATING SCOPE   The process of validating scope is responsible for obtaining the stakeholder's formal acceptance of the completed project scope and associated deliverables. Each individual deliverable should be formally accepted by the appropriate stakeholder, as identified during the stakeholder analysis process. The process should provide written documentation that explains how the deliverable has met each of its requirements for scope and quality throughout the project, not just at the end. Once the stakeholder agrees, he or she must sign the document either in person or electronically. If the stakeholder refuses to sign the document, then an RFC form should be filled out and the integrated change control process initiated.

CONTROLLING SCOPE   The scope control process is responsible for influencing the factors that create project scope changes and attempts to control the impact of those changes, making sure all changes are approved through the formal integrated change control process discussed previously in this chapter. If a project is allowed to change freely (without change control), the rate of change experienced on the project will certainly exceed the rate of progress. As mentioned earlier, change on an IT project is inevitable and needs to be formally managed. Scope creep (which happens during IT projects when the scope of the system is allowed to continually grow) is one of the key contributors to projects costing more than originally budgeted and lasting longer than originally scheduled. The following are some of the major sources of scope changes experienced on IT projects:

- Missed or misunderstood requirements
- Technology changes and complexities

- Human resources issues (for example, untrained resources, poorly assigned resources, turnover, productivity problems)
- Uncontrolled changes
- Evolving knowledge of the product being created
- Evolving knowledge of the project environment
- New mandates (from the organization, society, government, and so on)
- Customers' understanding of their needs evolving over time as more of the product is created
- Poor schedule development

To control scope, a project leader and the entire project team need to understand all of these scope-related issues, implement a formal integrated change control process, and document and communicate all scope issues from the beginning of the project until the end to avoid trying to understand how a project gets so far behind schedule at the end. A project manager must maintain control of all facets of a project, especially scope, every day of the project. Waiting until the weekly status meeting to find out about a scope issue may be too late, depending on the issue. Automating the process of scope management will help a project manager track scope issues daily and deal with any time management issues, discussed next.

PROVEN STRATEGIES AND HINTS TO SUCCESS

Forselius' (2007) article is a summary of the core concepts of two initiatives referred to as "Southern SCOPE" and "Northern SCOPE" by the Australian government and the Finnish Software Measurement Association, respectively. The reported success rates attributed to these two initiatives have been extraordinary for the Information and Communications Technology (ICT) industry according to Forselius. In both initiatives a new role is introduced, referred to as the project scope manager, with responsibilities to scope, quantify, manage and control, communicate, requirements articulation and documentation, and change management. The scope manager works with and many times for the project manager. "The scope manager is typically a metrics specialist who has excellent skills in business analysis, project estimation and functional size measurement," writes Forselius. The scope manager is generally independent from the project team, meaning he or she doesn't report to the lead software developer or to a specific business unit manager. The other major issue addressed in the article is the proper sizing of the project. Too large and it becomes unmanageable; too small and it doesn't deliver sufficient business value. The projects must be broken down into subprojects correctly.

The Time Management Knowledge Area

The time management knowledge area includes processes that are responsible for making sure the project completes in a timely fashion according to the initial schedule created plus any authorized changes. In this chapter, the processes concerned with monitoring and control are described: controlling the schedule.

CONTROLLING THE SCHEDULE   The schedule control process is concerned with determining the current status of all items currently being worked on, influencing factors that create schedule changes, determining whether the schedule has changed, and managing changes to the schedule by using a formal integrated change control process. Summarized below are best practices to follow in controlling schedule issues.

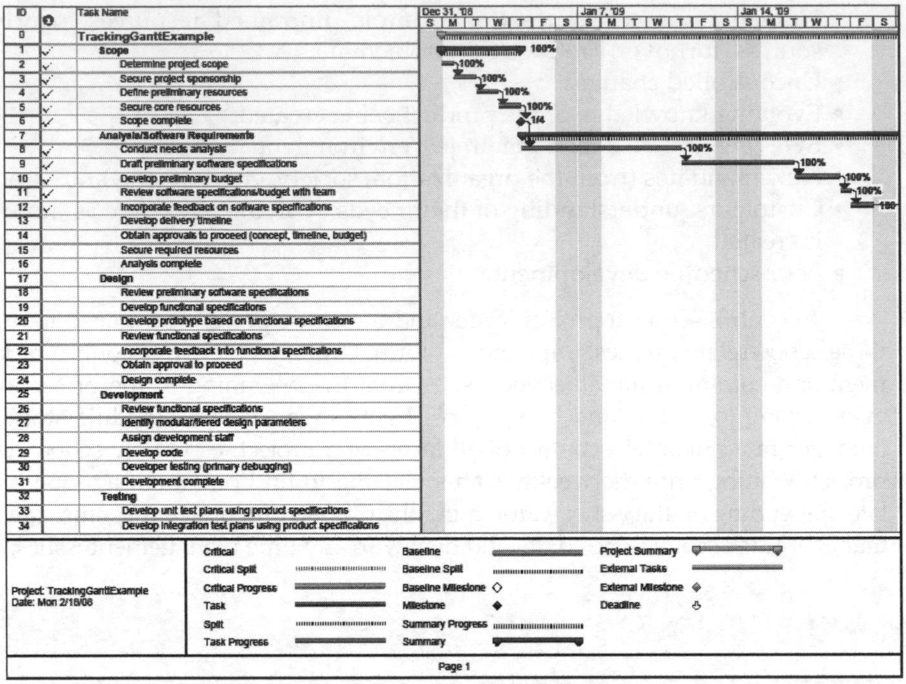

FIGURE 11-3 Microsoft Project Tracking Gantt Chart

- Build an accurate schedule in the beginning of the project, with known task dependencies.
- Follow a formal integrated change control process to determine if and when change that will affect the project schedule occurs.
- Foster an environment that allows and encourages honest, continuous communication among all project team members and stakeholders.
- Collect project status (via an automated system, if possible) in a timely manner (daily), especially near the end of the project.
- Determine early in the life of the project exactly what information needs to be collected and how often it might affect the schedule. Potential information to collect includes milestones achieved on time and on budget, hours worked on each task, hours remaining to complete each active task, resource availability issues such as turnover or health issues, cost information for resources and other budget items, risk information, quality information, scope changes, and vendor issues.
- Based on the stakeholder analysis, define the needs for data reporting of time and schedule issues. For an example of how to report the relevant information to the stakeholder, see the tracking Gantt chart shown in Figure 11-3.
- Be aware of the progress of parallel activities relative to each other.
- Conduct a formal risk management process.

Figure 11-3 shows a Microsoft Project tracking Gantt chart, which is used to quickly show project progress. The summary lines have an added bar beneath them, showing how much of the work has been completed. The chart shown also contains the percentage complete number that the project manager inserted. A chart such as this can give a stakeholder or a project manager a quick idea of how far along each task and summary task is toward completion. The chart is very easy to understand and can be tailored to fit each individual's need for information. The drawback to a tracking Gantt chart is that it has no ability to demonstrate the reason or root cause for being behind or ahead of schedule, and it doesn't provide a mechanism to show future projections for completions.

Controlling the schedule is best done on a continuous daily basis because once things begin to slip, the problems snowball into bigger and bigger issues. Time is a critical element on a project because no matter what you do, time passes, and when you lose it, it is very difficult to get back. Therefore, it's important to control time starting early in the life of a project and continuing throughout the project.

The Cost Management Knowledge Area

The cost management knowledge area is responsible for defining and controlling all project costs so that the project can be completed within the approved budget. In this chapter, the process concerned with monitoring and control is described—controlling cost.

CONTROLLING COST The cost control process is concerned with influencing the factors that create cost variances on a project and controlling changes to a project's budget. Like the other monitoring and control processes, cost control is a continual process of comparing the current actual project expenditures to the defined budget and determining when issues need to be dealt with to either bring the project back in line with the current budget or make the needed changes to the budget to reflect reality. Every change made on the project to scope, schedule, human resources, or quality will also affect cost, either positively or negatively. Very rarely will you add scope to a project or finish a project sooner and not affect the project budget. It is therefore important to learn to manage these changes, using the formal change control process, which includes process steps to evaluate cost impacts, and then communicate these impacts to all stakeholders.

A key tool used as input for the formal integrated change control process and the timely management of a project budget is the **earned value management (EVM)** technique. The technique helps a project team and stakeholders gain a better understanding of just how a project is performing. EVM provides needed information for the evaluation of project status simultaneously across time, cost, and work performance. Without EVM, many teams fail to evaluate performance properly. The following simple example illustrates the point. Tom, a newly promoted project manager, was preparing his weekly status report by reviewing the actual information that had been input by members of the team. The project team was scheduled to work on six different tasks during the previous week, and task 1 and task 4 were the only two tasks that should have been completed during the current reporting period. The current status of these six tasks was reported as follows:

- *Task 1*—Budget one resource, 16 hours effort; actual hours 10, task not complete
- *Task 2*—Budget two resources, 32 hours effort; actual hours 28, task not complete
- *Task 3*—Budget two resources, 40 hours effort; actual hours 8, task not complete
- *Task 4*—Budget two resources, 16 hours effort; actual hours 16, task complete
- *Task 5*—Budget four resources, 88 hours effort; actual hours 44, task not complete
- *Task 6*—Budget one resource, 24 hours effort; actual hours 8, task not complete

Tom reviewed the information and reported that everything was still on schedule except for task 1. For some reason, task 1 was scheduled to be worked on for 16 hours and then completed but only 10 hours was worked. Before Tom makes any assumptions about the current status of each of these tasks, one key piece of information is missing: Just how done are the tasks—really? The first mistake many new project managers make is to assume that just because task 5 had 44 hours of work reported that it was half done, or 50 percent complete. Two key additional pieces of information must be collected for each task from the resources working on them: an estimate of how much of the task is actually done and an estimate of how much work still remains. These two pieces of information are reported differently across organizations but generally are reported as percentage complete figures. For example, for task 5, the resources reported that they worked 44 hours on the task but that they were only about 25 percent done with all the work. If this is accurate, the budget and time information for this task will need to be changed. The original estimate of 88 total hours for four resources (22 hours each) will need to be changed to 176 hours, and the associated cost for this task will also need to be changed. This might also affect the project schedule if this item is on the critical path or becomes part of the critical path due to the change in time.

How resources determine a task's percentage complete may not be a trivial matter, depending on the size and complexity of the task. A small task requiring one resource just 8 hours to complete is much simpler than a task that requires four resources 40 hours to complete. In an IT project, some estimates of percentage complete are difficult to determine; think of the software testing phase for a newly developed application when the exact number of bugs or problems you will encounter is relatively unknown; coming up with an accurate percentage complete number is sometimes just an educated guess. A project team can use several tools to aid in making percentage complete estimates. Several are mentioned next:

- *0–100 percent rule*—No credit is given for any work completed until the task is completed. This rule makes it very difficult to obtain any meaningful information using EVM. The project will appear to always be running behind schedule.
- *50–50 percent rule*—When a task or work package is started, it is immediately assigned a 50 percent complete status until it is completed and then is set to 100 percent complete. This rule works well when assessing the percentage complete is extremely difficult. No estimate of completion is required, but as with the 0–100 percent rule, using EVM is not as useful.
- *Interval percent rule*—With this method, a team agrees to use a set of completion milestones such as thirds (33 percent, 67 percent, 100 percent) or fourths (25 percent, 50 percent, 75 percent, 100 percent). When the work package is started, it is quickly assigned a 25 percent complete status. When the resources working on the task estimate it to be half done, it moves to 50 percent complete, and when it is three-fourths complete, it moves to 75 percent done until it is complete.

Of the three rules, the interval percent rule comes closest to providing meaningful EVM output.

The following key terms and concepts are important to understanding how to use earned value to assess project performance and predict future project performance:

- *Planned value (PV)*—This is the budgeted cost for the work scheduled to be completed on a task, work package, or activity up to a given point in time. Also referred to as budgeted cost of work scheduled (BCWS).
- *Actual cost (AC)*—This is the total cost incurred in accomplishing work on a task during a given time period. It must directly correspond to the characteristics defined for PV and EV. Also referred to as actual cost of work performed (ACWP).
- *Earned value (EV)*—This is the budgeted amount for the work actually completed on a task during a given time period, or EV = (PV) * (Percentage complete). Also referred to as budgeted cost of work performed (BCWP).
- *Estimate to complete (ETC)*—This is the revised estimate for the work remaining, as determined by the project team. This should be an independent, non-calculated estimate to complete for all the work remaining, and it should consider the performance of the resources to date along with other factors, such as what tasks remain, risks, complexity factors, and learning curve theory.
- *Estimate at completion (EAC)*—This is equal to the actual costs reported to date plus the new ETC.
- *Budget at completion (BAC)*—This is equal to the planned total budget for the complete project.
- *Cost variance (CV)*—This equals earned value (EV) minus actual cost (AC), or CV = EV − AC.
- *Schedule variance (SV)*—This equals earned value (EV) minus planned value (PV), or SV = EV − PV.
- *Cost performance index (CPI)*—This equals the ratio of EV to the AC, or CPI = EV/AC. A CPI value less than 1.0 indicates a cost overrun of the estimates, and a CPI value greater than 1.0 indicates a cost under budget estimates.
- *Schedule performance index (SPI)*—This equals the ratio of EV to PV, or SPI = EV/PV. An SPI value less than 1.0 indicates a project behind schedule, and an SPI value greater than 1.0 indicates a project ahead of schedule.

The calculations for EV are fairly straightforward; the following simple example shows how EV can help a project team assess project performance. A systems development project has been planned using an iterative incremental systems development methodology that calls for the system to be developed in four iterations or releases. Each iteration is budgeted to cost $50,000 and take two months to complete. Table 11-1 summarizes the current situation at the end of six months of development.

As shown in Table 11-1, after six months of project execution, the first iteration or release has been completed, at the budgeted cost of $50,000; the second iteration's scope has also been 100 percent completed, but at a cost higher than budgeted, at $75,000; and the

TABLE 11-1   Earned Value Project Schedule Example

Iteration	Cost	Duration	Performance Results
Release 1	$50,000	2 months	Scope complete, at cost of $50,000
Release 2	$50,000	2 months	Scope complete, at cost of $75,000
Release 3	$50,000	2 months	Scope 50 percent complete, at cost of $40,000
Release 4	$50,000	2 months	Not started

TABLE 11-2   Earned Value Calculation Results

Formula	Results	Details
EV = PV* Percent complete	= ($150,000)* (5 / 6) = $125,000	Earned value = $50,000 + $50,000 + $25,000
AC	= $165,000	Actual cost = $50,000 + $75,000 + $40,000
CV = EV − AC	= $125,000 − $165,000 = (−$40,000)	Cost variance
SV = EV − PV	= $125,000 − $150,000 = (−$25,000)	Schedule variance
CPI = EV / AC	= ($125,000) / ($165,000) = .758	Cost performance index
SPI = EV / PV	= ($125,000) / ($150,000) = .833	Schedule performance index
BAC	= $200,000	Budget at completion: $50,000 + $50,000 + $50,000 + $50,000
ETC = (BAC − EV) / CPI	= ($200,000 − $125,000) /.758 = $98,945	Estimate to complete
EAC = AC + ETC	= $165,000 + $98,945 = $263,945	Estimate at completion

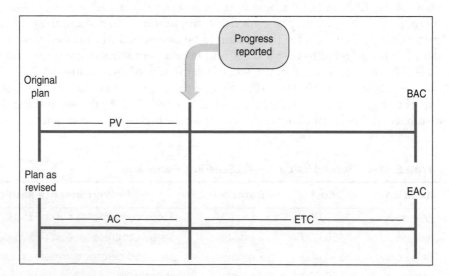

FIGURE 11-4   Earned Value Relationships

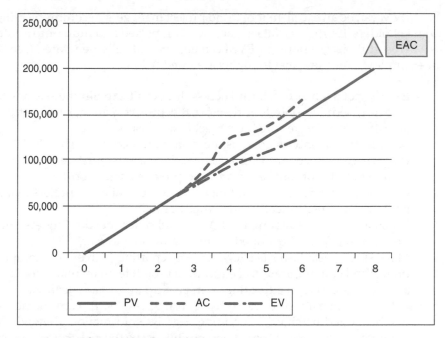

FIGURE 11-5 **Graph of Earned Value Calculations**

third release is only 50 percent completed at the end of two months, at a cost of $40,000. From these results, we can calculate the earned value information shown in Table 11-2.

Notice in Table 11-2 that the CV and SV are negative. Knowing nothing else about the project, a manager can look at these two numbers and quickly see that the project is overbudget and behind schedule at this point in time. A manager reviewing this information needs to understand that these values are only indicators of the current situation present when the performance measures were collected for this example at the end of month six. The numbers could be based on some anomaly that will be corrected in future work. The CPI and SPI reflect similar information in that they are less than 1.0. The ETC was calculated assuming that the numbers collected are typical performance measures that are not expected to change. If this were an atypical situation—meaning that in release 2 and 3 some exceptional events occurred that caused the schedule and cost to exceed the budget but this is not expected to affect the release 4 numbers—the ETC would be calculated as just the budget at completion (BAC) minus the earned value (EV). Figure 11-4 demonstrates the relationship between AC, ETC, BAC, and EAC.

When ETC is calculated, the number that most managers and stakeholders are interested in—the estimate at completion (EAC)—can be calculated. Table 11-2 shows that the BAC was $200,000, what the project was originally budgeted, and now with the cost escalation issues in release 2 and release 3, the estimated project budget has grown to $232,000. Figure 11-5 shows the values for PV, AC, and EV over time and where the project started going off course and what it will take to get it back to the original budget. During the first two months, the project was on time and on budget. During month 3 of the project, the scope was only half completed and at a higher-than-estimated cost. The graph reflects the higher costs and lower EV.

EVM can be an excellent tool to aid project managers in communicating project status to stakeholders. If progress data are accurately reported and input into a software tool such as Microsoft Project, reports on EVM can be automatically generated (see Appendix A for an example). A few key final thoughts are listed below:

- EVM is not a silver bullet for success. It doesn't explain the reasons for variances in cost or schedule—only that they exist. A project manager must still make the right adjustments to make sure the project is successful.
- The results are only as good as the data input accuracy. The old IT adage "Garbage in/garbage out" certainly applies here. The results must be based on accurate information both for original estimates and progress data reported.
- Generating the numbers in a timely fashion can allow a project manager to act in a proactive manner instead of in a reactive mode.
- When a team is calculating the EAC, stakeholders need to understand how the forecasted number was generated so they know how to react.
- Make sure to establish rules for progress reporting (percentage complete) early in the project and communicate and educate all project team members for consistency across all work tasks. When educating team participants, assure team participants that they will not be penalized for honestly reporting results. If team members feel that they will be judged harshly for reporting negative information, they will delay reporting accurate information, hoping they can still rescue the task from being late or overbudget, thus causing the EVM numbers to be inaccurate. The project manager won't have accurate information until the scheduled end of the task, when it isn't complete.
- EV information does not have to be gathered from every work package. Meaningful results can be obtained by estimating percentage complete information at the summary task level. For example, information can be collected for a subset of functionality instead of every detail item needed to create it. For example, say that adding new static contact information for an organization is just one of the new features being added to the public portion of the company's web site. Adding the static information requires many steps, including collecting the information, determining where to place it, determining the best font and size to use for the information, and updating any associated documentation. Instead of reporting percentage complete for each of these detail tasks, the team reports percentage complete for the task of adding static contact information.

This concludes the discussion of the tools and techniques used in the following monitoring and control processes: monitoring and controlling project work, performing integrated change control, validating scope, controlling scope, controlling schedule, and controlling cost. The next section discusses the general approach used to monitor and control project work.

THE PROJECT MONITORING AND CONTROL PROCESS

The process used to monitor and control project work varies, depending on the size, complexity, and location of resources and other factors. Listed below are general guidelines that should be followed during the monitoring and control process.

- Educate stakeholders and team members on the need for and use of progress information to foster an environment of honest and accurate reporting.
- Automate the collection of status information as much as possible.

- Frequency of collection is dependent on the size of the project and the location of participants. Regardless of the project characteristics, collection of project status information should never exceed one week, and if possible, it should be done daily.
- Frequency and formatting of reports are outlined in the stakeholder analysis described in Chapter 4.
- Figure 11-1 shows the process for integrated change control.
- Final deliverable approval must be formally obtained from stakeholders before any task can be declared complete.

HOW TO CONDUCT THE MONITORING AND CONTROL PROCESS, PART I

This last section of the chapter uses the processes outlined previously to provide examples of deliverables for the following monitoring and control processes: performing integrated change control, verifying scope, controlling scope, controlling schedule, and controlling cost. Before proceeding, review the information presented in the R & S Amusements Services case study. In Event 11, the project for R & S Amusements has been executing for some time and has experienced some familiar problems. Several of the identified issues are discussed next.

Educate Stakeholders and Team Members

Jeff and Kevin from PPMS met with each member of the project team and reviewed with them the process of reporting project status information and the importance of reporting accurate information. They stressed that in order for Reid Lewis and the other managers to understand the status of the overall project in terms of cost, scope, and schedule at a given time, the collection of the individual task status information was vital. The information about the tasks is combined to provide a complete picture of the project at a point in time. Management can review this snapshot and make adjustments, if necessary, to keep the project on track.

The employee status report template shown in Figure 11-6 was distributed to each team member, along with instructions on how to complete it. Each team member will submit a completed status report to Diana Brooks first thing each Monday morning. The template will be placed online so each member can submit an electronic copy to Diana via email.

Because of the need to receive timely and accurate status information, any issues that Diana cannot resolve will be sent to Reid Lewis, and disciplinary action may result if they cannot be resolved.

Steps 2 and 3: Define Frequency and Automate the Collection of Status Information

Diana Brooks will receive each member's status report and update the project repository using Microsoft Project by noon each Monday. The project management team has been trained to use Microsoft Project to view reports and perform queries.

Step 4: Distribute Management Project Status Reports

After collecting and inputting the weekly status information, Diana Brooks generates the management status report shown in Figure 11-7. This report is generated and distributed to the management team every Tuesday. Note that in addition to the financial calculations explained in the previous sections of this chapter, this report utilizes the red, yellow, and green

R & S Amusements Services

Employee Status Report

Employee Information

Employee Name: **Ashley Brooks**	Employee ID: **45007**
Department: **Business Operations**	Manager: **Diana Brooks**
Report Start Date: **4/2/08**	Report End Date: **4/8/08**

Project Tasks	Hours Worked	Status – Hours to Completion
Purchase Requisition – Laser and Bar Code Printers	4.5	Complete - 0
Contract Tracking	2.5	On track - 15

Next Week's Planned Tasks	Hours Planned	Concerns
Contract Tracking	3.0	

Accomplishments
Two HP laser printers and two bar code printers ordered.

Issues
HP laser printers will have a one week delivery delay.

FIGURE 11-6 **Example of a Team Member Status Report**

Project Performance Report   Asset Management   Week Ending 4/8/07

S#	Item Description	Budget		Earned	Actual	Cost		Schedule		Performance Index			Forecast			Average Index	Status
		Overall BAC ($)	PV ($)	EV ($)	AC ($)	CV ($)	CV (%)	SV ($)	SV (%)	CPI	SPI	ETC	EAC	VAC (%)	VAC ($)		
F.1	Asset Tracking	151600	99900	99200	96600	2600	3%	(700)	-1%	1.03	0.99	51027	147627	3%	3973	1.01	GREEN
F.1.1	Planning	102600	87400	87000	84300	2700	3%	(400)	0%	1.03	1.00	15116	99416	3%	3184	1.01	GREEN
F.1.2	Iteration 1	49000	12500	12200	12300	(100)	-1%	(300)	-2%	0.99	0.98	37102	49402	-1%	(402)	0.98	YELLOW

FIGURE 11-7   Example of a Project Performance Report

Request for Change

Project Name:	Asset Management	**Date Submitted:**	4/20/2008
Submitted by:	Elaine Henry - 491-5555	**Change Req. #:**	CR-AM-0012
(name, contact information)			
Priority	High	**Status:**	New

Description of Change:

Perform a physical inventory of all assets owned by R & S Amusements Services.

Category: Major

Business Reason for Change: (cost benefit analysis)

Physical inventory required in order to obtain and verify asset information to load into new Asset Management system because 30% of current data is found to be inaccurate or missing.
Required Resources:
3 - people for 10 days, 1 - person for 15 days - Total labor $4000.00
Travel Expenses - $.45 per mile at 2200 miles - Total Expense $990.00

Business Impact if Change Denied:

New system will be loaded with inaccurate date.
The management and tracking of assets will be suspect causing the expenditure of additional labor hours to validate information. This will also cause the system not to be trusted and prevent it from being used to its fullest potential.

Indicate Impact on:

Scope	X	Cost	X
Schedule	X	HR	
Risk		Quality	X
Other			

Suggested Implementation Schedule:

4/30/08 - Create inventory collection mechanisms and schedule
5/1/08 thru 5/15/08 - Collect asset inventory information
5/2/08 thru 5/18/08 - Verify & input asset inventory information

Required Approvals:

Name	Date	Approve/Reject
Diana Brooks	4/23/2008	Approve
Mark Lewis	4/23/2008	Approve
Reid Lewis	4/23/2008	Approve
Kevin Pullen	4/23/2008	Approve
Jeff Dunbar	4/23/2008	Approve

FIGURE 11-8 Example of a Request for Change

Project—Asset Management	

System Owner/Sponsor	Date
Reid Lewis	2/12/08

Approval signifies that the deliverable is accurate and represents a correct requirement of the project plan.

Operations Manager	Date
Mark Lewis	2/12/08

Business Manager	Date
Diana Brooks	2/12/08

Project Manager	Date
Jeff Dunbar	2/13/08
Kevin Pullen	2/13/08

FIGURE 11-9   **Example of a Stakeholder Signoff Sheet**

reporting mechanism to quickly draw management's attention to areas of concern. Items with a green status color are operating efficiently and need no attention. Items with a yellow status color are operating within tolerable limits but are showing some signs of problems and should be managed carefully. Items with a red status color are in immediate need of attention.

Step 5: Conduct the Integrated Change Control Process

After the project was initiated, Jeff and Kevin from PPMS held a group meeting instructing R & S about the change control process and specifically how to request a change. The CAB, consisting of Reid, Mark, Diana, Kevin, and Jeff, was introduced, and Diana was selected as the primary contact for submitting and requesting status of changes.

During the course of the project, as discussed in the opening case, Elaine Henry submitted one of the first changes to Diana Brooks, who serves as the change screener. She verified the viability of the change, logged the change, set up a meeting of the CAB, and then distributed copies of the RFC. When the CAB met and approved the request, the change was delegated to Kevin for management. On completion of the change, Kevin will report back to Diana, who will make the final notation in the change log. Figure 11-8 shows the approved RFC.

Step 6: Final Delivery Approval

Every task deliverable must be signed off on by the project management team (Reid, Mark, Diana, Jeff, and Kevin) before it is considered complete, and then Diana can update the project schedule. Figure 11-9 shows an example of the signoff sheet that will accompany each deliverable.

Chapter Review

1. Monitoring and control processes are used to continuously measure and report progress; handle changes to scope, time, cost, and quality; manage risk mitigation strategies; and administer procurement.
2. Successful monitoring and control processes depend on accurate and current project work performance information, such as daily raw numbers, frequency numbers, and qualitative assessments.
3. A formal integrated change control process helps ensure that only approved necessary changes are made to a project.
4. The change advisory board (CAB) is led by the stakeholders and consists of a cross-functional group of stakeholders and IT representatives. Their charge is to make sure the process is run optimally.
5. The configuration management process ensures that all the different components of the information system deliverable are coordinated such that the final product works as required.

6. The scope validation process involves obtaining a stakeholder's formal written acceptance of a product deliverable.
7. The scope control process is responsible for influencing the factors that create scope changes and controlling the impact of needed changes on the project schedule and budget.
8. The schedule control process is concerned with determining the current status of all items currently being worked on, influencing factors that create schedule changes, determining whether the schedule has not changed, and managing changes to the schedule using a formal integrated change control process.
9. The cost control process is concerned with influencing the factors that create cost variances on a project and controlling changes to a project's budget.
10. Earned value management (EVM) is a technique used to help determine and manage project progress and the magnitude of any variations from the planned values.

Glossary

earned value management (EVM)   A technique used to help determine and manage project progress and the magnitude of any variations from the planned values in terms of cost, schedule, and performance.

integrated change control   A formal process used to approve and manage any and all necessary project document and deliverable changes.

Review Questions

1. Explain the keys to making the monitoring and control process function properly throughout the project.
2. What is an integrated change control process?
3. Describe the key roles involved in the integrated change control process.

4. Describe the key activities performed during the integrated change control process.
5. Who should lead the integrated change control process? Explain.
6. List and define the data elements contained on the RFC form.

7. What is configuration management?
8. List and explain the steps involved in the configuration management process.
9. What is scope validation?
10. List and explain where many of the scope changes for IT projects originate.
11. Define *scope creep* and discuss the best methods for controlling it in IT projects.

12. What is the main purpose of the schedule control process?
13. What is EVM, and who on the project team should be trained to use it and understand it?
14. What is the formula for calculating earned value?
15. What are the cost performance index and scheduled performance index used for, and how are they calculated?

Problems and Exercises

1. The monitoring and control process occurs throughout the project life cycle. Explain when it begins and when it ends and how this process overlaps with the other life cycle phases.

2. Evaluate the following scenario and offer suggestions to Melissa, the project manager, on how to address the issues.

   Melissa has been a project manager for just two years, and the current customer relationship management (CRM) software implementation project is by far the largest IT project she has ever been responsible for running. Currently, there are five software developers working on configuring the new purchased software and integrating it with the current ERP application. The project has been experiencing some minor schedule delays. The actual costs reported are in line with the budget as well as the productivity numbers. Melissa is baffled at first as to why the project is falling behind schedule. After reviewing the numbers for several weeks, she decides the only way to find out what is going on is to interview each of the developers, so she proceeds to schedule appointments with each one in their office. During one of the interviews, Alonso, one of the lead software developers, takes a call from one of the most powerful project stakeholders. Melissa can hear only one side of the conversation but figures out that the stakeholder is asking Alonso to make some changes to a set of existing sales reports that will be deployed with the CRM software. Alonso finishes the conversation, say-

   ing that he will take care of the changes. Melissa asks Alonso why the stakeholder didn't go through the established integrated change control process. Alonso replies that he feels that due to the importance of the stakeholder, he couldn't tell him no. Melissa asks how often this has happened, and Alonso says that about once a week, the key stakeholder calls with minor changes he wants done, usually right away. Melissa is beginning to figure out why the project is experiencing some schedule delays.

3. Discuss the benefits and drawbacks of following a formal integrated change control process.

4. Discuss the best practices for schedule control described in the chapter.

5. Discuss what information is necessary in order to calculate an accurate earned value and explain what is meant by the statement "EVM is only as good as the information it is based on."

6. Discuss the different methods available for a project team to use when reporting how much work has been completed on a particular task and how much is left to do.

7. Discuss the benefits and drawbacks to earned value management.

8. Discuss the following project situations, using just the following schedule and cost information:
   a. PV = $10,000, AC = $12,000, EV = $10,500
   b. PV = $10,000, AC = $10,000, EV = $10,000
   c. PV = $10,000, AC = $9,000, EV = $10,000
   d. PV = $10,000, AC = $10,000, EV = $9,000

9. Use the following project status information to calculate each of the requested EVM numbers below (a–i). The project status is reported at the end of week 13.

Task	Budget Cost	Budget Duration	Status as of Week 13
A	$5,000	2 weeks	100 percent complete, $5,000
B	$8,500	3 weeks	100 percent complete, $9,000
C	$15,000	4 weeks	75 percent complete, $14,000
D	$10,000	4 weeks	50 percent complete, $9,000
E	$12,000	4 weeks	Not started
F	$15,000	5 weeks	Not started

a. Planned value
b. Actual cost
c. Cost variance
d. Schedule variance
e. Cost performance index

f. Schedule performance index
g. Budget at completion
h. Estimate to complete
i. Estimate at completion

10. Calculate values for a through i from problem 9, using the following table:

Task	Budget Cost	Budget Duration	Status as of Week 9
A	$5,000	1 week	100 percent complete, $4,000
B	$8,500	1 week	100 percent complete, $8,500
C	$15,000	2 weeks	100 percent complete, $14,000
D	$10,000	2 weeks	50 percent complete, $9,000
E	$12,000	3 weeks	50 percent complete, $12,000
F	$15,000	2 weeks	Not started

11. If the CPI on a project is .85 and EV is $10,000, what must the AC be?

12. The original plan for the project was for it to last one year at a cost of $100,000. Using the following information, calculate SPI, ETC, and EAC:

Planned value = $45,000

Earned value = $37,000

Cost variance = -$12,000

13. Recalculate your answers to problem 12 for SPI, ETC, and EAC, using the following:

PV = $45,000, EV = $47,000, cost variance = $10,000

14. Use the table below to calculate PV, AC, EV, CPI, SPI, and ETC for a project that is in its 11th week of execution.

15. For the data presented in problem 14 draw an earned value chart similar to the one presented in Figure 11-5.

Activity	Predecessors	Duration (Weeks)	Budget $	$ Spent	Percentage Complete
a	—	2	10,000	9,000	100 percent
b	—	2	12,000	14,000	100 percent
c	a	1	8,000	8,000	100 percent
d	b	3	15,000	22,000	75 percent
e	c	3	17,000	16,000	50 percent
f	d, c	2	10,000	—	
g	d	1	8,000	—	
h	e, f, g	2	20,000	—	

Projects and Research

1. Go to the Project Management Institute's web site, at www.pmi.org, and review the earned value management standard.

2. Search the Internet and find case studies related to how different organizations perform integrated change control. Map out their processes in a diagram similar to the process diagram provided in Figure 11-1.

3. Search the Internet and find case studies related to how different organizations apply earned value management techniques. How do they collect project status information? How to they report percentage complete.

MINICASE

1. *Background:* (Review the R & S case study material at the beginning of this chapter and Chapter 10.) We join the whole project team from R & S Amusements Services during the offsite face-to-face meeting, right after lunch. The agenda allows for an hour of open discussion about any concerns anyone is having about the way the project is going before the team-building exercises start.

   Current Situation 1: Laura Kimball, office supervisor, speaking with a slight edge in her voice, says, "I just don't understand why it takes so long to get the changes I asked for put into the software prototypes. I submit them in writing like we were told to do, but I haven't seen any of them yet. I have submitted at least 30 changes in just the last week, but nothing yet." The room is quiet for a moment and then Jeff from PPMS says, "All changes are submitted to the change advisory board for decisions on whether they should be included in the new system, and when a decision is made, someone from that group should reply to whoever submitted the change, but it will generally take longer than a week."

   Discussion: Put yourself in Jeff's place. How would you explain to Laura how the integrated change control process is supposed to work? Explain to the group what *scope creep* is and how it can affect the system under development and the entire project. Laura has been a very active participant, and many of her ideas are good ones because she is very knowledgeable about the way the work is currently done. How do you explain these topics to her in such a way that you don't discourage Laura's continued participation in the project?

Current Situation 2: When the discussion slows down, Mark Lewis, manager of West Lafayette operations, says, "I have another slightly different issue to bring up about the new software or, more to the point, about the guy (the consulting company hired to write the software) they sent out to interview me on what I thought the software needed to do. He didn't seem to know much about anything to do with our company and how we operate. He looked so young—like he had just gotten out of high school, let alone college. Shouldn't we have a say in who they use to do the work, and shouldn't they be sending people who are more familiar with what is going on?"

Discussion: Discuss how you would answer Mark's question. Should an organization have a say in who the seller uses to work on the project? Should the buyer of the services have the right to pick the individuals who will work on their project? Include as part of your answer how a company should go about deciding who should be chosen to work on a particular task.

Suggested Readings

Barr, Z. (1996, December). Earned value analysis: A case study. *PM Network*, pp. 31–37.

Brandon, D. (1998). Implementing earned value easily and effectively. *Project Management Journal* 29(2):11–18.

Flemming, Q., & Koppelman J. (1996). *Earned value project management*. Upper Darby, PA: Project Management Institute.

Forselius, P. (2007). Increase ICT project success with concrete scope management. PMI Global Congress Proceedings, Hong Kong.

Hatfield, M. (1996, December). The case for earned value. *PM Network*, pp. 25–27.

Lambert, L. (1993). Cost/schedule control system criteria (C/SCSC): An integrated project management approach using earned value techniques. In P. Dinsmore, ed., *The AMA Handbook of Project Management*. New York: AMACOM.

Project Management Institute web site, www.pmi.org.

Project Management Institute (PMI). (2004). *A guide to the project management body of knowledge,* 3rd ed. Newton Square, PA: PMI.

Project Management Institute (PMI). (2004). *Earned value management standard*. Newtown Square, PA: PMI.

Thamhain, H. (1987, August). The new product management software and its impact on management style. *Project Management Journal*, pp. 81–85.

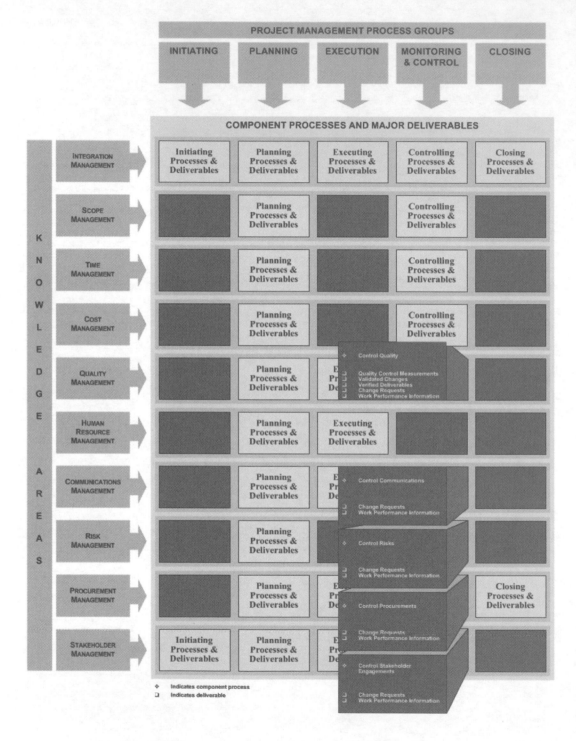

PROJECT MANAGEMENT PROCESS GROUPS

| INITIATING | PLANNING | EXECUTION | MONITORING & CONTROL | CLOSING |

COMPONENT PROCESSES AND MAJOR DELIVERABLES

KNOWLEDGE AREAS	INITIATING	PLANNING	EXECUTION	MONITORING & CONTROL	CLOSING
INTEGRATION MANAGEMENT	Initiating Processes & Deliverables	Planning Processes & Deliverables	Executing Processes & Deliverables	Controlling Processes & Deliverables	Closing Processes & Deliverables
SCOPE MANAGEMENT		Planning Processes & Deliverables		Controlling Processes & Deliverables	
TIME MANAGEMENT		Planning Processes & Deliverables		Controlling Processes & Deliverables	
COST MANAGEMENT		Planning Processes & Deliverables		Controlling Processes & Deliverables	
QUALITY MANAGEMENT		Planning Processes & Deliverables	Executing Processes & Deliverables	Control Quality · Quality Control Measurements · Validated Changes · Verified Deliverables · Change Requests · Work Performance Information	
HUMAN RESOURCE MANAGEMENT		Planning Processes & Deliverables	Executing Processes & Deliverables		
COMMUNICATIONS MANAGEMENT		Planning Processes & Deliverables	Executing Processes & Deliverables	Control Communications · Change Requests · Work Performance Information	
RISK MANAGEMENT		Planning Processes & Deliverables	Executing Processes & Deliverables	Control Risks · Change Requests · Work Performance Information	
PROCUREMENT MANAGEMENT		Planning Processes & Deliverables	Executing Processes & Deliverables	Control Procurements · Change Requests · Work Performance Information	Closing Processes & Deliverables
STAKEHOLDER MANAGEMENT	Initiating Processes & Deliverables	Planning Processes & Deliverables	Executing Processes & Deliverables	Control Stakeholder Engagements · Change Requests · Work Performance Information	

♦ Indicates component process
❑ Indicates deliverable

12

Project Monitoring and Control, Part II

R & S Amusements Services

Event 12

Setting *In Chapter 11, Event 11 focused on activities of the change advisory board in reviewing a request for change (RFC) submitted by Elaine Henry in response to the discovery of erroneous asset data residing in the legacy system. Event 12 focuses on the events that led up to the submission of the RFC. In a small conference room located outside Reid Lewis's office at R & S Amusements, several project participants (those associated with asset information) have convened for a quality analysis review of the asset data. Those in attendance include Elaine Henry, Kenny Jones, Brittany Lewis, Stephanie Crane (data collector), and Stephen Ironmant (service technician) from R & S and Jeff Dunbar and Kevin Pullen from Premier Project Management Services.*

KEVIN   Good morning, everyone. I hope you all had a good weekend. *[Everyone nods their approval]*

KEVIN   The reason for this morning's meeting is to review and analyze the findings that Elaine discovered when scrubbing the legacy asset data. I assisted Elaine in creating a Pareto diagram to present those findings. *[The diagram is presented later in the chapter.]*

JEFF   Kevin, if I may, for those of you not familiar with a Pareto diagram, it is a bar chart that displays, by frequency and in descending order, the most important errors that Elaine found.

KEVIN   Thanks, Jeff. *[Kevin distributes copies of the diagram to the attendees]* Now I will turn the meeting over to Elaine.

ELAINE   Thanks, Kevin. I analyzed the 6,500 asset records that currently exist in our old system. What you see in front of you is the results of that analysis. As Jeff said, the bars are ordered from left to right, with the most error occurrences being on the left.

KENNY   Elaine, are you saying we have 698 assets that have missing, duplicate, or invalid IDs?

ELAINE   That's correct, Kenny.

BRITTANY	What is an invalid ID?
ELAINE	It is an ID that does not represent a valid number. Remember that our asset IDs are supposed to be six-digit numeric values. We currently have IDs that begin with letters, consist of only three digits, and so on.
KENNY	Wow! How can that happen?
STEPHEN	I know one reason: kits.
KENNY	What do you mean, Stephen?
STEPHEN	Instead of buying a complete video game (cabinet, monitor, computer board, and so on) from a supplier, we can build our own using kits and different parts from different vendors.
KENNY	Okay. Your point?
STEPHEN	When you buy a complete game, it comes with a single set of specifications on a label somewhere on the cabinet. The label will have model number, serial number, and so on that you use for tracking and warranty information. When you assemble your own, you don't have that single set of specifications. You have specifications for each component you are using to assemble the game.
KEVIN	So you're saying that you'll have multiple serial numbers, model numbers, and so on when you build your own game, which makes tracking warranty information, as well as depreciation, a challenge.
STEPHEN	You got it. This is why people make up IDs and such, which sometimes result in duplicates, and, to be blunt, they are too lazy to see if the ID has already been used. We compound the problem when we convert one game to another when we switch out the computer board or kit. We . . .
JEFF	This is a great discussion, but can we hold off for a few minutes, and then we can formally address these issues? Please continue, Elaine.
ELAINE	You can also see in the diagram that we have 523 records that are missing critical vendor data, such as serial number. In addition, we have 163 records that are missing financial data, such as purchase cost, current value, and so on.
STEPHANIE	As you can see, everyone, this is a big problem. These data need to be accurate before we load them into the new system.
KEVIN	That's true, Stephanie, but just as important is figuring out how these data were corrupted in the first place. Basically, what are the causes of the errors, and how do we prevent them from happening in the new system? That's why we need to address the issues Stephen was talking about.
JEFF	That is the other reason we are here: to perform a cause-and-effect analysis on the problem, and I appreciate Kenny and Stephen's patience.
STEPHEN	I don't know what a cause-and-effect analysis is.
JEFF	It's pretty straightforward, Stephen. A cause-and-effect analysis is a systematic way of generating and sorting ideas about possible causes of an identified problem. When the root causes of problems are identified, we can try to fix those rather than just treat the symptoms.
STEPHEN	Okay. I think I understand.
KEVIN	You will. We will construct an Ishikawa diagram, better known as a "fishbone" diagram, to help depict the causes and effects.
KENNY	Did you say *fishbone*?
KEVIN	Yes. It is referred to as a fishbone diagram because it looks like a fish skeleton. You will see when we start constructing the diagram.
JEFF	Is everyone ready to get started?

(To be continued)

(This chapter provides instructions for constructing Pareto and fishbone diagrams, along with examples.)

CHAPTER PREVIEW AND OBJECTIVES

This chapter describes the tools and techniques required to perform the monitoring and control for the project management body of knowledge (PMBOK) Quality Management, Communications Management, Risk Management, Procurement Management, and Stakeholder Management knowledge areas. This is the second and final chapter covering the topic of monitoring and control. As mentioned in Chapter 11, the material is presented such that the techniques of monitoring are intertwined with the techniques of control. The two represent opposite functions: Monitoring is collecting and reporting information concerning previously defined project performance elements, and control uses the information supplied by the monitoring techniques in order to bring the project's actual results in line with stated project performance standards.

As you read this chapter, you will:

- Understand how to create and interpret the following tools used during quality control: control charts, Pareto diagrams, and cause-and-effect diagrams
- Create accurate, timely, and tailored performance and status reports
- Understand how to monitor and control risks
- Manage procurement seller relationships within the specifications described in the contract

AN INTRODUCTION TO PROJECT MONITORING AND CONTROL, PART II

This chapter is the second of two chapters covering the techniques used during the monitoring and control phase of the project life cycle. Chapter 11 covered the first four knowledge areas concerned with monitoring and control—Integration Management, Scope Management, Time Management, and Cost Management—and the three main areas of monitoring and control—scope, time, and cost. The continuous process of monitoring and control touches nine of the ten knowledge areas of the PMBOK. This chapter covers the remaining five areas: quality, communications, stakeholders, risk, and procurement management.

As in Chapter 11, it is important to remember that monitoring and control are two separate steps put together into one process group within the project life cycle. Monitoring is concerned with collecting and reporting information about project performance to all stakeholders and the project team. Control uses the information supplied by the monitoring process to bring the actual project performance in line with what was planned. The material in this chapter first identifies the data to be collected and presented (the monitoring process) and then describes the techniques used to alter project outcomes (the control process).

Much of the monitoring function in medium to large projects is generally done by a separate department that is specifically trained and unbiased—at least this is the goal. Such departments go by different names, such as quality control or quality assurance. In smaller projects or organizations, the monitoring is done by the same persons who are working on the project team, which introduces the potential issues of bias and reduces the productivity of the project team because it then has the added responsibility of supplying information required for the control process. Also, individuals doing their own reporting may be hesitant to report bad news on their progress and may hide the real numbers or report false progress. Therefore, care must be taken when allowing the persons responsible for creating the deliverable to also be responsible for monitoring and control.

A final note before discussing the tools and techniques used during monitoring and control: Experienced project managers know how difficult it can be to obtain accurate information about a project they are leading. For students, the information in this chapter may seem to be pretty cut and dried: You collect the information, make decisions based on what the information is telling you, and then affect change. In reality, it is much more difficult than can be expressed in the text. Getting accurate data, depending on the size and nature of the project, can be very difficult. Most project participants will feel as if they have more important things to do than continuously supply the project manager with details about how much work they have gotten done and how much is left to accomplish. If the project team is geographically dispersed, the task of collecting data is even more difficult. Decisions concerning project changes must be based on accurate data, so it is extremely important for a project manager to make it as easy as possible to collect the data by automating as much of it as possible. The easier the project manager makes it for the team to enter up-to-date information, the more accurate it will become, resulting in better decision making and more successful projects.

PROJECT MANAGEMENT CONCEPTS: PROJECT MONITORING AND CONTROL

Quality Management: Controlling Quality

The triple constraint of project management includes the scope of what is to be produced, the time it should take, and the cost of producing the product or service the project was initiated to create (see Chapter 1). A fourth item that also constrains all IT projects is quality. Throughout the history of IT projects, when money is running short or time is running out and the project must be completed, the quality of the end product is often sacrificed. Because of this, it is very important that the quality monitoring and control process be executed continuously throughout the entire project, from the time the project charter is signed until the project sponsor accepts the final deliverable.

The **quality control** process involves monitoring specific project results (artifacts) identified during the planning phase of a project to determine whether they comply with the relevant quality standards and identifying ways to eliminate causes of unsatisfactory results. The metrics a team chooses to monitor and control vary from project to project (see Chapter 7). For items that fall outside the range of acceptability, corrective actions need to be taken to bring them back into the range of acceptable quality standards. For example, say that a software development team has set quality standards of no more than 3 minor bugs for every 10 objects developed and 1 medium-sized software flaw for every 50 objects built. These standards apply to bugs found during object integration testing before the full system integration testing and long before the user acceptance testing. If reported software bugs or flaws begin to rise above acceptable standards, the team may need to take actions such as providing more training on the tools, hiring more senior software developer leadership, and programming in pairs to reduce the number.

The following are a few key terms that need to be understood before further discussion:

- *Prevention versus inspection*—Prevention attempts to keep errors out of a process, whereas inspection attempts to keep errors from reaching the final customer.
- *Sampling*—Attribute sampling looks at whether the collected result conforms to defined standards at a point in time. Variable sampling rates the result on a continuous scale, measuring the degree of conformity.

- *Sample size*—The sample size is the number of results needed to determine whether a process or result is performing to standard. Getting the sample size right is extremely important because choosing too many samples is a waste of time and money, and choosing too few will not yield accurate information. It is beyond the scope of this text to provide a complete discussion on statistical sample size, but it is important to understand the basic concept. For example, to determine whether a new accounts receivable application is producing accurate invoices for a company that produces and sends out thousands of invoices each day, it would be impossible to look at every invoice and make sure it was created correctly. The trick is to know how many invoices the quality control team should look at to be fairly confident they have tested a high percentage of the different types of invoices present in the application.
- *Tolerances and limits*—A result is acceptable if it falls within the range specified by the tolerance or stakeholder set specifications. The process is in control (operating within acceptable limits) if the result falls within the control limits.

Quality control is a process that occurs on a continuous basis, throughout the life of a project. Remember the continuous quality cycle for improvement—Plan, Do, Study, Act—presented in Chapter 7? Chapter 7 covers the "Plan" part of the process, and Chapter 10 covers the "Do." The Study and Act processes refer to the quality monitoring and control functions discussed in this chapter.

The next section of this chapter presents three tools used to monitor and control project quality: **cause-and-effect analysis**, process control charts, and Pareto analysis. Each of these tools graphically displays collected statistical results, helping a project team measure variances to aid in the continuous process of improving the quality of a product. These tools help a team to identify issues (Pareto analysis), discover root causes for the issues (cause-and-effect analysis), and then analyze improvement possibilities (control charts).

A cause-and-effect analysis—also called an *Ishikawa diagram* after the creator of the technique or a *fishbone diagram* based on what the final diagram resembles—is used when a problem or issue has been discovered and you need to determine its root cause so that the most appropriate actions can be taken. A cause-and-effect diagram identifies the relationship between an effect and its causes (see Figure 12-1).

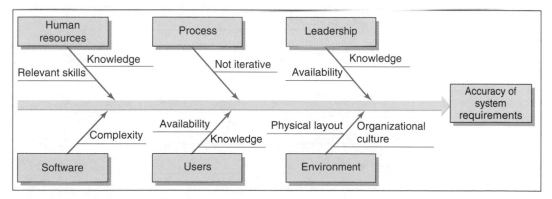

FIGURE 12-1 Cause-and-Effect Diagram

The effect, or problem, identified in Figure 12-1 is that the project team has had issues with the accuracy of system requirements collected from users of a new system by IT analysts and interpretations of these requirements by software developers. Each of the rectangular boxes represents a major category of suspicion: human resources, process, leadership, software, users, and the environment. The arrows connecting the categories to the central line have attached to them lines containing more detailed ideas of what might be the root cause for the problem. For example, the human resources category has two detailed causes identified: relevant skills and knowledge. It could be that the IT analysts doing the requirements capture lacked the skills or experience necessary to do the job, or maybe they lacked sufficient domain knowledge to understand the requirements. If this turns out to be the cause, then different analysts need to be selected or the currently assigned ones need to be given more training. The process to create the drawing is relatively simple and is generally done during a group brainstorming session. The steps are to:

1. Define the problem and obtain agreement from the group.
2. Put the problem on the drawing and draw the center line.
3. Brainstorm ideas for major categories to consider trying—but don't get into too much detail.
4. Put the categories on the diagram inside rectangles and draw an arrow connecting each to the center line.
5. Conduct brainstorming activities, concentrating on each category one at a time to focus the activity and list as many probable causes as possible. Add these to the connecting arrows and underline them.
6. Collectively identify corrective actions for each cause.

A **control chart** is used to prevent problems before they become major issues as opposed to inspecting a final product to find issues. Control chart analysis helps determine whether the process variability and the process average result are at stable (acceptable) levels and whether one or both are out of control (unacceptable). Another benefit of control chart analysis is that it helps determine whether variability is attributable to something that can be fixed or some random set of variables based on chance alone. Figure 12-2 is an example of a control chart that looks at the number of software bugs found during peer reviews.

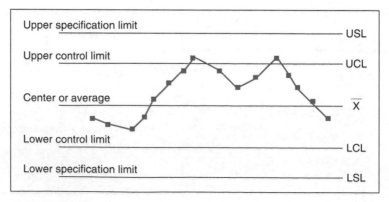

FIGURE 12-2   Control Chart

A control chart is made up of five straight lines that refer to the specification limits, the statistical control limits, and the mean or arithmetic average. The curved line is the plotted data results. Specification limits are used when specific parametric requirements exist for a process; they are generally the pass/fail limits determined by the organization. For example, say that management and stakeholders have determined that they will not tolerate any application development effort with more than 2 critical software bugs per 100 objects created. If during the monitoring of a systems development effort, the team reports 3 critical software bugs, this would demonstrate a process that needs attention. The upper and lower control limits are placed ±3 standard deviations from the mean. Because software development is mostly done by humans, a certain number of errors will always be made. For example, during the past several projects an organization has run, an average of 1.2 non-critical bugs have been documented per 100 objects created. The company has tried many different quality control techniques to move this number to zero, but none have been able to eliminate all errors. The end products created, even with the 1.2 non-critical bugs, have met stakeholder approval because the bugs are non-critical and are fixed in subsequent releases. Therefore, management has determined that setting control limits of 1.2 non-critical bugs is adequate and within the normal operating range of development. There are several possibilities for interpreting various kinds of patterns or runs on a control chart (results that may need intervention):

- A single point falling outside the upper or lower control limit
- Patterns which suggest that the observed data are not statistically independent:
  - Two successive points that fall on the same side and more than two standard deviations away from the centerline
  - Four out of five successive values that fall on the same side and more than one standard deviation away from the centerline
  - Eight successive values that fall on the same side of the centerline
- Runs of at least seven successive points lined up all on one side of the average line
- A trend—a continued rise or fall of at least seven data points in succession
- Any point outside a control limit or a specification limit

A control chart can be used for both project metrics (for example, the number of milestones hit on time) and product metrics (or example, the number of bugs per object created).

Pareto analysis uses a diagram (see Figure 12-3) based on a histogram that helps identify and prioritize problems. A **Pareto diagram** displays the frequency of issues so that project teams can focus on the problems that are occurring most often or are causing the biggest issues in terms of time and/or cost. Pareto analysis identifies the key few contributors that account for most quality problems in the target process or system. The Pareto principle states that 80 percent of the impact of a problem will show up in 20 percent of the causes. If this principle holds true for an issue under investigation, 80 percent of the total issues will appear on the far-left portion of the histogram. This comes very close to describing the results shown in Figure 12-3, which has 71 percent of the issues reported in the first two categories (inventory application objects and user interface objects). The values being plotted are arranged in descending order, and a line graph is added to show the cumulative totals of each category. Some diagrams also add the percentage contribution of each category. Figure 12-3 shows an example of a Pareto diagram generated from the number of software defects detected by type of object being developed. The chart shows that 41 percent of all errors reported occurred in inventory application objects and 30 percent occurred inside user interface objects. These two

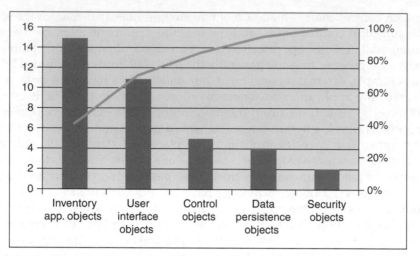

FIGURE 12-3   Pareto Diagram

categories account for 71 percent of the errors reported. Based on this information, the project team needs to look at what is going on with the teams involved in these two categories and see if it needs to arrange for more training, more time, more peer reviews, or different personnel.

PROVEN STRATEGIES AND HINTS TO SUCCESS

Heusser (2012) is reviewing work done by David J. Anderson and Dragos Dumitriu from Microsoft in an article they published at the TOCICO International Conference in November of 2005. Anderson and Dumitriu's case study article was titled "From Worst to Best in 9 Months: Implementing a Drum-Buffer-Rope Solution in Microsoft's IT department." The case study article referred to their methods as "Drum-Buffer-Rope," which is analogous to a more popular and well-known quality control process called "Kanban." In Japanese, "a Kanban is a board or visualization of inventory. Workers can request new parts only when inventory is extremely low, which leads to just-in-time assembly. The Kanban 'card' gives permission to build to the next operator in the process. Without the card, the operator must not complete their tasks, or else he or she creates more waste in the form of excess work in progress." Anderson and Dumitriu created the "virtual Kanban board" by making the work-in-progress visible, identified the constraints of the process as the programmers, limited their work-in-progress to one item at a time, and subordinated all work to those programmers. The programmers could focus only on writing the currently defined software code and nothing else. They were not given future work to be done in future iterations of the agile development process—only what was needed currently. Kanban moves from a "push" system to more of a "pull" process. Workers are given one assignment at a time. When they finish, they pull the next assignment from the stack. Instead of blaming the bottleneck, the rest of the staff views that bottleneck as the constraint on the system and moves to lessen its impact. Heusser uses the following example to make his point: If the quality assurance testers are behind, programmers are finishing code faster than it can be tested, then you may see developers writing test tools or doing some of the testing themselves, anything that will reduce the bottleneck.

Communications and Stakeholder Management: Control Communications

STAKEHOLDER MANAGEMENT: CONTROL STAKEHOLDER ENGAGEMENT Both the control communications and control stakeholder engagement processes involve the collection of project- and product-related data and the distribution of performance information to stakeholders. The control communications process focuses on maintaining communications with all stakeholders throughout the entire project to ensure the information needs of the stakeholders are met. The control stakeholder engagement process is focused on working with stakeholders to meet their needs and expectations and foster appropriate stakeholder involvement throughout the project.

Project-related data includes information from all areas of a project, including schedule, costs, quality, risks, human resources, and, if needed, procurement. The performance reports generally demonstrate how resources (human and other) are being utilized to achieve project objectives and cover project artifacts and product artifacts. The frequency of the reports (for example, daily, weekly, monthly) is determined by the type of report, the size of the project, and the importance of the project.

Some organizations produce four different categories of performance reports:

- *Performance reports*—These reports show physical progress to date and actual data versus planned data.
- *Status reports*—These reports identify where a project is at the time the report is prepared and the information from collected performance data to calculate schedule variance and cost variance.
- *Projection reports*—These reports calculate the following earned value numbers: estimate at completion (EAC), estimate to complete (ETC), schedule performance index (SPI), and cost performance index (CPI). These reports are forward looking, giving projections/forecasts of the project finish.
- *Exception reports*—These reports show exceptions, problems, and risks.

To simplify reporting, especially in medium to small projects, the performance report shown in Figure 12-4 combines all four types of information into one report.

The methods used to collect performance data vary from project to project, but in medium to large projects performance data are generally collected using an electronic tool. In a small project involving just a few people, data can be collected manually. But when a project involves many people spread out geographically, it becomes impossible to capture this information manually and produce timely reports. Many electronic systems (see Figure 12-5 for an example) allow each team member to enter his or her own information and have this data feed into a central database for reporting purposes. Most such tools interface directly with the project management software in use. Figure 12-5 is a snapshot of the timesheet entry screen from HMS Software's Time Control application, which can be directly linked to Microsoft Office Project 2007.

Project Risk Management: Monitoring and Controlling Risks

Monitoring and controlling risks is a continuous monitoring process for all previously identified risks and for any new risks. As stated in Chapter 8, the identification of risks is a continuous process—not just for the planning stage. A team must always be looking

---

Project Status Report Template

Project Name: _____

Period: _____

Project Manager: _____

Status this period:

- List each WBS item worked on during this time period with the following information
    - WBS number, task name, owner, planned time and cost, actual time and cost, schedule variance, and cost variance
    - Also note if the task completed, if not then estimate to complete

Activities for next period:

- List each WBS item to be worked on during the next reporting time period
    - WBS number, task name, owner, planned time, and cost

Projections:

- Present project level cost performance index and schedule performance index
- Discuss how CPI and SPI will be used to generate estimate at completion
- Provide estimate to complete (ETC) and estimate at completion (EAC)

Issues of concern:

- Review top risk items from the risk register by including them here as bullets and giving brief explanation of status
- Review any other issues that may affect project performance that need to be communicated to stakeholders.
- Review items dealt with during the last reporting period which were mentioned in this section

FIGURE 12-4   Periodic Project Performance Report Template

for risks that may affect the outcome of a project. The whole project team is involved in routinely reviewing the risk register and adding to it when necessary. Each risk owner is responsible for monitoring trigger conditions and updating the team on the status of mitigation strategies and their effectiveness (see Figure 12-4). This review should occur daily, if possible, but never longer than each week during the project. This process of monitoring risks can be more formalized into a risk audit. The risk audit is generally done by a separate group not currently connected with the project. It may help to obtain a more thorough and accurate look at the status of risks on the project. Finally, any updates needed to the project's contingency reserves for cost and schedule need to be communicated to stakeholders.

Project Procurement Management: Control Procurements

The procurement control process is carried out by both a seller and a buyer to make sure each party meets the respective contractual obligations. The seller is mainly concerned with creating deliverables that match stated specifications, managing communication with

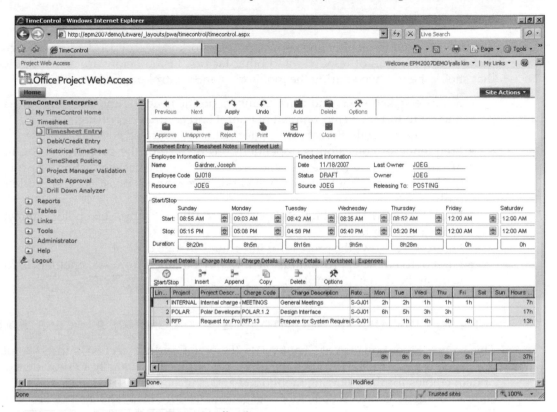

FIGURE 12-5   Project Data Entry Application

Source: Reprinted with permission from HMS Software.

the buyer, managing the budget, and managing risk. The buyer is concerned with communication with the seller, payment schedules (which are generally based on the acceptance of deliverables), timely quality reviews of deliverables, and risk management.

Due to the complexities involved in a legal contractual situation, many organizations have a professional contracts person handle or at least be heavily involved in the process of contract administration. If a project is large enough and has several different vendors involved, this management function can become very complicated. Whoever is assigned responsibility for managing a contract must also make sure that all outcomes associated with the work of each seller are formally documented with other project documentation so any future work possibilities with the same seller can be evaluated.

Finally, a contract or seller change control system needs to be in place to handle all changes to the contract and/or deliverables requested. In many cases, the system is an extension of the internal integrated change control process, as discussed in Chapter 11. The contract change control system should include procedures for handling any changes to deliverables, completing tracking of the change request and associated implications for cost and schedule, handling dispute resolutions, and getting required approvals to enact any contractual change. The system should also be able to track any associated warranty information by deliverable.

THE PROJECT MONITORING AND CONTROL PROCESS

The process used to monitor and control project work varies, dependent on the size, complexity, and location of resources and other factors. Listed below are general guidelines that should be followed during the monitoring and control process.

- Educate stakeholders and team members on the need for and use of progress information to foster an environment of honest and accurate reporting.
- Automate the collection of status information as much as possible.
- Frequency of collection is dependent on the size of the project and the location of participants. Regardless of the project characteristics, collection of project status information should never exceed one week, and if possible, it should be done daily.
- Frequency and formatting of reports are outlined in the stakeholder analysis described in Chapter 4.
- Figure 11-1 shows the process for integrated change control.
- Final deliverable approval must be formally obtained from stakeholders before any task can be declared complete.

HOW TO CONDUCT THE MONITORING AND CONTROL PROCESS, PART II

This section, a continuation of Chapter 11's "How to Conduct" section, addresses the areas not covered in Chapter 11. It uses the processes outlined previously to provide examples of deliverables for the following monitoring and control processes: quality control, control communications, control stakeholder engagement, control risks, and control procurements. Before proceeding, review the information presented in the R & S Amusements Services case study. In Event 12, the project for R & S Amusements has been executing for some time and has experienced some familiar problems. Each of the identified issues is discussed next.

Educate Stakeholders and Team Members

As in Chapter 11, Jeff and Kevin, or a representative from PPMS, conduct training sessions in relation to the following topics.

CONTROL QUALITY   As presented in the opening case, Jeff and Kevin met with employees of R & S Amusements Services in addressing the quality problems with the asset data. Initially, they met with Elaine Henry and assisted with the identification and classification of the data error. They instructed her on the use of Pareto diagrams and provided a tool to construct them. The diagram she constructed and presented to the team members is shown in Figure 12-6. In order for the team members to fully comprehend what the diagram communicates, Jeff instructed the team on the principles of Pareto analysis: 80 percent of the impact of a problem will show up in 20 percent of the causes. If this principle holds true, then 80 percent of the data quality errors will appear on the far left portion of the histogram. In looking at Figure 12-6, notice that missing IDs and invalid vendor data make up 76 percent of the data errors.

Using the Pareto diagram as a point of reference, the team next concentrated on the causes of the errors. Jeff next instructed the team on cause-and-effect analysis, using

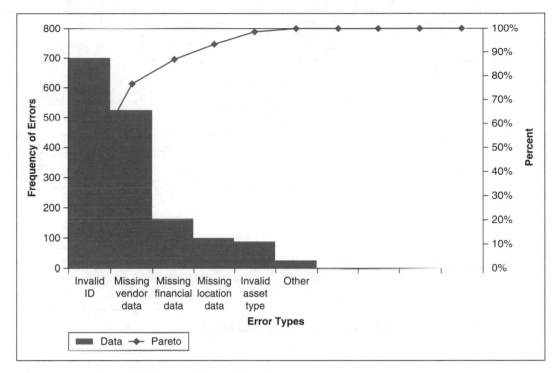

FIGURE 12-6 **Pareto Diagram of Asset Data Errors**

the Ishikawa (fishbone) diagram as the tool of choice. The team first identified the major categories and then brainstormed the detailed causes for each category. As shown in Figure 12-7, one of the root causes for the current data errors is that the legacy system did not perform data validation, nor did it have the capability to handle kit assemblies. Also, the diagram identified the individuals who capture and record the asset information as a potential issue. It was determined that they lacked the necessary process knowledge to understand the impact of not recording the information correctly, and in some cases they did not know how to capture and record it. The team showed these findings to Reid Lewis in order to initiate a task to define a new asset tracking process and then to create awareness by providing appropriate employee training. As a result, Jeff and Kevin were tasked with analyzing the impacts to cost and schedule.

COMMUNICATIONS MANAGEMENT AND CONTROL STAKEHOLDER ENGAGEMENT Refer to Chapter 11 in the "How to Conduct" section for examples of the project status reports used to aid the team in communicating the current project status to stakeholders.

CONTROL RISKS During the weekly status meetings, Jeff and Kevin made an effort to emphasize the importance of monitoring the risk list and identifying any changes that may occur. (Refer to Chapter 8 for the risk management plan.) Because of the data quality problems identified, a new risk—business process redesign—was identified and added to the current risk list (see Figures 12-8a and 12-8b).

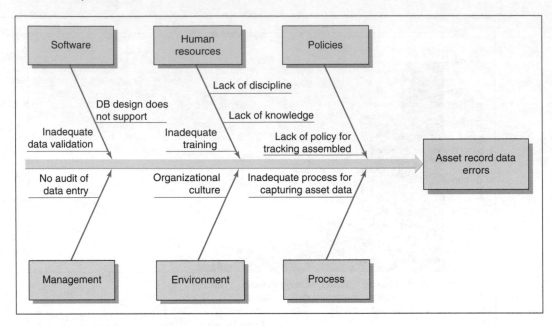

FIGURE 12-7   Fishbone Diagram of Asset Data Errors

The team assessed the risk exposure to be high, as shown in Figure 12-9, and assigned Jeff Dunbar as the owner of the risk.

Figure 12-10 shows the results of the analysis transferred to a probability and impact table. The shaded areas represent a risk exposure greater than .07, which is the threshold that the leadership team determined for mitigating risks. As indicated in Figure 12-10, risks ❶, ❹, ❻, and ❿ need to be managed.

Finally, the risk register was updated with the new risk. Figure 12-11 shows the risk register which documents the event that triggers the risk, the consequence of the risk happening, and the mitigation plan.

CONTROL PROCUREMENTS   When the shipment of the tablet PCs and thermal printers was received, Elaine Henry was responsible for verifying that the items received matched what was specified in the purchasing contract. If there had been any discrepancies, Elaine would have notified the vendor of the nonconformance and demanded that it be resolved. In either case, Elaine updates the project documentation and the contract status.

Steps 2 Through 6

These steps are covered in detail in Chapter 11.

Risk List

Risk No.	Category	Risk Description
1	Internal—Resources	Unavailable subject matter experts—the staff at R & S Amusements Services will not be dedicated to this project alone; they will still have to perform their regular duties.
2	Internal—Inexperience	Inexperienced team—Jeff and Kevin have many years of experience running IT projects but all of the R & S team members do not
3	Internal—Schedule	Schedule changes—with the possibility of scope changes and other issues, schedule changes may also be needed
4	Technical—Requirements	Poor scope definition—Because the workers at R & S are new to project management and the use of technology to aid them in their asset management process, Jeff and Kevin need to make sure that the requirements are captured accurately and reflect the true requirements of the project.
5	Project management—Scope risk	Scope creep—Jeff and Kevin need to make sure that a formal change control process is in place and is followed. This may be a challenge since the workers at R & S are new to project management practices.
6	Project management—Scope risk	Scope changes—due to the difficulties mentioned above in getting all of the requirements identified, scope changes will be inevitable
7	Project management—Plans	Unclear objectives—same issues as poor scope definition
8	Project management—Plans	Unclear SOW or WBS—same issues as poor scope definition
9	External—Vendors and suppliers	Because R & S management has directed that a package will be purchased to implement the Asset Management requirements, there exists a risk that the purchased solution does not meet management's expectations in terms of functionality, cost, technical feasibility, or support.

FIGURE 12-8a   Existing Asset Management Project Risk List

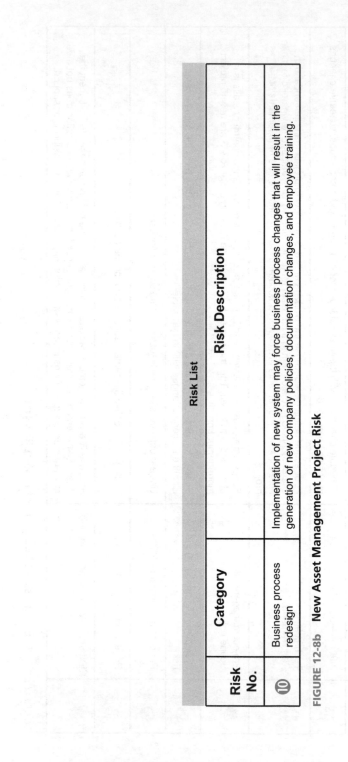

Risk List

Risk No.	Category	Risk Description
❿	Business process redesign	Implementation of new system may force business process changes that will result in the generation of new company policies, documentation changes, and employee training.

FIGURE 12-8b New Asset Management Project Risk

Risk Exposure

Risk No.	Assignee	Risk Probability (RP)	Risk Impact (RI)	Risk Exposure RP * RI
⑩	Jeff Dunbar	High (.9)	High (.9)	.81

FIGURE 12-9   **Risk Exposure for Business Process Redesign Risk**

Impact →	Low	Low med	Medium	Med. high	High
Probability Low		❼ ❽			
Low medium			❷ ❸ ❺		
Medium	❾		❹ ❻		❶
Medium high					
High					⑩

FIGURE 12-10   **Asset Management Project Prioritized Risks**

Risk Register

Project: R&S Asset Management   Date: October 21, 2007

Risk No.	Risk	Trigger Event	Responsible	Consequence	Probability	Mitigation
⑩	Implementation of new system may force business process changes that will result in the generation of new company policies, documentation changes, and employee training.	Current workflow differs from proposed workflow by 30%.	Jeff Dunbar	New process will impact team involvement which will impact cost and schedule.	High (.9)	Request executive approval to revise budget and schedule to accommodate implementation of process redesign

FIGURE 12-11   Updated Risk Register

Chapter Review

1. Quality control involves monitoring specific project results (productivity, time, and cost) identified during the planning phase of a project to determine whether they comply with the relevant quality standards and identifying ways to eliminate causes of unsatisfactory results.

2. Quality control is a process that should occur in a continuous fashion, starting the day the project charter is signed through the time when the final project lessons learned process is conducted at the end of the project.

3. Cause-and-effect analysis uses a diagram (referred to as Ishikawa or fishbone diagram) to identify causes for an identified problem.

4. A control chart is used to prevent problems before they become major issues. It is a graphical tool for monitoring changes that occur during the execution of a process.

5. Pareto analysis uses a diagram, a form of histogram, to display, by frequency and in descending order, the most important quality issues found or reported.

6. The Pareto principle states that 80 percent of the impact of a quality problem/issue will show up in 20 percent of the causes.

7. Performance reporting involves the collection of all project-related data and the distribution of performance information to stakeholders.

8. Risk control is a continuous process for the management of previously identified risks and for any new risks that develop during a project's execution.

9. Procurement contract control is carried out by both a seller and a buyer to ensure that each part meets the respective contractual obligations.

Glossary

cause-and-effect analysis   A systematic method of generating and sorting ideas about possible causes of an identified problem. Once the root causes of problems are identified, they—rather than just the symptoms—can be dealt with.

control chart   A graphical tool for monitoring changes that occur during the execution of a process, by distinguishing between variation of results that are inherent in the process (common causes) and variation that yields a change to the process (special/unique causes).

Pareto diagram   Reported performance information represented in a bar chart that displays, by frequency and in descending order, the most important issues/defects found or reported to aid a project manager in concentrating effort on the most important events.

quality control   A process that involves monitoring project results to determine whether they comply with the defined relevant quality standards.

Review Questions

1. What is a quality assurance or quality control department used for in many organizations?

2. What is the quality control process, and when is it used on the project?

3. Describe the difference between quality prevention and quality inspection.
4. Describe the difference between tolerances and limits.
5. What is cause-and-effect analysis, and how is it used in the context of quality control?
6. What is a control chart, and how is it used in the context of quality control?
7. List the types of patterns or runs found in a control chart that should be of concern to a project manager.
8. What is Pareto analysis, and how does a project manager use a Pareto diagram during quality control?
9. List the different types of performance reports and describe the key pieces of information used for each.
10. What is contract administration, and who performs it?

Problems and Exercises

1. Research and discuss reasons why it is better for the quality monitoring and control process to be conducted by a separate group that is not associated with the execution of the project.
2. Research and discuss reasons why it is difficult for project managers to obtain accurate project performance information.
3. Think of a recent project you were involved in, either at school or at a job, and describe a problem you encountered. Follow the steps to drawing a fishbone diagram and describe the problem you encountered.
4. Discuss any potential problems you see with the project represented by the following control chart:

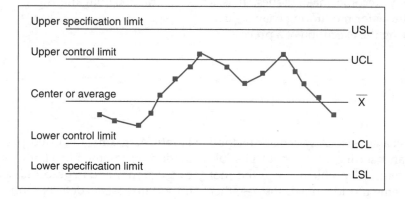

5. Discuss any potential problems you see with the project represented by the following control chart:

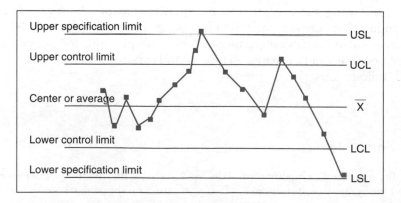

6. Draw a Pareto diagram similar to the one in Figure 12-3, based on the following information: The number of bugs found in security objects was 15; in data persistence objects, 3; in control objects, 12; in user interface objects, 4; and in inventory application objects, 4.

7. Discuss several methods for collecting project performance information from team members.

Projects and Research

1. Use the Internet to search for industry case studies that discuss how different organizations conduct quality audits. Include who is doing the audits and a list of the metrics tracked.

2. Use the Internet, your university, or your current organization to look for project status report templates. Compare and contrast what you find with what is presented in this chapter.

MINICASE

1. *Background:* (Review the R & S case study material at the beginning of this chapter.) Diana Brooks, business operations manager for R & S Amusements Services, has just gotten off the phone with COMPTEC, the computer supply store that was given the contract to deliver 20 tablet PCs for the asset tracking project. COMPTEC was given 60 days (via the contract) to deliver the 20 units to R & S or face financial penalties. Now, due to some unforeseen reasons, it appears that the computers will be delivered late.

Current Situation 1: After hanging up the phone, Diana makes a quick trip down the hall to Reid Lewis's office to give him the news. Diana explains the bad news. It seems that the company that manufactures the screens for the tablet PCs that R & S ordered from COMPTEC is located in Malaysia; a fire broke out at the company, which will now not be able to supply any screens for three months. The computer manufacturer from which COMPTEC was getting the tablets is currently searching for other vendors but is not sure when or if they will be able to deliver the machines for at least an extra three months.

Discussion: Put yourself in Reid's position and discuss your options for getting the needed computers. If the computers can't be obtained from COMPTEC, what other options do you have? Will the financial penalties spelled out in the contract help get this project done on time? Explain. What contingency plans should R & S have put in place earlier to aid in getting the project done on time, even with these delays from COMPTEC?

Current Situation 2: Reid Lewis calls Jeff Dunbar from PPMS, gives him the bad news about the delay in getting the computers, and asks for his advice. Jeff explains to Reid that getting the computers in 60 days was not on the critical path of the project schedule; the task had 45 days of slack.

Discussion: Knowing this new bit of information, how might your suggested decisions about what to do change?

Suggested Readings

Adams, J., et al. (1997). *Principles of project management.* Newtown Square, PA: Project Management Institute.

Afzalur, R. (1992). *Managing conflict in organizations.* Westport, CT: Praeger.

Besterfield, D., et al. (1999). *Total quality management.* Upper Saddle River, NJ: Prentice Hall.

Burton, J. (1980). *Conflict resolution and prevention.* New York: St. Martins.

Cohen, H. (1980). *You can negotiate anything.* Secaucus, NJ: Lyle Stuart, Inc.

FreeQuality.org web site, www.freequality.org.

Grossman, J. (1995, September). Resolve conflicts so everybody wins. *PM Network.*

Heusser, M. (July 30, 2012). How the Kanban method changes software engineering. *CIO.* Retrieved from http://www.cio.com/article/712449/How_the_Kanban_Method_Changes_Software_Engineering.

Jandt, F. (1987). *Win–win negotiating.* New York: Wiley.

Jarvis, A., & Crandall, V. (1997). *Inroads to software quality: "How to" guide and toolkit.* Upper Saddle River, NJ: Prentice Hall.

Kloppenborg, T., & Petrick, J. (2004). Managing project quality. *Quality Progress* 27(9):63–69.

Posner, B.Z. (1986). What's all the fighting about? Conflicts in project management. *IEEE Transactions on Engineering Management* EM-33: 207-211.

Project Management Institute web site, www.pmi.org.

Project Management Institute (PMI). (2004). *A guide to the project management body of knowledge,* 3rd ed. Newton Square, PA: PMI.

Robbins, S., & Judge, T. (2007). *Organizational behavior.* Upper Saddle River, NJ: Prentice Hall.

Thamhain, H., & Wilemon, D. (1997). A high-performing engineering project team. In R. Kats, ed., *The human side of managing innovation.* New York: Oxford Press.

Thamhain, H., & Wilemon, D. (1975). Conflict management in project life cycles. *Sloan Management Review,* 16(3):31–50.

Verma, V.K. (1996). *Human resource skills for the project manager.* Upper Darby, PA: Project Management Institute.

PART 4

Project Closeout Methods and Advanced Topics

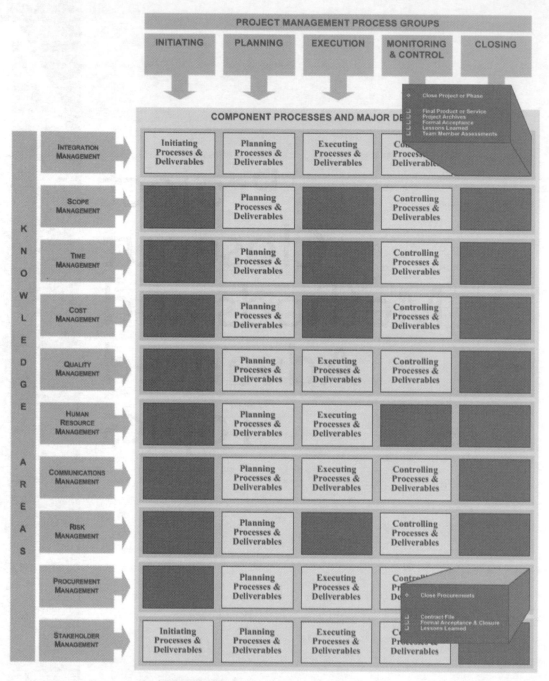

PROJECT MANAGEMENT PROCESS GROUPS

| INITIATING | PLANNING | EXECUTION | MONITORING & CONTROL | CLOSING |

COMPONENT PROCESSES AND MAJOR DE...

	INITIATING	PLANNING	EXECUTION	MONITORING & CONTROL	CLOSING
INTEGRATION MANAGEMENT	Initiating Processes & Deliverables	Planning Processes & Deliverables	Executing Processes & Deliverables	Controlling Processes & Deliverables	
SCOPE MANAGEMENT		Planning Processes & Deliverables		Controlling Processes & Deliverables	
TIME MANAGEMENT		Planning Processes & Deliverables		Controlling Processes & Deliverables	
COST MANAGEMENT		Planning Processes & Deliverables		Controlling Processes & Deliverables	
QUALITY MANAGEMENT		Planning Processes & Deliverables	Executing Processes & Deliverables	Controlling Processes & Deliverables	
HUMAN RESOURCE MANAGEMENT		Planning Processes & Deliverables	Executing Processes & Deliverables		
COMMUNICATIONS MANAGEMENT		Planning Processes & Deliverables	Executing Processes & Deliverables	Controlling Processes & Deliverables	
RISK MANAGEMENT		Planning Processes & Deliverables		Controlling Processes & Deliverables	
PROCUREMENT MANAGEMENT		Planning Processes & Deliverables	Executing Processes & Deliverables	Controlling Processes & Deliverables	
STAKEHOLDER MANAGEMENT	Initiating Processes & Deliverables	Planning Processes & Deliverables	Executing Processes & Deliverables	Controlling Processes & Deliverables	

KNOWLEDGE AREAS

Close Project or Phase
Final Product or Service
Project Archives
Formal Acceptance
Lessons Learned
Team Member Assessments

Close Procurements
Contract File
Formal Acceptance & Closure
Lessons Learned

◆ Indicates component process
❏ Indicates deliverable

13

Project Closure

R & S Amusements Services

Event 13

Setting   *The project has been completed, just 16 months after it started. The management team has convened in a small conference room located outside Reid Lewis's office at R & S Amusements. Those in attendance include Reid Lewis, Diana Brooks, Mark Lewis, Mike Lewis, Foster Hines, Elaine Henry, and Heidi Cosgray from R & S and Jeff Dunbar and Kevin Pullen from Premier Project Management Services.*

JEFF   Good morning, everyone. Thank you for taking time out of your busy schedules to attend this final project status meeting, as outlined in our communication plan. It has been a fun and exciting project. Here is the agenda for today's meeting:
[The following bullets are displayed on an overhead projector]

- Review of the project closeout checklist
- Final signoff on the asset tracking software implementation and the Premier Project Management Services contract
- Review of the final project report
- Lessons learned workshop

KEVIN   Let me start off by saying what a great job everyone has done on this project. I wish we always had such dedicated and committed people to work with.

REID   Well, I think I speak for all of us in saying thanks and the feeling is mutual. You two have done a great job in getting this project completed successfully. And most of the time I understood what you were talking about . . . *[Laughing]* But when we haven't understood exactly what was going on or what was next, you two have been very patient with us and did a great job of thoroughly explaining everything. So what next, now that everything is in place and operating?

JEFF   Well, we have just a couple items to finalize and then Kevin and I will leave you alone to do your jobs. We need two documents signed from the team. One is for the final project deliverables and the other is to officially end the contract with Premier Project Management Services.

HEIDI	Everything is done and working, and we are using the software and the new computers, so I guess everything is done. Why do we need to sign anything?
JEFF	It is a good practice to get a final deliverable signoff that all has been delivered for the project. Then, after we get the signatures on the completion documents, we would like to conduct one final activity—a "postmortem" review of the project.
DIANA	What is that? It sounds awful.
JEFF	Sorry about the "project speak" again. *Postmortem* is a way of looking at lessons learned. We will conduct an organized brainstorming workshop, with everyone's input, to review the highlights of the project.
KEVIN	We will highlight the key things that went well and those that didn't go quite as planned.
HEIDI	You mean like the software not automatically displaying the best route for the drivers but making them click that button before it displayed?
KEVIN	Yes, exactly. We have recorded all the events to review in the project management database and will be bringing up some of the highlights on the screen, one area at a time—for example, technology and then each key part of the software.
DIANA	Sounds like we could be here for awhile.
JEFF	Not really. We don't plan to spend much more than a couple hours at the most. We just want to review what we did well and note those things that could be improved for future projects. This will help us (Kevin and me) as well as help you the next time you execute a project.
KEVIN	Well, if everyone is ready, we can get the documents signed and get the lessons learned workshop under way . . .

(This concludes the project and the case study.)

(The details of conducting the lessons learned session are covered later in the chapter.)

CHAPTER PREVIEW AND OBJECTIVES

This is the final chapter on process elements of the project management body of knowledge (PMBOK) from the Project Management Institute (PMI). This chapter focuses on the activities conducted at the end of a phase of the project life cycle, the end of a contract with a seller, or the end of an entire project. The tools and techniques discussed here apply whether a project was cancelled before completion or was finished and deemed successful or unsuccessful.

As you read this chapter, you will:

- Understand the reasons projects are terminated
- Understand the tools and techniques of the closing project/phase process
- Understand how to lead a lessons learned exercise
- Understand how to close out a contract with a seller

AN INTRODUCTION TO PROJECT CLOSURE

Chapter 4 through Chapter 12 defined all the activities that occur before and during the execution of an IT project. This chapter covers the tools and techniques that project managers use at the end of a phase or project. Refer to the project **life cycle** diagram shown in Figure 2-2, back in Chapter 2, for help visualizing where we are in the life of the project.

One of the key items discussed in Chapter 1 about the definition of a project is that a project is a temporary endeavor—which means there must be an end. The end is either a termination due to some failure or a success in the eyes of the stakeholders. Many projects become what Ed Yourdon (1997) calls "death march" projects that never end. Even though everyone on such a project knows that the objectives will never be achieved, the project just keeps going. Project managers need to learn that it is okay if a project is cancelled before completion if there are valid reasons to abandon it, such as the technology selected becoming obsolete, sponsors of the project no longer supporting it, or the objectives of the project no longer matching the company's goals. In these and other similar circumstances, it is best to terminate the project and save the organization money that can be invested in better projects.

Put simply, projects terminate for two general reasons: The project is successful or the project is not successful in meeting scope, time, cost, and/or quality objectives. As stated earlier, terminating a project can be a positive thing for an organization, as the following examples illustrate:

- The FBI Virtual Case File system was supposed to allow better sharing of vital information inside the Federal Bureau of Investigation (FBI). It was proposed to be an improvement on the existing Automated Case Support System, which was seen as obsolete. The project, which was finally scrapped in 2005, had suffered from slowly evolving and poorly defined requirements. At the time it was scrapped, it contained over 700,000 lines of code and had an estimated worth of $170 million. The project deadline had been revised multiple times, and more and more money was being allocated. Scrapping the project was a good way of cutting losses, as there seemed to be little chance of salvaging it. The code was full of errors, and testing would have taken substantial resources in terms of time and money. Even then, the final product would not have met the requirements, as the expectations were overambitious. For example, there was a problem with deployment: The FBI wanted to deploy the system at once, but with the minimal amount of testing done, if the software failed, the FBI would have had no backup.
- The Texas Superconducting Super Collider was housed in a 54-mile underground tunnel beneath Waxahachie, Texas; the Super Collider was designed to accelerate beams of subatomic particles to fantastic speeds and then crash the particles into one another, purportedly generating huge amounts of energy. Researchers hoped to use the collider to simulate the conditions present during the Big Bang, thus providing new insights into the very nature of matter. The cost ballooned, however, from an original estimate of less than $5 billion to just under $12 billion. In 1993 Congress decided to cancel the project, with less than one-third of the tunnel finished. The closing of the project made sense because smaller and less expensive alternatives—particle accelerators, the largest of which is a mere 5 miles in diameter—achieve the same goals.

Not all projects have been as fortunate as these examples. For many reasons, including the following, projects aren't cancelled when they should be:

- Individuals don't want to admit that there are problems because they fear management retribution.
- Individuals with a "superman" or "superwoman" complex believe they can get the project done by pulling off the impossible.

- Sometimes individuals see only what they want to see; they don't want to face any bad information.
- Many times individuals don't want to be the one to "rock the boat" or be seen as the bearer of bad news.

The decision to terminate a project should be made by key stakeholders who have the authority to cancel the project.

The reasons that projects are terminated are varied. The following are some examples:

- The best scenario is that all project objectives meet with stakeholder approval.
- Key sponsor support is lost.
- During end-of-phase reviews, the project's financial incentives (for example, NPV, IRR, ROI) no longer meet organization or stakeholder requirements.
- Key project personnel are no longer available.
- Key project objectives are no longer obtainable or have changed drastically, such that a new project needs to be created and the current one terminated.
- The technology selected for the project doesn't work or has become obsolete.
- The project's forecasted budget at completion and estimate to complete are not acceptable.
- Other projects take priority and starve the current project of resources.
- The project is combined with another similar project to gain advantages not available with them remaining separate.

Terminating a project, regardless of reason, can be a difficult choice, especially for large, complex projects. Making the decision to cancel—for example, deciding to cancel a large ERP project when millions of dollars have been invested, hundreds of workers have been pulled away from their regular jobs and co-located with the IT team, new hardware and software have been purchased, seller contracts have been signed, and many promises have been made—is a very difficult thing to do. But continuing to spend organizational assets on a project that will not meet stakeholder needs must stop.

Regardless of how a project is terminated, the processes of project closure and contract closure should still be completed; there is just as much to learn from a bad project as from a good project. If a project manager and an organization want to avoid making the same mistakes over and over again, they must learn from the past; as the philosopher and poet George Santayana wrote, "Those who do not remember the past are condemned to repeat it." Resources assigned to a project will need to be reassigned to other duties, and any other material, such as hardware and software, will need to be dealt with, regardless of the reasons for project termination. The next section describes the closing project/phase process, followed by the closing procurements process.

PROJECT MANAGEMENT CONCEPTS: CLOSING A PROJECT

Integration Management—Closing a Project or Phase

The Integration Management knowledge area consists of the following processes: develop project charter, develop project management plan, direct and manage project work, monitor and control project work, perform integrated change control, and close project or phase. In this chapter we cover the final process: close project or phase.

PROVEN STRATEGIES AND HINTS TO SUCCESS

From Steve Hart, the practice manager responsible for project leadership and delivery services for the Cardinal Solutions Group, in an article entitled "4 Elements of an Effective Project Closure Reporting Process":

1. Limited Original Work—If the project execution process and the closure process activities have been effectively conducted, the project closure report should just be a summarization of related effort, versus any effort involving original work.
2. Executive Summary—Many of the concerned stakeholders, especially the higher up on the totem pole, are looking just for the executive summary information on the results of the project: what was delivered, what wasn't delivered, how effectively was it delivered, and finally, what did you learn from the project.
3. Variance Explanations—Include "fact-based" variance numbers along with detailed explanations for any significant variances. The fact that you went over budget 1% is probably not all that newsworthy, but run over budget 40% and you should be prepared to give explanations.
4. Next Steps—The closure report links the project performance to the lessons learned and any continuous improvement related next steps.

Project managers in most organizations rarely get much time off at the end of a project before they need to start the next one. In fact, in most cases, they are working on several projects at the same time, each in a different phase, so there isn't a break at all. Therefore, the tendency is often to leave a completed project as soon as possible and move on to the next, without conducting much of a project closing process. The closing process is extremely important to the continued success of an organization and a project team, and it must not be skipped, regardless of the size of the project. The closing process must be a part of the project schedule, with time and resources assigned. Project managers, in some cases, must fight to make sure this step is not skipped. Project managers can help ensure that the process is followed by including time and resources in the project plan for the closing process. As mentioned earlier, the project or phase closeout process must be completed, regardless of the size of the project or the reason for a project or phase termination. The terms *project* and *phase* are both used here because the closing process is needed at the end of each phase or iteration of a project as well as at the end of an entire project.

The formality, number of people involved, and time devoted to the closure process are based on the size of a project. A short one-month project involving 3 people will have a very short, informal closing process. A one-year project with 100 resources will need a more formal closing process, involving many of the resources that worked on the project, including the sponsor and key stakeholders. Each phase or project iteration needs a closing process.

The main goal of the closing process is to finalize all project activities across all process groups to formally close the phase or project and, if needed, transfer responsibility for the product to a support or operations department within the organization or perhaps to an external agency. Stakeholders are required to sign documents indicating their agreement that the deliverables of the project are completed. A good practice is to use a final checklist to make sure everything is completed. Figure 13-1 is an example of a checklist.

Task Description	Required	Date Scheduled	Responsible
Closeout meeting			
Determine attendees			
Communicate project termination			
Schedule meeting			
Conduct meeting			
Document and update all project data			
Prepare final status report			
Financial			
Close out financial records			
Audit financial records			
Prepare final reports			
Human resources			
Officially transfer team members			
Close out all work authorizations			
Prepare final performance reviews			
Obtain operational support acceptance			
Contracts			
Update seller performance information			
Obtain seller signature			
Obtain stakeholder signature			
Handle any contractual compliance issues			
Prepare final status report			
Site			
Close down site operations			
Handle software/hardware disposition			
Handle infrastruture material disposition			

FIGURE 13-1   Project/Phase Closeout Checklist

The checklist consists of the following elements: the short name of the activity to complete, whether the activity is required for this project, the date the activity is to be completed, and who is responsible for the activity. The activity categories are as follows:

- *Closeout meeting*—The closeout meeting can be used in a variety of ways. For example, it can be a brainstorming session to list/review the things that went right and those that went wrong during the project. It is also used to review the entire project and provide a help session so that future projects avoid the same pitfalls. So that everyone hears the same message, it is a good practice to get the stakeholders and the team together at the same time to share ideas and final thoughts on the project. This paves the way for collaboration on future projects.
- *Financial*—In some organizations the financial or accounting department requires official signatures in order to close out accounts. Closing the accounts ensures that erroneous charges don't appear and possibly signal the start of an audit. The audit is used to review project spending to find errors and possibly fraud.
- *Human resources*—In most medium to large projects, human resources are transferred to work on the project full time, leaving their previous assignments within

the company. Once the project terminates, these individuals need to be reassigned to new projects or back to similar jobs they had before they were transferred. A project manager may also be responsible for writing final performance appraisals for each team member, to be used in their annual reviews. The final task on the checklist is to get official acceptance of the system by the group that will support it during the normal life of the product; this is often a group called operational support or operations.

- *Contracts*—This category is discussed in the next section of the chapter.
- *Site*—If any special accommodations were required for the project team, such as rental of office space, the site will need to be closed and assets either returned to the organization or, if rented, returned to the owner.

As a part of the process "document and update all project data" in the checklist shown in Figure 13-1, an organization needs to make sure that all project-related information is electronically documented for future use. This information should be updated throughout the project, not just at the end. If it is left to the end, much of the information needed will be lost. During the closeout process, the information is finalized and moved to an archive status to protect it from being changed or deleted. The data consist of all planned and actual performance data, including schedule, cost, scope, quality, team performance, risks, and communication issues. Information generated from the lessons learned sessions should also be added before the database is archived. These data are then used to produce the final project report as well as for future projects. The final project report contains the following information:

- *Project performance*—This includes all actual results compared to plan as well as an examination of project methodology issues. How accurate were the initial time and money estimates? How well did the iterative project life cycle work? How well did the communications plan work? How well did the team identify potential risks and manage them?
- *Product performance*—This mainly concerns the quality of the product created. Did the product meet the defined quality standards? Was it fit for use?
- *Administrative performance*—How well did the decision makers perform on the project in terms of speed and accuracy, based on the quality of the information available for decisions? How well did the organizational structure aid the project or hinder the project? Did the decision makers have the correct levels of authority?
- *Team member performance*—How well did the team work together? Did the team motivation incentives work, or did the team-building exercises work? How well did this team's performance compare to the performance of other teams within the organization? Did the team have the right members assigned? If training was required, how well did it work, and was it done at the right time in the life of the project?
- *Benefits realized*—The project was selected based on some perceived benefits to the organization. Are these still achievable, based on the final product?

The closeout meeting, also referred to as the *lessons learned session* or *postmortem*, is very important and should never be skipped. As many of the team members as possible should be in attendance, as should the stakeholders. Having everyone in the same room is preferred, but having some participate in a virtual setting is permissible. As with the project kickoff meeting, having everyone hear the same message and have an opportunity to add to the conversation will benefit future projects and the participants. Depending on the size of the meeting, it may be necessary to have a skilled project manager organize and run the event to keep it on topic and offer everyone a chance to participate.

The lessons learned session should include a review of the following elements described in the checklist:

- The group should review the project's objectives met/unmet along with quality standards met/unmet.
- The group should review the planned versus actual performance, and if a large variance exists, the group should determine why and make adjustments for future projects.
- The group should review the integrated change control management process: Did it go correctly? Could it be improved? How did the accepted changes affect the project and the product? Could any of the changes have been avoided? If so, a detailed explanation should be drafted for future projects.
- Stakeholder assessment of and opinions about the project should be recorded because the determination of the success of a project rests with them.
- The group should review how well the project methodology worked for this type of project. What changes need to be made? Is additional training needed?
- The group should review the project organizational chart used for any improvements.
- The final output of the closeout process is a document list of activities/issues that went well and those that didn't, complete with explanations and action items for improvements for future projects.

Procurement Management: Closing Procurements

The Procurement Management knowledge area consists of the following processes: plan procurements, conduct procurements, control procurements, and close procurements. This section concentrates on the final process: closing procurements.

The closing procurements process supports the overall project closing process described in the previous section in that it verifies that all deliverables from the contract are acceptable (meet quality standards) and officially approved. This process may or may not be needed, depending on whether outside vendors were used. If the project is done completely in-house, then no contracts will exist to close. The closing process should finalize the archiving of all data related to how the contract was administered and how the seller performed for future contract work with this seller. The requirements for the formal written contract closing are generally defined in the terms of the contract. In many cases, all that is needed is a final signature from the project sponsor or key stakeholder that the provided services or product has been delivered. Any unresolved claims (unfinished or poorly finished work) may be subject to litigation after the contract closure.

As with project termination, contract termination can occur for many reasons: The deliverable may be completed and accepted, the technology required may have changed, the seller may have performed poorly, or the organization's priorities may have changed and the product may no longer be required. The conditions for terminating a contract early, before final deliverables, must be spelled out in the contract terms. Termination can be done by a mutual agreement of both parties or based on the seller or buyer defaulting on their part of the contract. Some reasons for early termination might include the seller missing key deadlines, the seller creating a product that doesn't meet minimal quality standards, the buyer missing payments, or the buyer continuously rejecting the seller's work and asking for changes.

Finally, a lessons learned session (which can be done as part of the session described earlier) should be held to review the procurements process. A procurement audit should be performed to document an honest appraisal of the contract from both sides—the buyer's side and the seller's side. With the aid of the data collected from the audit, the team can review the following:

- Was the right type of contract used?
- Were milestones achieved by both the buyer and seller? (Referred to as the milestone hit-rate)
- Was the change control process timely and effective, and was it followed?
- Were the deliverables of acceptable quality?
- Was the communications plan effective?
- How well did the project meet financial goals?
- Were the right human resources assigned by the buyer and seller?
- How effective were risk mitigation strategies?

The single best method project managers can use to improve how they run projects is to learn from past mistakes and past successes. These results must be documented and reviewed more than just at the end of the project. The project management database needs to be available to more than just the project manager who ran the project so others can learn from the same information. The next section describes the process used to conduct the closing project and closing procurements processes and is followed by an example of each, using the opening case study.

PROJECT CLOSURE PROCESS

The process for the project closure process and the contract closure process is listed here and shown in Figure 13-2:

1. Communicate final decisions and review the closure checklist.
2. Update the project schedule for any remaining work.
3. Obtain final approvals/signatures from stakeholders, management, and sellers.
4. Conduct final audits, if needed, of the project, product, contract, and personnel.
5. Schedule and hold a final lessons learned workshop.
6. Reassign any remaining personnel.
7. Return any leased/borrowed resources and vacate rented facilities.
8. Publish results across the organization.

The following section provides examples of each step, using information from the R & S Amusements Services case study.

HOW TO CONDUCT THE CLOSING PROJECT PROCESS

In this final section, the R & S Amusements Services case study that is presented at the beginning of the chapter is used to demonstrate the activities of the closing processes. This section provides examples and walks through many of the processes defined in the previ-

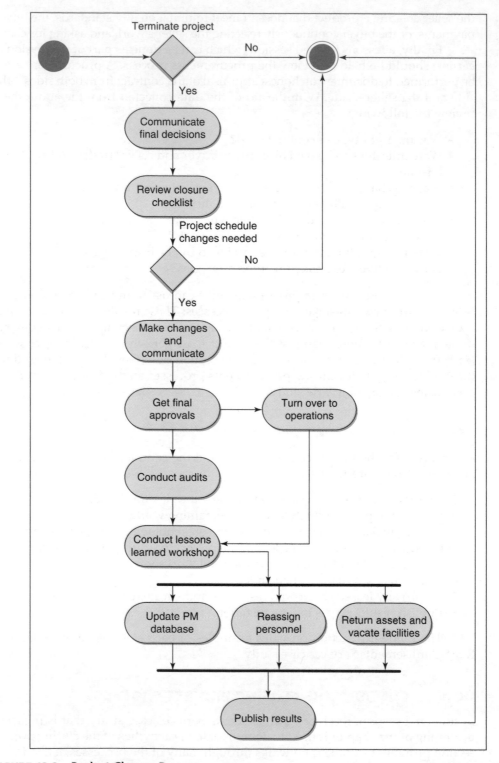

FIGURE 13-2 Project Closure Process

Task Description	Required	Date Scheduled	Responsible
Closeout meeting			
Determine attendees	yes	8/3/2008	Mark Lewis
Communicate project termination	yes	8/1/2008	Mark Lewis
Schedule meeting	yes	8/3/2008	Mark Lewis
Conduct meeting	yes	8/13/2008	Mark Lewis
Document and update all project data	yes	8/10/2008	Mark Lewis
Prepare final status report	yes	8/13/2008	Mark Lewis
Financial			
Close out financial records	yes	8/10/2008	Diana Brooks
Audit financial records	yes	8/10/2008	Diana Brooks
Prepare final reports	yes	8/13/2008	Diana Brooks
Human resources			
Officially transfer team members	no		
Close out all work authorizations	no		
Prepare final performance reviews	yes	8/10/2008	Mark Lewis
Obtain operational support acceptance	no		
Contracts			
Update seller performance information	yes	8/3/2008	Elaine Henry
Obtain seller signature	yes	8/3/2008	Elaine Henry & Reid Lewis
Obtain stakeholder signature	yes	8/13/2008	Elaine Henry
Handle any contractual compliance issues	yes	8/10/2008	Elaine and Reid
Prepare final status report	yes	8/13/2008	Elaine and Reid
Site			
Close down site operations	no		
Handle software/hardware disposition	no		
Handle infrastruture material disposition	no		

FIGURE 13-3   Asset Management Software Project Closeout Process Checklist

ous sections. The processes tend to follow the order shown here but can be varied. Before proceeding, take time to reread and review the R & S Amusements Services case study at the beginning of the chapter.

Step 1: Communicate Final Decisions and Start Working Through the Closeout Checklist

Jeff Dunbar and Kevin Pullen from Premier Project Management Services have presented the project closeout checklist shown in Figure 13-3 to the R & S project team to use as part of the agenda to bring the project to a close. The closeout meeting was scheduled and prepared by Mark Lewis, the lead project leader from R & S, with the help of Jeff Dunbar from PPMS. The meeting was scheduled for approximately two weeks after the delivery and testing of the project's final deliverable. In the financial section, an official close of financial records was performed by Diana Brooks, the business operations manager. The official close will prevent any new charges against accounts that were specifically set up for this project. Diana was also responsible for performing the financial audit and preparing the final financial report, which is part of the overall final project status report (shown later in this chapter). The one task that needs attention in the human resources area—preparing the final performance reviews—was done by the project leader, Mark Lewis. The team members' functional managers will use these reviews to help create the annual performance evaluations for the team members. In the contracts section, there were three major vendors used during the project: asset management software, hardware, and the project management consulting company PPMS. Each of these contracts needs to be officially closed, information about each one needs to be maintained, and a final status report needs to be prepared as part of the final project status report.

Step 2: Update the Project Schedule for Remaining Work, if Needed

At this point in the asset management software project, no additional work has been identified other than that listed in the closeout checklist which was listed in the original schedule. If additional work had been identified, the project schedule would need to be updated, along with associated budget information and resources assigned to perform the work.

Step 3: Obtain Final Approvals/Signatures

Jeff and Kevin from PPMS have brought the final project deliverable signoff documents for the key stakeholders to sign, and this will officially end the project. Figure 13-4 shows the signoff document for the asset management software project. The document is a very simple restatement of the agreed-to objectives from the current project charter and asks the stakeholders if they agree that all the objectives were met. Once it is signed, the project is officially ended and turned over to the group that will be responsible for daily operational support. For R & S, operational support will be done by a local IT services consulting company until a full-time IT person can be hired. The support will be supervised by Mark Lewis.

R & S Project Deliverable Signoff Document

Project Title: Asset Management

Description:

- Purchase an asset management software package that comes closest to meeting R & S needs.
- Then, perform a gap analysis and write custom code to deliver what is missing from the package.
- Finally integrate this software into the other software solutions of R & S.

Objectives:

- Ability to track the location of every amusement asset (onsite or in the field)
- Inventory: game machines, maintenance supplies, dollar bill changers, external speakers
- Inventory information is updated continually in real-time
- Generate purchase requisitions
- Ability to generate ad-hoc reports
- Track vendor information
- Track asset performance

By signing your name below, you agree that this project has satisfied all of the above objectives and can be closed.

Approvals

Mark Lewis _____   Elaine Henry _____

Reid Lewis _____   Kenny Jones _____

Diana Brooks _____

FIGURE 13-4 **Deliverable Signoff Document**

Step 4: Conduct Final Audits, if Needed

Diana Brooks was put in charge of organizing and running the financial audit of the project. Diana selected two employees from her department who had not, up to this point, been very involved in the project. Their main goal was to reconcile all project charges over $500 to make sure they were applied correctly to the project and that the final cost performance numbers are correct.

Elaine Henry and Reid Lewis were put in charge of auditing each of the seller contracts to make sure they complied with the particulars of the contract and to make sure that all elements listed in the statement of work were, in fact, delivered.

R & S Amusements Services
Final Status Report
Date: 8/13/08

Project Name: Asset Tracking   Prepared by: Mike Lewis
Current Project Phase: Project Closeout

Activity CTP	Budget $	Actual $	Completion Date Schedule	Actual
Total Project	153.6K	152.9K	8/1/07	8/1/08

Activity STP	Budget $	Actual $	Completion Date Schedule	Actual	%Complete
Final Meeting	10.5K	10K	8/13/08	TBD	90%

Current Earned Values

CPI = .989
SPI = 1.00

Project Status

	Red
	Yellow
✓	Green

Financial Audit Results

Description	Cost Impact	Time Impact
No discrepancies found		

Contract Audit Results

Description	Cost Impact	Time Impact
No discrepancies found		

FIGURE 13-5   **Final Project Status Report**

Step 5: Schedule and Hold a Final Lessons Learned Workshop

Mark Lewis along with Jeff Dunbar and Kevin Pullen put together the lessons learned workshop, using data from the current project management database and the completed project audits. Mark did the scheduling and made sure all the participants could attend. Jeff and Kevin conducted the workshop. The workshop was a simple brainstorming session focused on these key areas of discussion:

- Findings associated with the project plan and project methodology used
- Findings associated with vendor selection and the eventual vendor deliverables
- Findings associated with the budgeting process

- Findings associated with the selected hardware
- Findings associated with the selected software

Each of these topics was put on the whiteboard, and Jeff and Kevin then led the discussion about what worked and what didn't work and why. Suggestions for improvement were then solicited and documented. Discussion of each topic was limited to 25 minutes.

Step 6: Reassign Any Remaining Personnel, if Needed

No one on the team was assigned 100 percent to this project, but the two R & S employees who were temporarily relieved of part of their responsibilities working in the regional offices to work on this project were sent back to their prior job responsibilities at 100 percent. Everyone was reminded that the financial accounts had been closed, and they would not be allowed to charge any more of their time to the project.

Step 7: Return Any Leased/Borrowed Resources, if Needed

The project did not require any leased or borrowed resources. The R & S internal office space that was made available for Jeff and Kevin while they worked on the project is now available for other uses, as Jeff and Kevin have removed all of their belongings.

Step 8: Publish Results

Mark Lewis was put in charge of making sure that all employees were informed of the final disposition of the project. He was also responsible for making sure that all material discussed during the lessons learned workshop made its way into the final project documentation (see Figure 13-5 for an example of the final project status report).

Chapter Review

1. Projects are terminated for a variety of reasons, some bad and some good.
2. Terminating a project early when it should be terminated is not always done for several reasons, such as fear of management retribution, feeling that a miracle can be accomplished, selective sight, and not wanting to be singled out as a problem employee.
3. Regardless of project size, a closing project phase process should be executed.
4. Regardless of contract size, a closing procurements process should be executed.
5. The main goal of the closing project or closing phase process is to finalize all project activities across all process groups to formally close the phase or project and, if needed, transfer responsibility for the product to a support or operations department within the organization or to an external agency.
6. Many project managers use a closeout process checklist to make sure nothing is forgotten.
7. The final project report consists of the following sections: project performance, product performance, administrative performance, team member performance, and benefits realized.
8. The closing procurements process verifies that all deliverables from the contract are acceptable and are officially approved.

Glossary

life cycle   A prescribed order of phases (smaller segments of an entire project) that contain specific deliverables that collectively deliver a result.

Review Questions

1. List some of the reasons some projects are not terminated when they should be.
2. Who should be the one to terminate a project? Why?
3. List some of the reasons projects are terminated. Can you think of any others to add to the list?
4. Describe each of the major categories of items on the closing project process checklist.
5. Describe the reasons for having a closeout process meeting with all team members and stakeholders.
6. Describe the contents of the final project report.
7. List the main objectives of the closing procurements process.

Problems and Exercises

1. Think about a project you've done in class this semester or a previous semester. Perform a closeout process and create each of the deliverables mentioned in the final section of the chapter for your project: closeout checklist, final project deliverables report, and lessons learned session.
2. "The closing procurements process is used to review the performance of both the buyer and seller." Explain this statement.

Projects and Research

1. Use the Internet to find examples of terminated IT projects. Describe the circumstances surrounding the termination. Who made the decision?
2. Use the Internet to find examples of IT projects that probably should have been terminated or should now be terminated. Explain why you believe they should be terminated.
3. Research how organizations conduct their closeout sessions or lessons learned sessions. Explain their similarities and differences compared to the one presented in this chapter.

MINICASE

1. *Background:* (Review the R & S case study material at the beginning of this chapter.) The first hour of the R & S lessons learned workshop has gone extremely well, with minor comments as each major topic area has been explored. When the review comes to the topic of key software deliverable issues, the first highlighted item is the problem encountered with the first iteration of the inventory reporting software application. The firm hired to write the application was not told about the need to consolidate inventory from multiple bins within the main West Lafayette location, nor was it told to consolidate inventory from all three other warehouses so management could get a complete picture of current inventory levels. The oversight in the development of the requirements ended up causing many hours of rework and increased the cost for the project substantially.

Current Situation 1: When this discussion comes up, Kenny Jones, R & S warehouse manager, gets very defensive because he was in charge of this part of the application. Kenny was the key user working with the software development company to define the requirements for the inventory control module. Jeff Dunbar from PPMS tries to assure Kenny that this is not a blaming session but an attempt to learn for future projects. Kenny continues to be very upset and raises his voice, saying that he has never done anything like this before and can't be blamed.

Discussion: Discuss ways in which the lessons learned workshop should be run to minimize these types of reactions. Should these problems be brought up in large, open discussions or just in small groups? List and explain the types of processes that should be put in place to make sure the system requirements are defined and understood correctly by both the subject matter experts and the IT staff.

Current Situation 2: At the end of the lessons learned session, Kevin Pullen from PPMS puts up the last slide, which displays the final project results for scope, time, and cost. The scope was delivered 100 percent, the cost ended up 15 percent overbudget, and the completion date was 5 percent past the original deadline.

Discussion: Was this a successful project? Why or why not? What factors determine the success or failure of a project? Put yourself in the place of each of the major stakeholders (Reid Lewis, Diana Brooks, and Mark Lewis from R & S; Jeff Dunbar and Kevin Pullen from PPMS; COMPTEC, the vendor selected to supply computers; and the software company selected to build the custom software) and state, from that person's perspective, whether the project was a success.

Suggested Readings

Balachandra, R., & Raelin, A. (1990, July). How to decide when to abandon a project. *Research Management*, pp. 24–29.

Black, K. (1996, November). Causes of project failure: A survey of professional engineers. *PM Network*, pp. 21–24.

Chi, T., Liu, J., & Chen, H. (1997, February). Optimal stopping rule for a project with uncertain completion time and partial salvageability. *IEEE Transactions on Engineering Management*, pp. 54–66.

Cooke-Davies, T. (2001). *Project closeout management: More than simply saying good-bye and moving on.* In Knutson, J., ed., *Project management for business professionals.* New York: John Wiley & Sons, pp. 200–214.

Hart, S. (2012, December 15). "4 elements of an effective project closure reporting process. PM-Foundations. Retrieved from http://pm-foundations.com/tag/project-closure/.

Ingram, T. (1994, June). Managing client/server and open systems projects: A 10-year study of 62 mission-critical projects. *Project Management Journal*, pp. 24–36.

Keil, M., Truex, D., & Mixon, R. (1995, November). The effects of sunk cost and project completion on information technology project escalation. *IEEE Transactions on Engineering Management*, pp. 372–381.

Kumar, V., Persaud, A., & Kumar, U. (1996, August). To terminate or not an ongoing R&D project: A managerial dilemma. *IEEE Transaction on Engineering Management*, pp. 273–284.

Meredith, J., & Mantel, S. (2003). *Project management.* New York: Wiley.

Pinto, J., & Mantel, S. (1990, November). The causes of project failure. *IEEE Transaction on Engineering Management*, pp. 269–276.

Pritchard, C. (1998). *Project termination: The good, the bad, the ugly. Field guide to project management.* New York: John Wiley & Sons.

Project Management Institute web site, www.pmi.org.

Project Management Institute (PMI). (2004). *A guide to the project management body of knowledge, 3rd ed.* Newton Square, PA: PMI.

Staw, B., & Ross, J. (1987, March–April). Knowing when to pull the plug. *Harvard Business Review*, p. 71.

Yourdon, E. (1997). *Death march: The complete software developer's guide to surviving "mission impossible" projects.* Upper Saddle River, NJ: Prentice Hall.

14

Advanced Topics in Project Management

R & S Amusements Services

Event 14

Setting *The R & S Amusements Services project has been completed, and the management team is walking out the door after the lessons learned exercise. Reid Lewis, R & S's president, has lagged behind all the rest to have a final word with Jeff Dunbar and Kevin Pullen, consultants from Premier Project Management Services (PPMS).*

REID   Well, that session was certainly enlightening. I had forgotten about all those small issues that came up during the project. I have to confess that I didn't think this was going to be worthwhile, but it certainly was. Thanks for making us go through it.

KEVIN   You're welcome. This is not the first time we have had to convince people of the merits of holding a final lessons learned session.

JEFF   Well, it has been a pleasure working with you, Reid. Your team did an excellent job, and you now have a successful IT project already beginning to provide benefits.

REID   You're right, it seems to be working great. Thanks again, guys, for all your help. I don't think there would have been any chance for success without your project management guidance.

JEFF   There is no replacement for having trained project managers working on the project and having a dedicated team.

KEVIN   Well, take care, Reid, and let us know if we can be of service in the future.

(Jeff and Kevin leave R & S's offices for the last time.)

CHAPTER PREVIEW AND OBJECTIVES

This chapter presents some industry best practices and special topics as they relate to the field of project management. The topics covered are project management offices, outsourcing, ethics, virtual teams, and maturity models—namely the Capability Maturity Model Integrated (CMMI) and the Organizational Project Management Maturity Model (OPM3). In addition to the information presented earlier in the text, based almost exclusively on the Project Management Institute's project management body of knowledge (PMBOK), this chapter presents some additional tools and techniques that are essential for the long-term success of a project manager and an organization.

As you read this chapter, you will:

- Understand what a project management office is and how to set it up
- Understand the benefits to an organization and to each individual of acting ethically
- Understand why and when to use outsourcing
- Know how to define the benefits and drawbacks of outsourcing
- Understand how to manage a virtual project team
- Understand the benefits and drawbacks of maturity models

THE PROJECT MANAGEMENT OFFICE

The **project management office (PMO)**, also referred to as a project office, project support office, or center of excellence, is an organizational entity (for example, group, department, business unit) with full-time personnel assigned to provide a wide range of project management support and services across an entire organization. The number of organizations implementing some type of PMO is growing rapidly. According to PM Solutions' benchmark study (see www.pmsolutions.com/research) on the "State of the PMO 2012," PMOs decreased failed projects by 30%, delivered 25% of projects under budget and 19% ahead of schedule, and saved companies an average of $411,000 per project. The survey consisted of 554 high-level project management personnel from all size organizations in various industries. Of the organizations surveyed, 85% have a PMO in place, demonstrating a steady growth from 48% in 2000, 77% in 2006, and 84% in 2010. The reasons for this growth are many, including improved success rates, improved return on investment (ROI), and new government-mandated reporting requirements (for example, those contained in the Sarbanes-Oxley Act, which requires companies to report investments, such as large information technology [IT] projects, that may affect an organization's performance, for example the implementation and deployment of an ERP software project).

For help in understanding where the PMO exists in the organizational structure and its role, refer to Figure 1-8 in Chapter 1, which shows the organizational chart of a matrix structure. The example presented has the PMO reporting directly to the chief executive officer of the entire organization and shows the project leaders reporting to the management of the PMO. The tasks performed by the PMO vary widely, based on what is needed by the organization, the organizational structure, the staff, and other considerations. A PMO may perform one or all of the following functions:

- Provide project support when and where needed (for example, consulting, mentoring, technology)
- Aid in project selection and business case development

- Train all team participants, leaders, and stakeholders
- Function as a central library or documentation repository to improve communication
- Handle integrated change control management
- Provide methodology control, audits (for example, cost, time), and evolving maturity levels
- Act as an organizationwide resource repository to share and level resources across projects
- Constantly look at the industry for best practices and add them to the methodology
- Aid in portfolio management
- Aid management in go/no go decision points on projects
- Perform quality assurance reviews/audits
- Lead post-implementation "lessons learned sessions"

Kent Crawford (2002), in his book *The Strategic Project Office*, defines three broad levels at which the PMO might operate. Level 1, which is the individual project level, helps add value to individual projects by defining basic processes and recording results that can then be adopted by other projects. At Level 2, the PMO helps to diffuse the processes and uniform methodology to other projects generally within the same department, division, or business unit. Finally, a Level 3 PMO, which is the corporate level, manages the entire collection of the organization's projects, maintaining information on strategic goals, project metric history, and current progress on all ongoing projects.

Depending on the functions performed and the level of PMO created, the PMO may consist of many of the following resources (whose titles will vary between organizations).

- *Chief project officer*—Owns project management for the enterprise, business unit, or department. Expert and mentor in all areas of project management.
- *Project manager*—Directs and coordinates project activities.
- *Project planner*—Handles consolidating and managing of project plans, including schedule development, budgeting, and resources.
- *Project librarian*—Maintains a repository of project knowledge (records, standards, methods, and lessons learned).
- *Best practice expert*—Develops and maintains project management methodology and processes.
- *Process improvement manager*—Prepares and executes process quality assurance plans. Documents and maintains project processes and standards.
- *Resource manager*—Works with human resources in providing job descriptions, roles and responsibilities, and how to measure performance against those roles and responsibilities.
- *Communications controller*—Handles external and internal communications related to projects within the PMO.
- *Change control expert*—Is responsible for organizational change management, developing and maintaining issue resolution, and change control processes.
- *Executive administration*—Provides secretarial support and performs back-office tasks.
- *Technology services*—Manages and coordinates technology issues, maintains central software configuration management for teams on all projects, and supports and maintains the PMO software, database, and all other technical needs.

The most successful implementation of PMOs have started small at Level 1, proven successful and moved up to Level 2, and then advanced to Level 3. The following is a list of implementation strategy best practices:

- Establish the business need for a PMO and get agreement from key stakeholders. Never do it just because it can be done.
- Develop the PMO slowly, evolving functions over time. Start small.
- Determine at the outset at what level the PMO should ultimately operate—the individual project, business unit, or corporate level.
- Ensure that executive management support is in place before starting.
- Establish written descriptions of positions, responsibilities, and authority distributions.
- Get buy-in from all operating units affected.
- Put your best and brightest in the PMO.
- Realize that the PMO need not be involved in every project.
- Allow some guided flexibility in the standard methodology used across all projects.
- Do not take on any of the roles within the project team other than project leader or resource leader.
- Manage stakeholder expectations just as you should in any project.

Organizations have attributed many benefits to their PMO, but many experts caution that reduced cost should not be a selling point. In most cases, cost will actually increase in the early stages of implementation. It takes time for the benefits to become reality after organizations learn to efficiently run projects using the PMO. The following are some of the benefits:

- Standardization of operations/processes
- More efficient and effective operations/processes
- Elimination or reduction of company silos (getting different departments to cooperate), better shared knowledge
- Better resource allocations across all projects
- Better and quicker decision making
- Quicker access to higher-quality data that is centrally stored
- More realistic prioritization of work
- Better training and improvement for project management and project leaders
- More accurate cost and schedule estimates
- Better visibility and support for project management practices and project managers
- Improved stakeholder satisfaction levels
- Higher project success rates

Project management offices are not without issues or drawbacks. A PMO is not a "silver bullet" that, once implemented, will fix all of the organization's project issues. Establishing a well-functioning PMO requires a culture change across the organization. Some departments or divisions need to give up some control or authority to the PMO. A PMO requires upfront expenses and training, sometimes for long periods, before it begins to show a positive ROI. Finally, implementers need to make sure that the PMO doesn't become a bureaucracy of paperwork that ultimately gets in the way of getting projects completed successfully. But even with some of these hurdles, organizations that have met the challenge and established PMOs have been very successful.

OUTSOURCING

Outsourcing transfers project activities and certain decision rights to an external entity, by contract, with specific performance measures, related rewards (generally monetary), penalties (again generally monetary), and exit clauses defined. (Refer to Chapter 9 for an explanation of contracts and exit clauses.) Contracts should include detailed service-level agreements (SLA) to help define the buyer/seller relationship (see Chapter 9). Outsourcing has become a necessity for many organizations to compete in a global economy and to find needed resources. Researchers have estimated that an average Fortune 1000 company spends 30 to 35 percent of its budget on outsourcing. Forrester, a leading IT research and consulting company, estimates that by 2015, 3.3 million jobs, representing $136 billion in wages, will be outsourced outside the United States. Forty percent of Fortune 500 companies outsource part of their IT functions. From a 2012 survey conducted by Bluewolf, a global IT consulting company (see www.bluewolf.com), the top drivers for IT outsourcing in 2012 are: productivity and profitability, flexibility to turn resources on and off, and access to experts and hard-to-find talent. Other information collected from the survey: $0.48 of every outsourcing dollar is spent on application services, in the next 12 to 18 months 32% of the responding organizations will increase IT outsourcing investments, 73% outsource application services at least partially, 48% will hire more contractors rather than full-time staff, and 16% of data center operations are managed in the cloud.

Many different alternatives are available for outsourcing, some of which are listed below:

- *Offshoring*—Offshoring is the movement of a business process (in whole or in part) done at a company in one country to another company in another, different country.
- *Rural sourcing*—Rural sourcing is the movement of a business process (in whole or in part) done at a company to another company located in a lower cost setting within the same country. In the United States, there are large differences between the salaries paid to IT workers depending on where they live and work. As reported from the Robert Half 2009 salary survey a software developer's salary ranges from $60,000 up to $100,750 depending on the exact skill set they posses and where they work. Larger cities such as Boston and San Francisco pay on average 30 to 35 percent more. (Robert Half, 2009) Companies can save money by outsourcing to sellers located in lower-cost markets.
- *Nearshoring*—Nearshoring is the movement of a business process (in whole or in part) to companies in a nearby country, often sharing a border with the company's own country. In the United States, nearshoring generally describes work sent to Canada and Mexico. Nearshoring is becoming a popular alternative for companies that don't want to deal with the cultural, language, and time zone differences involved in offshoring to faraway places.
- *Multisourcing, or best-of-breed sourcing*—Outsourcing can involve a number of different types of outsourcing (for example, nearshoring, offshoring, and rural sourcing); this is called multisourcing, or best-of-breed sourcing. A company chooses the services of a large outsourcing partner, such as IBM or EDS, and then, based on costs and other features, the company can decide where the work will get done. IBM and EDS have offices and/or partners in all corners of the globe, which allows them to offer a best-of-breed approach. The company signs one contract with the seller, but the work is done at many different locations—programming in Canada, help desk in India, and so on.

TABLE 14-1   Average IT Salary Comparison

Country	Average Salary
United States	$75,000
India	$7,779
Argentina	$9,478
Brazil	$13,163
Mexico	$17,899

- *Insourcing*—Insourcing, the opposite of outsourcing, is the movement of a business process within a company to an internal entity (inside the same company) that specializes in that operation.

Organizations looking for competitive advantages are outsourcing for a variety of reasons. The number-one reason is cost. Hiring IT workers outside the United States offers cost advantages in terms of salaries. Table 14-1 lists the average IT worker salaries from various countries (King, 2008).

Other common reasons for outsourcing include the following:

- Transferring the risk to a seller
- Flexibility in resource management (that is, freeing up internal resources to work on other projects or to aid in completing a task more quickly)
- Access to expertise not available in-house
- Allowing the organization to concentrate on its core competencies
- Disaster recovery

Not all processes or job functions are being outsourced. While many organizations have found success and cost advantages in outsourcing business operations that have direct impact, such as call centers, help desks, and some software development, a number of key processes, such as the following, still need to be owned by the company:

- *Project management*—The organization must have someone on its side managing the relationship. This is especially crucial when dealing with outsourcing relationships.
- *Functional knowledge*—Some functions require intricate knowledge of how the business operates.
- *Process knowledge*—The organization must have someone with intimate knowledge of the process from end to end.
- *Process design*—Making corrective actions to a process requires intimate knowledge of the entire process.
- *Systems analysis and design*—These functions require intimate knowledge of the business that can take long periods of time to acquire.
- *Change management*—As with project management, someone needs to be managing the changes that occur during the project or relationship.

Offshoring has become a popular and beneficial form of outsourcing, but if not managed properly, it can fail to deliver a successful solution. Before embarking on an offshoring relationship, organizations should explore the following list of topics:

TABLE 14-2 Weighted Scoring Model Outsourcer Selection

Category	Weight
Language	10 percent
Government support	5 percent
Labor pool	5 percent
Infrastructure	10 percent
Educational system	5 percent
Cost	30 percent
Political and economical stability	10 percent
Culture compatibility	10 percent
Globalization maturity (including legal system)	5 percent
Security and privacy	10 percent

- Investigate the political stability of the country.
- Understand the copyright laws and be sure to have written into the contract the rights to any intellectual property created.
- Be sure to create an accurate cost picture when calculating ROI. Organizations should factor in a least a 15 percent overhead cost to deal with added management and communication issues.
- Factor in the time and cost required to transfer needed knowledge.
- Understand security issues and how the outsourcing company will protect your organization's information.
- Travel costs can become a significant part of the equation, depending on the number of trips needed. Working with an outsourcing company from China could easily cost the organization $3,000 or more for each person for each trip.
- Additional issues with travel and working with virtual teams is covered in the next section on virtual teaming.
- Gartner, a leading IT industry research organization, offers the suggestions (Table 14-2) for building a weighted scoring model for the selection of an outsourcing partner. (Cohen, 2002) The following is a list of off-shoring best practices:

  - Find the right vendor (in terms of culture, experience, quality record, employee turnover rates, and so on), using the weighted scoring model shown in Table 14-2.
  - Sign the right type of contract, which shares the risk to and benefits of each participant.
  - Clearly spell out penalty and reward (incentives) clauses in the contract.
  - Follow a documented formal integrated change management process.
  - Establish early in the relationship a communications management plan, especially when dealing with multiple time zones.
  - Follow a documented formal monitoring and control plan with established metrics.
  - Include in the contract clearly stated contract cancellation criteria.
  - Establish clearly who owns what when the contract is done.
  - Be sure to create a clear and complete statement of work (SOW).

- Include clear and complete SLAs.
- Build a detailed risk management plan that includes contingency plans and reserves.

WORKING IN VIRTUAL TEAMS

Learning to work in a **virtual team** has become a necessity in today's organizations. Project managers must learn to deal with project teams that are not co-located. A virtual team is a team whose members are unable to regularly meet face-to-face, so instead they must use various technologies to communicate. A virtual team could be a small group of people on different floors of the same building or a large group spread across the globe that need to communicate to get their jobs finished successfully. This might also include people who are working from home in the same country or even the same city.

The use of virtual teams is on the rise for many reasons: Due to the growing trend of outsourcing, discussed in the previous section, the positive economics of allowing some people to work from home, the rising cost of travel, location of corporate offices, and the need for more scarce specialized skills are all driving companies to invest in technologies to support virtual teams. It is estimated that more than 60 percent of employees in large companies—those with more than 500 employees—have participated in virtual project teams. According to the Telework Network, telecommuting grew by 61% between 2005 and 2009, and based on current trends, the organization estimates the number of telecommuting workers will grow to nearly five million by 2016—a 69% increase (Lister and Harnish, 2011).

Working in a virtual team has some issues that need to be overcome to make these teams successful. In many cases, the project manager is the one who needs to solve them. The key issues are listed next:

- Rewards and punishment are more difficult to assess and deliver, so using either for team improvement is limited.
- Researchers estimate that 90 percent of communication is nonverbal, transferred by body language and facial expressions. A message can be difficult to understand when you can't see the person you are communicating with, and it can be difficult to know whether your message was understood without visual confirmation. Also, it can be difficult or nearly impossible to assess commitment of the listener without seeing the person's body language.
- Cultural awareness is necessary when part of the team is located in another country.
- The technology a virtual team needs to use to communicate can be complex or may not work when needed.
- Time zone differences make it difficult to work, regardless of the technology, when part of the team is 8 to 10 hours different.
- Language barriers can crop up, even when everyone is speaking English. Depending on the clarity of the technology and the speaker, it can be very difficult to understand each other.

To overcome many of these issues, project managers should follow these best practices:

- Remember that nothing is a replacement for good project management in all aspects of the job.
- Create a space for open dialogue without management interference.
- Be careful when trying to convey emotion using text; it's better to just stick to facts.
- Be culturally aware of all who are on the team and help the whole team understand the cultural differences present. Specific cultural training for all should be mandatory, which goes for both the company in the United States and the offshore partner.

- Use a formal standard project methodology and communicate it to all participants. This does not mean you can't use a more agile or iterative methodology approach as described back in Chapter 2.
- Pick the right technology for the situation (email, phone, instant messaging, blog, teleconferencing, videoconferencing, etc.) and be sure it is stable and everyone is trained on its proper use.
- Host regularly scheduled status meetings.
- Find ways to build trust—which is especially difficult in a virtual setting—by hosting virtual social events such as virtual gaming competitions or virtual social hours, using a tool such as Second Life and with no management personnel involved.
- Establish a security policy for all communication and project artifacts.
- Remember that successful virtual teams are based 90 percent on people and only 10 percent on the technology.
- Communicate, communicate, communicate.

The following is a brief list of some of the technologies being used today to facilitate virtual communication:

- Virtual workspaces (discussion forums, intranet):
  - Microsoft Tools—Lync, Windows Meeting Space, NetMeeting, SharePoint
  - Google Apps
  - Novell GroupWise
  - Lotus Notes
- Social networking:
  - MySpace
  - Facebook
  - Second Life
  - You Tube
- Instant messaging (IM) programs, which are good for both one-on-one communication and creating a virtual room with many people in it to allow everyone to talk:
  - Skype
  - Yahoo Messenger
  - AOL Instant Messenger (AIM)
- Audioconferencing:
  - No visual cues (body language)
  - Easier to become a "wall flower"
  - Groupthink issues to deal with
- Videoconferencing:
  - Time delays
  - Distracting
  - Cost
  - Great at the beginning of project and then periodically
- Email:
  - Banned by many groups as a means of communication about project issues
  - Not instant; can be delayed or missed due to the amount of spam most receive
  - Can forget to include someone on the distribution list
  - Can make members feel left out of the group and lead to dysfunction

PROJECT MANAGEMENT–RELATED MATURITY MODELS

A **maturity model** is a structured collection of elements (best practices, processes, activities) that describe characteristics of effective processes (see Chapter 7). A maturity model provides a place for an organization to start when thinking of how to improve its processes, the benefit of a collection of prior experiences, a common language and a shared vision, a framework for prioritizing actions, and a documented way to define improvement metrics for an organization. A maturity model might also be used as a benchmark for assessing other like organizations for comparison. The philosophy behind maturity models in general is in line with W. Edwards Deming's idea that an organization must first define and understand a system before it can improve the system. (Refer to Chapter 7 for a review of Deming's work in quality.) This chapter describes two maturity models: the CMMI from the Software Engineering Institute at Carnegie Mellon University and the OPM3 from the Project Management Institute.

Note that both the maturity models discussed in this chapter have a few drawbacks. First, an organization will not produce a high-quality product just because it follows one of these models. Maturity models deal with process only and are models, not solutions. Second, maturity models are not a "silver bullet" that, once implemented, will address all the ills of the organization. Finally, once an organization is certified at a certain level of maturity, there is no mandatory process or audit procedure that monitors the organization to ensure that it remains at that maturity level. However, research has begun to show that these maturity models described here can deliver a very favorable ROI for organizations. In fact, the ROI grows significantly at each higher level of maturity.

The Capability Maturity Model Integrated (CMMI)

The CMMI was created at the SEI at Carnegie Mellon University, a federally funded (by the U.S. Department of Defense) research and development center. Due to the strategic importance of software in all U.S. defense systems, the SEI was created to advance the practice of software engineering. CMMI is based on the premise that the quality of a production-ready system is highly influenced by the quality of the process used to acquire, develop, and maintain it. CMMI will no longer exist within the SEI but will continue to be owned and operated by Carnegie Mellon University (CMU) through a start-up entity created in 2012 called the "CMMI Institute," which will formally assume operation of CMMI on 1 January 2013. This entity will be able to be more market-focused and industry-driven, according to Carnegie Mellon. Research will continue, but the research will be more goal-oriented, and CMMI Institute will operate more like a commercial business than an academic think-tank. CMMI can provide the following benefits:

- Help integrate disparate organizations
- Help establish process improvement goals and priorities
- Provide a benchmark for appraising current practices
- Provide a substantial reduction in systems integration time and cost
- Foster higher levels of collaboration among the various engineering and technology functions
- Increase the use of and improve the quality of software engineering standard practices across all projects
- Learn from previous process improvement initiatives

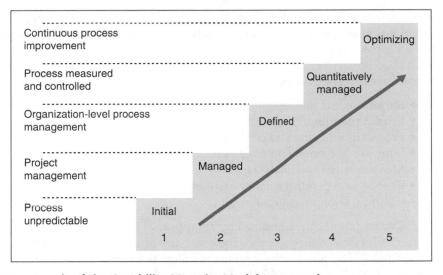

FIGURE 14-1 Levels of the Capability Maturity Model Integrated

CMMI consists of five levels of maturity: initial, managed, defined, quantitatively managed, and optimizing (see Figure 14-1). Within these five levels are 22 process areas with numerous generic and specific practices attached to them to aid organizations in improving their ability to create software. A process area identifies a cluster of related activities that, when performed collectively, achieve a set of goals considered important for that level of maturity. The five levels are defined as follows:

- *Initial*—At this level, development follows little to no rules. The project may go from one crisis to the next. The success of the project depends on the skills of individual developers and other team participants. At this level, it is impossible to repeat successes because everything is reinvented with each project.
- *Managed*—This level is characterized by requirements management, project planning, project tracking and oversight, subcontract management, quality assurance, and configuration management.
- *Defined*—This level is characterized by decision analysis and resolution, integrated project management, maintenance of a usable set of organizational process assets and work environment standards, development of skills and knowledge to perform roles effectively and efficiently, risk management, validation, and verification of the end product.
- *Quantitatively managed*—An organization at this level establishes and maintains a quantitative understanding of the performance of the organization's set of standard processes in support of quality and process–performance objectives, and it provides the process performance data, baselines, and models to quantitatively manage the organization's projects.
- *Optimizing*—This level is characterized by casual analysis and resolution as well as organizational innovation and deployment.

An organization gets rated at one of the five levels, with every organization starting at Level 1. Achieving a particular maturity level means that an organization, when appraised, was found to be achieving the goals required by that level. Those goals are a combination of specific and generic goals from a specific set of process areas. Each maturity level has a specific set of process areas associated with it, and each process area in turn has a specific set of goals. Maturity Level 2 (Managed), for example, requires the following process areas be performed:

- Requirements management
- Project planning
- Project monitoring and control
- Supplier agreement management
- Measurement and analysis
- Process and product quality assurance
- Configuration management

Organizations are appraised by an appraisal team led by an SEI-authorized lead appraiser, who determines whether the company or department is performing the practices of the CMMI. The process the appraisers follow is referred to as *SCAMPI*, which stands for Standard CMMI Appraisal Method for Process Improvement.

According to the CMMI Institute, there are over 5,000 businesses that use CMMI models from over 70 countries. Of the 5,159 organizations that participated in the latest survey sponsored by the Institute (19% USA companies, 81% non-USA): 22% are at level 2 Managed, 67% are at level 3 Defined, 1.6% are at level 4 Quantitatively Managed, and 5.4% are at level 5 Optimizing. The leading countries reporting CMMI activity are: China (number one), USA (second), and India (third).

The Organizational Project Management Maturity Model (OPM3)

The OPM3, first published in 2003, was created after 5 years of development by a team consisting of more than 800 project managers from more than 30 countries, brought to-

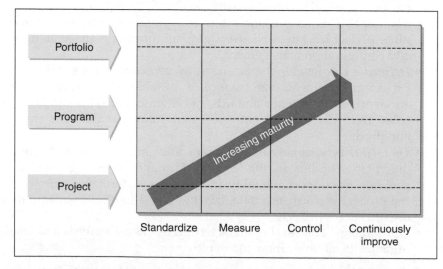

FIGURE 14-2   Organizational Project Management Maturity Model (OPM3) from PMI

gether by PMI. PMI defines *organizational project management* as "systematic management of projects, programs, and portfolios to achieve an organization's strategic goals." OPM3 applies to all organizations and industries in all countries, regardless of size. OPM3 focuses on three elements: improvement, knowledge, and assessment.

The knowledge element of the model provides a basic template for how to use the model and its relative structure. The assessment element enables the user to determine the current level of maturity of the organization. It reveals the organization's strengths and weaknesses and where it stands relative to standards of excellence and comparable industry competitors. The improvement element, which is utilized after the assessment is complete, provides the user with the ability to map out an improvement plan for complying with best practices.

The application of the OPM3 begins with first understanding the model and all its components. Then an assessment of how well the organization's processes coincide with the model must be conducted. The organization must plan how it can improve its process and implement the plan. After the improvements are made, another assessment is conducted, in which the current level of capability/maturity is determined. This process continues iteratively until the organization reaches its desired level of maturity. The process is similar to Deming's work on quality (see Chapter 7) and the Plan, Do, Study, Act process. Acknowledgement of achieving a certain level of maturity is gained by demonstrating that the organization is capable of producing an expected outcome of the best practice in question. Key performance indicators are used to measure the ongoing existence of an outcome. It is only through understanding and defining the organization's processes and educating all human resources on those processes that the system can be improved.

OPM3's maturity structure is shown in Figure 14-2. The model contains four levels of maturity: standardize, measure, control, and continuously improve. An organization may reach each level of maturity at three levels of project management: at the project level, at the program level, and at the portfolio level. An organization or a business unit within an organization may be at the control level of maturity for individual projects but at a standardize level of maturity for programs and portfolios. Remember that a *program* is a group of related projects, managed in a coordinated way to obtain benefits and control not available from managing them individually, and a portfolio is a collection of projects and/or programs grouped together to facilitate effective management of that work to meet strategic objectives. The maturity levels are defined by the set of best practices that exist in each one. The path to maturity involves these general levels:

- *Standardize*—This level is characterized by standardization of the entire project life cycle and by artifacts, metrics, and an adequate number of trained resources assigned.
- *Measure*—An organization at this level is able to measure and analyze actual performance against standards.
- *Control*—An organization at this level is able to monitor and control performance and the stability of the process.
- *Continuously improve*—An organization at this level is able to continuously improve project performance based on process improvement recommendations.

The benefits attributed to using the OPM3 to measure project maturity are:

- More efficient and successful execution of projects
- A better link between business strategy and its projects created to implement the strategy
- Delivery of more projects on time, on budget, on scope, and with higher quality

As mentioned earlier, maturity models have several drawbacks that an organization needs to consider before it begins a CMMI or an OPM3 initiative, but the ROI from such an initiative may be substantial.

PROJECT MANAGEMENT ETHICS

Corporate and project ethics has gained a new and more important significance in the past several years due to some highly publicized events involving questionable behavior. Some of the most notable examples are listed below:

- *Enron*—Enron was forced in 2001 to file for the largest corporate bankruptcy in U.S. history (which was eclipsed shortly later by WorldCom) after their accounting practices were found to be hiding the real value of the firm. As the scandal became known, Enron's stock fell from $90 a share to less than 50 cents. The financial scandal also forced Enron's accounting firm, Arthur Andersen, at the time a Big Five accounting firm, to dissolve and also led to the investigation of other Andersen clients, with which similar issues were found. This case led to the 2002 formation of one of the most significant federal securities laws in recent memory: the Sarbanes-Oxley Act (SOX). SOX imposes more severe penalties for fraud and requires public companies to avoid making loans to management, to report more information to the public, to maintain stronger independence from their auditors, and to report on and have audited their financial internal control procedures.
- *Adelphia Communications Corporation*—Adelphia was the fifth-largest cable company in the United States before it filed for bankruptcy in 2002 because of internal corruption. The founders of Adelphia were charged with securities violations: Five officers were indicted, and two were found guilty.
- *Tyco International*—The former chair and chief executive as well as the former chief financial officer were accused of the theft of $600 million from Tyco. During their trial in March 2004, they contended that the board of directors had authorized the theft as compensation. In 2005, after a retrial, both were convicted on all but one of the more than 30 counts against them. The verdicts carry potential jail terms of up to 25 years in state prison.
- *WorldCom*—At one time WorldCom was the second-largest long-distance phone company in the United States. Beginning in 1999 and continuing through May 2002, the company used fraudulent accounting methods to hide its declining earnings by painting a false picture of financial growth and profitability to prop up the price of WorldCom's stock. WorldCom's internal audit department uncovered approximately $3.8 billion of the fraud in June 2002, during an examination of capital expenditures. By the end of 2003, it was estimated that the company's total assets had been inflated by around $11 billion.

From these examples, it is clear that companies must pay special attention to ethical issues. Most large organizations have created new management positions (such as a corporate ethics officer) to deal specifically with managing internal **ethics** issues and training. Other reasons for the increased awareness of ethical issues are related to the increasing globalization of many organizations. Globalization has created a more complex work environment, spanning diverse cultures and societies, each with its own idea of what constitutes **ethical behavior**.

Ethical behavior refers to human behavior that conforms to generally accepted social norms. On many issues, what constitutes ethical behavior is influenced by family, friends, education, and life experiences. *Ethics* are defined as beliefs regarding right and wrong behavior. For organizations, coming up with one definition of ethical behavior is becoming more and more difficult. But even with the difficulties, all organizations are finding benefits, including the following, in creating ethics programs:

- Helps protect the organization and its employees from legal action. (Review the examples at the beginning of this section.)
- Helps create an organization that operates consistently because workers have guidelines to follow and a place to go with questions.
- Helps avoid unfavorable publicity, which is especially important in these days of instant news via the Internet across the globe.
- Helps gain the goodwill of the community.

Organizations that want to establish an ethics program can follow these steps:

1. Appoint a corporate ethics officer.
2. Have the board of directors or the highest-ranking body within the organization establish ethical standards.
3. Establish a corporate code of conduct that is written and disseminated to all staff that covers all areas of the enterprise. This is a dynamic document that should be updated as the organization and society change.
4. Conduct social audits to ensure that the code of conduct is being followed by all. It is especially helpful if the audit is done by a non-biased external group.
5. Require employees to take ethics training yearly, not just once and forgotten.
6. Include ethical criteria in employee appraisal/reward systems.

So, how does all this talk of ethics apply specifically to the field of project management? Project managers need to understand an organization's code of conduct and follow it throughout a project. Ethical dilemmas for a project manager may emerge at each phase of the project: at project selection time, when making sure the weighted scoring model is created with honest numbers; when building the plan, to not build in larger-than-needed contingencies; during project execution, reporting honest progress or lack thereof on the project to stakeholders; and during monitoring and control, again making sure audits are done honestly, providing accurate quality, performance, and progress numbers. Another major area for issues comes up during the procurement phase, if needed, and the selection of the most qualified sellers. Project managers should follow these suggestions for ethical decision making:

- Get the facts via accurate reporting.
- Identify the stakeholders and their positions (stakeholder analysis).
- Consider the consequences of a decision for yourself, your team, and the organization.
- Weigh various guidelines and principles (according to the company's code of conduct). Approach the corporate ethics officer with questions.
- Develop and evaluate options.
- Review your decision.
- Evaluate the results of your decision and conduct a lessons learned session.

The following are some other ethical issues that many IT workers deal with:

- *Software piracy*—Software piracy in a corporate setting is sometimes directly trace-able to IT people: Either they are allowing it to happen or are actively engaging in it. Often, piracy is done to reduce IT-related spending to meet challenging budgets. Some countries have different perspectives on software piracy. It is estimated that as high as 90 percent or higher of all software in use in some countries is obtained illegally.
- *Trade secrets*—A trade secret is a piece of information used in a business, generally unknown to the public, that a company has taken strong measures to keep confiden-tial. All of the examples (WorldCom, Enron, etc.) at the beginning of this section dealt with this issue of illegally sharing of company trade secrets.
- *Project status*—IT project managers might want to inaccurately report project status in order to keep the resources flowing into the project, hoping that the problems can be corrected before anyone notices.
- *Bribes from suppliers*—Suppliers strive to maintain positive relationships with project managers (or decision makers, as the case may be) in order to make and increase sales.

Professional societies and other groups, such as PMI, the Association for Computing Machinery (ACM), the Association of Information Technology Professionals (AITP), and the Institute of Electrical and Electronics Engineers (IEEE), have recognized the importance of ethics and created codes of ethics for their members. "A professional code of conduct states the principles and core values essential to the work of a particular occupational group." (Reynolds, 2003) In addition to IT-related professional societies, many other professions and organizations maintain codes of conduct. All the professional societies' codes of conduct have similar sections to address all facets of their actions. IT-related state-ments generally cover the areas of acting ethically toward the profession, to one's organi-zation, and to one's community and society. The Project Management Institute's code of ethics is shown in Figure 14-3a and 14-3b.

Chapter 1. Vision and Applicability
    1.1 Vision and Purpose
    1.2 Persons to Whom the Code Applies
    1.3 Structure of the Code
    1.4 Values that Support this Code
    1.5 Aspirational and Mandatory Conduct

Chapter 2. Responsibility
    2.1 Description of Responsibility - is our duty to take ownership for the decisions we make or fail to make, the actions we take or fail to take, and the consequences that result.
    2.2 Responsibility: Aspirational Standards
        2.2.1 We make decision and take actions based on the best interests of society, public safety, and the environment.
        2.2.2 We accept only those assignments that are consistent with our background, experience, skills, and qualifications.
        2.2.3 We fulfill the commitments that we undertake - we do what we say we will do.
        2.2.4 When we make errors or omissions, we take ownership and make corrections promptly. When we discover errors or omissions caused by others, we communicate them to the appropriate body as soon they are discovered. We accept accountability for any issues resulting from our errors or omissions and any resulting consequences
        2.2.5 We protect proprietary or confidential information that has been entrusted to us
        2.2.6 We uphold this Code and hold each other accountable to it
    2.3 Responsibility: Mandatory Standards
        2.3.1 We inform ourselves and uphold the policies, rules, regulations and laws that govern our work, professional, and volunteer activities
        2.3.2 We report unethical or illegal conduct to appropriate management and, if necessary, to those affected by the conduct
        2.3.3 We bring violations of this Code to the attention of the appropriate body for resolution
        2.3.4 We only file ethics complaints when they are substantiated by facts
        2.3.5 We pursue disciplinary action against an individual who retaliates against a person raising ethics concerns

Chapter 3. Respect
    3.1 Description of Respect - is our duty to show a high regard for ourselves, others, and the resources entrusted to us. Resources entrusted to us may include people, money, reputation, the safety of others, and natural or environmental resources.
    3.2 Respect: Aspirational Standards
        3.2.1 We inform ourselves about the norms and customs of others and avoid engaging in behaviors they might consider disrespectful
        3.2.2 We listen to others' points of view, seeking to understand them
        3.2.3 We approach directly those persons with whom we have a conflict or disagreement
        3.2.4 We conduct ourselves in a professional manner, even when it is not reciprocated
    3.3 Respect: Mandatory Standards
        3.3.1 We negotiate in good faith
        3.3.2 We do not exercise the power of our expertise or position to influence the decisions or actions of others in order to benefit personally at their expense
        3.3.3 We do not act in an abusive manner toward others
        3.3.4 We respect the property rights of others

FIGURE 14-3a   PMI Code of Conduct retrieved from www.pmi.org//PDF/ap_pmicodeofethics.pdf

---

Chapter 4. Fairness

4.1 Description of Fairness - is our duty to make decisions and act impartially and objectively. Our conduct must be free from competing self interest, prejudice, and favoritism

4.2 Fairness: Aspirational Standards
4.2.1 We demonstrate transparency in our decision-making process
4.2.2 We constantly reexamine our impartiality and objectivity, taking corrective action as appropriate

4.2.3 We provide equal access to information to those who are authorized to have that information

4.2.4 We make opportunities equally available to qualified candidates
4.3 Fairness: Mandatory Standards
4.3.1 We proactively and fully disclose any real or potential conflicts of interest to the appropriate stakeholders

4.3.2 When we realize that we have a real or potential conflict of interest, we refrain from engaging in the decision-making process or otherwise attempting to influence outcomes, unless or until: we have made full disclosure to the affected stakeholders; we have an approved mitigation plan; and we have obtained the consent of the stakeholders to proceed.
4.3.3 We do not hire or fire, reward or punish, or award or deny contracts based on personal considerations, including but not limited to, favoritism, nepotism, or bribery
4.3.4 We do not discriminate against others based on, but not limited to, gender, race, age, religion, disability, nationality, or sexual orientation
4.3.5 We apply the rules of the organization (employer, Project Management Institute, or other group) without favoritism or prejudice

Chapter 5. Honesty

5.1 Description of Honesty: is our duty to understand the truth and act in a truthful manner both in our communications and in our conduct.
5.2 Honesty: Aspirational Standards
5.2.1 We earnestly seek to understand the truth
5.2.2 We are truthful in our communications and in our conduct
5.2.3 We provide accurate information in a timely manner
5.2.4 We make commitments and promises, implied or explicit, in good faith
5.2.5 We strive to create an environment in which others feel safe to tell the truth
5.3 Honesty: Mandatory Standards
5.3.1 We do not engage in or condone behavior that is designed to deceive others, including but not limited to, making misleading or false statements, stating half-truths, providing information out of context or withholding information that, if known, would render our statements as misleading or incomplete

5.3.2 We do not engage in dishonest behavior with the intention of personal gain or at the expense of another.

FIGURE 14-3b   PMI Code of Conduct retrieved from www.pmi.org//PDF/ap_pmicodeofethics.pdf (continued)

Chapter Review

1. A project management office (PMO) is an organizational entity with full-time personnel assigned to provide a wide range of project management support and services across the entire enterprise.

2. A PMO may exist at three different levels: single project, department business unit or division, and enterprise.

3. Outsourcing transfers project activities to an external entity by contract with specific performance measures, rewards, penalties, and contract exit clauses.

4. Forty percent of Fortune 500 companies outsource part of their IT functions.

5. The number-one reason most organizations outsource is to obtain a cost savings over doing the work internally.

6. A virtual team is a team whose members are unable to regularly meet face-to-face, so instead they must use various technologies to communicate.

7. Virtual teams communicate using many different technologies, including virtual workspaces, instant messaging, audioconferencing, videoconferencing, and e-mail.

8. A maturity model is a structured collection of elements (for example, best practices, processes, activities) that describe characteristics of effective processes.

9. Maturity models provide a place for organizations to start when thinking of how to improve their processes, the benefit of a collection of prior experiences, a common language and a shared vision, a framework for prioritizing actions, and a documented way to define improvement metrics for an organization.

10. The Capability Maturity Model Integrated (CMMI) is based on the premise that the quality of a production-ready system is highly influenced by the quality of the process used to acquire, develop, and maintain it. The Organizational Project Management Maturity Model (OPM3) aids an organization in the systematic management of projects, programs, and portfolios to achieve its strategic goals.

11. Ethical behavior refers to human behavior that conforms to generally accepted social norms. Ethics has taken on extra importance of late for all organizations. Many organizations have created a new role called a corporate ethics officer.

Glossary

ethical behavior: Human behavior that conforms to generally accepted social norms.

ethics Beliefs regarding right and wrong behavior.

maturity model A structured collection of elements that describe characteristics of effective processes.

outsourcing The process of transferring project activities and certain decision rights to an external entity, by contract, with specific performance measures, related rewards, penalties, and exit clauses defined.

project management office (PMO) An organizational entity with full-time personnel to provide a wide range of project management support and services across an entire organization.

virtual team A team whose members are unable to regularly meet face-to-face, so instead they must use various technologies to communicate.

Review Questions

1. List and describe the three levels at which a PMO may operate.
2. What is the purpose of setting up a PMO? What are the benefits and drawbacks to doing so?
3. List the functions that a PMO may perform.
4. List the resources that work within a PMO and their functions.
5. List the reasons organizations outsource project activities and other functions within the IT department.
6. Describe these different types of outsourcing: offshoring, rural sourcing, nearshoring, multisourcing, and insourcing.
7. List the different types of jobs that are not currently being outsourced.
8. Describe what it means to work in a virtual team.
9. Why are virtual teams becoming more prevalent for all organizations?
10. Describe some the issues associated with working in virtual teams that organizations must overcome in order to be successful.
11. What is a maturity model?
12. Describe the benefits and drawbacks of using a maturity model.
13. Describe the maturity steps associated with the CMMI and the specific benefits of using it.
14. Describe the maturity steps associated with the OPM3 and the specific benefits of using it.
15. Define *ethical behavior*.
16. Why has ethical behavior become a major concern for organizations?
17. How might ethical behavior affect the work done by a project manager?
18. What best practices should project managers follow to make better ethical decisions?

Projects and Research

1. Use the Internet to compare the codes of ethics from several large public companies.
2. Research ethical issues besides the ones mentioned in this chapter that organizations have gotten themselves into.
3. Research several organizations and describe the PMO in place: At what level is it operating, what functions is it performing, and how is it staffed?
4. Research the current statistics on organizations outsourcing different IT department activities. How many companies are doing this? What types of functions are being outsourced?
5. If you have had experience working in a virtual team, write a paper that describes your experiences. Did it work well, or were there problems? What technology was used? Why did you need to use a virtual team?
6. Write a paper describing the differences and similarities between the CMMI and OPM3 maturity models.
7. Compare the ethical codes of conduct of PMI (see Figure 14-3a and b) with another professional society.

Suggested Readings

Abrams, F., Fahrenkrog, S., Haeck, W., & Whelborn, D. (2003). *Project Management Institute's Organizational Project Management Maturity Model*. PMI North American Congress, Baltimore, MD.

Bernstein, S. (2000, December). Project offices in practice. *Project Management Journal* 31(4):14.

CBP. (2008). The state of the PMO: 2007-2008. Retrieved from www.cbponline.com.

Chesbrough, H., & Teece, D. (1996, January–February). When virtual is virtuous? Organizing for innovation. *Harvard Business Review*, pp. 65–73.

Chrissis, M., Konrad, M., & Shrum, S. (2003). *CMMI guidelines for process integration and product improvement*. Reading, MA: Addison-Wesley.

Cohen, L. & Berg, T. (2002). Marketplace realities in strategic outsourcing. Retrieved from www.gartner.com/pages/story.php.id.8733.s.8.jsp.

Crawford, K., & Pennypacker, J. (2002, October). Put an end to project mismanagement. *Optimize*, pp. 73–78.

Crawford, K. (2002). *The strategic project office.* New York: Marcel Dekker, Inc.

Elkins, W. (2003, February 17). Maximize ROI with a project office. *Computerworld*. Retrieved from www.computerworld.com/manageementtopics/ roi/story/0,10801,78517,00.html.

Fleming, Q., & Koppelman, J. (1997). Project teams: The role of the project office. *AACE International Transactions*, p. 157.

Hoffman, T. (2003, July 21). Value of project management offices questioned. *Computerworld* 37(29):7.

Kerzner, H. (2004). *Advanced project management—Best practices on implementation.* Hoboken, NJ: John Wiley & Sons, Inc.

Kerzner, H. (2003, June). Strategic planning for a project office. *Project Management Journal* 34(2):13.

King, R. (2008, April 7). The new economics of outsourcing. *BusinessWeek*. Retrieved from www.businessweek.com/technology/content/apr2008/tc2008043_531737.htm.

Kwak, Y., & Dai, C. (2000). Assessing the value of project management offices. PMI Research Conference 2000. Retrieved from http://home.gwu.edu/~kwak/PMO_Value.pdf.

Lister, K., & Harnish, T. (2011, June). The state of telework in the U.S. Telework Research Network, Carlsbad, CA.

Melymuka, K. (1999, August). Project office: A route to better performance. *Computerworld* 33(31):44.

Project Management Institute web site, www. pmi. org.

Project Management Institute (PMI). (2003). *Organizational Project Management Maturity Model.* Newtown Square, PA: PMI.

Project Management Institute (PMI). (2004). *A guide to the project management body of knowledge,* 3rd ed. Newton Square, PA: PMI.

Reynolds, G. (2003). *Ethics in information technology.* Boston: Course Technology.

Robert Half (2009). Robert Half Technology 2009 Salary Guide. Retrieved from www.rhi.com/salaryguides.

Rose, K. (2002, Dec). The advanced PMO: A comprehensive look at function and implementation. *Project Management Journal* 33(4):69.

Santosus, M. (2003, July 1). Office discipline: Why you need a project management office. *CIO.* Retrieved on October 10, 2005, from www.cio.com/archive/070103/office.html.

Souder, W. E. (1983). Project evaluation and selection. In Cleland, D. I., and W.R. King, eds., *Project management handbook.* New York: Van Nostrand Reinhold.

PART 5

Appendixes

APPENDIX A

Microsoft Project Help Guide

1.0 MICROSOFT PROJECT INTRODUCTION AND OVERVIEW

1.1 WHAT IS A PROJECT?

A *project* is a temporary endeavor undertaken to accomplish a unique purpose. All projects are subject to the triple constraint of scope, time, and cost. A project must produce something—a product or service—within time and budget (cost) restrictions. A fourth constraint that must be dealt with on all information technology (IT) projects is quality.

1.2 WHY USE PROJECT MANAGEMENT SOFTWARE?

Project management software assists a project manager and a team in the functions of managing a project, including making a schedule, assessing which resources are available and when, communicating project progress, and determining the critical path, among other functions. Project management software allows a user to easily create and modify documents created for a project while documenting the effects of those modifications and the impact they might have on the success of the project.

Microsoft Project 2010 is one of the most widely used project management software applications on the market, and it is used here to demonstrate some of the benefits project management software, if used correctly, can provide. All Microsoft Project 2010 screenshots in this appendix are reprinted with permission from Microsoft Corporation.

1.3 HOW TO START THE APPLICATION

To start Microsoft Project, navigate to Start | All Programs | Microsoft Office | Microsoft Office Project 2010.

Note: This path will vary, depending on the operating system you're using.

1.4 HOW TO START A NEW PROJECT

By default, Microsoft Project will open with a blank screen showing an empty list of tasks and an empty Gantt chart (see figure A1-1). To create a new project, click on the File tab at the top of the application screen and you should see something very similar to figure A1-0. Microsoft project will create a project in several ways: from scratch with all fields blank, from a stored template, from Microsoft at office.com, or somewhere else, from an excel spreadsheet, or from a Microsoft SharePoint task list.

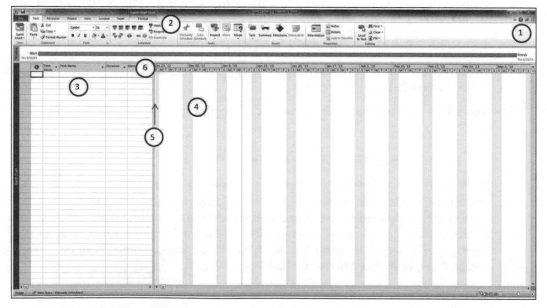

1.5 WORK AREA OVERVIEW

This section describes the basic layout of the Microsoft Project window (see Figure A1-1) and associated names this appendix uses when describing how to use the features of the software. Not all Microsoft Project displays look exactly like this one, but the basics of how the different parts are laid out are the same:

1 = Ribbon toolbar
2 = Ribbon tabs (File, Task, Resource, Project, View, Format)
3 = Project task data displayed in rows and columns
4 = Graphical representation of data such as Gantt charts and histograms
5 = Movable split bar
6 = Timeline; a high-level view of the project

FIGURE A1-1 Overview Screen

1.6 MICROSOFT PROJECT DEFAULT OPTIONS

Figure A1-2 shows the Options screen, from which you can change all the Microsoft Project configuration options. To reach the screen, navigate to "File" tab on the ribbon, then choose "Options." The options are broken down into several categories that you can reach by selecting the appropriate menu tab. The Display tab, which is displayed in Figure A1-2, allows you to define how the different views appear onscreen. For example, the first option, "Calendar Type," is used to select the type of calendar (Gregorian, Hijri, or Thai Buddhist) the project will use to schedule tasks.

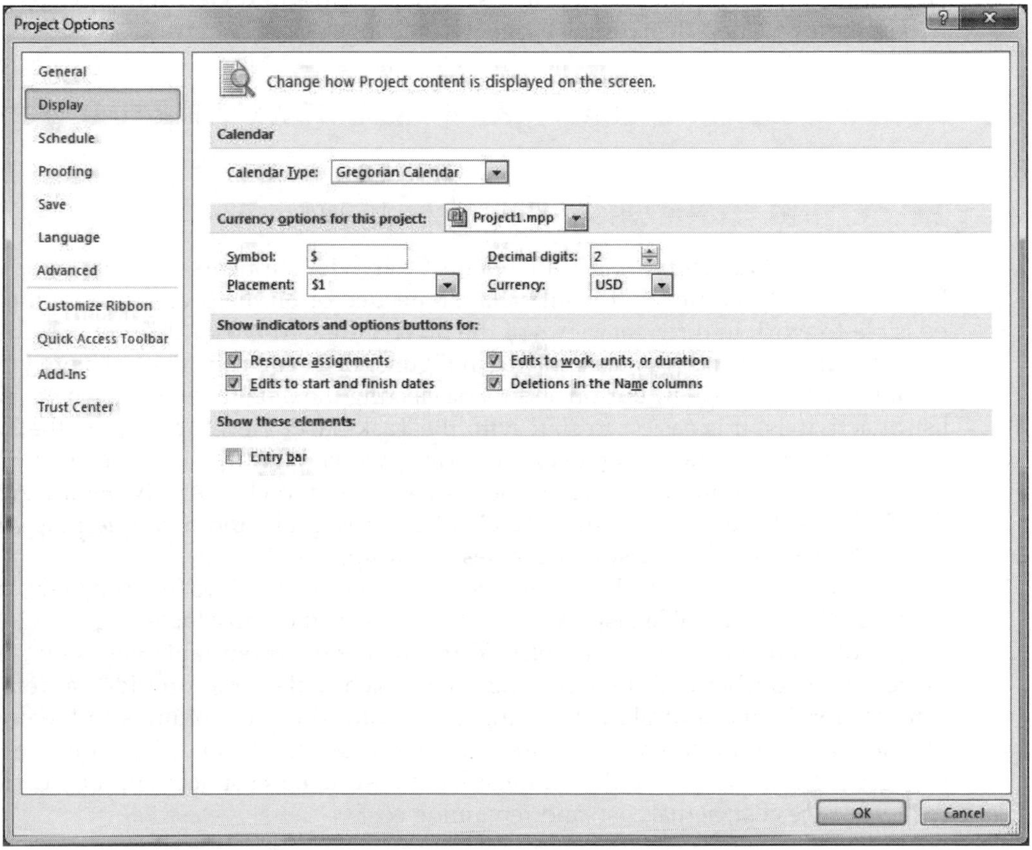

FIGURE A1-2   **Options Screen**

1.7 GETTING HELP

When you select Project Help, a new pane appears, with a search function you can use to find the topic needed. Simply type your help question into the search box, and a list of related topics appears. This function works the same as in other Microsoft applications.

Unit 1 Exercises

A. Open Project and get familiar with the menu system and each of the display areas.
B. Turn off.
C. Change the default view page to Task Sheet from the options page.
D. With the Options screen open, invoke Project help and review the explanations.
E. Close Project and then restart to see what changes have occurred.

2.0 CREATING A BASIC WORK BREAKDOWN STRUCTURE (WBS)

2.1 GETTING TO THE WBS OR TASK SHEET VIEW

After starting Microsoft Project, the Gantt Chart view appears by default, as shown in Figure A2-1. Depending on the information needed or on the preferences of the user, it is possible to work in different views of the project data. Microsoft Project provides several predefined views of the data, as shown in Figure A2-2. You can create custom views of the data by clicking the New button and then selecting the data to view. When starting a new list of activities, it is easiest to start with the Task Sheet view. To display the Task Sheet view, or the WBS view, navigate to View Tab | Other Views | More Views. A new screen appears, as shown in Figure A2-2. Select Task Sheet and click Apply. Figure A2-3 shows the Task Sheet view. Notice that the Gantt chart is gone, and a couple new columns of data—Predecessors and Resource Names—now appear.

Microsoft Project provides predetermined column displays for each view, referred to as *tables*. The default table displayed in Figure A2-3 is the Entry table. Figure A2-4 displays the list of available predefined tables. You can create custom table views by clicking the More Tables option and then clicking New. Each table view provides a default set of columns for display, but all can be changed; you can add some columns and remove others. The default columns follow the theme of the view name; for example, under the table cost, you get the following default columns: fixed cost, fixed cost accrual, total cost, baseline cost, variance cost, actual cost, and remaining cost.

2.2 ENTERING THE PROJECT TITLE

To set the title for the project, you should navigate to the File tab on the ribbon, then select Save As and give the project a name, which also will give the project file a name on your storage location. The name will then be reflected on all reports and across the top of the application screen. You should assign your file the name "GeoffGourmetGrocery" now.

Note: Throughout this appendix, we'll use a case study that focuses on automating a retail chain of gourmet grocery stores and electronically linking them back to the corporate office.

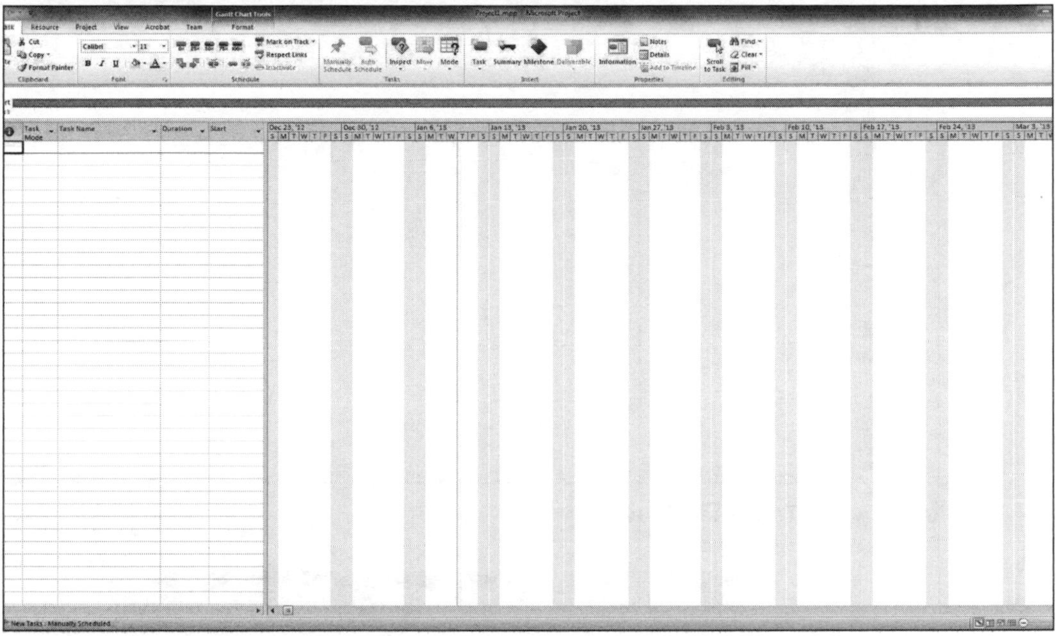

FIGURE A2-1   Gantt Chart View

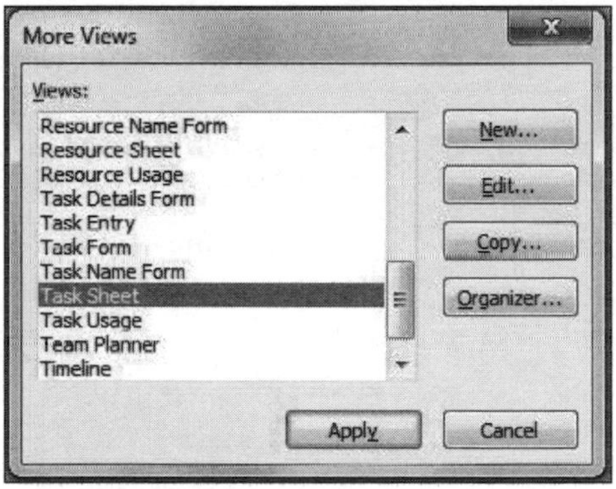

FIGURE A2-2   Selecting the Task Sheet View

FIGURE A2-3   **Task Sheet View**

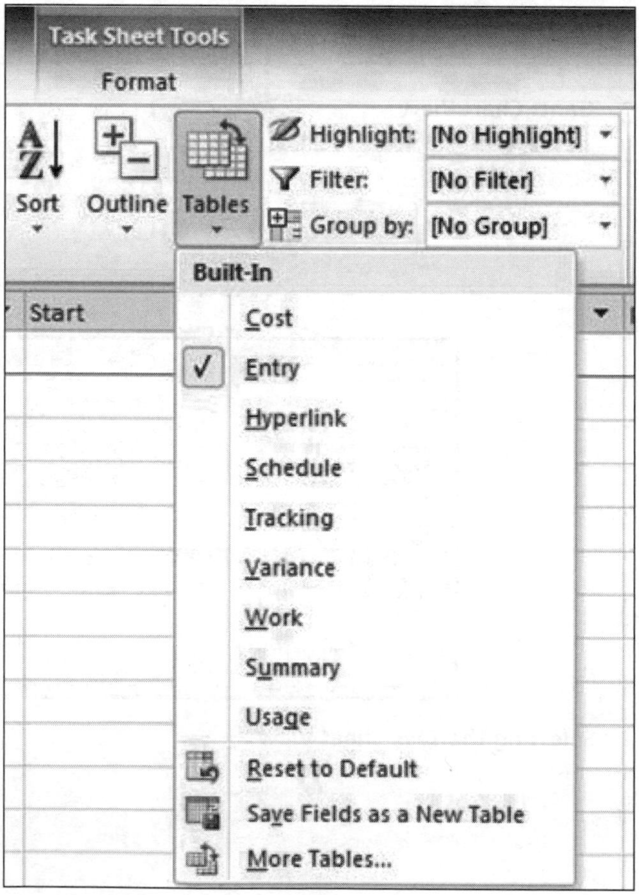

FIGURE A2-4   **Table View Options**

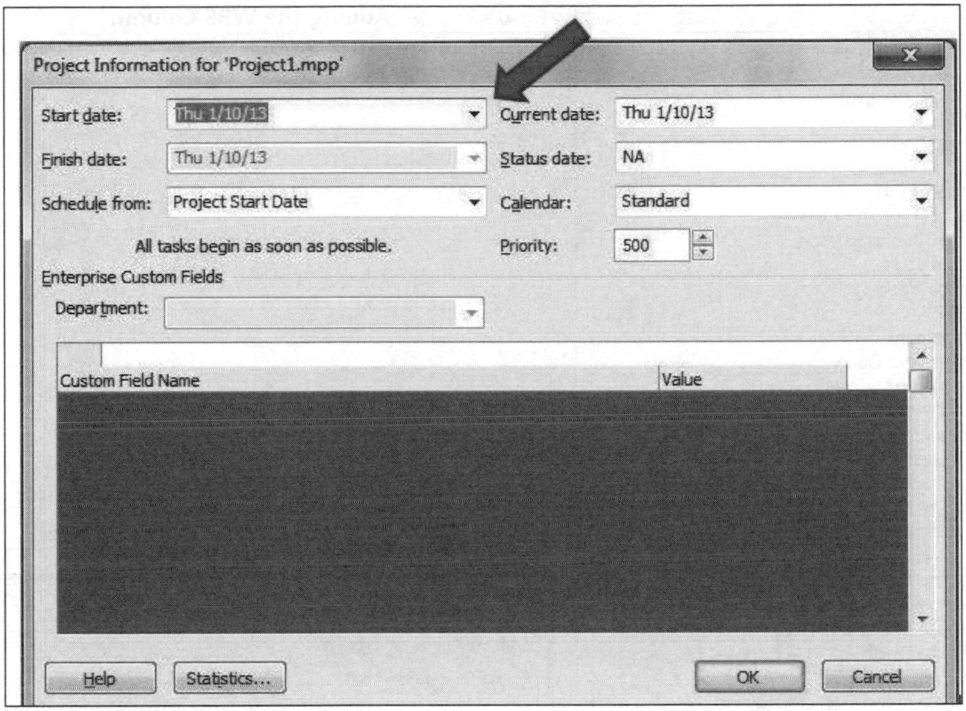

FIGURE A2-5   **Entering the Start Date**

2.3 ENTERING A PROJECT START DATE

The next activity is to set a start date for the project. Navigate to Project Tab | Project Information. A new screen appears, as shown in Figure A2-5, where you can type in the start date or click the drop-down arrow to select the date. Click OK to continue.

2.4 INSERTING A NEW COLUMN ON THE TASK SHEET

You can change the task sheet by removing and adding any fields (columns) that Microsoft Project keeps track of. A useful column to include in the display of tasks is a column for WBS code. To add the WBS code column into the task sheet, click "Add New Column," displayed in Figure A2-3. Once clicked, the list of available fields will appear (see Figure A2-6). Scroll down, find "WBS," and select it. The screen will now include the WBS code column and create a new "Add New Column" for future use. The next operation is to create the format for the WBS code covered in the next section.

2.5 CREATING A UNIQUE WBS CODE

After you add the WBS code to the viewable columns on the Task Sheet view, the next step is to create the WBS codes. Project Tab | WBS | Define Code. A new screen appears, as shown in Figure A2-7. You can now add a code that will prefix the number sequence. You

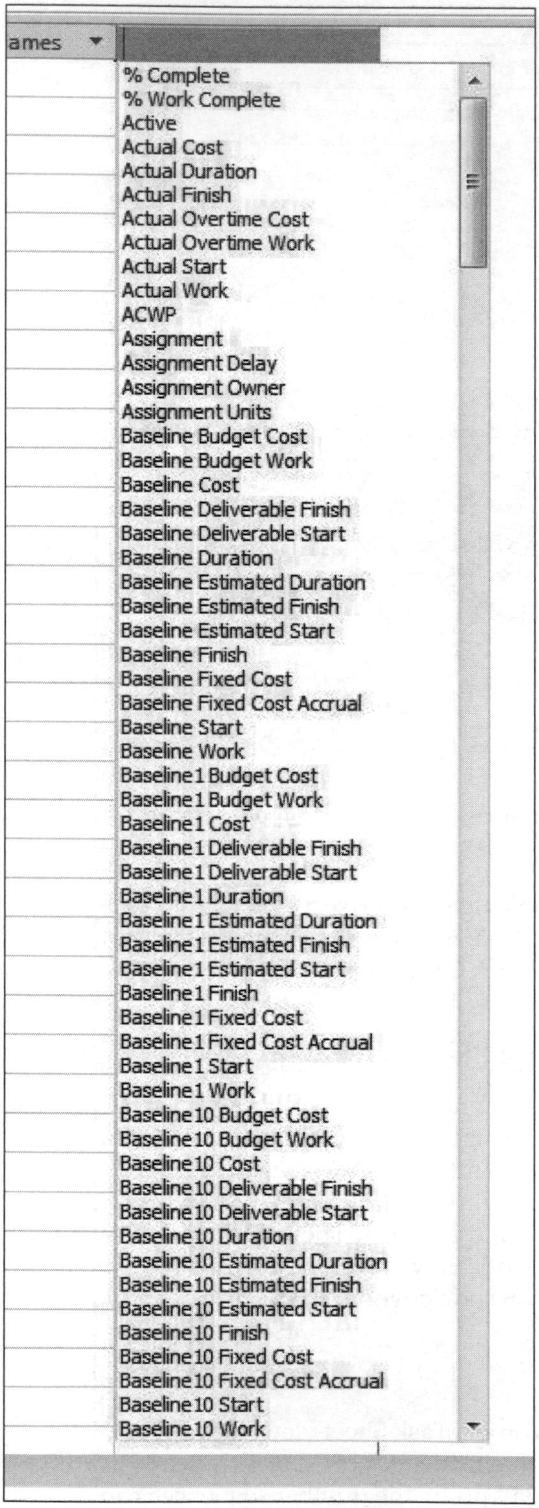

ames ▼	
	% Complete
	% Work Complete
	Active
	Actual Cost
	Actual Duration
	Actual Finish
	Actual Overtime Cost
	Actual Overtime Work
	Actual Start
	Actual Work
	ACWP
	Assignment
	Assignment Delay
	Assignment Owner
	Assignment Units
	Baseline Budget Cost
	Baseline Budget Work
	Baseline Cost
	Baseline Deliverable Finish
	Baseline Deliverable Start
	Baseline Duration
	Baseline Estimated Duration
	Baseline Estimated Finish
	Baseline Estimated Start
	Baseline Finish
	Baseline Fixed Cost
	Baseline Fixed Cost Accrual
	Baseline Start
	Baseline Work
	Baseline1 Budget Cost
	Baseline1 Budget Work
	Baseline1 Cost
	Baseline1 Deliverable Finish
	Baseline1 Deliverable Start
	Baseline1 Duration
	Baseline1 Estimated Duration
	Baseline1 Estimated Finish
	Baseline1 Estimated Start
	Baseline1 Finish
	Baseline1 Fixed Cost
	Baseline1 Fixed Cost Accrual
	Baseline1 Start
	Baseline1 Work
	Baseline10 Budget Cost
	Baseline10 Budget Work
	Baseline10 Cost
	Baseline10 Deliverable Finish
	Baseline10 Deliverable Start
	Baseline10 Duration
	Baseline10 Estimated Duration
	Baseline10 Estimated Finish
	Baseline10 Estimated Start
	Baseline10 Finish
	Baseline10 Fixed Cost
	Baseline10 Fixed Cost Accrual
	Baseline10 Start
	Baseline10 Work

FIGURE A2-6   Adding the WBS Column

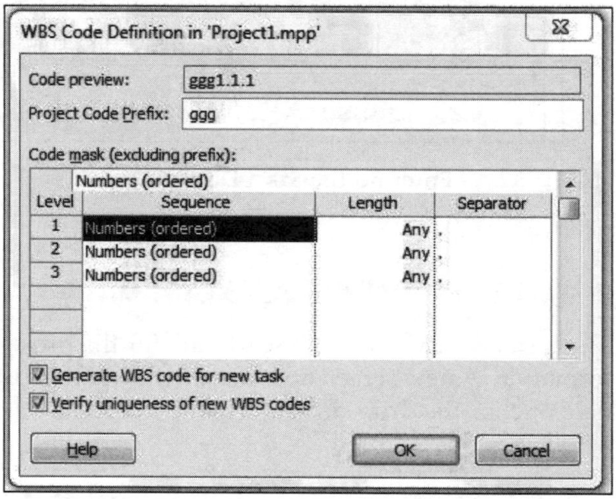

WBS Code Definition in 'Project1.mpp'

Code preview: ggg1.1.1

Project Code Prefix: ggg

Code mask (excluding prefix):

Level	Sequence	Length	Separator
1	Numbers (ordered)	Any	.
2	Numbers (ordered)	Any	.
3	Numbers (ordered)	Any	.

☑ Generate WBS code for new task
☑ Verify uniqueness of new WBS codes

Help   OK   Cancel

FIGURE A2-7   Making a Unique WBS Code

can also create the numbering hierarchy. To create three levels of a numbered hierarchy, for example, select Numbers (Ordered) in the first three rows of the Sequence column of the WBS Code Definition dialog (see Figure A2-7). To separate the numbers using periods, select a period in the Separator column. Leave the two items on the bottom of the screen checked. The code preview at the top of the screen provides an example of what the finished code will look like. The WBS code will be created each time a new task is created or when tasks are moved around in the task list. On occasion, the numbers can get out of sequence due to the number of changes or types of changes. To rebuild the WBS sequence, select Tasks | Project | WBS | Renumber. You can renumber just a set of highlighted tasks or all tasks for the entire project.

2.6 ENTERING A TASK

You can now start entering project tasks. There are several ways to enter a task, and we don't need to show them all here, but let's look at the most frequently used techniques. To enter a task, click the empty task name column once and start entering the name or double-click the task name field to show the Task Information Screen and enter the information. As shown in Figure A2-8, the Task Information screen appears. After entering the name of the task, click OK to return to the Task Sheet view. You can change the task name at any time by clicking on the Task Name column in the Task Sheet view and changing the name.

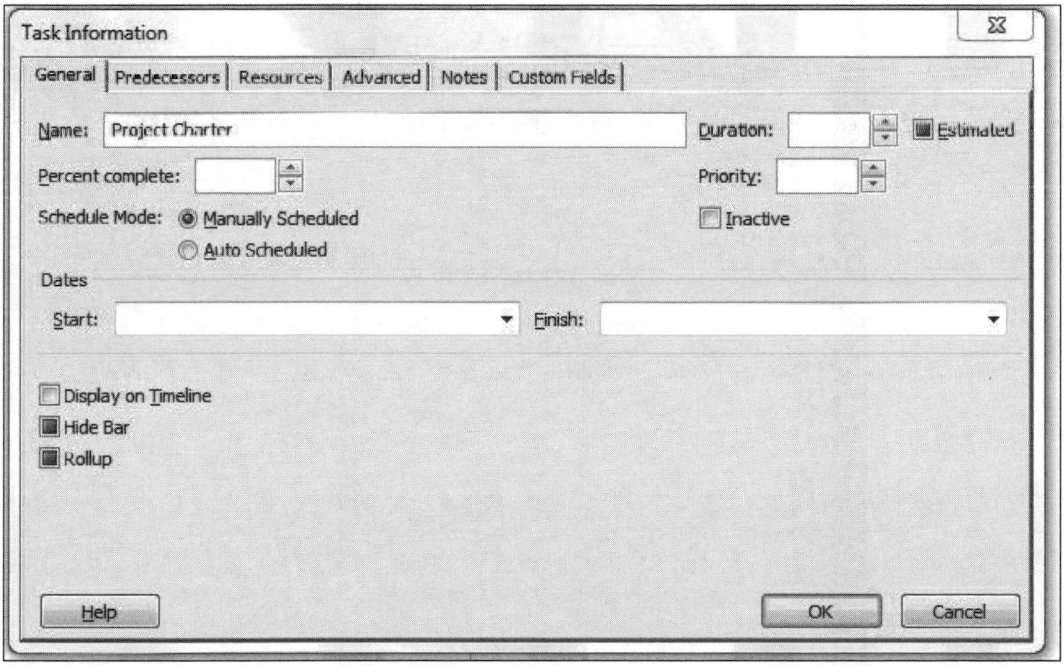

FIGURE A2-8   Task Information Screen

2.7 MAKING A MILESTONE

A *milestone* is a task that has zero duration; it is generally used for tracking purposes. To make a task a milestone, you change the Duration field for the task to 0 days, as shown in Figure A2-9. You can also accomplish this by double-clicking the task, changing the Duration field to 0 days, and clicking OK to apply the change. A third way of setting a milestone is to double-click the task, select the Advanced tab, and then select Mark Task as Milestone, as shown in Figure A2-10. When you view this task in Gantt Chart view, the milestone will appear as a solid diamond, as shown in Figure A2-9. You will set up some milestones later in this appendix.

2.8 ENTERING RECURRING TASKS

Microsoft Project has a feature to enter recurring tasks (for example, the project team will conduct a weekly status review meeting). To use this feature, select Task Tab |Task | Recurring Task. A new screen appears, as shown in Figure A2-11. Enter the frequency (daily, weekly, monthly, or yearly) and the day of the week the task will occur. You can also specify a date range to mark the start and end of the recurring task or just enter the number of times the task will repeat. Click OK to save and continue. This feature works very similarly to the recurring appointment feature in Microsoft Outlook.

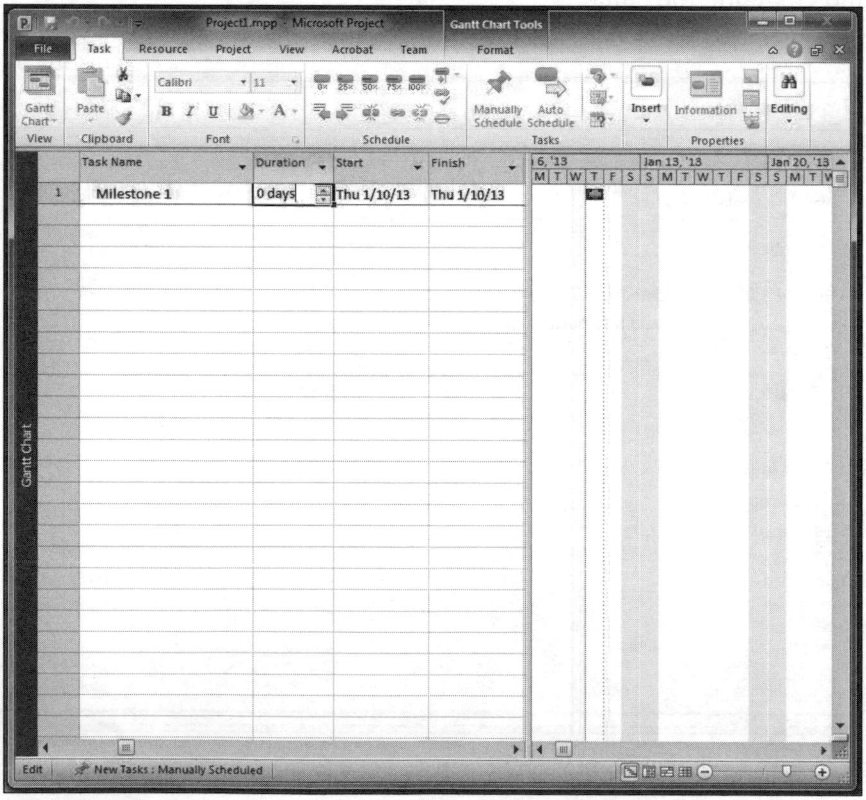

FIGURE A2-9   Setting the Task Duration to 0 Days to Create a Milestone

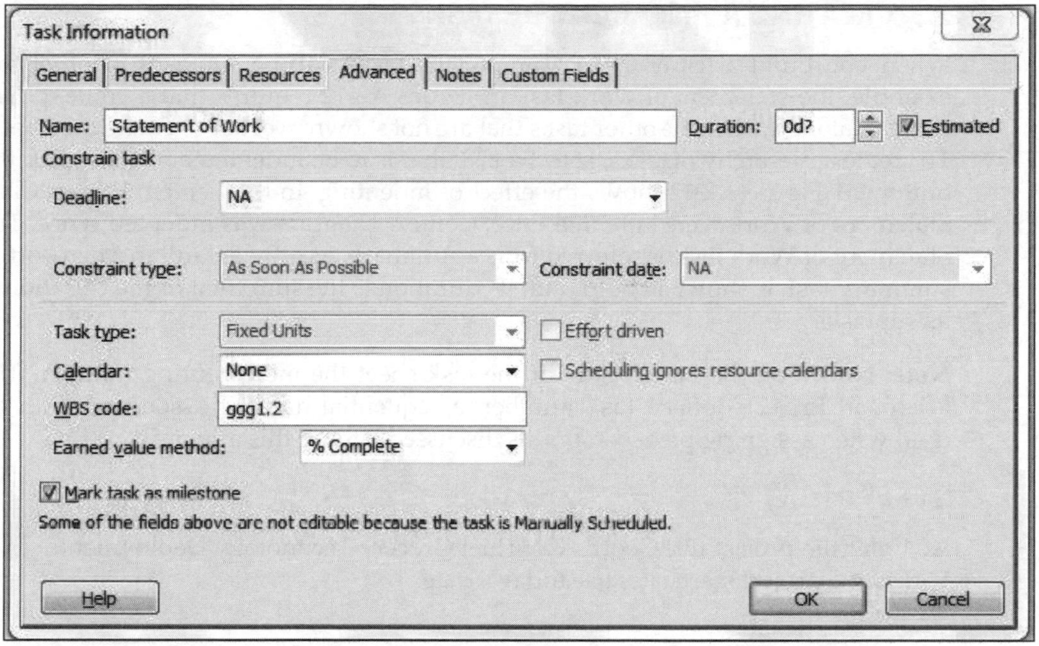

FIGURE A2-10 Making a Task a Milestone by Using a Different Method

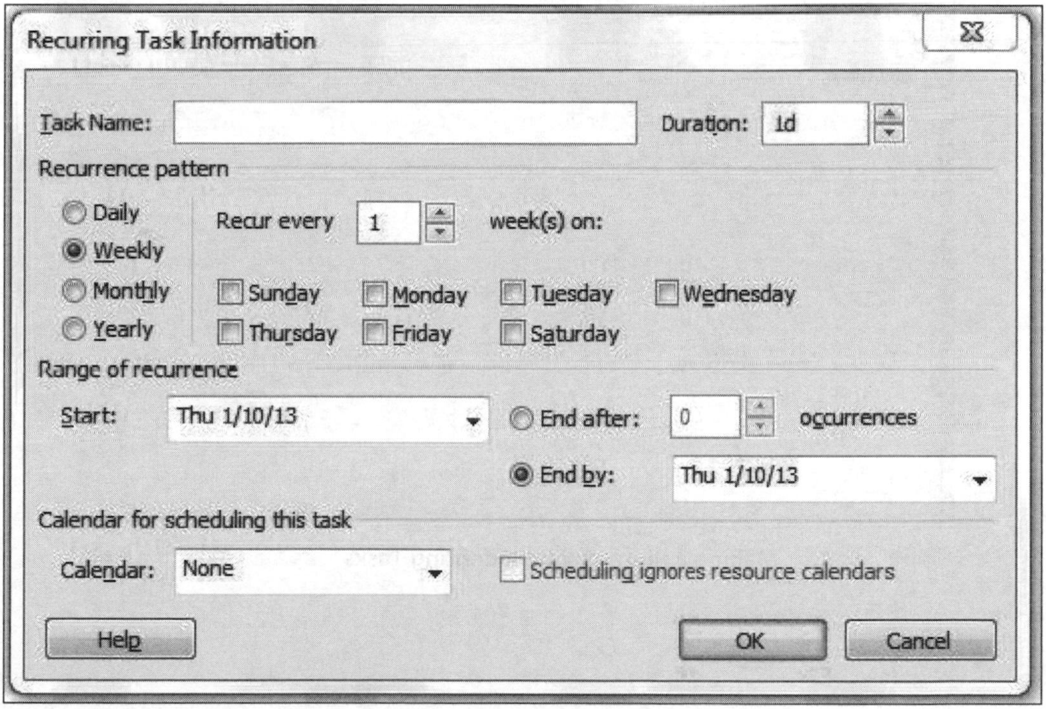

FIGURE A2-11 Entering Information for a Recurring Task

2.9 CREATING A HIERARCHY OF TASKS

When you build a list of tasks, some of the tasks will be subtasks of other items. For example, the statement of work task in Figure A2-12 requires that a context diagram be created, along with some other tasks that are not shown in order to create the final product. To create a hierarchy of tasks, select a task that is to be indented and then click the indent button ⬌. Figure A2-12 shows the effect of indenting. In this screen, Project Charter and Statement of Work were indented once. Context Diagram was indented twice. Task 3, the Statement of Work task, is referred to as a summary task. By default in Microsoft Project, a summary task is shown in bold and, its duration is the sum total of the durations of all of its subtasks.

Note: Notice on the far left side of the task sheet the incrementing number. This is the Microsoft Project–defined task number, a sequential number associated with each task used when assigning predecessors, as discussed later in this appendix.

Unit 2 Exercises

A. Enter the project title Geoff's Gourmet Grocery Technology Deployment.
B. For the project start date, use today's date.

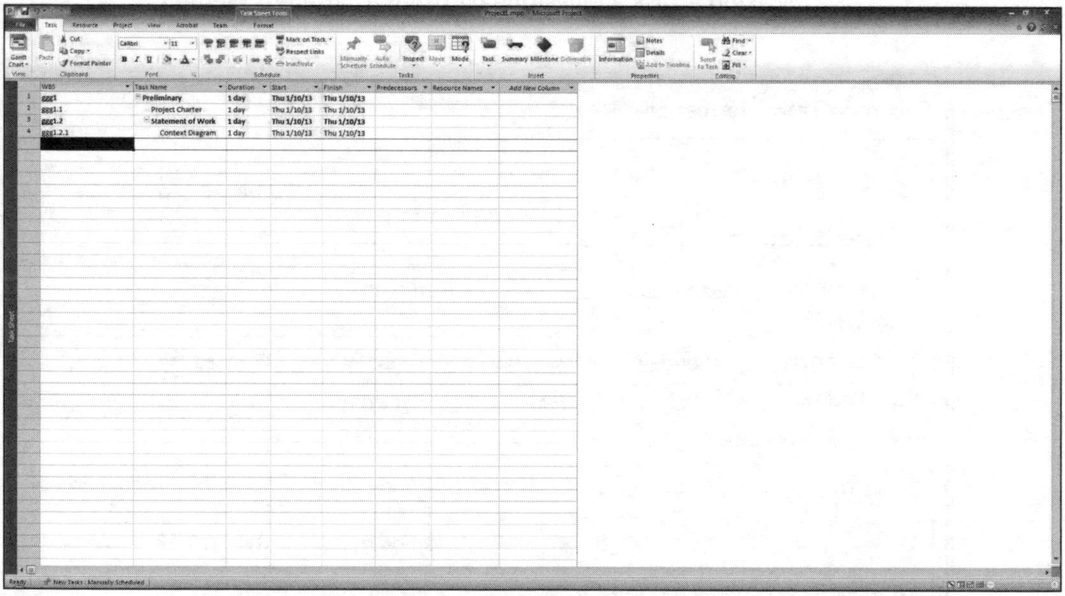

FIGURE A2-12   Making a Hierarchy by Indenting Tasks

C. Enter the following tasks, in the hierarchy shown here. Do not enter the numbers—just the task names.

1. Project Initiation

    1.1 Develop Project Charter

    1.2 Develop Statement of Work

    1.3 Develop Preliminary Scope Statement

    1.4 Develop Preliminary Architecture Model

    1.5 Project Initiation Complete

2. Project Plan

    2.1 Develop Scope Management Plan

    2.2 Develop Change Management Plan

    2.3 Develop Initial Descriptive Budget

    2.4 Develop Schedule

    2.5 Develop Quality Management Plan

    2.6 Develop Human Resource Plan

    2.7 Develop Risk Management Plan

    2.8 Project Plan Complete

3. Project Execution

    3.1 Release 1

        3.1.1 Analysis Phase

        3.1.2 Design Phase

        3.1.3 Construction Phase

        3.1.4 Validation Phase

        3.1.5 Deployment Phase

        3.1.6 Closeout

        3.1.7 Release 1 Complete

    3.2 Release 2

        3.2.1 Analysis Phase

        3.2.2 Design Phase

        3.2.3 Construction Phase

        3.2.4 Validation Phase

        3.2.5 Deployment Phase

        3.2.6 Closeout

        3.2.7 Release 2 Complete

    3.3 Execution Complete

4. Project Closeout

5. Project Complete

D. Create the WBS code GGG1.1.1, where GGG is the prefix, and display it in the Task Sheet view.

E. Set the following tasks as milestones: 1.5, 2.8, 3.1.7, 3.2.7, 5.

3.0 ADDING MORE DETAILS TO THE WBS

3.1 ENTERING THE DURATION FOR A TASK

It is important to specify the duration for only the lowest-level tasks—those without indented children. The summary tasks will inherent their duration from their child tasks. It is also important to know that the duration of a task does not equate equally with the amount of effort put forth in most tasks. *Effort* refers to the amount of time it will take to complete a task, and *duration* refers to the amount of total time it will take, including other activities. For example, you estimate that a task will take 16 hours of effort to complete, but most IT workers must work on more than one task at a time, so it will take longer than 2 days to complete this task. The resource assigned to work on this task works 4 hours the first day, works 6 hours the second day, doesn't work on the task at all on day 3, and works 6 more hours to finish the task on the fourth day. The duration would be shown as 4 days in the Duration column. To add the duration for a task, modify the Duration column for the given task by double-clicking a task to bring up the Task Information screen shown in Figure A3-1, specifying the duration, and click OK. You can simply type in 4d to indicate 4 days or use the spin buttons to increment 1 day at a time. Duration can be tracked in the following increments: minutes, hours, days, weeks, and months.

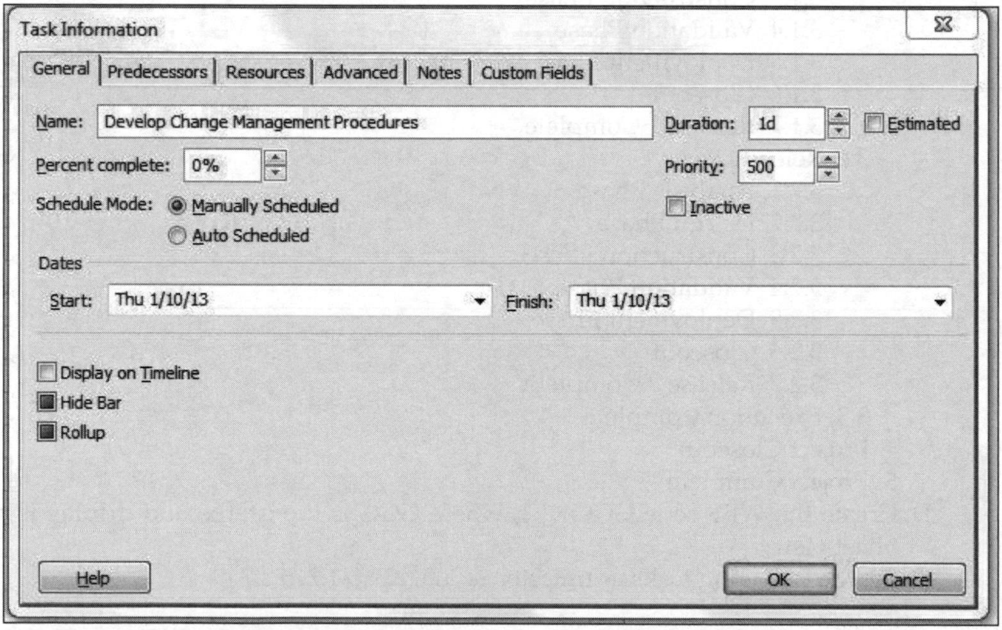

FIGURE A3-1   Adding the Duration to a Task

3.2 ASSIGNING PREDECESSORS TO TASKS

Assigning predecessors to tasks allows for the use of dependencies in the WBS. Understanding dependencies helps in determining a schedule and better organizes the project. Dependencies between tasks occur for a variety of reasons: One task's output is the input for another, only one resource exists that can do both tasks so one will need to wait on the other, and so on. To add a predecessor to a task, double-click the task that needs the predecessor, select the Predecessors tab from the Task Information screen, enter in the ID for the task on which the selected task is dependent, and then select the type of dependency needed (see Figure A3-2).

Four dependency types could be used, based on the task relationships. Finish-to-Start (FS), the default, is used most often. With this dependency, the second task cannot be started until the first task is completed. With the Start-to-Start (SS) dependency, the second task cannot start until the first task starts. With the Finish-to-Finish (FF) dependency, the second task cannot finish until the first task has completed. With the Start-to-Finish (SF) dependency, the second task cannot finish until the first task has been started. Figure A3-3 shows a Gantt chart with predecessors assigned between tasks. The arrow joining Tasks 16 and 17 is connected to the left side of the task and enters the left side of the successor task, demonstrating a Start-to-Start relationship. The arrow joining Tasks 17 and 18 leaves the

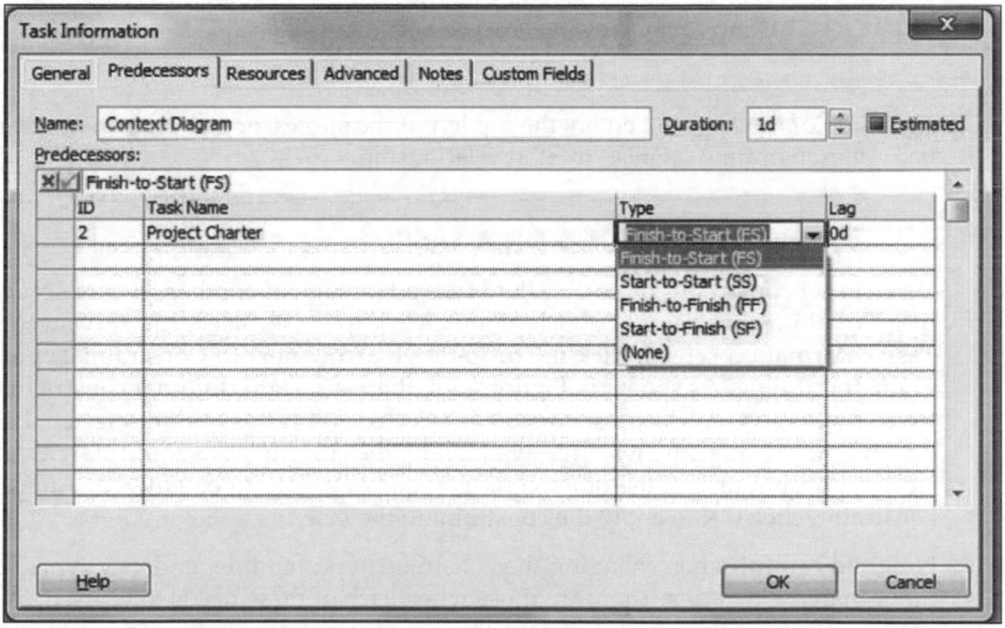

FIGURE A3-2   Specifying a Predecessor and the Type of Dependency

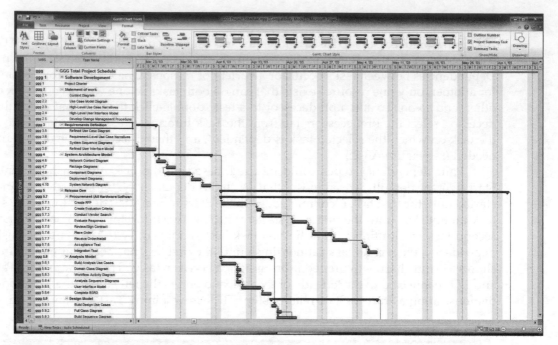

FIGURE A3-3   Gantt Chart Showing Predecessors

right side of the task and enters the top left of the successor task near the beginning of the task, demonstrating a Finish-to-Start relationship.

3.3 SETTING CONSTRAINTS ON A TASK

You can set constraints on each task to take advantage of another level of scheduling control. To add a constraint to a task, double-click the task, select the Advanced tab on the Task Information screen, click the drop-down arrow next to Constraint Type, and select a constraint type. As shown in Figure A3-4, there are eight different constraints to choose from. By default, As Soon As Possible is selected. With this option selected, based on the dependency chosen and resource availability, the current task should start as soon as possible. Choosing any of the other choices requires a date to be entered. After choosing a constraint, click OK to apply the constraint to the task.

Note: Be careful when changing the constraint types and dependency types to anything other than the defaults. There are times when each of these needs to be used, but be aware of their effects on the schedule before changing them. If you're new to project management software, it is best to leave these two options set to the defaults.

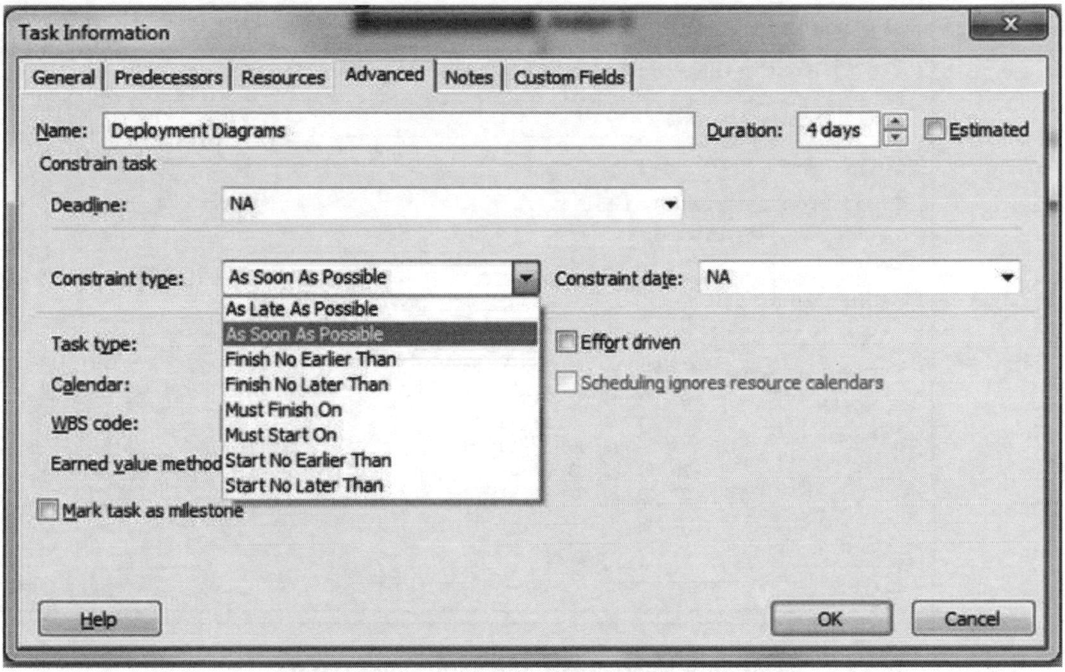

FIGURE A3-4   Selecting the Constraint Type to Be Used for a Task

3.4 ENTERING THE EARLY START AND EARLY FINISH DATES

To display the early start and early finish dates on the task sheet, right-click a column, select Insert Column, and add the Early Start and Early Finish columns. You can now change the early start and early finish dates on the task sheet by using the appropriate drop-down boxes. You can also easily set the dates by double-clicking the task and changing the start and finish dates, using the Start and Finish drop-down boxes (see Figure A3-5).

Unit 3 Exercises

A. Enter the following durations for each task, leaving them as estimates (that is, leave the question mark following the duration amount); the information is provided in the following format for each task (task name, duration, predecessor):

   1. Project Initiation
      1.1 Develop Project Charter (5 days, none)
      1.2 Develop Statement of Work (7 days, 1.1)
      1.3 Develop Preliminary Scope Statement (3 days, 1.2)
      1.4 Develop Preliminary Architecture Model (4 days, 1.1)
      1.5 Project Initiation Complete (0 days, 1.1, 1.2, 1.3, 1.4)

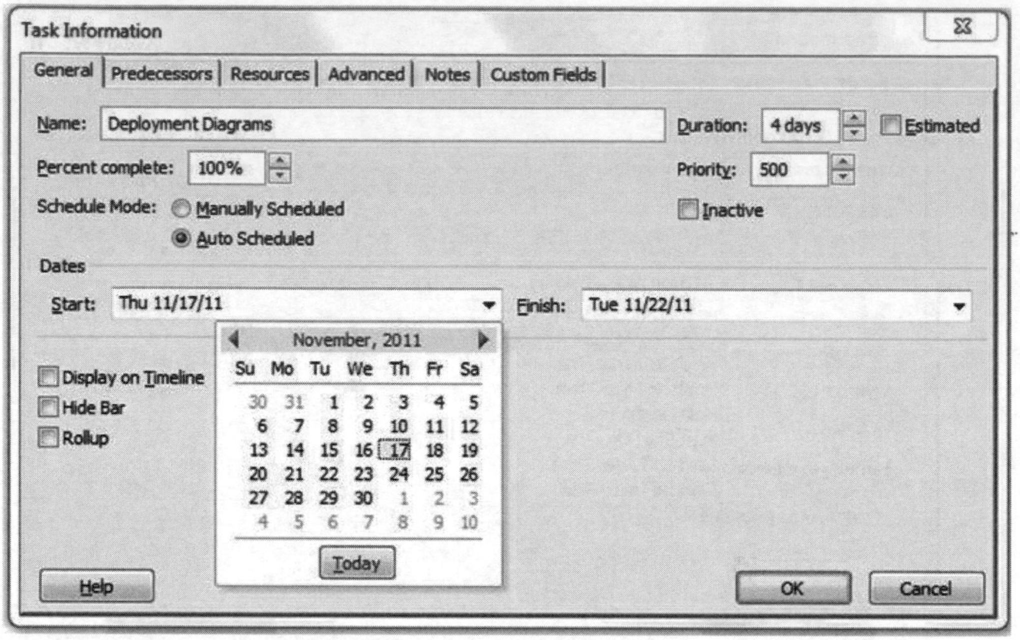

FIGURE A3-5   Entering the Early Start and Early Finish Dates

2. Project Plan
   2.1 Develop Scope Management Plan (1 day, 1.0)
   2.2 Develop Change Management Plan (2 days, 1.0)
   2.3 Develop Budget (10 days, 2.1)
   2.4 Develop Schedule (2 days, 2.1)
   2.5 Develop Quality Management Plan (2 days, 1.0)
   2.6 Develop Human Resource Plan (3 days, 2.1)
   2.7 Develop Risk Management Plan (2 days, 2.1)
   2.8 Project Plan Complete (0 days, 2.1–2.7)
3. Project Execution
   3.1 Release 1
        3.1.1 Analysis Phase (18 days, 2.0)
        3.1.2 Design Phase (15 days, 3.1.1)
        3.1.3 Construction Phase (12 days, 3.1.2)
        3.1.4 Validation Phase (12 days, 3.1.3)
        3.1.5 Deployment Phase (3 days, 3.1.4)
        3.1.6 Closeout (1 day, 3.1.5)
        3.1.7 Release 1 Complete (0 days, 3.1.6)
   3.2 Release 2
        3.2.1 Analysis Phase (18 days, 3.0)
        3.2.2 Design Phase (15 days, 3.2.1)

    3.2.3 Construction Phase (12 days, 3.2.2)
    3.2.4 Validation Phase (12 days, 3.2.3)
    3.2.5 Deployment Phase (3 days, 3.2.4)
    3.2.6 Closeout (1 day, 3.2.5)
    3.2.7 Release 2 Complete (0 days, 3.2.6)
  3.3 Execution Complete
4. Project Closeout (1 day, 3.0)
5. Project Complete (0 day, 4.0)

B. Enter the recurring task Status Review Meeting every Friday morning at 9:00 AM eastern standard time, duration 1 hour, start when project starts, and end when project ends.
C. Set up predecessors as defined in exercise A.
D. Set the constraint type for all relationships to As Soon as Possible.

4.0 ADDING RESOURCES TO THE WBS

4.1 DISPLAYING THE RESOURCE SHEET

To add resources for a project, the resources and information for each resource needs to be completed on the resource sheet. To view the resource sheet (see Figure A4-1), navigate to View Tab | Resource Sheet or use the Resource Tab in the Ribbon. You can now enter resources.

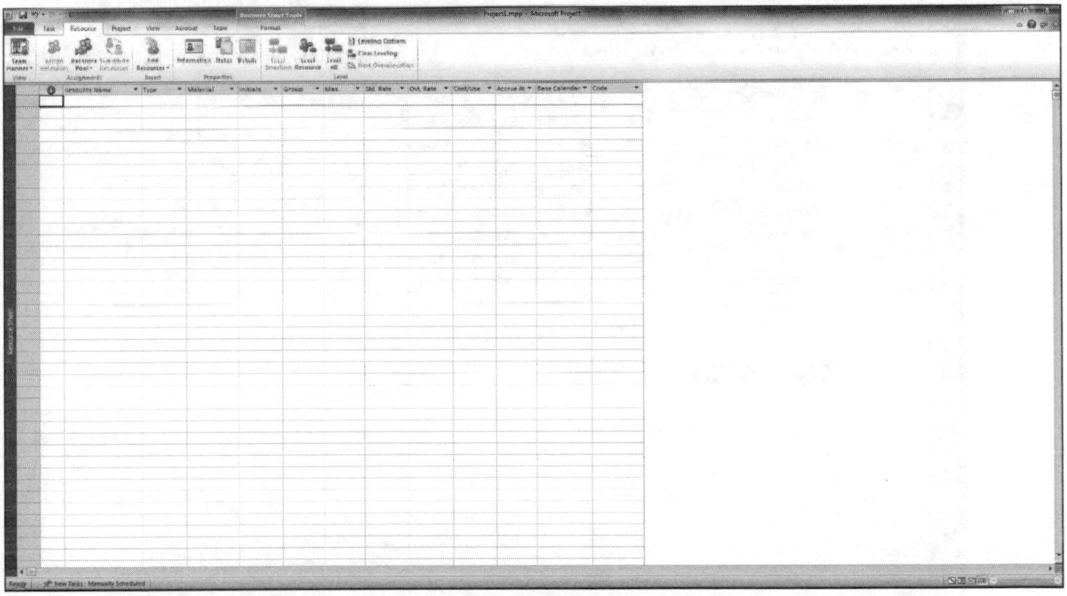

FIGURE A4-1   Displaying the Resource Sheet View

4.2 ADDING RESOURCE ATTRIBUTES

When you're in the Resource Sheet view, adding resources to be displayed and hiding others involves the same process mentioned earlier with the Task Sheet view. To begin, you use the Resource Name, Max Units, Std. Rate, Ovt. Rate, and Base Calendar fields, as shown in Figure A4-2. Resource Name is the title of the resource to be used, such as Network Analyst 1 or John Doe. Max Units is entered as a percentage and represents the maximum capacity for which a resource is available to accomplish a task. By default, this is set to 100 percent, but if you have three resources named Analyst 1, the Max Units field could be adjusted to 300 percent for the single resource to show that there are three of these analysts available for work on the project (see Figure A4-2). Std. Rate is the rate at which the resource is normally paid for work on the project. Ovt. Rate is the overtime for which the resource is paid for working overtime on the project. Base Calendar is the normal schedule the resource will follow. There are three standard schedules that can be specified using the drop-down box in the column for Base Calendar: Standard (the default), 24 hours, and Nightshift.

4.3 ENTERING MULTIPLE PAY RATES

You can establish multiple pay rates by double-clicking a resource and displaying the Resource Information screen, navigating to the Costs tab (see Figure A4-3), and either changing the rates for a given date range or specifying another pay rate for another calendar

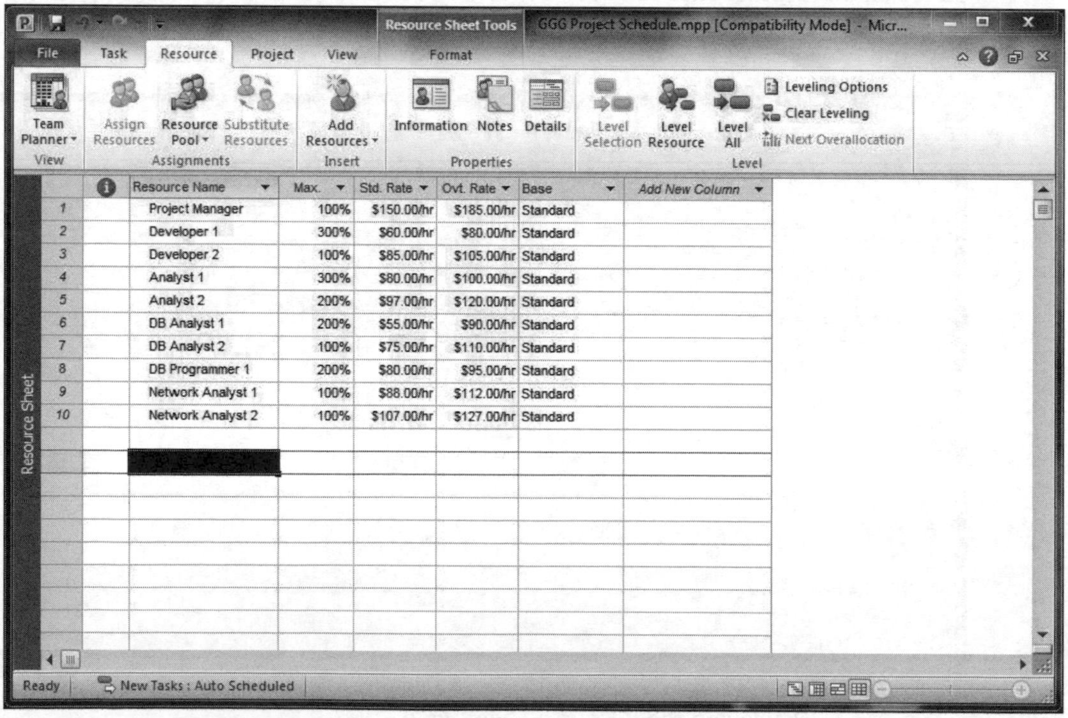

FIGURE A4-2   Adding Attributes to a Resource

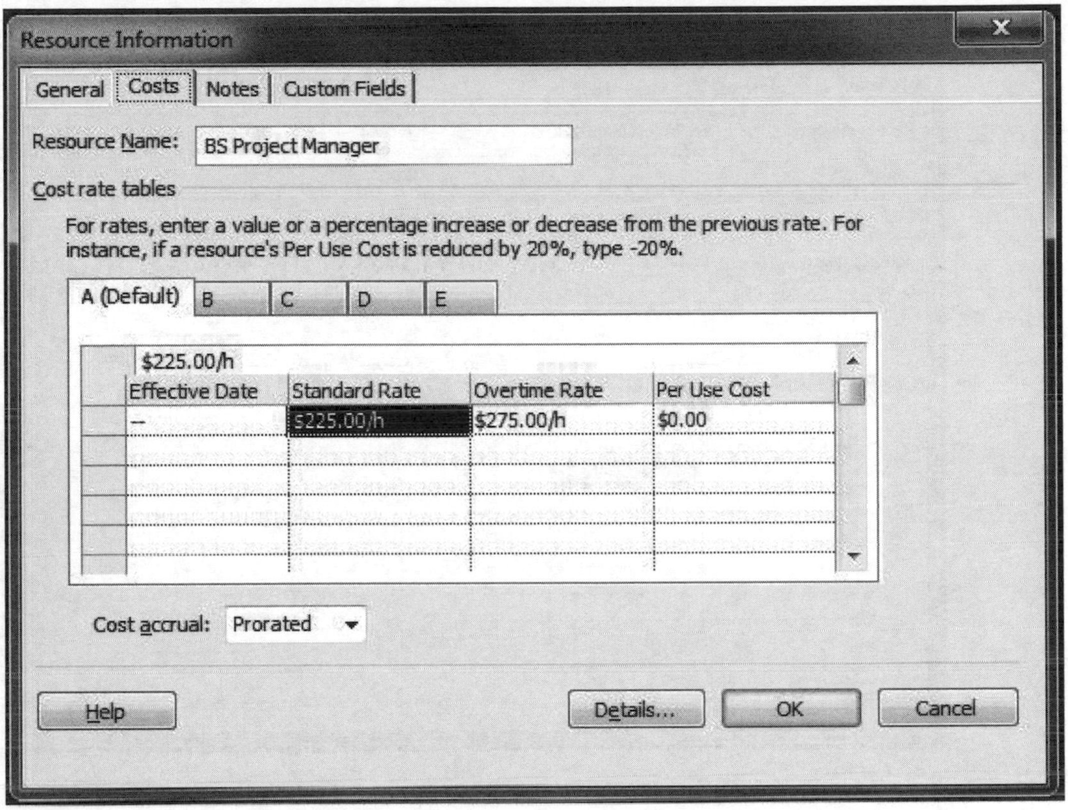

FIGURE A4-3 **Creating Multiple Pay Rates**

by selecting one of the other lettered tabs (A, B, C, D, or E) in the Cost Rate Tables section and modifying the attributes.

4.4 ENTERING EQUIPMENT AND MATERIAL RESOURCES

To enter information for equipment or material costs, double-click an open row in the resource sheet. When you do this, the screen shown in Figure A4-4 appears. To change the type of resource from the default, Work, click the drop-down box in the Type field and select Material, such as rented computers or telephony equipment. You can now also add Material Label, below the Type field. Adding material to the project schedule has several advantages, such as adding the ability to track the schedule of when the material is needed and how long it will be used for cost purposes.

4.5 EDITING THE RESOURCE CALENDAR

As noted earlier, there are three options for the base calendar of a resource. For the standard calendar, the normal working times are 8:00 AM to 12:00 PM and 1:00 PM to 5:00 PM,

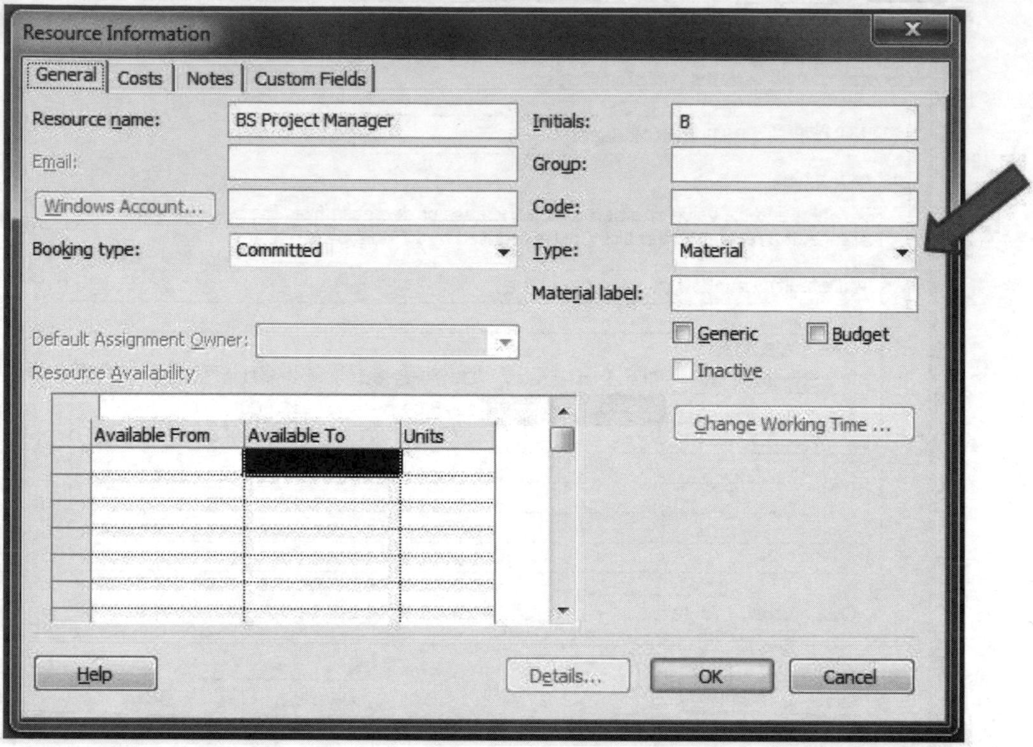

FIGURE A4-4 **Entering a Material Resource**

Monday through Friday. However, you can add specific working times and days by double-clicking the resource to modify, selecting the Change Working Time button in the new window that appears (see Figure A4-5), and then specifying the new work times. You can enter vacations, holidays, and other non-working times by typing in an exception just for this resource or for all resources. If you get to this screen by first going to the resource, the changes will affect only that resource; if you first use the Tools menu, the change will affect all resources assigned to this project.

4.6 ASSIGNING RESOURCES TO A TASK

To assign resources to a task, return to the Task Sheet view. Next, double-click the task that needs a resource assigned to it. The Task Detail Information screen appears. Select the Resources tab, as shown in Figure A4-6. To assign a specific resource, click the drop-down box below Resource Name and select a resource. By default, the percentage of units assigned to the task is 100 percent, which means the resource will work on this task as much as possible, depending on the allocation set up in the Resource Information screen, but you can change this amount by using the Units field. For example, if the resource is assigned 50 percent in the Resource Information screen and then assigned 100 percent to a task, that person would be working half time, or 4 hours of an 8-hour day, on this task.

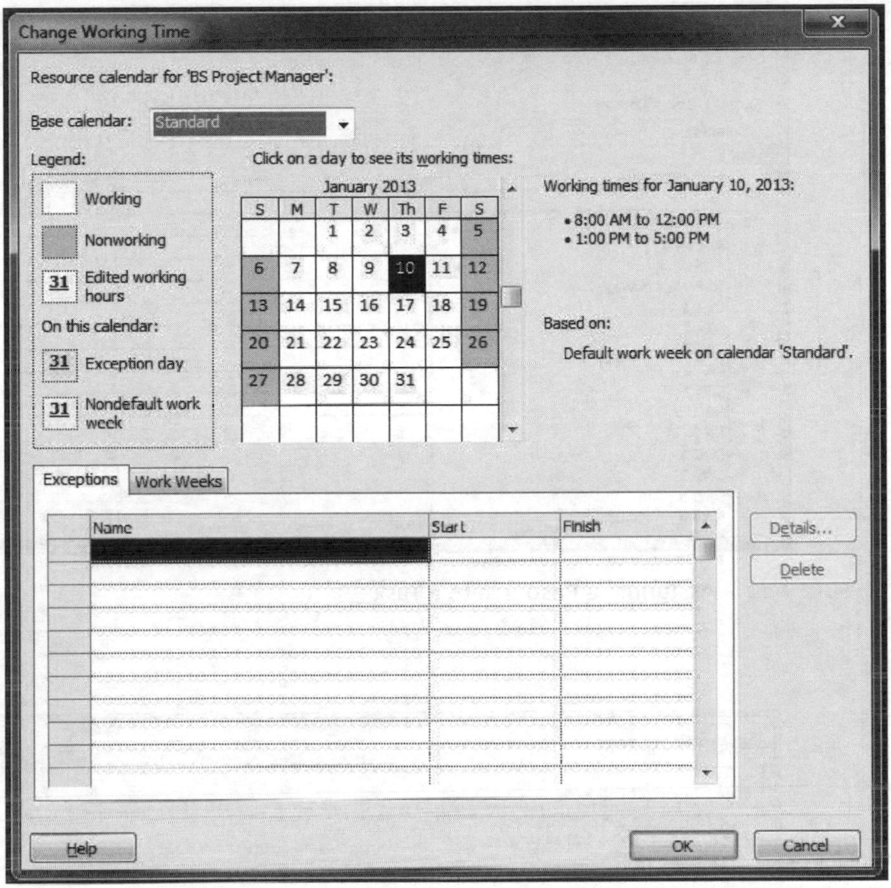

FIGURE A4-5   Editing the Resource Calendar

You can also add resources by using two other methods. The first method involves displaying the Resource Names column on the task sheet. To choose a resource for a task, simply click the drop-down box for the task and select the resource(s). Another alternative is to select the task to add a resource to, navigate to Resource Tab | Assign Resources. The screen shown in Figure A4-7 appears. Select the resource to be used and click Assign to add the resource to the task. By default, the maximum units will be set to 100 percent.

4.7 DEALING WITH OVERALLOCATED RESOURCES

When you assign resources to a task, a resource may become overallocated, meaning that the person is assigned to work on more tasks than he or she has time available. To determine whether a resource is overallocated, navigate to Resource Sheet or Resource Usage. If there are any overallocated resources, they will appear in the list in a different color with a note in the indicators column. To remedy a problem with overallocated resources, you need to assign other resources to tasks to take pressure off the resource that is overal-

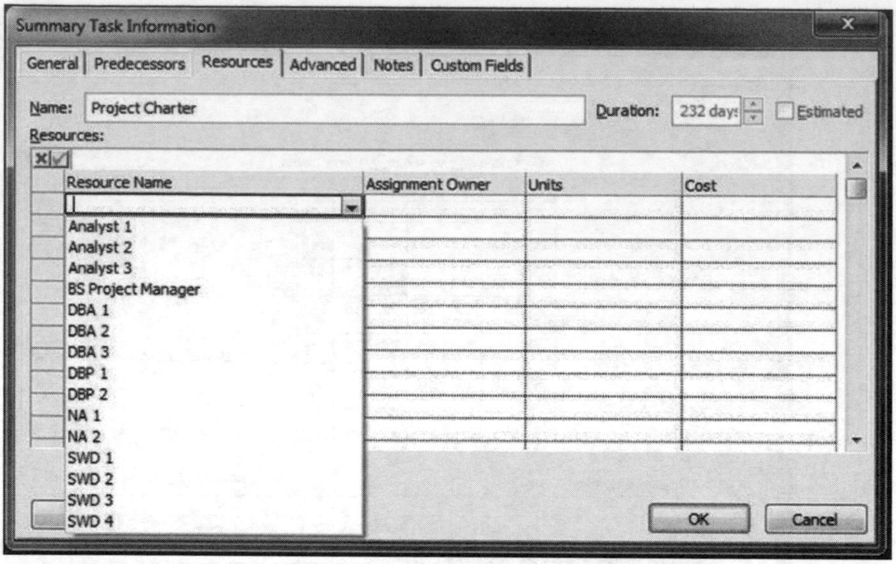

FIGURE A4-6 Assigning a Resource to a Task

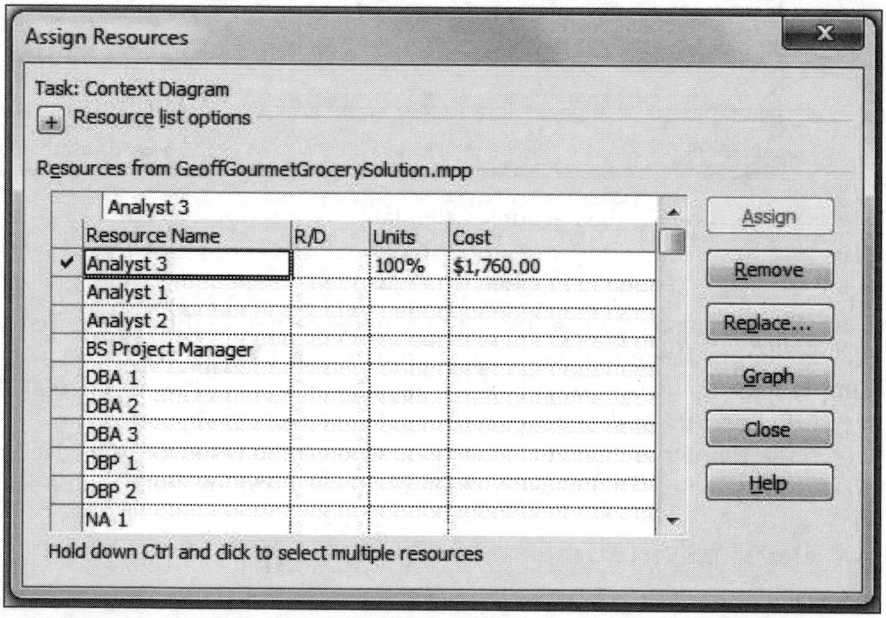

FIGURE A4-7 Assigning a Resource to a Task

located or you must extend the time to complete the task. You can do this by assigning another resource to a task, assigning a different resource to a task, or using the automated resource leveling function in Microsoft Project, as explained next.

4.8 LEVELING RESOURCES

When you level resources, the Project either splits tasks (meaning work is stopped on a task and resumed later) or adds a delay to a task until the overallocated resource can complete the task, based on his or her schedule. To have Microsoft Project level resources, navigate to Resource | Resource Sheet | Level Resources. The screen shown in Figure A4-8 appears. Click Level Now to level the resources.

Figure A4-8 offers the following settings for leveling resources:

- *Automatic or Manual*—Manual is default and should be used. Automatic levels resources every time something is changed in the schedule, and if the project is large, it will get quite annoying to wait on the software every time a change is made.

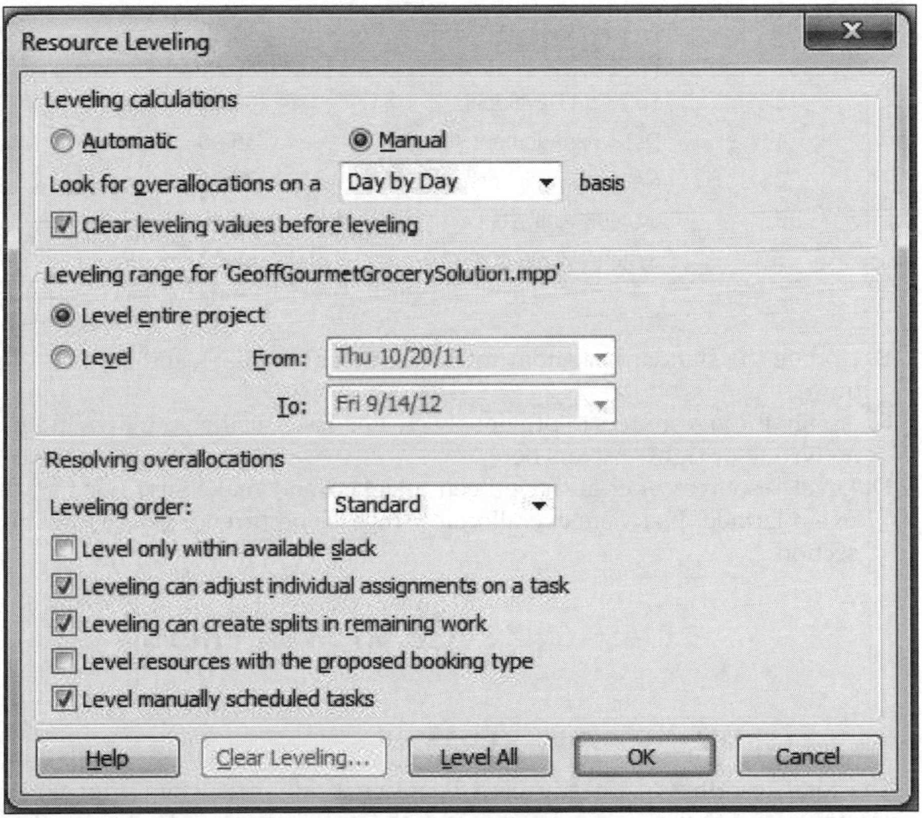

FIGURE A4-8   Setting the Resource Leveling Specifications

- *Look for Overallocations on a Day by Day Basis*—Most schedules are set up to monitor activity on a day-by-day basis; other options are minutes, hours, weeks, or months.
- *Clear Leveling Values Before Leveling*—If you check this option, delays previously entered as a result of leveling are cleared.
- *Leveling Range*—You can level an entire project schedule or a selected date range.
- *Level Only Within Available Slack*—This option delays a task only if it has slack available. If no slack is available, the resource remains overallocated.

Note: Before you level resources, be sure to save the project schedule first and/or make a backup copy of the schedule. Leveling can sometimes produce unwanted changes to the schedule that can be difficult to find and repair.

Unit 4 Exercises

A. Create the following resources with associated costs:

Number Available	Title/Name	Standard Rate ($/hr)	Overtime Rate ($/hr)
1	Project Manager– Maria Ramos	150.00	200.00
3	Software Developers	60.00	80.00
1	Data Management Analyst	55.00	75.00
2	Network Engineers	75.00	95.00
3	Systems Analysts	75.00	95.00
1	System Architect	85.00	105.00

B. Update the standard calendar for U.S. national holidays and set them to non-working times.

C. Assign these resources to previously created tasks, using your own judgment. There are no wrong or right answers here.

D. Level resources after all have been assigned and make sure none of the resources is overallocated. If any are overallocated, fix each occurrence before moving on to the next section.

5.0 ASSIGNING COST INFORMATION TO A TASK

5.1 DETERMINING PROJECT COST

The total resource cost of a project is automatically calculated after you assign costs to resources and then assign resources to each lower-level task. To display the cost, insert the Cost column in Task Sheet view. You can also enter and track material in Microsoft Project. The screen shown in Figure A5-1 shows how you add the Cost column. Figure A5-2 shows the task sheet with relevant cost descriptors associated with the default table view for cost.

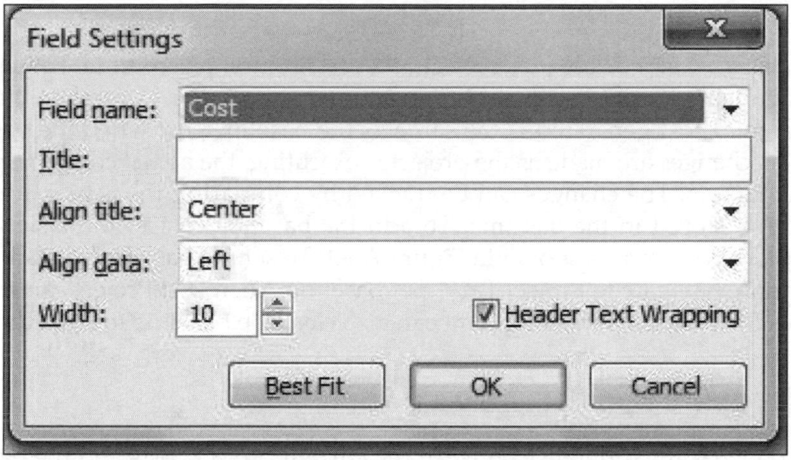

FIGURE A5-1 **Inserting the Cost Column**

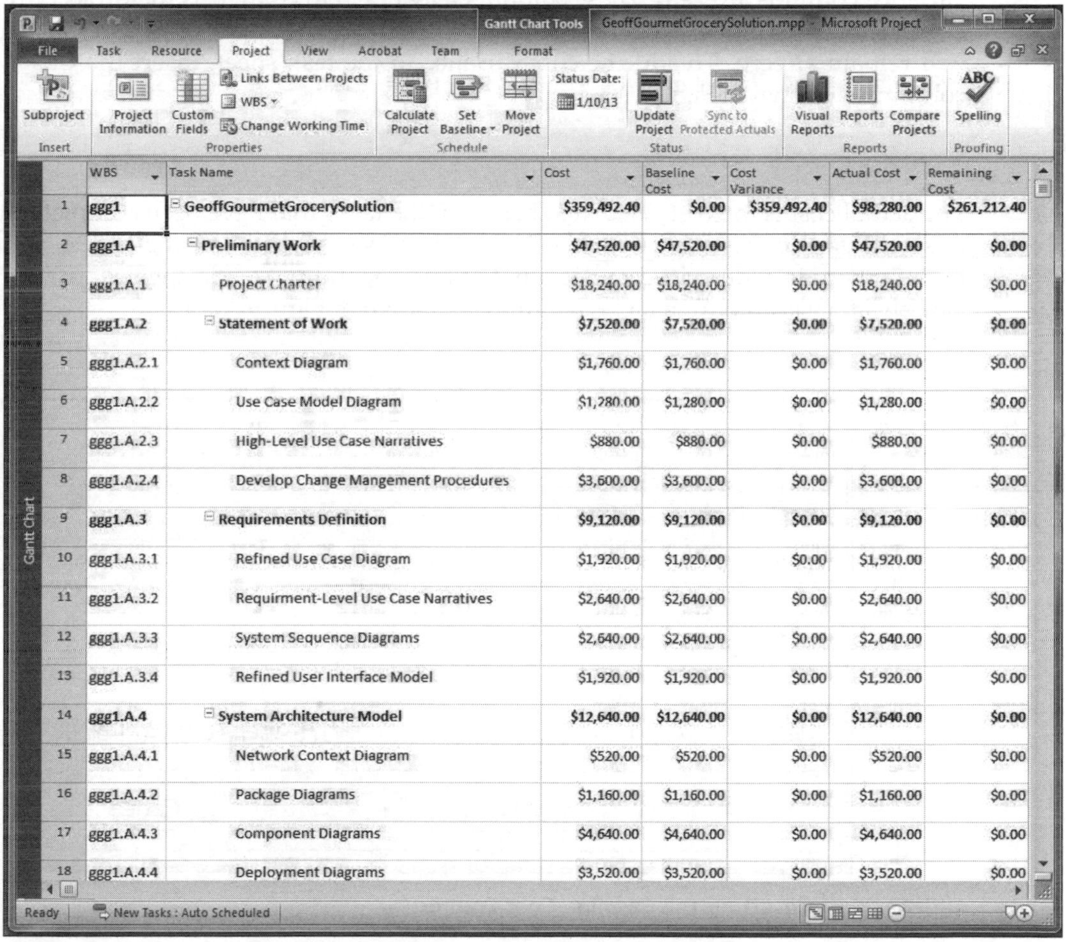

	WBS	Task Name	Cost	Baseline Cost	Cost Variance	Actual Cost	Remaining Cost
1	ggg1	GeoffGourmetGrocerySolution	$359,492.40	$0.00	$359,492.40	$98,280.00	$261,212.40
2	ggg1.A	Preliminary Work	$47,520.00	$47,520.00	$0.00	$47,520.00	$0.00
3	ggg1.A.1	Project Charter	$18,240.00	$18,240.00	$0.00	$18,240.00	$0.00
4	ggg1.A.2	Statement of Work	$7,520.00	$7,520.00	$0.00	$7,520.00	$0.00
5	ggg1.A.2.1	Context Diagram	$1,760.00	$1,760.00	$0.00	$1,760.00	$0.00
6	ggg1.A.2.2	Use Case Model Diagram	$1,280.00	$1,280.00	$0.00	$1,280.00	$0.00
7	ggg1.A.2.3	High-Level Use Case Narratives	$880.00	$880.00	$0.00	$880.00	$0.00
8	ggg1.A.2.4	Develop Change Mangement Procedures	$3,600.00	$3,600.00	$0.00	$3,600.00	$0.00
9	ggg1.A.3	Requirements Definition	$9,120.00	$9,120.00	$0.00	$9,120.00	$0.00
10	ggg1.A.3.1	Refined Use Case Diagram	$1,920.00	$1,920.00	$0.00	$1,920.00	$0.00
11	ggg1.A.3.2	Requirment-Level Use Case Narratives	$2,640.00	$2,640.00	$0.00	$2,640.00	$0.00
12	ggg1.A.3.3	System Sequence Diagrams	$2,640.00	$2,640.00	$0.00	$2,640.00	$0.00
13	ggg1.A.3.4	Refined User Interface Model	$1,920.00	$1,920.00	$0.00	$1,920.00	$0.00
14	ggg1.A.4	System Architecture Model	$12,640.00	$12,640.00	$0.00	$12,640.00	$0.00
15	ggg1.A.4.1	Network Context Diagram	$520.00	$520.00	$0.00	$520.00	$0.00
16	ggg1.A.4.2	Package Diagrams	$1,160.00	$1,160.00	$0.00	$1,160.00	$0.00
17	ggg1.A.4.3	Component Diagrams	$4,640.00	$4,640.00	$0.00	$4,640.00	$0.00
18	ggg1.A.4.4	Deployment Diagrams	$3,520.00	$3,520.00	$0.00	$3,520.00	$0.00

FIGURE A5-2 **The Task Sheet View, Displaying the Relevant Costs**

5.2 DETERMINING THE BASELINE COST

The *baseline cost* is the cost of a project at a certain moment in time. Baseline information is also available for start and finish dates for each task. For example, when a project begins, the total cost generated is the same as the baseline cost when the baseline has been set, but as changes are made as the project is executing, the actual costs could change, based on many factors. The changes can be tracked by comparing the actual information to the information stored in the baseline. To add the baseline cost to the task sheet, insert the Baseline Cost column, as shown in Figure A5-3. To set the baseline cost and other baseline information, navigate to Project Tab | Set Baseline. Microsoft Project can track 11 separate baselines for variance reporting. You can also clear the baseline to reset the values.

5.3 DETERMINING THE COST VARIANCE

Cost variance is the difference between the current project costs and the baseline costs. As described in Section 5.2, at the beginning of the project, when the baseline is first set, the variance columns are zero. These columns may begin to change as the project progresses. If the project executes exactly as planned (which never happens), the variance amounts will remain at zero. To add the cost variance to the task sheet, insert the Cost Variance column, as shown in Figure A5-4.

5.4 DETERMINING THE ACTUAL COST

The actual cost is the cost calculated based on the tasks that have been completed thus far. It is a measure of costs accrued thus far in the project. Adding actual progress information to the schedule is described in Section 7 of this appendix. To add the cost variance to the task sheet, insert the Actual Cost column, as shown in Figure A5-5.

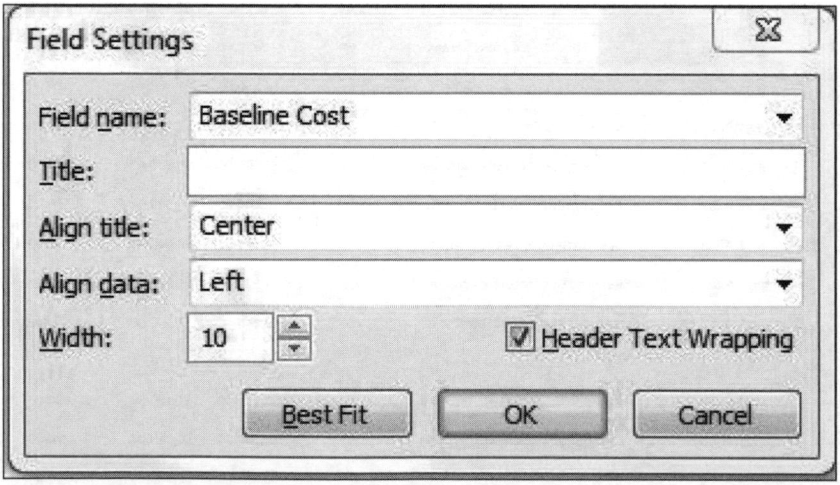

FIGURE A5-3   Inserting the Baseline Cost Column

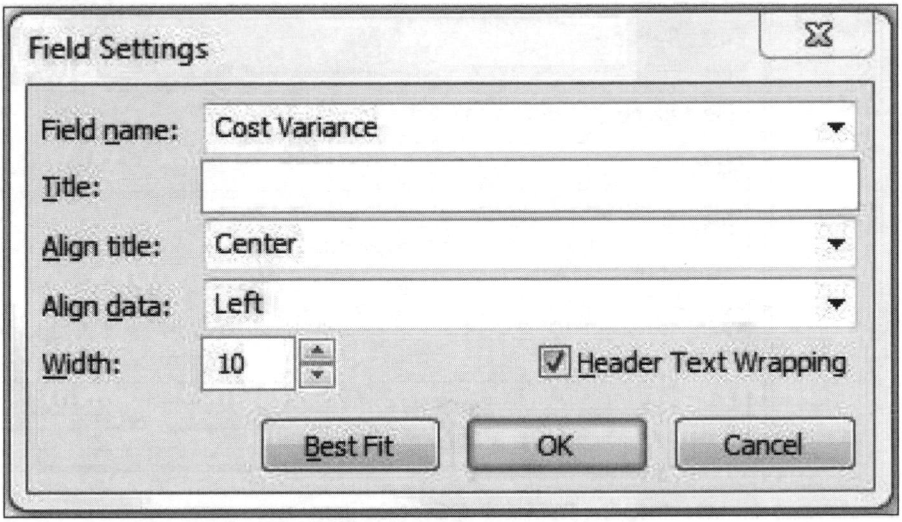

FIGURE A5-4 **Inserting the Cost Variance Column**

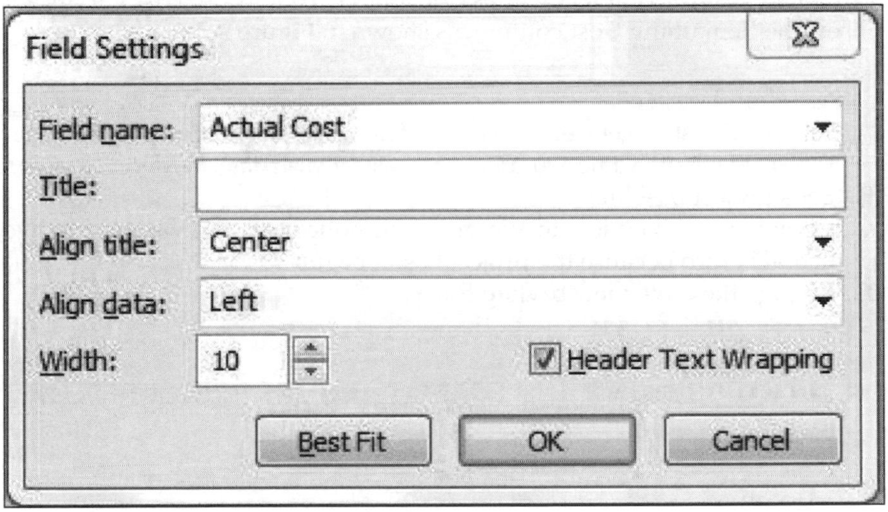

FIGURE A5-5 **Inserting the Actual Cost Column**

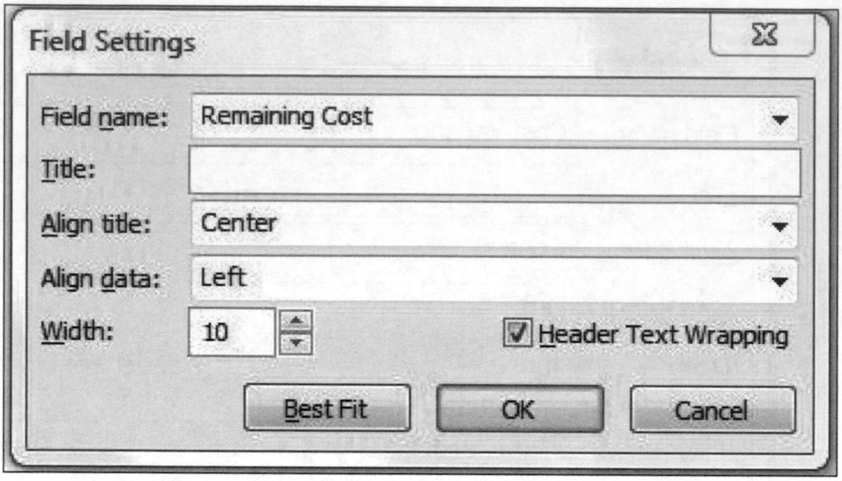

FIGURE A5-6   Inserting the Remaining Cost Column

5.5 DETERMINING THE REMAINING COST

The remaining cost is the difference between the total cost and the actual cost. It is the estimated cost to complete the task or project. To add the cost variance to the task sheet, insert the Remaining Cost column, as shown in Figure A5-6.

Unit 5 Exercises

A. Set up the Task Sheet view to have the following information displayed, in the order shown: WBS Code, Task Name, Duration, Start date, Finish date, Predecessor, Resource Name, Cost.
B. Set a project baseline.
C. Change the table view to Variance and notice that the variance between baseline and actual is zero because the project hasn't begun yet.
D. Change the table view back to Entry.

6.0 PRINTING AND FORMATTING THE PROJECT INFORMATION

6.1 USING A GANTT CHART

To switch to the Gantt Chart view, select Task Tab | Gantt Chart. You can now use several options, as shown in Figure A6-1. To adjust the timescale shown, select View Tab | Timescale, then select the pull down menu and select Timescale. The screen shown in Figure A6-2 appears. In this screen, you can specify the start date for the Gantt Chart view, and you can specify the timescale, which is visible across the top of the Gantt chart, such as minutes, hours, weeks, thirds of months, months, quarters, half years, and years. Several other options can be used as well. Figure A6-2 can also be accessed by hovering the mouse over the timescale above the Gantt chart and clicking your right mouse button.

FIGURE A6-1 Gantt Chart Options

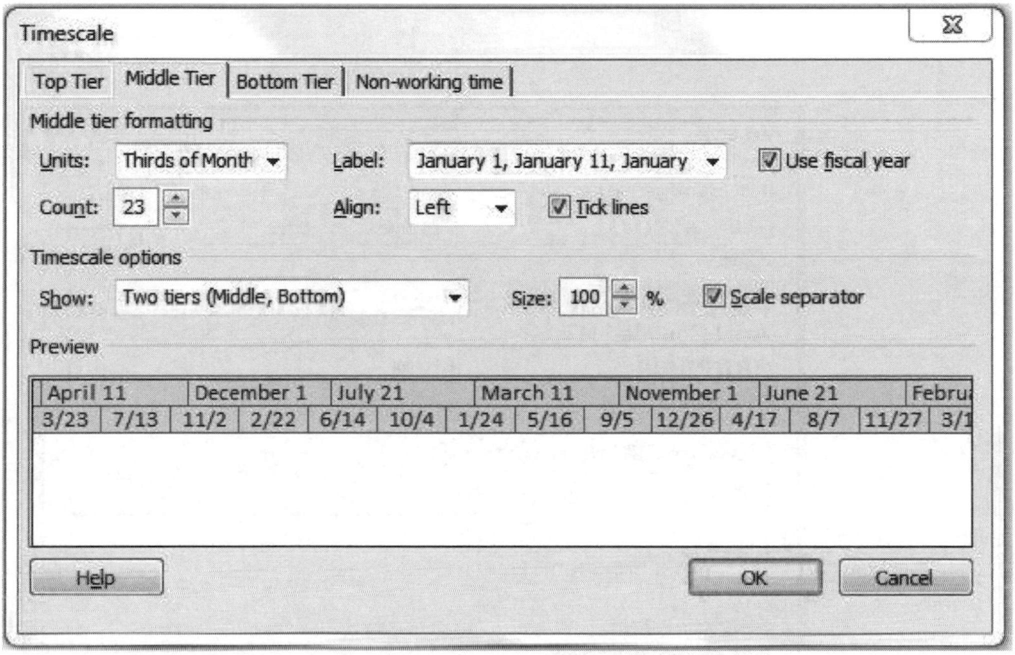

FIGURE A6-2 Setting the Timescale to Show on a Gantt Chart

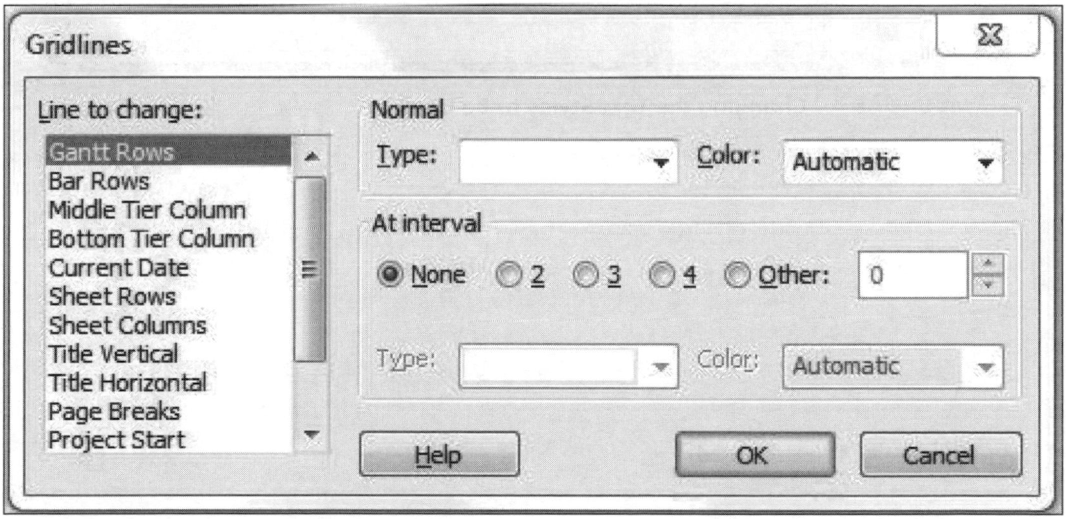

FIGURE A6-3 Changing the Gridlines to Be Used

To format the color or the type of gridlines used on the chart, select the Gridlines option located on the Format tab to open the dialog shown in Figure A6-3.

To change the text used on the Gantt chart, select the Text Styles option located on the Format tab to open the screen shown in Figure A6-4. To format the bar styles used on the chart, select the Bar Styles option, located on the Format Tab | Format Option, and the screen shown in Figure A6-5 appears. In this figure, only the summary tasks and project summary bars are shown.

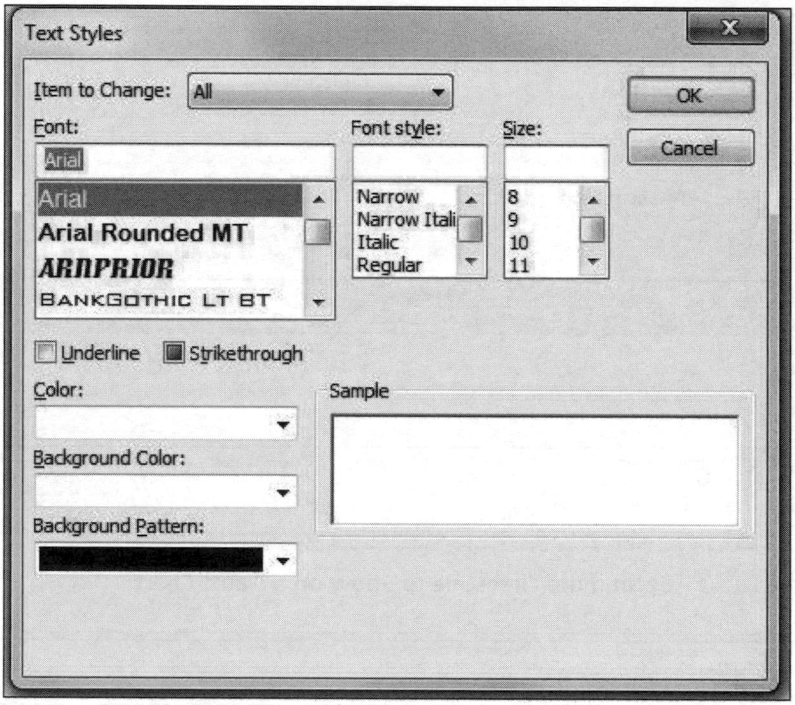

FIGURE A6-4   Changing the Text Styles to Be Used

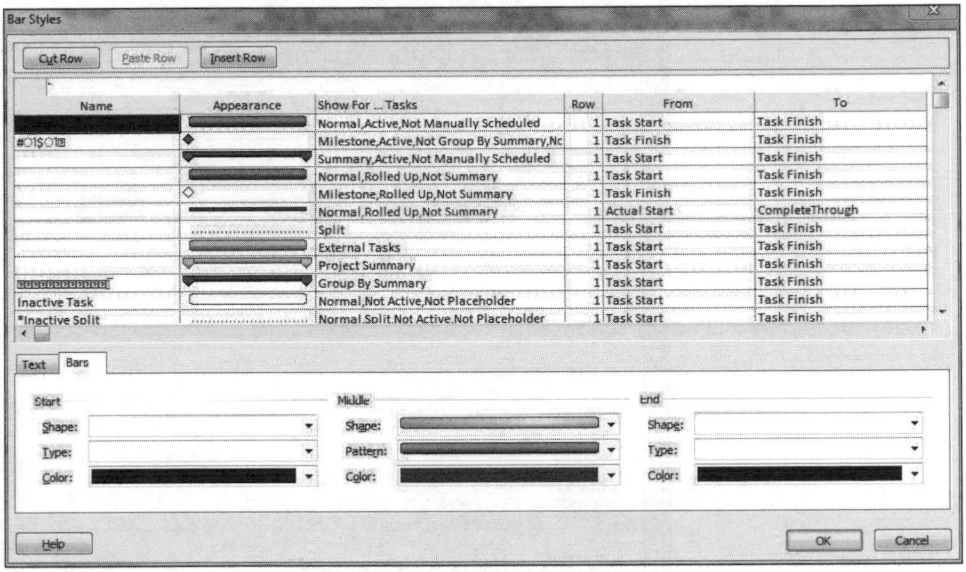

FIGURE A6-5 Selecting the Bar Styles to Use for the Tasks

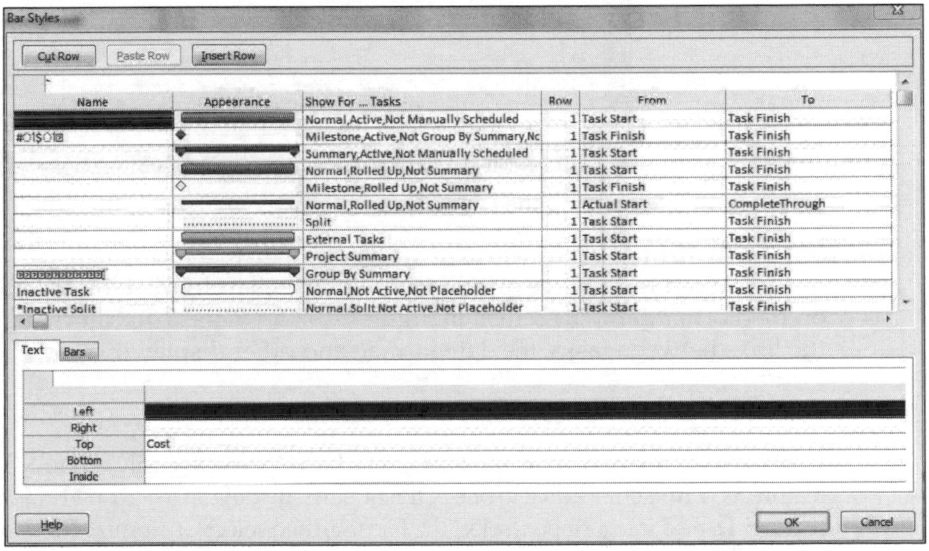

FIGURE A6-6 Choosing the Display Text Associated with Each Bar

Select the Text tab to change where and what text appears by each bar. In the example shown in Figure A6-6, only the actual cost will be displayed to the center and above each summary task bar.

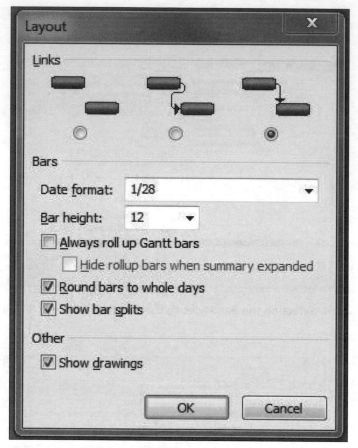

FIGURE A6-7   **Specifying the Layout**

You can modify the overall layout of the chart by clicking the Layout option located on the Format tab. The screen in Figure A6-7 appears. You can change the formatting for the links between tasks, the date format, and other display options.

6.2 USING THE GANTT CHART WIZARD

In Microsoft Project, you can use the Gantt Chart Wizard to easily create a Gantt chart. To use this feature, you must first add it to one of the ribbons. By default Microsoft Project does not include this feature. To add it to a ribbon, select the File tab, then select Customize Ribbon. The series of screens displayed in Figures A6-8 through A6-13 show the process of using the Gantt Chart Wizard.

6.3 EXPORTING THE PROJECT INFORMATION

An important feature in Microsoft Project is the ability to export the project information along with charts, such as a Gantt chart. You do this simply by selecting File Tab | Save As. The screen shown in Figure A6-14 appears. As you can see, the file can be saved to a number of different formats.

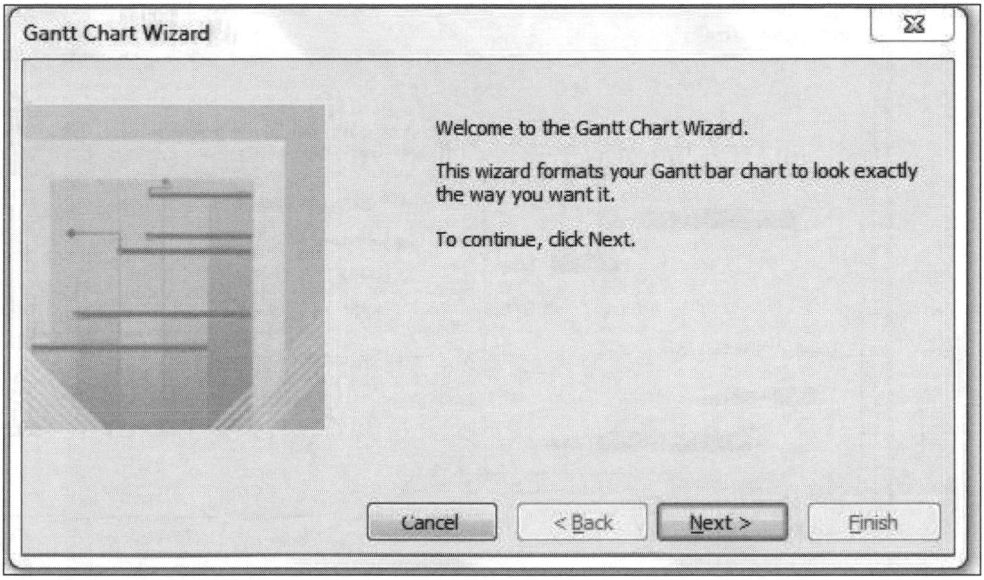

FIGURE A6-8   Starting the Gantt Chart Wizard

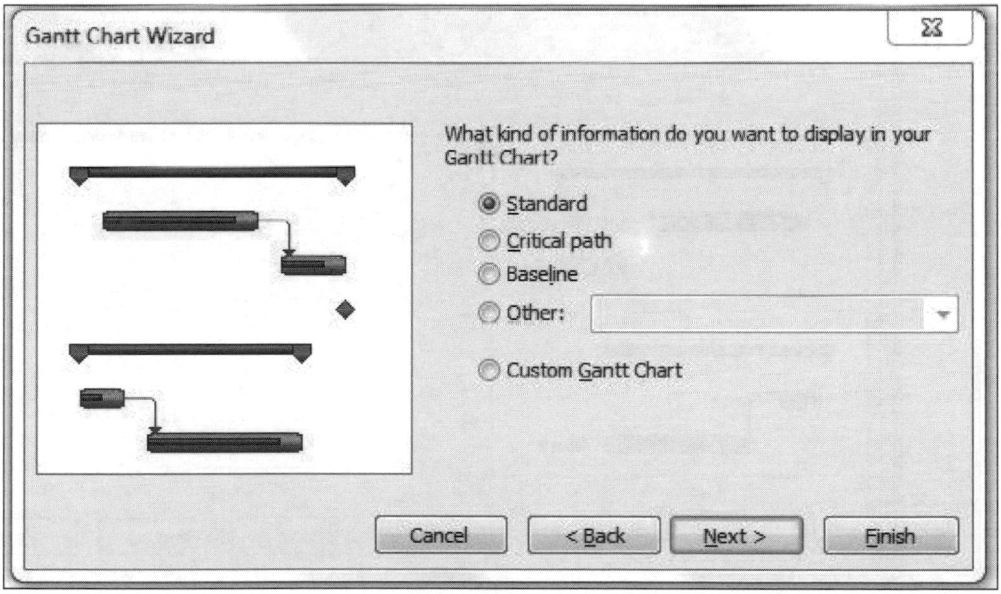

FIGURE A6-9   Choosing the Information to Display

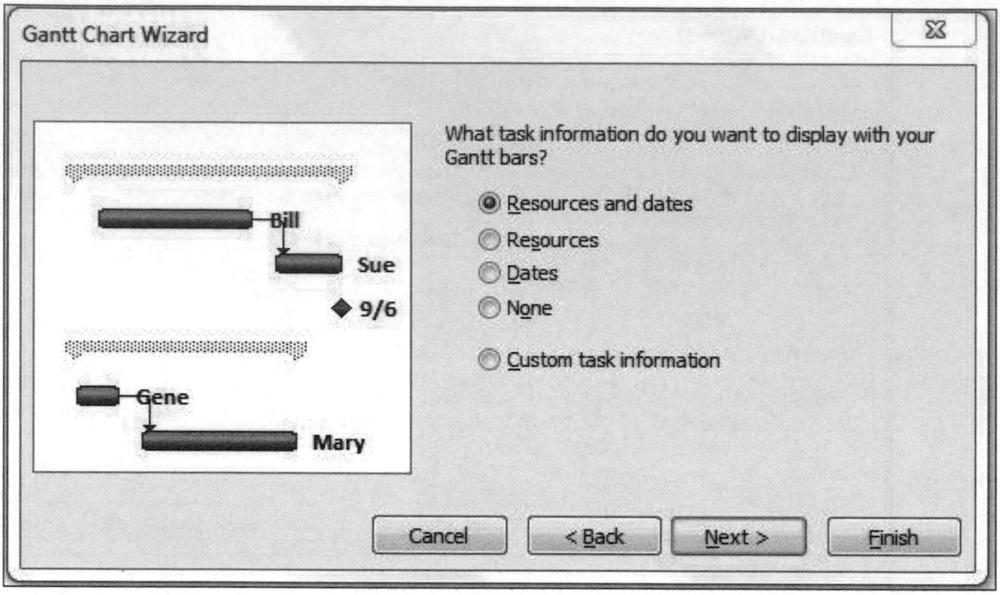

FIGURE A6-10   Choosing the Task Information to Display with the Bars

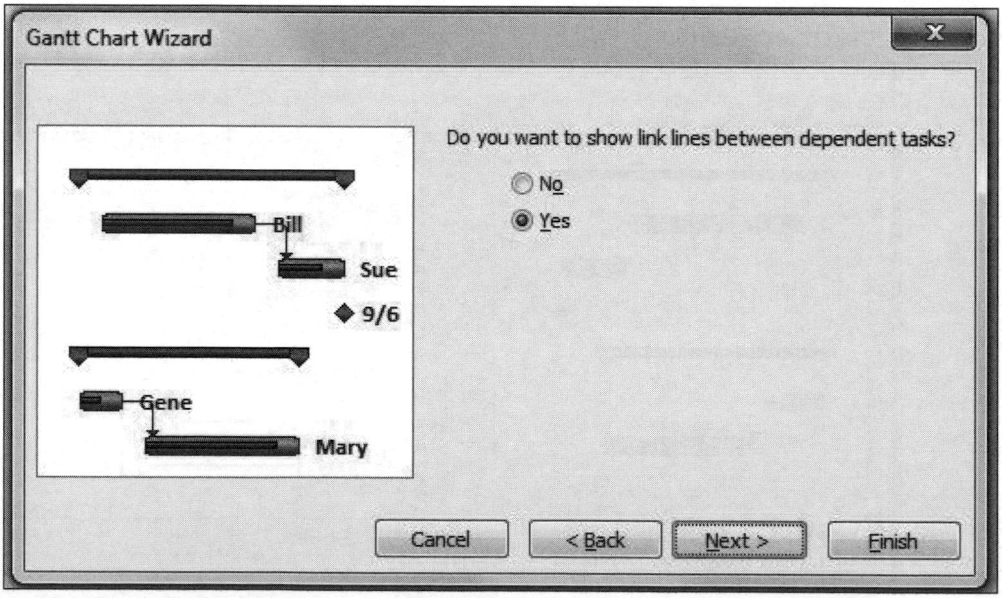

FIGURE A6-11   Choosing Whether to Show the Links Between Dependent Tasks

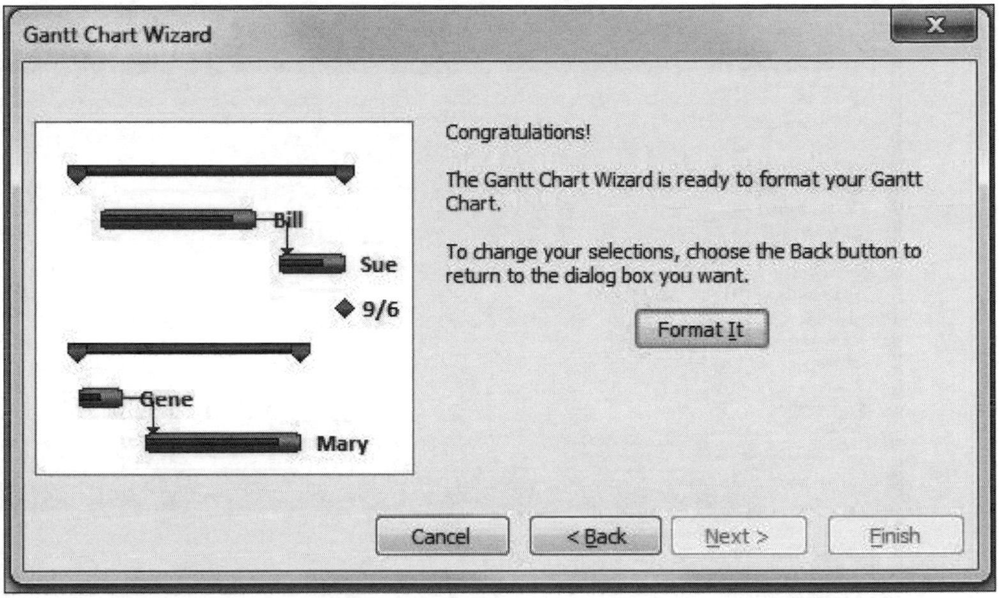

FIGURE A6-12   Finishing the Wizard

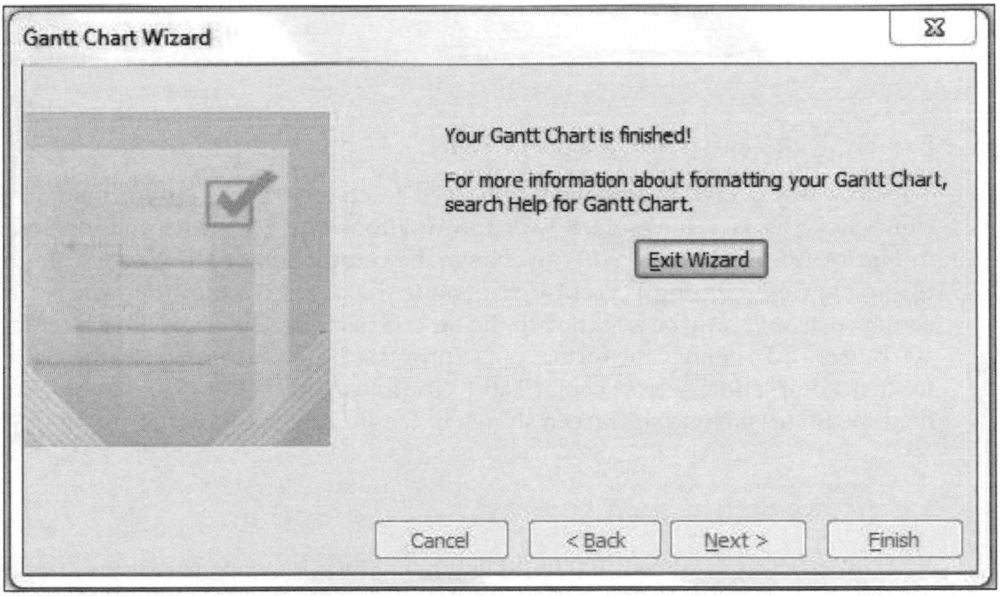

FIGURE A6-13   Exiting the Wizard

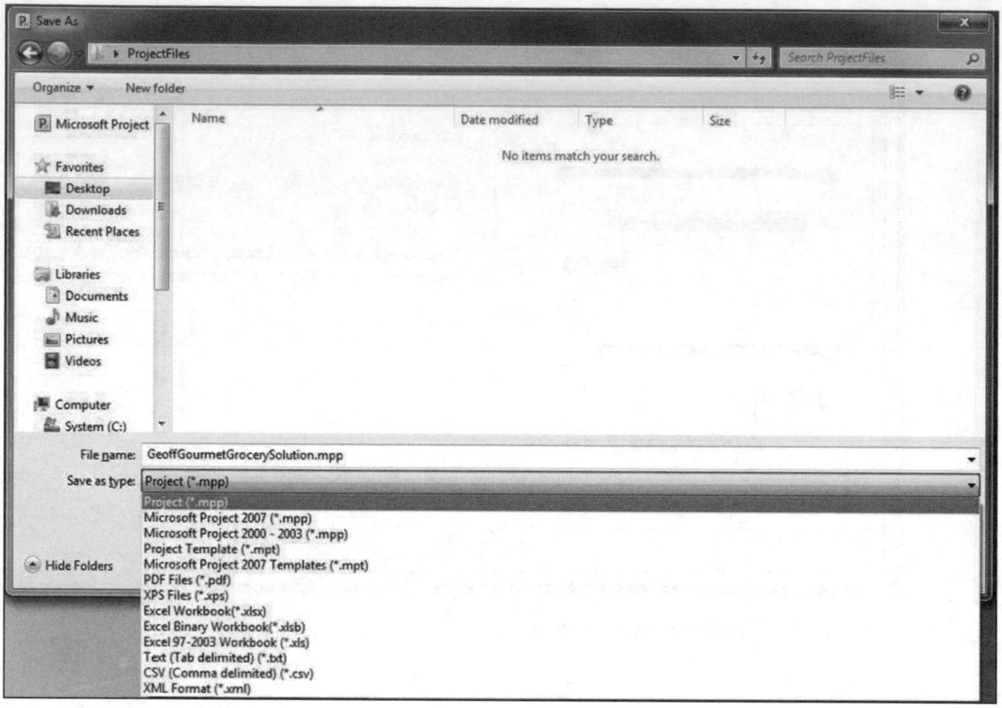

FIGURE A6-14   Exporting Project Files to Different Formats

6.4 DISPLAYING TASK COMPLETION

To show that a task is complete, you need to change the task information. To do this, right-click the task and select Task Information. The Task Information screen, shown in Figure A6-15, appears. You can change the completion of the task by using the Percent Complete field. Setting Percent Complete to 100% shows that the task is finished, and actual costs will now be assigned to the task. (This is done even if the percentage is below 100 percent.) To change the format of the progress lines that appear on the Gantt chart bars for task completion, select Format Tab | Gridlines, then select Progress Lines. Next, select the Line Styles tab and the screen shown in Figure A6-16 appears.

6.5 USING PREDEFINED REPORTS

You can generate several different predefined reports by using Microsoft Project, including earned value management reports. To create one of these, select Project tab and then either Visual Reports or Reports from the ribbon. The report categories are displayed: Overview, Current Activities, Costs, Assignments, Workload, and Custom (see Figure A6-17). To select

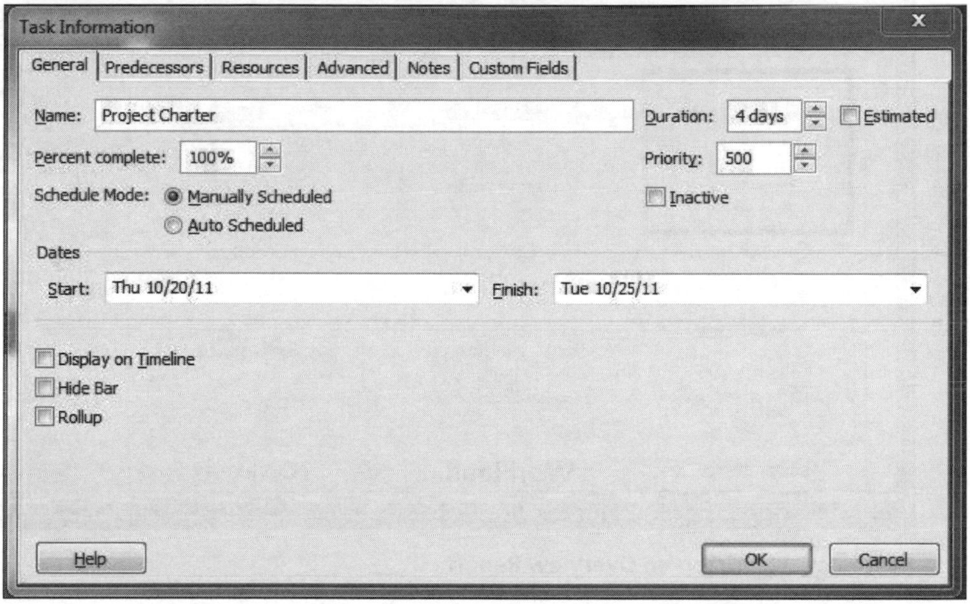

FIGURE A6-15 Changing the Percent Complete Field

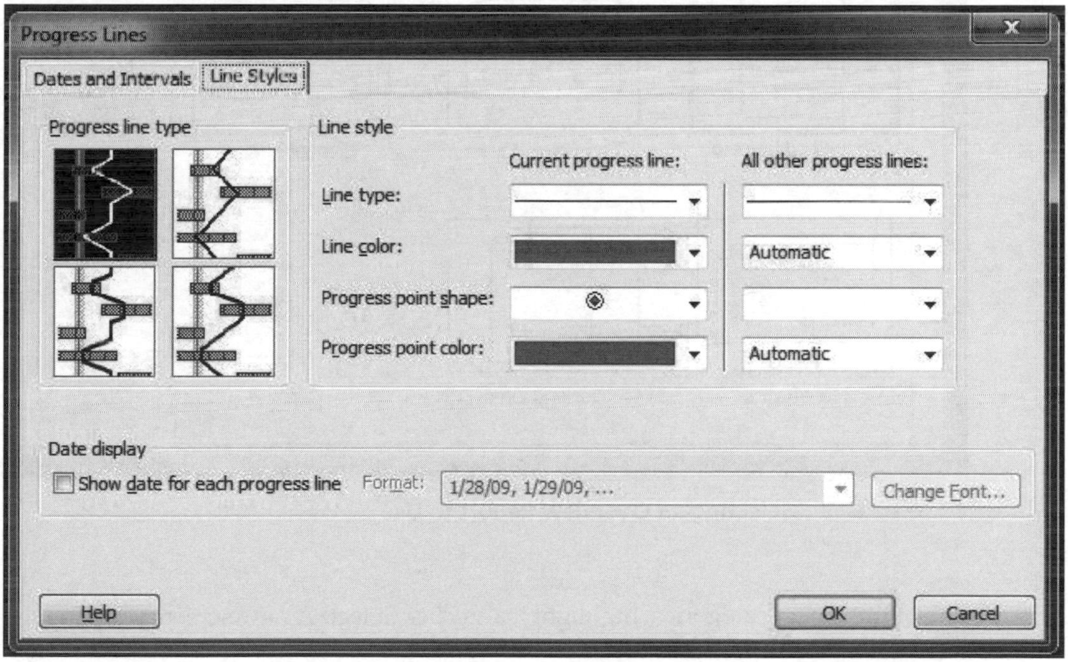

FIGURE A6-16 Choosing the Progress Lines

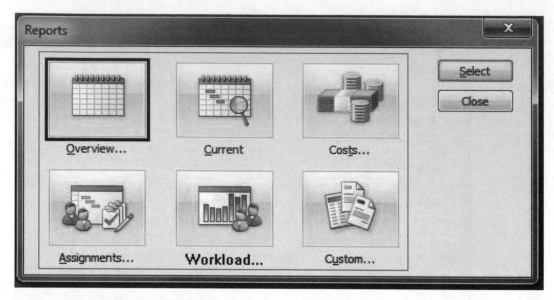

FIGURE A6-17   Using an Overview Report

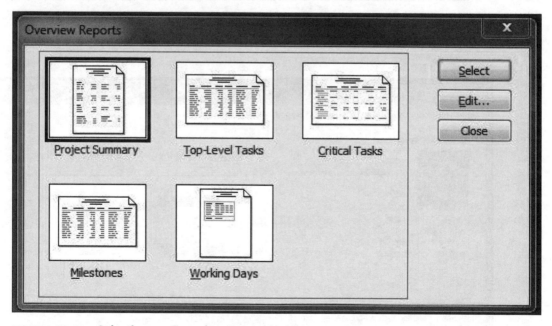

FIGURE A6-18   Selecting an Overview Report to Use

one of the report categories, highlight it and click Select. A new screen, showing the various reports that are available within each category, appears. Highlight the specific report to use and click Select to display the report. Figure A6-18 shows the reports available in the Overview category, and Figure A6-19 shows the reports available in the Assignment category.

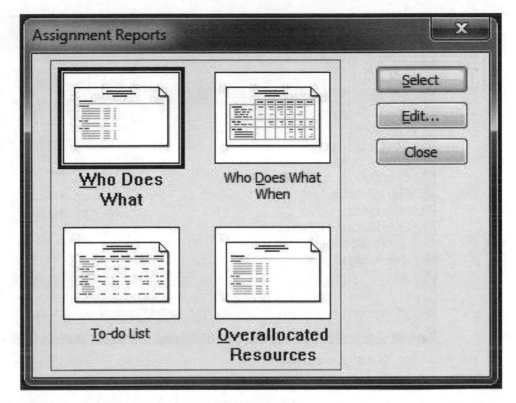

FIGURE A6-19 **Selecting an Assignment Report to Use**

6.6 CREATING CUSTOM REPORTS

The Custom report option, shown in Figure A6-17, contains many different options. After you select the option to use a custom report, the screen shown in Figure A6-20 appears, displaying custom report options that offer default formats that can be customized. Clicking the Setup button allows you to make changes to the page, margin, header, and footer formatting on the report. Clicking the Edit button allows you to change the data on the report. Clicking the Organizer button allows you to change many different options related to organization of the report. Clicking New allows you to select four different reports: task report, resource report, monthly calendar report, and crosstab report. Figures A6-21 through A6-25 show the selection of settings that can be changed for each type of report.

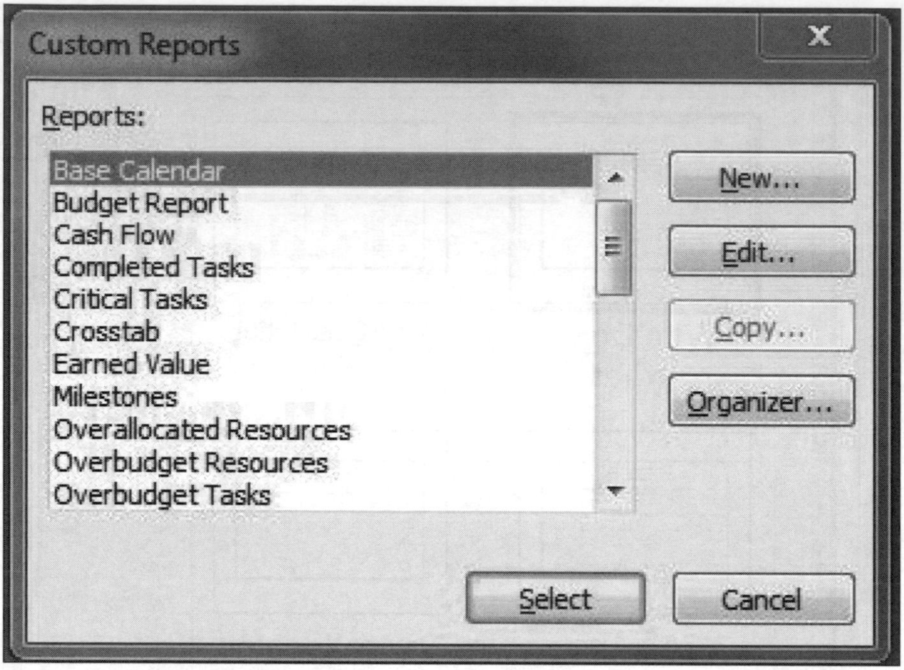

FIGURE A6-20   **Selecting the Report to Use**

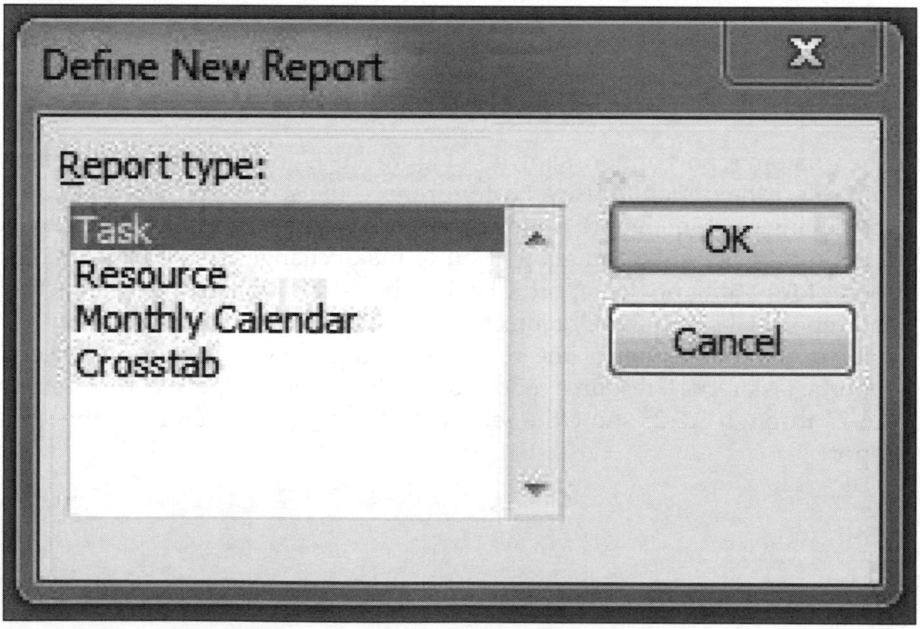

FIGURE A6-21   **Selecting the Type of Report to Generate**

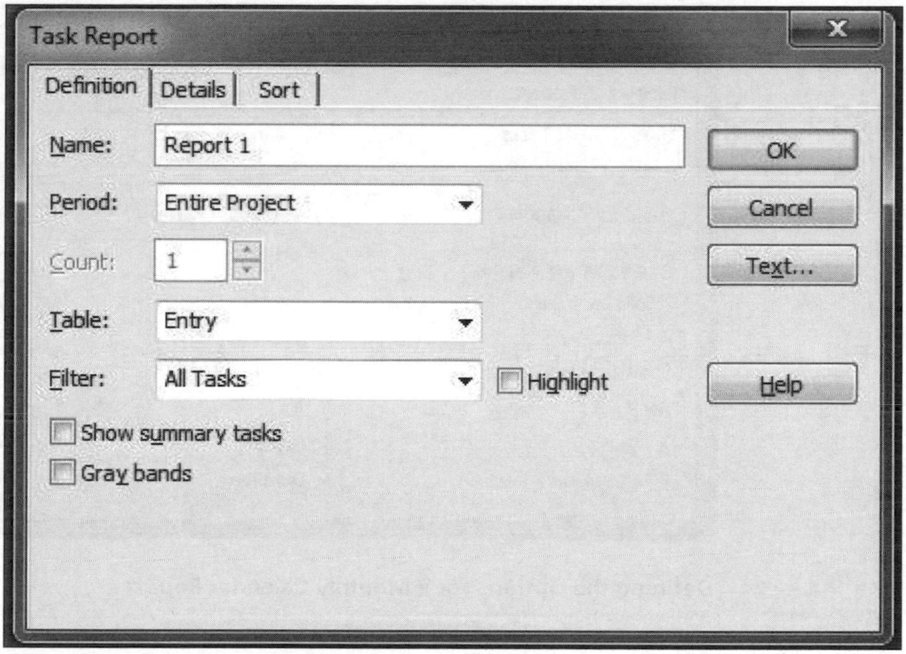

FIGURE A6-22   Defining Options for a Task Report

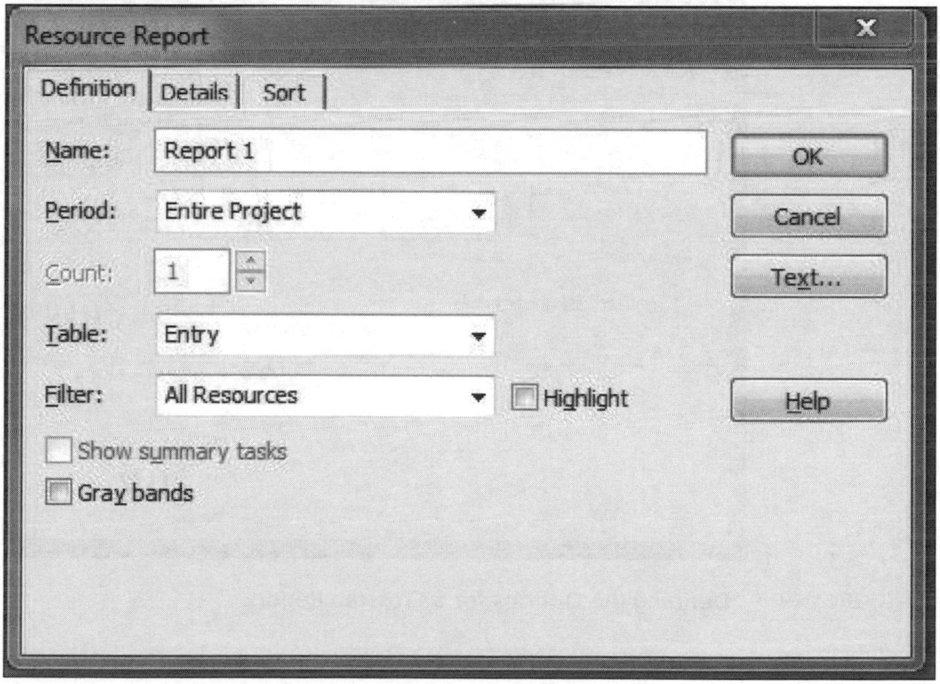

FIGURE A6-23   Defining Options for a Resource Report

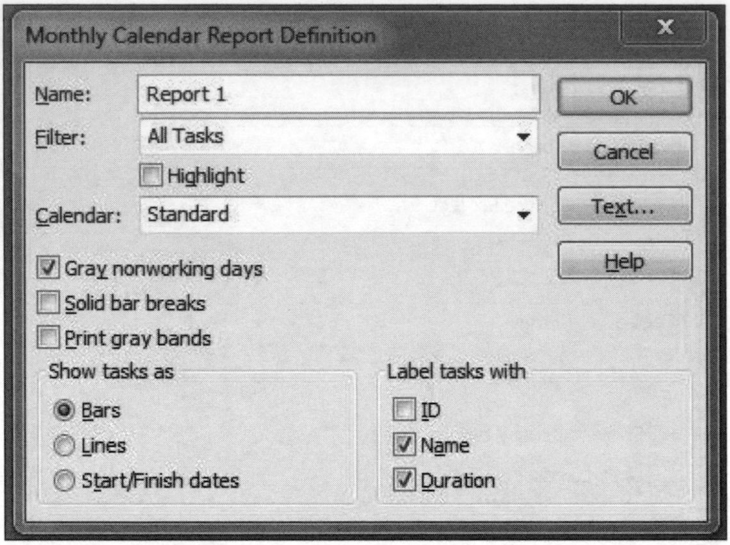

FIGURE A6-24   Defining the Options for a Monthly Calendar Report

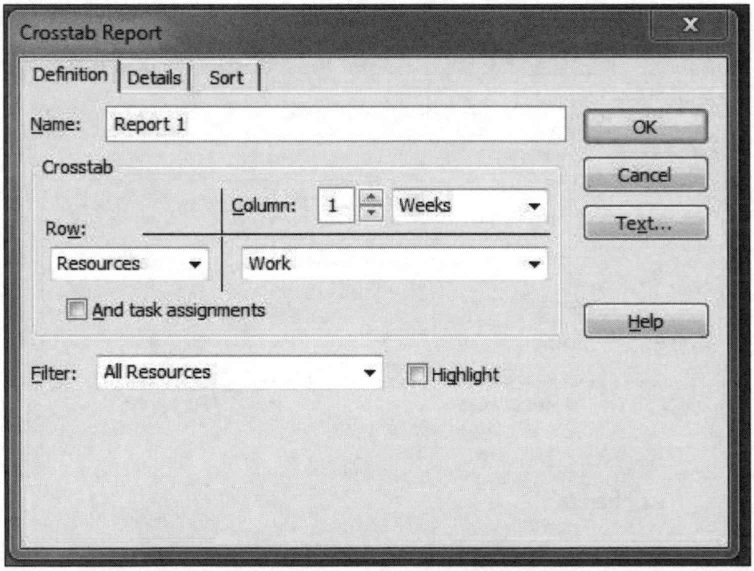

FIGURE A6-25   Defining the Options for a Crosstab Report

Selecting the Visual Reports option will display the screen shown in Figure A6-26. The reports are broken down into topic areas such as Task Summary or Resource Summary, or you can just view them all using the "All" tab. The reports, once generated, will launch either Microsoft Excel and present the results or Microsoft Visio.

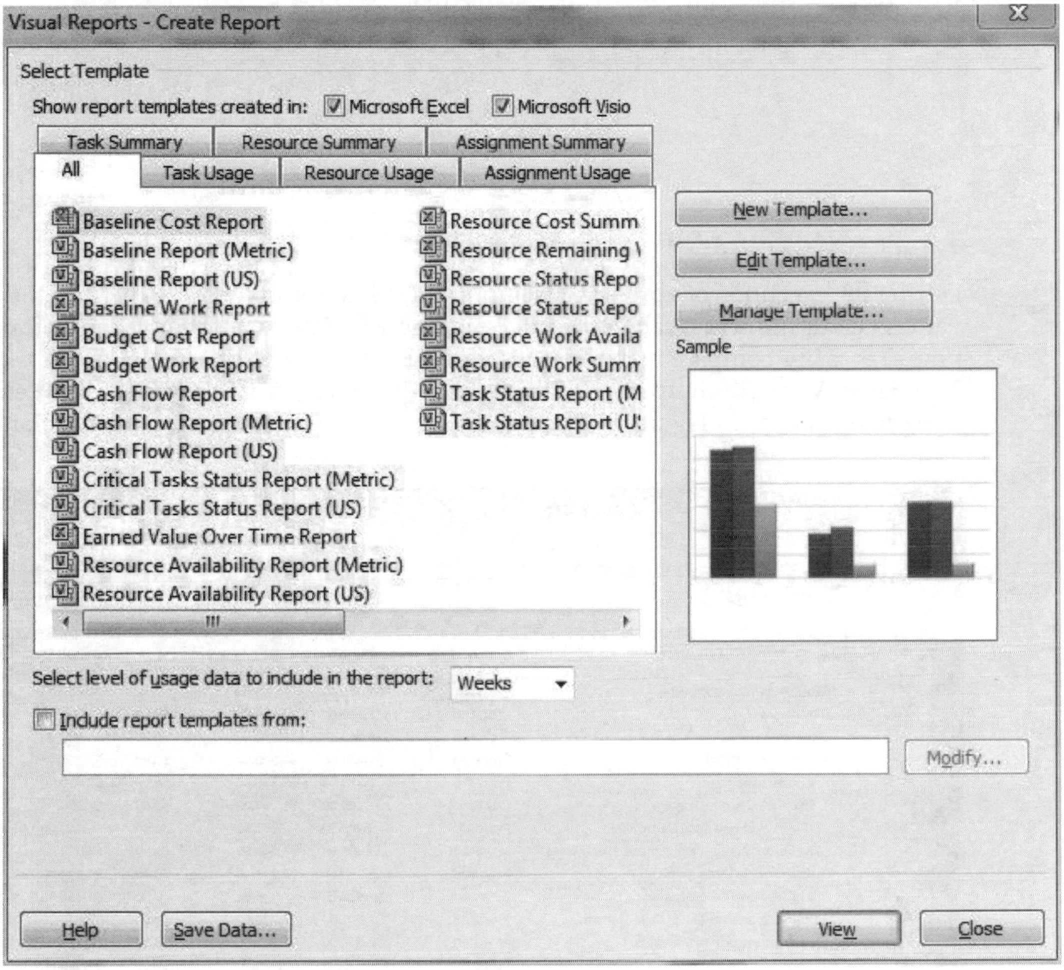

FIGURE A6-26   Displaying the Cost Table

Unit 6 Exercises

A. Display the Gantt Chart view and then make the following display changes:
  1. Ensure that the chart fits on one landscape-oriented 8.5 × 11 page when printed and is readable.
  2. Display only Level 1 and Level 2 tasks.
  3. Change the timescale to accommodate the chart being printed on one page.
  4. Display the total cost column amount above each bar in the Gantt chart.
B. Export a picture of the Gantt chart to a GIF image file.
C. Generate a standard Assignments report called Who Does What When and review it.

7.0 TRACKING PROGRESS

7.1 PLANNED VERSUS ACTUAL AMOUNTS

During the execution of a project, it is important to know and consistently track the planned values versus the actual values to understand why variances may be occurring for cost and time. To easily compare planned costs against actual costs, select View Tab, then select Task Sheet View. Then select the Tables pull down menu from the ribbon and select Cost. The screen shown in Figure A7-1 appears. To compare the variances among planned and

	Task Name	Fixed Cost Accrual	Cost	Baseline Cost	Cost Variance	Actual Cost	Remaining Cost
1	⊟ GeoffGourmetGrocerySolution	Prorated	$359,492.40	$0.00	$359,492.40	$98,280.00	$261,212.40
2	⊟ Preliminary Work	Prorated	$47,520.00	$47,520.00	$0.00	$47,520.00	$0.00
3	Project Charter	Prorated	$18,240.00	$18,240.00	$0.00	$18,240.00	$0.00
4	⊟ Statement of Work	Prorated	$7,520.00	$7,520.00	$0.00	$7,520.00	$0.00
5	Context Diagram	Prorated	$1,760.00	$1,760.00	$0.00	$1,760.00	$0.00
6	Use Case Model Diagram	Prorated	$1,280.00	$1,280.00	$0.00	$1,280.00	$0.00
7	High-Level Use Case Narratives	Prorated	$880.00	$880.00	$0.00	$880.00	$0.00
8	Develop Change Mangement Procedures	Prorated	$3,600.00	$3,600.00	$0.00	$3,600.00	$0.00
9	⊟ Requirements Definition	Prorated	$9,120.00	$9,120.00	$0.00	$9,120.00	$0.00
10	Refined Use Case Diagram	Prorated	$1,920.00	$1,920.00	$0.00	$1,920.00	$0.00
11	Requirment-Level Use Case Narratives	Prorated	$2,640.00	$2,640.00	$0.00	$2,640.00	$0.00
12	System Sequence Diagrams	Prorated	$2,640.00	$2,640.00	$0.00	$2,640.00	$0.00
13	Refined User Interface Model	Prorated	$1,920.00	$1,920.00	$0.00	$1,920.00	$0.00
14	⊟ System Architecture Model	Prorated	$12,640.00	$12,640.00	$0.00	$12,640.00	$0.00
15	Network Context Diagram	Prorated	$520.00	$520.00	$0.00	$520.00	$0.00
16	Package Diagrams	Prorated	$1,160.00	$1,160.00	$0.00	$1,160.00	$0.00
17	Component Diagrams	Prorated	$4,640.00	$4,640.00	$0.00	$4,640.00	$0.00
18	Deployment Diagrams	Prorated	$3,520.00	$3,520.00	$0.00	$3,520.00	$0.00
19	System Network Diagram	Prorated	$2,800.00	$2,800.00	$0.00	$2,800.00	$0.00

FIGURE A7-1   Displaying the Cost Table

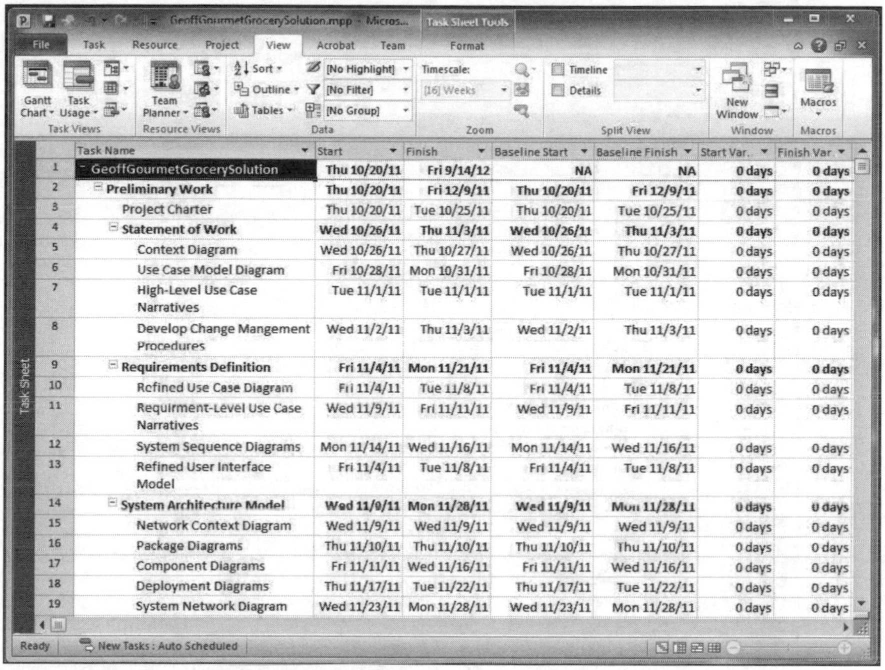

	Task Name	Start	Finish	Baseline Start	Baseline Finish	Start Var.	Finish Var.
1	GeoffGourmetGrocerySolution	Thu 10/20/11	Fri 9/14/12	NA	NA	0 days	0 days
2	Preliminary Work	Thu 10/20/11	Fri 12/9/11	Thu 10/20/11	Fri 12/9/11	0 days	0 days
3	Project Charter	Thu 10/20/11	Tue 10/25/11	Thu 10/20/11	Tue 10/25/11	0 days	0 days
4	Statement of Work	Wed 10/26/11	Thu 11/3/11	Wed 10/26/11	Thu 11/3/11	0 days	0 days
5	Context Diagram	Wed 10/26/11	Thu 10/27/11	Wed 10/26/11	Thu 10/27/11	0 days	0 days
6	Use Case Model Diagram	Fri 10/28/11	Mon 10/31/11	Fri 10/28/11	Mon 10/31/11	0 days	0 days
7	High-Level Use Case Narratives	Tue 11/1/11	Tue 11/1/11	Tue 11/1/11	Tue 11/1/11	0 days	0 days
8	Develop Change Mangement Procedures	Wed 11/2/11	Thu 11/3/11	Wed 11/2/11	Thu 11/3/11	0 days	0 days
9	Requirements Definition	Fri 11/4/11	Mon 11/21/11	Fri 11/4/11	Mon 11/21/11	0 days	0 days
10	Refined Use Case Diagram	Fri 11/4/11	Tue 11/8/11	Fri 11/4/11	Tue 11/8/11	0 days	0 days
11	Requirment-Level Use Case Narratives	Wed 11/9/11	Fri 11/11/11	Wed 11/9/11	Fri 11/11/11	0 days	0 days
12	System Sequence Diagrams	Mon 11/14/11	Wed 11/16/11	Mon 11/14/11	Wed 11/16/11	0 days	0 days
13	Refined User Interface Model	Fri 11/4/11	Tue 11/8/11	Fri 11/4/11	Tue 11/8/11	0 days	0 days
14	System Architecture Model	Wed 11/9/11	Mon 11/28/11	Wed 11/9/11	Mon 11/28/11	0 days	0 days
15	Network Context Diagram	Wed 11/9/11	Wed 11/9/11	Wed 11/9/11	Wed 11/9/11	0 days	0 days
16	Package Diagrams	Thu 11/10/11	Thu 11/10/11	Thu 11/10/11	Thu 11/10/11	0 days	0 days
17	Component Diagrams	Fri 11/11/11	Wed 11/16/11	Fri 11/11/11	Wed 11/16/11	0 days	0 days
18	Deployment Diagrams	Thu 11/17/11	Tue 11/22/11	Thu 11/17/11	Tue 11/22/11	0 days	0 days
19	System Network Diagram	Wed 11/23/11	Mon 11/28/11	Wed 11/23/11	Mon 11/28/11	0 days	0 days

FIGURE A7-2 Displaying the Variance Table

actual amounts for the time on the project, select Table pull down once again and select the Variance option. The screen shown in Figure A7-2 appears.

7.2 TRACKING PROJECT PERCENTAGE COMPLETION

To view the percentage of completion for a project, insert the % Complete column on the task sheet. Figure A7-3 displays this column and the detail it provides. As shown in the figure, this project is 25 percent complete. This column can also be used to enter the task completion percentage. You can also view the project completion information by selecting Table pull down menu from the ribbon and select Tracking. The screen shown in Figure A7-4 appears, for displaying tracking information for the project.

7.3 TRACKING ACTUAL HOURS WORKED

To see the actual hours worked on the task sheet, you need to insert the Actual Work column, which displays the actual hours worked for each task and the whole project, as shown in Figure A7-5. You can view this, along with other work information, by displaying the Work table (see Figure A7-6). You open the Work table by selecting the Table pull down menu from the ribbon and select Work.

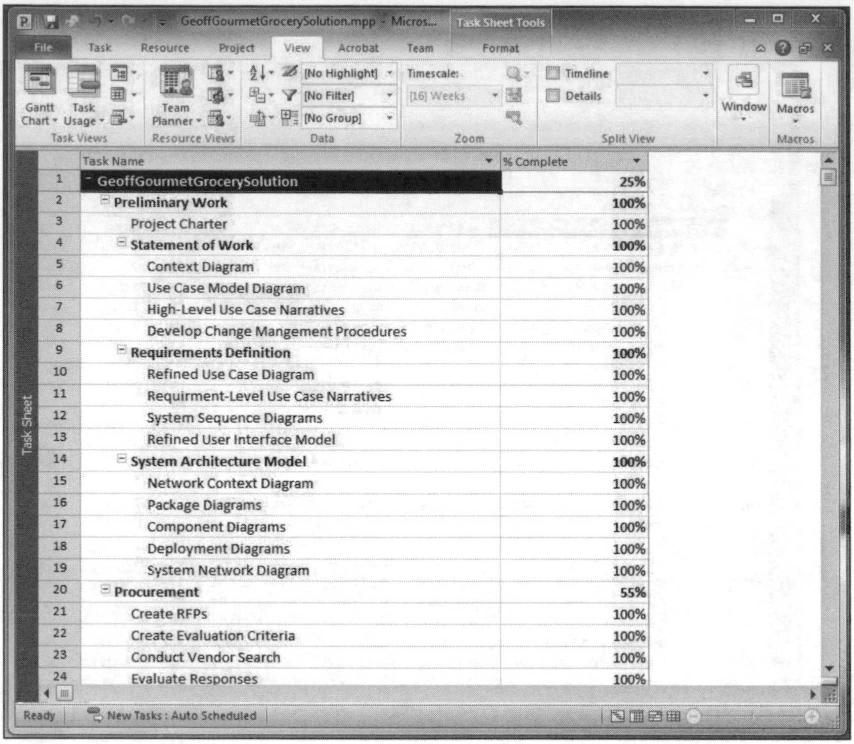

FIGURE A7-3   Displaying the % Complete Field

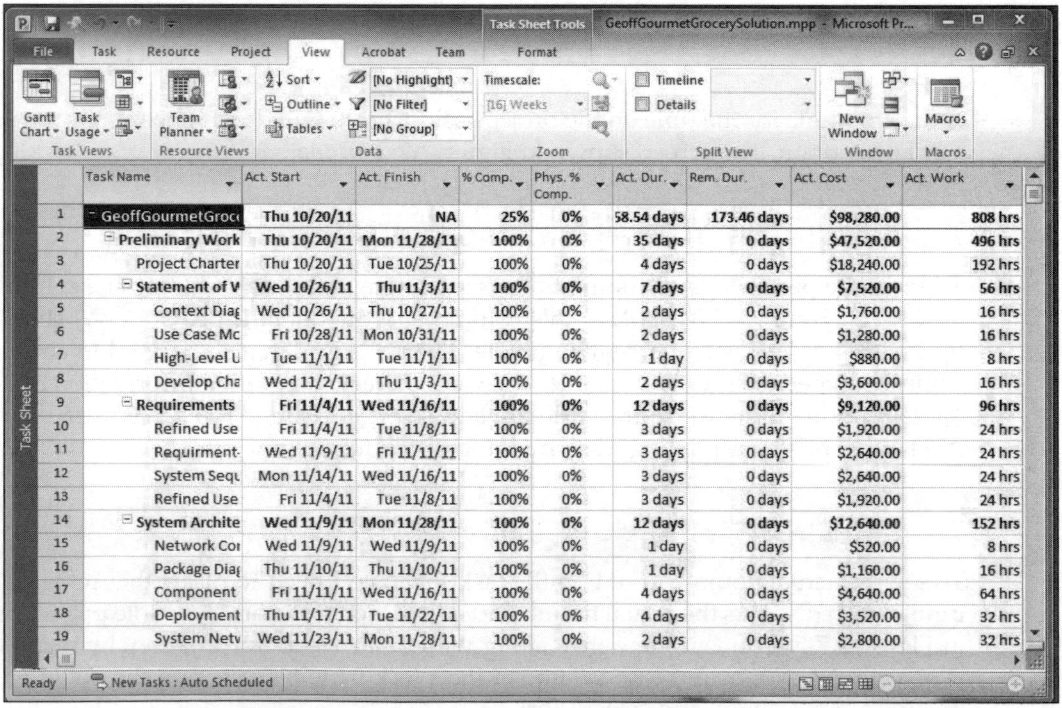

The Task Sheet view showing the % Complete field:

	Task Name	% Complete
1	GeoffGourmetGrocerySolution	25%
2	Preliminary Work	100%
3	Project Charter	100%
4	Statement of Work	100%
5	Context Diagram	100%
6	Use Case Model Diagram	100%
7	High-Level Use Case Narratives	100%
8	Develop Change Mangement Procedures	100%
9	Requirements Definition	100%
10	Refined Use Case Diagram	100%
11	Requirment-Level Use Case Narratives	100%
12	System Sequence Diagrams	100%
13	Refined User Interface Model	100%
14	System Architecture Model	100%
15	Network Context Diagram	100%
16	Package Diagrams	100%
17	Component Diagrams	100%
18	Deployment Diagrams	100%
19	System Network Diagram	100%
20	Procurement	55%
21	Create RFPs	100%
22	Create Evaluation Criteria	100%
23	Conduct Vendor Search	100%
24	Evaluate Responses	100%

FIGURE A7-4   Displaying the Tracking Table

The Task Sheet view showing the Tracking Table:

	Task Name	Act. Start	Act. Finish	% Comp.	Phys. % Comp.	Act. Dur.	Rem. Dur.	Act. Cost	Act. Work
1	GeoffGourmetGroce	Thu 10/20/11	NA	25%	0%	58.54 days	173.46 days	$98,280.00	808 hrs
2	Preliminary Work	Thu 10/20/11	Mon 11/28/11	100%	0%	35 days	0 days	$47,520.00	496 hrs
3	Project Charter	Thu 10/20/11	Tue 10/25/11	100%	0%	4 days	0 days	$18,240.00	192 hrs
4	Statement of V	Wed 10/26/11	Thu 11/3/11	100%	0%	7 days	0 days	$7,520.00	56 hrs
5	Context Diag	Wed 10/26/11	Thu 10/27/11	100%	0%	2 days	0 days	$1,760.00	16 hrs
6	Use Case Mc	Fri 10/28/11	Mon 10/31/11	100%	0%	2 days	0 days	$1,280.00	16 hrs
7	High-Level U	Tue 11/1/11	Tue 11/1/11	100%	0%	1 day	0 days	$880.00	8 hrs
8	Develop Cha	Wed 11/2/11	Thu 11/3/11	100%	0%	2 days	0 days	$3,600.00	16 hrs
9	Requirements	Fri 11/4/11	Wed 11/16/11	100%	0%	12 days	0 days	$9,120.00	96 hrs
10	Refined Use	Fri 11/4/11	Tue 11/8/11	100%	0%	3 days	0 days	$1,920.00	24 hrs
11	Requirment-	Wed 11/9/11	Fri 11/11/11	100%	0%	3 days	0 days	$2,640.00	24 hrs
12	System Sequ	Mon 11/14/11	Wed 11/16/11	100%	0%	3 days	0 days	$2,640.00	24 hrs
13	Refined Use	Fri 11/4/11	Tue 11/8/11	100%	0%	3 days	0 days	$1,920.00	24 hrs
14	System Archite	Wed 11/9/11	Mon 11/28/11	100%	0%	12 days	0 days	$12,640.00	152 hrs
15	Network Cor	Wed 11/9/11	Wed 11/9/11	100%	0%	1 day	0 days	$520.00	8 hrs
16	Package Diag	Thu 11/10/11	Thu 11/10/11	100%	0%	1 day	0 days	$1,160.00	16 hrs
17	Component	Fri 11/11/11	Wed 11/16/11	100%	0%	4 days	0 days	$4,640.00	64 hrs
18	Deployment	Thu 11/17/11	Tue 11/22/11	100%	0%	4 days	0 days	$3,520.00	32 hrs
19	System Netv	Wed 11/23/11	Mon 11/28/11	100%	0%	2 days	0 days	$2,800.00	32 hrs

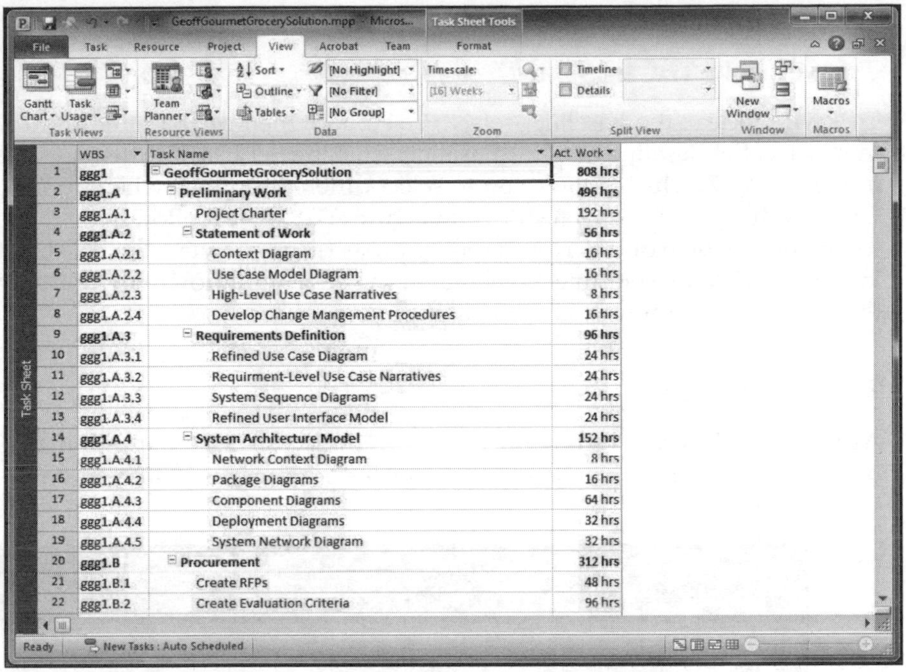

	WBS	Task Name	Act. Work
1	ggg1	GeoffGourmetGrocerySolution	808 hrs
2	ggg1.A	Preliminary Work	496 hrs
3	ggg1.A.1	Project Charter	192 hrs
4	ggg1.A.2	Statement of Work	56 hrs
5	ggg1.A.2.1	Context Diagram	16 hrs
6	ggg1.A.2.2	Use Case Model Diagram	16 hrs
7	ggg1.A.2.3	High-Level Use Case Narratives	8 hrs
8	ggg1.A.2.4	Develop Change Mangement Procedures	16 hrs
9	ggg1.A.3	Requirements Definition	96 hrs
10	ggg1.A.3.1	Refined Use Case Diagram	24 hrs
11	ggg1.A.3.2	Requirment-Level Use Case Narratives	24 hrs
12	ggg1.A.3.3	System Sequence Diagrams	24 hrs
13	ggg1.A.3.4	Refined User Interface Model	24 hrs
14	ggg1.A.4	System Architecture Model	152 hrs
15	ggg1.A.4.1	Network Context Diagram	8 hrs
16	ggg1.A.4.2	Package Diagrams	16 hrs
17	ggg1.A.4.3	Component Diagrams	64 hrs
18	ggg1.A.4.4	Deployment Diagrams	32 hrs
19	ggg1.A.4.5	System Network Diagram	32 hrs
20	ggg1.B	Procurement	312 hrs
21	ggg1.B.1	Create RFPs	48 hrs
22	ggg1.B.2	Create Evaluation Criteria	96 hrs

FIGURE A7-5 Displaying the Actual Work Column

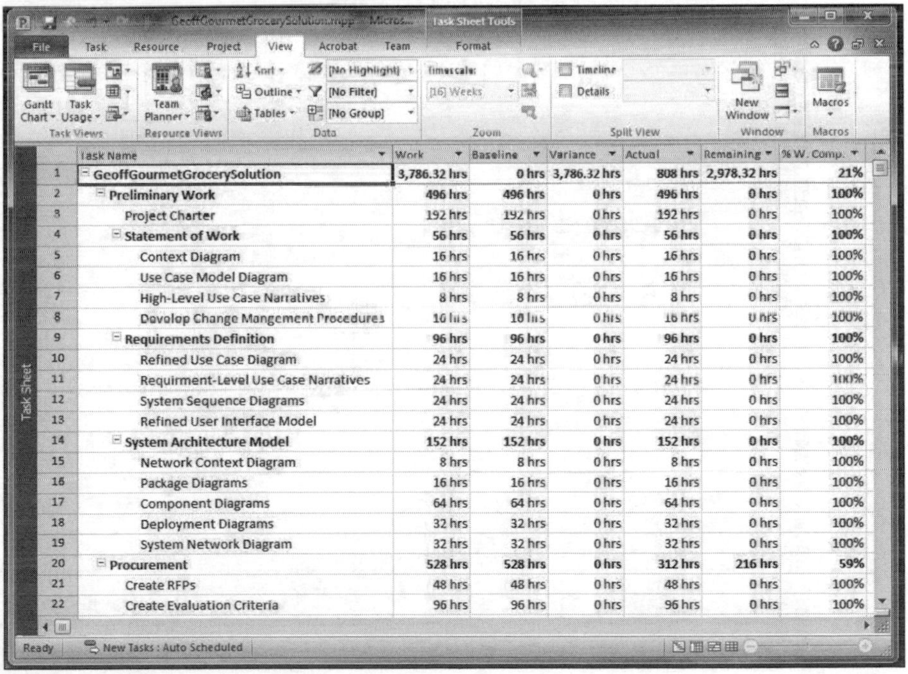

	Task Name	Work	Baseline	Variance	Actual	Remaining	% W. Comp.
1	GeoffGourmetGrocerySolution	3,786.32 hrs	0 hrs	3,786.32 hrs	808 hrs	2,978.32 hrs	21%
2	Preliminary Work	496 hrs	496 hrs	0 hrs	496 hrs	0 hrs	100%
3	Project Charter	192 hrs	192 hrs	0 hrs	192 hrs	0 hrs	100%
4	Statement of Work	56 hrs	56 hrs	0 hrs	56 hrs	0 hrs	100%
5	Context Diagram	16 hrs	16 hrs	0 hrs	16 hrs	0 hrs	100%
6	Use Case Model Diagram	16 hrs	16 hrs	0 hrs	16 hrs	0 hrs	100%
7	High-Level Use Case Narratives	8 hrs	8 hrs	0 hrs	8 hrs	0 hrs	100%
8	Develop Change Mangement Procedures	16 hrs	16 hrs	0 hrs	16 hrs	0 hrs	100%
9	Requirements Definition	96 hrs	96 hrs	0 hrs	96 hrs	0 hrs	100%
10	Refined Use Case Diagram	24 hrs	24 hrs	0 hrs	24 hrs	0 hrs	100%
11	Requirment-Level Use Case Narratives	24 hrs	24 hrs	0 hrs	24 hrs	0 hrs	100%
12	System Sequence Diagrams	24 hrs	24 hrs	0 hrs	24 hrs	0 hrs	100%
13	Refined User Interface Model	24 hrs	24 hrs	0 hrs	24 hrs	0 hrs	100%
14	System Architecture Model	152 hrs	152 hrs	0 hrs	152 hrs	0 hrs	100%
15	Network Context Diagram	8 hrs	8 hrs	0 hrs	8 hrs	0 hrs	100%
16	Package Diagrams	16 hrs	16 hrs	0 hrs	16 hrs	0 hrs	100%
17	Component Diagrams	64 hrs	64 hrs	0 hrs	64 hrs	0 hrs	100%
18	Deployment Diagrams	32 hrs	32 hrs	0 hrs	32 hrs	0 hrs	100%
19	System Network Diagram	32 hrs	32 hrs	0 hrs	32 hrs	0 hrs	100%
20	Procurement	528 hrs	528 hrs	0 hrs	312 hrs	216 hrs	59%
21	Create RFPs	48 hrs	48 hrs	0 hrs	48 hrs	0 hrs	100%
22	Create Evaluation Criteria	96 hrs	96 hrs	0 hrs	96 hrs	0 hrs	100%

FIGURE A7-6 Displaying the Work Table

7.4 SETTING THE BASELINE

To save or clear the baseline, select Project tab, then set Baseline from the ribbon, and then select Set Baseline or Clear Baseline. Clicking Set Baseline displays the screen shown in Figure A7-7, which allows you to select different options when saving. Clicking Clear Baseline displays the screen shown in Figure A7-8, which allows you to clear the baseline for an interim plan or tasks for the entire project. You can view the Baseline table, as shown in Figure A7-9, by selecting View tab on the Table pull down menu from the ribbon and then select More Tables and then Baseline.

7.5 VARIANCES

As mentioned earlier, Project provides a premade Variances table that allows you to view the variance information. Refer to Section 7.1 for more information on viewing variance information.

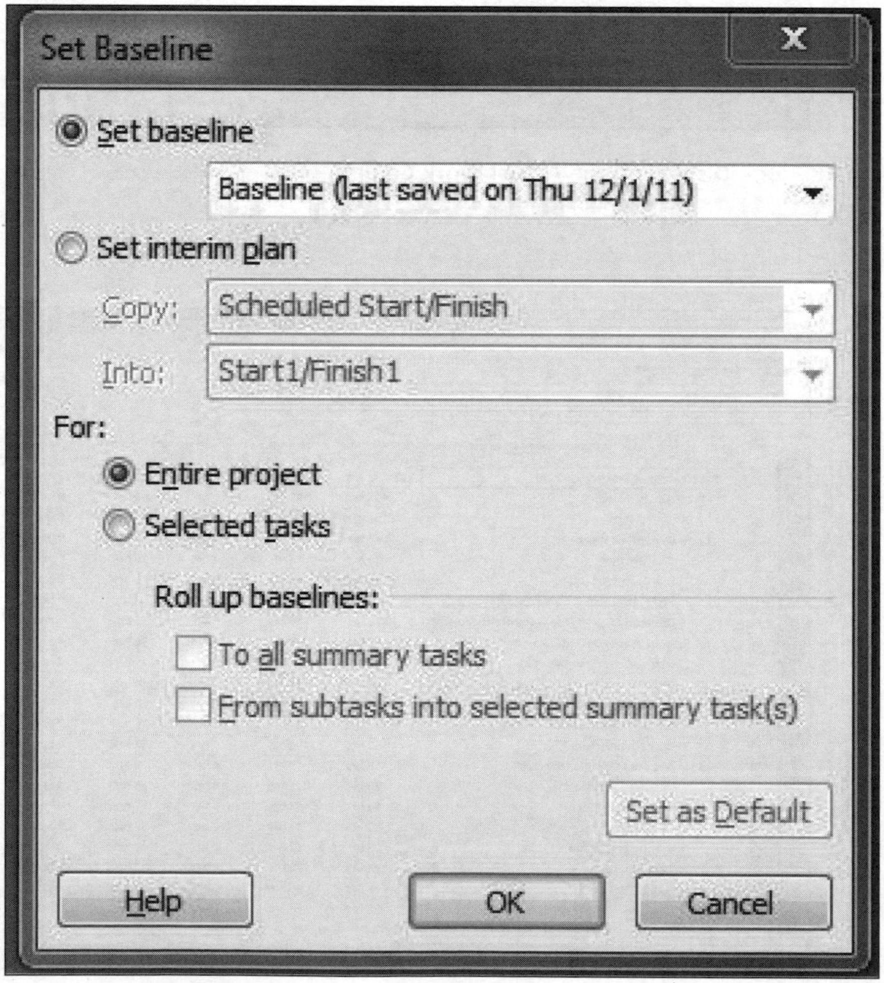

FIGURE A7-7   Saving the Baseline

Clear Baseline

○ Clear baseline plan   Baseline (last saved on Thu 12/1/11) ▼

○ Clear interim plan   Start1/Finish1 ▼

For   ● Entire project   ○ Selected tasks

       [OK]   [Cancel]

FIGURE A7-8   **Clearing the Baseline**

	Task Name	Baseline Dur.	Baseline Start	Baseline Finish	Baseline Work	Baseline Cost
1	GeoffGourmetGrocerySolution	0 days	NA	NA	0 hrs	$0.00
2	Preliminary Work	35 days	Thu 10/20/11	Fri 12/9/11	496 hrs	$47,520.00
3	Project Charter	4 days	Thu 10/20/11	Tue 10/25/11	192 hrs	$18,240.00
4	Statement of Work	7 days	Wed 10/26/11	Thu 11/3/11	56 hrs	$7,520.00
5	Context Diagram	2 days	Wed 10/26/11	Thu 10/27/11	16 hrs	$1,760.00
6	Use Case Model Diagram	2 days	Fri 10/28/11	Mon 10/31/11	16 hrs	$1,280.00
7	High-Level Use Case Narratives	1 day	Tue 11/1/11	Tue 11/1/11	8 hrs	$880.00
8	Develop Change Mangement Procedures	2 days	Wed 11/2/11	Thu 11/3/11	16 hrs	$3,600.00
9	Requirements Definition	12 days	Fri 11/4/11	Mon 11/21/11	96 hrs	$9,120.00
10	Refined Use Case Diagram	3 days	Fri 11/4/11	Tue 11/8/11	24 hrs	$1,920.00
11	Requirment-Level Use Case Narratives	3 days	Wed 11/9/11	Fri 11/11/11	24 hrs	$2,640.00
12	System Sequence Diagrams	3 days	Mon 11/14/11	Wed 11/16/11	24 hrs	$2,640.00
13	Refined User Interface Model	3 days	Fri 11/4/11	Tue 11/8/11	24 hrs	$1,920.00
14	System Architecture Model	12 days	Wed 11/9/11	Mon 11/28/11	152 hrs	$12,640.00
15	Network Context Diagram	1 day	Wed 11/9/11	Wed 11/9/11	8 hrs	$520.00
16	Package Diagrams	1 day	Thu 11/10/11	Thu 11/10/11	16 hrs	$1,160.00
17	Component Diagrams	4 days	Fri 11/11/11	Wed 11/16/11	64 hrs	$4,640.00
18	Deployment Diagrams	4 days	Thu 11/17/11	Tue 11/22/11	32 hrs	$3,520.00
19	System Network Diagram	2 days	Wed 11/23/11	Mon 11/28/11	32 hrs	$2,800.00
20	Procurement	60 days	Tue 11/29/11	Thu 2/23/12	528 hrs	$74,400.00
21	Create RFPs	6 days	Tue 11/29/11	Tue 12/6/11	48 hrs	$10,800.00

Ready   New Tasks : Auto Scheduled

FIGURE A7-9   **Displaying the Baseline Table**

7.6 THE TRACKING GANTT CHART

To view the tracking Gantt chart for the project, select View tab, then select Tracking Gantt Chart from the list of views. The screen shown in Figure A7-10 appears, displaying the percentage completion of tasks.

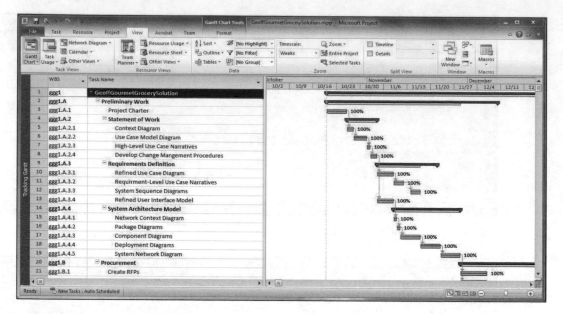

FIGURE A7-10   Displaying the Tracking Gantt Chart

7.7 EARNED VALUE

Earned value (EV) is calculated as the project percentage completion multiplied by the worked scheduled to be performed, or planned value. EV is what the project is worth at this point in the project life cycle. EV can be viewed in Microsoft Project as budgeted cost of work performed (BCWP). To view information for the EV on a project, select View tab, then the Table pull down menu from the ribbon and select more tables, then select Earned Value. The screen in Figure A7-11 appears, showing all the EV information.

Note: Actual cost and ACWP are the same thing.

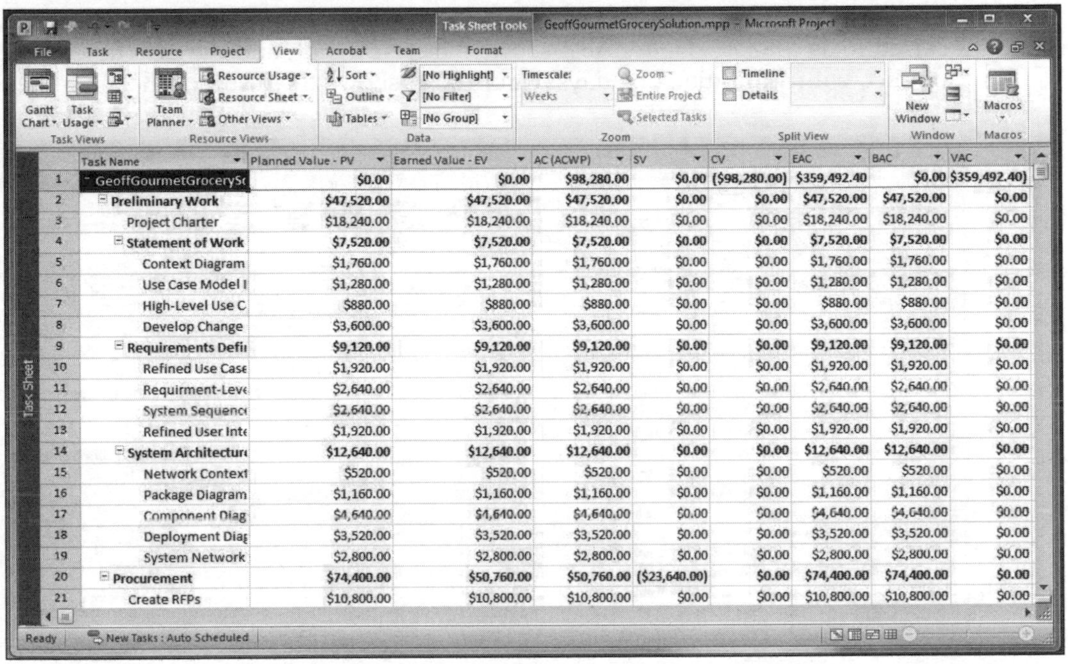

	Task Name	Planned Value - PV	Earned Value - EV	AC (ACWP)	SV	CV	EAC	BAC	VAC
1	GeoffGourmetGroceryS	$0.00	$0.00	$98,280.00	$0.00	($98,280.00)	$359,492.40	$0.00	$359,492.40)
2	**Preliminary Work**	**$47,520.00**	**$47,520.00**	**$47,520.00**	**$0.00**	**$0.00**	**$47,520.00**	**$47,520.00**	**$0.00**
3	Project Charter	$18,240.00	$18,240.00	$18,240.00	$0.00	$0.00	$18,240.00	$18,240.00	$0.00
4	**Statement of Work**	**$7,520.00**	**$7,520.00**	**$7,520.00**	**$0.00**	**$0.00**	**$7,520.00**	**$7,520.00**	**$0.00**
5	Context Diagram	$1,760.00	$1,760.00	$1,760.00	$0.00	$0.00	$1,760.00	$1,760.00	$0.00
6	Use Case Model I	$1,280.00	$1,280.00	$1,280.00	$0.00	$0.00	$1,280.00	$1,280.00	$0.00
7	High-Level Use C	$880.00	$880.00	$880.00	$0.00	$0.00	$880.00	$880.00	$0.00
8	Develop Change	$3,600.00	$3,600.00	$3,600.00	$0.00	$0.00	$3,600.00	$3,600.00	$0.00
9	**Requirements Defi**	**$9,120.00**	**$9,120.00**	**$9,120.00**	**$0.00**	**$0.00**	**$9,120.00**	**$9,120.00**	**$0.00**
10	Refined Use Case	$1,920.00	$1,920.00	$1,920.00	$0.00	$0.00	$1,920.00	$1,920.00	$0.00
11	Requirment-Leve	$2,640.00	$2,640.00	$2,640.00	$0.00	$0.00	$2,640.00	$2,640.00	$0.00
12	System Sequenc	$2,640.00	$2,640.00	$2,640.00	$0.00	$0.00	$2,640.00	$2,640.00	$0.00
13	Refined User Int	$1,920.00	$1,920.00	$1,920.00	$0.00	$0.00	$1,920.00	$1,920.00	$0.00
14	**System Architectur**	**$12,640.00**	**$12,640.00**	**$12,640.00**	**$0.00**	**$0.00**	**$12,640.00**	**$12,640.00**	**$0.00**
15	Network Context	$520.00	$520.00	$520.00	$0.00	$0.00	$520.00	$520.00	$0.00
16	Package Diagram	$1,160.00	$1,160.00	$1,160.00	$0.00	$0.00	$1,160.00	$1,160.00	$0.00
17	Component Diag	$4,640.00	$4,640.00	$4,640.00	$0.00	$0.00	$4,640.00	$4,640.00	$0.00
18	Deployment Diag	$3,520.00	$3,520.00	$3,520.00	$0.00	$0.00	$3,520.00	$3,520.00	$0.00
19	System Network	$2,800.00	$2,800.00	$2,800.00	$0.00	$0.00	$2,800.00	$2,800.00	$0.00
20	**Procurement**	**$74,400.00**	**$50,760.00**	**$50,760.00**	**($23,640.00)**	**$0.00**	**$74,400.00**	**$74,400.00**	**$0.00**
21	Create RFPs	$10,800.00	$10,800.00	$10,800.00	$0.00	$0.00	$10,800.00	$10,800.00	$0.00

FIGURE A7-11 Displaying the Earned Value Table

Unit 7 Exercises

A. Return to the Task Sheet view and insert the % Complete column.

B. Enter the following % Complete numbers for the schedule created in earlier units: Tasks 1.1 through 1.5: 100%; Tasks 2.1 through 2.4: 100%; and Tasks 2.5 through 2.7: 25%.

C. Display the Cost table view and review it.

D. Display the tracking Gantt chart and make the same modifications to it as you made to the standard Gantt Chat in Unit 6 by altering the timescale, adding cost information above each bar, and changing the list of displayed tasks to just the summary tasks so the chart fits on one printed page.

8.0 ADAPTING THE WBS TO CHANGE

8.1 CHANGES IN COMPLETION DATE

The finish date of a project cannot be changed. Instead, the duration of tasks needs to be changed in order to affect the finish, or completion date, of the entire project. Changes to the task duration might mean that more resources need to be used in order to prevent overallocation. In addition, more tasks that had been scheduled to run sequentially may need to be done concurrently in order to finish on time; this is referred to as *fast tracking*. It may also be possible to shorten the completion date by adding more resources to a project, which is referred to as *crashing*. Figure A8-1 shows the critical path and the 24th task, Review/Sign Contract, with a duration of 4 days. Figure A8-2 shows the result of changing the duration

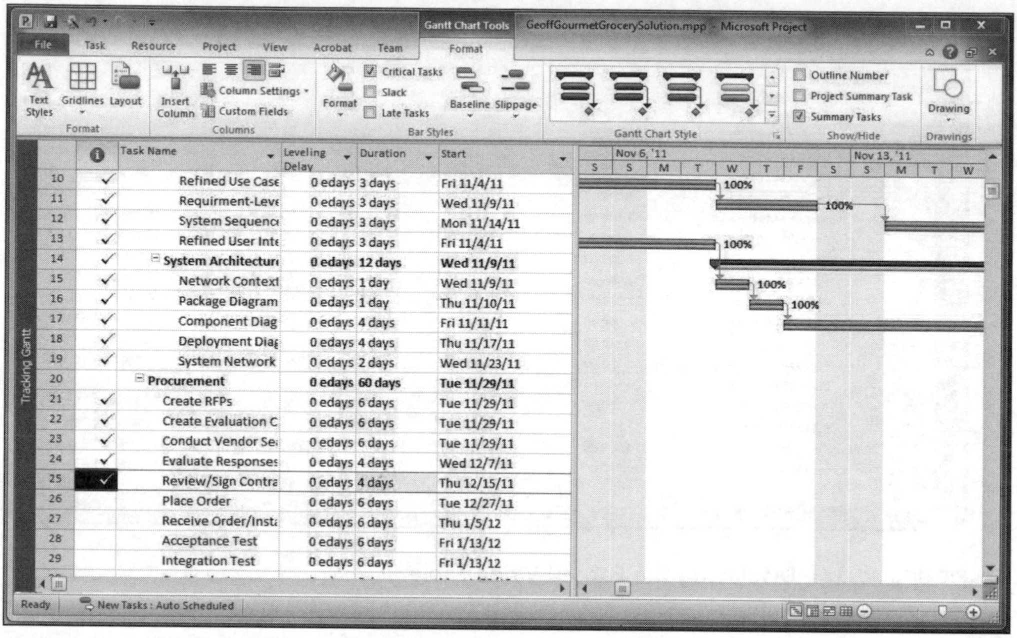

FIGURE A8-1   Displaying an Unaltered Critical Path

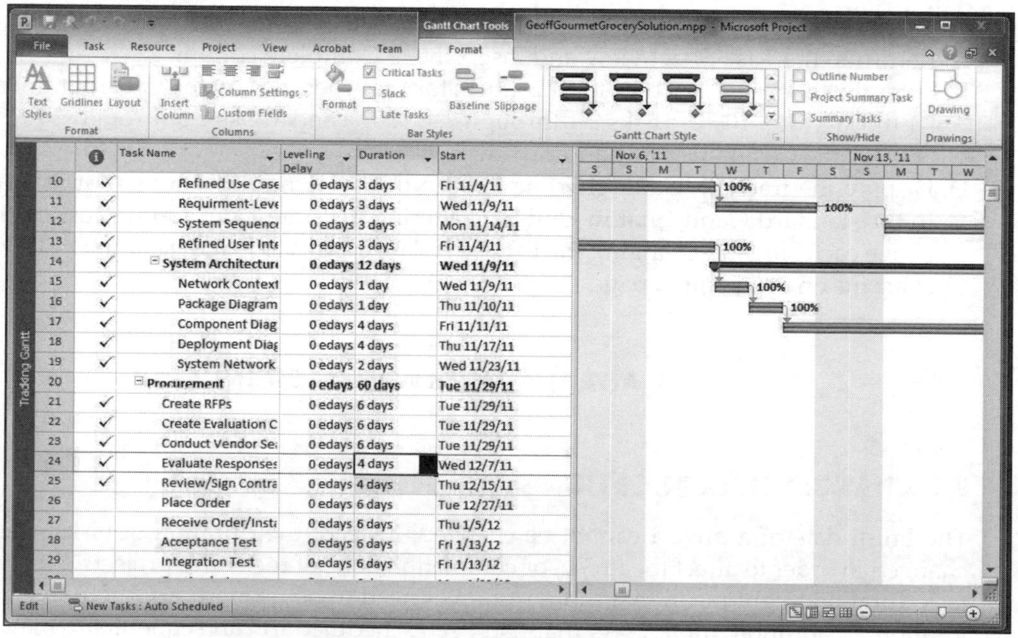

FIGURE A8-2   The Result of Changing Task Duration on the Critical Path

of this task to 10 days: It changes the project completion date from 172 days to 178 days and delays the start of the succeeding tasks because this task is on the critical path.

8.2 CHANGES IN COST

Changing the rates for a resource will affect the cost of the project. These variations can be seen in the difference between the actual and baseline costs. A change in cost can also be due to the change in the duration of a task. Figure A8-3 displays the Context Diagram task, without any variance and with a duration of 2 days. Figure A8-4 shows the effect of changing the duration of that task to 10 days, which results in a variance of $7,040 from the original cost, which is added to the total cost of the project.

8.3 CHANGES IN TASK DURATION

Changing the task duration affects the completion date of a project as a whole. A small diamond sign with an exclamation point (⬦) appears when a task duration is changed to alert the user that the change will have further effects. Clicking the small arrow next to this diamond displays several options, as shown in Figure A8-5. Selecting Work Required to Do This Task Has Increased, so It Will Take Longer results in a variance; on the other hand, selecting Resources Will Work Fewer Hours per Day, so the Task Will Take Longer option does not create a variance. Selecting the Show Me More Details option displays a screen similar to the one shown in Figure A8-6. The actual cost will be adjusted as the duration changes. For example,

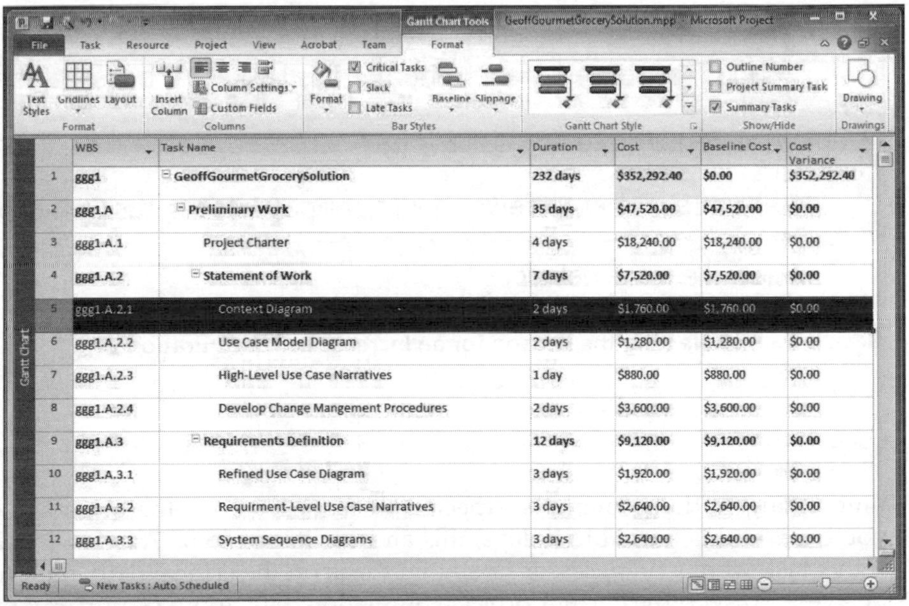

FIGURE A8-3 **Displaying a Task Without a Variance**

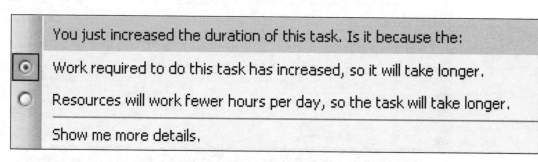

FIGURE A8-4   Displaying the Resulting Variance from a Change in Duration of a Task

You just increased the duration of this task. Is it because the:

Work required to do this task has increased, so it will take longer.

Resources will work fewer hours per day, so the task will take longer.

Show me more details.

FIGURE A8-5   Selecting the Reason for an Increase in Task Duration

unit testing in the example is expected to cost $4,480 for the original 4-day period. If you expand this period to 7 days, this amount jumps to $5,760, for a $1,280 difference. If this task were a predecessor for another task on the critical path, the project would be delayed. To keep the current project completion date, more resources would need to be assigned, and tasks might need to be run concurrently.

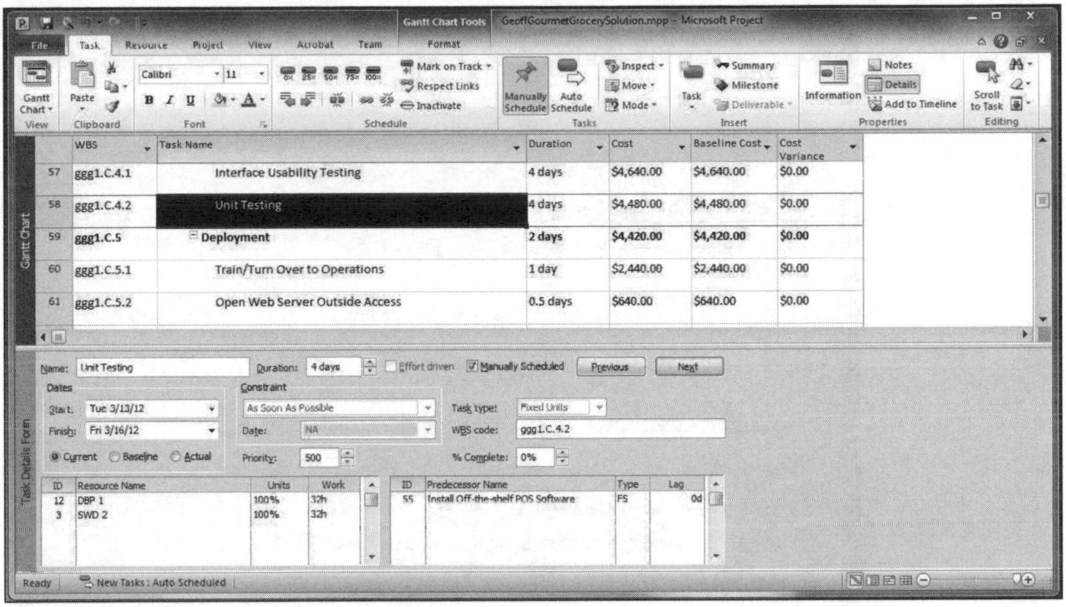

FIGURE A8-6   The Result of Clicking Show Me More Details

8.4 CHANGES IN AVAILABLE RESOURCES

As resources become available or unavailable, they may need to be reassigned. This reassignment may also cause a change in the cost of the project as resources are paid for the amount of work they do. The best and easiest way to change resources in Microsoft Project is by going to the Task Information screen or the resource sheet. To get to the Task Information screen, double-click a task and select the Resources tab, where you can change the resource assigned to the task. To display the resource sheet, select View tab, then Resource Sheet. This view allows you to change all of the attributes of a resource, including availability.

8.5 LEVELING RESOURCES TO AVOID OVERALLOCATION

During the course of a project, it may be necessary to level resources to avoid overallocation. As explained in Section 4.8, you do this is by selecting Resource tab, then Level Resources. The screen shown in Figure A8-7 appears. You can select the Clear Leveling Values before choosing the Leveling option to erase all previous leveling. In the Leveling Range section of this screen, there is the option to level the entire project or to level

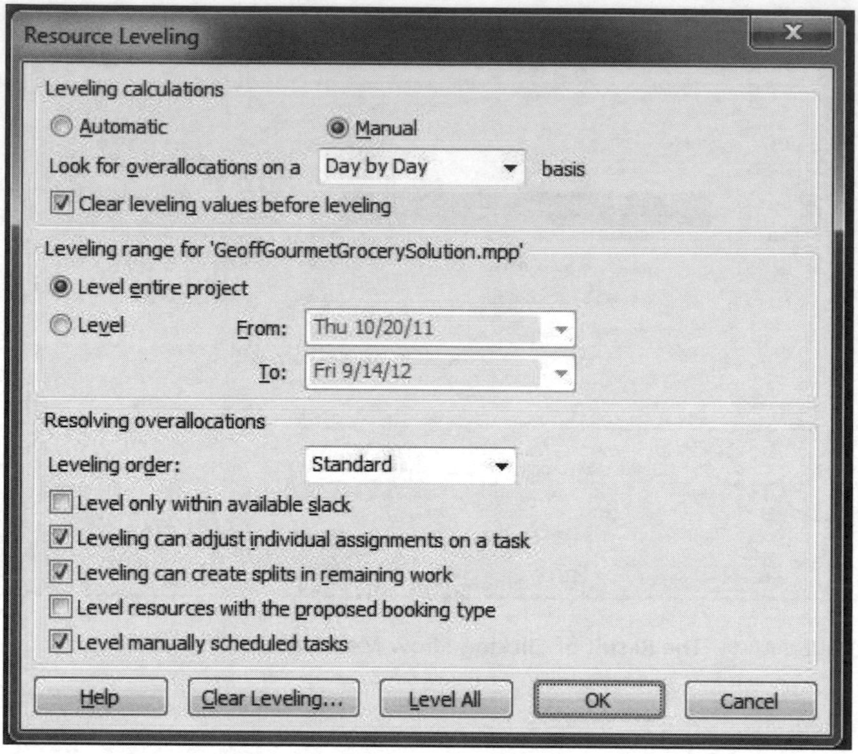

FIGURE A8-7   Leveling a Project

between a specified start date and finish date. When you level an entire project, all tasks are open for leveling. When you specify a range of dates in which to level, tasks are leveled only in that time period.

8.6 DISPLAYING THE CRITICAL PATH

There are many ways of viewing critical path information for a project. To view the critical path on a Gantt chart, select View tab, then More Views, then select Detail Gantt. When you use the normal Gantt chart, you can see the tasks on the critical path by selecting View tab, then Gantt Chart, then for the filter option on the ribbon select Critical. Figure A8-8 shows the drop-down list of filter options after you select Filter For. Selecting the AutoFilter option results in a screen similar to the one shown in Figure A8-9. This allows each field to be filtered using values in the drop-down boxes. In the Gantt Chart Wizard, the critical path is an option that you can add. To show multiple critical paths, if they exist, select File tab, then Options and then select the Advanced tab. Scroll down to the Calculate Multiple Critical Paths check box and click OK.

Built-In

[No Filter]

Active Tasks

Completed Tasks

Critical

Date Range...

Incomplete Tasks

Late Tasks

Milestones

Summary Tasks

Task Range...

Tasks With Estimated Durations

Using Resource...

⟨K⟩ Clear Filter

⟨Y⟩ New Filter

⟨Y⟩ More Filters...

⟨Y⟩ Display AutoFilter

Show Related Summary Rows

FIGURE A8-8 The Drop-Down List of Filter Options

	WBS	Task Name	Cost	Baseline Cost	Cost Variance	Actual Cost	Remaining Cost
1	ggg1	GeoffGourmetGrocerySc	$359,332.40	$0.00	$359,332.40	$91,080.00	$268,2!
2	ggg1.A	⊞ Preliminary Work	$54,560.00	$47,520.00	$7,040.00	$47,520.00	$7,04
20	ggg1.B	⊞ Procurement	$67,200.00	$74,400.00	($7,200.00)	$43,560.00	$23,64
31	ggg1.C	⊟ Release One	$52,000.00	$52,000.00	$0.00	$0.00	$52,0(
32	ggg1.C.1	⊟ Analysis Model	$19,800.00	$19,800.00	$0.00	$0.00	$19,80
33	ggg1.C.1.1	Build Analysis Us	$1,280.00	$1,280.00	$0.00	$0.00	$1,28
34	ggg1.C.1.2	Domain Class Dia	$2,720.00	$2,720.00	$0.00	$0.00	$2,72
35	ggg1.C.1.3	Workflow Activit	$2,320.00	$2,320.00	$0.00	$0.00	$2,32
36	ggg1.C.1.4	Analysis Sequenc	$1,760.00	$1,760.00	$0.00	$0.00	$1,76
37	ggg1.C.1.5	User Interface M	$1,040.00	$1,040.00	$0.00	$0.00	$1,04
38	ggg1.C.1.6	Complete Design	$10,680.00	$10,680.00	$0.00	$0.00	$10,68
39	ggg1.C.2	⊟ Design Model	$12,820.00	$12,820.00	$0.00	$0.00	$12,82
40	ggg1.C.2.1	Build Design Use	$520.00	$520.00	$0.00	$0.00	$52
41	ggg1.C.2.2	Full Class Diagrar	$1,160.00	$1,160.00	$0.00	$0.00	$1,16
42	ggg1.C.2.3	Build Sequence [	$680.00	$680.00	$0.00	$0.00	$68
43	ggg1.C.2.4	Operation Activit	$1,120.00	$1,120.00	$0.00	$0.00	$1,12
44	ggg1.C.2.5	User Interface M	$680.00	$680.00	$0.00	$0.00	$68
45	ggg1.C.2.6	Database Schema	$2,160.00	$2,160.00	$0.00	$0.00	$2,16
46	ggg1.C.2.7	Build Componen	$760.00	$760.00	$0.00	$0.00	$76
47	ggg1.C.2.8	Build Deploymer	$1,040.00	$1,040.00	$0.00	$0.00	$1,04
48	ggg1.C.2.9	Training Model	$560.00	$560.00	$0.00	$0.00	$56
49	ggg1.C.2.10	Test Model	$1,120.00	$1,120.00	$0.00	$0.00	$1,12

FIGURE A8-9 Displaying the Results of Choosing the AutoFilter Option

8.7 INTERRUPTING WORK ON A TASK

Sometimes it is necessary to stop work on a task and move resources to something else for a short time, either because you are waiting on something or some other task needs more resources. For example, you could be waiting on new computers to come in and therefore need to delay a task in the middle of execution. Microsoft Project can delay a task so it does not appear that you are continuing to work on the task while you're waiting. There are several ways to delay a task. On the Gantt chart, you can hover over a bar and right-click and select Split Task, as shown in Figure A8-10. You can also use the icon from the Task ribbon for splitting a task ⚏ . In either case, the split task tool appears, as shown in Figure A8-11.

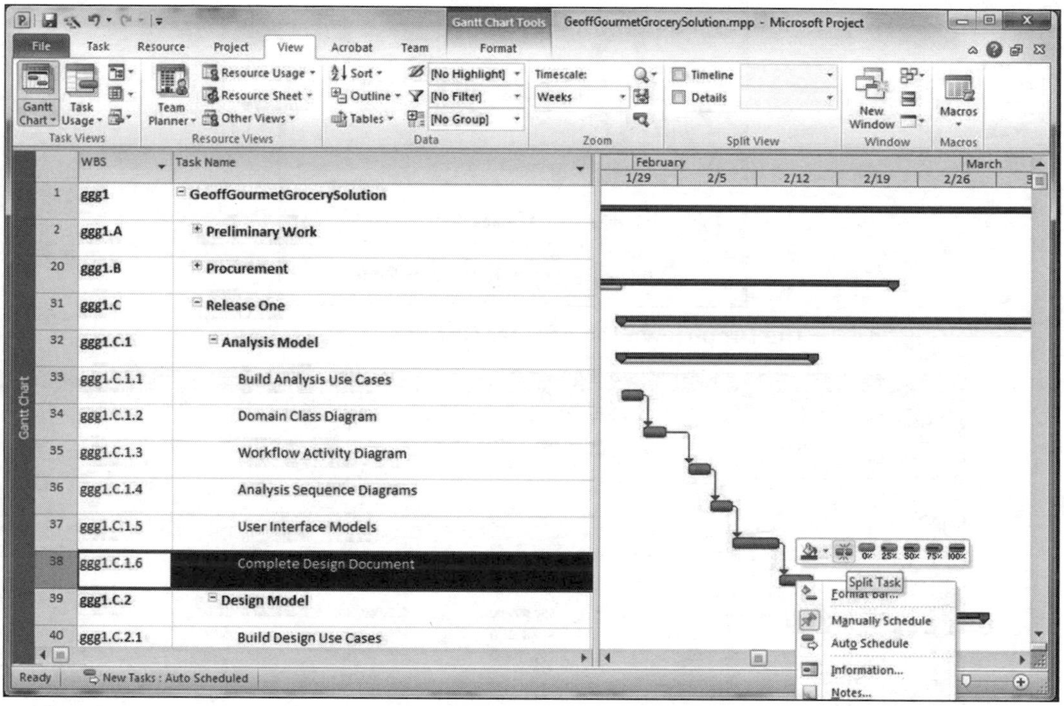

FIGURE A8-10   Splitting a Task

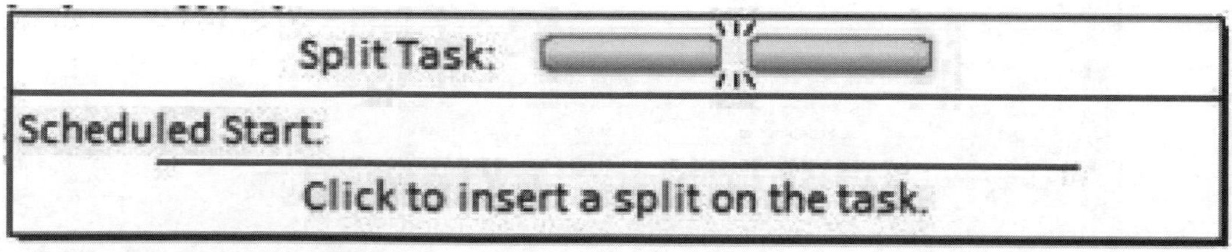

FIGURE A8-11   Using the Split Task Tool

Unit 8 Exercises

A. Return to Task Sheet view and make the following changes to task durations: Task 2.5 is now estimated to take 4 days; Task 2.6 will take 6 days; and Task 2.7 will take 5 days.
B. Display the Variance table view and observe changes to Tasks 2.5, 2.6, and 2.7.
C. Display the tracking Gantt chart.
D. Print an earned value cost report.
E. Return to the Task Sheet view and filter to show just the critical path.
F. Change the filter back to show all tasks.
G. Change resource availability by removing one of the system analysts and one of the software developers by reducing their respective availability numbers to 0 percent from this day forward.
H. Level resources to make sure these changes do not create any overallocated resource situations. If overallocations occur you should fix them.

9.0 PROJECT SERVER

9.1 WHAT IS PROJECT SERVER, AND WHAT DOES IT DO?

Microsoft Project Server is a project management server solution that allows for project information to be stored in a central location and offers a great number of capabilities in addition to what Microsoft Project offers by itself. When you need to link several projects together or manage them from one location, you need Project Server. Project Server allows for resources to be allocated and tracked from a central location. Templates and guides are also available to enable processes to be repeatable.

9.2 LINKING PROJECTS WITHOUT PROJECT SERVER

To link projects without Project Server, you can link predecessors to outside projects. To do this, double-click a task to add a predecessor, navigate to the Predecessor tab, and then enter the absolute path to the other project file, along with the ID number of the task. Figure A9-1 shows the linking of projects using predecessors.

9.3 PROJECT SERVER FUNCTIONS

As mentioned earlier, Project Server has many different functions. Project Server has a Reporting Data Services section, which allows for information to be shared with business reporting tools, such as SharePoint. Project Server also provides a central location for monitoring, finding trends, and identifying and managing risks. Project Server allows for multiple members of a team or other teams to work together from different locations with the use of Project Web Access, which is made possible with Project Server. As mentioned earlier, this tool provides the capability to manage resources effectively from a central location. The entire project life cycle can be managed and implemented, from proposal to project completion. As also mentioned earlier, Project Server provides templates and guides to

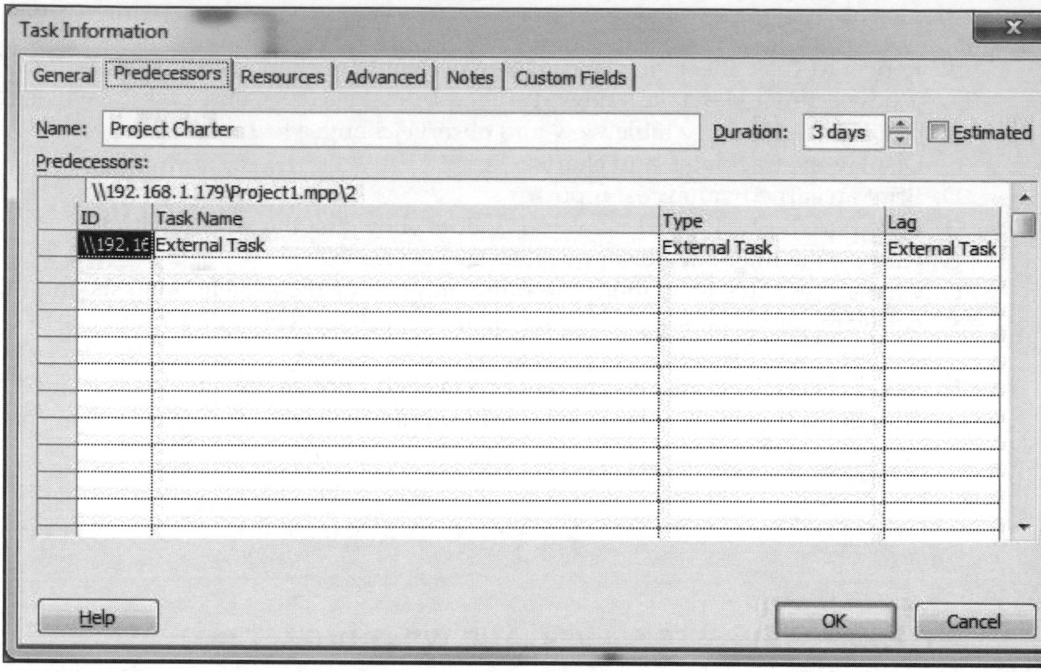

FIGURE A9-1   Linking Two Projects Using Predecessors

aid in creating repeatable processes, thus increasing future efficiency and effectiveness. These are just a few functions that are possible with Project Server. For more information, see the following Microsoft web site.

A complete list of Project Server capabilities can be found at:
http://office.microsoft.com/en-us/projectserver/FX101759381033.aspx

APPENDIX B

Project Management Templates

The templates listed in this appendix are available on the publisher's web site for the text.

CHAPTER 4

Project Selection Weighted Scoring Model Using Microsoft Excel

			Project		
Criterion		Weight	1	2	3	4
1	Market Share affect	10%	70	70	50	30
2	Competition	5%	30	70	70	70
3	Risk	10%	10	30	50	30
4	Product Fit	5%	70	70	50	0
5	Strategic Plan Alignment	15%	50	50	70	30
6	Customer Support	20%	50	50	30	30
7	Payback	10%	70	70	30	10
8	NPV	15%	70	50	30	30
9	ROI	10%	50	50	30	10
	Totals	100%	53	54	43	26.5

FIGURE B-1 **Project Selection Weighted Scoring Model**

Business Case

```
Business Case Template

Key Objectives

    •
    •
    •

Methods

    •
    •
    •

Benefits to the Organization if the Project Is Successful

    •
    •
    •

Consequences if the Project Is Not Done

    •
    •
    •

Full Life Cycle Costs


Qualitative Model Results


Quantitative Models



Top 10 Identified Risks with Probability and Impact Estimates

    1.
    2.
    3.
    4.
    5.
    6.
    7.
    8.
    9.
    10.
```

FIGURE B-2   Business Case

Project Charter

Project Title: _____   Date: _____
Version: _____

Description:

```
```

Project Manager: _____   Authority Level: _____

Objectives:

-
-
-

Major Deliverable Schedule:

-
-
-

Critical Success Factors

-
-
-

Assumptions/Constraints/Risks

-
-
-

Key Roles and Responsibilities

-
-
-

Approvals

```
```

FIGURE B-3   **Project Charter**

Stakeholder Assessment Matrix

Stakeholder	Interests	Influence	Unique Information	Role	Approach Strategies

FIGURE B-4   Stakeholder Assessment Matrix

Roles and Responsibilities Matrix

Responsible Party					
Activity	Project Manager	Database Analyst	Accounting Supervisor	CFO	Lead Systems Analyst	Inventory Control Supervisor
Task 1	R	I	A	A	C	C
Task 2	A	C	C	R	C	C
Task 3	R	C	C	A	I	C
Task 4	R	C	C	C	R	I
Task 5	C	R	I	C	I	I

Legend: R = Responsible
A = Approval
C = Consult or Review
I = Inform or act as subject matter expert

FIGURE B-5 Roles and Responsibilities Matrix

CHAPTER 5

Scope Statement

Project Objectives

-
-
-

Success Criteria

-
-
-

Constraints/Assumptions

-
-
-

Project Resource Organization (roles and responsibilities matrix)

-
-
-

Complete WBS

Cost Estimate

Integrated Change Control

<<identify the change control plan that will be used>>

Risks, Who Is Responsible, Mitigation Strategies

1.
2.
3.
4.
5.
6.
7.
8.
9.
10.

FIGURE B-6   Scope Statement

REQUIREMENTS TRACEABILITY MATRIX

Project Name: <optional>

Project Manager Name: <required>

Project Description: <required>

Requirement ID	Requirement Description	Status	Architectural/ Design Document	Technical Specification	System Component(s)	Software Module(s)	Test Case Number	Verification	Additional Comments
001									
002									
003									
004									
005									
006									
007									
008									
009									
010									
011									
012									
013									
014									

FIGURE B-7   Requirements Traceability Matrix

CHAPTER 7

Fishbone Diagram

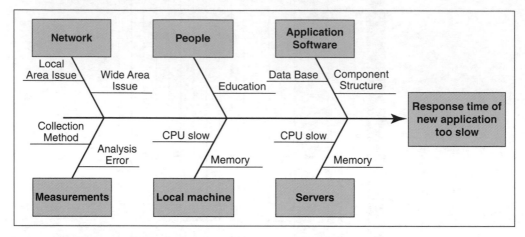

FIGURE B-8   Fishbone Diagram

Stakeholder Communications Matrix

Stakeholder	Document	Detail Level	Delivery Format	Frequency	Team Contact
John Smith	Status Report	Summary—2	Email—PDF	Monthly	Laura Smith
Mike Dunbar	Status Report	Detail	Email—PDF	Weekly	Laura Smith
Becky Ploss	EVM Report	Summary—1	Intranet	Weekly	Larry Cosgray
Dir. Finance	Budget/Actuals	Detail	Hard Copy	Monthly	Carlos Rodriguez
Dir. Human Resources	Staffing Plan	Detail	Email—PDF	Weekly	Larry Cosgray

FIGURE B-9   Stakeholder Communications Matrix

Project Status Report

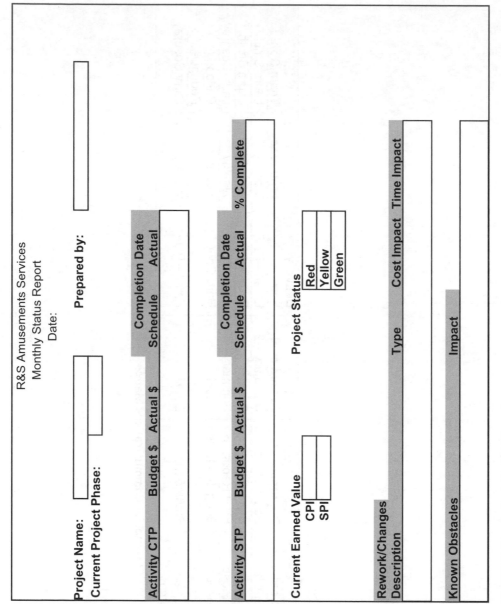

FIGURE B-10   Project Status Report

CHAPTER 8

Risk Register

Project: Project Name					Date: Current Date
Risk	**Trigger Event**	**Responsible**	**Consequence**	**Probability**	**Mitigation**
(name and short description)	(action(s) preceeding the risk occurring)	(person or group responsible for monitoring and mitigation)	(key project impact if risk occurs)	(qualitative or quantitative probability of occurrence)	(strategy being used to reduce liklihood)

FIGURE B-11 Risk Register

Probability and Impact Matrix

Impact ➜	Low	Low Med	Medium	Med. High	High
Probability Low				▓	▓
Low Medium				▓	▓
Medium			▓	▓	▓
Medium High	▓	▓	▓	▓	▓
High	▓	▓	▓	▓	▓

FIGURE B-12   **Probability and Impact Matrix**

Risk Management Plan

Risk Management Plan template   *10/31/07*

TABLE OF CONTENTS

Brewer/Dittman "Methods of IT Project Management"   Page: 2

FIGURE B-13   **Risk Management Plan**

CHAPTER 9

Statement of Work

TABLE OF CONTENTS

Brewer/Dittman "Methods of IT Project Management"   Page: 2

FIGURE B-14   Statement of Work

RFP/RFQ Procurement Document

Table of Contents

FIGURE B-15   RFP/RFQ Procurement Document

CHAPTER 11

Request for Change

Project Name: [ ]	**Date Submitted:** [ ]
Submitted by: [ ]	**Change Req. #:** [ ]

(name, contact information)

Priority: [ ] (E,H,M,L)   **Status:** [ ]

Description of change:

[ ]

Category: [ ] (Major, Significant, Minor, Operational)

Business Reason for change: (cost benefit analysis)

[ ]

Business Impact if change denied:

[ ]

Indicate Impact on:

Scope	[ ]	Cost	[ ]
Schedule	[ ]	HR	[ ]
Risk	[ ]	Quality	[ ]
Other	[ ]		

Suggested Implementation Schedule

[ ]

Required Approvals:

Name	Date	Approve/Reject

FIGURE B-16   Request for Change

CHAPTER 12

Project Performance Report

Project Name: _____

Period: _____

Project Manager: _____

_____

Status this Period:

- List each WBS item worked on during this time period with the following information
  - WBS Number, Task name, Owner, planned time and cost, actual time and cost, schedule variance and cost variance
  - Also note if the task completed, if not then estimate to complete

Activities for next Period:

- List each WBS item to be worked on during the next reporting time period
  - WBS Number, Task name, Owner, planned time and cost

Projections:

- Present project level cost performance index and schedule performance index
- Discuss how CPI and SPI will be used to generate estimate at completion
- Provide Estimate to complete (ETC) and Estimate at Completion (EAC)

Issues of concern:

- Review top risk items from the Risk Register by including them here as bullets and giving brief explanation of status
- Review any other issues that may affect project performance that needs to be communicated to stakeholders
- Review items dealt with during the last reporting period which were mentioned in this section

FIGURE B-17 **Project Performance Report**

CHAPTER 13

Project Closeout Checklist

Task Description	Required	Date Scheduled	Responsible
Closeout meeting			
Determine attendees			
Communicate project termination			
Schedule meeting			
Conduct meeting			
Document and update all project data			
Prepare final status report			
Financial			
Close out financial records			
Audit financial records			
Prepare final reports			
Human resources			
Officially transfer team members			
Close out all work authorizations			
Prepare final performance reviews			
Obtain operational support acceptance			
Contracts			
Update seller performance information			
Obtain seller signature			
Obtain stakeholder signature			
Handle any contractual compliance issues			
Prepare final status report			
Site			
Close down site operations			
Handle software/hardware disposition			
Handle infrastruture material disposition			

FIGURE B-18   Project Closeout Checklist

APPENDIX C

Project Management Professional (PMP) Certification Help Guide

At the time this text was published, the new version of the *Guide to Project Management Body of Knowledge* had just been released, version 5. Unfortunately, the corresponding changes to the PMP certification exam were not yet available, but you can still use this section to practice as the authors don't believe there will be substantial changes to the format and types of questions.

This appendix will help you obtain the Project Management Institute's (PMI's) Project Management Professional (PMP) certification. This appendix can also help prepare you for PMI's Certified Associate in Project Management (CAPM) certification. Much of the material in this appendix was obtained from the PMI web site, located at www. pmi. org. As mentioned in Chapter 3, there has been explosive growth in the number of people obtaining PMP certification. At the end of 2007, PMI reported that there were 267,367 active PMPs, up from 216,200 at the end of 2006. The content of this appendix, as well as the content of the entire text, is based on the most recent edition of A Guide to the Project Management Body of Knowledge (PMBOK), 4th edition, from PMI. The PMP certification exam is based on the 4th edition as of June 30, 2009.

PMI first started offering the PMP certification exam in 1984. PMI's certification process is accredited under ISO 9001, and PMI was the first professional organization in the world to achieve this distinction. Individuals pursue the PMP credential for a variety of reasons:

- When looking for a job or trying to win a contract, the credential is a great differentiator.
- According to a study funded by PMI, PMPs earn on average 20 percent higher salaries than similarly qualified but uncertified project managers.
- Certification demonstrates proof of professional achievement and the ability to be a lifelong learner.
- Certification improves skills, knowledge, and abilities due to the time spent studying for the exam and continued study to retain the credential.
- Certification provides peer recognition and self-confidence.
- Certification creates opportunities for advancement.
- Certification improves customer confidence.

To be eligible for a PMP credential, you must be able to document that you meet specific guidelines (outlined below) that objectively measure experience, education, and professional knowledge:

- You must have 35 hours of specific project management education.
- With a bachelor's degree (or the global equivalent), you must have a minimum of three years' professional project management experience, with 4,500 hours spent leading and directing project tasks, within eight years from the time of application.
- Without a bachelor's degree (or the global equivalent), you must have a minimum of five years' professional project management experience, with at least 7,500 hours spent leading and directing project tasks, within eight years from the time of application.

- You must pass a four-hour examination composed of 200 multiple-choice questions, which measures your ability to apply project management knowledge, skills, and techniques.
- You must pay the credential fee.

THE PMP CERTIFICATION PROCESS

To obtain the PMP certification, you need to follow this process:

1. Fill out the lengthy online application at www. pmi. org, which requires detailed eligibility documentation, with dates. Be prepared to spend some time filling out this information.
2. Agree to abide by PMI's code of conduct.
3. Pay the exam fee. At the time of this writing, the fee is $405 for a PMI member and $555 for a nonmember.
4. PMI will review your application and notify you about whether it has approved you. If it has, you have one year to schedule a time to take the online exam at a testing center.
5. At the testing center, you are permitted to bring nothing in; the testing center provides scratch paper, a calculator, and pencils. The exam may last up to four hours and consists of 200 multiple-choice questions. At the conclusion of the exam, you must return all materials before leaving. The online exam is scored immediately, and you are notified about success or failure. To pass the exam, you must answer 141 questions correctly. Only 175 of the 200 questions are scored; the other 25 questions are considered pretest questions that test the validity of future examination questions.
6. If you pass the exam, PMI mails your certificate and associated information.
7. To maintain the credential, every three years, you must earn a total of 60 professional development units (PDUs) over the course of that three-year period.
8. If you do not pass the exam, you can retake it up to three times during the following one year of eligibility. Each time you retake it, you must pay an additional fee and reschedule time at a testing center.

THE EXAM FORMAT AND OBJECTIVES

The 200 multiple-choice questions on the PMP certification exam are written in English and cover the following process groups and general knowledge areas:

- Initiating (11 percent of the exam)
- Planning (23 percent)
- Execution (27 percent)
- Monitoring and Control (21 percent)
- Closing (9 percent)
- Professional and social responsibility (9 percent)

  The following are the exam objectives, by process group or knowledge area:

- Initiating:
  - Conduct project selection methods

- Define scope (understand customer needs and expectations)
- Document project risks, assumptions, and constraints, using historical data and expert judgment
- Identify and perform stakeholder analysis, using a variety of methods
- Develop the project charter
- Obtain project charter approval

- Planning:
  - Define and record detailed requirements, constraints, and assumptions
  - Identify project team and define roles and responsibilities, creating a project organizational chart
  - Create the work breakdown structure with team involvement
  - Develop the change management plan
  - Identify risks and define risk strategies in preparing the risk management plan
  - Obtain plan approval from the sponsor and key stakeholders
  - Plan and conduct a kickoff meeting
- Executing:
  - Execute tasks defined in the project plan to meet project objectives
  - Ensure common understanding and manage stakeholder expectations
  - Implement the procurement plan for project resources
  - Manage resource allocation for the plan
  - Implement a quality management plan to meet established quality standards
  - Implement approved changes, following the formal integrated change control process
  - Implement approved actions and workarounds to mitigate risk
  - Improve team performance
- Monitoring and control:
  - Measure project performance, using a variety of tools, identifying variances and performing required corrective actions
  - Verify and manage changes to the project
  - Ensure that all project deliverables conform to quality standards
  - Monitor the status of all identified risks
- Closing:
  - Obtain formal final acceptance for the project from the sponsor and stakeholders
  - Obtain financial, legal, and administrative closure, both internally and externally
  - Release project resources in accordance with organizational policies
  - Identify, document, and communicate lessons learned
  - Create and distribute final project report
  - Archive and retain project records
  - Measure customer satisfaction, using appropriate surveys and interviews
- Professional and social responsibility:
  - Ensure personal integrity (legal, ethical standards, and social norms)
  - Contribute to the project management knowledge base, sharing lessons learned
  - Enhance professional competence
  - Promote interaction among stakeholders and team members by respecting personal and cultural differences

Tips for Preparing and Taking the PMP Certification Exam

- Because all unanswered questions on the exam are scored as wrong answers, guess at an answer rather than leave it blank.
- Memorize the name of each process, its primary purpose, and the deliverables.
- Make sure to memorize the terms used by PMI and not the ones you might have used in the past.
- Arrive at the testing center early so you can relax and prepare.
- Take advantage of the many resources available to help you prepare to take a multiple-choice exam of any kind.
- Use study guide material similar to this appendix. Many authors have written entire books that can help you pass the exam and teach courses whose focus is to help you pass the exam.
- After being seated for the exam, use your scratch paper to quickly write down any formulas or definitions you need so you can relax when they come up during the exam.
- Review the *PMP Credential Handbook*, the *PMP Examination Specification*, and the *PMP Sample Questions* document.
- Study *A Guide to the PMBOK*, fourth edition, and other texts that discuss the management of communications, cost, human resources, integration, procurement, quality, risk, scope and time, and a project manager's social and professional responsibilities. The exam covers more material than just what is presented in *A Guide to the PMBOK*, especially in the Professional and Social Responsibility section.

Sample Questions from Each Section of the PMP Certification Exam

The following sections contain questions that are similar to the questions contained in the actual PMP certification exam. At the time of the writing of this text, the PMP exam is still based on the 3rd edition of the PMBOK.

INITIATING

1. The amount of authority a project manager has to make decisions on a project can be
   A. Associated with the organizational structure
   B. Associated with the project manager's personality
   C. Associated with the personal relationship between the sponsor and the project manager
   D. Elected by the project team
2. Which of the following is a document that authorizes the start of all projects and the first document put under configuration control?
   A. Scope statement
   B. Project charter
   C. Statement of work
   D. Business plan

3. What are the key inputs to the identify stakeholders process?
   A. Project charter, organizational chart, stakeholder analysis, organizational process assets
   B. Vendor requirements, project statement of work, enterprise environmental factors
   C. Project charter, project statement of work, approved change requests, organizational process assets
   D. Project charter, procurement documents, enterprise environmental factors, organizational process assets
4. Which form of organizational structure affords the project manager the greatest amount of authority?
   A. Functional
   B. Strong matrix
   C. Weak matrix
   D. Project
5. You are a project manager and have been asked to review projects for selection. The financial information presented is listed below:

   Project A, NPV is $2500, IRR is 15%, payback period is 15 months
   Project B, NPV is $5000, IRR is 16%, payback period is 17 months

   Which project do you select?
   A. Project A because it has a shorter payback period
   B. Project B because it has a higher NPV and a higher IRR
   C. Project A because it has a lower NPV, a lower IRR, and a shorter payback period
   D. Project B because it has a longer payback period

PLANNING

1. Which of the following is not a tool or technique of the scope definition process?
   A. Templates, forms, standards
   B. Product analysis
   C. Alternatives identification
   D. Expert judgment
2. You're the project manager for a company's new portal application. You are tasked with creating a document that describes, in detail, the project's deliverables and the work required to create those deliverables. This document is called the
   A. Project scope management plan
   B. Project scope statement
   C. WBS
   D. Scope baseline
3. Using the analogous approach to creation of a WBS means
   A. Using a WBS supplied by an outside vendor
   B. Conducting a brainstorming session to create the WBS from the bottom up
   C. Starting at the top of the hierarchy and breaking down the WBS into smaller and smaller units of work
   D. Using the WBS from a previous similar project as a template

4. When you have 10 individuals on a project team, this equates to how many channels of communication?
   A. 20
   B. 45
   C. 10
   D. 100

5. As a project manager, which tool should you use to communicate to all team members and stakeholders what their respective roles on the project activities will be?
   A. Responsibility assignment matrix
   B. Organizational chart
   C. Role activity assignment matrix
   D. Stakeholder responsibility matrix

EXECUTION

1. As a project manager with a tight schedule but stakeholders who are interested in good results, your best approach to resolving conflict on the team is
   A. Withdrawal
   B. Compromise
   C. Confrontation
   D. Smoothing

2. All except which of the following are tools and techniques used during the acquire project team process?
   A. Pre-assignment
   B. Negotiation
   C. General management soft skills
   D. Virtual teams

3. Which of the following is the one key input into the information distribution process?
   A. Communications management plan
   B. Project scope statement
   C. Project management plan constraints and assumptions
   D. Enterprise environmental factors

4. The quality assurance process is best described by which of the following?
   A. Identifying which quality standards are relevant to the project and determining how to satisfy them
   B. Applying planned, systematic quality activities to ensure that the project will employ all processes needed to meet the key sponsor's needs
   C. Monitoring specific project results to determine whether they comply with relevant quality standards and identifying ways to eliminate causes of unsatisfactory results
   D. Applying planned, systematic quality activities to ensure that the project will employ all processes needed to meet requirements

5. All except which of the following are tools and techniques to use while selecting sellers?
   A. Weighting system
   B. Bidder conference
   C. Screening system
   D. Expert judgment

MONITORING AND CONTROL

1. Monitoring and control is a process that should occur throughout the life of a project. Continuous monitoring of project performance aids a team in identifying project issues before they become serious problems. The monitoring and control project work process is concerned directly with all except which of the following?
   A. Comparing actual project performance against the project management plan
   B. Implementing risk mitigation activities
   C. Providing forecasts to update current cost and current schedule information
   D. Monitoring implementation of approved changes when and as they occur

2. As a new employee just hired into Geoff's Gourmet Grocery Store's corporate office as project manager, you have been asked to consult on an ongoing project that is having difficulties meeting its scope, time, and cost goals. After some investigation, you discover that the project is experiencing large amounts of scope creep and little to no formal control of changes. Your first task is to implement an integrated change control process. You explain to the project team and upper management that an integrated change control process offers all except which of the following capabilities?
   A. Guarantees that all changes are effectively implemented
   B. Identifies that a change needs to occur or has occurred
   C. Provides a formal process to review and approve requested changes
   D. Provides a formal process to review and approve all recommended corrective and preventive actions

3. Which of the following statements is true regarding scope control?
   A. It is concerned with making sure that once the detailed scope statement is created, it doesn't change while the project is executing
   B. It is concerned with influencing the factors that create project scope changes and their associated costs
   C. It is concerned with influencing the factors that create project scope changes and controlling the impact of those changes
   D. It is concerned with making sure that all of the proposed changes are made by upper-level management stakeholders

4. Which of the following is not part of the control schedule activities during the integrated change control process?
   A. Progress reporting
   B. Schedule change control system
   C. Variance analysis
   D. Status review meetings

5. The current project manager for a company's web site redesign project has left the company for another job, and you have been brought over to finish the project. You ask for the earned value reports to see how the project is doing so you can concentrate on the most important areas first. The report lists the following values: SPI = 79%, CPI = 98%. How do you react?
   A. Review the cost baseline and actual costs to see why costs are surpassing the budget
   B. Review the schedule baseline and actual schedule results to see why the project is behind schedule
   C. Call a meeting of the project team and congratulate them on being ahead of schedule and below budget

D. Schedule a meeting with the stakeholders and upper management and tell them the project is going to run way over schedule and budget and ask for more time and more money to get it completed

CLOSING

1. Which of the following processes are performed in the closing process?
   A. Close the project or phase and close procurements
   B. Verify final deliverables, close the project, and close procurements
   C. Close the scope, close the budget, close the project, and close procurements
   D. Close integration management and close procurement management
2. Which of the following is not an output of the project closing process?
   A. Organizational process assets updates
   B. Final product transition
   C. Contract evaluation
   D. Final service transition
3. All except which of the following are activities addressed by the project closing or phase closing procedure?
   A. Actions and activities to define the stakeholder approval requirements for changes and all levels of deliverables
   B. Actions and activities required by the project team members, customers, and other stakeholders involved to ensure the successful contract closing process
   C. Actions and activities necessary to satisfy completion or exit criteria for the project
   D. Actions and activities necessary to confirm that the project has met all sponsor, customer, and other stakeholder requirements
4. As one of the best project managers in the company, you have been asked to sit in on a lessons learned session to review the results and make recommendations for improvements. Currently under review is a work product that was outsourced to a vendor in India. You are reviewing the results of the procurement process from the purchase and acquisition planning process all the way through to the contract administration process. The results you are reviewing were generated by which technique?
   A. Procurement performance review
   B. Outsourcing contract audit
   C. Outsourcing performance review
   D. Procurement audit
5. In order to conduct the procurement closing process, all except which of the following information is used as input?
   A. Project management plan
   B. Procurement documentation
   C. Contract documents
   D. Procurement qualified sellers list

PROFESSIONAL AND SOCIAL RESPONSIBILITY

1. The PMI code of conduct consists of which five chapters?
   A. (1) Vision and Applicability, (2) General Moral Imperatives, (3) Professional Responsibilities, (4) Fairness, and (5) Honesty
   B. (1) Vision and Applicability, (2) Responsibility, (3) Respect, (4) Fairness, and (5) Honesty
   C. (1) General Moral Imperatives, (2) Professional Responsibilities, (3) Organizational Leadership Imperatives, (4) Respect, and (5) Integrity
   D. (1) Adherence to Social Norms, (2) Respect, (3) Integrity, (4) Fairness, and (5) Honesty

2. Which of the following should be your response if you discover that one of your co-workers is claiming to be a PMI-certified PMP, but you know for a fact that he or she never renewed the credential and let it lapse?
   A. Inform the individual that you know he or she is not still a PMP and ask the person to stop using the credential
   B. Inform PMI and management of the firm that this individual is claiming to be a PMP and is not
   C. Do nothing; just because they are no longer certified doesn't mean they can't run a project
   D. Send an email to the person's boss, informing the boss of the issue and to leave you out of it

3. You are the project manager for a large system upgrade for all of the distributed servers in the company. The company is spread out across the United States in 40 different states. The upgrade will affect 200 servers. You are in the middle of reviewing seller responses to the issued RFQ to perform the system upgrades, when one of the sellers stops by, unannounced, saying he just happened to be in town and wants to take you to lunch. How do you respond?
   A. Thank him for the offer but decline because this could call your personal integrity into question.
   B. Thank him for the offer and accept because you see no conflict of interest because a simple lunch is not expensive compared to the total dollar amount of the contract.
   C. Thank him for the offer and accept because you told your boss that you were going to lunch and this would have no bearing on your final decision.
   D. Thank him for the offer but decline because this could be a conflict of interest because a final decision on the seller has not been reached.

4. The PMI code of conduct applies to all except which of the following individuals?
   A. All PMI-certified individuals
   B. All PMI members
   C. All practitioners who have project management titles
   D. Nonmembers of PMI who serve as volunteers

5. As a PMP, you are required to contribute to the project management knowledge base by doing all except which of the following?
   A. Sharing lessons learned from just the successful projects
   B. Sharing best practices from all projects
   C. Sharing research results
   D. Transferring knowledge through coaching, mentoring, and training

ANSWERS TO THE MULTIPLE-CHOICE QUESTIONS:

Initiating

1. A
2. B
3. D
4. D
5. B

Planning

1. A
2. B
3. D
4. B
5. A

Execution

1. C
2. C
3. A
4. D
5. B

Monitoring and Control

1. B
2. A
3. C
4. D
5. B

Closing

1. A
2. C
3. B
4. D
5. D

Professional and Social Responsibility

1. B
2. B
3. D
4. C
5. A

GLOSSARY

A

activity definition The process of identifying and documenting the work that needs to be performed to deliver a product.

activity duration estimate A quantitative assessment of the likely number of work periods (for example, hours, days, weeks) that will be required to complete an activity.

activity list A list that includes all the activities that will be performed on the project.

activity resource estimating The process of estimating the number of work units (for example, hours, days, weeks) required to complete each activity.

activity resource requirements The hours available from each resource for each task.

activity sequencing A process that involves identifying and documenting interactive logical relationships—that is, identifying the sequence in which activities must be performed in order to produce a realistic and achievable project schedule.

adjusted baseline A revised and reissued baseline that reflects approved changes and forms the new baseline for future changes.

administrative, or process, conflict Conflict associated with disagreements on reporting relationships or who has authority to make decisions.

affinity diagram A group decision-making technique designed to sort a large number of ideas, concepts, and opinions into a set of organized groups.

analogous estimating An estimating method that bases a current work package time estimate on the actual time of a work package from a similar project already completed.

appraisal costs Costs associated with ensuring that all requirements have been met (for example, customer acceptance tests, demonstrations, lab tests).

attributes Individual characteristics that are part of systems and subsystems. Defining a new software system involves defining attributes such as business requirements and database schemas. Project management involves defining attributes such as budgets, schedules, and activities or tasks.

B

balanced scorecard An approach for managing and measuring business performance that takes into consideration factors beyond the typical financial metrics.

benchmarking The study of a competitor's product, service, or business practice for the purpose of improving your own performance.

boundary A limit that surrounds a system and separates it from the environment.

brainstorming A nonstructured or semi-structured method of eliciting ideas from a group, with the goal of generating a complete list of ideas.

burden rate The cost of a human resource, which takes into consideration more than just the person's salary or hourly rate, including benefits, vacations, holidays, and so on.

business case A document composed of a set of project characteristics—costs, benefits, risks, and so on—that aids organization decision makers in deciding what projects to work on.

C

Capability Maturity Model Integration (CMMI) A framework used to assess and evaluate an organization's processes.

cause-and-effect analysis A systematic method for generating and sorting ideas about possible causes of an identified problem. Once the root causes of problems are identified, they (rather than just the symptoms) can be dealt with.

change advisory board (CAB), or change control board (CCB) A cross-functional group consisting of key members of the user and IT management teams that has the authority to either accept or reject a requested change.

change request A request to change the project scope, change project costs (budgets), or change the project schedule.

checklists Specific lists that are used to verify that a set of required steps has been performed.

close procurements A process that involves completion and settlement of a contract, including resolution of any open items.

closed system A system that is completely self-contained. To understand a closed system, you merely look on the inside, without regard to the external environment. For example, a machine is a closed system; to understand how it works, you simply open it up and study the internal mechanisms.

closing processes Processes that consist of formal acceptance of a project or a phase and updating of the project information base with lessons learned.

communications management The processes necessary to ensure timely and accurate generation, distribution, storage, retrieval, and disposition of project information.

communications management plan A formal or informal document that specifies:

- What methods will be used to gather and store the various types of information
- To whom information will flow and what methods will be used to distribute the various types of information
- A description of the information to be distributed
- Methods for accessing information between scheduled communications
- A method for updating and refining the communications management plan as the project progresses and develops

communications planning A process that involves determining the information and communication needs of stakeholders—who needs what information, when they will need it, how it will be given to them, and by whom.

component process An organized set of tasks designed to fulfill an explicit outcome within a process group.

conduct procurements A process that involves obtaining quotations, bids, offers, or proposals, as appropriate, and choosing solutions from among potential sellers.

conflict management A process that seeks to prevent, manage, or resolve conflicts as they occur throughout the life of a project.

conformance to requirements/specifications A product's conforming to written specifications.

constraints Limitations forced on a system by internal forces or external forces or that are self-controlled. Examples of constrains are scope, time, and cost.

contingency reserves Excess amounts of time, money, resources, and so on that are approved for a project and are only used if necessary in order for the project to finish as originally planned.

contract A mutually binding agreement entered into by two or more parties that is enforceable in a court of law. It obligates the seller to provide the specified products, services, or results. It also, in most cases, obligates the buyer to provide financial compensation.

contract file A complete set of indexed records to be included with the final project records.

control chart A graphical tool for monitoring changes that occur during the execution of a process, by distinguishing between variation of results that are inherent in the process (common causes) and variation that yields a change to the process (special/unique causes).

controlling processes Processes that consist of monitoring of project variances from what was planned to actual progress.

corrective action Anything done to bring expected future project performance in line with a project plan.

cost–benefit analysis A technique used to determine the trade-off between the costs of building a quality product or service and the benefits obtained from a product that meets defined quality standards.

cost budgeting A process that involves allocating overall cost estimates to individual activities or work packages to establish a cost baseline for measuring project performance.

cost control A process that involves controlling changes to a project budget.

cost estimate A quantitative assessment of the likely costs of the resources required to complete project activities.

cost estimating A process that involves developing an approximation (estimate) of the costs of the resources needed to complete project activities.

cost management The processes and methods required to create and manage a project budget.

cost of nonconformance Total costs incurred by an organization because a product does not meet user requirements (for example, rework, poor user productivity).

cost of quality Total costs incurred by an organization to prevent a faulty product or to avoid developing a system that does not meet system requirements.

cost performance baseline A time-phased budget that is used to measure and monitor cost performance on a project.

cost-reimbursable contract A contract that involves the reimbursement (payment) of the seller's actual costs, plus a fee typically representing the seller's profit.

crashing A schedule compression technique in which cost and schedule trade-offs are analyzed to determine how to obtain the greatest amount of compression for the least incremental cost.

critical chain method A network schedule analysis technique that examines the changes to the schedule that are needed based on limited resources.

critical path The list of activities that, if delayed, will delay the completion date of a project. By definition, these activities have zero slack. The duration of the critical path determines the duration of the entire project.

critical path method (CPM) A method that identifies the set of tasks, when performed in sequence, that total the longest overall duration of time, which is the shortest time to complete the project.

D

decomposition The act of breaking down a task into smaller and smaller parts until the component parts are at a level that can be assigned, monitored, and controlled.

deliverable A tangible and verifiable product, result, or capability to perform a service that is a requirement to produce the end result product of a project.

design of experiments A statistical method to help identify which factors have influence on the quality of a product or process.

direct costs Costs that are directly attributable to the activities of the project (for example, purchasing hardware or software, labor cost of workers on the team).

document package A buyer-prepared formal statement of work sent to each seller which forms the basis of the seller's response in the form of a proposal.

E

earned value management (EVM) A technique used to help determine and manage project progress and the magnitude of any variations from the planned values in terms of cost, schedule, and performance.

element The smallest part of a system. What is defined as an element varies, depending on the level of understanding needed at a point in time. While investigating the detailed workings of an order processing software subsystem, for example, you need to break it down into smaller pieces, such as entering new orders, checking inventory, and checking customer addresses. These pieces become the elements for the order processing software subsystem.

environment Everything that exists outside a system or outside the control of a project manager.

estimate at completion (EAC) A forecast of most likely total project costs, based on project performance and risk quantification.

ethical behavior Human behavior that conforms to generally accepted social norms.

ethics Beliefs regarding right and wrong behavior.

evolutionary prototyping model An approach to systems development that focuses on gathering correct and consistent requirements and that involves building a system incrementally through a series of gradual refinements or prototypes.

executing processes Processes involving coordinating all resources (people and material) during the implementation of a project plan.

expected monetary value (EMV) analysis A statistical technique for calculating the average outcome when dealing with unknown future scenarios.

external failure costs Costs associated with defects in a system that has been fully deployed (for example, scrap, rework, returns, market share, lawsuits).

Extreme Programming (XP) An agile approach to systems development that includes short development cycles, frequent updates, separation of business and technical priorities, and assignment of user stories. XP has four key values—communication, feedback, simplicity, and courage—plus a dozen practices that are followed during XP projects.

F

fast tracking A schedule compression technique that looks specifically for activities that can be done in parallel if the necessary resources are available.

finish-to-finish (FF) dependency A type of precedence diagram method dependency where the completion of a task is dependent on the completion of all its predecessors.

finish-to-start (FS) dependency A type of precedence diagram method dependency where the beginning of a task is dependent on the completion of all its predecessors.

fitness for use Satisfactory quality of a product so that it can be used as it was originally intended to be used.

fixed costs Costs that are expenses whose total does not change in proportion to the activity of a business or project, within the relevant time period or scale of production (for example, rent, insurance).

fixed-price, or lump-sum, contract A contract under which the seller is obligated to complete 100 percent of the work at the negotiated contract value.

flexibility options Options that give a company the ability to change its plans in the future.

forecast An estimate of conditions in a project's future, based on information available at the present time.

formal acceptance Stakeholders' formal acceptance (via signatures) of a product.

formal acceptance and closure A formal written notice that a contract has been completed.

framework A set of assumptions, concepts, values, and practices that constitutes a way of viewing reality.

free slack The difference between the earliest time an activity can begin and the latest time an activity can begin without changing the completion date of any successor task.

function point A measurement of the size of a business function that a new system needs to have, such as an input screen or a report.

G

Gantt chart A chart that shows the dependencies of some tasks on other tasks and that can aid in building a good project schedule.

growth options Options that give a firm the ability to increase its future business.

H

human resources management The processes and methods required to use the people associated with the project effectively.

human resources planning A process that involves identifying, documenting, and assigning project roles, responsibilities, and reporting relationships.

I

indirect costs Costs that are not directly attributable to the activities of a project (for example, overhead rates such as management salaries, energy costs, rents).

information distribution A process that involves making needed information available to project stakeholders in a timely manner.

initiating processes Processes that consist of authorizing the beginning or ending of a project or phase.

insourcing The opposite of outsourcing, the movement of a business process within a company to an internal entity (inside the same company) that specializes in that operation.

integrated change control A formal process used to approve and manage any and all necessary project document and deliverable changes.

integration The effective working together of all subsystems and elements that is necessary for a system to reach its objectives.

Integration Management A PMBOK knowledge area that describes the processes and methods required to identify, define, combine, unify, and coordinate the various processes with all of the other eight knowledge areas.

internal failure costs Costs associated with defects in a system before it is fully deployed (for example, scrap, rework).

internal rate of return (IRR) The discount rate at which NPV is zero.

International Organization for Standardization (ISO) Based in Geneva Switzerland, a consortium of more than 100 of the world's industrial nations. The American National Standards Institute (ANSI) is the U.S. representative.

interpersonal, or relationship conflict Conflict associated with personality differences between project team members, such as work ethics, egos, or individual personalities.

iterative and incremental model An approach to systems development that is an intuitive approach to the waterfall model. This model involves multiple development cycles, and the cycles are divided up into smaller, more easily managed iterations. Each iteration passes through the standard life cycle phases. A working version of software is produced during the first iteration, so you have working software early on during the project life cycle. Subsequent iterations build on the initial software produced during the first iteration.

K

knowledge area From the PMBOK, a description of project management knowledge in terms of component processes.

L

lessons learned Documentation that details the causes of variances, the reasoning behind the corrective action chosen, and other types of lessons learned.

life cycle A prescribed order of phases (smaller segments of an entire project) in which the phases contain specific deliverables that collectively deliver a result.

life cycle costs All costs incurred over the life of a product or service.

list of analyzed risks (register) A list (or multiple lists) that include prioritized qualitative and quantified risks and risks for additional analysis and management.

M

maintainability The time and expense needed to restore a product to an acceptable level of performance after the product has failed or begun a trend toward failure.

make-or-buy analysis A process used to determine whether a product team should produce a product or service itself or purchase it.

matrix organizational structure An organizational structure that seeks to combine the benefits of the functional structure and the benefits of the project structure in one organization. The matrix structure takes three general forms: weak, balanced, and strong.

maturity model A structured collection of elements that describe characteristics of effective processes.

mitigation strategy A process that attempts to reduce the likelihood and/or impact of a risk on the success of a project goal.

monitoring and controlling risks A process that involves monitoring residual risks, identifying new risks, executing risk reduction plans, and evaluating their effectiveness throughout the project life cycle.

Monte Carlo simulation A technique used to randomly generate specific end values for a variable with a specific probability distribution.

multisourcing, or "best of breed sourcing," or crowd sourcing A form of outsourcing that involves a number of different types of outsourcing (for example, nearshoring, offshoring, and rural sourcing).

N

nearshoring The movement of a business process (in whole or in part) to companies in a nearby country, often sharing a border with the company's own country.

net present value (NPV) A method of calculating the expected net monetary gain or loss from an investment (project) by discounting all future costs and benefits to the present time.

nonrecurring costs Costs that appear only once (for example, initial purchase cost of hardware and software).

O

objectives The things that an open system is designed to do in order to change an input into an output via an internal process.

offshoring The movement of a business process (in whole or in part) done at a company in one country to another company in another, different country.

open system A system that is not self-defining; to understand an open system, you must understand its environment. The human body and organizations are examples of open systems. They can affect and be affected by their environments and adapt.

opportunity costs A measure of the anticipated return against the anticipated return an organization would receive on a highest-yielding alternative investment that contains a similar risk assessment.

organization A system composed of human and physical resources working together to achieve shared goals.

organizational chart A graphical display of project reporting relationships that communicates who works for (or reports to) whom among project team members and stakeholders.

organizational project management The application of knowledge, skills, tools, and techniques to organizational and project activities to achieve the strategic goals of an organization through projects.

Organizational Project Management Maturity Model (OPM3) A framework within which organizations can reexamine their pursuit of strategic objectives via best practices in organizational project management.

outsourcing The process of transferring project activities and certain decision rights to an external entity, by contract, with specific performance measures, related rewards, penalties, and exit clauses defined.

P

Pareto diagram Reported performance information represented in a bar chart that displays, by frequency and in descending order, the most important issues/defects found or reported to aid a project manager in concentrating effort on the most important events.

payback period The amount of time it takes for the accrued benefits of a project to surpass accrued costs, or how much time an investment takes to recover its initial cost.

payment schedule A formal schedule of when and how much payment is due. It should also include acceptance criteria before payment is approved.

performance measurements The schedule variance and schedule performance index values for selected WBS activities.

performance report A document that organizes and summarizes the information gathered and that presents the results of a performance analysis.

performance reporting A process that involves collecting and disseminating performance information, such as status reporting, progress measurement, and forecasting.

planning processes Processes related to ensuring that the objectives of a project are achieved in the most appropriate way.

portfolio A collection of projects and/or programs that are grouped together to obtain benefits and control not available by managing them individually.

portfolio management Control and monitoring of an organization's mix of projects to match organizational objectives for risk and investment returns.

precedence diagram method (PDM) A method of constructing a project network diagram that uses boxes to represent activities (nodes) and lines with arrows to represent dependencies.

prevention costs Up-front costs associated with satisfying customer requirements (for example, design reviews, all forms of system testing, training, surveys).

process group A collection that consists of one or more component processes.

process improvement The process of identifying non-value-added procedures and outputs and eliminating them as much as possible.

procurement The purchase or acquisition of products, services, or results needed from an entity outside a project team to perform work defined on the project, possibly under a contract.

procurement documents Documents such as RFPs used to solicit proposals from prospective sellers.

procurement management The processes and methods required to acquire and manage goods and resources from a source outside the project team.

procurement management plan A document that describes how the remaining procurement processes (from solicitation planning through contract closeout) will be managed.

procurement planning A process that involves determining what to procure, when to procure it, and a list of potential sellers.

program A group of related projects, managed in a coordinated way to obtain benefits and control not available when managing them individually.

program evaluation and review technique (PERT) chart A schematic display of project activities and the logical relationships (dependencies) among them.

project A temporary sequence of related activities that must be completed to create a unique product or service.

project archives A complete set of indexed project records.

project assumptions Factors that for planning purposes are considered to be true, real, or certain.

project authority The delegated, earned, legal, or rightful power to command, act, or direct the activities of others.

project-based organizational structure A structure that is organized completely around projects and sometimes exists only for one particular project.

project charter A document that formally authorizes the work to begin on a project and provides an overview of objectives and resource requirements.

project closure Confirmation that a project has met all customer requirements for the product of the project.

project constraints Factors that limit a project management team's options.

project initiation The process of formally authorizing a new project or an existing project to proceed into its next phase.

project management The process of applying knowledge, tools, and techniques to a project's activities to deliver stated project requirements within agreed-upon scope, time, cost, and quality constraints.

project management body of knowledge (PMBOK) Describes the sum of knowledge within the profession of project management, including knowledge of proven traditional practices that are widely applied as well as knowledge of innovative and advanced practices.

Project Management Institute (PMI) An international professional society created to guide the development of project managers and researchers.

project management office (PMO) An organizational entity with full-time personnel to provide a wide range of project management support and services across an entire organization.

project network diagram A schematic display of project activities and the logical relationships (dependencies) among them. The most common type of project network diagram is called a PERT chart.

project plan A formal approved document used to manage project execution.

project planning A process that involves establishing a predetermined course of action, team participants, and delivery dates, based on a project's goals and objectives.

project presentations Presentations made by a project team to provide information formally and informally to any and all project stakeholders.

project records Records including correspondence, memos, and documents describing a project.

project reports Formal project reports on project status and/or issues.

project schedule A deliverable that includes, at a minimum, the planned start and expected finish dates for each activity. The project schedule can be presented in tabular form or graphically, using a project network diagram or using Gantt charts and milestone charts. The schedule should include a management plan that defines how changes to the schedule will be managed.

project team development A process that involves developing individual and group competencies to enhance project performance.

project team management A process that involves tracking each team member's performance during a project and coordinating changes.

proposal A seller-prepared response to a buyer's document package.

Q

qualified sellers list A list of sellers asked to supply a proposal.

qualitative analysis A process that involves using subjective methods to qualify each risk for impact and probability of occurrence.

qualitative model A model that involves making selection decisions based on subjective evaluation using nonnumeric values of project characteristics.

qualitative risk analysis A process that involves performing a qualitative analysis of risks and conditions to prioritize their effects on project objectives.

quality The degree to which a product satisfies both stated and implied requirements.

quality assurance The application of planned activities to ensure that a project will employ all processes needed to meet stated quality requirements.

quality audit An independent review of executing processes to ensure that they are being followed and that they will enable the project team to meet the established quality standards.

quality control A process that involves monitoring project results to determine whether they comply with the defined relevant quality standards.

quality control measurements Collected results of quality control activities for evaluation against quality standards.

quality improvement A process that involves taking action to increase the effectiveness and efficiency of a project to provide added benefits to project stakeholders.

quality management Processes and methods implemented to ensure that a project delivers the stated and implied needs for which it was designed.

quality management plan A formal or informal document that describes how a project management team will implement its quality policy.

quality metrics What something is and how it is measured by the quality control process.

quality planning The process of identifying which quality standards are relevant to a project and an organization and determining the activities necessary to meet the established standards in order to deliver the product fit for customer use.

quantitative model A model that involves making selection decisions based on objective evaluation involving numeric values of project characteristics.

quantitative risk analysis A process that involves measuring the probability and consequences of risks and estimating their implications for project objectives.

R

rational unified process (RUP) An iterative process that identifies four phases of a software development project: inception, elaboration, construction, and transition. Each phase contains one or more iterations where an executable is produced, but perhaps an incomplete system (except possibly in the inception phase). During each iteration, you perform activities from several disciplines (workflows) in varying levels of detail.

real options An approach that allows an organization to value IT projects in a manner similar to the way we value stock options. A stock option lets us make a small investment today in order to reduce our risk later on. At the same time, it keeps open the possibility of making a bigger investment later, if the future goes the way we expect.

recurring costs Costs that appear more than once throughout the life of the project (for example, annual hardware and software maintenance costs).

reliability The probability of a product performing as specified without failure over a set period of time.

requirements plan A document that describes how each requirement meets a business need for a project.

return on investment (ROI) The percentage return expected over the life of a project.

rework Repetition of a task to correct an identified error.

risk An event that, if it occurs, will have a negative impact on one or more of the following: project scope, time, cost, quality, or resources.

risk acceptance The act of accepting the consequences should a risk occur without trying to control it.

risk avoidance The act of eliminating a specific threat or risk, usually by eliminating its causes.

risk identification A process that involves determining which risks might affect a project and documenting their characteristics.

risk management The processes and methods used to identify, quantify, and control risks associated with a project.

risk management plan A document that describes how risk identification, qualitative and quantitative analysis, response planning, monitoring, and control will be structured and performed during a project's life cycle.

risk management planning A process that involves deciding how to approach and plan the risk management activities of a project.

risk mitigation The act of reducing the impact of a risk event by reducing the probability of its occurrence.

risk register An artifact that contains the outcomes from the risk identification and assessment analysis processes.

risk response plan A document that describes the actions that will be performed for each risk identified.

risk response planning A process that involves developing procedures and techniques to enhance opportunities and reduce threats to a project's objectives.

risk transference The act of shifting the consequence of a risk and responsibility for its management to a third party internal or external to the organization.

rural sourcing The movement of a business process (in whole or in part) done at a company to another company located in a more rural setting within the same country.

S

schedule control A process that involves controlling changes to a project schedule.

schedule development The process of analyzing activity sequences, activity durations, and resource requirements to create a project schedule.

schedule update Any modification to schedule information that is used to manage a project.

scope change Any modification to the agreed-upon project scope, as defined by the approved WBS.

scope control A process that involves controlling changes to a project's scope.

scope creep The unanticipated gradual growth of information systems requirements during the life of a project, causing budget and time overruns.

scope management The processes and methods used to ensure that a project delivers exactly what the customer requested and only what the customer requested to create a successful project.

scope statement A statement that describes the characteristics of a product that a project was created to deliver.

scope verification The process of formalizing acceptance of a project's scope.

Scrum approach An approach for managing the system development process that is based on the concept that software development is not a defined process but an empirical process with complex input to output transformations that may or may not be repeated under differing circumstances.

seller performance evaluation A document that describes the performance of the seller during the length of the contract for future consideration.

Six Sigma A rigorous and disciplined methodology that uses data and statistical analysis to measure and improve a company's operational performance by identifying and eliminating defects in manufacturing and service-related processes.

Software Engineering Institute (SEI) Located at Carnegie Mellon University and sponsored by the U.S. Department of Defense through the Office of the Under Secretary of Defense for Acquisition and Technology, an organization created in 1984 to aid organizations in the advancement of software engineering practices.

special interest group (SIG) A group organized around a common interest or issue. Examples of current PMI SIGs include Aerospace & Defense, Human Resources, Information Systems, and Women in Project Management.

spiral model An approach to systems development that emphasizes the need to go back and reiterate earlier stages a number of times as a project progresses. This model is actually a series of short waterfall cycles, each producing an early prototype that represents a part of the entire project.

staffing management plan A formal or informal document that describes when and how human resources will be brought onto and taken off a project team. It also describes the resources' available time to work on the project, any training needs, any pertinent human resources policies or regulations, and any safety guidelines.

stage gate A decision-making opportunity between phases or iterations in the project life cycle to determine whether the project should proceed as is, proceed with changes, or be terminated.

stakeholder analysis A process used to identify the influence and interests of the various stakeholders and to document their needs, wants, and expectations.

stakeholder management strategy A document that outlines specific strategies needed to ensure that a project manager maximizes positive stakeholder influences and minimizes negative stakeholder influences.

stakeholder register A document that summarizes all the stakeholders (people or organizations) that are affected by some part of a project.

start-to-finish (SF) dependency A type of precedence diagram method dependency in which the completion of a task is dependent on the start of all its predecessors.

start-to-start (SS) dependency A type of precedence diagram method dependency in which the start of a task is dependent on the start of all its predecessors.

statement of work (SOW) A document that describes 100 percent of the work or services required to be completed under contract by a seller.

strategic plan A formal plan generally spanning three to five years for an entire business entity that defines its mission, vision, goals, strategies, and measures of progress.

subject matter expert (SME) A person who has the level of knowledge and/or experience in a particular facet of the business needed to support decision making.

subsystem Smaller systems that are part of a larger system. For example, the human heart is a subsystem of the human body, and the accounts receivable subsystem is a part of the financial software system of an organization.

sunk cost A cost expended on a product or service that cannot be retrieved.

SWOT analysis An analysis of strengths, weaknesses, opportunities, and threats; an information gathering and analysis technique to evaluate external influences against internal capabilities.

system A set of interacting, interrelated, or interdependent elements that work as part of a whole.

system development life cycle (SDLC) An approach to building IT systems that consists of a standard set of phases, each of which produces a prescribed set of deliverables.

systems analysis A problem-solving technique that decomposes a system into its component pieces for the purpose of studying how well those component parts work and interact to accomplish their purpose.

systems approach A process of examining a problem or an issue by first understanding its environment and then reducing the problem or issue into smaller components and finally managing the resolution of the problem or issue.

systems management Management of a whole system, including objectives, the environment (both internal and external), constraints, resources (both human and nonhuman), and the culture and social environment of an organization.

systems theory A philosophy of or a way of looking at the world; a language or set of principles and interventions for thinking and solving problems.

T

task-oriented conflict Conflict associated with disagreements regarding end results or outcomes.

time and material contract A contract under which the seller is reimbursed for all previously defined costs and additional material costs of the seller to complete the product.

time management The processes and methods required to create and manage appropriate schedules to complete a project.

time value of money The concept that a sum of money is more valuable the sooner it is received: A dollar today is worth more than the promise of a dollar tomorrow. The worth is dependent on two variables: the time interval and rate of discount.

total quality management (TQM) The culture, attitude, and organization of a company that strives to provide customers (internal and external) with products and services that satisfy their needs.

traditional organizational structure A structure that is organized based on one of the following characteristics: job function, end product, customer groups, a specific process, or geographic locations.

triple constraint Scope, time, and cost objectives that have to be balanced in order to deliver successful projects.

V

variable cost Costs that change based on the activity of a business or project (for example, project employee costs).

virtual team A team whose members are unable to regularly meet face-to-face, so instead they must use various technologies to communicate.

W

waterfall model A traditional approach to systems development that describes a development approach that is linear and sequential and that has distinct objectives for each phase. In this model, the output of one phase is the input for the next.

WBS (work breakdown structure) An outcome-oriented list of tasks executed by a project team to accomplish the stated project objectives.

WBS dictionary A document that supports a WBS with further details of the work packages and control accounts.

work package A document that describes the work needed to produce a deliverable at the lowest level of a WBS.

INDEX